REREADING THE BLACK LEGEND

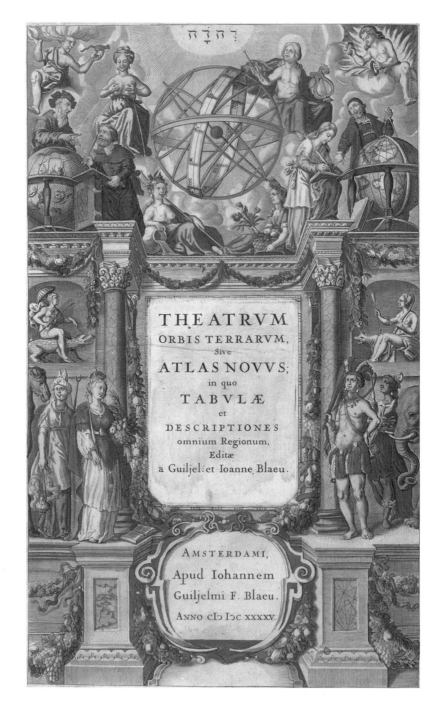

THEATRVM
ORBIS TERRARVM,
Sive
ATLAS NOVVS;
in quo
TABVLÆ
et
DESCRIPTIONES
omnium Regionum,
Editæ
a Guiljel: et Ioanne Blaeu.

AMSTERDAMI,
Apud Iohannem
Guiljelmi F. Blaeu.
ANNO cIɔ Iɔc XXXXV.

REREADING THE BLACK LEGEND

*The Discourses of Religious and Racial Difference
in the Renaissance Empires*

Edited by

Margaret R. Greer,

Walter D. Mignolo,

and Maureen Quilligan

THE UNIVERSITY OF CHICAGO PRESS
Chicago and London

MARGARET R. GREER is professor of Spanish and chair of the Department of
Romance Studies at Duke University. WALTER D. MIGNOLO is the William H.
Wannamaker Professor of Romance Studies and director of the Center for Global
Studies and the Humanities at Duke University. MAUREEN QUILLIGAN is the
Florence R. Brinkley Professor of English at Duke University.

The University of Chicago Press, Chicago 60637
The University of Chicago Press, Ltd., London
© 2007 by The University of Chicago
All rights reserved. Published 2007
Printed in the United States of America

16 15 14 13 12 11 10 09 08 07   1 2 3 4 5

ISBN-13: 978-0-226-30721-3 (cloth)
ISBN-13: 978-0-226-30722-0 (paper)
ISBN-10: 0-226-30721-2 (cloth)
ISBN-10: 0-226-30722-0 (paper)

Frontispiece: Willem Blaeu, title page from *Theatrum orbis Terrarum* (1645).
Theatrum Orbis Terrarum, sive Atlas Novus in quo Tabulae et Descriptiones Omnium Regionum,
editae a Guiljel: et Ioanne Blaeu. *Theater of the World, or a New Atlas of Maps and*
Representations of All Regions, edited by Willem and Joan Blaeu, Henry J. Bruman Map
Collection, UCLA Library.

Library of Congress Cataloging-in-Publication Data
Rereading the Black Legend : the discourses of religious and racial difference in the
Renaissance empires / edited by Margaret R. Greer, Walter D. Mignolo, and
Maureen Quilligan.
    p. cm.
  Includes bibliographical references and index.
  ISBN-13: 978-0-226-30721-3 (cloth : alk. paper)
  ISBN-10: 0-226-30721-2 (cloth : alk. paper)
  ISBN-13: 978-0-226-30722-0 (pbk. : alk. paper)
  ISBN-10: 0-226-30722-0 (pbk. : alk. paper)
  1. Black Legend (Spanish history). 2. Spain—Civilization—1516–1700.
3. National characteristics, Spanish. 4. Imperialism—History—16th century.
5. Spain—Foreign public opinion. I. Greer, Margaret Rich. II. Mignolo, Walter.
III. Quilligan, Maureen, 1944–
  DP48 .R44 2007
  940.2'1—dc22
                                                                    2007030140

CONTENTS

ACKNOWLEDGMENTS

Many of the essays in this book were first presented as part of a conference entitled "Rereading the Black Legend: The Discourses of Racial Difference in the Renaissance Empires," held at Duke University in April 2003. We wish to thank the vice provost for Interdisciplinary Studies and the dean of the Humanities of Duke University and the Josiah Charles Trent Memorial Foundation for their assistance in supporting that conference.

We thank Hillary Eklund for her work in compiling the bibliography and Cathy Knoop for her expert work in formatting the manuscript copy, tracking down illustration permissions, and helping keep the manuscript moving forward in other ways.

Our gratitude also goes to William J. Kennedy and David Carrasco for their thoughtful reading of the entire manuscript and for their useful suggestions for improving it, and to our editor, Randy Petilos, for his enthusiastic reception of the book and patient guidance in dealing with all three of us and our contributors.

Portions of chapter 6, written by Irene Silverblatt, are excerpted from *Modern Inquisitions: Peru and the Colonial Origins of the Civilized World,* copyright 2004, Duke University Press. All rights reserved. We thank the publisher for granting permission to include it in this volume.

CHAPTER ONE

INTRODUCTION

Margaret R. Greer, Walter D. Mignolo, and Maureen Quilligan

M odern western European practices of racialized discrimination developed in the late medieval and early modern periods, but the concept of "race" has a much longer history in the West. This history, while unique to Europe and its territories, is important to consider even as we attempt to pay new attention to other geographical notions of difference between peoples, if only because the West has been the self-appointed culture of "modernity." The idea of the Black Legend as a specific name for Spain's colonial brutality in the Americas during the sixteenth and seventeenth centuries dates from the early twentieth century.[1] A Spanish journalist, Julián Juderías, coined the phrase "Black Legend" in 1912, protesting the characterization of Spain by other Europeans as a backward country of ignorance, superstition, and religious fanaticism that was unable to become a modern nation. Juderías rightly points to envious sixteenth-century Protestant hostility within Europe as the primary origin of such anti-Spanish sentiment, and it is the long-lasting legend of Spain's *unique* brutality in the conquest of the New World that we seek to reconceptualize. Spain was not the only European power to carve an empire out of the New World; it was merely the first. A comparative study of the Dutch and Portuguese engagements in India as well as English projects in America allows us to put Spain's actions into a new context. To add to that context the wider consideration of Chinese, Mughal, and Ottoman imperial arrangements before and during the western European expansions of the sixteenth century makes possible a global rereading of the very different racism of western European Renaissance empires. It was a racism that was subtended by religious differences and that not only helped to structure the imperial programs of sixteenth-century western European societies but also continued to structure western Europe's thinking into the time of Emmanuel Kant, whose rehearsal of some of Las Casas's sixteenth-century prescriptions about barbarians reveals how reverberant the concepts have been.

The Black Legend owes its own genesis to the course of three simultaneous events: the expulsion of the Moors and Jews from the Iberian Peninsula; the so-called discovery of America and the domination and exploitation of Indians and African slaves; and the privileged position in which Christianity found itself to create a classification in which Christians were one of the groups classified and, simultaneously, possessors of the privileged discourse that created the classification. Christianity's originally nonexclusionary evangelism could be used to pointed imperial effect, as, for example, at the moment when the Inca Atahulapha threw down a religious book a Spanish priest had handed to him; because of his apparent rejection of the Christian God, the Spanish felt free to attack, firing into a crowd of unarmed people, ultimately overtaking the empire and enslaving the population. Ganzalo Lamana in chapter 7 chronicles the remarkable import of the varying redactions of this iconic moment in Spanish aggression against Peru. In contrast, as Leslie Peirce reveals in chapter 2, Ottoman rulers were required by Islamic law to protect the religious freedom of foreigners within their realms. While Ottoman emperors did force some conquered Christians to convert and also enslaved them, they drew Janissaries—their highest imperial administrators and their royal consorts—from this group. Both the Ottomans and the Chinese used castration to render conquered men useful for their imperial administrative purposes; in mid-fifteenth-century China, Muslim eunuchs rose to great power, but the famous maritime commander Zheng He, for example, a eunuch serving Emperor Zhu Di, was never required to relinquish his Islamic faith. Eastern empires were not without their repressive brutalities; they simply operated on very different axes from the Western empires.[2]

The links between religiously coded racism and color-coded racism were the consequences of early modern European imperial expansion in Africa, the subjugation of the indigenous populations of America, and the evolution of the ancient practice of slavery practiced by virtually all ancient peoples into the hugely profitable transatlantic slave trade, later monopolized throughout the eighteenth century by the British. Slavery had existed from time immemorial but had not been associated with color or had ever generated so much capital. The discourses of religious and racial difference in the European Renaissance became naturalized in the subsequent centuries and established the epistemic foundation of modern colonial racism. Although antecedents of the concept of race may be found in the remote history of humankind, the drastic qualitative conceptual shift in the sixteenth century (which in the eighteenth century was universalized as race and racism) is unprecedented. The history of racism as we know it today began to be articulated right then, in the sixteenth century, and there, in the Atlantic world.

By seeking to revisit the processes of global colonial domination in the context of the European debate about Spain's New World empire, we hope to locate a historical intersection for the creation of stereotypes, classifications, or what Foucault called "dividing practices"—practices of enormous ideological and practical consequence in forging, justifying, and maintaining early modern regimes of domination and exploitation, whose shifting combinations continue to shape how we think and act in the world we inhabit today. We approach this intersection via a rereading of the Black Legend about the Spanish conquest of the Americas, itself a manifestation of imperial conflicts within Christian Europe. Placed in the wider context of a global system of imperial expansion that included Turkey, China, India, and Russia, we are in a better position to see how the distinct form of western European imperialism is marked by capitalist effects not much in evidence elsewhere: where the Chinese chose to extract tribute from newly contacted countries and showered the ambassadors with gifts often of greater value than the tribute, the massive appropriation of land on new continents by the Spanish, Portuguese, French, Dutch, and finally the English, along with the massive exploitation of the labor of indigenous and imported nonindigenous peoples, created the conditions of a proper capitalist global market in newly valuable commodities (not merely the gold and silver found in the Americas but also the labor of extracting them itself). When seen in this global context capitalism clearly is not, properly, the creation of the industrial revolution but rather of the commodification of labor attendant upon western European colonial expansion into the Americas.

We do not in any way seek to downplay the devastating consequences for native populations in the Americas of European invasions of their lands, but we do seek to explore from a variety of perspectives how the concept of race as we understand it today began to emerge in the discourses of colonial otherness fostered by the global contest for empire. By juxtaposing the ways in which non-European sixteenth-century empires of the east—Chinese, Mughal, and Ottoman—constructed hierarchical differences within their own newly conquered or reorganized territories to those of the Western regimes, we hope better to understand the differential structures of empire and therefore also its distinctive means for compelling complicity in conquered populations. While Mughal and Ottoman emperors enslaved religious and ethnic others, and also transported and exploited the labor of specific ethnic populations, they did so to build their own dynastic power, not in the service of a widely dispersed search after monetary profit, open to any freelance adventuring individual as was the case with many of the Spanish conquistadors and, later, northern European colonists. The Ottomans decided not to invest in New World exploration, and in the fifteenth century, the Chinese, while more capable than any empire of global conquest by their sheer maritime and technological superiority, chose not to extend their trade network and, indeed, elected to shut down the massive fleet of treasure ships they had built and to focus inward on internal developments. While free-lance Chinese traders sailed the Indian Ocean both before and after the massively government-financed voyages of the early fifteenth century, commanded by the famous Muslim navigator Cheng He, their activities were mostly illicit and of little lasting consequence. The Eastern empires, in short, were not individualistically entrepreneurial and capitalistic, while the Western empires can be seen, in contrast, to be clearly so. In Shakespeare's *The Tempest*, for example, a clownish character comments that when Londoners would not "give a doit to relieve a lame beggar they will lay out ten to see a dead Indian. Any strange beast" in England "makes a man." In direct opposition to the cast of mind Trinculo reveals when he speculates on the money he could earn by making a profitable spectacle of the New World creature Caliban, the Chinese invited ambassadors from Africa to bring tribute directly to the emperor, including exotic animals such as giraffes. These ambassadors were lavishly entertained on luxurious ships the size of which would have allowed all three of Columbus's galleons to be easily stored on deck (fig. 1.1). The ambassadors would have been received with great and elaborate ceremonies, allowed to trade with the populace, and received gifts in return from the emperor. In celebration of the success of the imperial treasure fleets under Zheng He, Emperor Zhu Di had a 240-foot-high porcelain pagoda built, costing 2.5 million ounces of silver. "Each story was fashioned with exactly the same number of tiles and the tiles became smaller as the graceful structure narrowed to a point. The base of the gilt finial at the top was twelve feet in diameter and was decorated with 152 porcelain bells that chimed in the wind. The finial itself, covered in gold leaf, shone brilliantly in the sun. Around the temple were beautiful gardens and exotic trees that Zheng He had brought back from his voyages."[3]

And, of course, like the Ottomans, the Ming emperors finally decided they had little interest in trade with territories so far removed from what they considered to be the center of the universe.[4] The discourses constructed to deal with the differences Europeans perceived in the New World profoundly affected the way western Europe, at least, looked back at other Old World regimes and formed the basis for many orientalizing ideologies, completely misrecognizing the histories of their different imperial structures. By going back to the sixteenth-century site of the instantiation of so many imperial projects, we hope to be in a better position to critique the ideological after-

1.1   Zheng He's treasure ship as compared with Columbus's Santa María. Illustration by
      Jan Adkins. From Louise Levathes' *When China Ruled the Seas.*

effects of their shared history, specifically the very different racist discourses
constructed by the processes of empire in different places, to unravel their
blindness to each others' histories.

LAS CASAS

It is one of the first ironies of this history that the condemnations of the barbarity of Spain's conquest were based from the mid-sixteenth century forward on its own questioning of the legitimacy of its imperial enterprise in
America. The first important critiques of the conquest for its injustice and
brutality to indigenous populations in the western hemisphere were actually
voiced by Spanish missionaries in the New World. The most famous of them
was the Dominican priest and bishop of Chiapas, Bartolomé de las Casas,
who, after the failure of his legal arguments against the *encomienda* system of
slave labor for the conquered indigenous peoples, published in Seville in
1552 the *Brevísima relación de la destrucción de las Indias* (A very short account
of the destruction of the Indies). This volume would quickly become a cornerstone of the Black Legend, to be translated and republished over the centuries with each new conflict involving Spain and its European rivals or American colonies. The first translation, into French, as *Tyrannies et cruautez des
Espagnols, perpetrees ès Indes Occidentales* by the Fleming Jacques de Miggrode,

appeared in Antwerp in 1578 with a notice that it was "To serve as example and warning to the seventeen provinces of the Low Countries," where Philip II's governors, particularly the Duke of Alba, had been dealing out harsh punishments for religious dissent and separatist rebellion against Spanish rule. Anti-Catholic and protonationalist sentiments fed the growth of the Black Legend in England. The repetition of the Black Legend would serve the interests of the rival Dutch and English empires belatedly contesting Spanish imperial dominance in the Americas.[5] It was, as Fernández Retamar (1989, 63) points out, a weapon in an interimperial struggle.[6] The Black Legend would have another revival in the early nineteenth century, inspired by the wars of independence against Spain by the Latin American colonies, and yet again in 1898, now centering in the United States and connected to the so-called Spanish-American War.

Translated into English as *The Spanish Colonie* in 1583, Las Casas's own Spanish and Catholic identity was ignored so that the tract formed the basis of a wholesale denunciation of the Spanish imperial project. A century later, when at the treaty of Utrecht in 1714 England gained the Asiento and took over the monopoly of the African slave trade, Spain still carried on its shoulders the imprint of the cruelty so famously denounced by Las Casas. It was African ex-slaves who testified to the fact that northern European colonists were just as vicious as their Iberian counterparts. Published in 1787, Quobna Ottobah Cugoano's *Thoughts and Sentiments on the Evil of Slavery* made clear that from the point of view of the colonial subject there was no difference between Spanish and British domination. He observed, "The French and English, and some other nations in Europe, as they founded settlements and colonies in the West Indies or in America, went on in the same manner, and joined hand in hand with the Portuguese and Spaniards, to rob and pillage Africa, as well as to waste and desolate the inhabitants of the western continent" (1787, 73).

If we can say that Las Casas's tract formed the basis of an anti-Spanish tradition among other European powers—which resistances like Cugoano's did little to change—we can also trace a second important strand of European discourse about racial difference to Las Casas as well. This second text by Las Casas provides the context for understanding what we normally think of as racial difference in the Renaissance empires. In his epilogue to the *Apologética Historia Sumaria* (1552), Las Casas defines four types of "barbarians." Briefly, the first and third types of barbarians are very similar. The first places greatest emphasis on ferocious individuals, while the third underlines communities living close to a state of nature, a point similar to the bases on which Hobbes and Locke will build their political theories—but that could also be found in Aristotle's *Politics*. The second and fourth types of barbarians clearly establish the foundation of modern/colonial and Western racism. They are defined by one main criteria and described as *barbarie negativa* (negative barbarism): all those who "lack" some key civilizing element — or sometimes have it in excess — are barbarous. All non-Latin empires, as well as the Inca and Aztec empires, may have been in Las Casas's mind when defining this second type, for such barbarians are characterized by the lack of "literal locution," by which Las Casas means a lack of "Latinity." Deploying the full force of the humanist Renaissance recovery of Roman imperial power, Las Casas here instantiates a key point in Renaissance consolidation of European superiority by means of alphabetic writing and of Latin as the language closest to God. The conjunction of both ruled out Turkic, Arabic, Hebrew, and Russian and because, although they may all be alphabetic languages, none of them derive directly from Latin (English may pose a special case, being of Germanic base but having been conquered by French, a Latin tongue).[7] The consequences of this move by Las Casas were profound: in casting aside ancient languages such as Arabic, Turkic, Hebrew, and Chinese, as well as non-Christian and noncapitalist empires, it cast aside the Islamic and the Ottoman empires. He may not have realized that he was also casting aside the emerging Russian empire, at that moment consolidating itself with Ivan the Terrible's rise to power — curiously enough, during the very same years that Elizabeth I and Philip II took over Spain and England. More to the point, neither the Aztecs nor the Incas had literal locution, and so in this respect, both could be classified/categorized as the second type of barbarians.

Although Las Casas is not clear about it, none of the four types of barbarians seem to be found in western Christendom, which was quickly being transformed into Europe. In this respect, Las Casas's barbarians in the age of Christian imperialism became one template for Immanuel Kant's racial classification of the ethnocontinental tetragon, this time based essentially on skin color: yellow Asia, black Africa, red America, and white Europe. For Kant as for Las Casas, none of the people inhabiting the globe outside of Europe — beyond Germany, France, and England — were apt to understand a central literary tradition, which for Kant was understood to be the beautiful and the sublime; the level of all non-Europeans' rationality thus becomes questionable. Such is the Kantian version of Las Casas's second type of barbarians — those lacking literal locution. In the later half of the eighteenth century Kant said, following Hume, "Hume challenges anyone to cite a single example in which a Negro has shown talents, and asserts that among the hundreds of thousands of blacks who are transported elsewhere from their countries, although many of them have even been set free, still not a single one was ever found who presented anything great in art or science or any other praise-worthy quality, even though among the whites some continually rise aloft from the lowest rabble, and through superior gifts earn respect in the world" (1991, 111).

Las Casas's fourth type of barbarian—comprising all those who did not have the right religion (such as the Moors, the Chinese, and all those living in South Asia)—was equally central for the Renaissance invention of colonial difference. They could not have religion because their infidel souls had been taken and dominated by the devil, the prime example of which were the Indians of the New World. That is why conversion was the necessary imperial "civilizing" mission. The four types of barbarian "comprende todos aquellos que carecen de verdadera religión y fe cristiana, conviene a saber, todos los infieles, por muy sabios y prudentes filósofos y políticos que sean. La razón es porque no hay alguna nación (sacando las de los cristianos) que no tenga y padezca muchos y muy grandes defectos, y barbaricen en sus leyes, costumbres, vivienda y policias [. . .]" (1967, 2:645). [include all those who lack true religion and Christian faith; in other words, all infidels, however wise and prudent philosophers or politicians they might be. The reason is that there is no nation (apart from Christian ones) that does not have and suffer many great defects and barbarities in its laws, customs, housing and policies.] There is thus a double implication of the racial underpinnings of the Black Legend. One is the superiority of European culture to the rest of the world, and the other is the construction of an imperial difference, internal to Europe, that Immanuel Kant also articulates when he argues how civilized the British are and how absurd and leaning toward the uncivilized the Spanish are. Kant argues, for example, in his papers *On the Beautiful and the Sublime* and in *Anthropology from a Pragmatic Point of View,* that the Spanish possess a second-class European national character only slightly better than the Orientals: "The Spaniard, who evolved from the mixture of European blood with Arabian (Moorish) blood, displays in his public and private behavior a certain solemnity; and even the peasant expresses a consciousness of his own dignity toward his master, to whom he is lawfully obedient" (1978, 231). That is for Kant the "good" side of the Spaniards. As for the bad side, "The Spaniard's bad side is that he does not learn from foreigners; that he does not travel in order to get acquainted with other nations; that he is centuries behind in sciences. He resists any reform; he is proud of not having to work" (1978, 231). Sentiment against Spaniards for being "tainted" by Moorish and Semitic blood predated the Renaissance conquests and also the completion of Spain's reconquest, so Kant's assumption of the Spanish mixed-blood origins is of longer duration than the Renaissance prejudice.

Spain had long served as Europe's racialized internal other. For example, Geoffrey of Monmouth's twelfth-century formulation of the legend of King Arthur in the *Historia Regum Britanniae* works to distance a painful episode in Christian history, the desperate degradation of the Christian forces' practice of cannibalism in Syria during the first Crusade.[8] He transforms the crusaders' cannibalism into a battle Arthur wages with two anthropophagous giants who invade Europe, one of whom is of Spanish origin. According to Geraldine Heng (2003, 5), this constituted a double writing to indict Islam, relating Muslim Spain with Syria to distance the memory of cannibalism from England and from Christians.[9] Fernández Retamar (1989) notices the persistence of the racial othering of Spain and its extension to Latin America when he cites Alexandre Dumas's classic formulation of the cliché, "Africa begins at the Pyrenees." Retamar points out the persistence of this form of the Black Legend itself as a form of racism, evident in the common use in the United States of the words "Hispanic" and "Latino" as classified with other "people of color."

A vivid illustration of the "denigration" of the Spanish can be seen in Theordor de Bry's engraving for the frontispiece of Part V of *America* (fig. 1.2). Printed in 1595, the volume published John Benzoni's narration of Spaniards' cruelty to the Indians and their use of slaves imported from Africa. As Patricia Gravatt carefully argues in chapter 12 of this volume, de Bry actually had a more nuanced view of the Spanish than the engraving itself reveals. But the engraving does make clear the way in which the Spanish soldiers are seen to become indistinguishable from their Negro slaves as they all toil, with bulging buttocks, up the left side of the engraving. Perhaps even more pertinently than the shared toil, the Africanized features, including the flattened nose of one of the Spanish conquistadors scrambling down the right side of the mountain, differs markedly from the Spanish noblemen at the base of the engraving, where the pope divides up the New World between Portugal and Spain. So too, the cross being planted on top of the mountain, seen slanted backward as if in perspective, radically distorts the Christian symbolism of the Catholic civilizing process as seen by the hostile Protestant eye.

RACE AND RELIGION IN SPAIN BEFORE AND AFTER THE RECONQUEST

Spain is indeed a crucial site in the history of the concept of race and the practice of racial discrimination, from the late medieval period on through its empire building and colonization. Race in medieval Spain was not color coded, however, but was defined as a descent group or lineage, or as a given

AMERICÆ
PARS QVINTA.

Nobilis & admiratione plena
Hieronymi Bezoni Mediolanensis,
secundæ sectionis Hispanorum, tūm in
Nigrittas seruos suos, tum in Indos crudelita-
tem, Gallorumq, piratarū de Hispanis toties
reportata spolia; Aduentū item Hispanorū
in Nouam Indiæ continentis Hispaniam,
eorumq, contra incolas eius regionis
sæuitiam explicans.
Addita ad singula fere Capita scholia, in quibus
res Indiæ luculenter exponuntur.
Accessit præterea Tabula Chorographica Nouæ
Hispaniæ in India Occidentalj.
AD
Invictis RVDOLPH. II. ROM. IMP. AVG.
Omni elegantibus figuris in aes incisis expressa à
Theodoro de Bry Leod. ciue Franc. A. cb b xcv.

1.2   Theodore de Bry, frontispiece to Volume V of *America* (Frankfurt, 1595). Yale
Collection of Western Americana, Beinecke Rare Book and Manuscript Library.

religious identity. The religiously based definition assumed an increasingly racialized character by the late Middle Ages, and a categorization by class or estate would be added to definitions of race by the late seventeenth century.

Whether or not the *convivencia* (literally, "living together") of Muslims, Christians, and Jews in medieval Spain constituted a culture of tolerance or cohabitation of convenience or one of necessity remains a matter of dispute. María Rosa Menocal (2002) paints southern Spain under the Islamic Umayyad dynasty as a "first-rate place" of tolerance, in which Islamic respect for *ðhimmi* (people of the Book) fostered beneficent interfaith relations that were acknowledged and to an extent perpetuated by Christian kings from Alfonso VI to Alfonso X even as the Christian reconquest advanced. David Nirenberg (1996) and Joseph Pérez (2000), however, discount the existence of real tolerance between the three religious communities, each of which believed itself the possessor of the one true faith, which it was obliged to defend. Religious affiliation in medieval Europe meant membership in the community into which one was born, as a Muslim, Jew, or Christian, and ethnic and religious strife were generally inseparable. Nevertheless, intermarriages did occur, and Nirenberg (1996) maintains that at least in the Crown of Aragon, prior to the 1391 wave of anti-Semitic violence, there is little evidence of anxiety about the conservation of racial purity.[10] According to Christian doctrine, all human beings were children of Adam and Eve, and the objective was their conversion.

Just what caused the breakdown of this at least relative tolerance? Menocal's (2002) narrative implies that a key factor was the successive invasion of two fanatic groups of North African Berbers into southern Spain after the breakup of the Umayyad caliphate when the domains of the *taifa* (party) kings were shrinking before the Christian advance.[11] Under the repressive Berber regimes, not only *mozárabes* (Christians living in Arab realms) but also Jews migrated north into the Christian realms. Jews—at their maximum point comprising close to 5 percent of the population of Iberia, the largest contingent of Jews in medieval Europe—were welcomed and valued for their learning, for their language skills, and as a financial and administrative resource for the royalty. Jews lived under the direct jurisdiction of Christian royalty and were dependent on their protection. In the fourteenth century, a series of bad harvests, the Black Death that ravaged all Europe, and political turmoil set the scene for a devastating wave of anti-Semitic violence in 1391.[12] Economic resentment and something like class warfare played a part in the scapegoating of Jews for their role as lenders to Christians; they were accused of causing the plague by poisoning wells, of alliance with the devil, of ritual killing of Christian children, and similar atrocities. As large-scale conversions of terrified Jews followed, the same suspicions and resentments would eventually be turned against *conversos* (converted Jews). The infamous statutes of *limpieza* (purity of blood) that denied public and church offices to those of Jewish and Muslim ancestry were also rooted as much in class interests as in religious concerns, as the aristocracy sought to limit competition for the positions it had traditionally dominated and as commoners who had risen by dint of talent and education retaliated by requiring proof of blood purity of an aristocracy that had intermarried with wealthy *converso* families.[13] The "Catholic kings" had continued to protect Jews and rely on Jewish financiers, who bankrolled the last stages of the reconquest. Yet, a mere two months after the capitulation of Granada in 1492, on the grounds that their continuing presence encouraged secretive practice of Judaism on the part of the *conversos*, Isabela decreed the expulsion of all Jews in Spain who did not convert.

A similar process of a shifting balance of power and the difficulty of integrating a large Muslim population under Christian authority led to the revocation of protection for newly conquered Muslims, when it was only the owners of large landed estates in Aragon and Andalusia who depended on their labor. Forced conversion proved even less effective than it had in the case of the Jews, and the *moriscos* (converted Muslims) rebelled at mounting pressure to abandon their language and culture as well as their religion. So too, large-scale resettlement of *moriscos* among northern Christian populations also caused economic resentment. Fears that they were a fifth column within Spain who might call on assistance from North African Muslims and the Turks culminated in the 1609 expulsion of the *moriscos*, against the objection of numerous theologians and two popes, who argued that they were at least technically Christians and that they represented no real danger to Spain.

DICTIONARY DEFINITIONS OF RACE

The historical context of the publication of the first Spanish dictionary of Sebastian de Covarrubias Orozco in 1611 was therefore fraught with a profoundly negative attitude toward converted Jews and Muslims. In this dictionary we find *raza* defined as, "La casta de caballos castizos, a los cuales señalan con hierro para que sean conocidos. . . . Raza, en los linajes se toma en mala parte, como tener alguna raza de moro o judío." [The breed of thoroughbred horses, which are branded with an iron so that they can be known. . . . Race in [human] lineages is understood pejoratively, as having some Moorish or Jewish race.] As this reference to the branding of thoroughbred horses implied, there was in fact no truly reliable way of distinguishing pure breeding that was visible to the naked eye, hence the need for making a visible mark by branding.[14] Men are distinguished only by a "lineage" centered on religious "race," where race is the inmixing of something other and equally invisible.

The expanded definition of *raza* in Real Academia Española's 1734 *Diccionario de Autoridades* demonstrates the further development of the concept of a religioethnically based notion of race and reveals the same hardening of genealogical attitude as Kant's. It repeats the definitions given by the early seventeenth-century dictionary but further emphasizes the threatened nature of "pure breeding": "Casta o calidad del origin o linage. Hablando de los hombres, se toma mui regularmente en mala parte. Es del Latino *Radix*. Latino *Genus. Stirps. Etiam generis macula, vel ignominia.*" [Breed or quality of origin or lineage. In speaking of men, it is regularly used pejoratively. From Latin *Root. Genus. Stock. Even a stain on the breed, or ignominy.*] The examples that this early eighteenth-century dictionary provides are telling. The first is drawn from the statutes of the Order of Calatrava, one of the military-religious orders founded in the twelfth century to advance the Christian reconquest of Muslim lands in Spain: "Ordenamos y mandamos que ninguna persona, de qualquiera calidad y condición que fuere, sea recibida a la dicho Orden, ni se le dé el Hábito, sino fuere Hijodalgo, al fuero de España, de partes de padre y madre y de abuelos de entrambas partes, y de legítimo matrimonio nacido, y que no le toque *raza* de Judío, Moro, Hereje, ni Villano." [We order and decree that no person, of whatever quality or condition, be received in the said Order, nor be given its Habit, unless he be of noble descent, according to the law of Spain, on the part of father and mother and grandparents of both, and born of legitimate marriage, and not tainted by the *race* of Jew, Moor, Heretic, or Lowborn.]

The second example is drawn from the 1600 *History of Spain* of the Jesuit historian Juan de Mariana and makes equally clear the problem of intermixture and bastardization: "No de otra manera que los sembrados y animales, la *raza* de los hombres, y casta, con la propiedad del Cielo y de la tierra, sobre todo con el tiempo se muda y se embastarda." [Not differently from sown fields and animals, the *race* and caste of men, with the influence of the heavens and the earth and above all over time, changes and is bastardized.] Such definitions, discounting the possibility of true religious conversion or full assimilation to the dominant culture, register a religioethnic racism, as Frederickson (2002) has defined it: "when differences that might otherwise be considered ethnocultural are regarded as innate, indelible, and unchangeable . . . a racist attitude or ideology can be said to exist." Some scholars have attributed the anxiously inquisitorial society of early modern

Spain in the wake of the expulsion and/or forced conversion of Jews and Muslims to the deeply problematic invisibility of true faith.[15] The Inquisition then becomes a futile attempt to read in the bodies of the converted any tell-tale sign of impurity, in body and blood as well as in religious practice. Black skin, despite the symbolic linkage of black with death and evil, carried few generalized negative connotations for a medieval Europe with little contact with blacks. As the representation of one of the Magi as black and the legend of Prester John demonstrate, blackness was exotic and could be coded positively.[16] The very lack of visible signs that so troubled the Inquisition indeed shows the difference between this earlier instantiation of religiously raced difference and later versions of racism attendant upon the hugely profitable African slave trade.

SUMMARY

Although not named until the twentieth century, the Black Legend was created when Spain's enemies took Spain's own internal debates about its identity and "purity of blood" and the morality of its behavior in the New World and constructed an image of the Spanish as violent and close to barbarians. The image of the Spaniards that the Black Legend helped to create was similar to the first type of barbarian described by Las Casas. But of course, it was impossible for Las Casas to think that Christian Spaniards would belong to any category of barbarian, as he was operating on the premise of the superiority of Western Christians. For Las Casas, the problem the Spaniards had in the New World was an in-house problem that needed to be cleared up, but it could in no way confuse them with the "barbarians out there." From the perspective of the northern Europeans, in contrast, the difference was more imperial than colonial (although the Dutch, colonized by Spain, had a different motive and used Spanish New World barbarity to legitimate their political rebellion). For England it was a difference among equals, even if those in the south were Catholic. There was, however, a fifth type of barbarian belonging to a category Las Casas termed the "barbarie contraria." To the fifth type belong, states Las Casas, all those who hate Christianity and want to destroy it. Las Casas may well have included northern Christians, the Lutherans and Calvinists, in this category, along with the followers of Islam. Las Casas wrote the *Apologética Historia Sumaria* in defense of the Indians during the years of the Council of Trent, so that the Counter-Reformation moment is a clear context for his thinking about "differences" among barbarians around the globe.

Yet even a barbarian of the fifth sort, such as Suleyman the Magnificent, would not yet have been racially denigrated. There would have been no doubt in the minds of the Spaniards living in the first half of the sixteenth century that Suleyman the Magnificent had the same stature as Charles V. Both men came to prominence during the same years and established the imperial foundations of both the Ottoman and the Spanish empires. If we consider the history of their two empires after Suleyman and Charles V, we see the multiple uses of Las Casas's rhetoric: in time, both the Ottoman and Spanish empires succumbed to the growing power of a capitalist Anglophone imperial project. Five centuries later, Spain elected to withdraw from the war against Islam being waged by Anglophone powers facing the menace of Islam in present-day Iraq. Which is the "barbarie contraria" of the twenty-first century?

❊   ❊   ❊

The book begins with the section on empires in the East because the two empires in question offer a remarkably different perspective on imperial organization from that based on western New World conquests; thus they offer a usefully "estranging frame" for our rereading of the Black Legend. The two chapters in part I, titled "Two Empires of the East," one on the Ottoman Empire and the other on the Mughal Empire, provide this useful frame — but it would be irresponsible not to offer some comment on the vast expansion China also undertook at this time and from which they inexplicably turned away. Under emperor Zhu Di in the first decades of the fifteenth century, seven expeditionary navies were sent out around the world, commanded by Zheng He, a Muslim eunuch captain loyal to the emperor, to set up an elaborate tribute system and to map all the oceans of the globe. The records for four of these expeditions reveal that the treasure ships reached Africa (Kenya and Somalia), India, Arabia, Indonesia, Japan, and Korea and carried ambassadors back and forth to China as part of a vast trading system. Apparently, the records from two of the last voyages were destroyed, according to Gavin Menzies (2002), because the Mandarins turned so violently against Zhu Di's costly programs of internal and external expansions.[17] He had moved the Chinese capital to Beijing and built the Forbidden City, had rebuilt and lengthened the Grand Canal between Beijing and Nanking, and had vastly enlarged the navy, including the construction of the treasure ships themselves. Built of teak and mahogany, the ships were huge, each requiring three hundred acres of forest to be felled. Zhu Di's policies meant that

China's colony Vietnam was deforested, causing a major uprising and the loss of the colony. Carrying between five hundred and one thousand sailors, the expeditionary galleons stretched 400 feet in length and were 160 feet wide; they easily dwarfed Columbus's ships[18] (see fig. 1.1). Zhu Di commissioned more than two hundred fifty treasure ships, making the Chinese fleet by far the largest in the world.[19]

Menzies (2002) argues that it was only Zhu Di's fleet that had the capacity to map the entire world and to produce the maps that clearly predate Columbus's voyages; he provocatively argues that on the two missing voyages, the Chinese did map all the ocean shores—as the emperor had commanded—and had reached the west coast of the Americas (from Oregon to Tierra de Fuego), rounded the Cape of Good Hope, sailed to western Africa, and built a navigational tower in Newport, Rhode Island.[20] While such a hypothesis remains as yet unproven, there is some evidence to suggest that contact was made between South America and the Chinese before Columbus arrived. If it is ever proven to be so, Columbus's lifelong insistence that he had found China will make a bit more sense. And even if the Chinese did not make contact with the Americas, it is certain that they had explored a major part of the world and that, like western Europe during the fourteenth century, they had experienced huge economic and social shifts that included outward reaching into an unknown world. With its government-planned expeditions, requiring vast outlays of men and resources, China finally decided that the effort to maintain trade with the underdeveloped (compared to China) world was not worth it, thus leaving the way clear for the tiny, ragged, individualistic, and entrepreneurial "conquests" of the western Europeans. As a Muslim, Zeng He was allowed to make one last voyage to Mecca in 1433 in deference to his naval achievements under the former emperor. But after that, the Chinese fleet faded into oblivion. We begin, then, with a section on empires in the East not only because their modern offspring today offer a powerful challenge to the hegemony of the west but also because their sixteenth-century imperial structures are so different from the organization of dominance based on western New World conquests and on the emergence of modern/colonial capitalism.[21]

In chapter 2, titled "An Imperial Caste: Inverted Racialization in the Architecture of Ottoman Sovereignty," Leslie Peirce argues that the Ottomans, far from abjecting subjugated colonial others, instead used enslaved, converted Christians from the borders of their empire to create an elite ruling caste with which the Ottomans continuously intermarried for six centuries of remarkably stable rule. The Ottoman rulers, however, never married out to other royal dynasties; this endogamous and self-perpetuating unit bureaucratically controlled an expanding polyglot empire, which allowed the conquered kingdoms to retain their various cultural differences unconverted and so remained densely hybrid in nature. This super-elite "kul" class of enslaved Christians was forced to convert to Islam and then trained in the arts of Ottoman rule; such a process produced the pool from which all the administrative pashas, elite Janissary troops, and royal concubines were drawn. Peirce argues that by such a means, the Ottomans avoided the specter that in 1556 broke up, for example, the European Hapsburg Empire into its Austrian and Spanish halves. In forcing the conversion of Christian slaves, the Ottomans freely transgressed the Islamic law that required Muslim rulers to protect people of different faiths within their domains. This single instance of such illegality freed the Ottomans to obey the rule throughout the rest of the empire, where people of radically divergent devotional practices were protected and embraced. Peirce points out that, had the Ottomans extended their rule to the New World (which they specifically declined to do), they would have been required by their customary structures to allow, for example, Aztec and Inca rulers to reign as Ottoman magistrates. It would also have been illegal to convert indigenous peoples from their native religions. Self-conscious inheritors of the legacy of the Roman empire — so much so that they called their domains "Rumi" — the Ottomans ruled in a manner that projects, as Peirce puts it, an "inverted" mirror image of racial and religious hierarchy from the western Renaissance empires.

Addressing the similarly multicultural nature of the Mughal Empire in India during the sixteenth century, Ruby Lal argues in chapter 3 that the increasing invisibility — and number — of women in the imperial harem in Mughal India marked the changing claims by the sultan to a differentiating divinity. A hegemonic withdrawal symbolized by the architecture of the harem building itself, the secreting of the women (and the sultan's power) allowed Hindu and Muslim ritual practices to coexist so that the two cultures could be connected, out of sight but joined within the most powerful center. This mixing of cultures, and the dominance of one over the other, took place behind the mystifying screens of the harem itself, as the hiddenness of gender became a suitable discourse for the occlusion of cultural conflict.

Part II, "Spain: *Conquista* and *Reconquista*," concerns the Iberian Peninsula and its global reach to the New World, with the Spanish conquests of Mexico and Peru. Before beginning a discussion of those outward conquests, however, it is necessary to understand the medieval prehistory of the Iberian Renaissance empires, especially with respect to the question of racial difference. David Nirenberg thus opens part II with a discussion of the medieval problem of the Jews: were they, in fact, a separate race, or were they simply a different religious ethnicity or caste? Deftly summarizing the modern question of race and racialization, Nirenberg works to conserve the term for use in the Middle Ages—however different its use might have been then—in order to understand the history of race and how, indeed, medieval people worked to "naturalize" their own histories of social conflict.

Further complicating the question of racial difference within the peninsula itself, in chapter 5, titled "The Spanish Race," Barbara Fuchs argues for an enduring fascination with Moorish culture in the construction of Spanish identity itself. So persistent was "maurophilia"—even in the face of the violent expulsions of the *reconquista*—that a hidden "Orient within" continuously reveals itself in multiple identifications of Spanish with specifically Moorish dress and cultural fashions. "Turkish" or Islamic turbans, for example, as Fuchs points out, were worn as part of Spanish national costumes, and the endurance of many other Muslim cultural styles (of eating, of interior decoration, etc.) enabled an "orientalizing" of Spain. Other emerging European nations could use the cultural persistence of Muslim "blackness" within Spain to ward off its looming imperial and cultural threat. The Black Legend could be used in Fuchs's careful formulation, then, "to stigmatize Spain, in Spain's own terms, by reinscribing the presence of the Moors as a racial taint." Northern Europe then was able, through time, to use the complicated persistence of Moorishness within Spanish self-identity to denigrate Spain as the black other of its northern European self.

Irene Silverblatt in chapter 6 demonstrates the power of racialized peninsular thinking as it was transformed by Spain's colonial experiences in the New World. In 1639 in Lima, Peru, two different individuals were burned at the stake: a wealthy merchant and a female mulatta slave. Both were accused of "unholy" relations with the native Andeans. In the case of the wealthy merchant, Perez, suspicion fell on him because he was a "New Christian," a Jewish convert. Silverblatt points out the typical paranoid blending of Judaic ritual and native practice in the inquisitorial mind when Perez was accused of engaging in Jewish rituals with tobacco and cola nuts. The case of the woman, burnt as a witch, pointed to fears among colonial administrators that women would "go native," adopting Indian dress, manners, and, ultimately, worship of Incan deities. The etiology of fear and blame created by colonial administrators in Peru used a racialized vision to confuse the differences among caste categories, religious practices, and nationalist sentiments.

By revisiting the many different printed versions of Pizarro's confrontation with the Inca emperor Atahualpa in the plaza of Cajamarca on November 16, 1532, Gonzalo Lamana in chapter 7 argues for the evolving—and contrasting—perspectives on the catastrophic moment from the point of

view of the Spanish conquistadors, of the Inca elite themselves, and of subsequent propagandistic deployments in the Anglophone world.

Taking as their focus the persistence of indigenous culture, particularly
in Mayan and Mexican contexts, SilverMoon and Michael Ennis argue in
chapter 8 that one assumption of the Black Legend—that the Spanish conquest utterly annihilated indigenous culture—is wrong and that the postconquest period can usefully be thought of as a moment when Mexican and
Mayan elites actively collaborated in the creation of postconquest Indian
cultures. Paying close attention to the process by which the famous Florentine Codex was created, SilverMoon and Ennis argue that its author relied
on a Nahua elite—leaders, informants, interpreters, and scholars—who collectively managed to tell their side of the story. The story was slanted toward
the interests of those who had been earlier conquered by the Aztecs and
who were, therefore, critical of them. SilverMoon and Ennis name the individual men who were educated at the famous school in Mexico City, who
commented from their own indigenous perspective and with cosmopolitan
sophistication on many global matters, including England's Protestant Reformation under Henry VIII. As SilverMoon and Ennis point out, "Nahua
culture survived [during the Renaissance] in forms exceeding the stereotype
of a provincial peasantry."

Using Raymond Williams' schematic formula for social change—of dominant, residual, and emergent cultural forms—Yolanda Fabiola Orquera argues in chapter 9 that it is possible to see three distinct periods of cultural development in Central and South America after the Spanish conquest. The
first period is of imperial peninsular consolidation out of the initial conflicts
articulated by the Sepulveda/Las Casas debates—Sepulveda's humanist-
based, protocapitalist, and modernizing understanding of the indigenous
American populations as profit-based labor power versus Las Casas's more
medieval sense of the people as fellow humans, capable of conversion, with
their own undeniable rights. After the ideology of domination was consolidated, a second phase occurred in which indigenous residual forms began to
play a part. Orquera locates the residue in the distinctive manner by which
indigenous peoples sought to interweave themselves into the fabric of the
dominant Spanish ideology, much as they had earlier handled ethnic conflict
and difference among themselves before the conquest. In this mode of appropriation, just as before the conquest when the victors in a war had "interwoven" the myths of the conquered into their own rituals, various indigenous writers created alphabetical texts that simultaneously deployed older
pictorial techniques to imagine real agency for the impoverished Indian subject. The final period of "emergence" goes beyond our period of the Renais-

sance, but, Orquera argues, the emergent forms of colonial and postcolonial expression owe much to the earlier "residual" attempts of interweaving indigenous cultural practices.

Kathryn Burns, in chapter 10, titled "Unfixing Race," examines the persistence of racism by focusing on the supposedly fixed categories of race as shifting markers whose evolution responds both to very local conditions and tensions and to far-flung imperial rivalries as well as to the drive to consolidate a Spanish absolutist state grounded on a militant and intolerant Christianity. Arriving in America fresh from the end of the reconquest of Granada, Columbus described the Indians by reference to Moors, and early modern Spanish dictionaries, as discussed above, defined "race" in terms of impurity of both breeding and religious faith. Yet the very terms shifted according to who used them and when and where they did so. Burns examines the use in colonial Peru of the words *creole, mestizo, mulato,* and *puka kunka* (red neck) from the perspective of the subjects wielding them rather than in relation to the human object whom they purportedly labeled.

To begin part III, "Dutch Designs," Carmen Nocentelli turns her attention in chapter 11 to the Portuguese trading empire in India to describe a Portuguese version of the Black Legend there. The creation, at least at first, of a Dutch traveler, Jan Huygen van Linschoten, in his *Itinerario* (1596), the Portuguese Black Legend concerned the marked decline in the Portuguese maritime empire due to the tendency of the colonists to go native, pushed to the brink of moral bankruptcy by "Oriental" influences and especially by the allure of native women. At first the Portuguese Crown had encouraged interethnic unions as a means for creating stable colonial societies, but toward the end of the sixteenth century such practices had become suspect, leading to an effeminization and degeneration of the colonial population, causing even *castiços,* or creole, native-born European children, to acquire a different skin color. Nocentelli notes that as a Protestant Dutchman, Linschoten unsurprisingly insists upon the need of all Europeans, not merely the Portuguese, to remain constantly vigilant in disciplining the self against the dangers of foreign seduction, a program Nocentelli finds most compellingly offered in the foreign techniques of Indian *sati* and Chinese foot binding, each of which Linschoten praises and which represent, she argues, "training procedures that supercede mere repression."

Patricia Gravatt in chapter 12 explores the work of another Dutchman, Theodore de Bry, whose majestic, multivolume folio printing of *America* became a major purveyor of images of the New World for Europeans. Published throughout the 1590s and into the first decade of the next century, de Bry's book has been generally assumed to be a major source of the Black

Legend, offering visual proof that Spain had profoundly abrogated its human responsibilities in the conquest of the Americas. Gravatt takes exception to this assumption and shows that, in fact, some of de Bry's pictorial representations owe their particular cruelty to exemplars drawn from the representations of civil conflict in France during the wars of religion. De Bry specifically cautions, "Let us not be too quick to condemn the Spaniards and let us first seriously examine ourselves, in order to see if we are truly better than they are."

Save its troubled conquest of Ireland, in the sixteenth century England had no overseas empire. Such a situation does not mean that it was not engaged with the European project of nation and global empire building, or that its concerns were less racial. Part IV's chapters devote themselves to the peculiarities of England's idiosyncratically belated and imaginary sixteenth-century empire.

In chapter 13, titled "West of Eden: American Gold, Spanish Greed, and the Discourses of English Imperialism," Edmund Campos argues for the complications inherent in England's belatedness in New World conquest and most particularly its envy of Spanish gold. Beginning with a discussion of Richard Eden's mid-sixteenth-century description of his alchemical creation of an island of silver, Campos traces England's envious emulation of Spain, with its fabulous gold and silver mining wealth. The problem for England was, according to Campos, how to emulate Spain's success without descending into the immorality of forced labor so infamously a part of the Black Legend. The most heinous cruelties were caused by Spain's mining for New World gold and silver. Campos shows how the dramatist Lyly places the problem of gold-mining wealth back into classical times with the tale of Midas, who lusts after the island of Lesbos (a cover for England). So too, Campos shows how Edmund Spenser reveals to Guyon the fountain of all the world's wealth by means of demonic mining activity. Spenser makes Guyon proof against the temptation, revealing the crucial English disdain for wealth gotten by forced labor. As Campos also points out, however, Guyon's "freelance" heroism also legitimates the piracy on the open seas whereby men like Francis Drake were authorized to relieve the Spanish galleons of their gold without also incurring the guilt of the labor that produced it. In such a way, England used the Black Legend of Spanish enslavement of local populations to differentiate and authenticate its own piratical imperial policies.

Like Campos's discussion of Eden's alchemical experiment, Linda Bradley Salamon in chapter 14 traces how Roger Ascham's completely imaginary construction of "The Turk" form his experiences at the Hapsburg court in Germany during a similar mid-sixteenth-century moment. Viewing the Ottomans through the lens of the Hapsburg court makes Ascham's sense of the Turk a completely imaginary enounter with a colonial other figured as an orientialized icon rather than an individual. While, as Salamon observes, all other contemporary rulers are specifically named, only Suleyman the Magnificent remains "The Turk." Salamon argues that Ascham's midcentury imaginings before any real contact between England and Istanbul anticipate the orientalizing figurations Edward Said analyzes in later colonial discourse. Salomon points out that the startling cruelty of anecdotes associated with feeding of human flesh to animals by the Turk retains a remarkable consistency that goes throughout the discourse of contact with America. Perhaps more surprisingly, "The Turk" is imagined to be a geopolitical other, not a religious other, perhaps (as Salamon suggests) because the more important religious differences for Ascham held between English Protestants and Hapsburg Spanish Catholics. Indeed, as she argues, the cruelty of the Turks is, in Ascham's text, sutured to the cruelty of the Spaniards and becomes a hallmark of the English version of the Black Legend in service of the increasingly violent war with Spain, during which Elizabeth made a temporary peace with the Ottoman empire.

In chapter 15, titled "Nations into Persons," Jeffrey Knapp explores the means by which Elizabethan writers characterized English national identity as "motley," that is, as a mixture of many other cultures, languages, and peoples. Rather than reaching out to imagine the conquest of other realms, Knapp argues that Lyly, Shakespeare, and Spenser reach back into history to remember when England was itself a conquered territory, first by Rome, then by the Danes, and of course by the Normans. So often tracing England's mythological origin from Troy, Elizabethan writers turn England into the quintessentially vanquished civilization. Insisting that such a tradition of loss allows for a powerful disintegration and intermixing, Knapp argues that Spenser in particular claims that no European nation is of pure blood. Shakespeare's Hal exemplifies such a personal character, which is, as he declares himself, to be "of all humors." The intermixed nation, then, is not figured as a multicultural social unit, but as a single person who embodies in himself or herself the complexity of the social formation. Hal as future monarch is a case in point: the complicatedly intermixed nature of a realm is not merely identified with the person of the monarch but is continually figured in Elizabethan literature by persons. Such persons (Britomart, Lyly's heroines, Richard II), by means of their often erotic self-alienation, can act as able carriers of the possibility of imperial inclusion. In such a way, Spenser can base his sense of England's imperial destiny in *A View of the Present State of Ireland* on the very inclusiveness of the flexibility of English personhood to which different nations, gathered into a peaceful empire, may aspire.

Everywhere in this history of racial difference, violent domination, and barbaric cruelty we see interstices of desire for peace and tolerance. Before we can ever get to a new world order that allows such a thing, we must understand the inordinate pressures that history places upon us. The Black Legend emerged as part of the racial organization of the world and contributed to founding the racial imperial difference within and outside Europe itself. Racism, we should remember, is not a question of skin color, blood proportions, or the shape of one's nose. Racism is a discursive classification of the chain of human beings, their distance from the ideal model.

In assembling the chapters in this book, we have by design used the term "Renaissance" rather than "early modern" to locate our study in time for two reasons. First, a number of the empires touched on in the following chapters — Aztec, Inca, Maya — did not survive as politically organized structures into the era that calls itself modern, although the lure of the mythical Aztec homeland, Aztlán' the emergence of Mayan organizations in Guatemala, and the present growth of indigenous political forces in the Andean region demonstrate their continuing power. Second, the notion of modernity itself imposes a teleological narrative that privileges the narrative about western European dominance. If we name the period with the word that calls up comparison with the classical past — Greek and Roman empires — we do not thereby banish Eurocentrism, but we are at least in a better position to see the construct of empire as a conceptually different form of social organization, specific to a local site and history and not in the service of current (postmodern) Anglophone world dominance and global capitalism. By using a term that privileges the past as a past, which understands its crucial informing pressure on the present, we have tried to resist (however successfully) the way modernity itself colonizes previous human experience, turning it into a primitive version of the present.

Imperum, which originally meant sovereignty, was the word used to name the Roman social organization. In other similar social organizations, the word referred to the head of the organization. Therefore, a better name for what is called the Inca empire would be "Incanate," as Inca was the name of the ruler; similarly, we should use "Sultanate" instead of Ottoman Empire and "Tzarate" instead of Russian Empire. We should recognize, nevertheless, that *imperum* became the name imposed by the affirmation and expansion of western European capitalist and Christian empires (primarily Spanish and English).

The Renaissance imposed a racial classification in which, as Las Casas stated, Christians served as the model and point of reference, and western Christianity (on its way to becoming Europe) as the self-legitimated locus of enunciation. There is no doubt that race and racism are social constructions. But the questions are, who constructed them, when, for whom, and why? We hope to have answered some of these questions in this introduction and in the chapters that follow. If we are to understand the possibilities for our global future, we need to apprehend the varieties of historical experience, each with their own very different pressures on myriad locales. China, Muslim and non-Muslim South Asia, Turkey, North and South America, England, and Europe are all in play at this new millennial moment. By looking back half a millennium, we may be better able to deal with where we are today.

PART I

TWO EMPIRES OF THE EAST

CHAPTER TWO

AN IMPERIAL CASTE
Inverted Racialization in the Architecture of Ottoman Sovereignty

Leslie Peirce

This chapter explores the self-fashioning of the Ottoman dynasty and the unusual pattern of recruitment employed in the construction of the Ottoman ruling class. The latter in particular—the creation of a governing caste made up of converted Christians—is one of first things the student of Ottoman history encounters. I revisit this aspect of Ottoman rule to see what it might tell us about attitudes toward conquered peoples and about the ways in which "difference" was defined and exploited. In the case of the Ottoman sultans, because they were not protonational rulers in the manner of a king of Spain, the construction of sovereignty vis-à-vis both subject peoples and rival polities was a trickier and possibly more critical matter.[1] On the other hand, their frontier geography and the long season of their empire building gave the Ottomans opportunity to draw selectively on the several imperial models at hand: Roman (Byzantine), Islamic, Persian, and Turco-Mongol. These traditions were combined in a new and energetic synthesis under the rubric of "Ottoman," a dynastic label derived from the name of the individual, Osman, recognized by historical tradition as the first leader of what was to become a ruling house of extreme longevity.

If racialization in the context of empire—a theme of this volume—means ascribing a nonmutable, culturally genetic profile to a group in order to marginalize it, then I am doubtful that concepts of race and racialization have meaning in the Ottoman context, at least until the territorial dissolution of the empire in the early twentieth century. The one exception, arguably, is the architecture of Ottoman sovereignty, that is, the shaping of the governing elite and the assumptions and rationales behind it. I use the term "inverted racialization" to suggest that the Ottomans created a kind of imperial ethnicity, a ruling caste comprising Christian slaves converted to Islam and trained in the arts of government. This "Ottoman" caste, conceived as a vast royal household headed by the sultan, had the purpose and effect not of marginalizing but of isolating and elevating the dynasty above its various subject peoples. Rule through an imperial caste was a phenomenon of Ottoman expansion; it gave way to less strict recruitment practices when, toward the end of the sixteenth century, the limits of expansion were realized. But by then the hegemony of the House of Osman, as the dynasty was termed, was so firmly established that it weathered challenges for another three hundred years.

A RULING CASTE

Let us begin with a brief sketch of this governing class, which began to evolve in the later fourteenth century, at a time when conquests in western Anatolia (Asia Minor) and the Balkans had turned Ottoman tribal chieftans into local rulers of some stature. It reached maturity under Mehmed II, whose conquest of Constantinople in 1453, the second year of his thirty-year reign, crowned the expanding Ottoman domains with an imperial capital. The import of this conquest was incalculable: Constantinople was the New Rome, capital of the eastern Roman empire (dubbed Byzantine only in the sixteenth century[2]), and the unattained object of Muslim ambition since the generation following the Prophet Muhammad. The flowering of the imperial slave caste went hand in hand with this achievement of empire. Mehmed used his victory to execute the grand vezir Halil Çandarli, scion of an aristocratic Muslim Turkish family that had monopolized the office for one hundred years. Çandarli had opposed the conquest.

The Ottoman governing class, including its famed Janissary infantry corps and the imperial cavalry, was made up of Christian recruits who were brought to the capital, converted to Islam, and trained to serve the sultan. The most promising male recruits received an extensive education within the imperial palace, where they constituted the personal retinue of the sultan. They were then "graduated" to take up the highest offices of the state as the pashas and the vezirs (the highest pasha rank) who commanded armies and navies, governed provinces, and made policy in the Council of State. These recruits were acquired in three ways: as prisoners of war, through purchase on the slave market, and through the systematic levy of Christian peasant subjects of the sultan.[3] This last — a kind of superrogatory tax on Christian subjects — has been taken as particularly emblematic of Ottomanism; it was also technically illegal.

Less well known than the recruitment of males is its female counterpart.[4] By the late fourteenth century, the consorts of the sultans were almost exclusively concubines of Christian origin. Like their male counterparts, these concubines were converted to Islam. The most promising received training within the palace to prepare them for their roles as mothers of Ottoman princes and princesses. Female recruits who were not among the chosen few to be groomed as concubines served the royal harem as managers, attendants, and servants or were married to male palace graduates. Female recruits were also acquired in three ways: captured in battle or in raids on their homes; purchased on the slave market; or given as gifts to the sultan, his sons, his sisters, or his mother.

To sum up, the reproduction of Ottoman political power depended on Christian converts—both biologically (producing new royal generations) and administratively (translating the sultan's military and executive authority to the provinces). Moreover, the dynastic household's reach was extended through satellite households established by married palace graduates, male and female. This model held true for most of the premodern period. It was not a static model, to be sure: the systematic levy on Christian peasants, for example, tapered off over the seventeenth century. Recruitment to imperial service continued, but more Muslims penetrated the echelons of administration.[5] And in the seventeenth century new frontiers—the Caucasus and southern Russia—brought recruits of different ethnic origins.

Nor were all top officials originally peasants, especially in the seventy-five years or so following the conquest of Constantinople. Balkan princes from Byzantine, Serbian, Bosnian, and Herzegovinian royal or noble houses entered the service of the sultans, some through capture, some voluntarily. A measure of the importance of these princely recruits is the fact that they served as grand vezirs for thirty-five of the sixty-three years from 1453 to 1517.[6] In a quirk of history, one of these vezirs was a nephew of Constantine XI Paleologus, the Byzantine emperor who went down with Constantinople. Had the empire not fallen, this childless emperor might have been succeeded by the scion of the Palaeologus line who went on to serve Mehmed II as Mesih Pasha.

The precise status of the Christian recruits, male and female alike, is the subject of some debate. They are generally viewed as slaves of the dynastic household, their weighty responsibilities a feature of the Islamic legal category of slaves licensed to act on their master's behalf.[7] However, the Ottoman term for them, *kul*, was ambiguous in its general connotation of "servant," and some scholars have begun to use this term instead of "slave," as the situation of the *kul* did not entirely conform to the treatment of slaves in Islamic jurisprudence.[8] The principal violation was in the levy of Christian peasant youth: forcibly conscripting Christian subjects and converting them to Islam violated the legal mandate of a Muslim sovereign to protect the religious autonomy of his non-Muslim subjects (*dhimmi*s, "protected ones," in the language of jurisprudence). This legal nicety does not seem to have bothered the Ottoman regime, which often violated Islamic strictures in the management of the royal household, although honoring them in the treatment of ordinary subjects.

Why such a ruling caste? The "slave institution" was an old and seasoned practice of Muslim states, originating with the famed Abbasid caliphate in the ninth century.[9] Its purpose was to create a loyal governing class wholly dependent on the sovereign for its status and honors, as opposed to a native nobility whose members might pose limits on the sovereign or, worse, aspire to his overthrow. It is not surprising that, under the Ottomans, the practice was initiated in the late fourteenth century, when they were struggling to assert primacy over other Turkish warrior lineages in the Balkans; indeed it may have been adopted from these lineages.[10] There were other reasons as well, both practical and symbolic. Practically, it was useful, especially in the decades following acquisition of Balkan territories, to have administrators familiar with the languages, religion, and customs of new subjects in a new frontier. Symbolically, the reduction of former princes and peasant boys to servants of the sultan, no matter how exalted their ultimate station, stood for the hegemony of the Ottoman regime.

HISTORICAL LEGACIES

The complex history of the centuries during which the Ottoman polity emerged and gradually expanded provides the context that gave rise both to the characteristic Ottoman inclusiveness toward the various peoples and territories that would make up the empire and to the unique structures of the dynastic household. The Ottoman empire was hardly the first polyglot[11] empire in the eastern Mediterranean, but it was notable for its devotion to keeping all of its pieces—all of its subject peoples—on the game board. I argue that the character of the Ottoman empire—its territorial limits, its ideological posturing through the sixteenth century, the management of its polyglot population—was strongly influenced by the legacy of past empires, especially Rome, in both its classical and then its Byzantine Christian incarnations. This focus in no way challenges the importance of other legacies the Ottomans adopted and adapted—the Persian, Turko-Mongolian, Anatolian, and of course Islamic. But the *longue durée* historical continuities in the eastern Mediterranean region have generally been overlooked.

The mature Ottoman empire was truly a Eurasian phenomenon, with its territories in the Balkans, Anatolia, the Aegean islands, greater Syria, Egypt, North Africa, the Crimea, and the Caucasus anchored around the arc of eastern Mediterranean shores and around the Black Sea. It is wrong to think of the empire as "Middle Eastern," a modern Eurocentric conception that is anachronistic when applied to the Ottoman domains except in their last decades. The Ottoman polity originated as an Aegean state, with one foot in western Anatolia and the other in the Balkans. It was from this territorial base, secured with the linchpin of Constantinople, that the sultans marched eastward, in the footsteps of Byzantine emperors, Roman emperors, and most famously of all, Alexander. It was only with the Congress of Berlin in 1878 and then the Balkan wars of 1912–1913 that this core foundation was irreparably fragmented, and with it the centuries-old understanding of what constituted the Ottoman empire.

The Ottomans were heir to eastern Mediterranean imperial legacies in concrete ways, most obviously in the limits to their territorial ambitions. Past empires taught lessons about the viable size for an eastern Mediterranean empire and the dangers of overreaching. The Ottomans never ventured to establish an overseas empire, nor did they seriously pursue Alexander's vision of uniting Persia (Iran) with an Aegean- or Mediterranean-based polity. The Ottomans exceeded the frontiers of the eastern Roman and Byzantine empires only in their conquests of Hungary, the western coast of Arabia (including Yemen), and Mesopotamia; Hungary and Yemen were the least permanent of major Ottoman possessions, and Mesopotamia remained something of a backwater in Ottoman times.[12] The dynasty did not waste resources in fruitless efforts to expand beyond this historically certified domain, so to speak. That this was a conscious decision is suggested in a legend recounted by the seventeenth-century traveler Evliya Çelebi: two priests, a Spaniard and a Portuguese, announce to Bayezid II (r. 1481–1512) that they have discovered a rich New World; when they offer it to him, he replies, "Mecca and Medina and this Old World are enough to conquer, we don't need to cross the ocean and go tremendous distances."[13] The enduring geopolitical reality of the Ottoman empire was as a revived eastern Roman empire, with the addition of the Prophet Muhammad's Arabia.

The continuities are striking. The Ottomans fought many of the same battles that the Byzantines and their predecessors had, protecting roughly the same borders against the same territorial enemies. In the east, ancient Greeks, Romans, early Byzantines, and Ottomans alike confronted various Persian empires and their powerful institutions of kingship. The rhetoric of rivalry was also striking in its continuity: from an Aegean perspective, just as the "freedom" of the ancient Greeks was pitted against Persian "royal decadence," so in the sixteenth century the Sunni Islamic "rectitude" of the Ottomans was pitted against the "moral corruption" of Safavid Iran's Shiite "heretics."

As the new caesars of the eastern Mediterranean, the Ottomans also took up the mantle of rivalry with the west. As in the east, here also the geography of rivalry remained fairly constant (the boundary roughly the Adriatic Sea) while identities shifted over time: Greece/Rome, eastern Rome/western Rome, Orthodox church/Latin church, and so on. Relations between east and west were severely damaged by the Latin occupation of Constantinople in 1204 (the Fourth Crusade) — an occupation that lasted until 1261. The west continued to assemble "crusades" through the sixteenth century, and the Ottomans parried with "holy war" (although the popular term was not *jihad* but rather *ghaza*, "border raids"). Religious rhetoric was probably addressed more to internal audiences, while "caesarism" was a language of competition among dynasties. But the intertwining of the two discourses — religion and territorial might — is eminently visible in the lavish posturing of Charles V and Suleyman, rival "Roman" emperors, in the 1530s and 1540s.[14]

It is important to recognize that the Ottoman encounter with western Europe was conditioned by territorial rivalries of ancient vintage. It was not motivated merely by Islamic holy war, just as western assaults on the Ottomans were not driven merely by Christian crusade. In any event, the confrontation lost much of its propagandistic steam by the later sixteenth century, in part a result of the demise of universalist posturing by Mediterranean rulers. One-upsmanship had characterized the rivalry between the Ottomans and Hapsburgs earlier in the century: if Charles' elaborate investiture in 1530 as Holy Roman Emperor compelled Suleyman to react with his own staging of imperial glory, the sultan appeared to gain the upper hand in 1547 when Charles and his brother the Archduke Ferdinand sued for peace — Charles was demoted to "the king of Spain" in the language of the treaty and Ferdinand humiliated by the imposition of an annual tribute to the sultan for the remnant of Hungary he managed to hold. Suleyman now had greater license to style himself the sole Roman emperor, a pretention that perhaps inspired the plans for the great mosque whose first stone the sultan laid in 1550 — it was modeled on Haghia Sophia, the great church built by Justinian, whose status as "emperor of the Orient and the Occident" had waited a millenium, in Ottoman eyes, to be matched.[15] But the end of the century saw the contest end in a draw. During the 1606 treaty negotiations ending a long and enervating war between the Ottomans and the Hapsburgs, Ahmed I would not concede the title "caesar," but the Ottomans now had to recognize their imperial rivals as equals: the treaty hailed the Holy Roman Emperor Rudolph as "emperor" (if not holy or Roman).[16]

The Ottomans were arguably better defenders of the eastern Roman legacy than the Byzantines had been. This was mainly because they assembled and maintained a larger territorial domain, which in turn yielded more resources and greater defensive capability. Selim I's conquest of Syria and Eygpt in 1516–1517 meant that the eastern Mediterranean was united for the first time since the 630s, when Muslim armies took Syria and Egypt from the Byzantines. Moreover, the Ottomans were bigger players in European politics, as a result of the enlarged world of early modern times and the complex religious and territorial rivalries in Europe. Notable was the periodic liaison between France and the Ottoman empire, which was useful in hedging the power of Spain and the Austrian Hapsburgs. But perhaps the most significant component of Ottoman success was the dynasty's talent in exploiting the talents of its subject peoples, who, in the realm of international relations, contributed to diplomacy, global finance, and the acquisition of new technologies. Why this was so is a legacy of the eastern Mediterranean world of late medieval times.

THE ROOTS OF OTTOMAN POLYGLOTISM

In the early fourteenth century, it was no doubt unexpected that the founders of a small inland principality in northwestern Anatolia would come to be "masters of the two continents [Eurasia] and the two seas [Mediterranean and Black], the shadow of God over the orient and the occident," as Suleyman was hailed by his grand vezir Ibrahim Pasha in a letter to Charles V.[17] The Ottoman polity arose in the context of late Byzantine fragmentation and the extraordinarily fluid politics it generated in the eastern Mediterranean of the thirteenth, fourteenth, and fifteenth centuries. Competing for economic and political control were several Byzantine Greek principalities, Serbs, Bulgarians, Genoese and Venetian trading colonies, Turks, and various lesser players, many of whom disappeared over the course of the fourteenth century, including Mongols, Norman remnants, and the *Tourkopouloi* ("sons of Turks"), a Christianized Byzantine cavalry corps (some of whom were to join Catalan mercenaries in betrayal of the emperor[18]).

At first a bit player in this contest for eastern Mediterranean dominion, the Ottomans were the newcomers, with no ancestral claim to any piece of this landscape. Indeed, the most persistent of their legends of origin emphasized their outsiderness as new tribal migrants from central Asia. Turks had begun to appear in the eastern Mediterranean in the late eleventh century after a resounding Byzantine defeat in eastern Anatolia at the hands of the Seljuk sultans, at the time the rulers of the most powerful (if unstable) empire in the Islamic Middle East. While the new Seljuk state established in Anatolia adopted Persian courtly culture, many of its subjects were Turkmen, that is, Turkish-speaking tribal groups who traced their lineage back to central

Asian Turkestan. Demographic and political upheaval reccurred in Anatolia
when new waves of Turkmen (and some Persians) fled the Mongol advance
of the 1250s. Several tribal chieftains (presumably including Osman's ancestors) proceeded to exploit the vacuum left by the Byzantine return in 1261
to Constantinople from their refuge in western Anatolia. By 1331 the famous
Moroccan traveler Ibn Battuta could comment that Osman's son Orhan was
"the greatest of the kings of the Turkmens and the richest in wealth, lands,
and military forces."[19] These local "kings" (*beys* in Turkish) profited in the
form of slaves and booty from alliances with various Byzantine contenders
for the emperorship. Ottoman mercenaries did not come cheap: Orhan's marriage in 1346 to Theodora, daughter of the usurper John VI Kantakuzenos,
sealed the alliance that brought the first Ottoman soldiers to Europe. But
still only *primus inter pares*, the Ottomans would eliminate the last Anatolian
Turkmen principality only in the 1520s.

We should not be fooled by the westward vector of celebratory origin
mythologies (Osman's ancestors may or may not have been recent immigrants, although many of their followers no doubt were). The early Ottomans
received their political tutelage and acquired mastery in an Aegean environment evolved during two centuries of cultural familiarity, tension, and fusion
among Turks, Greeks, and others.[20] Contact took many forms. Trade among
Aegean players persisted despite official bans and military conflict.[21] At the
level of royalty, wives were exchanged between courts, as were political hos-
tages (to say nothing of mercenaries). Hybrid religious culture manifested itself in a number of ways—from the shrines dotting Anatolia, where St. George
was translated into the Muslim prophetic figure Khidr, to village families
whose uncertain religious identity was reflected in the mix of names they
carried, Muslim ones alongside others drawn from the calendar of Christian
saints.[22] Late Byzantine icons represented the saints Sergios and Bakchos,
Roman soldiers martyred for their Christian faith, as *Tourkopouloi*.[23] All this
is unsurprising because Anatolia was historically a great crossroads of soldiers, traders, artisans, and scholars and thus a melting pot of cultures.

The point here is that we can speak of an *eastern Mediterranean pluralism*
that emerged during the long season of Byzantine disintegration and embodied itself as a regional politics acknowledging (if tacitly) the legitimacy of
multiple players—including, by 1350 or so, the leading Turkish principalities. Muslim identity certainly mattered (the Church anathematized Islam,
although it rationalized the presence of Muslims on Byzantine soil).[24] But
the historic tension between the Latin and Orthodox churches mitigated any
systematic vilification or "racialization" of Turks, whose religious proclivities
in this period were in any case less than rigorously orthodox.

What implications does this early history have for the mature Ottoman empire's attitudes and policies toward those Balkan nations that, one by one, would become subject peoples over the course of the fifteenth century? Eastern Mediterranean pluralism meant that the Balkan states, as well as long-standing "Frankish" trading colonies, were too numerous, too diverse, and too solidly in place historically and culturally to permit their reduction to a status of racial or cultural inferiority (except in hierarchy with the new imperial culture). If nothing else, the Ottomans had as warning the long and unsuccessful struggle of the Byzantine emperors to tame these same groups. It might be thought that the polyglotism of the Ottomans was inescapable, given Islamic policy on the treatment of non-Muslims in a Muslim-ruled state, but like numerous Muslim sovereigns before them, the Ottomans violated the rules "protecting" *dhimmis* when it suited them. More than ideologically or legally, the Ottomans were *pragmatically* motivated to recognize, and then exploit, the multiple populations under their rule. Perhaps they had no other choice. They could hardly ignore the sheer numbers of Christians in the Balkan half of the Ottoman heartland (indeed, the burgeoning empire was predominantly Christian until the conquests in 1514 and 1516–1517 of eastern Anatolia, greater Syria, and Egypt). Perhaps another caution against attempting to subordinate or erase historic identities was the futility of the Byzantines' periodic efforts to force conversion on Jewish subjects. The Ottomans did offer incentives for individual conversion, to the point that they sometimes undermined *dhimmi* expectations of religious independence, but they never directly took on the millenium-old cultural hegemony of the Church—in fact, they benefited from exercising authority over Christian subjects through their patriarchs (as they did Jewish communities through the rabbis). In short, rather than weaken or erase local cultural sovereignties, the Ottomans sought to exploit them.

LAYERED IDENTITIES

These realities determined Ottoman self-definition. Until the conquest of Constantinople—that is, during a formative period of one hundred fifty years—the Ottoman presence in the eastern Mediterranean, however strong militarily and tactically, was weak ideologically. The Ottomans could assert no historic claim that might justify hegemony over other regional players. On the other hand, this very absence of legitimation through overlordship of a nation, founded either on a people or a territory, gave them a free hand to create a kaleidescope of royal imagery and propaganda.

The Ottomans played dynastic identity against territorial identity. The vocabulary of imperial titulature was primarily eastern, a layered language that invoked the shahs of ancient Persia, the caliphs and sultans of the Islamic past, and the khans of central Asia. In contrast, the Ottoman heartland was a Roman landscape: the capital in official parlance was the Arabized "Kostantiniyya" ("Istanbul" remained the popular name for the city, as it was in Byzantine times). The widely used term "Rum" had a range of contemporary meanings, primarily "Rome" (the empire, classical and Byzantine) but also "Anatolia" (a key component of the empire); the Ottoman term for the core Balkan region was "Rumeli" (land of Romans); and the adjective *Rumî* could mean "Roman," "imperial," or "Anatolian."[25] This interleafing of dynastic and territorial identities made the point that the Roman empire of the Ottomans, like its European counterpart, was holy—it was, finally, Muslim. Mehmed II's first act after taking the city in 1453 was to convert the nine hundred–year-old cathedral of Haghia Sophia to the premier mosque of the capital.

This ideological opportunism was a key element in the extraordinary longevity of the Ottoman dynastic regime, one of the longest lived in history. Ottoman rulers governed for roughly six hundred years in a succession of thirty-seven generations, disrupted by forced depositions and even regicide, but never broken. Loyalty to the dynastic house was tenacious: the Byzantine diplomat and historian Doukas, who observed the Ottomans at close quarters in the first half of the fifteenth century, commented that "a subject easily transfers his allegiance from one ruler to another so long as both the old and the new sovereign [are] descended from the line of Othman."[26]

At this point, it may be useful to comment on the Ottoman dynasty's Turkishness. It is appropriate for the fourteenth century to think of the Ottomans as Turks or, more accurately, as one of several Turkish-speaking lordly lineages in western Anatolia. But once the empire was established, the dynastic family did not present itself as Turkish. Europe may have called the sultan "the Grand Turk," but to the sultan, an *Ottoman*, Turks were now just one more group in the subject population. Mehmed II's Book of Laws echoed the age-old urban bias of the eastern Mediterranean by distinguishing between city dwellers and "Turks," unsophisticated rural folk. Turkishness did become a featured component of Ottoman identity in the later fifteenth century, but the aim here was to challenge rival states to the east claiming hegemony on the basis of descent from great Turkic or Mongol khans. Like the language of caesarism, this Turkishness was a discourse of power among rulers, a story of noble descent and not a populist ideology to consolidate a subject population. The point always was to fabricate a wholly new dispensation justified by a new incarnation of eastern Mediterranean imperial traditions. The sultans were Ottomans (rulers), not Turks (subjects).

The most common phrase that the Ottoman sultans came to use in describing their empire was *memalik-i mahruse*, "the well-protected domains" (protected by God first but also by the dynasty). This label emphasized the plurality of domains, not their unity or their "Ottomanness." When the sultan wished to proclaim his own legitimacy, most volubly expressed to other rulers, he announced his several imperial titles and then enumerated the kingdoms, principalities, and ancient metropolises subsumed under his dominion.[27] The point was that in acquiring all these lands, the sultans defeated ruling houses, not peoples. This view of what empire meant is reflected in one of the titles used by the sultans—the Persian *shehinshah*, king of kings. Had the Ottomans gone to the New World, they would have had to valorize Inca and Aztec rulership in order for the conquest of these kingdoms to count. Surely one reason they did not build an overseas empire was that remote kingdoms had no historical resonance in the Eurasian geography of their "old" world.

A CHEMISTRY OF DIFFERENCE

The notion that the Ottoman dynastic household was not "of" any people that it ruled but rather reigned over many former kingdoms is key to the structures of Ottoman sovereignty. This aloofness freed the dynasty to design an administration best suited to accomplishing its two key goals: perpetuating the dominance of the lineage of Osman and controlling the collection of former principalities. Management of a polyglot empire went hand in hand with a carefully constructed ruling elite.

The eclectic set of ruling-class mores and tastes that made up Ottoman identity was clearly posed as the superior social and cultural model in the empire and one that all subjects had to acknowledge with respect, at least tacitly. But it was imposed only on members of the ruling caste. The Ottoman regime in early modern times was rarely persecutorial (with the exception of schismatic Turkmen groups who supported the Iranian shahs). On the contrary, it was happy to let existing groups and cultures remain in place. Indeed, the dynasty exploited the wide spectrum of talent under its command: local specializations; multiple forms of artisanal, commercial, and fiscal expertise; varieties of religious and secular learning; and regional merchant networks each linked to a different global economic zone. The empire was a huge crazy quilt of cultures stitched together by Ottoman networks of integration and control.

Ottoman practice was basically to allow no group to assert hegemony over another, unless it suited the interests of the sultanate to arrogate extraordinary status to a particular group, for example, Genoese tax farmers in the fifteenth century, Jewish financiers of Iberian origin in the sixteenth, Muslim preachers in the seventeenth, and Phanariot Greek diplomats in the eighteenth. This is not to say that the empire was a harmonions "garden" of peoples, to use a favorite Ottoman trope. It experienced all the ethnic and religious stereotypes and intercommunal tensions that go with a polyglot polity. Subjects of the empire had no trouble using racializing epithets to distinguish themselves from others of different religion, ethnicity, lifestyle, and so on. Balkan Christians referred to Muslims as "Hagarenes," descendants of Abraham's slave woman Hagar and her son Ishmael—in other words, a race of slaves. Muslims simply called Christians *kafir*, "infidels." Greeks disdained Bulgarians and vice versa; Istanbulites disdained Cairenes; urban Muslims disdained tribal Turkmen, Kurds, and Beduins; Sunni Ottomans denigrated Persian Shiites as shifty, dissolute heretics. Rather than enforcing a regime of surveillance and repression, the Ottomans chose to govern by playing groups against each other. When intercommunal violence erupted, peace was generally negotiated or imposed by the state: the dynasty and its household of servant officials, the army of judges, and even local Christian and Jewish authorities.

In sum, the dynasty can be said to have fostered a chemistry of difference that generated competition for its goodwill and thus nurtured dependence on the imperial center. And so the sultans were able to strike a pose of neutrality toward their polyglot population, except for a generic privileging of Muslims over non-Muslims. This style of governance worked reasonably well, at least from the dynasty's point of view, until the nineteenth century. One solution to the burgeoning ideologies of nationalism and religious equality was to invite everyone to think of himself as Ottoman—in other words, to offer citizenship in what had been an exclusive imperial identity. But it was too late to ask people to think outside the box of polyglotism. The multiethnic empires of Europe and Asia—Ottoman, Hapsburg, Romanov, and Qing—were over by 1920.

SERVANT AND SULTAN

Through the sixteenth century, the principal mechanism of Ottoman absolutism was the exercise of executive authority by *kul* stationed around the empire. To be sure, the *kul* establishment was not the only arm of imperial government, although it was the first to be molded into an instrument of administration: existing judicial and bureaucratic cadres were not organized under the dynasty's control until the mid-sixteenth century. This sequence reflects the evolving orientations of the sultanate, first to a long period of expansion and consolidation, then to administration of a settled empire. What the presence of the *kul* accomplished, both publicly and within the palace, was to isolate and insulate the sultanate, enabling it to govern without favoring any one of its subject peoples as accomplices. As generals and admirals, elite *kul* were the bodyguards of the empire. As governors of provinces, their command of police powers reminded faraway subjects that the sultan provided local peace but also demanded obedience.

Who were these servants of the sultans, and what was it about the dynasty's interpretation of the classic slave institution that contributed to Ottoman longevity? Two points, noted earlier, demand comment: first, the number of recruits, especially those populating the highest offices, who were subjects of the empire, and second, its corollary, the systematic nature of Ottoman recruitment. Earlier Muslim states typically sought slaves outside their borders. In the closest models in space and time, the Anatolian Seljuks recruited from beyond their frontiers in Trebizond, Cilicia, the Caucasus, and the Crimea,[28] while the Mamluk state in Egypt took Qipchak Turks and Circassians from the Caucasus region. Nor was the use of outsiders unfamiliar to Roman and Byzantine rule: "barbarian" generals frequently commanded armies.[29] Another early influence was the practice of exogamy prevalent among Turkish and Mongol tribes: raiding parties provided wives of different tribal or ethnic origin, and builders of tribal confederations, most famously the Mongols, deployed the talents of conquered elites to administer their domains. Ottoman comfort with foreign servants thus had many precedents. On the other hand, pragmatic reasons for systematizing recruitment abounded, beginning with the early sultans' need to secure a solid share of the flood of Byzantine war captives before their rivals and followers appropriated the lot. Later, the very success of Ottoman expansion in the Balkans threatened a shortage of foreign manpower. The levy imposed on Christian subjects ensured a steady supply of recruits (the Mamluks had suffered when blocked trade routes diminished the flow of new recruits). Moreover, as noted earlier, the levy provided the sultans with "expert knowledge" of newly conquered regions. In sum, the *kul* system grew up as a mechanism for mastery over newly acquired territories, particularly in the Balkans. Mastery meant control both of new subjects and of rival Turkish *beys*.

The logic of the *kul* system is further revealed by the geography of *kul* origins, particularly of high-ranking officials. Through the sixteenth century, recruits came overwhelmingly from the Balkan region, especially its western half (today's Albania, Bosnia, Serbia, and Croatia, to a lesser extent Greece, Macedonia, and Bulgaria). What stands out here is that recruits were not drawn from all around the empire, but only from areas that fell along either side of the advancing Ottoman frontier. In contrast, the sultans did not recruit Christians who had long been subject to Muslim rule in greater Syria, Egypt, and, for the most part, Anatolia; there, they dutifully protected their non-Muslim subjects. In the seventeenth century, *kul* officials began to appear in more than occasional numbers from the Caucasus, Ukraine, and southern Russia, that is, from the territorial ring around the northern half of the Black Sea. Recruitment of "eastern" *kul* reflected both the dwindling supply of war prisoners from the Balkans and a new focus of military action in the Caucasus (which brought the empire to its greatest territorial extent around 1590). The novelty of this shift was reflected in the fact that the origins of vezirs from these areas were broadcast in their names, for example, "So-and-so Pasha the Georgian/Circassian/Abkhasian/Armenian." By midcentury, two rival *kul* blocks had emerged, the "westerners," primarily Albanian and Bosnian, and the "easterners."[30] But it is noteworthy that the interlude of "Black Sea" grand vezirs was terminated with the assignment in 1656 of extraordinary power to Köprülü Mehmed Pasha, a "westerner" of Albanian origin whose own sons and household scions controlled the office for the rest of the century.

But there is more to the story of the Ottoman *kul* than can be told by this multiplicity of factors, tactical and legal. It is hard not to see in the Ottoman practice of elite slavery a means of "bottling," even in a diluted form, the energizing mix of persons and cultures that fueled early expansion. It is well known that the first Ottoman leaders collaborated with Greek sympathizers and opportunists, no doubt necessarily. Indeed, the heroic roles in Ottoman expansion of local Greek Christian lords—for example, Mikhal "the beardless"—were celebrated in early Ottoman chronicles. The *kul* system in a sense institutionalized this collaboration. In a parallel fashion, the fluid religiosity of early times was preserved through the adoption of the heterodox Bektashi sufi order, famously friendly to Christians, as the patron order of the Janissaries, the formidable Ottoman infantry made up of Christian recruits. That Bektashi heterodoxy was later toned down only highlights its earlier syncretic function.[31]

Collaboration was clearly the work of a frontier society, incubated during two centuries of neighborly competition and cooperation preceding the Ottomans' emergence onto the stage of history. That the region had long been preoccupied with frontier hybridity is demonstrated in the eleventh-century Byzantine epic poem *Digenes Acritas*, which recounts the exploits of the "two-blooded" son of an Arab emir and a Byzantine noble woman (the emir converted to Christianity). Although Digenes defended the Byzantine emperor with devotion, he refused to leave his station on the Euphrates, so the em-

peror came to him. The Ottomans staked much of their identity on this notion that dynamism, both military and cultural, is found on the frontier, hence
their popular reputation as *ghazi*s, frontier fighters for Islam. But the early
intimacy of cultural fusion and tension was threatened after 1453, when
frontier eclecticism inevitably gave way to protocols of imperial governance
and the legal architecture of Islam. Moreover, there was the constant danger
that others might claim the frontier, not only rival warlords but also chal-
lengers within the dynastic family. What the *kul* system did was enable the
sultans to adopt rituals of imperial removal and yet sustain the heady energy
of frontier fusion. The seventeenth-century prominence of Caucasian *kul*
surely had something to do with that region's emergence as a new frontier
(with a revitalized Iran), whereas the European frontier was now one of un-
ending desultory conflict.

The *kul* did more than help the sultans expand the empire and defend its
borders. They were also pivotal in the formation and dissemination of the
new imperial culture. The message of royal benevolence was broadcast
through their monopoly of patronage outside the capital: to them belonged
the prerogative of commissioning the major mosques, colleges, baths, cara-
vansarays, and soup kitchens that populate every major Ottoman city. Royal
mothers were prominent in this endeavor, especially in cities with a religious
prominence. Civic philanthropy had another function, of course. The aniconic
nature of Islamic representations of authority meant that urban centers lacked
statues of the monarch; nor were marketplaces alive with sovereign images,
as coins carried only inscriptions. Rather, the imperial signature was written
most prominently in the reconfiguration of urban skylines, most spectacu-
larly in the capital.[32] An esthetic canon was developed for the exclusive use
of the ruling class in the decorative programs of the monuments they constructed.[33] Not surprisingly, this metropolitan style was commonly known as
Rumî, or "Roman," a term that by the sixteenth century must have conveyed
a weighty sense of an imperial Ottoman identity that subsumed the grand
history of the region.[34] The collaboration of servant and sultan in building an
imperial culture also took the form of literary patronage, and aspiring poets
and chroniclers dedicated their works to pashas as well as to princes and sultans. Of the four leading centers of literary patronage in Mehmed II's time,
one was the circle around Mahmud Pasha, the celebrated grand vezir from
the Byzanto-Serbian noble house of Angelovič; the others were the courts of
the sultan and two of his sons.[35]

The potential exuberance of the imperial master-slave collaboration can be
sensed acutely in the staging of Suleyman's "magnificence" by the sultan and
Ibrahim Pasha, his intimate and grand vezir, a Greek from Parga in Epirus

who was well versed in both ancient history and current rivalries among European monarchs.[36] Yet in 1536, at the moment of the pasha's greatest
power—following his masterminding of a huge military campaign against
Iran that captured Baghdad—the sultan abruptly ordered his execution by
strangling. Ibrahim was not the first celebrated grand vezir done away with
by his creator, for Mehmed II executed Mahmud Pasha after twenty years
of service. Gianmaria Angiolello, an Italian serving one of Mehmed's sons,
thought it was fear of Mahmud's influence among the army: "The reason
why the Grand Turk executed Mahmud Pasha was jealousy, more than anything else."[37]

The relationship of sultan and servant was fraught with ambiguity and,
for the male *kul*, with obvious danger. Through most of the sixteenth century,
pashas and vezirs could pass on to their offspring neither their offices nor
their wealth, for an intrinsic feature of the *kul* system was the constant influx
of new recruits to serve new sultans. The stature of the *kul* was merely on loan
from the sultan, although their household establishments could be grand
(Ibrahim allegedly had 1,700 slaves of his own). The contingent nature of
sultanic largesse was publicly demonstrated in the confiscations of the *kul*'s
possessions that often followed their dismissal from office or, more dramatically, their execution.

There was some compensation for these deprivations. Powerful officials
garnered enormous prestige, so much so that their activities were carefully
tracked by European ambassadors. Codes of ritual permeated relations between the sultan and his slave recruits. Indeed, so compelling was the dynamic of honor that Suleyman's fourth-ranked vezir, the Bosnian Hüsrev
Pasha, starved himself to death from shame when the sultan dismissed him.[38]
This sense of a special relationship trickled down to the rank-and-file military: in 1622, on the occasion of the first regicide, the English ambassador
Sir Thomas Roe noted that the rebels "first tooke a generall oath, not to sack
the imperiall throne, which they call their house and their honor."[39]

Although in theory *kul* were "reborn" to a new identity and new loyalty,
their origins were not erased. Ottoman biographical dictionaries typically give
the origin, then the service career, and finally the good works of pashas and
vezirs. Indeed, this advertisement of *kul* origins valorized a self-consciously
polyglot ruling household, united under the banner of Ottomanism. Sokollu
Mehmet Pasha, one of the most powerful grand vezirs, was known by his Serbian patronymic Sokolović, "from the town of Sokol," or Sokollu in Turkish.
The pasha exemplified the benefit that the dynasty derived from the *kul*'s
ability to mediate two identities: Sokollu Mehmed set up numerous charitable foundations in his Bosnian homeland and is also thought to have been in-

strumental in the reestablishment in 1557 of the Patriarchate of Peć, to which office his nephew (in some sources, his brother) was assigned. Other members of Mehmet Pasha's family, including his father, converted to Islam and found high office in the service of the Ottomans (an early but telling instance of *kul* family establishments).[40] Similarly, the queen mother Nurbanu's contacts with her native Venice and with the French regent Catherine de Médicis helped maintain relations with powers whom the sultan was not himself currently cultivating.[41]

THE FEMALE *KUL* AND THE POLITICS OF REPRODUCTION

There is still a major question waiting to be answered. What does all this have to do with the nexus of empire building and racialization? It is when we turn to the female *kul* that we must ask questions about racialized differentiation as a mechanism of imperial control. Were we to confine our inquiry to male *kul*, we could explain the slave system as an essentially political phenomenon whose principal aims were to free up rulers from their natural competitors, subordinate the conquered, exploit their local knowledge, and propagate a new imperial culture. It is the politics of biological reproduction, both in the dynastic family itself and in the slave cohorts of the imperial household, that wants a vocabulary to name the reproduction of dynastic power.

The gendered structures of the imperial household make clear that the deployment of female recruits was central to imperial control. Dynastic reproduction was founded on the practice of concubinage. By the early fifteenth century, if not earlier, the mothers of royal children were *kul* recruits, Christian born and mostly (to judge from the spotty evidence) from the Euro-Asian fringes of the empire. The Ottomans would seem to be the only Muslim dynasty to confine reproduction to concubine consorts rather than legal wives, a phenomenon that underscores the unrelenting attention they paid to the architecture of their sovereignty. There is little that is doctrinally Islamic in this practice except its permissibility: a male enjoyed licensed sexual use of his female slaves and, unlike Roman law, his children with a slave concubine were considered freeborn. Even when the sultans made diplomatic marriages with foreign princesses, as they did until the conquest of Constantinople, these marriages appear to have been intentionally sterile. According to the Byzantine statesman George Sphrantzes, one of the concerns in a proposed marriage alliance between the Serbian princess Mara and the (last) Byzantine emperor Constantine XI was that Mara had already been married: she was the widow of Sultan Murad II (r. 1421–1451). This was no problem, Sphrantzes contended, because "she, it is generally believed, did not sleep with [the sultan]."[42]

If one definition of race is a group of people related by common descent, then the sultans created a purely patriarchal Ottoman lineage through the erasure of their consorts' origins. However, these women did not lack stature, at least those who rose to the top. Rather, their considerable wealth and political power stemmed from their "retroactive" membership in the House of Osman as royal mothers. From the dynasty's point of view, it was safer to share power with a concubine than with a princess-wife who carried another state's or another noble's power in her train. It is this retroactive lineage that accounts for the relative obscurity of female *kul* origins, and also sometime of their identities, as they were publicly named as mother of a particular prince or princess. The seal of Hüsnüşah, one of Bayezid II's consorts, identified her as the "Mother of Sultan Şehinşah"; it was with this seal that she signed the letter she wrote to inform the sultan of his son's death in 1511.

That the dynasty was engaged in propagating a unique imperial ethnicity becomes more arguable when we turn to the marriages that it routinely contracted between male and female palace servants. Through ties of clientage with these now-manumitted former slaves, the royal household spawned a whole ruling class whose social and educational practices replicated those of the imperial establishment. This elite was far larger than anyone has thought to calculate. It is easy to assume that the aim of these marriages was to provide wives for public figures. This is certainly true, since *kul* were to avoid outside allegiances that might erode their dependence on the sultan. But an additional dynamic was at work, namely, that men were marrying in, that is, husbands were being provided for women. Take, for example, the marriage made for a minor vezir of Suleyman, Pilak Mustafa Pasha: as the historian Peçevi tells it, "after he rose to the rank of governor-general, he was married to a lady named Shahhuban, one of the slave women of the imperial harem, and because of this he was graced with the vezirate."[43] The dynamic of marrying men in is even more visible in the marriages arranged for Ottoman princesses, who from the late fifteenth century on had vezirs as husbands (Ibrahim was married to Suleyman's sister and Sokollu Mehmed to his granddaughter Ismihan). These male consorts were formally known as *Damad*, Son-in-law. Initiated by strong sultans, royal damadship was clearly one more bond that restrained while it honored. But it also became a manipulable tool as the dynamics of power sharing in the dynastic household grew more complex: there was now the potential for an alliance among *damad*, princess-wife, and the latter's mother.[44]

With sultans and their sons reproducing with female recruits, and royal women with male recruits, the dynasty was reproductively self-sufficient. Practicing a kind of household endogamy, it ran few of the risks that European monarchical marriages entailed. I suspect the Ottomans must have been dumbfounded at the way in which whole countries could be gained or lost through the marriage of a single prince or princess. From their point of view, Charles V's "crushing inheritance"[45] was bound to fragment, as it did in 1556 into its Spanish and Austrian halves, for it lacked the kind of organic unity that the Ottomans themselves had painstakingly attended to in the two centuries it took to assemble their own empire. On the other hand, the concentration of so much power in the Ottoman household was increasingly beset by its own inherent risks.

In contemplating the vocabulary of caste, race, and ethncity in relation to Ottoman politics of reproduction, I find myself veering scarily close to the views of H. A. Gibbons, who argued in 1916 that the creative spirit in the Ottoman enterprise was not "Asian" (Turkish) but rather "European," by virtue of the presence of former Byzantine Greeks in the new "race" generated by the Ottomans.[46] Ottoman politics of reproduction may at first glance seem a subordination of Turkish lineage to Balkan blood, as if a new Roman ruler had to be "of" the subject peoples in order to rule them. But the semiotics of domination were too ritualized not to send an unmistakable message of sultanic supremacy, at least to an Ottoman audience.

Perhaps the most explicit staging of dominance was the sultan's control of the sexuality of both his male and female servants. The use of *kul* as both female and male consorts enabled the dynasty to craft a parthogenetic form of royal authority. The symbolism of the sultan's virility as a marker of sovereign authority was rife. The spatial dynamics within the imperial palace built by Mehmed II (the Topkapi Palace) communicated his sexual dominance: he was the only person who carried his male identity intact across the threshold of the inner quarters. The eunuch guards of the inner palace were physically degendered. The recruits in training were reduced to an arrested state of manhood and symbolic, if not actual, sexual passiveness: they were confined to their quarters, forbidden to grow beards (a sign of manhood), and taught not to speak in the sultan's presence but rather use a special sign language. It would be wrong, however, to see these males as desexed or feminized, as their martial skills, intellectual acumen, and physical vigor were cultivated by the sultan. Their latent virility, activated when they were graduated from palace to public service, was all the more a reflection of the sultan's own mastery over his household, and by extension over his empire.

EPILOGUE

If the reproduction of political power through a caste of trained servants of the sultan was a durable feature of Ottoman rule, it was also mutable. Originating as a product of late-medieval frontier expansion, the *kul* institution evolved in predictable and unpredictable ways as it adapted to changing times. The principal motivational forces in its evolution were the shifting orientation of the sultanate, from expansion to administration of a finite territory, and pressures from within the growing and increasingly differentiated ranks of the *kul* themselves. The practices described above constituted the heyday of an imperial household controlled by charismatic, authoritarian sultans who led their armies and had personal relations with the pashas to whom they delegated authority. By the late sixteenth century, the constitution of ruling elites was more complex, and more groups, including the *kul,* claimed a voice in the disposition of the empire.

The distance between "elite caste" *kul* and rank-and-file soldiers becomes more apparent in this period. The households of pashas grew larger and more politically engaged, to the extent that some took up arms against the sultan, to make a policy point or to broker more power. Replicating the politics of the imperial household, pashas recruited their own forces (sometimes from local subject populations) and placed their followers in positions of authority. Household patronage could favor the pasha's relatives and also *kul* of his own ethnic background. In other words, there were now multiple household channels for entry into the governing class. However, this was not a case of the servant ruling the master, for two reasons. First, the dynastic household itself was expanding rapidly, and moreover propagating new networks of patronage stemming from new players at court, most notably the queen mothers. Second, while sultans no longer loomed large in the manner of Mehmed II or Suleyman, the weight of three hundred years of dynastic success provided political capital to even the weakest of the sultans. The sultanate was still the ultimate source of legimate power.

It was the rank-and-file *kul* who played the role of praetorian guard in the Ottoman empire. More than fickle soldiers whose potential disloyalty could inspire the execution of a Mahmud Pasha or an Ibrahim Pasha, by the seventeenth century the imperial troops had become a body demanding "constitutional" rights and exerting its own collective force in the political arena. Numbers counted, as enrollments in military corps multiplied under the pressure brought by *kul* to enroll their sons (military status was now claimed as a hereditary right). Like pashas, the rank and file used force of arms to oppose disagreeable policies, particularly devaluation of the coinage with which they were paid. Starting in 1584, several insurrections in the capital protesting these damaging fiscal measures prepared the way for the first regicide in 1622, which was perpetrated by the imperial troops. Their legitimacy as kingmakers came in part from their ability to ally with leading members of the Muslim religious establishment, now a powerful voice in its own right, claiming the duty to rule on the illegitimacy of sultanic acts and even of individual occupants of the Ottoman throne. The effectiveness of these uprisings also came from the support of the Istanbul marketplace, in which numerous *kul* now had commercial interests.

By the seventeenth century, the *kul* had clearly become more than a household of imperial servants. The regicide of Osman II was a showdown over the evolution of *kul*-hood from select personal service to the sovereign to a more porous and broad-based government service.[47] As the caliber of recruits and their training were diluted through a kind of "democratized" access, the sultans forfeited the strict meritocracy that Machiavelli had written about admiringly. Osman II, however, objected to this accommodationism: he was angered by the poor performance of his troops and so canceled some of their entitlements.

But the regicide was about more than obstinacy on both sides in the negotiation over rights and duties. It was also about the "Rumî" identity of the empire. Under the guise of making the pilgrimage to Mecca (something no sultan had ever done), Osman was allegedly planning to assemble a new military force in Anatolia, Syria, and Egypt and then eliminate the *kul* corps stationed in Istanbul. It was even rumored that the capital was to be transferred to Damascus or Cairo, thereby abandoning the "Roman" city that bridged "the two lands and the two seas." Nor were female *kul* to be spared: Osman intended to get rid of his concubines and take Muslim wives.[48] In short, the sultan envisioned the overthrow of a two hundred fifty–year-old formula that was the foundation of the empire. The *kul* would not stand for it. With one exception, the major Ottoman historians of the seventeenth century agreed that Osman had transgressed fundamental Ottoman traditions. What was at stake, of course, was the status quo that favored not only the *kul* but other groups enmeshed in the structures and patronage networks surrounding the sultanate (including the historians). But also at stake were the core geography of the empire and the central place within it of the "servants" without whom the House of Osman could not have become what it was.[49]

CHAPTER THREE

HIERARCHIES OF AGE AND GENDER IN THE MUGHAL CONSTRUCTION OF DOMESTICITY AND EMPIRE

Ruby Lal

What is the significance of the three hundred wives or five thousand women—depending on one's source[1]—that the Mughal emperor Akbar (1556–1605) is supposed to have had in his *haram*? While the emperor's chroniclers differ in reporting the number of women, they are unanimous in writing about the large size of the *haram*. Babur, the first Mughal king, even with his wanderings and establishment of many homes, is said to have had no more than ten wives. Humayun, the second king, probably had five.[2]

In order to answer this question, it will help to consider a few examples of Akbar's marriages, which are extensively discussed in the chronicles of his reign. According to Abu-l Fazl's *Akbarnama*, the officially commissioned history of the empire, when Akbar was in Delhi in 1556, he married the elder daughter of Jamal Khan, "one of the great zamindars [landed elite] of India." Bayram Khan Khan-i Khanan, Akbar's guardian, and later *vakil*, or vice-regent, of his empire,[3] married Jamal Khan's younger daughter.

In January 1562, Chaghatai Khan, an intimate courtier of Akbar, discussed with him the exceptional loyalty of Raja Bihari Mal, the head of the Kachwaha clan.[4] Bihari Mal was brought into Akbar's presence and was elevated as one of the distinguished members of the court.[5] To cement this political alliance, the raja offered his daughter in marriage to Akbar. Other such matrimonial alliances followed. In his *Muntakhab-ut-Tavarikh*, 'Abd al-Qadir Badauni notes that in 1562–1563, when Akbar was pursuing Shah 'Abdul Ma'ali, a rebel, it was in Delhi that the emperor's "intention of connecting himself by marriage with the nobles of Dihli was first broached." Thus, "Qawwals and eunuchs were sent into the harems for the purpose of selecting daughters of the nobles, and of investigating their condition."[6]

In 1568, according to Nizam al-Din Ahmad's *Tabaqat-i Akbari* (another member of Akbar's court), several *zamindars* expressed their allegiance to Akbar, including Miran Mubarak Shah, the ruler of Khandesh.[7] Later on, an imperial *farman* (decree or order) was sent to Miran Mubarak "that he should send one of his daughters whom he may consider to be deserving of doing service to the emperor [sic] to the court."[8] Miran Shah was overjoyed, according to Nizam al-Din Ahmad, and considered the proposal to be a great honor.[9] In 1570–1571, Akbar married the niece of Raja Kalyan Mal of Bikaner and the daughter of Raja Har Rai of Jaisalmer.[10]

Akbar and his close associates entered into many kinds of marital alliances. Some of the earliest reinforced links with noble families of central Asian background, while others established connections with major communities in the subcontinent. Akbar's marriage, on the above-mentioned death of Bayram Khan in 1560–1561, to the latter's wife, Salimeh Sultan Begum, is one prominent example that signaled Akbar's loyalty and commitment to those who were close to the Mughal court. It can have done his cause no harm that the Begum was also the daughter of Nur al-Din Muhammad Chaghaniyani and the granddaughter of Babur.[11]

Several historians have stressed the political importance of Mughal marriages.[12] Many of Akbar's marriages are recorded as having taken place in the early part of his reign when the need to cement his power was greatest: his kingdom was not yet a dominant power in the region, and its general circumstances were fluid. Marital alliances, required for production of royal heirs, as is clearly recorded in imperial regulations on matrimony, were also key to forging political partnerships.

Akbar's marriages might perhaps also be read in another way: symbolically demonstrating that the world was under the emperor's protection. They served as an important mark of the empire's new vision, and of its strength and virility—as a symbol of its regality and new imperial position, in other words. In the *Akbarnama* and other contemporary chronicles, Akbar is constructed as the center of the realm upon whom was premised the making of other domains of his empire.[13] It was likely that those who married him were seen as blessed simply by the fact of such union. As Abu-l Fazl tells us, imperial marriages were exalted because of the emperor. It is as if the emperor was accommodating the entire world through a marital grid. Daughters of kings and nobles of all cultures and every domain were seeking his protection, and Akbar was extending his sheltering umbrella far and wide.[14]

The ambition of imperial monarchs, with aspirations to "take in" the world through marital alliances and war, is not an unusual phenomenon. There are numerous examples from different parts of the world (and different ages) of the large *harams* maintained by royalty as a sign of imperial power and dominance. However, the presence of the large number of women in Akbar's *haram* might also be specifically read as a sign of the supremacy of the monarch as the center of the empire. The reach and protection of Akbar's empire comes to be enlarged through his marriages in extraordinary terms. Kin, fellow-believers, and people of the Book mattered, but the rest of the world—non-believers, kafirs, other races, subjects—came to be of crucial importance too. Thus Akbar's marriages with the Rajputs and other Hindu nobles become an index of a power that incorporated the universe in unprecedented ways.

I begin with examples of Akbar's marital alliances in order to elaborate the new imperial vision, and to underscore the argument that the Mughal empire was not a ready-made regime nor fully formed from its birth. Its establishment was processual, as well as troubled and multitonal. A great deal of trial and error, negotiation, and conflict went into its emergence. Abu-l Fazl's construction of a genealogy sought to make Akbar the fulcrum of Mughal life: the commissioned histories; the extended rules and regulations that were established for the court and the *haram;* the physical grandeur of the court; the court laureates; the presence of distinguished clerics, Jesuit priests, ambassadors, and other dignitaries; and the hunts, feasts, and other paraphernalia are all examples of new institutions that were developed as part of the building up of a new imperial polity.[15] The changes that occurred under Akbar's rule did not mark a complete break from the practices of his immediate predecessors; nonetheless, they signaled the establishment of a much more confident and secure regime.

Central to the making of the new imperial vision were new relationships and hierarchies—and not least among these were the hierarchies of gender. This was the first time in the reign of the Mughals that an official regulation on the royal household was issued. The women were officially designated *pardeh-giyan,* the veiled ones. This development needs to be seen in the context of the routinization of imperial spaces and practices and the creation of new subjects (especially female) in the making of Akbar's new regime. I have elaborated elsewhere[16] the processes that went into the making of Akbar's monarchy and empire by probing how Abu-l Fazl constructed the imperial monarch as sacred, sovereign, and masculine and conjured up the empire and its structures around the figure of this awesome center. The following discussion focuses specifically on the ordering of domestic life that was central to the wider restructuring of the imperial regime under Akbar.

THE ORGANIZATION OF THE *HARAM*

The construction of order in different arenas and activities—what Abu-l Fazl, in the preface to the *A'in-i Akbari* describes as the proper order of the household, army, and empire—was a major hallmark of Akbar's reign.[17] In the drive to coordinate all aspects of imperial life, domestic life too was carefully regulated.

Indeed, one of the most striking developments of Akbar's reign was the institutionalization of the *haram*, both in its physical laying out at Fatehpur-Sikri and in its conceptual framework. Courtly and domestic spaces came, for the first time, to be distinctly separated from each other.[18] A neatly compartmentalized *haram* (*shabistan-i Iqbal*) was designed to place women in a strictly segregated space—for "good order and propriety," as Abu-l Fazl has it. As part of the process of the institutionalization, the term "haram" itself came to be the most common description of the women's sphere, signifying important changes in the Mughals' domestic life.

This marks a change in the meaning and resonance of the word from its usage in Babur and Humayun's time.[19] "Haram," in Akbari chronicles, refers both to physical structures—the secluded quarters where royal women lived—and to the women themselves who lived in those dwellings. Akbari chronicles mark a return to the origins of the term in early Islamic history (*haram* as a sanctum sanctorum) and to the sanctity that extends not only to the inner quarters but also to the *haram* folk: this is not altogether surprising, given the divine connections now repeatedly drawn up for the emperor.

> His Majesty is a great friend of good order and propriety in business . . . For this reason, the large number of women [*pardeh-giyan*]—a vexatious question even for great statesmen—furnished his Majesty with an opportunity to display his wisdom, and to rise from the low level of worldly dependence to the eminence of perfect freedom. The imperial palace and household are therefore in best order. . . . His Majesty has made a large enclosure with fine buildings inside, where he reposes. Though there are more than five thousand women, he has given to each a separate apartment. He has also divided them into sections, and keeps them attentive to their duties. Several chaste women have been appointed as daroghas, and superintendents over each section, and one has been selected for the duties of writer. Thus, as in the imperial offices, everything is here also in proper order.[20]

In this discussion of the new sanctity that was to be created through the seclusion of women, Abu-l Fazl also lists the arrangements for the security of the *haram* by what he calls "sober and active women." According to him, the most trustworthy women were placed at the quarters of Akbar. The eunuchs guarded the outside enclosure, and at some distance from them, the Rajputs formed another line of watchmen. In addition, on all four sides of the complex were "guards of Nobles, Ahadis."[21] Abu-l Fazl then gives the salaries of the women guards: the women of "highest rank" received 1,610 to 1,028 rupees per month, and those of the servants varied between 51 rupees and 2 rupees. If a woman wanted anything "within the limit of her salary," she had to apply to the cash-keepers (*tahwildars*) of the *haram*. It was the general treasurer, however, who made the payments in cash.[22]

As far as visitors were concerned, Abu-l Fazl says, whenever "the wives of the nobles, or other women of chaste character" desired to visit the *haram*, they had to convey their wish to the servants of the *haram* and wait for a reply. From there the requests were sent to the officers of the palace, and "those who . . . [were] eligible" were given permission to enter the *haram*. Some women "of rank" could be given permission to remain in the *haram* for a whole month.[23]

The public pronouncement of separated living arrangements of the imperial women is a first step in Abu-l Fazl's narrative; from here he anticipates the ascription of the veiled status, and the careful allocation of women's quarters, as a vital hallmark of the grand empire. There are various ways in which he follows this declaration.

While recording the events of the thirty-ninth year of Akbar's reign, Abu-l Fazl notes that Akbar had sent a letter addressed to the emperor of Persia.[24] The letter, incorporated in the *Akbarnama,* is prefaced with praises of the glorious prophets and apostles "who led mankind to better ways."[25] Akbar draws subtle connections between bounteous God and the rulers on earth (himself as well as the Persian monarch) as "shadows of Divinity" or God's representatives who were to discipline and guard mankind.[26] In one of the passages to the Safavid king, he says, "Let us proclaim in the pulpits of publicity; firstly, their glorious condition [of divine humans, with the help of divine aid], and secondly . . . let us tell of the bounties and noble qualities of the 'members of the household' [*Ahl-i-bait*] who are confidants of the great secrets, and unveilers of the mysteries of the prophets, and let us, relying thereupon, implore new mercy!"[27]

The citation evokes the sacredness of Prophet Muhammad's family and, by extension, of his earthly descendents—a significant parallel in the context of what is presented as the holy empire of Akbar. This ideal of the prophet's household, it has been argued by several scholars, became key in the assertions of Muslim monarchs who vied with each other to appropriate genealogical legitimacy as descendents of the prophet's family.[28]

Ahl-i bayt, the Persian term used for "household" in Akbar's letter, incorporates two words, *ahl* and *bayt. Ahl* may be understood as companion or relative, persons, people of distinction, servants, and attendants. In the plural, the word means kinsmen (*kisan*), relatives (*khvishavand*), race or tribe (*qawm*), and friends (*payruvan, yaran, ashab*).²⁹ *Bayt* means a house, a temple, an edifice, or fabric.³⁰ As a compound word, *ahl-i bayt* renders the sense of a household—an expression that is also found in Babur's autobiography in the context of extended familial structures.

The term *bayt* is used fifteen times in the Quran to describe God's house: aside from a simple house, it is also designated as "the first house," "the ancient house," and the "sacred house" (*al-bayt al-haram*).³¹ Most of these Quranic references to God's house derive from the period after Muhammad and his followers had settled in Medina³²—the time after the revelations when the prophet's new religiopolitical community (*ummah*) was being formed. The phrase *ahl-i bayt* occurs only three times in the Quran, and in each instance, it is connected with the household of a major prophet and involves references to female members of the household. Eduardo Juan Campo tells us that the "most important aspect of the 'people of the house' phrase is not its use in the Quran per se, however, but what Muslims later made of it." After Muhammad's death, the term came to designate the prophet and his family, as well as his "noble" descendents.³³

Abu-l Fazl too seems to be invoking a prophetic-familial association for Akbar. The emperor is represented as making this connection alongside a community of divine monarchs, thereby enhancing what Abu-l Fazl refers to at one point as the "spiritual relationship" between Akbar and the Safavid king, both of whom are described as the members of the *ahl-i bayt*.³⁴

Once the spiritual connection with the *ahl-i bayt* was spelled out, the virtues of such a "divine household," (the members of which are "confidants of the great secrets") highly praised by the monarch would then become the model for his own, earthly household—both in expectation and portrayal. The term *ahl-i bayt* is not frequently used in the contemporary chronicles of Akbar's time. Its spirit, however, is amplified by other terms used to project Akbar's domestic world. These terms include *dudman-i quddusi* (holy family),³⁵ *dudman-i vala* (sublime family),³⁶ and *dudman-i dawlat* (illustrious family), to take only a few examples.³⁷

The word *dudman* is of some interest. In relation to Babur's domestic life, we come across the word *khandan*, which pertains to an illustrious family. For Babur, who emphatically called on his Timurid lineage, *khandan* was an important term; it entailed the following meanings: *dudman* or genealogy, *tabar* or extraction, *dudeh* or genealogy; as a compound noun (*khanivar*), *khandan* indicates the people of the same house.³⁸ The invocation of *dudman* or genealogy was of a different order in the construction of Akbar's empire: here, the imperial chronicler called on the prophetic ancestors (not Timurid) to establish close connections with them.

None of the terms discussed above are encountered as frequently as the *haram*, officially designated as the *Shabistan-i Iqbal* (literally, the fortunate place of sleep or dreams) in the *A'in-i Akbari*, the imperial gazetteer and accompaniment to the *Akbarnama*.[39] The etymology of the word "haram" is critical to understanding its various associations, some of which Akbari chroniclers may have had in mind. R. B. Serjeant informs us that closely linked with the holy family is the institution known in ancient Arabia as the *haram* (and in contemporary South Arabia as *hawtah*).[40] He explains that in ancient Arabia, at the top of the social stratification were the armed tribes, ranging from camel-owning desert tribes to tribesmen living in settled villages. Customary law was central to how these tribal units governed their relationships. Because there were always times when tribesmen needed greater authority than their own, they turned to the holy family, which derived its power from the divine—perhaps through the medium of a prophet or a saint. According to Arabic hagiologies, a member of the holy family declared a certain piece of land a sacred enclave, a *hawtah*. It was incumbent upon people to show it respect (*ihtiram*), and any infringement on or violation of the sanctity of this domain was likely to bring "condign punishment."[41] In and around this sacred, sanctified space, authority reposed clearly in the creator of that space. Serjeant explains that if the Medinean tribes ("self-governing but linked to the *haram*") disagreed at any point, the disagreement was to be referred to the Prophet Muhammad who knew the law.[42]

Among the Bedouin, *haram* was "a sacred area around a shrine; a place where the holy power manifests itself." As an adjective, the term represented "everything that is forbidden to the profane and separated from the rest of the world. The cause of this prohibition could be either impurity (temporary or intrinsic) or holiness, which is a permanent state of sublime purity."[43] The *haram* subsequently came to accumulate many more meanings. Aliakbar Dehkhoda's *Loghatname* lists these: those behind the curtain, not to be seen (*pardeh-giyan*); that which is inside, internal, within, intrinsic (*andarun, andaruni*); house where the wives and the household live (*haramsara*); place of sleep (*shabistan*, used as a synonym for *haram*); Mecca, Medina, the area around the Ka'ba, and the garden of the Prophet Muhammad (Ruzayi Rasul).[44]

The fabric of invocations for Akbar's dwellings and of its habitants is woven around the prophet, including the holy sites associated with him: his garden, Mecca, Medina, and the Ka'ba. In this construction, the centrality of Akbar in the *haram* is absolute, like that of Muhammad in his *haram*. The parallel between Muhammad and Akbar is significant. This is yet another component of the claim to be a hallowed and "blessed" empire—here, premised upon domestic order. The frequent use of a vocabulary resplendent with divine invocations is therefore hardly unexpected.

One other thing must be said of this vocabulary—including the less commonly used expressions for Akbar's domestic world—that the sacred adjectives used as prefixes or suffixes often appear to overshadow the word indicating the familial. Thus *quddusi* (holy), *vala* (sublime), or *dawlat* (illustrious)—advertising the purity and sanctity attached to the notion of the familial—capture our attention first, rather than the substantive *dudman*.[45]

The veiled status of imperial women was now officially encoded in the imperial regulations.[46] The publicly declared, "required" veiling of women fits in with the larger rendering of them as perfect and hence secluded. The veiled women thus serve as icons of the sacred empire, and their veiling preserves the sanctity of that empire. We need to pause here, however. The Mughal *haram* becomes forbidden or invisible, but only for the greater impact—invisibility—it thus had on the rest of the world. Its sanctity is very much part of an immediate display of worldly power. In this new elaboration, the emperor also represents empire—but as its most visible symbol, the focus of all matters, spiritual and mundane, of institutions, as well as of other people's lives. As if to balance this intensely visible, omnipresent hallmark of a new power, the *haram* emerges as a particularly secluded, sacred space—which also signifies imperial majesty.[47] In other words, Akbar appears to sanctify the secluded space as well as draw sustenance from the segregation of imperial women subjects and their quarters.

BIRTHS IN THE *HARAM:* THE ABSENCE OF MOTHERS

In the making of Akbar's empire and his *haram*, women were honored and cloistered at the same time. An aspect of this development was the invisibility of the Mughal women, or of most of them, in the public pronouncements and activities of the empire—a situation that seems to contrast sharply with the elevated status accorded to them.

Consider the reverential titles and forms of address for the imperial women commonly deployed in the Akbari chronicles. The *Akbarnama* and the *A'in-i Akbari* are particularly resplendent with honorifics for the women of Akbar's *haram*. The elder women were evidently the most revered ones. Hamideh Banu Begum, the mother of Akbar; Maham Anageh, his foster mother; Haji Begum, his stepmother; Gulbadan Begum, Mughal memoirist and the emperor's aunt, Gulchihreh Begum, also his aunt; and Salimeh Sultan Begum, his older (and therefore senior) wife—all elder relatives of Akbar—were referred to with illustrious titles. But while the women were revered and invoked as chaste and pure, they were at the same time (explicitly) referred to as the *pardeh-giyan,* the veiled ones.

Hamideh Banu Begum was addressed as Maryam-Makani. There is some uncertainty about the date of Hamideh Banu's new name.[48] Maryam means Mary, and the epithet may be rendered in various ways — she who dwells with Mary, is of the household of Mary, and is of equal rank with Mary. She was also referred to as the "veil of chastity"[49] and "pillar of purity."[50] Maham An-ageh was called the "cupola of chastity," and Akbar's stepsister "the chaste" Bakht-un-Nisa Begum.[51] Similarly, Haji Begum was also called "the cupola of chastity,"[52] and Gulbadan Begum, Gulchihreh Begum, and Salimeh Sultan Begum were all "connections of the noble family."

In contrast, we are confronted with the general invisibility of Mughal women in the contemporary records. This is especially striking in the case of Akbar's wives, including the mothers of his sons. Abu-l Fazl's account of the "auspicious birth of the world-illuminating pearl of the mansion of the dominion and fortune, the night-gleaming jewel of the casket of greatness and glory, viz., of Prince Sultan Selim [the future emperor, Jahangir]"[53] is a telling example. The chronicler begins by writing about the keen desire of Akbar for the "great boon"[54] of a son and successor. Before Salim's birth, several children had been born to Akbar, "but they had been taken away for thousands of wise designs, one of which might be the increasing joy in the acquisition of the priceless pearl."[55] Salim was conceived with the blessings of Shaykh Salim Chishti, a Sufi *shaykh* who lived near Fatehpur-Sikri. The pregnant wife was taken to repose in the shelter of the *shaykh*'s hospice, where she gave birth to Akbar's son.[56]

So when "the unique pearl of the Caliphate," Salim, was born in Fatehpur-Sikri, great joyousness and celebration followed.[57] The prisoners of the imperial domains were released, horoscopes were cast, and poets composed congratulatory odes: "a pearl of Shahinshah's mansion," "a pearl of Akbar Shahi's casket" (*gawhar-i-durj-i Akbar Shahi*).[58]

Yet in this extended narrative of Salim's birth, bursting with superlatives, the name of the mother of Salim never appears. Indeed, nowhere in the official history is her name mentioned. Salim's birth was splendidly cast in the visual folios of the *Akbarnama*.[59] In these folios, the attention to detail in imagining the birth chamber and describing the postnatal care of the mother and infant are all crucial manifestations of the act of reproduction and the centrality of the mother in childbirth.

In the congratulatory notes, however, it is Akbar alone who is glorified in the birth of his son; Salim is "*gawhar-i-durj-i Akbar Shahi.*" In monarchical societies, the reproductive power of a wife was recognized as a major contribution. It is all the more noteworthy that even in the performance of that single act of consequence, Akbar's mother is missing from the records. There are metaphorical references to her: "shell of her womb"; and then, ". . . it was determined that the matrix of the son of fortune [the pregnant mother of Salim] together with several of the officials attached to the Zenana should be conveyed to Fathpur and should enjoy repose in the vicinity of the Shaikh."[60] The only contemporary document that names the mother of Jahangir is a later *hukm* (edict) issued by Maryam-uz-Zamani.[61] The seal on the *hukm* says, "Vali Ni'mat Begum, valideh Nur al-Din Jahangir,"[62] thus clearly identifying Maryam-uz-Zamani with Vali Ni'mat Begum and unequivocally declaring her the mother of Jahangir.[63]

This is an extraordinary moment in imperial history. The wife remains unnamed even at the birth of the imperial heir. Most chronicles of the time tell us that Salim was the long-prayed-for son and the first surviving child of Akbar. While encomiums were composed in praise of this event, the person glorified was only the king. Thus:

> God be praised for the glory of the King
> A splendid pearl came ashore from the ocean of justice . . .
> The just and perfect Muhammad Akbar, Lord of Conjunction
> The renowned King, seeking and attaining his desires . . .
> May our King be permanent and also the Prince
> For countless days and unnumbered years. (Khvajeh Husain of Marv)[64]

Abu-l Fazl recounts some other births in the *Akbarnama*. In these instances too, noble wives remain unnamed producers of noble children. Two-and-a-half months after Prince Salim was born, in November 1569, a daughter was born in Akbar's *haram*. The girl was named Khanum, and Akbar "ordered rejoicings."[65] No other details of the celebration are available to us. The name of the mother is not given. Similarly in recording the births of Shah Murad and Prince Danyal,[66] the mothers remain unnamed. In discussing the birth of Murad, Abu-l Fazl emphasizes the union of "celestial fathers" and "the terrestrial mothers" that results "every spring [in] a fresh flower [that] blooms in the garden of fortune." "Celestial" or "terrestrial," the adjectives say it all, even if there is thus a reference to the mother as the necessary instrument in this royal birth. In June 1570, once again, a noble son "whose forehead the lights of high fortune were visible, appeared in the fortunate quarters of Shaykh Selim in Fathpur." He was named Shah Murad. Encomiasts composed verses and chronograms for this birth and received rewards for their efforts.[67]

There is another point to be made in regard to the celebration of royal births. In what might at first appear as similar descriptions, a fine difference runs through the narratives of the births of Salim and Murad on the one hand and that of Khanum on the other. The birth of a daughter was not of the same order as that of a son. The casting of horoscopes, the celebratory odes, and the general environment of overflowing joyousness is absent in the writing on Khanum's birth. The moment of birth is simply recorded, not anticipated as an important event for the dynasty and its future. Adjacent to the composition of Khanum's birth is the trace of the "uneventful" birth of Aram Banu Begum in December 1584, one that simply "glorified the harem of the Shahinshah . . . and the world's lord conferred on her that great name."[68]

In line with the culture of the courts as it was developed under the first two Mughal kings, certain aspects of the lives of senior and junior women remain unchanged. They remain partners in the production not only of heirs but also of imperial genealogies, new royal rituals, the establishment of new traditions, and even the practice of governance. Paradoxically, however, the women are depicted as being so invested in the future of the empire—in the form of giving birth to illustrious progeny and in the maintenance of "established" traditions—that their own present tends to be erased in the very performance of their royalty and womanhood. They do not need to be named at the moment of the birth of royal heirs.

Royal mothers continued to be significant presences in the public-political affairs, as we shall see presently, but this was markedly so only in the case of the elders, especially the mother of the emperor. Active participation of younger women in the consolidation and prolongation of the empire was rendered entirely trivial. They were present but hidden away, crucial to the maintenance of the empire but unnamed in its annals.

HARAM FOLK SPEAK

The new arrangements increased the invisibility of the royal women, now more elevated and at the same time more secluded than before. However, the prescription of the new imperium, which was to find tangible form in the sacred, incarcerated *haram*, was never so successful as to wipe out contradictions, tensions, human volition, or unexpected departures. Although in the changing environment of Akbar's reign a great deal happened to alter domestic arrangements, there is (as one would expect) considerable evidence to show how women and men continued to negotiate the prescribed and the everyday.

The first part of this chapter illustrated how Akbari chronicles put into play a certain set of domestic arrangements and norms as a pivotal component of the increasing glory of the Mughal kingdom. In the next three sections, I consider how Mughal women responded to the new imperial constructions of the normative, and how women's negotiation of the publicized ideals was to be a key element in the making of the monarchy—at times, in the very following of those ideals.

THE EMPEROR'S MOTHER

There were several areas of tension and instability in the new dispensation under Akbar. Not least among these were the activities of the older imperial women. Hamideh Banu, the revered mother of the emperor, was not inappropriately christened "Empress Dowager" in W. H. Lowe's translation of Badauni's *Muntakhab-ut-Tavarikh*. Every so often in the Akbari accounts, one finds fragments related to Hamideh Banu Begum, about how her opinion was sought on many matters and how her intervention counted for a great deal. These fragments are scattered all over the imperial chronicles. On their own, they appear marginal. When put together, they make for an instructive statement.

On July 20, 1580, Father Rudolf Acquaviva, a Jesuit priest at Akbar's court, wrote to Rui Vicente Provincial regarding Akbar's "inadequate attention to the word of God."[69] He discussed the opposition of Akbar's own people to Christian leanings, including the king's immediate family and other close associates: "On the one hand he has his mother, wives and friends to importune him, and on the other are those who wish him ill."[70] Again, on July 30, 1581, Rudolf Acquaviva wrote to Father Everard Mercurian informing him of the benefits they had received from the emperor and his mother: "To us the king grants many favours and so do the Queen Mother, and the princes."[71]

Even though sketchily narrated, the exalted status and frequent public appearances of Hamideh Banu Begum is highlighted in the records time and again. Note the anticipation of Akbar's responses toward Hamideh Banu at several junctures. In April 1578 when the emperor was hunting in the neighborhood of the town of Bhira, near Shahpur district of Punjab, it was announced to him that his mother had arrived at the camp and was anxious to see him. Akbar was much delighted, says Abu-l Fazl, and "made arrangements for doing her honour." He also ordered that Salim should go and meet her, along with other officers. After that Akbar went to receive the "visible God [Hamideh Banu Begum], an act of worship of the true Creator."[72] The etiquette and the delight of the emperor in honoring his "visible God" intensify the mother's status.

In September–October 1581, when Akbar visited the tomb of Humayun and went on to visit his stepmother Haji Begum, Hamideh Banu Begum followed him. At the end of the day, Akbar was informed that his mother had arrived. Akbar treated her with great respect. This time Prince Danyal was in attendance on her.[73] On another occasion, Hamideh Banu Begum arrived while Akbar was on an expedition to Punjab. Abu-l Fazl records that "on account of her great love" for Akbar, Hamideh Banu Begum could not remain (*niyarastand*) in the capital. Akbar is said to have been delighted at this news of her arrival, and he welcomed her with the utmost respect.[74]

During Akbar's expedition to Afghanistan in 1589, Hamideh Banu Begum, in her "desire to behold" Akbar, set off for Kashmir, along with Gulbadan Begum and several other women. When they heard that Akbar had gone to Kabul, they followed him there. On being given the news of the arrival of women, Akbar first sent Prince Danyal and some officers to meet the women, and afterward Prince Murad, and finally Prince Salim. Then he himself went and received the Begums near Begram.[75]

Hamideh Banu Begum's persistent, unannounced journeys to see her son are not the only indication of her central presence in the imperial order. The English traveler Thomas Coryate noted Akbar's devotion to his mother in the following eye-catching instance. Coryate says that Akbar never denied her anything except once. At some stage Hamideh Banu demanded of Akbar that the Bible should be hung around the neck of an ass, which should be paraded around Agra. This arose because on a Portuguese ship a copy of the Quran had been found tied around the neck of a dog. Akbar apparently denied her request by saying "that if it were ill in the Portugals to doe so to the Alcoran, it became not a king to requite ill with ill, for that the contempt of any Religion was the contempt of God, and he would not be revenged upon an innocent Booke."[76]

Alongside the clear visibility of the matriarchs in the records is a corollary: a declining mention of the public presence of younger and less centrally placed women. This is not altogether surprising, given that there were now hundreds of royal women in the *haram* and that their activities were more regimented than before. These are conditions that stand out against the peripatetic Mughal domestic life of Babur and Humayun, in which the smaller groups of women in the *padshah's* (king's) camp—more dispersed and less permanently settled—probably had greater opportunities for initiative and intervention.

It is notable that we find no trace of a loved one or a favorite wife associated with Akbar, in legend or in the contemporary literature. The presentation of the emperor on a sanctified pedestal meant that he could not be reached by a single, mortal woman—in the public narrative at any rate.[77] Instead, the woman who emerges as an outstanding figure—an elder, a matriarch, and an authority in her own right — is the mother of the emperor. Yet the mother of the emperor was not the only privileged senior in the *haram*.

OTHER SENIOR *HARAMAN*

It is recorded in the *Akbarnama* as well as the *Muntakhab-ut-Tavarikh* that one Khvajigi Fathullah "reposed for a while in the shelter of the imperial women, who were returning from the Hijaz [the pilgrimage to Mecca undertaken by a number of royal women]. Now by their intercession he was pardoned, and laid hold of the skirt of daily-increasing fortune."[78] Khvajigi Fathullah's offense was that he had gone off to Mecca without leave.[79]

On another occasion, even the *ṣadr* (chief judge) of the empire, Shaykh 'Abd-un-Nabi, had sought "protection from the secluded ladies."[80] 'Abd-un-Nabi was the grandson of 'Abdul Qaddus Gangohi,[81] a great saint of his time. Akbar had appointed 'Abd-un-Nabi the *ṣadr* of the empire but found cases of bribery and murder against him.[82] Therefore Akbar gave his position to Sultan Khvajeh,[83] and 'Abd-un-Nabi was banished to Mecca. It was after his return that he sought refuge with the women. In due time Akbar gave orders for his arrest "in such a manner that the ladies should not know of it." 'Abd-un-Nabi was later put to death.[84] It is notable that Akbar had to do all this quietly, without crossing swords with the senior women of his *haram*. According to the decrees of the empire, Akbar was to be at the center of everything; in the everyday life of the empire, however, he was inevitably not the only point of initiative and control.

Another thought-provoking discussion in relation to the privileges of senior women in the *Akbarnama* centers on Salim's plotting against and putting to death of the distinguished courtier and chronicler Abu-l Fazl.[85] It was hard for anyone to speak in favor of Salim, having committed what Shaikh Ilahdad Faizi Sirhindi referred to as great faults owing to "loss of prudence" and because of "the intoxication of youth and of success."[86] But "the great lady of the age" Maryam Makani, Hamideh Banu, and "the Khatun of the chamber of chastity," Gulbadan Begum, pleaded forgiveness for the prince from the emperor. Akbar granted their wishes and gave an order that the prince be brought to court. He also ordered that "the cupola of chastity," Salimeh Sultan Begum, should give Salim the news of forgiveness and bring him to court. Salimeh Begum, "in order to soothe the prince's apprehensions," took from Akbar an elephant named Fath Lashkar, a special horse, and a robe of honor and went to fetch the prince.[87] This is one more example of the authority of the senior royal women.

Sakineh Banu Begum, another senior woman of Akbar's *haram,* gave counsel to Hakim Mirza.[88] Sakineh Banu Begum and Mirza Hakim were both children of Humayun and Mah-chuchak, hence stepbrother and stepsister of Akbar. Sakineh Banu was married to Naqib Khan Qazvini, "a personal friend of Akbar."[89] Akbar's relations with Mirza Hakim require a little elaboration. For most of his life, Mirza Hakim was the ruler of Kabul. This is in itself of some significance. Mirza Kamran (also son of Babur) had operated in much the same area, and "as such it remained poorly incorporated into Mughal territories."[90] On two occasions Mirza Hakim had allied with rebels in Akbar's Hindustan, and at one time, the *khutba* was read in his name. In both instances, Akbar had marched against him.

Sakineh Banu Begum was sent to Kabul in 1578, before Akbar's second march on that city. The *mirza* at that point seemed to have conducted negotiations with the Abulkhairi Uzbek state of Mavra-un-nahr and with the Safavids, "who treated him as a sovereign ruler," as well as with another Timurid potentate, Mirza Sulayman.[91] The "veiled one of the palace of chastity,"[92] Sakineh Banu Begum, was sent to pacify the *mirza* and was advised to offer Prince Salim in marriage to his daughter as an incentive.[93]

The jostling for position between Mirza Hakim and Akbar continued for a long period. Father Monserrate, a Jesuit missionary at Akbar's court, has a passage in his memoir about the significant intervention of another woman later on in these proceedings. At the time of the defeat of the *mirza,* Bakht-un-Nisa (also called Najib-un-Nisa and Fakhr-un-Nisa[94]), the *mirza*'s sister, went up to Akbar and "asked for pardon, and begged him [Akbar] to have mercy on his conquered brother and to give him back his kingdom, for he [Mirza Hakim] was sorry for what he had done. The result of her interceding was that the king, in reliance on her virtue, faithfulness and tact, handed over the kingdom to her charge." Having thus obtained the kingdom of Kabul through her intercession, Bakht-un-Nisa quietly handed it back to her brother.[95]

The handing over of Kabul to Bakht-un-Nisa is a fact of no little significance. It portrays the extremely high profile of some of the senior Mughal women and the power they could sometimes wield. Among such examples of Mughal women's initiative and influence is another prominent case: Hamideh Banu Begum's charge of Delhi when Akbar marched to Kabul in order to suppress a conspiracy, led by several rebels, to install Mirza Hakim as the ruler of Hindustan.

Monserrate comments on the arrangements made by Akbar before his departure. Hamideh Banu Begum remained at Fatehpur-Sikri with her youngest grandson Danyal. 'Aziz Kukeh was made the viceroy of Bengal and Qutub al-Din Khan of Gujarat. "The king's mother was to be superior to both of

these, and was to have charge of the province of Indicum or Delinum [Delhi]."
Ten thousand cavalry were left as a garrison in Gujarat and twelve thousand
with the king's mother. Akbar also left his infant daughter (Ximini Begum,
according to Monserrate[96]) with her grandmother at Fatehpur-Sikri. He
took with him a few of his principal wives and his older daughters. "On the
day of his [Akbar's] departure his mother set out with him, and spent two
days in camp with her son, in his immense white pavilion."[97]

Senior imperial women thus stand out as leaders and independent actors
on several counts. They took over positions of public authority at crucial
junctures. They counseled and mediated between dissenting kinsmen. Their
advice was constantly sought, and they frequently arbitrated and made suggestions on public matters. Although many senior women were the privileged participants in the running of the empire, the emperor's mother, the
"Queen Empress," seems to have inhabited an especially honored position
during Akbar's reign. Her tenure as the governor of Delhi in 1581 is only the
most striking illustration of this.

HARAM TRAVELS

In 1578, Gulbadan Banu Begum led several women of Akbar's *haram* to
Mecca on a *hajj*.[98] There are only brief allusions to this arresting moment in
the histories of the time. Yet this is a journey that raises many questions
about the hierarchies in Akbar's new regime, the centrality of the emperor,
the making of the *haram*, and, paradoxically in a confined *haram*, the unusual
initiatives of women. I shall therefore conclude this chapter with a discussion
of this privilege by imperial Mughal women from Akbar's *haram*.

Abu-l Fazl discusses the "visit to the Hijaz of the veiled ladies of the
Caliphate."[99] He explains that Gulbadan Begum, Akbar's paternal aunt, had
"long ago made a vow to visit the holy places."[100] She had not been able to
fulfill this vow owing to the insecurity of the route to be traveled (this refers
especially to Gujarat). However, when there was relative calm in Gujarat,
and after the "masters of the European islands, who were a stumbling block
in the way of the travellers to Hijaz" became submissive, Gulbadan Begum
discussed her desire for a pilgrimage with Akbar.[101] Abu-l Fazl says Akbar
sent Gulbadan Begum a large sum of money and goods and gave her permission to proceed.[102] The caravan left on October 8 or 9, 1575,[103] and stayed
for three-and-a-half years in Mecca.[104]

The cortege of royal women accompanying Gulbadan Begum included
mainly elder members of the Mughal *haram*:[105] close connections of the early
Mughal kings, including 'Askari (a son of Babur), as well as reliable servants.

On such a special and privileged occasion, a pilgrimage to Mecca organized
for — and by the royal women, it is conspicuous that Hamideh Banu Begum
and a long-time servant and intimate, Bibi Fatimeh, did not take part.[106] Prince
Sultan Murad, age six, was directed to lead the pilgrims up to the shore of the
southern ocean[107] — the clearest possible statement on assumed (or rather,
advocated) hierarchies of age and gender. In a hierarchical and patriarchal
world, a little boy was, by virtue of his gender alone, "senior enough" to escort the seniormost women of the dynasty to lands across the seas. It is noteworthy, however, that, on hearing of this proposal, Gulbadan Begum requested that the prince might be kept back, precisely on account of his
tender age.[108] Akbar agreed. Three older men accompanied the convoy along
with some servants: Baqi Khan, the elder brother of Adham Khan (both foster brothers of Akbar); Rumi Khan of Aleppo, possibly an artillery officer
under Babur who accompanied the group perhaps as an interpreter;[109] and
'Abdur Rahman Beg, a nephew of Haydar Mirza (Babur's cousin), who had
married one of Mirza Kamran's (another son of Babur) daughters.[110]

The composition of the women pilgrims' party once again points to the
significance and privileges of senior women: mothers, aunts, and other older
women in the Mughal family. Gulbadan Begum conducted the *hajj*. No young
wife of Akbar accompanied the pilgrims. While this may be another illustration of the special status of senior women, it could as well be that the elders
felt a more urgent need to go on the pilgrimage and might also reflect the
view that younger women needed to be kept at home for their protection.

The *hajj* of the senior women indicates very clearly the multitude of concerns and interests that animated the activities and initiatives of the *haraman*.
Historians who notice it tell us only of Akbar's generous support to women
for this journey.[111] The details of the journey in the chronicles show that
the women themselves took a large part in planning the trip. Gulbadan,
while working out the arrangements for the journey to Mecca, was staying
at Surat.[112] In order to ensure safety and friendly treatment from the Portuguese, she went as far as to give them the town of Butsar (Bulsar, or Butzaris,
as Monserrate calls it).[113] Gulbadan's decision not to include Prince Murad
as their escort, Hamideh Banu Begum's (and Bibi Fatimeh's) resolve to stay
back — one that may be read as a consensus decision among the *haraman,* and
indeed the shipwreck and the consequent stay of the royal women in Aden
for one year on their return journey (no details of which are recorded in the
contemporary texts) are all signs of a most unusual enterprise.

Badauni comments that the two possible routes through which the *hajj*
could be undertaken were inaccessible at the time.[114] One of these lay through
Shi'a Iraq, and the other through Gujarat, across the Arabian Sea, which re-

quired a pass that "bore the idolatrous stamp of the heads of the Virgin Mary and of Jesus Christ ('on whom be peace')."[115] Other chroniclers also discuss the difficulties of this journey. Abu-l Fazl notes that Akbar was concerned about these difficulties; he had, in fact, instructed the *amirs*, the officers of every territory, the guardians of the passes, the watchmen of the borders, the river police, and the harbor masters to perform "good services" for the travelers.[116] In such circumstances, the permission to perform the *hajj* came perhaps because it served a crucial political purpose, but also, surely, because the elder women expressed their keenness in no uncertain terms.

In order to fully appreciate the character of Gulbadan's *hajj*, its narratives have to be placed alongside the accounts of the debates on religious traditions that were at their peak in the 'Ibadat Khana (literally the house of worship, instituted by Akbar to hold discussions among representatives of various faiths) in the 1570s. Badauni's *Muntakhab-ut-Tavarikh* underscores some resentment regarding Akbar's growing interest in different religions and the nature of religious-social-legal debates in the 'Ibadat Khana. Given the panegyric nature of the imperial history and Abu-l Fazl's laudatory account of the emperor's policies, Badauni's chronicle becomes even more important for an alternative view of Akbar's eclectic interests more generally. At such a time, Gulbadan's pilgrimage is likely to have helped reinforce the Islamic face of the empire. It is interesting to note that Haji Begum, a wife of Humayun, had also undertaken a pilgrimage to Mecca and Medina in 1564. Her return from the *hajj* in 1567 is recorded by Abu-l Fazl,[117] but the visibility and the importance attached to the organization and finer details of Gulbadan's *hajj* is missing in the case of Haji Begum.

Gulbadan's *hajj* was organized as a spiritual journey for the participants, the records tell us. But it was perhaps more than that. What the *hajj* seems to mark is a moment of critical change in the structures of Mughal rule: from relatively fluid political structures to a more settled, consolidated government. The *hajj* was one among the many pietistic activities supported by the emperor—part of a series of moves that he and others in his court may have found necessary for the consolidation of Muslim support in this uniquely polyglot empire. The undertaking (and the imperial sanction for it) may thus be seen as another sign of the ideological tension that marked this stage of the formation of the Mughal empire. This tension is evident again in Badauni's comments on the debates in the 'Ibadat Khana.[118] The empire was seeking different forms of legitimacy. The imperial women's *hajj* presumably helped to signal its "Muslim" character.

In addition, the *hajj* serves as a crucial marker of the volition of women. At the time of the making of Akbar's empire, when its mechanisms and philosophy were still being drawn, a group of the seniormost royal women was able to travel across the seas as pilgrims. Although women continued, individually, to make trips to Mecca,[119] such a *hajj* by a large group of imperial women was never heard of again—either later in Akbar's reign or under any of his grand successors.

The *hajj* in the late 1570s is an extraordinary statement in the Mughal chronicles. It is a comment on the exceptional enterprise of royal women in rather restrictive circumstances. A royal women's *hajj* was no mean venture, its organization no meager task. The women's initiative and decision making lay not only in their urging of the emperor to let them undertake the pilgrimage but also was seen all along in its arrangements and in the way that the women faced the ensuing hazards. And there is another inference to be drawn from this evidence of collective royal women's pilgrimage to Mecca: a dream moment for a historian of premodern courtly societies and gender relations. While Akbar and Abu-l Fazl were perhaps successfully fabricating a carefully circumscribed *haram* world to project the sanctity of the empire, the *haram* folk were responding to those constructions in rather unexpected ways. The *hajj* of Gulbadan Begum, alongside other undertakings of royal women, may be considered one of those unpredictable rejoinders.

FINAL THOUGHTS

The institutionalization of the *haram* and the more general regulation of the Mughal domestic world that mirrored the making of a new imperial order under Akbar is a provocative statement—not only about the Mughal construction of institutions and practices but also in relation to the considerable element of uncertainty and experimentation that marks the establishment of all new regimes.

It is clear that the inhabitants of the *Shabistan-i Iqbal* (Akbar's *haram*) were pivotal in a move toward glorification of the empire and its majesty. But there is something more to be emphasized about the texture of the Akbari *haram* and its accompanying arrangements. The imperial regulations now marked a move toward elevating women in the records in extraordinary terms. Ironically, this revered attribution came along with the confinement of the royal women and a constriction of the space available for their activities and agency. The honoring and seclusion, or perhaps one should say, honoring by seclusion, of the *haraman* became a major aspect of the new imperial order. The remains of the grand complex of women's quarters in Fatehpur-Sikri stand testimony to that.

A development that is surely no less striking is that the *Shabistan-i Iqbal* came to have hundreds of women. I have said that this development may be seen in many ways, not just the fact noted by numerous historians that these multiple marriages were contracted for political aggrandizement and ascendancy. There is no doubt that the need for political alliance was at the heart of several of Akbar's marriages. More crucially, I argue, the several marriages of the emperor speak to a vision of empire in which the emperor was the center of the universe: by a marital union with this near-divine ruler, women were marvelously blessed—as were all others who came under the protection of the imperial umbrella.

In this period of imperial consolidation under Akbar, the presence of and exercise of power by imperial women, especially the seniors, is repeatedly noted in the records of the time. Recall the matriarchs: Hamideh Banu Begum, Gulbadan Begum, Salimeh Sultan Begum, Bakht-un-Nisa, Sakineh Banu Begum, and others. Yet in spite of the ascription of unusual influence and authority to particular Mughal women, one's overwhelming sense remains that of their profound invisibility, more striking of course in the case of junior women. This is especially so once Akbar's statute and institutions come into place. The absence of the name of the mother of the emperor Jahangir, the much-longed-for and (according to the chronicles) miraculously conceived son of Akbar, is perhaps the most telling example of this breathtaking silence.

The names of Jahangir and his imperial male siblings (like those of Babur, Akbar, and Humayun) reverberate through the records of the time and through subsequent histories. Some senior women also traverse these writings. Hamideh Banu Begum, Akbar's mother, is conspicuous in this tradition—advising, guiding, even substituting for her son in government and maintenance of imperial power—perhaps a forerunner of the "Empress" Nur Jahan of later Mughal times. It should be clear, however, that Hamideh Banu and Nur Jahan emerge as shining examples only because of a certain patriarchalism—of their and our times—that privileges exceptional, malelike, older, wise women. Other royal women, the mothers and sisters and daughters of kings and princes, remain hidden behind the walls erected by the patriarchs—the kings, their male advisors, and their male recordkeepers.

PART II

SPAIN: *CONQUISTA* AND *RECONQUISTA*

CHAPTER FOUR

RACE AND THE MIDDLE AGES

The Case of Spain and Its Jews

David Nirenberg

I n one of a series of lectures at the College de France in 1976, Michel Foucault insisted that racism was a uniquely modern phenomenon, the product of particular state formations and binary representations of society that
did not exist before the seventeenth century. Clearly his audience was not
convinced, for he began his lecture of February 4 by addressing their objections. "During the last week or two, people have sent me a number of objections, both oral and written," to the previous lectures, asking in particular,
"what does it mean to have racism originate in the sixteenth or seventeenth
century, to attach it only to problems of state sovereignty, when we well
know, after all, that religious racism (anti-Semitic racism in particular) has
existed since the Middle Ages?" Foucault did not respond to these objections. He merely restated his conviction and concluded with the greatest evasion available to a professor: "Come see me during office hours."

The proceedings of Foucault's office hours, unlike those of his lectures,
have not been transcribed and published, so we cannot say whether or how
he engaged the question. It is, however, a question worth asking seriously. A
century ago, few historians would have hesitated before describing medieval
and early modern conflicts between Christians and Jews (or Muslims) as
"racial." Today the situation has so reversed itself that any invocation of the
vocabulary of race by premodernists is an invitation to polemic. Foucault did
not bring about this consensus: to the contrary, in his restriction of race and
racism to modernity, at least, he was completely orthodox. What is at stake
in this orthodoxy? What work does it do for us in the present, and with what
effect on our understanding of the past? On what grounds might a critical
"reformation" of this orthodoxy be undertaken, and what devotional costs
and opportunities might such a reformation offer?

Less than a lifetime ago many believed that racial theories offered reasonable explanations of the differences they perceived between Jews and

Europeans, as well as among many other populations. The turning point in the fate of race as a scientific concept, especially vis-à-vis Jews and Judaism, is not difficult to find: it came at mid-twentieth century, with the German National Socialists' adoption of an explicitly racial ideology and of an exterminationist policy. The Second World War thoroughly discredited race as a mode of discourse in the biological and social sciences (though not in popular usage), so that today few reputable scholars would state that race is a concept capable of providing an acceptable explanation for the existence of cultural, economic, and social difference, or for the persistence of such difference through time. Indeed for the past half-century social scientists have been struggling, with mixed success, to supercede the older vocabulary and find new terms and theories with which to describe the persistence of group identity and group difference across time and space.[1]

For historians, however, the problem is a little different, for their interest is not primarily in the empirical validity or usefulness of racial ideas and ideologies, but rather in the role that these may have played in the thinking of their historical subjects. Nineteenth- and twentieth-century historians therefore speak without second thought about "racial anti-Semitism." Scholars of premodern European societies have had to ask additional questions. Can people writing before the development of modern evolutionary theories be said to think in terms of "race"? If not, then racism is a misleading anachronism when applied to discriminations between Jew and Christian before the modern age.

Precisely this question began to be posed with urgency after the rise of National Socialism. Some historians, such as Cecil Roth, saw real affinities between premodern ideologies (particularly those of late medieval Spain toward Christians descended from Jews) and modern (particularly German) ones, affinities he explored in an essay published in 1940, entitled "Marranos and Racial Anti-Semitism: A Study in Parallels." Others, like Guido Kisch, categorically denied any racial element in premodern anti-Judaism and criticized those who thought otherwise for "reading modern racist conceptions into medieval sources."[2] Yosef Haim Yerushalmi took up the debate in 1982, comparing late medieval Spanish ideologies that posited the immutability of Jewishness (i.e., that claimed Jewishness was carried in the blood and could not be erased by conversion) with nineteenth-century German anti-Semitic ideologies, and understanding both as recognizably racial.[3] More recently Jonathan Elukin used a similar logic to argue for an "incipient racial ideology" in medieval Europe.[4]

The polemic has grown into a heated one, with important consequences at stake. Did medieval systems of discrimination lead inexorably to modern exterminations? There are some for whom the gravitational pull of Auschwitz is so great that medieval ideologies about Jews become early coordinates in a trajectory clearly spiraling toward destruction. Such historians (Benzion Netanyahu is an example[5]) make free use of the words "race" and "racism" in their work on premodern attitudes toward Jews. Or was modern racial anti-Semitism the specific and contingent product of the intersection of capitalism, imperialism, and post-Enlightenment natural science, a phenomenon radically discontinuous with other histories? Most have preferred this position, perhaps because it erects a historical *cordon sanitaire* around an ideology that has come to stand for all that is evil in western Europe. The Reformation historian Heiko Oberman, for example, assures us that Reuchlin, Erasmus, and Luther were not racist in their many negative comments about Jews, about converts from Judaism, and about their descendents, for theirs was a purely theological understanding, not a biological one, which we might term anti-Judaism but not anti-Semitism.[6] The point is made more generally by Robert Bartlett: "while the language of race [in medieval sources] — gens, natio, 'blood,' 'stock,' etc. — is biological, its medieval *reality* was almost entirely cultural."[7] In other words, though there may be a biological tone to some of the language medieval people used to describe difference, the differences they were describing were cultural, not biological, and therefore their ideology cannot be described as racial.

Whatever their respective merits, these positions pay little attention to the modern theorizations of race and racism whose relevance they are either embracing or rejecting. Even if, for example, the convictions of Jewish immutability on which advocates of medieval racism focus were due to biological ideas (rather than to ideas about the educational influence of parents upon their children, about pollution and infection, about sin and divine will, about climactic influence, etc.), this would not suffice to make them racial in a modern sense. Many racial theories and ideologies allowed for a great deal of mutability, drawing their power precisely from the way they represented the risks of change, hybridity, and decline. Similarly, few of those who deny the possibility of a medieval racism have taken seriously the task of understanding in a suitably complex way the concept they seek to dismiss.[8] Some have taken refuge in nominalism, arguing (for example) that because the word *Rasse* did not enter the German language until the eighteenth century and the word *Anti-Semitismus* until the nineteenth, we need not look for these concepts in the earlier history of German-speaking lands. (As we shall see, the argument will not work for the romance languages, where the word *raza* has a medieval etymology.) Others have embraced narrow definitional strategies, which succeed not in solving the problem but in rendering it uninteresting. It is not surprising, for example, that those who define race as the application of eighteenth- and nineteenth-century vocabularies of biological classification to human populations differentiated by skin color are certain that it cannot be found in earlier periods.[9] Such definitions fail to make sense even of modern racial ideologies, which are themselves not only tremendously diverse but also change a great deal over time.

Finally, too many of the arguments against premodern racism still depend on the demonstrably false assumption that there exists a truly biological racism against which premodern forms of discrimination can be measured and judged innocent. What does it mean to say that although a premodern ideology was expressed in biological terms, it was not racial because the differences it reinforced were not really biological? This could be said of any racial ideology. All racisms are attempts to ground discriminations, whether social, economic, or religious, in biology and reproduction. All claim a congruence of "cultural" categories with "natural" ones. None of these claims, not even the most "scientific" ones of the twentieth century, reflect biological reality.[10] From the point of view of population genetics there are of course some real differences between sub-Saharan African populations and, say, Swedish ones, just as there are between Jewish and non-Jewish populations (as any student of breast cancer or Tay-Sachs disease knows), but none of these biological differences have any obvious or natural relationship to the cultural work they are asked to do in systems of racial discrimination, systems that are products of culture, not of nature.[11] If this lack of congruence does not suffice to make modern racist ideologies less "racial," then it cannot suffice to excuse premodern discriminations from the charge.[12]

I am not making these admittedly general criticisms in order to claim that race did exist in the Middle Ages, or that medieval people were racist. Such statements would be reductive and misleading, obscuring more than they reveal. But the same is true of the opposite, and far more common, assertion. The underdetermined and easily exorcised specter of a "true racism" against which premodern discriminations can be measured and exonerated has negatively affected both the medievalist and the modernist. Among medievalists it has stifled investigation of the strategies by which premodern people sought to make their own cultural classifications appear natural. Among modernists it has reinforced a tendency to think of modern ideologies as radically discontinuous from those of the distant past. In other words, the practice of defining race reductively for the purpose of summarily dismissing it from the premodern has effectively short-circuited the very processes of comparison and analogy upon which any argument about the relationship of past and present forms of discrimination must depend.

What might such a process of comparison and analogy look like? Let us focus on one particular geography and historiography, that of the Iberian Peninsula. Iberian history has long served as a focal point for arguments about premodern race because, as is well known, large populations of Muslims and Jews made the peninsular kingdoms the most religiously diverse in medieval western Europe. The late fourteenth and fifteenth centuries witnessed massive attempts to eliminate that diversity through massacre, segregation, conversion, Inquisition, and expulsion. In one sense these efforts toward homogeneity were successful. Over the course of the hundred years from 1391 to 1492, for example, all the Jews of Spain either converted or were expelled.[13]

But the conversion of a large number of people whom Christians had perceived as profoundly different transformed the old boundaries and systems of discrimination rather than abolished them. Categories that had previously seemed primarily legal and religious were replaced by the genealogical notion that Christians descended from Jewish converts (*Cristianos nuevos, confessos, conversos, marranos*) were essentially different from "Christians by nature" (*Cristianos de natura, cristianos viejos, limpios*). Moreover, the ideological underpinning of these new discriminations claimed explicitly to be rooted in natural realities, as is most evident in the doctrine of "limpieza de sangre." According to this doctrine, Jewish and Muslim blood was inferior to Christian; the possession of any amount of such blood made one liable to heresy and moral corruption; therefore any descendent of Jews and Muslims, no matter how distant, should be barred from church and secular office, from any number of guilds and professions, and especially from marrying Old Christians.

The debate over the utility of concepts such as race and racism in explaining these conflicts, discriminations, and ideologies has been heated. It has remained, however, bedeviled by the fiction of true race. In the early years of history as *Wissenschaft*, of course, this fiction enabled racial analysis, because historians themselves believed in the racial logic they were attributing to their historical subjects. In writing of conflict between Christians, Muslims, and Jews, historians constantly employed the vocabulary of race, although they meant very different things by it.[14] An early example is that of Leopold von Ranke, who believed that the Old Christian refusal to intermarry with New Christians was an extension of the ancient abhorrence that the "Germanic" and "Romanic" races felt toward amalgamation with "Semitic" Jews and Muslims.[15] Half a century later (ca. 1882) the great historian Marcelino Menéndez y Pelayo, in whose honor Spain's Real Academia de la Historia is named, could echo Darwin unselfconsciously: "It is madness to believe that battles for existence, bloody and century long struggles between races, could end in any way other than with expulsions and exterminations. The inferior race always succumbs. . . ." Elsewhere he opined that "the matter of race [by which he meant the existence of "Semitic" Jews and Muslims] explains many phenomena and resolves many enigmas in our history" and "is the principal cause of decadence for the [Iberian] Peninsula." At much the same time, though an ocean and an ideology away, Henry Charles Lea also adopted racial categories in order to make more or less the opposite argument, that the Spanish Inquisition was an instrument of racism.[16]

But as we have already seen from the debate between Cecil Roth and Guido Kisch, such certainties began to fade in the mid-twentieth century. Within the ambit of Spanish historiography, Américo Castro became perhaps the most influential critic of racial vocabulary. Castro was interested in debunking not just notions of Jewish or Muslim racial identity but the idea of a "raza hispanica" as well. As he put it in one of his later works, "faith in the temporally uncertain biological continuity of the Spaniard has inspired the works both of respected men of wisdom and of superficial scholars."[17] His task, as he saw it, was to demonstrate the falsity of any model of Spanish identity based on such a faith. To this end, Castro began nearly all of his books with an attack on the relevance of the concept of race to Spanish history.[18] In the opening of *The Spaniards*, for example, he explains that he speaks of Muslim, Jewish and Christian "castes," not races, "for in that Spain of three religions everyone was light-skinned, with horizontal eyes, except for a few black slaves brought in from Africa," (v) Similarly in the introduction to the 1965 edition of *La realidad* he writes, "A much wider detour will be necessary in order to include in future historiography the positive and decisive presence of the Moorish and Jewish castes (not races!). Because the resistance is notable to the acceptance that the Spanish problem was of castes, and not of races, [a term] today only applicable to those distinguished, as the Dictionary of the Academy has it, 'by the color of their skin and other characteristics.'"[19]

When Castro made these arguments he was engaging many Spanish scholars who maintained that Jews and Muslims were members of races inferior to the "raza hispanica."[20] By repudiating the vocabulary of race, he helped bring these groups back into the mainstream of Spanish history and culture. That repudiation, however, depended on familiar strategies: first a nominalist focus on the *Diccionario*'s definition of race as referring only to skin color (he ignored the ominous "Y otros caracteres"), then the conjuration of an easily dismissed "true" biological racism based solely on external physical characteristics.[21]

Castro's approach to race is the one point of his *oeuvre* with which nearly all Spanish and French scholars of peninsular history agree. In the words of a devoted "Castrista," F. Márquez Villanueva, "The problem of the New Christians was by no means a racial one; it was social and in the second line religious. The *converso* did not carry in any moment an indelible biological stigma. . . ." Historians with less enthusiasm for many of Castro's broader arguments agree. As Adeline Rucquoi recently put it, "Loin d'être lié à des concepts plus ou moins biologiques de 'race,' loin aussi d'être un simple mécanisme d'exclusion d'un groupe social par un autre, le problème de la pureté du sang nous paraît être un problème ontologique, lié dans l'Espagne du début des Temps Modernes au problème du salut." [Far from being linked to more or less biological concepts of "race," and far from being a simple mechanism for exclusion of one social group by another, the problem of purity of blood seems to us to be an ontological problem, linked in early modern Spain to the problem of health.] The fact that the few dissenting voices are mostly American has perhaps contributed to the polarization, as Spanish scholars have sought to distance themselves from what they perceive to be a polemical Anglo-Saxon historiography.[22]

As these examples make clear, the trajectory of Iberian historiography on the subject of race is parallel to that of other European historiographic traditions, though of course it has its own particular history. What might a counterhistory look like? To begin with, it might emphasize, rather than elide, the medieval vocabularies through which "naturalizations" of difference were expressed. The history of the Romance word "raza" (from whence came the English word "race") provides an obvious starting point. The Castilian word does cover a broad semantic field,[23] yet certain corners of that field deserve closer cultivation than they have received. Castro's invocation of the Real Academia's modern definition of "raza" in order to dismiss the possibility of premodern "Spanish" racism is in fact a startling procedure, given that Castro was a philologist who had elsewhere, for example, deployed the history of the word "Español" to suggest that the concept of "Spanishness" was a late import to Spanish culture. *Raza* too is a word with a suggestive history in the various romance languages of the peninsula.

Already in the early fifteenth century "raza," "casta," and "linaje" were part of a complex of interchangeable terms that linked both behavior and appearance to nature and reproduction. Some of these terms, like "linaje," had a long history that was only tangentially related to Judaism, even if they could be used to tie character to lineage. By about 1435, for example, it made sense for Gutierre Díez de Games to explain all treason in terms of Jewish "linaje": "From the days of Alexander up till now, there has never been a treasonous act that did not involve a Jew or his descendants."[24] The Castilian word "raza" was newer, and it seems to have emerged as a way of describing defects linked specifically to Judaism. Francisco Imperial's exhortatory poem addressed to the king in 1407 provides an early but ambiguous example: "A los tus suçessores claro espejo/ sera mira el golpe de la maça./sera miral el cuchillo bermejo/que cortara doquier que falle Raza." [It shall be a clear example to your successors to see the blow of the mace, to see the roseate knife that will cut wherever it finds a flaw ("raza")]. Scholars have not seen in this early use an association of "raza" to "lineage of Jews." But the poet's condemnation of the "bestia Juderra" a few lines before (line 321) suggests otherwise, as does his echo of the exhortation, commonly addressed to Trastamaran kings of Castile, that they defeat that Jewish beast.[25]

In any event the relationship soon became more obvious. Alfonso Martínez de Toledo, writing around 1438 in the midst of an evolving conflict over converse office holding in Toledo (discussed below), provides a clear example of the emerging logic of *raza*. You can always tell a person's roots, he explains, for those who descend from good stock are incapable of deviating from it, whereas those of base stock cannot transcend their origins, regardless of whatever money, wealth, or power they may obtain. The reasons for this, he asserts, are natural. The son of an ass must bray. This can be proven, he suggests, by an experiment. If one were to take two babies, one a son of a laborer, the other of a knight, and rear them together on a mountain in isolation from their parents, one would find that the son of the laborer delights in agricultural pursuits, while the son of the knight takes pleasure only in feats of arms and equestrianship: "Esto procura naturaleza." "Thus you will see every day in the places where you live, that the good man of good raça always returns to his origins, whereas the miserable man, of bad raça or lineage, no matter how powerful or how rich, will always return to the villainy from which he descends . . . That is why when such men or women have power they do not use it as they should, as the old refrain says: 'Vídose el perro en bragas de cerro, e non conosçió a su compañero.'"[26]

Not everyone agreed with such ideas; indeed they were subject to strenuous debate (just as there were many who doubted the claims of eighteenth- and nineteenth-century racial theories). But there is no doubt that this language was saturated, then as now, with resonance to what contemporaries held to be "common sense" knowledge about the reproductive systems of the natural world.[27] To confirm this we need only open a medieval manual on animal husbandry like that of Manuel Diez. His popular manual on the care of horses (written ca. 1430) admonished breeders to be careful in their selection of stock: "For there is no animal that so resembles or takes after the father in virtues and beauties, nor in size, or coat, and similarly for their contraries. So that it is advised that he who wishes to have good race and caste of horses that above all he seek out the horse or stallion that he be good and beautiful and of good coat, and the mare that she be large and well formed and of good coat."[28] The relevance of knowledge about horse breeding to an understanding of the application of *raza* to the descendents of converts from Judaism and Islam was noted already by scholars in the early modern period. Sebastian de Covarrubias, in the famous Spanish dictionary he published in 1611, defined "raza" as "the caste of purebred horses, which are marked by a brand so that they can be recognized. . . . Race in [human] lineages is meant negatively, as in having some race of Moor or Jew."[29]

The natural science upon which such wisdom was based was not that of the nineteenth century, but it was nonetheless capable of generating conclusions startlingly similar to those of a later age.[30] Nor, I hasten to add, was this logic in any way particular to Spain. In 1538 Jacobus Sadoletus would urge the readers of his child-rearing manual "that what is done with horses and dogs should also be done with men . . . so that out of good parents there might be born a progeny useful to both the king and the fatherland." Joachim du Bellay (ca. 1559) admonished the French parliament in a similar vein:

> For if we are so careful to preserve the race
> Of good horses and good hounds for chase
> How much more should a king carefully provide
> For the race, which is his principal power?[31]

The point, in short, is that words like *raza* and *linaje* (and their cognates in the various Iberian romance languages) were already embedded in identifiably biological ideas about breeding and reproduction in the first half of the fifteenth century.[32] Moreover, the sudden appearance of this vocabulary and its application to Jews precisely coincides chronologically (the 1430s) with the appearance of anti-*converso* ideologies that sought to naturalize religious categories and hierarchies and to legitimate their reproduction. One of the earliest examples comes from 1433. It was on January 10 of that year that Queen María decreed on behalf of the converts of Barcelona that no legal distinction could be made between "natural" Christians on the one hand and neophytes and their descendants on the other, a decree which implies that some people were attempting to make precisely those distinctions.[33] The following year the Council of Basel decreed that ". . . since [the converts] became by the grace of baptism fellow citizens of the saints and members of the house of God, and since regeneration of the spirit is much more important than birth in the flesh . . . they enjoy the privileges, liberties, and immunities of those cities and towns where they were regenerated through sacred baptism to the same extent as the natives and other Christians do."[34]

Such proclamations had suddenly become necessary. A few months later King Alfonso of Aragon rejected attempts in Calatayud to impose disabilities on neophytes; in 1436, the councilors of Barcelona moved to bar converts and those whose parents were not both "christianos de natura" from holding the office of notary; in 1437 the town council of Lleida attempted to strip *conversos* of broker's licenses.[35] The converts of Catalonia and Valencia felt compelled to appeal to the pope, and in 1437 Eugene IV condemned those "sons of iniquity . . . Christians only in name," who suggested that recent converts be barred from public office and who "refuse to enter into matrimony with them."[36] Similar attempts took place in Castile. In Seville, an antimonarchical rebellion may have planned to murder the *converso* population in 1433–1434, and ten years later, still in the midst of civil war, King Juan II felt obliged to instruct the cities of his kingdom that the *conversos* were to be treated "as if they were born Christians," and admitted to "any honorable office of the Republic."[37]

As we can see from these examples, a naturalizing vocabulary was beginning to be applied to converts and their descendants. The "christiano de natura" mentioned by Queen María became a common (though by no means exclusive) term of reference for old Christians. The exclusionary genealogical logic of the term was perfectly clear to *conversos*, some of whom coined a rebuttal: "cristianos de natura, cristianos de mala ventura" (Christians by nature are Christians of bad fortune). By this they meant (or at least so they told the Inquisition decades later) that *conversos* shared the lineage of the Virgin Mary, whereas old Christians were descended from idol-worshiping gentiles.[38] The topic is too complicated to address here, but such evidence suggests that the converts, under the pressure of the Old Christian *Naturgeschichte*, were beginning to see their own identity in increasingly genealogical terms.[39] In any event the wide extension of such vocabulary in the 1430s and following decades makes clear that the role of lineage in determining character, which had become an increasingly important aspect of chivalric and aristocratic ideology in Iberia in the decades following the Trastamaran civil war, was now becoming more explicitly biological and being applied extensively to converts from Judaism.[40] As the *conversos'* rebuttal makes clear, the logic of lineage was not *a priori* prejudicial to converts, and indeed was often deployed in defense of *converso* rights. Many writers argued, as did Diego de Valera around 1441, that the *conversos'* descent from the chosen people ennobled them.[41] But in fact throughout the middle decades of the fifteenth century, these naturalizations came increasingly to be deployed against *conversos*.

The Toledan revolt of 1449 against the monarchy and its perceived agents, the *conversos*, provides a good example of such deployment. The Toledans and their sympathizers were clearly anxious about the reproduction of social and political status, an anxiety they transposed into a sexual key. Thus they claimed that converts were motivated only by ambition for office and "carnal lust for nuns and [Christian] virgins," and that Marrano physicians poisoned their Christian patients in order to get hold of their inheritance and offices, "marry the wives of the old Christians they kill" and stain their "clean blood" (*sangre limpia*).[42] Arguing that Jewish ancestry (somatically expressed in terms of Jewish blood) predisposed people to corruption and viciousness (cf. the passage from the *Arcipreste* cited in note 26 above), the Toledans proposed to stem this tide of sexual and economic competition with what later would come to be called a purity of blood statute: descendants of converts were to be banned from holding public office.[43]

The texts produced by the rebels and their allies in defense of their position, and by opponents like Alonso de Cartagena, Lope Barrientos, and Fernán Díaz de Toledo against it, became central texts in the Spanish debate over the "Jewishness" of converts and their descendents. The eventual victory of the anti-*converso* genealogical arguments in the debate was not obvious or easy, for medieval people had a great many ways of thinking about the transmission of cultural characteristics across generations without invoking nature and sexual reproduction. Pope Pius II, for example, authorized an annulment for Pedro de la Caballeria in 1459, on the grounds that his wife was a heretic who had been taught to "judaize" by her mother. ". . . Pedro, a true Catholic, is prepared to endure . . . every danger of death rather than consummate a marriage of this sort, lest [any] begotten offspring follow the insanity of the mother, and a Jew be created out of a Christian." Though this text has been interpreted as exhibiting a sense of hereditary Jewishness, its logic appears quite different once we realize that Pedro de la Caballeria was himself almost certainly a *converso*. The problem here is one of pedagogy and nurture, not inheritance.[44]

Nevertheless the genealogical turn was taken, and it proved to be one of extraordinary power. The reasons for its success are many and complex, but one which should not be underestimated is the power of its appeal to medieval "common knowledge" about nature. Consider, for example, the language of a treatise like the *Alborayque* (ca. 1455–1465). The treatise maps moral attributes and cultural practices of the *conversos* onto diverse body parts of the Alborayque, the Qur'anic composite beast (part horse, part lion, part snake, etc.) that carried Muhammad to heaven. The use of this hybrid to stand for the converts, though often treated by modern critics as a mere conceit, is in fact a systematic strategy of argument from nature. The converts are not only Alborayques. They are bats, unclassifiable as animal (wings) or bird (teeth); they are a weak alloy rather than pure metal; and above all, they are a mixed lineage, a mixture of Edom, Moab, Amon, Egypt, and more. These unnatural mixtures support the conclusion (and here is the leap to culture) that the *conversos* can never be classified as Christian, for "si los metales son muchos ... segun la carne, quanto mas de metales de tantas heregias"[45] [if the alloys are many ... according to the flesh, how many more the alloys of so many heresies]. Similarly the negative imagery of mixed species in the treatise leads ineluctably to its conclusion: a prayer that the "clean" lineages of the Old Christians not be corrupted through marriage with the New.[46]

Like a number of polemicists before him, the author of the *Alborayque* chose to focus on the corruption of the Jewish lineage in historical time, but other approaches were possible.[47] Writing at about the same time, for example, Alonso de Espina verged on a polygenetic approach when he related the lineage of Jews to the offspring of (1) Adam with animals and (2) Adam with the demon Lilith. As a result of these unions, he wrote, Jews are of the lineage of demons and of monsters, the mule and the sow their adoptive mother.[48] Such genealogies doubtless seemed as fantastic to many medieval readers as they do to us. They provided an important theoretical underpinning, however, for the doctrine of "limpieza de sangre," or purity of blood: the idea that the reproduction of culture is embedded in the reproduction of the flesh. It is upon this logic that new boundaries would be built between Christian and "Jew" in Spain. These new boundaries were enormously controversial.[49] I know of no more extensive premodern discussion about the relationship between biology and culture than that in the literature produced in the debate over *converso* exclusion between 1449 and 1550.[50] But the logic of the *Alborayque*, with its mapping of Judaizing behavior onto Jewish genealogy, was eventually victorious, and the consequences of that victory were momentous. The argument that *converso* morals were habitually corrupt, for example, led to the establishment of the first "proto-Inquisition" under Alonso de Oropesa in the 1460s. Oropesa, a prominent opponent of discrimination against descendents of *conversos*, found little evidence for these charges, but their increasingly effective reiteration was used to justify the establishment of the Inquisition itself in 1481. And this Inquisition operated according to a logic strikingly similar to that of the *Alborayque*. Judaizers were to be identified by their behavior, but that behavior only gained meaning in light of their genealogy.

Already in 1449 Fernán Díaz, the relator of Juan II, had pointed out the dangers of such a genealogical system. There was scarcely a noble house in

Spain that had no *converso* in its family tree. If Jewishness were attached to blood, the relator warned, the nobility of Iberia would be destroyed.[51] Moreover, because the effects of genealogy were primarily expressed culturally, the religioracial classification of cultural practice became an important part of the accusational economy. Virtually any negative cultural trait could be presented as Judaizing. We have seen the *Alborayque*'s list, and there were many others, each sounding more and more like Borges's Chinese encyclopedia. Jewish characteristics, according to the bishop of Cordoba in 1530, included heresy, apostasy, love of novelty and dissension, ambition, presumption, and hatred of peace. The list of traits grew ever longer, and all of them could be encoded, at least in theory, in the smallest drop of blood. The effectiveness of such claims in attracting the attention of Inquisitional courts made them strategically useful and thereby judaized ever more extensive cultural practices. By 1533, even Rodrigo Manrique, son of the then inquisitor general, could write to the self-exiled humanist Luis Vives, "You are right. Our country is a land of . . . barbarism. For now it is clear that no one can possess any culture without being suspect of heresy, error, and Judaism."[52]

We have seen that fifteenth-century Spaniards utilized a vocabulary of race grounded in theories of animal husbandry that posited the biological reproduction of somatic and behavioral traits. We have also seen how this vocabulary underwrote a set of strategies that explained and legitimated the creation and perpetuation of certain hierarchies and discriminations through the language of reproduction. We cannot, however, therefore conclude that we are justified in speaking of modern "race" and "racism" in fifteenth-century Spain. All we have shown is that one influential family of arguments for dismissing the relevance of "race" to medieval Spain, that of Américo Castro and his disciples, makes inadequate sense of the "natural histories" available to residents of the Iberian Peninsula in the fifteenth and sixteenth centuries.

The humility of this conclusion can be defended on a number of grounds. Perhaps the least rigorous (though not necessarily the least important) is previous experience with the risks of certainty. Américo Castro's easy isolation of race in the epidermis, for example, blinded him to the ways in which his methodology simply displaced the naturalizing and essentializing functions of race unto the less charged term of "caste" (much as many speakers today use "ethnicity"). There is a close kinship between Castro's "Semitic caste" and "Semitic culture" and Ernest Renan's "Semitic race." Both posited stable, essential, and inescapable forms of group identity continuously reproduced across time. Castro, like Renan, combed "Jewish" texts beginning with the Old Testament for Semitic characteristics whose entrance into Spain he then attributed to Jews and *conversos*. He found a number of them. "Inquisitorial fanaticism and recourse to slandering informants — what one might call in Spanish 'malsinismo' — frantic greed and plundering, the concern over purity of blood . . . the concern with public reputation . . . the desire of everyone to be a nobleman . . . somber asceticism . . . the negative view of the world . . . disillusionment, and the flight from human values," all of these were the "poisons . . . that seeped into Spanish life, Spanish Christendom, in the increment of forced converts."[53]

These "cultural" traits of Jews and converts are startlingly similar, not only to those "racial" ones listed by Renan or his disciples (which on this score included Claudio Sánchez Albornoz[54]) but also to those of fifteenth- and sixteenth-century anti-*converso* tracts advocating *limpieza.* Nor are the means of their reproduction so very different, for though Castro and his students rejected biological explanations for cultural transmission, they relied heavily on genealogical ones, frequently mapping a particular intellectual position or literary style onto a family tree in order to prove the "Semiticness" of either the idea or its exponent, a type of logic that has turned the Iberianist into a disciple of the inquisitor.[55] Like many other historians and philologists, Castro fled from the horrifying embrace of race straight into the arms of another genetic fantasy. Small wonder that, far from having banished race and racism, he found himself accused of replicating it under another name.[56]

There are more methodological arguments for humility. It is an ancient tendency of the historical imagination to think of ideas and concepts as having a discrete origin in a particular people, whence they are transmitted from donor to recipient cultures across space and time. There may be some concepts whose histories are well described by such etymological and genealogical approaches.[57] In this chapter, however, we are concerned with the conviction that culture is produced and reproduced in the same way as the species procreates itself. This conviction, which we might call the enabling condition of racial thought, is so venerable and widespread that Giambattista Vico elevated it to a universal in his *Principles of the New Science.* Moreover it is also infinitely diverse. Even when restricted to modernity, "race" and "racism" encompass too heterogeneous a set of discourses and outcomes to be understood as a "concept" or a "theory." Given this range and diversity, any history of race's origin and transmission can only be the product of our (generally inadvertently) constrained recognition of significance. Foucault famously illustrated the limitations of such "histories of knowledge" by quoting from Borges's Chinese encyclopedia. Frege put it in very different but still useful terms: "What is known as the history of concepts is really a history either of our knowledge of concepts or of the meaning of words."[58] Taken too seriously, such Platonism would paralyze the writing of history. Its warning becomes more relevant, however, the more generalized our topics. Specifically, when historians relate diverse "natural histories" to each other in an evolutionary genealogy, they are not so much clarifying the histories of these discourses as reproducing their logic.

None of this means that histories of race should not be written. There will always be strategic reasons for choosing to represent the relationship of ideas about the natural reproduction of culture that are scattered across time and space in terms of filiations or, conversely, in terms of disjuncture. Yet the choice can only be situational and polemical, in the sense that its recognition of significance springs from the needs and struggles (political, philosophical, theological, historiographic, etc.) of a specific moment. The polemics produced by such choices are invaluable when they stimulate us to self-consciousness. If, however, we treat them as anything but strategic, we simply exchange one lack of consciousness for another.

As an example of this last point, let us return to the conceptualization of race with which we began, that of Michel Foucault. Foucault's treatment of race (which came only late in his career) derived from his understanding of other transformations more central to his *oeuvre*, particularly those from "regimes of blood" to "regimes of sex." Foucault understood the emergence of racism as a consequence of a struggle for sovereignty. According to him, medieval sovereignty was organic and corporatist. It was of course hierarchical and therefore potentially conflictual, but the potential for conflict was always contained by a ritual regime and a historical discourse that were celebratory and inclusive. Even warring nations never forgot their common ancestry, going back, if not to Rome then to Troy. And from this memory sprang as well a common historiography. "What is there in [medieval] history," Foucault asked, quoting Petrarch, "that is not in praise of Rome?"[59]

Foucault believed that race arose out of the collapse of this system. By the early seventeenth century, society was no longer thought of as an organic system, but as a binary. The governing metaphor was no longer that of society as a harmonious body, but of society as a war between two irreconcilable groups or bodies. And although those groups could be characterized and classified in a number of ways (e.g., as classes), the symbolic logic underlying these classifications was always racial, in that it imagined one group as polluting and the other pure, one to be isolated or exterminated, the other to be protected and reproduced. The emerging nation-state was at first the venue for this struggle between groups, then eventually its arbiter, the chief guarantor of racial purity. This final nineteenth-century stage Foucault referred to as "state racism." And just as history in the Middle Ages had been a reflection of the symbolic order that articulated power in terms of organic unity, in modern history it became a battlefield, an accounting of losses and victories in the eternal war of the races.

Foucault's "history" of race, like his other histories, was explicitly strategic. It was designed to counter the fantasies of lineage that he perceived as seducing prevailing history. "History," he therefore insisted, "is for cutting." Perhaps because these cuts were meant to denature the workings of modern discourse, the premodern often fell on their far side, as it does here, in the case of race. How should premodernists confront such a history?[60] Remaining within the example of Spain and its Jews, we might be inspired to ask if medieval Christian understandings of sacred history also took the form of a binary opposition between Christian and Jew, and if so, how the cultural work of such a binary in the Middle Ages differed from or was similar to the work Foucault had in mind in the modern age. We might note the formal similarities with the "racial antisemitism" of later periods that so struck scholars like Netanyahu, Yerushalmi, Frederickson, and Waltz. But we might also note how different the uses, functions, and effects of these medieval ideologies were from modern ones. We might, in other words, use Foucault's history as a stimulant best expressed by the almost untranslatable German term "Auseinandersetzung."

What we should not do, however, is take its dictates too seriously. On the one hand, if we embrace its disjunctures as sufficient evidence for the irrelevance of race and racism in the Middle Ages, then we are replicating Foucault's strategic use of the premodern as an unhistoricized foil for the modern. If, on the other hand, we argue from similarity in order to establish the identity of the premodern with the modern, we simply reverse the polemic. Kathleen Biddick, for example, finds in medieval texts a simultaneous insistence on the importance of blood and of pedagogy and concludes that Foucault's insistence on the modernity of blood regimes and disciplinarity is therefore incorrect. "Disciplinarity (pedagogy) was always already folded within this colonial symbolics of blood."[61] With this discovery she claims to have uncovered the "banality" of Foucault's periodization, though to my mind her "always already" threatens to substitute a more dangerous one in its place.[62]

Race demands a history, both because it is a subject both urgent and vast and because its own logic is so closely akin to that of the disciplines (etymology, genealogy, history) with which we study the persistence of humanity in time. For these same reasons, any history of race will be at best limited, strategic, and polemical and at worst a reproduction of racial logic itself. In either case, histories of race are best read by premodernist and modernist alike not as prescriptive but as provocations to comparison. There is energy to be drawn from the collision of such polemics with our own particles of history, and new elements of both past and present to be found in the wreckage. Put another way, we might read such histories as metaphors. I mean metaphor not in the sense of model or map, as some anthropologists and scholars of comparative religion have recently championed, but in the medieval sense articulated by Albert of Monte Casino: "it is the function of metaphor to twist, so to speak, its mode of speech from its property; by twisting, to make some innovation; by innovating, to clothe, as it were, in nuptial garb; and by clothing, to sell, apparently at a decent price."[63] As in Albert's understanding of good metaphor, good histories and theorizations of race are a source of productive deceit. The associations they provoke are seductive, communicative, startlingly revealing, but also in some sense fraudulent. We cannot reject their power without impoverishment, but neither can we accept their suggestions without suspicion.

The same is true, of course, in reverse. Just as modernity provokes the medievalist, so should medieval encounters disturb the troubled certitudes of the modernist. The latter will, however, not travel without guides: yet another reason why it is important that premodernists (or at least those interested in specific problems, such as the transformations of religious categories in fifteenth-century Spain) confront their subjects' natural histories, rather than hiding behind a nominalist rejection of race. But it is equally important that we not confuse the strategic comparisons and heuristic polemics produced by such confrontations with a history of "race" or "racism." The suggestion that we can benefit from the systematic juxtaposition of various strategies of naturalization need not imply that these strategies can be arranged into an evolutionary history of race, just as the argument that we can learn from the similarities we discover between, say, fifteenth-century ideologies and twentieth-century ones need not suggest that one followed from the other.[64] Admittedly the danger of such a fallacy is great, for the subject of race tends to bewitch its historians with the same philogenetic fantasies and teleological visions that underwrite racial ideologies themselves.[65] But if we wish to study how medieval people sought to naturalize their own histories while at the same time attempt to denaturalize our own, it is a risk worth taking.

CHAPTER FIVE

THE SPANISH RACE

Barbara Fuchs

This chapter considers the construction of Spanish identity, both within and outside Spain, in relation to "maurophilia"—the cultural fascination with Moors in early modern Europe. I use the term "Moor" rather than a more ethnographically precise alternative both because its ambiguity is useful for my purposes and because it reflects early modern usage. The term could refer both to light- and dark-skinned people, to Muslims in Spain as well as in North Africa, and even, occasionally, to Turks or sub-Saharan peoples. The capaciousness of the category made it particularly useful for early modern discourses of race, which oscillated among biological, genealogical, ethnic, and cultural definitions.[1] As I will show, these malleable discourses became particularly effective in the construction of the Black Legend.

I am particularly intrigued by the domestic side of maurophilia—that is, the enduring and intense negotiation of Moorish culture within Spain after the fall of Granada, as the emerging nation attempts to solidify its identity. As will become clear, however, this negotiation is closely connected to the representation of Spain elsewhere in Europe, so that the national problem quickly becomes international in scope. We are used to thinking of Spain's self-definition in the sixteenth century as a process of excising the Semitic—both Jewish and Moorish—elements from its culture. The fall of Granada in 1492 and the concurrent expulsion of the Jews are taken as signal events in its nation formation. Yet after 1492 Spanish culture in fact retains and even celebrates the Arabic culture of al-Andalus; in many cases, particularly where popular culture is concerned, the Spanish and Andalusi cultures come together in hybrid forms. Moreover, even as Spain goes to great pains to contain the influence of al-Andalus by racializing and othering *conversos* and *moriscos*—Jews and Moors who had undergone forced conversion—rival European states busily construct Spain as precisely the racial other of Europe.

I find this conflictive negotiation a central problem for two reasons. First, because a more balanced history of Spanish national identity requires us to reexamine its enduring fascination with Moorish culture as well as the persecution and expulsion of the Moors. If we reconstruct this affinity without taking the exclusionary nation as a given, we find a far more nuanced and often contradictory situation than what the shrillest denunciations of the Semitic presence in Spain would suggest. Second, because of the increasing sense within early modern studies that the models of postcolonial theory—in this case, primarily Said's *Orientalism*—should be refined to consider earlier encounters and situations in which Europe bears a very different relationship to the East. Though medievalists have recently countered Said's claim that medieval orientalism was a purely textual phenomenon, they have not adequately addressed the problem of Spain and its peculiar relationship to an Orient within.[2] Scholars of early modern England, for their part, have challenged Said's model for its anachronism but have not tackled the specific, very different modes of conceiving the East across Europe.[3]

Consider two admittedly impressionistic pieces of evidence for just how complex Spain's institutional relation to its Moorish past is today. The city of Cáceres, in Extremadura features among its attractions a "Casa-Museo Arabe," which reproduces the inside of a house "as it might have looked under Arab domination," with a clear emphasis on the exotic; incense and colorful silks are found everywhere.[4] The reconstruction produces Moorishness as a difference within. Although the museum, in a city famed for its Renaissance palaces, clearly attempts to remind us of how widespread Moors and *moriscos* were throughout Spain, it paradoxically circumscribes the Moorish influence to one highly fanciful interior. My second piece of evidence is the much more sober house of Lope de Vega, the most canonical of Spanish Golden Age playwrights, in Madrid. Lope's house, which displays furnishings from the period, nonetheless features braziers, pillows on the floor, and a number of elements of what is clearly a Moorish heritage, yet there is no acknowledgment that the high Spanish culture here being celebrated owes anything to al-Andalus. Hybridization either goes unremarked or is swept under the rug.

The juxtaposition of these two very different institutions suggests an attempt to quarantine Moorish influence, which clearly pervaded Spanish culture well into the early modern period, while mainstream Spanish culture, whether wilfully or unconsciously, ignores its Moorish side. The presence of Moors is recognized, of course, but not as an integral, hybridized facet of Spanishness. The critical recovery of hybrid practices, I would suggest, provides one way to challenge the highly artificial boundaries, such as the touting of Moorish exoticism for tourists, within which Spain manages the legacy of al-Andalus. This seems particularly urgent in present-day Spain, moreover, as the celebration of Moorish heritage in the official discourse of tourism co-exists with a marked racism against North African immigrants.

The distinctions established in the national imaginary are often chrono-logical, as though with the fall of Granada Moors and their culture had dis-appeared from Spain. That story of supersession and split temporality is one I would like to complicate here: the place of Moorish culture within Spanish national identity continues to be a central quandary well after 1492; some might say that the issue is far from resolved today. There is also, of course, a different kind of split temporality in the frequent recuperation of a glorious Moorish past for the nation within a contemporary climate of intolerance and racial prejudice and of closed borders. The role of the Moors in Spain in this respect is reminiscent of the place of the mestizo in the imaginary of many Latin American nations, marked by the idealization in a sanitized national mythology of groups consistently marginalized or persecuted in the present.[5]

FROM LITERATURE TO CULTURE

The term "maurophilia" was first proposed by the French historian Georges Cirot in a series of articles that appeared in the *Bulletin Hispanique* from 1938 to 1944. Cirot largely circumscribes the fascination with Moorish culture as a literary phenomenon (his actual term is *maurophilie littéraire*) and dismisses it as a fashion of no particular cultural significance.[6] This same impetus lies behind the diminutive *novelita morisca*, the term used by some critics to sug-gest the limited significance of the genre—which includes such pointedly political texts as *El Abencerraje, Las Guerras Civiles de Granada*, and "Ozmín y Daraja"—as a *divertissement* or trifle. Yet some earlier scholars noted well the larger significance of maurophilia. As Ramón Menéndez Pidal pointed out fifty years ago in his *España y su historia*, the broad pervasiveness of the Moor-ish fashion and its larger implications for understanding early modern Spain demand further study.[7]

My own argument relies on the expansion of maurophilia from literary curiosity to cultural phenomenon. The prolonged attachment to Moorish culture in not just literary texts but the culture at large highlights the com-plex relation of Spanish national identity to that which it attempts to deny. Beyond the culture's psychic investment in the other, we need to examine the material investment manifested in clothing, jousting games, and other forms that Spain adopts whosesale from al-Andalus. Whereas the fine work of Stally-brass and Jones[8] is concerned largely with the cultural value of dress as an intra-European phenomenon, here I examine "national costume" as one in-dex of the enduring trace of al-Andalus in Spain, for the ways in which it complicates the category of Europe itself.[9] For if Spain's self-representation continually invokes Moorish culture, in both a domestic and an international context, when other nations rehearse Spain's maurophilia they often transform it into an essentialized discourse of racism and xenophobia that negates Spain's place within Europe. The very different valence of maurophilia from a domestic and a foreign perspective signals its central importance for the construction of national identity.

Costume presents a particularly interesting problem. Historian Carmen Bernís has traced the wide acceptance of Moorish fashions among Christians in Spain, both before and after 1492.[10] Bernís notes the gradual dissemination of Moorish costume throughout a widening swath of society. While initially adopted as an extravagant fashion by the upper classes, who prized Moorish textiles for their showiness and often wore them for ceremonial occasions, certain items, such as the *toca* or headdress, were eventually worn by plain folk in the Castilian countryside. The negotiation between the exotic and the quotidian is particularly intriguing here. The initial, ceremonial uses mark Spain as an exotic, impressive presence for early observers, as in the royal jousting games — *juegos de cañas* — held to celebrate the arrival in Spain of Princess Margarita of Austria, witnessed by an Italian traveler soon after the fall of Granada:

> La regia magesta et il principe montati in su cavalli velocissimi, con le targe loro, vestiti a la morescha de salii et manti de brochato, cum diversi rechami et gale, con la testa velata al modo moresco.
>
> Il conestabili, duchi de Alva, Biegera, Alburchech et marchese de Villafrancha vestiti a la modesima foglia ma tutti de varii colori, et tanto richamente quanto sia posibile . . . Cum epsi erano multi altri conti et cavalieri, tutti cum salii et manti de brocato et seta sopre seta, cum tanti recami de oro et argento, con si varie et bella fogie, che era cosa de maraveglia.[11]
>
> [His royal majesty and the prince rode on their very swift horses, with their shields, dressed in the Moorish fashion with brocade mantles and doublets, with various embroideries and ornaments, with their head veiled in the Moorish fashion.
>
> The Constable, and Dukes of Alva, Biegera, Albuquerque and Marquiss of Villafranca dressed in the same fashion but all in different colors, and as richly as possible. With them were many other counts and knights, all with brocade doublets and mantles and silk over silk, with so much embroidery in gold and silver, with such varied and beautiful fashions, that it was a marvelous thing.]

In many *juegos de cañas*, unlike the mock combats between Moors and Christians, all participants dressed in Moorish clothes. It thus seems difficult to dismiss this particular embrace of Moorish finery as simply a reenactment of Christian superiority over Islam—the performance is staged exclusively by ersatz Moors to awe a foreign audience. A similar ceremonial instance of Spanish self-fashioning as the exotic occurs at Charles V's imperial coronation in Aix-la-Chapelle, with Spanish pages "tocados a la morisca" (in Moorish headdress) in the emperor's train.[12] Here, Moorish headdress sets the Spaniards apart from the Germans, the Flemish, and the Burgundians.

Within Spain, such headdress was hardly exotic. The Moorish *toca*, which we would call a turban, was virtually, Bernís claims, "un tocado nacional" (a national headdress).[13] Initially adopted in the mid-fifteenth century, by the early 1500s it had become widespread. The Flemish courtier Laurent Vital, in his chronicle of the future Charles V's first trip to Spain, describes the *toca* of a peasant as both old-fashioned and common:

> Ce bon viellard, au moyen de son accoustrement, sembloit estre l'ung des trois roys qui vindrent adorer nostre sauveur Jésus, en tel arroy estoit triumphamment venu. Il estoit tocquiet par la teste à la mode turquoyse ou judayque que Turcqz et Sarrazins se coiffent: c'est un habillement de teste qui se torteille, tout de linge, entour de la teste, comme en Castille on souloit user: mais a présent il s'y délaisse fort, si ce ne sont les anchiens, qui envys délaissent leurs anchiennes costumes et manières de faire, comme j'ay vu par dechà aulcuns anchiens entretenir les souliers à poulaine, ainsy font les aulcuns ces tocques . . . Je ay veu plusieurs gens campestres en porter.[14]

> [This good old man, by his costume, seemed like one of the three kings who came to adore our savior Jesus, so triumphantly was he dressed. His head was covered in the Turkish or Jewish fashion that Turks and Saracens use: it is a headdress wound several times around the head, all made of cloth, such as they used to wear in Castile, but now it is largely abandoned, except for the old people, who regretfully leave their ancient customs and ways of doing things; just as I have seen [in our country] some old people wearing their *poulaine* shoes, so do some of these with this headdress . . . I have seen many country people wearing them.]

Vital's primary frame of reference for the *toca morisca* is the artistic representation of the exotic Three Kings.[15] Notice how the Castilian custom, albeit on its way out, is conflated with all manner of "Oriental" garb, as worn by Turks, Jews, and Saracens. Vital's observation is as telling for its temporal specificity as for its geographical imprecision: though he stresses that the custom is increasingly abandoned, he nonetheless manages to connect Spain with the exotic East. The quotidian, old-fashioned headdress of the countryside both marks the survival of Moorish culture within Spain well into the sixteenth century—Bernís finds additional evidence of its use into the 1540s—and feeds into the European construction of an exoticized Spain.

One could read these moments, as I have done elsewhere, as ethnic cross-dressing—the performance of ersatz Moorishness to construct a "fictive ethnicity"[16] for Spain as a nation that has conquered Islam by fetishizing its visible manifestations in the context of ceremonial performances. This is a similar argument to that offered by Claire Sponsler and Robert L. Clark to explain the staging of Jews in medieval drama.[17] These performances, the argument goes, enable the construction of identity by staging otherness; the theatrical representation of the exaggerated other bolsters the development of a cohesive self. Yet it is striking how late Spain continues to present itself in Moorish guise, and how it does so in international contexts where the exact nature of the relation between representer and represented is less easy to control. In Spain, the greeting of foreign dignitaries with a "Moorish" spectacle makes sense in a kind of metonymic model: where before we had Moors, now we have only their appurtenances. And the mock battles, of course, stage Moorish defeats. But the Moorish pages at Charles' coronation abroad pose a greater problem. They identify Spain with the Moors in a less elliptical fashion: in this context, Moor stands for Spaniard. This elision was in fact common in representations of Spain in early modern Europe, well after the fall of Granada—consider for example Ariosto's emphasis on Saracen Spain in *Orlando Furioso* (1516, 1532):[18] there are no Spanish Christian champions in the poem because Spaniard *means* Moor in the world of the text. Spain's liminal position vis-à-vis Europe, as recorded in such texts, must thus necessarily inflect any reading of its relationship with the Moorishness within.

It is also important to remember that there are significant differences between medieval representations of Moors (often called Saracens) and Jews in northern Europe (as in the Croxton *Play of the Sacrament* that concerns Sponsler and Clark) and the sixteenth-century representation of Moors in Spain. First, there seems to have been no particular emphasis, at least in the instances I am describing here, on the bodily difference of the other. When Spaniards represent Moorishness, they do so in their own bodies, as a typical cultural practice, with no exaggeration or deformation. In the dances, the jousting games, but also in everyday costume, difference is embraced, even *embodied*, so that we are forced to ask whether it really is difference. Those presumably alien cultural forms that mark the outer limit of Christianity also, paradoxically, constitute Spain. In some cases, one must even wonder to what extent the practices are recognized as anything but Spanish. Take, for example, the custom of sitting on pillows on the floor, which so struck me in Lope de Vega's house. In describing the palace of the Infantado, in Guadalajara, home to the powerful Mendoza family, Helen Nader writes, "Until late in the seventeenth century, Christian women sat on the floor Muslim style; to accommodate this custom, in the women's salon, a low platform (estrado) covered with carpets and cushions occupied most of the floor space."[19] Located as it is in an irreproachable noble household, the practice is clearly not controversial, indeed, not even noted as exotic, yet it marks both Spain's difference vis-à-vis Europe and the undeniable hybridity of early modern Spanish culture.

BLACK SPAIN

While within the Iberian Peninsula the idea of the nation's pure, "gothic" identity was constantly complicated and challenged by a variety of cultural investments, whether self-conscious or inadvertent, Spain's enemies abroad ruthlessly exploited the connections between Spain and the Moors to construct that nation as a racial and religious other. Paradoxically, even in the sixteenth century the westernmost reaches of what is geographically Europe remained, at least for some observers, part of the Orient or Africa, and thus similarly savage, cruel, or tyrannical. It is important to note, first, that what is thus constructed is emphatically not the Orient, however marked it might be by the Moorish occupation, and, second, that unlike in Said's model the Orientalist construction does not lead to colonial domination. Instead, Spain is deliberately represented as "Oriental" in an effort to combat its imperial and cultural domination over other emerging European nations.

Particularly in anti-Spanish propaganda—the *leyenda negra* that this volume examines—Spain is consistently associated with Islam, with Africa, with dark peoples. It is important to recover the essentializing "blackness" of this cultural mythology: critics typically read it metaphorically, as a figure for Spain's cruelty and greed in the New World, yet it often refers in unambiguous terms to Spain's racial difference, its *essential* Moorishness. While this usage in no way counters the frequent association of blackness with evil in the early modern period,[20] it pointedly conflates the metaphorical with a literal sense, in an attempt to render Spain visibly, biologically black. This effort is particularly striking for its deliberate misrepresentation of the racialization of difference within Spain. Although a racism based on physical appearance did exist, and blacks were singled out for their color, Moors were not reliably identifiable in this way.[21] The phenotypical notion of race was emphatically not the main focus for Spaniards in the sixteenth century, particularly where Moors were concerned. As the grim documents that inventory the sale and redemption of slaves during the Moorish rebellion in the Alpujarras (1569–1571) demonstrate, Moors came in all shades, from "color moreno" (tawny) or "color negra" (black) to "color blanco que tira un poco a membrillo cocho" (white tending to cooked quince) and even, frequently, "color blanca" (white).[22] Sympathetic depictions of Moorish women in literary or historiographical texts occasionally portray them as blonde, Petrarchan beauties indistinguishable from their European counterparts.[23] Thus, even if outside Spain skin color is enlisted to essentialize difference, blackness emphatically does not equal Moorishness within Spain. Instead, Spanish racial hysteria focused on covert cultural and religious practices, and on the much more ambiguous register of blood. *Limpieza de sangre* (blood purity) was defined as the absence of Jewish or Moorish forebears for a particular person or family, yet there was a widespread consensus within Spain—amply reflected in satirical texts— that it was almost impossible to determine in any authentic fashion whether anyone was free of the Semitic taint.[24] This ambiguity suggests the possibility of assimilation, or "passing," and other challenges to the official rhetoric of essentialized difference, so that within Spain Moors sometimes escaped othering—not because, as the Black Legend suggests, Spain was "Moorish" or "African" in any uncomplicated way, but because the nuances of racial difference in the Iberian Peninsula differed markedly from English, French, or Dutch accounts of it.[25]

While the temporal dynamics of the *leyenda*'s construction of a black, African Spain, and Spain's response in its official self-presentation as Defender of the Faith, are undoubtedly complex, I am struck by the exacerbation of anti-Moorish rhetoric in Spain precisely as the Black Legend reaches a feverish pitch under Philip II. The animosity against the *moriscos*, despite their supposed inclusion as New Christians, peaks in the early seventeenth century, when they are summarily expelled from Spain despite their conversion. To what extent can we connect this pronounced increase in anti-Moorish sentiment with the Black Legend attacks on Spain? The evidence is certainly intriguing: critics have recently begun to trace the deliberate English construction of Spain as a racialized, essentialized other in the later decades of the sixteenth century.[26] The colorful anti-Spanish pamphlets that were widely produced, translated, and circulated throughout the Netherlands, France, and England in the 1580s and 1590s moved from a rhetoric of religious difference to a far starker vision of essential otherness.[27]

In these texts, Spain becomes conflated with the Moors, despite its own considerable ambivalence about Moorish culture and its powerful self-construction as vanquisher of Moors and victor in the *reconquista*. While from a certain perspective one might embrace these pamphlets as a corrective to Spain's own "blood" racism and denial of its Semitic heritage, they were not penned in any humanist attempt at tolerance. Instead, they represent an attempt to stigmatize Spain in Spain's own terms, by reinscribing the presence of Moors as a racial taint.[28] As Eric Griffin points out, the pamphlets are also effective at strengthening English identity in contradistinction to Spain, in a context of great anxiety about foreign influence or even invasion.[29] In this sense, their emphasis on the essential difference of Spain may say more about English anxieties concerning recusants—*English* others capable of assimilating or passing—who might easily cross over to Spain, whether physically or in their intimate allegiance, than about Spain itself. Yet the pamphlets nonetheless have powerful consequences for Spain, for its perception throughout Europe, and even for its inclusion therein.

Thus "The Coppie of the Anti-Spaniard," translated from the French in the same year, urges the nations of Europe to rally around France "and with one breath to goe and abate the pride and insolencie of these Negroes,"[30] invoking European racial solidarity against an African, black Spain. Conflating "Moors" and "Negroes" in this way is a powerful rhetorical gesture. Not only does it construct Spain's difference as essential and easily identifiable but it substitutes the peoples of sub-Saharan Africa for the encroaching powers of North Africa and the Levant. As Nabil Matar usefully reminds us, English (and European) relations with these two groups were very different: "England's relations with sub-Saharan Africans were relations of power, domination, and slavery, while relations with the Muslims of North Africa and the Levant were of anxious equality and grudging emulation."[31] Here, then, the specific substitution of "Negro" for Moor seems not merely a question of misunderstanding, but a deliberate rhetorical ploy in an attempt to diminish Spain.

Some of the pamphlets negotiate the apparent sameness of the Spaniards—after all, many English subjects would have seen Phillip II and his entourage during his brief marriage to Mary Tudor, or more recent envoys from Spain—as the product of miscegenation: though they may appear white, they are tainted with Moorishness.[32] Edward Daunce's "Brief Discourse of the Spanish State" (1590) foregrounds the accusation of racial impurity by claiming that Spaniards are genealogically "mingled with the Mores cruell and full of trecherie."[33] The theme of miscegenation is underscored when he argues, in a striking moment of innuendo, that during the eight centuries of the Moorish occupation "we must not think that the Negroes sent for women out of Aphrick."[34] This genealogical and racialist discourse appears often: as Griffin notes, *The Spanish Colonie, or briefe chronicle of the acts and gestes of the Spaniardes*, the first English translation of Las Casas's *Brevísima relación de la destrucción de las Indias* and a central document in the creation of the Black Legend, ascribes the Spaniards' behavior to their "firste fathers the Gothes" and "their second progenitors the Saracens."[35] Thus the more sophisticated texts echo Spanish anxieties about hidden differences while mounting at the same time more blatant accusations of an essential, visible otherness.

The references to an Islamic Spain appear not only in the Black Legend pamphlets but in literary texts centrally concerned with questions of national identity, such as Spenser's *The Faerie Queene*, in which Philip II is famously figured as "Souldan,"[36] and, more obliquely, in Shakespeare's *The Merchant of Venice*. As Lynda E. Boose cogently asks of Portia's Spanish suitor, "Is Arragon to be understood as merely another member of the multitude of failed European suitors, or does his structural placement between the black Morocco and the white Bassanio, a Spaniard between a Moroccan and a Venetian, geographically imply that he occupies the space of the 'white Moor'"?[37] In Boose's reading, the Spaniard is not necessarily marked by color, but his full participation within Europe is cast into doubt by his imputed miscegenated blood.

The identification of Philip II in particular with Islam returns in histories such as Fulke Greville's *Life of Sir Philip Sidney* (ca. 1612), in which the Spanish monarch makes an appearance as "Suleiman of Spain."[38] (The irony in this case is striking, since Greville's own subject is named after his godfather, the monarch vilified here.) The demonization of Spain through conflation with a threatening Islam—in these cases not the Moors but the encroaching menace of Ottoman Turks, who also represent tyranny—coexists uneasily with Elizabeth's overtures toward both the Porte and Morocco in the 1580s and 1590s, as England desperately sought commercial outlets and allies against Spain. The condensation of both Catholic Spain and the Islamic powers into a single figure for tyranny paradoxically complicates England's attempts to position itself advantageously within Mediterranean religious and political triangles. Yet these varying approaches toward both Spain and the Muslim world recall the peculiar dynamics of maurophilia, and its violent refusal, within Spain: whether embraced or stigmatized, Moorishness becomes an essential component in the construction of national identity. The process is not one of simple othering but a more complex negotiation between past and present, intra- and extra-European pressures, and fictive identities crafted both at home and abroad. The racialized, essentialized distinctions that might serve in the rhetorical, figurative register of Black Legend pamphlets or in nationalist epic may be very different from the more strategic representation of commonalities between England and Morocco, for example, as part of diplomatic negotiations.[39]

Given the Black Legend disourse of Spanish "blackness" and "Moorishness," it seems difficult to imagine early modern Spain espousing the models of Orientalism that critics have developed for northern Europe. Most often, the European orientalist gaze seems to have considered Spain as one more instance of the East, or of Africa. As I have tried to show, the problem of reconstructing the valence of Moorish culture in this context is (at least) twofold: how does Spain, in its development as a nation-state, negotiate its often contradictory identifications with Moorishness, and how does this relationship change over the course of the sixteenth century, as al-Andalus recedes and the Counter-Reformation puts pressure on all forms of cultural difference? Conversely, how does the rest of Europe represent Spain's connection to the Moors, and how is this connection exploited for particular political goals? Rather than a two-way connection between "Europe" and "Islam" (if we could ever imagine such simplified actors), the real interest lies in the strategic characterizations of Spain as Moorish, by Spaniards themselves, and by other Europeans at a time of striking political and religious upheaval. Maurophilia is an unstable and often risky proclivity, which makes its embrace all the more intriguing for a cultural history of the encounters between East and West. Yet that history cannot be separated from intra-European pressures and from the discourses that enlist both race and religion to construct legends of national distinction.

CHAPTER SIX

THE BLACK LEGEND AND
GLOBAL CONSPIRACIES

Spain, the Inquisition, and the Emerging Modern World

Irene Silverblatt

I n most American imaginations Spain, and particularly the Spanish Inquisition, represent the opposite of modernity: examples of the horrors,
barbaric irrationalities, cruelty, and ruthlessness people were forced to endure before our modern way of life claimed victory over the planet.[1] American imaginations were not the first to have made Spain and the Spanish Inquisition into foils against which modern successes could be judged. Both
nation and institution have served as counterpoints to civic virtues for centuries—and they did so in the service of America's Anglo forbearers.

From its beginnings, England was obsessed with Spain. England had to
confront Spain before it, too, could become a player in the West's new political order, and their battles were fought on both religious and secular grounds.
Protestantism became a badge of English nationalism once the Church of
England broke from Rome; during the last decades of the sixteenth century,
England saw itself as the bearer of the true faith, a chosen people, with Catholic Spain as its nemesis. The Inquisition—the defender of Catholicism and
false arbiter of heresy—became in England's propaganda wars—or Black
Legend—the emblem of Spain's moral and political degeneracy.[2]

In the hands of British propagandists, the Inquisition represented Spain's
most glaring affront to the standards of civilization, and, in familiar vitriol,
the British pilloried the Inquisition for its abuse of law and contempt for justice.[3] John Foxe called it "this dreadful engine of tyranny" and, in international comparison, praised England as a country "not cursed with such an
arbitrary court."[4] The tribunal was not only a model of government gone
wrong but a throwback to the past: proof that Spain disdained the political
principles of a modern nation.[5] In these tracts, Spain's backwardness was

made all the more evident by the progressive light of England's modern, "legitimate" (i.e., more free market) approach to power.[6]

This chapter argues, contrary to Black Legend propaganda, that the Spanish Inquisition was a modern institution and that Spain was an emerging modern nation. Moreover, it argues that from the sixteenth century through the mid-seventeenth, Spain was, in fact, in the vanguard of the modern world, installing cutting-edge bureaucracies and race-thinking designs—crucial to its global civilizing mission—in its widely dispersed colonies.

This particular view on modernity takes its lead from Hannah Arendt and her struggles to account for the vexing question of how the civilized world could display such despicable brutality. Puzzling over the rise of fascism, Arendt searched for a precedent in Western history—a form of government supporting the worldwide dominance of a master race—that would have eased the way for "civilized" peoples to embrace barbarity. She found it in nineteenth-century imperialism, when northern European nations, like England, were putting machinery in place to rule colonies around the globe. That machinery included an organization for absolute political control and an ideology of social superiority: nineteenth-century imperial powers governed colonies as despotic bureaucrats, argued Arendt, and racial ideologies turned bureaucrats into members of a superior, white-European caste justified in their dominion. Her fear was this: intertwined, race-thinking, and bureaucratic rule could unleash "extraordinary power and destruction," destruction all the more terrible because it was bathed in the aura of "rationality" and civilization. Life in the seventeenth century was very different from life in the nineteenth, of course, but it was Spain's colonial efforts that spearheaded the mix of "civilizing," bureaucracy, and race thinking at the heart of modern experience.[7]

This chapter broadly explores what happens to our sense of modernity once we trace its elementary forms from the nineteenth century back to the seventeenth. If we take the first wave of European empire as the origin of what Arendt called the civilized world's "subterranean stream," we are forced to recognize the importance of colonialism to the making of our modern ways of life. We also get a better grasp of the irrationalities and illusions confounding us. Colonial Peru and, in particular, the Lima office of the Spanish Inquisition will serve as our case in point.

STATE AND INQUISITION

Castilian monarchs, learning from the obstacles to absolutist control encountered on the Iberian Peninsula, kept the colonies (at least in principle) under a tight rein. They established political institutions connecting Spain to the Andes that were meant to ensure the supremacy of royal authority over both settlers and natives. In addition to the *cabildos* (municipal councils), royal *audiencias* (courts), the viceregal apparatus, and, eventually *corregidores* (state-appointed regional authorities), the Crown instituted measures to investigate the beliefs and ethics of its subjects. The Spanish Inquisition, responsible for vigilance over internal heresies, set up an office in Lima at the end of the sixteenth century. Although not allowed to stand in judgment over natives (that was a diocesan affair), the Inquisition was the only royal institution with authority over all of the Spanish empire's colonies and kingdoms—with offices in the Philippines, Mexico, Columbia, Basque country, Catalonia—virtually anywhere Spanish settlements could be found. And it was a *state* bureaucracy: the Spanish Inquisition was not under the supervision of the Church or Rome, but of the Crown.[8] With jurisdiction over pivotal dimensions of religious life—in a country in which Catholicism was akin to a nationalist ideology—the Spanish Inquisition was a commanding political presence. And, as befitted one of the most advanced bureaucracies of its day, the Spanish Inquisition generated an amazing amount of paperwork. Much of this presentation is based on the Lima tribunal's record-keeping compulsions.

Like any bureaucracy, the Inquisition was run according to procedures and rules, and its workings were overseen by bureaucrats, that is, credentialed *letrados* (learned men, university graduates). The ideal Lima inquisitor was to be "circumspect, judicious . . . not greedy or covetous, understanding, very charitable . . . and experienced and informed about life in the Americas"; he was *pacifico*—tranquil, unperturbed, and not a hothead better suited to be a swashbuckling conquistador.[9] The ideal inquisitor, bureaucratically disposed, was immersed in rules, and the tribunal seemed to have rules for everything: office holders (each local tribunal had twenty—inquisitor, attorney general, defense attorney, notary, constable, office manager, accountant, pharmacist, porter, among others); job descriptions and requirements (inquisitors had to be university graduates, preferably with a degree in law, and have extensive professional experience). There was even an ecclesiastic career ladder (inquisitor was higher than prosecuting attorney); and most believed that an American posting was a rung on the stairway to bureaucratic success.[10] While not precisely a court of law (the Inquisition was established to "meet a perceived national threat"), the Inquisition had much in common with the secular and ecclesiastical courts of the day. In principle, its practices were guided by regulations designed to promote equity and justice as well as limit the powers of officeholders according to an established hierarchy of command.[11] Inquisition manuals gave specific instructions about evidence needed for arrest and for conviction, methods for conducting interrogations, and criteria for determining sentences. Like most European courts, the tribunal assumed that the accused were guilty unless shown otherwise. And although the burden of proof remained squarely on their shoulders, defendants were supported by a number of statutes: they were entitled to a lawyer (appointed by the tribunal), to name corroborating witnesses, and to provide a list of enemies who might testify out of spite.[12] Procedures notwithstanding, however, assumptions of guilt coupled with the (also regulated) use of torture seemed to make the fight for innocence almost hopeless.

Like their twenty-first century counterparts, Lima's inquisitors learned to fudge. They were practiced in the art of bending or subverting the rules—something they could do judiciously by taking advantage of their months' long distance from headquarters. And, like their twenty-first century counterparts, Lima's inquisitors justified their actions with appeals to reasons of state and national security.[13]

COLONIAL CULTURAL POLITICS

The Spanish Empire was at the vanguard of early modern state making, building bureaucracies as it established colonies around the globe. It was also at the vanguard of the cultural politics infusing the nascent modern world. Spain's imperial enterprise was rooted in the construction of the new social beings at modernity's core: (1) the racialized triad—Indian, Spaniard, black—and (2) bureaucratized beings—created in tandem with institutions of state.[14] The Spanish Inquisition was the institution responsible for certifying the nature of the "blood" coursing through colonial veins, weighing its purity along with supposed heresy that impurities might foretell. We will be exploring, then, aspects of emerging modernity through the lens of cultural changes at the heart of Spain's efforts to convert the Andean region into a dependency. Colonial conspiracies are our focal point.

One of the Lima Inquisition's most important functions was to clarify cultural blame; it was to specify and bring to judgment those among the viceroyalty's inhabitants who held contrary beliefs or engaged in life practices perceived to threaten the colonial state. Accordingly, inquisitors, ready to quash heretical dangers to the public weal, legitimized their most brutal acts—infamous torture sessions and punishments—in the name of the state's welfare and security. In the middle of the seventeenth century, inquisitors expressed deep-seated fears that Peru's moral fabric—and political stability—was being undermined by two principal culprits: hidden Jews, glossed frequently as New Christian/merchant/Portuguese, and the colony's ubiquitous witches.

Both, according to tribunal calculations, had significant ties to Peru's indigenous or slave populations, and their purported relationships, crossing the
racialized divides of colonial rule, suggest the empire's confused fears, its
strikingly conspiratorial bent, as well as broader struggles over political and
social legitimacy.

Coca-Chewing, Inca-Worshiping Non-Indian Women Called Witches

Writing in the 1620s from Lima to Inquisition headquarters in Madrid, the
inquisitor Juan de Manozca bemoaned the colony's abysmal lack of faith.
He assessed Peru as a degraded country and, in his letter, blamed a good part
of Peru's degradation on the ubiquity of witches—Spanish, *mestiza* (mixed
Indian and Spanish), or *mulata* (mixed Spanish and black) women—who,
while not Indians, were immersed in the customs and knowledge of the
colony's natives.[15] In 1628 Manozca's concerns were taken up by an unusual
edict of faith. Following inquisitorial tradition, this edict, or statement of the
heresies and immoral habits that Catholics were obliged to report to the Holy
Office, was read in Peru's churches and publicly displayed on church doors.
The Peruvian version, however, was different in one respect from every other
edict read in every church throughout the Spanish empire: the Peruvian edict
also had this warning directed to the particular problem of women: ". . . and
when they are worshiping the devil they wait for images of the future to appear . . . for which the aforesaid women . . . go to the countryside and . . .
drink certain potions of herbs and roots, called *achuma* and *chamico*, and *coca*
with which they stupefy the senses."[16] This emphasis on the dangers of witchcraft was highly unusual. The Spanish Inquisition, in the eyes of most historians, tended to minimize the dangers provoked by witchcraft, not emphasize them.[17] What stands out both in the edict and in Manozca's letter is
concern over the insidious attraction of all things Indian to Peruvian women
who were not. Tagging witches, like tagging hidden Jews, was part of the
Inquisition's efforts to assign cultural blame, and the cases against accused
witches present the broad strokes of a *tableaux* of social fears.

In the first years of the Inquisition's presence in Peru, witches were accused of unholy practices similar to their peninsular sisters: chanting spells,
reciting prayers (like the *credo*), and mixing herbs and powders to foretell
events and intervene in life's chances. And, like their peninsular sisters,
witches' special skills addressed the daily stuff of life—in love and justice:
they could foretell if much-missed husbands would be coming on the next
fleet and if they would arrive married to another.[18] They could ensure that
lovers remain passionate;[19] that men treat their kinswomen well;[20] and, in a

foray into the field of social justice, that royal officers be impeded from carrying out a sentence.[21]

In this early period, some of the accused flirted with more dangerous sources of potency, turning to the imputed "powers" of Catholic Iberia's first enemies within. In the 1590s, Jewish symbols and *morisca* (converted woman of Moorish descent) insights were not uncommon ingredients in devilish brews, where they joined myriad saints, sacred relics, stars, and items of nature.[22] Ten accused women from the "Potosi conspiracy," residing in Bolivia and Cusco at the time of their arrest, were led by the Sevilian, dona Francisca Maldonado, in a series of chants in which Jewish themes did—but not always—appear. And so we find prayers and incantations like "Our lady saint Martha . . . loved by the queen of the angels . . . with the sea and the sand and the sky and the stars and the Eucharist from the altar, and the Holy Trinity" along with prayers to Saint Erasmus that spoke of "the moon and the sun, with the Mountains of Zion, with the seven tribes of Israel" or "the Incantation of the Lights" that invoked "the Holy Trinity . . . with the sacred Eucharist . . . and with the altar stone, and with the priest . . . and with the Tablets of Moses. . . ."[23] Living in the colonies opened up a Pandora's box of knowledge—herbal cures, divining tricks, and potions for love and power—rooted in the wisdom of three continents. The same women who were accused of conjuring with the Tablets of Moses and the Tribes of Israel were also experimenting with indigenous lore, using it as a complement to their own traditions. Dona Maria de Aguilar, a well-heeled *mestiza* from Cochabamba, married to Potosi's *procurador* (chief fiscal agent), was condemned with two "Indian related" counts. She was said to "speak in Indian" with some of her cohorts and, more damaging, was charged with actively seeking native *hechizeras* (witches) to assist in "sorcery" sessions.[24] Francisca Gomez, a *mestiza* married to a Spaniard and not part of the Potosi conspiracy, was also rumored to be lured by Indian doings and denounced for running off to join native pilgrimages for the purpose of learning "Indian witchcraft."[25] By the mid-1590s, seeking out the knowledge of Indian women was a suspicious act. It was the "Indianness" that was so disquieting, as inquisitors (along with their objects of investigation), found themselves increasingly drawn to the dangers of native wisdom.[26]

Records also tell us about the followers of accused witches. One group was particularly notorious and threatening to authorities: these were the "women from all backgrounds and ranks" who would attend witchcraft sessions "cloaked in veils." These women were actually famous throughout Peru. Known as *tapadas*, they would mask their public activities—and their "backgrounds and ranks"—by carefully and seductively draping shawls over their faces. Although serenaded in poetry, they were condemned by secular and religious authorities over the course of decades for "enjoying improper liberty, promoting public scandal and disgrace."[27] We encounter *tapadas* in colonial witchcraft trials throughout the seventeenth century. Flaunting as they did the political and cultural hierarchies at the heart of the colonial enterprise, it should not be surprising then that "witchcraft" involving *tapadas* could get blamed for inciting all kinds of political havoc.[28]

Things Indian were taking on a more potent and frequent share of witchcraft paraphernalia as the decades passed, and by the time the 1629 edict of faith was hung on church doors, their impact was palpable. Now, not only were witches' special skills addressing the stuff of life, witches were also engaging questions of justice: it was said that they could stop royal officers from carrying out a sentence or even stop inquisitors from pursuing a case.[29]

Catalina de Baena was one of nearly a dozen women chastised in the years after the edict's first appearance. Born in Jerez de la Frontera, Spain, and living in Potosí, Catalina's was a hybrid lore, drawing on Christian items—special masses, prayers, and Indian rites—using native herbs and poultices. However, there was another native object, frightening and dangerous, on her list, one that must have ratcheted up the perils of Indian *hechizos* (spells). Catalina was accused of searching old Indian burials, or *guacas*, for the bones of *gentiles*—native peoples who, never baptized, had never been touched by the Christian world.[30] Spaniards were robbing pre-Columbian graves for their spells, and this represented a formidable turn in Andean witchcraft.

In keeping with the cross-ethnic character of Andean witchcraft, Catalina de Baena was guided by two Indians, had a black accomplice, and was schooled by a *mulata*. In her words, "[she] went to some *guacas* (graves) in the company of an Indian man and woman . . . and brought back a sack full [of bones] . . . and left them in the home of a "*negra*," Isabel . . . who then told the *mulata*, Francisca, who was supposed to prepare them as she had promised."[31] All who testified against Catalina agreed that she had brought back "bones and the skulls of two bodies"[32] from the Indian burial grounds, around twelve miles away. But the women attending this "coven" were more than grave robbers; they were students of native traditions. One witness testified that "in order to take the bones from the tombs [Catalina] had put some cloth with gold, chambray, pearls, and taffeta inside the [burials]."[33] This was subject to dispute: Catalina de Baena denied leaving an offering but confirmed, regardless, her trek to get native bones.[34] In any case, either Catalina or the witness (an accomplice/client) or both knew enough about native custom to confess they had left several items of worth behind in a gesture of *ayni,* the bedrock Andean principle of reciprocity. No matter who did or said what, *Peruanas* were becoming fluent in distinctly Indian ways.

Like the other accused witches, Catalina de Baena denied ever making a pact with the devil, adding "she didn't know what that was and . . . this thing about pacts seemed like Latin to her."[35] She insisted she would never use Indian bones for maleficent ends. But that is not how witnesses saw it, or better said, how they declared it. They claimed that Catalina had unearthed these bones for an evil deed, "to bewitch a woman named dona Isabel de Mendia," and according to several, "[she] was desperately ill in bed as a result."[36] Regardless of its intended purpose, Indian magic had developed a reputation that was to shroud it throughout the century: Indian magic was dangerous magic.[37]

Race thinking framed Peruvian culture, and it showed its hidden ambiguities in Catalina de Baena's witchcraft trial. Over the course of her confessions, Catalina de Baena not only declared Francisca, the *mulata,* to be the region's preeminent witch but affirmed that it was Francisca who had "ordered her" to bring the Indian bones to Potosi. And when one of Catalina's slaves was caught giving writing material to another inmate, Catalina was charged with breaking the tribunal's pledge of secrecy. In her defense, Catalina insisted she did so while under duress, cowed by a noted witch by the name of Maria Martinez. Maria Martinez, born in Portugal and the offspring of an affair between the village priest and his slave from Guinea, had a fierce reputation for straightening out questions of love and justice. She was *zahori,* "could see right into peoples insides,"[38] and because of her gifts she was sought after by Spaniards, "donas," free blacks, slaves, and "women with cloaked faces."[39]

Colonial circumstance brought together women from a variety of ranks and "races"; colonial circumstance also marked the breaches between them. In line with the official dictates of Peru's racial hierarchy, Catalina de Baena, "well born and of honorable [Spanish Old Christian] descent," was spared the public penance and corporal punishment meted out to the *mulata,* Maria Martinez. There are analogous racial divisions in the illicit worlds of sorcery and divination, except the hierarchy is inverted: Catalina de Baena could be intimidated by the daughter of a slave; Catalina sought out the special magic of Indian grave sites. The colonial racial hierarchy cut both ways: it gave dominance to *espanoles* in the realm of official politics, but when it came to the subterranean powers of shamans and witches, it put authority in the hands of Peru's subordinates.[40]

By 1645 and through the century's close, trials against non-Indians accused of witchcraft—whether Spanish, *mulata, mestiza,* or *negra,* free or slave—show a remarkable turn in "Indianness." Coca was becoming the center piece of (witches') collective conjuring rites, paired with a new group of personages in the colonial *hechizo* repertoire. Now joining saints and credos, we find the Inca, and sometimes the Coya or Inca queen.[41]

Cusco royalty first appear in the trial of Ana Maria de Contreras, penanced by the Inquisition in the Gran Auto of 1639.[42] This *mulata* slave explained that the great numbers of women who sought her out, lavishing money and food, pushed her return to old "deceits and tricks." Ana Maria de Contreras's "deceits" and "tricks" included "having worshiped the mountain peaks and rocks in memory and signification of the Inca and his wife."[43]

Dona Maria de Cordoba's coca readings—always conducted with several friends, *maestras*, (teachers/mentors), and relatives of the person to be healed— were built around deciphering images made from wads of coca leaf. Although she denied ever praying to the devil or even seeing his figure in her porcelain bowl,[44] she did venerate the Inca as the pagan king of the pagan Indians who had lived in the Andes before the coming of Spaniards. Witches drew on these *gentile* powers for insight and strength: "I conjure you with the *palla* (noblewoman) and with your ancestors, with the idols whom you believed in, my father, I drink to you with this wine, [and] with this coca that you used in your sorcery."[45]

Dona Maria de Cordoba was chewing coca with dona Luisa de Vargas when the tribunal's bailiff knocked on her door. Dona Luisa de Vargas could also be called dona Luisa *la quarterona* or Luisa Blanca (White).[46] Like her sometime accomplice, dona Luisa was expert in love matters: a specialist in "domesticating" (*amansar*) men, and occasionally in domesticating women, she was the preferred sorcerer of one of Lima's magistrates.[47] Dona Luisa, also schooled in more political conjures, was the witch who gave moral support to a friend about to appear before the inquisitors. "[H]ave womanly valor . . ." (*valor de muger*), she told her *comadre*, and then "taught her a special charm against Inquisitors to give her strength to face the judges when called in front of the tribunal."[48]

Dona Luisa used a variety of ingredients in her ceremonies to fix love lives or facilitate justice, including wine and the holy water from three churches and special "unguents for the shameful parts (*partes vergonzosas*),"[49] but at the core of this *blanca/quarterona de mulata*'s recipes were Indian herbs, Indian drinks, and Indian chants. Coca was the centerpiece, chewed for its effects, for its secrets, and for its uncanny way of bringing together the ritual players, but other items, like *chicha* (Andean corn beer), *palla palla* (an herb whose name refers to women of the Inca nobility), tobacco, and guinea pig were also part of dona Luisa's mending kit.[50] Dona Luisa, like so many of the accused, intoned the common orations to Saint Martha; however, her sacred language was inspired by Quechua, with chants often "spoke[n] in the Indian language."[51]

How did dona Luisa find out about these orations, plants, and cures? She told how she first learned about certain herbs and ointments for love magic from *una negra,* about other plants from *indios,* about *"coca* and the drink Indians call 'chicha' from a *negra,"* and sacred altar stone from a *mulato* sacristan.[52] In turn, dona Luisa would teach her knowledge to others. Sometimes she would even write out prayers and send them to acolytes — to the inquisitors' great surprise, as she claimed to be illiterate.[53] And dona Luisa, like most of the accused, boasted a clientele as diverse as her teachers.

While coca was her principal conjuring instrument, the Inca was her principal object. Dona Luisa, at least according to the testimony of twenty-four witnesses, would appeal to several figures, but it was the Inca whom she ultimately implored to intervene in life's destinies (". . . and blowing some tobacco smoke into the porcelain, and calling . . . the Inga, saying strength and vigor I give you, my Inga so you reveal the future and the truth"[54]). The Inca, the former Indian king, possessed all the power and authority attached to royalty. Joined by her colleagues, dona Luisa would chant, "o my *coca,* I conjure you with the Inca, with all his vassals and court. . . ."[55]

The Inca, the Indian king (*el rei indio*) was also *el rei gentil,* the pagan king, the king of Andeans before the Spanish conquest and the advent of Christianity.[56] The *rei gentil* had never been baptized; Peru's clerics, controversially, decided the Incas and their ancestors were fated, then, for an eternity in hell. Dona Luisa and her colleagues, on the other hand, did not condemn the Inca; they believed the Inca possessed special powers precisely because he was an unbaptized pagan.

By now coca was irrevocably tied to colonial concepts of Indian and Inca. Before the Spanish conquest, most native peoples living in the Andes did not consider themselves to be the Inca's descendents; many, in fact, detested the Inca for usurping their labor, lands, and political sovereignty. Nor did they consider themselves part of one encompassing ethnic group — like "Indian." It was colonial Peruvians who were transforming that pre-Columbian past, painting Indians/Inca in broad strokes and making coca the key to a merging Indian/Inca domain.

The colonial Inca, promising fortune and power over human beings, sparked colonial imaginations. Ana Maria de Ulloa, in prayers to fix the outcome of a civic trial, implored, "O my coca, o my princess, o my Inca, I beg you, since for you nothing was impossible. . . ."[57] During the middle decades of the seventeenth century and the years to follow — when the strength of Spanish imperial dominion was battered by internal dissension, economic downturns, and foreign challenges—the Inca's powers in love, luck, and even government began to grow.

Witchcraft accusations and incantations were inseparable from the broader contests over power infusing the colonial world. Royal officials, ever wary that the Dutch or British would form allegiances with "Indian" subjects, only enhanced the cachet of native Peruvians and their power as the potential "enemies within." During the period when witchcraft loomed as a threat, clerics and royal authorities were increasingly concerned that natives were abandoning Christianity and returning to the idolatrous, pagan ways of their ancestors. And idolatry, they reckoned, was the first step in the slippery slope to sedition.

Catholic missionaries twinned Indian idol worship with witchcraft, and once clerics found witchcraft in native religious practices, they were quick to discern *indias* doing the devil's work. Assumed capable of the darkest of witchcraft, of using the black arts to cause death, native women were accused of making diabolic pacts that could wreak all kinds of havoc in love and in politics.[58] Churchmen feared that women's heresies—Indian and non-Indian—were beginning to crisscross cultural boundaries; all the more reason to see non-Indian women, turning to Indian habits, as growing threats to the colonial enterprise.

Inquisitor Manozca's concerns over witchcraft and "Indianness" were tied to imperial efforts to build a sustaining hegemony. Colonial rule, inseparable from colonial cultural hierarchies, was jeopardized by witchcraft ideologies that polluted the norms of imperial politics. Witches were charged with practicing an Inca-centered, nativist, possibly even anticolonial form of sorcery. And the perceived danger of colonial witchcraft surged as it absorbed other fears—including those engulfing converted men and women of Jewish descent, called New Christians.

The Jewish Threat

Juan de Manozca, who wrote to Madrid from Lima about the dangers of women engaged in witchcraft, was also spearheading a drive to arrest members of the viceroyalty's New Christian community. He believed that they too were undermining the viceroyalty through unsavory associations with Indians and blacks. Like the accused witches, accused Judaizers bore an extraordinary ideological weight; like the accused witches, it was their reputed tie to Indians and blacks that ballooned Spanish fears. New Christians were also involved in conspiracies.

Perhaps the bloodiest episode in Lima's inquisitorial history was the *auto-da-fe* of 1639, the *auto* when members of the so-called "great [Jewish] conspiracy" were punished. Out of the seventy-two individuals who were penanced for Judaizing, ten were burned at the stake. Among the condemned were men like Manuel Bautista Perez, rich and powerful merchants, who refused to confess to heresies. Aghast at the broad sweep of arrests and the harsh sentences imposed by the Lima office, Madrid headquarters demanded an explanation.[59] The Lima tribunal justified their severity by appealing to the dangers crypto-Jews posed, not only to the ethical foundation of the colony but to its very political security.[60]

Accusations against "Judaisers" in the New World were similar to charges against Jews and New Christians throughout Europe and the Iberian Peninsula.[61] The "Jewish problem" in seventeenth-century Peru—the distorted rhetoric of the viceroyalty's conspiracy theories—had a centuries-long, continental pedigree, and beliefs turning Jews into societal threats framed a broad climate of suspicion pervading much of the Old World. Nonetheless, the outrage and fear provoked by Peru's New Christians were, in addition, tied to the contradictions of the early modern colonial world. The terrors that Jews seemed to provoke were an integral part of the turbulent cultural politics generated by and shaping Spain's imperial state-making designs.[62]

Thus, the Lima tribunal's take on the Jewish menace elaborated a familiar set of charges, but with a twist appropriate to the emerging social conditions of a global, colonial order: New Christians were said to usurp trade and merchandizing to the detriment of Castillians; New Christians were said to commit treachery through alliances with Spain's foreign foes; New Christians were said to commit treachery through alliances with the potential enemies within (Indians and Black slaves); and New Christians were said to be able to plot treachery because of their remarkable ability to conspire in secret languages. Seventeenth-century Jewish conspiracies had a long history, but they were chiseled in the geopolitics of the New World empire—with its expanding mercantile networks and new, racialized, social beings.

Anti–New Christian sentiments were not preordained. We should remember that conflicting attitudes toward New Christians vied for prominence in Peru of the 1620s and 1630s. On the one hand, the wealthiest New Christian merchants, en route to becoming colonial aristocrats, were championed in the highest places of ecclesiastical and secular government. At the same time, however, Lima's inquisitors were appalled that men of suspect origins were entering the highest places of ecclesiastic and secular government. The Lima tribunal, with Manozca leading the charge, began to step up its campaign against New Christians. They were bolstered in this endeavor by Spain's purity of blood laws, decrees that formally prohibited New Christians—the inheritors of "stained" blood because of Jewish or Moorish ancestry—from holding office, entering university, or engaging much of Spanish public and professional life. So, when stories began to spread about the growing number of hidden Jews living in the viceroyalty, Lima's inquisitors came to the fore, promising to find a cure for this "plague"[63] that was devouring Peru.

This "plague," we discover, had several facets—all contributing to a growing viceregal anxiety over Jewish conspiracy. One was economic: in line with stereotype, New Christians were accused of mercantile chicanery. "Since about six or eight years," the Lima tribunal wrote to Madrid, "it is said that many [New Christians] have found a footing in Peru . . . commanding almost exclusively all the commerce of the kingdom; they owned all the dry goods stores; and monopolized the retail trade and traffic so that from gold brocade to sackcloth, and from diamond to cumin seed, and from the lowest black slave from Guinea to the most precious pearl passes through their hands."[64] "A Castilian of pure stock," they added, "has not a ghost of a chance."[65]

These anxieties over a colonial economic conspiracy were compounded by political plots. Again in line with stereotype, New Christians were accused of treachery. By the end of the sixteenth century, Castilians merged Portuguese with the categories of Jew and New Christian[66]—a new alignment with significant impact on imperial assessments of New Christian duplicities. New Christians were now judged against the backdrop of Spain's often ambiguous relationship with Portugal. Tensions with these two countries coalesced in 1580, when Spain assumed the Portuguese crown, took over the defense of Portugal's New World colonies, and therefore had to fight Holland for control over northeast Brazil.[67] The Dutch were Spain's principal enemies in European battles for dominion over South America, and during the first half of the seventeenth century, Dutch forces were invading port towns (like Pernambuco in Brazil), establishing footholds on South American soil, and generally wreaking havoc with Spanish trade.[68] It was a Castilan commonplace that Portuguese New Christians were secret allies of the Dutch, and Spaniards blamed them for Castile's initial loss of Bahia in 1624 (recaptured in 1625), as well as for the Spanish defeat in Pernambuco six years later.[69] It is not surprising that Spanish officials harbored gnawing—if not truly justified[70]—qualms about New Christian loyalties. New Christians and crypto-Jews could escape Spain's intolerance by settling in Holland,[71] and, to Spain's chagrin, once the Dutch settled northeast Brazil (1630–1654), the observant Jewish population—consisting of Dutch immigrants and former colonial New Christians—ballooned in size.[72] Peru's inquisitors were well aware of the possible dangers presented by a Dutch colony—where

Judaism could be freely practiced—so close to its borders. They feared that a vibrant Jewish center in Brazil could renovate crypto-Jewish practices on the rest of the continent, facilitate Dutch political objectives, and perhaps even encourage seditious New Christians to migrate to the viceroyalty of Peru.[73] Thus, Jewish ancestry redounded in suspicions: as New Christians, they were mistrusted for being hidden Jews; as Portuguese, they were mistrusted for their fidelity to Lisbon and then Holland. These doubts were compounded by the Dutch victory over Spain (and Portugal) in northeast Brazil.

The "Jewish problem" in early seventeenth-century Peru clearly had long-standing roots in Iberian history and prejudice; however, equally striking is the fact that its character was honed by the global politics of imperial rule. "Jew" (or "New Christian," or "Portuguese") marked a new kind of conspiracy, one born in the Americas: a pact with Spain's enemies, foreign and internal, to undermine Iberian sovereignty over its transatlantic possessions. Enemies could be outside competitors over colonial territory, or, perhaps even more treacherously, they could be residing within the boundaries of imperial rule. New Christians were accused of cultivating subversive ties with the enemies within—*indios* and *negros*—as well as with Spain's external adversaries, like the Dutch.

After the arrest of Perez and other principal merchants precipitated a collapse in trade and credit, inquisitors were called by the Supreme Council to account for their actions. They did so by arguing that the threat that "New Christians" posed to religious orthodoxy had extended into the political arena. The colony's very survival was in jeopardy, claimed Lima. A plot had been uncovered in the jail cells of the Inquisition: Perez and others caught in the *conspiracion grande* were charged with stockpiling gunpowder earmarked for a second Dutch invasion of Peru's major port city, Callao.[74] And anxieties that New Christians were promoting a Dutch invasion of the Pacific Coast were compounded by fears that New Christians were conspiring with slaves and Indians.

Viceregal authorities in general were concerned about the loyalties of African and native Peruvians. Spaniards recognized that they themselves, the colony's privileged elite, were unpopular; they also recognized that they were vastly outnumbered.[75] One viceroy wrote of the need to keep ever vigilant: "There are over twenty-two thousand *negros* living in Lima and its surroundings, and if they were ever to see the Spanish losing in [battles with the enemy] there is little to assure us of them, because . . . generally they love liberty . . . and for similar reasons one has to be suspicious of '*indios*,' thus, everywhere, in these occasions, danger grows."[76]

Fears that New Christians were plotting religious sabotage only intensified Spanish suspicions of political complots. As far back as 1602, a royal decree sent to the king's representative in Buenos Aires warned of the corrupting influence: "created by the presence of many foreigners, and particularly Portuguese who have entered the country . . . 'Judaisers' . . . [And, vigilance must be maintained] . . . so that no error and evil sect is sown among the *indios* who are barely certain and instructed in our faith and vulnerable to any novelty . . ."[77] Solorzano, in his masterwork, a compilation of the laws of the Indies, also warned that the Portuguese might undermine the faith of Peru's "simple people," new to Catholicism, and that heresy would entail political consequences.[78] Blacks and Indians, Christian acolytes, were ripe for sedition, he argued, particularly so because New Christians were determined to undermine their faith.[79]

New Christians were said to communicate their heresies in the thriving mercantile spaces of colonial life. Here Indians, blacks, and New Christians could engage in illicit conversation; moreover they could do so secretly, for all were conversant in languages unintelligible to Old Christian ears. In fact "they could speak their languages in front of Old Christians, and Old Christians wouldn't have a clue"—or so went the charges.[80] ". . . [it was] a secret language . . . [and] Old Christians just heard normal words, not that out-of-the-ordinary language, [and New Christians spoke with] duplicity and scheming, so that the prisoner and the rest of his ancestry and kin could converse about conspiracies and heresies."[81]

Not only did Spanish conspiracy theories presume rather fantastic linguistic infiltrations between Indians, Africans, and Jews but they made customs of indigenous or African origin into heretical Judaic rituals. Manuel Bautista Perez, for one, stood accused of using tobacco and cola nut in the practice of Jewish rituals.

According to testimony, when Manuel Bautista would give his *compadre* and fellow Jew tobacco, "he would say, taking it with his fingers and pressing it to his nostrils, senor *compadre*, this tobacco is very good and he would scatter it on the ground or blow on it. Then the *compadre* would say to Manuel Bautista Perez, isn't there some *colilla* to drink with water (a root or fruit from Guinea, which becomes sweet by drinking water after putting it in the mouth) and Manuel Bautista Perez would order his servants to bring it." And, as if to reinforce the Jewish derivations of taking tobacco and drinking *colilla*, the witness added, "the compadre and Manuel Bautista would then speak to each other in a language only understood among themselves, talking about the Law of Moses."[82]

Of course, Manuel Bautista Perez emphatically denied these allegations. He strongly objected to charges he made ritual offerings to the god of the Old

Testament, let alone with cultural artifacts from South America and Africa. He was, however, the head of an international trading enterprise whose agents traversed the globe—including Africa and the Andes.

How striking that goods associated with processes at the heart of Spain's colonial endeavor, the conquest of *indios* and the expansion of the African slave trade, were conflated with the practices of Judaism. Global commerce and cheap labor anchored Spain's colonial enterprise, and New Christians along with Indians and African slaves were key figures in this equation. At least according to stereotype, New Christians dominated international trade, and in keeping with colonial reality, Indians and blacks embodied the vice-royalty's sources of cheap labor. Both groups were needed for the success of Spain's global endeavors, and both were distrusted. New Christian merchants, slaves, and colonized Indian vassals were outside of the traditional institutions that had structured life in the Iberian Peninsula before colonialism began to change the rules. In different cultural and economic ways, each signaled the novel social relations of the emerging modern world. This version of cultural finger pointing hints at the tensions animating nascent modern/colonial economics and politics, as well as the tensions animating the cultural order on which they both rested.

Manuel Bautista Perez was inscribed by the social contradictions of his times, contradictions that pit appeals to lineage and traditional hierarchy against appeals to worthiness based on a modern order rooted in commercial wealth. This renowned, prosperous, and powerful merchant surely felt that aristocracy, or at least full "Spanish" status, was his due. Of course, Manuel Bautista Perez believed in and defended the legitimacy of a political structure that enslaved *negros* and coerced Indian labor, but he also believed in the right of good Christian subjects, regardless of ancestry, to be justly recognized for their contributions to nation/empire and church. It was in this regard that he challenged Castile's racial definition of Jewishness and of Spanishness, along with its accompanying social hierarchy governed by purity of blood laws and an aristocratic ethos.

COLONIAL CONSPIRACIES

The idolatry campaigns against native Peruvians, which fanned concerns about a conspiracy of coca-chewing, Inca-loving witches, also had a direct bearing on concerns about Indian-loving, hidden Jews. In the early seventeenth century, inquisitors were laboring to purify the Iberian Peninsula from Jewish contaminants, just as some Peruvian clerics were rekindling drives to extirpate the native idolatries said to destroy the Andes. Spaniards coupled

Jews with *indios* when they assessed their long-standing mission to evangelize the faith. Missionaries sent to indigenous communities perceived their efforts in light of Spain's tumultuous religious past, understanding early church
strategies to convert pagan gentiles, and especially later attempts to convert
Moors and Jews, as rehearsals for ventures in the Americas. The "disease of
the Indians" (their reluctance to denounce native religion for Catholicism),
said one of Peru's most infamous missionaries, was not "so deeply rooted a
cancer" as that of Moors and Jews.[83] Nevertheless the disease of the Indians—so rampant in Peru—amplified concurrent anxieties over the New
Christian presence, as it did over Peru's proliferating witches.

Inquisitor Manozca's twin anxieties about witchcraft and "Indianness"
and about New Christians and Indians were tied to the cultural work of Spanish colonialism. Colonial dominion, inscribed in cultural terms and structured
through cultural hierarchies, was menaced, or so the inquisitors thought, by
witchcraft ideologies and New Christian conspiracies that reached into the
heart of imperial cultural politics. The imagined threats of colonial witchcraft and New Christian sabotage swelled as they pulled in fears surrounding idolatries, native subversions, the allegiance of slaves, the disorderliness
of women, and the power of foreign enemies. And vice versa.

Peru's inquisitors intertwined stereotypes of New Christians, Indians,
African slaves, and women as part of an etiology of fear and blame. This etiology was built on a racialized vision that confused nationalist sentiments,
religion, and the caste categories of colonial rule. It also promoted some of
the extraordinary irrationalities that have accompanied the modern age—irrationalities made all the more dangerous by their coating in the rhetoric of
reason and in the rhetoric of reasons of state. Seventeenth-century Peru provides a glaring example of how fears—in this instance about New Christians,
witches, and Indians—could coalesce, develop, and ultimately balloon into
absurd conspiracy theories, all with the help of government officials.

GLOBAL CONSPIRACIES AND THE BLACK LEGEND

Colonial conspiracies were spawned by the modern world's confusions of
race and nation, culture and religion, ethnicity and treachery: confusions in-
stantiated and institutionalized by the emerging bureaucracies of the nacient
modern world. And Black Legend denunciations of Spanish brutality, especially brutality in the Americas, were an added dimension to the conspiracies
of the times. British outcries went hand in glove with British anxiety over
Spain's global pretensions. England, however, had global designs of her own.
British apologists were in a bit of a bind: they wanted to stake a claim to the

world's riches yet at the same time distance themselves from Spain. They did so by deprecating the Spanish model—that is, colonialism, or direct state control over conquered populations. Their weapon of choice was trade, and their not-so-innocent rhetoric was to guarantee the creation of a world of sovereign nations united by the free market.

Hakluyt suggested the arguments. The "effects" produced by "tyrannical ambition" were "contrary to the profit which those shall receive which only are affectioned to the common benefit . . . to the general policy of all men, and endeavor to unite them one with the other as well by traffic and civil conversations . . ."[84] In other words, although the creation of a universal monarchy would lead to "ruin," the creation of a universal market would not. Trade relations, the search for common profits, would be "an end so much more commendable as it is far from all tyrannical and cruel government."[85] As we might have expected, Hakluyt, nevertheless, went on to write that if the "savages will not yield unto the endeavors so much tending to their profit," the conquest by "military virtues and force of arms" would be justified.[86] If the natives would not oblige voluntarily, then England would have no choice but learn something from Spain about political coercion.

Thus began an Anglo slight of hand, born in the Black Legend, that would elevate British colonial activities—principally the free market and free trade—as the modern way of conducting colonial business.[87] The United States is this ideology's most notable heir.

Hannah Arendt found the convergence of bureaucratic administration and race thinking a horrifying, modern danger; we can add, especially in these troubled times, so is our blinded ignorance of their workings and their appeal.

CHAPTER SEVEN

OF BOOKS, POPES, AND *HUACAS;* OR, THE DILEMMAS OF BEING CHRISTIAN

Gonzalo Lamana

"In all the kinge of Spain['s] domynyons . . . our men are dryven to flinge their Bibles and prayer bookes into the sea."

— Richard Hakluyt, 1584

"Speaking with great majesty . . . the . . . Ynga Atagualpa flung the book [friar Valverde had given him] from his hands."

— Felipe Guamán Poma de Ayala, ca. 1615

T his chapter examines questions of difference and authority at the inter- section of religion and politics that took place mainly in the sixteenth and nineteenth centuries and that have current echoes. It traces the emer- gence of the external and internal imperial borders of the modern/colonial dual world we live in through the changing narratives of a single event. The event is the encounter between Spaniards and Incas in the plaza of Caja- marca on November 16, 1532. That day Francisco Pizarro's conquest com- pany captured the Inca Atahualpa in a bloody attack after the exchange of a book and words between the Inca ruler and Fray Vicente de Valverde, head clergyman of the company. The narratives whose successive versions of these events I examine are those of conquerors who wrote soon after it; those of Spanish chroniclers writing some twenty years later; those of English politi- cians and explorers in the 1580s; that of an influential U.S. scholar who wrote in 1847; and finally, those of border thinkers, authors of Andean descent. I close by drawing parallels with the current neocolonial moment in an attempt to show how these questions of difference and authority from a distant past allow us to critically understand the present.

This approach helps to present the emergence of current geopolitical con- figurations born with the Black Legend from yet another point of view: that of subversion, mimicry, hesitancy, and transculturation. The argument is that the narrative of Cajamarca helps identify certain dilemmas of being Christian that were shaped by the emergence of the Atlantic as center of the first world system. This emergence entailed the definition and redefinition of values, epistemologies, and national projects on both sides of the ocean, until a solid hierarchy evolved in which native American peoples remain at the bottom, English at the top, and Spaniards somewhere in between. This still-current hierarchy began to develop at the end of the sixteenth century, and it involved the emergence of internal, imperial borders, which came into being once the ascendancy of the second, northern European modernity (English in this case) displaced the first, Mediterranean modernity (Spanish in this case).[1] This process, I suggest, was not linear and resulted more from politically driven blindness than from self-evident superiority.

Tracking this displacement through narratives of the relations between Spaniards and Incas is particularly illuminating because Spaniards and English in their own rivalries had nevertheless to agree on their superiority over native peoples, and both the superiority and the rivalries in the sixteenth century were related to "being Christian." The Spanish conquerors' concern was being able to respond to the internal Spanish critiques, which were as fierce as those of the English would be, and threatened their sense of righteousness by depicting the conquerors as resembling their more despised enemies, the Turks. The conquerors' quest for self-justification ended up being, in turn, intrinsically related to the Black Legend (Juderías 1967 [1914]), as the English co-opted the elements that the conquerors used to build difference, Christianity being a key one, and used them to their own ends. However, in doing so the English faced the dilemma of having to find the terms that enabled them to condemn those who were, even to their own eyes, though inferior to themselves, superior to the natives. It took them some time to be able to effectively do so. Finally, Andean intellectuals attempted to intervene in the formation of the Atlantic by renarrating Cajamarca in yet another way, and in doing so also had to face the dilemmas of being — by then — Christians. The same dilemmas, I suggest, condition some of the most salient world conflicts today, such as the U.S. occupation/liberation of Iraq.

The study shows that all these attempts to define values, epistemologies, and political projects tangled with each other and built on a succession of borrowings, intellectual hijackings, and erasures. It suggests in particular that the processes of distinction through which Europe made itself (including events so typically European as the Reformation and the Counter-Reformation) responded in part to the actual dynamics of the colonial encounter, which was powered by native Peruvian border thinkers. It was through debates and conflicts that took place in peripheral, colonial scenarios that England and Spain shaped their national/imperial differences. In this prebourgeois, colonial-metropolitan circulation of "grammars of difference" (Stoler 1995, Cooper and Stoler 1997), at stake were not the principles of decency but the grounds for reality making. The starting points of my analysis are the accounts of the Peruvian conquerors, which were expressions of the glory of a civilizing empire.

BEING CHRISTIAN IN THE 1530s

Among the first-hand accounts of the conquest of the Incas, the most well known is Francisco de Xérez's *Verdadera relación de la conquista del Perú (True account of the conquest of Peru)*. Xérez was the secretary of the would-be governor of Peru, Francisco Pizarro. He took active part in the capture of the Inca Atahualpa in Cajamarca on November 16, 1532, and returned to Spain after the Inca was executed in July 1533. Xérez arrived in Seville in June 1534; a month later his nineteen-page account was issued from the press. The book was a success, and not just in Spain; two Italian translations appeared in 1535, it was reprinted in Spain four times in 1540 and three times in 1547, and it was reprinted once in Italy in 1556 (Bravo Guerreira 1985).

As Lockhart (1972, 276) points out in his extensive study of Cajamarca, Xérez's 1534 account, together with that of his successor as Pizarro's secretary, Pero Sancho (1986 [1535]), forms the backbone of modern histories of the conquest of Peru. Its official character and detail makes it coherent and authoritative, even "objective" (Porras 1986, 97). It is only recently that this privilege has been questioned. In her path-breaking study of Cajamarca's encounter scene, Seed (1991, 14–19) shows the political goals and narrative strategy informing Xérez's account. *Verdadera relación*, Seed argues, expresses the Spanish belief in the transparency and universality of its values — Christianity and literacy. These beliefs organize the crucial scene, the exchange of the book and words between the Inca Atahualpa and Fray Vicente de Valverde. After the Inca completed his spectacular entry into the plaza, sitting in his gold *andas* carried by a large retinue and escorted by several thousand of his men, the clergyman approached him on foot and alone but for a translator, a cross he carried in one hand and a Bible he carried in the other. Choosing to tackle the first-contact uncertainty with a speech, the friar told the Inca, "I am a priest of God's, and I teach Christians the things of God, and thus I come to teach you all. What I teach is what God talked (sic) to us, which in is this book. Therefore, in God's and the Christians' behalf I beg you to be his friend, because God thus wants it, and good will come to you from it; and go talk to the Governor, who is waiting for you" (Xérez 1985, 111).[2]

Valverde's speech presents the offer of enlightenment and explicitly estab-
lishes a connection between God's words and the book. This connection implies not only the sacredness of the object but the certainty of superiority that
writing encodes. Xérez skillfully deploys both elements in the scene's de-
nouement, justifying the ensuing Spanish attack. After the friar delivered his
careful speech, "Atabalipa asked him to give him the book so that he could
see it, and he [Valverde] gave it to him closed; and not getting Atahualpa to
open it right, the clergymen extended his arm to open it, and Atahualpa with
great disdain hit him in the arm, not wanting him to open it; and struggling
to open it, he opened it; and not marveling at the letters or the paper as other
Indians did, he threw it five or six paces away from him."[3] As Seed (1991, 17)
points out, the Inca is doubly at fault. On the one hand, he rejects Christianity; on the other, "Atahualpa not only fails to be fascinated by the paradox of
an object containing speech but also fails to be awed by the Spaniards' cultural achievements, unlike 'other Indians.'" This double failure is an expression of the Inca's "arrogance" (*soberbia*), which also drove him to ask for all
that the Spaniards had taken to be returned. Valverde then went back to inform Pizarro of what had happened, how Atahualpa "had thrown the sacred
scripture to the ground" (Xérez 1985, 112); without uttering a word, the
Spanish conquistador took his arms and went after the Inca.

Although Xérez's narrative of the avenging Spanish attack focuses on
Pizarro and his men, the reader is soon reminded of the right order in the *mise
en scène:* the conquerors are only second-order actors; the main one was God
himself. After the capture, Pizarro addressed Atahualpa at length and listed
the benefits that would come to him from the fact that the conquest was God's
and the emperor's—the universal lord's—mission. The head of the Spanish
conquest company closed his enlightening words by making rationales explicit: despite Valverde's offer of peace "you threw to the ground the book
where God's word is, that is why our lord allowed your arrogance to be
brought low [*abajada*] . . . that no Indian could offend the Spaniard" (Xérez
1985, 113).

Although Xérez's account receives much attention from current scholars
(albeit for different reasons), this privilege does not necessarily reflect its
primacy or popularity in 1530s Europe. Xérez's was neither the first nor
the most widely available account of the Inca conquest in the 1530s—not by
chance did he title his text "true account." Two other publications preceded
it: a letter by a high-ranking Spanish officer in Panama, the *licenciado* Espinosa, and a narrative by a member of Pizarro's expedition, Captain Mena.
The comparison of all three that follows will show the escalating interventions and reveal the dilemmas that Cajamarca posed.

When Xérez's ship docked in Seville in June 1534, loose printed sheets that described summarily the conquest of Peru were already circulating in Europe. These short accounts focused on the capture of Atahualpa and the fabulous ransom that followed it. The first one appeared in February 1534, in German, in Nuremberg; two Italian editions followed by June in Venice, and soon a French one appeared in Lyon (Porras Barrenechea 1937, 28–44).[4] In the very brief German and Italian accounts, which were derived from translations of their common Spanish original, Espinosa's letter, Valverde, with translators, approached the "cacique" (Indian lord—an Antillean term) to negotiate peace with him, which he did, "and talking [sic] the friar the things of God, he gave him a breviary book he carried open, saying to look at it and kiss it, that it contained the things of God and of our faith; and the said cacique took it and very angrily cast it and threw it to the ground, beginning to show much anger because they have entered his land" (Porras Barrenechea 1937, 38).[5] Then the friar, having "seen [the cacique's] contempt for the things of God," exhorted the conquerors to attack.

Captain Mena's *La conquista del Peru, llamada la nueva Castilla* (The conquest of Peru, called the New Castille), the second account preceding Xérez's, published in Seville in the same print house Xérez's would be four months later, was also a success: it appeared in Italian in Rome and Venice in May and December 1534, in France in 1545, and again in Italy in 1556 (Pogo 1930). As scholars have pointed out, Mena was bitter because of receiving what he considered an unfair share in the distribution of Atahualpa's ransom. What is relevant here is that Mena's account of Cajamarca's scene shows transformations. Valverde approached Atahualpa with a cross in his hand to tell him "the things of God" and said through an interpreter that "the Christians were his friends and that the Governor loved him very much and that he should enter his house to see him. The Cacique replied that he would advance no further until the Christians returned all they had taken in all the land and after that he would do all he wished. Leaving those matters aside, with a book he held in his hands [the father] began to tell him the things of God which were convenient, but he did not want to accept them; [the cacique] asking for the book the father gave it to him thinking he wanted to kiss it; and he took it and threw it over his retinue" (Sinclair 1929, 9).[6] The interpreter then picked up the "book" and gave it to Valverde, who went back to Pizarro calling for the attack: "come out, come out, Christians, and come to these enemies, dogs who do not want the things of God . . . he has thrown . . . to the ground the book of our holy law" (Sinclair 1929, 9).

Although all three narratives share the same authoritative anchor—sacredness and reactions to it—there are differences. Espinosa relates that Valverde

asked Atahualpa to kiss the book; Mena improved the act by introducing expectations: Valverde thought he would. Both accounts stress Atahualpa's expressions of contempt toward a holy object, and through them his rejection
of Christianity. The Inca's disdain for the faith has to be understood not only
in religious terms, I suggest, but also as a refusal to recognize reality as it was.
True in "true faith" meant a claim about reality and about who had access to
it. In this all accounts, early and late, Spanish and English, agree. It is this connection that makes the expectation that Atahualpa would kiss the book reasonable, and the failure to do so punishable.

Xérez's account would seem to be but a more detailed version of the same
events, something reasonable given that Espinosa was a second-hand writer.
There are, however, significant differences among accounts. According to Espinosa, Valverde gave Atahualpa a breviary he carried open in his hands. Xérez
changes the details in a crucial way. In his account, the first sign of problems
is that Atahualpa has trouble in opening the book; therefore, the book had to
be closed, not open. Xérez edited the scene and chose precise words to describe the event: "no acertando." *Acertar* in Spanish means to get right, for instance, "to find what is true in what is uncertain, ignored, or hidden."[7] The
word choice gives Atahualpa's attempt something of a comic air—a strategy
with inheritors across the globe and across time. The Inca in *Verdadera relación*
resembles highland Papua New Guineans, who in the 1930s tried to find the
man inside a gramophone and—unlike Atahualpa—could not help being mes-
merized by the device. While the Leahy brothers, the Australian gold seek-
ers who set out onto the High Plateaus, took cameras to amuse their fellow
men with the recording, Xérez could only narrate it, but to the same effect:
make superiority evident *to the reader.*

Xérez's second innovation concerns the book itself. While Espinosa relates that Valverde carried a breviary, Xérez says it was a Bible. The difference may seem irrelevant, but to a sixteenth-century reader it was not; that
is, it was not to all sixteenth-century readers. The authority effect comes from
Atahualpa's rejection of God, embodied in the book. While to a Spaniard
whether Valverde carried the Bible or a breviary likely made not much of a
difference, it did to a Protestant. One of the basic tenets of Protestantism was
scriptural authority—the word of God, contained in the Bible, was the supreme authority; the word of man (much of the substance of a breviary) was
imperfect at best, at worst popish superstition. As Lutheranism was already
in full swing in the 1530s, amending Espinosa's account was recommend-
able. After all, as we saw, the conquistadors claimed not to be the main actors in Cajamarca scene; it was God himself.

And God acted for good reasons. Alleged demonstrations of divine favoritism were directed not only toward the internal Spanish critiques—which I will analyze shortly—but also toward the external, Christian ones. Espinosa closes his account of the news of Peru by enumerating the marvelous riches of the new land—a place whose inhabitants "keep the silver in a pen because they do not know where to put it." Those in Panama believed these marvels, Espinosa tells his king, because they had it "for certain" that it was God's will that Peru was discovered during Charles V's reign, "because Your Majesty is *in viam domini* serving him and defending his Christian republic and church . . . so that in a more spirited manner and with more chances he can continue the holy enterprise and war against the Turk and Luterio [Luther] and the other enemies of the faith" (Sinclair 1929, 39).

The religious changes in the European arena had forced a change in accounts of the Spaniards' conquest that have gone undernoticed. The conquerors of Peru call themselves, by and large, "Christians." The label may seem natural; after all, to borrow Anderson's (1991) well-known terms, Europeans' imagined community was at that time Christendom. Nation-states were far from being active identities; they were still undermined by the disruptive forces of kingdoms whose sovereigns changed according to the rules of dynastic inheritance and local political and legal structures and senses of loyalty. In Spain different kingdoms with particular laws, customs, and even languages coexisted in the early 1500s, making "Spain" a political label (Kamen 2004). Besides, conquests are so closely tied in Spanish accounts with evangelization that the label "Christian" seems only natural.

Yet it was not. In his famous *Cartas de relación*, written between 1519 and 1524, Hernán Cortés, the conqueror of Mexico, calls his own men "Spaniards," not "Christians." Peru's conquerors' way of self-identifying was clearly a choice, not just the natural way of doing it. It did not respond to the Indians they were interacting with but was an attempt to shape the way in which they were perceived back home; their audiences were Spanish and European. The same can be said of Xérez's narrative of Cajamarca. As I have argued elsewhere (Lamana 2005), rather than expressing a belief in the self-evident superiority writing expressed, Xérez's strategy responded to clear political needs: to protect his boss's career and honor. I do not argue against the *pretension* of self-evidence, as the claim to know reality is a fundamental component of any imperial project. However, something is self-evident only if there is no discrepancy about it. Such was not the case here, not because any Spaniard doubted the superiority of Christianity and literacy embodied, but because they doubted of their being evident to others. Examining the arguments of the Spanish dissidents reveals the limits of both Xérez's strategy and the internal Spanish critique.

THE INTERNAL CRITIQUE

Despite—or perhaps because of—its success, since the 1511 critical sermon that Fray Antonio de Montesinos delivered to the Spanish settlers in Santo Domingo, there was a long and fierce debate among Spaniards over the rights, forms, and procedures of Spanish colonialism. The debate was not simply a matter of intellectual dissent, but it had concrete effects. The Crown's zig-zagging course from Columbus's time to at least 1570 reflected the varied opinions and changing composition of the fledging body regulating Span-ish colonial affairs, the *Consejo de Indias*. The debate, a politicophilosophical struggle, had as its main adversaries those conceiving the Spanish task as one of pacific conversion and therefore advocating the rights of native American populations, and those conceiving it as a conquest by whatever means nec-essary and therefore advocating the conquerors/settlers' right to profit from Indians' labor—a modest reward for bringing the light to those who were little more than animals (Hanke 1965, 1985). While the arguments of the set-tlers' party went hand in hand with the narratives of heroic conquest just ex-amined, the arguments of the so-called "party of the Indians" debased in dif-ferent ways the world of glory and wonder the conquerors wanted to inhabit.

Two months after Peruvian conquerors arrived in Seville with the king's share of Atahualpa's fabulous ransom (the royal fifth), Francisco de Vicente the Vitoria, an eminent professor of theology at the University of Salamanca, questioned the heroic tale. First, he straightforwardly challenged the justifi-cation: "I do not understand the justice of that war . . . from what I have un-derstood of those that were in the . . . battle with Tabalipa [Atahualpa], never had Tabalipa nor his people done any offence to the Christians, nor a thing because of which they should wage war on him" (1947, 24). Second, even if that conquest was justified, a main obstacle remained: "even if the Emperor had just titles to conquer them, the Indians do not know it nor can know it" (Vitoria, 1947, 24); therefore they cannot be punished for defending them-selves "because they . . . think that the Spaniards tyrannize them and wage unjust war on them" (Vitoria, 1947, 24).

Vitoria continued to develop his critical ideas during the following years while he taught in Salamanca (Beltran 1929–1930). His thinking about colo-nial affairs reached its maturity in his famous *De Indis* and *De Juri Belli* lec-tures, delivered in early 1539 (Beltran 1928, 144–51), when the conquerors were still fighting Inca resistance. The lectures, which set the basis of inter-national law, examined in detail the rights of Indian peoples and the circum-stances under which the Spaniards' acts could be considered Just War.[8] I fo-cus here only on what relates directly to the events in Cajamarca.

First, Vitoria rejected all authorities and justifications Xérez invoked: the papal donation of the newfound lands had no validity (Vitoria 1947, 74–80), the emperor was no universal lord (Vitoria 1947, 66–73), and rejecting the Christian religion was no ground for just war (Vitoria 1947, 82–93). In the latter case, of particular importance here, the key lay in "invincible ignorance" (Vitoria 1947, 86). The Indians ignored the faith—they did not reject it like the Moors—and therefore could not be punished on religious grounds. More to the point, refusing to believe Christ's message when first communicated was no basis for dispossession; rather, it expressed some wisdom. Except in extraordinary cases, such as when the message is transmitted together with the occurrence of miracles, Indians could not be expected to tell which religion was the true one. Otherwise, Vitoria pointed out, had the Turks reached the Indians instead of the Christians, the former would have become Muslims. Thus, "if the faith has been proposed to barbarians in the said way [in the rush of conquests] and they do not accept it, the Spaniards cannot wage war on them for such reason" (Vitoria 1947 [1534], 90).[9] In short, as there was no affront in Cajamarca, there was no basis for just war—a war the conquerors were still waging.

This sort of questioning of a putatively self-evident truth does not end the political struggle in which the truth was enlisted; rather, the opposite occurs. Much as today in the United States, where those opposed to the war in Iraq are labeled "antipatriotic," in sixteenth-century Spain the pressure to support the glorious colonial epic resulted in questioning the allegiance of the dissidents: "if you condemn it [the conquerors' acts in Peru] straightforwardly, it scandalizes them, and some invoke the Pope, and say that you are schismatic because you question what the Pope does; and others invoke the Emperor, [saying] that you condemn His Majesty and the conquest of the Indies"[10] (Vitoria 1947, 23). While Vitoria decided to fight his battles in the relatively private space of the academy,[11] others in the party of the Indians chose the political arena and militantly persisted in arguing in the highest arenas of Spanish imperial politics. The most salient and outspoken among them was the indefatigable Fray Bartolomé de Las Casas.

Las Casas not only declared the conquests illegal but, in stark contrast to the Peruvian conquerors' celebratory accounts, challenged their alleged morality; rather than the work of Christians, the conquests were the work of Moors.[12] In a letter written to a member of the court in 1535, a year after Espinosa's and Xérez's accounts were published, Las Casas characterized Atahualpa's capture and execution as "cruel and tyrannical" acts done by "Pizarro and his sainted disciples," who were guided "by the law of stealing, in which they believe, and in that land are predicating and sowing" (1995,

89), to the extent that they are destroying it. The religious language not only attempted to use the conquerors' rhetoric against itself and thus denaturalize it, but it also responded to Las Casas's main political argument: the kings of Spain have the Indies by papal donation, but only to convert others, and to do so, "the only way" is the love of Christ, a point he developed at length in his 1534 treatise (titled *The Only Way*), which circulated widely in Spain and America (Casas 1992, 34–56). The dilemma for a Christian advocate like Las Casas was that the conquerors' (the Christians') violence not only thwarted the work of conversion but exposed the thinness of the Spaniards' own Christianity.

Conversion being so clearly the task, Las Casas asks in his 1535 letter, "why does everything end up up-side down? How does such just reason as our king's lordship . . . turn so suddenly . . . into eternal damnation?" (1995, 90). Foreshadowing the debate concerning the current war in Iraq, he questioned the choice of means used to achieve the end and argued that the conquerors' non-Christian (noncivilized) acts made the Indians' resistance legitimate. There was no *casus belli.* "I confess before the . . . Holy Trinity that in those lands there is no one who does more damage or opprobrium to his holy and catholic faith, or who impedes or defames it, but the Christians" (Casas 1995, 91). And in line with Vitoria, "no war, from the time the Indies were discovered until today, was just on the Christians' part," but all clearly have been from the Indians' as they defended themselves (Casas 1995, 93). Unlike Moors, who resist the faith, the Indians are infidels only out of ignorance, they "hold no foreign lands [as the Moors allegedly did] but their own; they do not exit their lands to go rob and infest us, rather we come and invade theirs, [and] we expel them from them." He closes, "this is not, sir, the way of Christ . . . but the way of Mahoma," the way of war (Casas 1995, 97), therefore unjust and contrary to God's service.

The similarities Las Casas worked against did not end there. It was not only that the conquerors' acts did not help spread Christianity and were those of Moors, the anti-Christians *par excellence,* but the Crown's legal discourse also had Muslim imprints. Las Casas openly condemned the *Requerimiento,* the 1513 text that the Crown mandated all *compañías* read to native lords when first encountering them.[13] Because the task was not conquest, a "satanic . . . Mahometic, abusive, improper and infernal word," but spreading God's message, "the damned *requerimientos* that until today have been done are not necessary" (Casas 1995 [1542], 117). In a well-known passage, the friar relates that when he first saw the *Requerimiento* he did not know whether to laugh or to cry (Casas 1965, II: 28) — I suggest that his uncertainty expressed no only the fact that the text was wrong in all respects but also the fact that it was heavily indebted to Moorish legal forms (Lemistre 1970; Seed 1995, 68–99).

After the relative success of the Indians' party during the early 1540s, the 1550s saw a renewed, direct debate at court over the destiny of the *encomiendas*, the cornerstone of the conquerors/settlers' existence. By then, an *encomienda* was a royal grant that entitled its holder (*encomendero*) to receive tribute and labor from a certain group of Indians and in exchange mandated that he should care for their conversion and be ready to defend the king. It was a reward for such services. The question in the 1550s was whether the *encomiendas* should be abolished and all Indians pay tribute directly to the king, as Las Casas advocated, or whether *encomiendas* should be given to the settlers in perpetuity with civil and criminal jurisdiction, as Juan Ginés de Sepúlveda advocated (Zavala 1992, 141–68).

In 1550–1551 a well-known debate took place before judges appointed by the Crown between Las Casas and Sepúlveda. The core issue was defining the nature of the Indians: if they were rational beings capable of self-government, they should be free and require just Christianization; if not, that is, if they were closer to natural slaves, then *encomiendas* in the settlers' way were entailed (Hanke 1988). As the judges never passed sentence the struggle continued. In 1552 Las Casas published a number of treatises against the conquerors/settlers' position. Among them was his most incendiary and famous text, *Brevísima relación de la destrucción de las Indias* (*Very short account of the destruction of the Indies*).

The book is what its title suggests: a hammering narrative of the acts of the Spanish conquerors in which they are portrayed as monsters guided by an appetite for gold, lust, and destruction, who decimate one native group after the other, inflicting on them the most horrifying forms of violence imaginable. There is no glory in the conquerors' acts; they serve neither to the king nor God. Rather, through them Indians learn to hate Christianity and to associate it with violence and injustice. All conquest wars were illegal while the natives' were justified; Cajamarca was no exception. Las Casas narrated a very short scene: Atahualpa, the rightful lord of his kingdom, surrounded by his naked, unarmed entourage, went to meet the Spaniards; in arriving, he asked for all that they had stolen and destroyed to be satisfied; then the attack and the massacre followed (Casas 1966, 101–2).

The fact that there is no Valverde and no book in the account shows the limits of the internal critique: it was based on the unquestionable superiority of Christianity and its symbols. The question was not one of goals and agency but one of means and agents. The particular manner in which the events took place in the plaza of Cajamarca posed a dilemma even to those arguing for a

Christianizing mission in a pacific way. Having a sophisticated critical apparatus in place and proving that the conquerors resembled Moors rather than
Christians was not enough to counteract the import and emotional weight of
the symbols involved. Las Casas found it necessary to remove them from
sight to make his account compelling.

The attempt by the heretics that challenged the pope and the emperor and
discredited Spain's name to produce a legitimate Christian man in contradistinction to the Moorish-seeming conquerors did not achieve a final political triumph, but it clearly unsettled the latter.[14] After twenty years of con-
servative perseverance, in the 1550s new accounts of Cajamarca appeared.
In an attempt to respond to the internal imperial critiques, the new versions
improved several elements of the scene. They did not alter the basis of the argument in a fundamental way, they just perfected it; in doing so they opened
a little-examined door for the Black Legend to enter the scene—an unfore-
seeable *tour de force* that announced the second modernity.

INTERNAL CLARIFICATIONS

No new narratives of Cajamarca were published during the 1530s and 1540s.
Showing that the available ones were deemed sufficient, Xérez's account was
republished in Spain three times in 1547, once jointly with a new edition of
the Crown's official chronicler Gonzalo Fernández de Oviedo's *Historia general y natural de las Indias*.[15] The situation changed soon. In the 1550s two new,
detailed accounts appeared, written not by conquerors but by chroniclers:
Lope de Gómara (1552) and Augustin Zárate (1555).[16] The scenario in Cajamarca is constructed of the same acts as in Xérez's: Valverde approached the
Inca, they exchanged words and a book, Atahualpa threw the book down,
the attack followed. The authoritative elements on which both 1550s accounts
build also follow closely Xérez's choices: on the one hand, Atahualpa's rejection of Christianity, which is made visually compelling by his throwing of the
sacred book to the ground; on the other, his barbarism, which his ignorance
of literacy made evident.

To justify the conquerors' attack, however, Gómara and Zárate take a
number of steps Xérez does not. Some are small. For instance, the reader is
informed of Atahualpa's intentions before the meeting—to capture the Spaniards. To that effect, he had a "general" with five thousand men in an attempt
to secure the conquerors from their eventual escape from the "trap." Other
changes signal a fledging imperial circulation of ideas. During the meeting
between Hernando Pizarro and Atahualpa the day before Cajamarca, they
have the Inca tell Hernando that he was going to meet them the next day to

order how they should leave the land. This innovation, which contradicts all other accounts of the meeting—including that of Hernando Pizarro himself (1952 [1533])—points to a circulation of intraimperial colonial knowledge: it suggests a borrowing from Cortés' second letter (1985 [1520], 79–182), in which the Aztec ruler Moctezuma repeatedly asks the Spaniards to leave his country.

The main difference with Xérez and all earlier accounts is that Zárate and Gómara improve them by adding a long, detailed exchange of words between Valverde and Atahualpa. I quote it at length because this addition, which I suggest was introduced to placate the internal Spanish critiques, ended up opening the door for cooptation and subversion by English authors. Valverde approached the Inca with a cross and the breviary "or the Bible, as some say" (Gómara 1991, 171), and told him that

> God trine and one made the world out of nothing and made man out of earth, whom he called Adam, of whom we all have origin and flesh. Adam sinned against his creator because of his disobedience, and all that after him were born and will be, except Jesus Christ, who, being true god, came down from the sky to be born in Mary, virgin, to redeem the human lineage of sin. He died on a cross like this one, and because of it we adore it. He was resurrected the third day [and] went up to the sky in forty days, leaving Saint Peter as his vicar in the earth and his successors, called popes; who have given to the very potent king of Spain the conquest and conversion of those lands; and thus now Francisco Pizarro comes to beg you to be friends and tributaries of the king of Spain, emperor of the Romans, monarch of all the world, and to obey the Pope and receive Christ's faith, if you believed it, which is very holy, and the one you have is very false. And know that doing the opposite we will wage war on you and take the idols so that you will leave the delusional religion of your many false gods.[17] (Gómara 1991, 171)

Atahualpa, "very angry," responded with an equally detailed speech. The Inca said that

> he did not want to pay tribute being free, nor hear there was another lord greater than he; yet, that he would rejoice to be the emperor's friend and to know him, who had to be a great prince since he sent so many armies as they said across the world; that he would not obey the pope, because he gave what was foreign to him, and to not leave to who never saw it the kingdom that was his father's; and about religion, he said that

very good was his, and that very well he was with it, and did not want, less ought to put into question something so old and proved; and that Christ died and the Sun and the Moon never did.[18] (Gómara 1991, 171)

From this intricate dialogue followed Atahualpa's question of authority — how did Valverde know all that he had said? Valverde responded that "that book said it," and gave it to him. The Inca "opened it, looked at it, flipped its pages, and saying that it [the book] did not tell him anything of that [Valverde's words], he threw it to the ground" (Gómara, 1991, 171). The outraged friar picked up the breviary, went back to Pizarro, and asked him to avenge the insult: "the gospel on the ground; vengeance, Christians; to them, to them, who want neither our friendship nor our faith" (Gómara, 1991, 172). The attack followed.

Gómara's addition introduces *before* the scene of the book a dialogue that clarifies and makes explicit what in Xérez's version was implicit: a request for religious conversion and political submission. Valverde's speech becomes — with minor variations — an abridged version of the *Requerimiento*. The source of authority legitimating the request is God, following whom is the chain of authorities that includes the papal donation and eventually reaches Pizarro. He was sent by the right authority and for good reasons to bring Christianity to those living in darkness. Although most contemporary readers may find the legal frame risible, a sixteenth-century reader would not necessarily do so. On the one hand, the peculiar history of the world Gómara crafted was the actual history of the world. Sixteenth-century scholars made considerable efforts to accommodate the existence of American peoples to biblical texts (for instance, trying to identify from whom its inhabitants descended and when they went astray). On the other hand, at the peak of the Reformation and Counter-Reformation, with the Council of Trent in full swing, doubting the pope's authority could be grounds for inquisitional action and charges of antipatriotism.

By making Valverde's words fit the *Requerimiento* Gómara set the legal frame of the encounter. The same reasons guide his version of Atahualpa's response. For the reading of the *Requerimiento* to have a legal effect, its message had to be understood by its alleged addressees, the Indians.[19] If in more violent circumstances this requisite could be waived, in a paradigmatic contact scene such as Cajamarca it was a must. Atahualpa's clear, explicit response indicates that the understanding took place, making its aftermath logical and the only possible outcome. The response follows the two propositions in the *Requerimiento*, political and religious submission. Addressing temporal matters, the Inca claims that he does not want to have an overlord, being free as he is;

there is no evident reason why he would wish to, which leads him to deny the authority of the pope, a man who gives away lands that are not his. Then Atahualpa shows that he understands and rejects the source of it all, God; he claims his own deities and creators to be not only true but more powerful and reliable than Christ.

The verbal exchange is doubly effective. The Inca not only refuses to accept the offer of recognition and submission but questions the order of things it invokes: there is no single god, and political authorities have diverse places of origin. The account of the response shows the Inca's ignorance and pride, the same effects Xérez mastered. The dialogue also anticipates the scene's second act, Atahualpa's incomprehension and dismissal of the sacred book. While in Xérez' account Atahualpa has trouble opening the book, in Gómara's the Inca's incompetence is even more laughable: he holds the book expecting it to talk.

There could be therefore no doubts whatsoever, either about the legality of the conquerors of Peru's acts or about their Christian character. Zárate's and Gómara's responses to the Spanish internal critique were an editorial success. In the sixteenth century, Gómara's account was published in Spanish in Zaragoza in 1552, and in Spain and Ambers in 1553 (twice) and 1554 (twice); in Italian in 1556, 1557, 1560, 1565, and 1576; in French in 1569, 1584, and 1587; and in English in 1578 and 1586. Zárate's was published in Spain in 1555 and 1573, in Dutch in 1563, 1564, and 1573; in Italian in 1563; and in French in 1581 (Pease 1995b, 413–17, Hampe Martínez 1995).

What neither of the successful chroniclers could imagine is that their elaborations on Cajamarca's scene would serve a purpose totally other than the one they planned: in a curious case of transculturation, their improvements ended up being co-opted and subverted in the service of a bitter critique of Spanish colonialism; this time not by concerned Spanish clergymen but, even worse, by what had by then become the staunchest enemy of Spain: England. And yet again, even to the forefathers of the Black Legend, Cajamarca posed a dilemma.

HESITANT DIFFERENCE

As is well known, the writing of the Spanish internal critics ended up being one of the main sources of inspiration and information for the Black Legend (Juderías 1967; Maltby 1971; Gibson 1971). Making the Spaniards evil, hypocritical creatures helped the nations of the second modernity (England, France, Holland, etc.) build their fledging counterhegemonic projects. In particular, Las Casas's *Brevísima relación* gave them the elements with which to criticize the Spaniards in what they claimed to be best at: enlarging the Christian faith. But if the fact that one empire's internal critique ends up fostering others' political programs is not surprising, what has often not been stressed is that the rejoinder to the internal Spanish critique was also food for external, imperial ones. Gómara's and Zárate's improvements fell prey to the enemies of Spain as much as Las Casas's assaults did. Using them to build the Black Legend required more effort, however, and the reasons why illuminate the limits of the imperial reason, either of the first or second modernity, and the dilemmas of being Christian.

In 1584, twenty-six years after Spain's alliance with England faltered with the death of the Catholic Queen Mary, Richarde Hakluyt presented to Mary's sister, the Anglican Queen Elizabeth, an elaborate work titled *A Particuler Discourse Concerninge the Greate Necessitie . . . by the Westerne Discouries Lately Attempted, Written in the Yere 1584*, designed to convince her of the convenience of establishing permanent English settlements in North America (Hakluyt 1993). The text is foundational to the next hegemonic project that would manage the center of the emerging world system: in an era when America was mainly a Spanish colony, Hakluyt's larger agenda was to launch England as a worldwide colonial power that could overpower Spain (Quinn and Quinn 1993).

Discourse advances in detail the reasons why England should have colonies, ways they should be run, and profits that would come from them, both material and spiritual. Its nineteenth (and longest) chapter was entirely dedicated to undermining Spain's colonial titles, which Hakluyt considered to be the papal donation bulls. The choice is telling, as there were varied opinions in Spain about the "just titles," not all pointing to the bulls and some openly critical of them, as we saw. It shows a first movement of unforeseen reappropriation: Hakluyt focuses on the bulls because such is the title Gómara gives — and transcribes in its entirety — in his *General History of the Indies* (perhaps by chance, in its nineteenth chapter).

To prove that the donation was of no legal force Hakluyt presents a number of arguments. The main one is, tellingly, the same one Vitoria had argued forty-five years earlier: that the pope had no temporal authority to grant land. And to back his point Hakluyt piles a number of quotations from Christian savants and the Bible (Hakluyt 1993, 96–97), of which the key one is Christ's words to Pilate: "that his kingdomme was not of this world" (Hakluyt 1993, 96). These are the exact same words Vitoria (1947, 71) had chosen as key testimony. It is important to notice that there is no evidence that the English critic read the Spanish, and that Las Casas, whom Hakluyt read, did not agree on this point.[20] In other words, Hakluyt had limited options to build his project of difference. He had to resort to the same sources of authority a Spaniard would, and make the same exegetic effort to derive clues from texts produced during medieval times about a world those texts absolutely ignored.

On the other hand, *Discourse* explicitly appropriates the Spanish internal critique. Las Casas's *Brevísima relación*, translated and published in England as *The Spanish Colonie* a year before (Casas 1583), is quoted extensively in *Discourse*'s eleventh chapter to prove the Spaniards' cruel character, and in the nineteenth to argue why Spain's colonial titles were void: even if the pope had the authority to give the lands, the donation was void because he did it on condition that the king "shoulde sende thither sober and godly men, and cause the Inhabitantes of those Contries discouered . . . to be instructed in the catholique faithe, and noseled in goodd manners, and thath they shoulde carefully applye themselues thereunto" (Hakluyt 1993, 108), which Las Casas took care to publicize they did not.

A consequence of the fact that the English project of difference was trapped by Spanish forms is that, even if the ones suffering the absurdity of the papal bull were native American lords, the argument against the Spanish titles is absolutely Western-centric. Hakluyt can use the colonial other to point out the failures of the Spanish argument, exposing its arbitrariness, but cannot go beyond this because, I suggest, to do so would expose that of his own. This limitation constrained his account of the only actual example of the effects that the "vnjuste and wrongfull dealings of the Pope" (Hakluyt, 1993, 107) — "the great inchantor or counser, and troubler of the world," as Hakluyt's master, Sir Walter Raleigh, called him (Raleigh 1928 [1595], 142)[21] — had on non-European peoples: the scene in the plaza of Cajamarca.

The narrative strategy is revealing. First, Hakluyt gives a quick summary of Valverde's speech: the friar told Atahualpa "that he shoulde becomme a Christyan and that he shoulde obey the Pope and the Emperor to whome the Pope had geuen his kingdomme" (Hakluyt 1993, 108). Then he presents in detail Atahualpa's response: "Atabalipa beinge greately insensed replied that seeinge he was nowe free he woulde not becomme tributarye, nor thincke that there was any greater Lorde then himselfe, but that he was willinge to be the Emperours frende and to have his acquaintaunce, for that he muste needes be somme great Lorde that sente so many armies abroade into de worlde: He answered moreover that he woulde not in any wise obey the Pope seinge he gaue away that which belonged to another, moche lesse that he woulde leave his kingdomme that came vnto him by inheritance to one which he had neuer seen in his life" (Hakluyt 1993, 108). If the dialogue sounds familiar it is because Hakluyt is following Lope de Gómara's account. Although the passage is true to Gómara's text — Atahualpa rejected both the emperor's and the pope's authority — the way in which the dialogue acquires meaning changes

180 degrees. While in Gómara's narrative Atahualpa's response showed his irreverence and ignorance, as befitting the barbarian he was, in the midst of Hakluyt's argument, which had proved the pope to have no authority whatsoever to donate any lands, Atahualpa is Rousseau's *noble sauvage* speaking the truth: the pope was, in fact, a fool. By the same token, Atahualpa's response did not express arrogance, as all Spanish accounts maintain, just a reasonable anger anyone would feel if exposed to an outrageous proposition as he was. Instead, it was Valverde who showed arrogance; after hearing Atahualpa's response, the friar "beinge displeased at his replye was gladd to seeke any waye to wreake his anger vpon him, in somoche as when Atabalipa lett his portresse falle to the grounde, he was so testye, that he sett Pizar and his souldiers forwares crynge, 'vengeaunce Christians vengeaunce, giue the charge vpon them'" (Hakluyt 1993, 108). The order of the events changes the meaning of the scene: Valverde, furious at Atahualpa because of his refusal to recognize the pope's authority, "gladly seeks" any way to lay his anger upon the Inca; when the latter "let" the breviary "fall," Valverde found the way. That is, he used the falling as an excuse to get the revenge he longed for. To efface the shift, there is neither a clear connection between the sacred book and Atahualpa (one does not know why or how it ended up in his hands) nor a clear intent behind the event. Unlike in Espinosa, Xérez, or Gómara, in Hakluyt's account, Atahualpa did not "throw" Valverde's breviary (not a Bible anyway), he merely let it "fall" to the ground; it was almost an accident. As a result, the scene revolves not around God or Christianity but around the pope and his absurd authority claims. Unreasonable emotions control Valverde, whose reasons and argument were foolish, not Atahualpa; the Inca, despite being logically incensed, responded with a clear argument, showing control.

I want to stress that Hakluyt needed the Spanish response to its internal critique to craft his account. First, he could not have written it based on Espinosa's, Mena's, or Xérez's text; only Gómara's (or Zárate's) augmented versions of the encounter, in which the dialogue is developed to include the abridged version of the *Requerimiento* and Atahualpa's studied response, gave him the resources. Second, it allows Hakluyt to use the voice of the colonial other, which mirrors Hakluyt's own denunciations but saves him the risks. By taking a native lord's words from a Spanish text, the demonstrative power of his *Discourse* was doubly enhanced. On the one hand, he could withdraw and let the sources speak for themselves; on the other, the fact that a barbarian could speak the truth to a Spaniard tears apart the Spanish claim of superiority—with which the English were very familiar,[22] and in particular its claim of universality, which affected both Incas and English, although in completely different ways; I will return to this topic below.

Hakluyt managed to subvert Zárate's and Gómara's main accomplishment (their proof that Atahualpa understood well), but he had to avoid the Spaniards' second strategy of justification: Atahualpa's inferiority, manifested in his incapacity to understand a book. *Discourse* erases the connection between God's words—what he said—and Atahualpa holding the book, as well as his incapacity to understand the object (recall Atahualpa's inability to open the book in Xérez and his foolish attempt to listen to it in Gómara). By omitting any reference to the act Hakluyt also erases the connection between God's words and the text, which could redirect the plot away from the pope and toward Christianity.

I do not suggest that the English did not celebrate the manifest superiority of literacy as the Spaniards did, rather the opposite; it is precisely because the two imperial projects resembled each other too much that they needed to mark stark distinctions. The tension between similitude and difference becomes clear in a key scene in Hakluyt's account that mirrors the events at Cajamarca. The center of the scene is, again, a sacred book, although in this case the people behind its mistreatment were the Spaniards.

Chapter two of *Discourse* argues that English foreign trade was at risk because of Spain's extensive power. The opening example in the chapter is the seizing of English ships found in areas the Spaniards considered under their jurisdiction. In those cases, not only were ships and merchandise confiscated but, even worse, the crews were given to the Inquisition. As a result, Hakluyt tells, in the Spanish king's domains "our men are dryven to flinge their Bibles and prayer books into the sea, and to forsweare and renownce their Relligion and conscience, and consequently their obedience to her maiestie" (Hakluyt 1993, 12). The defenders of the "true and sincere religion" were forced by the "superstitious" (Hakluyt 1993, 11), "barbarous" in their "sauvage" (Hakluyt 1993, 60) customs, to "fling" the Bible. This provides a perfect mirror of Cajamarca, as in both cases religion and sovereignty went hand in hand, and in both cases the reader can identify who were the foolish ones who based their acts only on force and who were the sound underdogs who suffered it. As a consequence of this offense the English were forced to renounce their religion and adopt that of the Catholics, attending Mass. However, the point was not simply violence but fear of similarity: some actually did convert and even sent their children to Spain to hear Mass (Hakluyt 1993, 15). In other words, if Las Casas was concerned with Christians acting like Turks, so was Hakluyt concerned with Anglicans acting like Catholics.

The passage exposes the fledging beginning of the second modernity, in terms not only of political power—Anglicanism was very fragile—but of self-imaginings; the borders between religions were porous. No wonder that *Dis-*

course's first chapter tried to convince the queen that one of the main benefits of establishing permanent settlements was to give the Church of England the chance to effectively outdo the papists in the task of saving souls. If they "in their superstition" had achieved so much, what could the defenders of the "true religion" not do? I suggest that the colonial scenario was also a chance to prove (to other European countries, not to Indians) divine favoritism; to make manifest that, as the would-be bishop of London put it in 1559, "God is English" (Hillgarth 2000, 361). In other words, the colonial other was seen as one more piece in the European chessboard. (This does not mean, though, that he or she complied.)

The last scenario in which I will examine the similitude between Spaniards and English and the imperial and colonial borders' role in it is that of the English confronting a colonial other. This will show that if the scene in Cajamarca, as he narrated it, enabled Hakluyt to undermine the Spaniards' aspirations of (self-evident) superiority, it also posed a dilemma and remained a source of anxiety, as it mirrored (and frustrated) English aspirations.

At the same time that Hakluyt was writing his discourse, Walter Raleigh, Hakluyt's master, was actively engaged in making the English colonies a reality. After a scouting trip in 1584, Raleigh equipped a colonizing expedition that left England in early 1585. The expedition reached the U.S. coast at North Carolina and soon established contact with native groups. Assessing the natives' mores in his account of the expedition, one of the settlers-to-be concluded that the English superiority would come to be manifest: "by howe much they vpon due consideration shall finde our manner of knowledges and craftes to exceed theirs in perfection . . . by so much the more is it probable that they shoulde desire our friendship & loue, and haue the greater respect for pleasing and obeying vs" (Hariot 1590, 24). This "greater respect" would ensure, Hariot continued, that the natives "may in short time be brought to ciuilitie, and the imbracing of true religion" (Hariot 1590, 24)—that is, Protestantism.

The natives' admiration for the Englishmen's knowledge was to facilitate conversion; it was through simple communication that things would happen, as "through conuersing with vs they were brought into great doubts of their owne, and no small admiratio~ of ours" (Hariot 1590, 26). Religion and literacy blended perfectly. Among the things the English had that made the natives marvel, Hariot mentions "bookes, writing and reading," which the natives thought "were rather the works of gods then of men, or at leastwise they had bin giuen and taught vs of the gods" (Hariot 1590, 26).

It would seem that Hariot got from the North Carolinians what Xérez and Valverde sought from Atahualpa; not quite though. The high esteem the books did receive had an immediate impact upon preaching, but not exactly in the way Hariot expected. After he "made declaration of the contentes of the Bible" to the natives, the latter, despite Hariot's repeated attempts to clarify things, mixed content and form: "although I told them the booke materially & of itself was not of anie such vertue, as I thought they did conceiue, but onely the doctrine therein co~tained; yet would many be glad to touch it, to embrace it, to kisse it, to hold it to their brests and heades, and stroke ouer their bodie with it" (Hariot 1590, 26). The natives' expression of a "hungrie desire of that knowledge which was spoken of" (Hariot 1590, 26) followed less the "virtuous doctrine" contained in the book—"what God had told us"—than the object itself. What seems not to have made Hariot wonder is that the germs the English carried caused striking mortality among the native groups they encountered, who, reasonably, concluded that they must have displeased their visitors' god—"the god of England" (Hariot 1590, 27). It was not about the message, or about literacy, it was about divinities, and the powerful/dangerous English one was a book.

Despite the awe, then, the North Carolinians reacted to the foreigners in a way that was not so different from Atahualpa's—he too was more interested in the book than in the words. Although Hariot considered it the fruit of a "conceptual" confusion, I suggest that the one confused was Hariot, because only from his epistemological standpoint was there a distinction between one thing and the other (a characteristic he shared with the Spaniards, in both ways). I will return to this "confusion" between the book and the god, and to the local nature of deities, when analyzing Cajamarca's scene through accounts from the Spanish colonial borders. For the time being, I just mention that the English certainty of superiority, its way of establishing reality in the colonial encounter, encountered other problems. The fledging colony lasted less than a year, among other reasons because of the open war with native groups who became reluctant to feed the foreigners, reluctance that, according to the latter, entitled them to ransack local peoples' supplies. The *coup de grâce* to the making of an English difference is revealed in the 1590 edition of Hariot's *True Report*. In it, Hariot added a preface aimed at discrediting unidentified circulating accounts of his (failed) colonizing enterprise, which said that it was doomed to fail because of the absence in the new lands of gold (Hariot 1590, 5). That is, the Spaniards' "true God" was lurking behind the English ideals of trade and conversion to the true religion.[23]

Leaving aside the fact that the English did not claim to have the pope's blessing to carry out their colonial expansion, and despite their claims of indisputable difference from the superstitious Spaniards, in both cases colonial titles were self-referential and authoritative. Queen Elizabeth's March 25,

1584, grant to Ralegh to establish the aforementioned colonies strikingly re-sembled any of the early Spanish king's grants: "Elizabeth by the grace of God of England . . . Queene, defender of the faith . . . [We] have given and graunted, to . . . Walter Ralegh Esquire . . . free liberty & licence . . . to dis-cover, search, finde out, and view such remote, heathen and barbarous lands, countreis, and territories, not actually possessed of any Christian prince, nor inhabited by Christian people . . . and . . . to have, holde, occupy & enjoy to him, his heires and assignes for ever, with all prerogatives, commodities, ju-risdictiõs, royalties, privileges, franchises and preeminences" (Quinn 1955, 82). The Queen also gave Raleigh the right to "expulse, repell and resist aswell by sea as by lande . . . all and every such person [who] . . . shall attempt to inhabit within the sayde Countreys" without recognizing his authority (Quinn 1955, 84). There is not a single word about native inhabitants.

Thus it is clear that despite the claims of evident difference from Spaniards, the founders of the second modernity had much in common with them. At a time when Protestant Englishmen were still struggling to define a distinctive national/imperial ethos (Helgerson 1991; Griffin 2004), the particular dy-namics and elements of the scene at Cajamarca proved difficult to control discursively. The Spaniards' claims of superiority and self-evidence could be counteracted only at the risk of undermining the English ones. Furthermore, one could argue that the "grammars of difference" (Cooper and Stoler 1997, 2) that enabled the second modernity to invent itself as different from the first were crafted in the colonial encounter. Only once the men of the second modernity produced what they considered clear boundaries with the first one could the scene at Cajamarca finally be narrated in a way that did not threaten the new hegemonic claim. This was accomplished not on the north-ern European side of the Atlantic but on the North American one.

SUCCESSFUL DIFFERENCE

In all likelihood, during the past two centuries the most influential work on the events in the plaza of Cajamarca has been William Prescott's *History of the Conquest of Peru*. Published originally in 1847, the book has long outlived its author. There have been more than 245 editions in multiple languages, the latest English one in 2006. By comparison, there are 174 editions of Karl Marx's *Capital*, volume 1, and fifty-six editions of Max Weber's *The Protestant Ethic*.[24] Prescott's work signaled a scholarly shift. Unlike most of his prede-cessors, who wrote histories of the Inca conquest using a relatively reduced number of published accounts, he built his narrative on a large amount of archival material, largely unknown at his time.[25] In addition to using this new documentary corpus, Prescott departed from the standard practice of his times of using the narratives of sixteenth- and seventeenth-century historians and instead used first-hand accounts written by the conquerors of Peru. Thus, the names of Lope de Gómara [1552], Zárate [1555], Herrera [1610–1615], and Garcilaso [1617] are replaced by those of Hernando Pizarro [1533], Mena [1534], Xérez [1534], Estete [1535?], and Pedro Pizarro [1571].[26] The result is a lively narrative that often transports the reader to the emotion of the original events.

There is, however, a notorious exception: to narrate the scene in the plaza of Cajamarca Prescott follows the account of Friar Naharro. The choice is odd, because Naharro is a third-hand source of no repute whose writings are placed at best guess in the 1600s and are based on a text collectively made by his order, the Mercedaries.[27] Prescott chose to follow Naharro's account, he says, because Naharro "collected his information from the actors in the tragedy, and whose minuter statement is corroborated by the more general testimony of both the Pizarros and . . . Xerez" (Prescott 1998, 291, n. 16). However, Naharro's (1917) account does not resemble either of them; it is, rather, a free version of Gómara. Why the choice then? The answer, I suggest, illuminates the change that had taken place in the configuration of the Atlantic from Hakluyt to Prescott. Far from the anxiety of the former, Prescott's choice expresses the certainty of a second modernity that has achieved power and crafted an identity that made itself different from and superior to both Spaniards and Indians. Like Hakluyt, Prescott needed the augmented version of the dialogue between Valverde and the Inca; unlike him, he did not need to edit it. The key to Prescott's solution lay in showing that both Incas and Spaniards deluded themselves, which gives the reader the privilege of knowing what none of those in Cajamarca could.

As in all other accounts, Atahualpa entered a plaza with no Spaniard in sight. When his men halted, Valverde came forward "with his breviary, or, as other accounts say, a Bible in one hand" and a crucifix in the other, and delivered his speech (Prescott 1998, 290). Prescott chooses the long, elaborated version of the dialogue, but unlike Hakluyt presents it in full. Valverde explained the Trinity, the creation of man, his fall, Christ's role in his salvation, and the power transfer from the apostles to the popes until the last pope commissioned the "Spanish emperor" to conquer and convert the natives of the "Western hemisphere"—Pizarro's task. Finally, the friar asked Atahualpa to receive Pizarro kindly, give up the errors of his own faith and embrace the Christians', and recognize Charles V as overlord (Prescott 1998, 291).

In a creative version of the speech, Prescott has Valverde present the entire edifice of Catholicism (and inevitably some of Protestantism) to the Inca.[28] Atahualpa's response encapsulates half of Prescott's solution:

> The eyes of the Indian monarch flushed fire, and his dark brow grew darker as he replied, — "I will be no man's tributary. I am greater than any prince upon earth. Your emperor may be a great prince; I do not doubt it, when I see that he has sent his subjects so far across the waters; and I am willing to hold him as a brother. As for the Pope . . . he must be crazy to talk of giving away countries which do not belong to him. For my faith . . . I will not change it. Your own God, as you say, was put to death by the very men whom he created. But mine," he concluded, pointing to his Deity, — then, alas! sinking in glory behind the mountains — "my God still lives in the heavens, and looks down on his children." (Prescott 1998, 291–92)

Although in quotation marks, Atahualpa's response is quoted from no text; it is a collage of sources with some parts created by Prescott.[29] The creation shows coincidences and differences with Hakluyt's text. Like the latter, by choosing the long version Prescott made the popish Spaniards' foolishness manifest. The pope enters the picture thinking he is able to give away what is not his and the Spaniards follow suit — a self-deluding duet. As in Hakluyt's account, the absurdity of the argument legitimizing the conquerors' acts is exposed by having Atahualpa speak the truth to Valverde: the pope is a "crazy man" (an improvement of Gómara by Naharro, which in his text is meant to give an even clearer proof of the Inca's insolence and ignorance[30]).

The coincidences end there. Unlike in Hakluyt's account, in Prescott's Atahualpa rejects the faith on grounds that have nothing to do with the pope. The Inca questions not just the Spaniards' superiority but their god's: Christ died, the Sun was still shining. Here Prescott improves on Gómara's version: the historian of the second modernity has Atahualpa say that the Sun (his god) was looking after him. The addition is allegorical, and revealing: Prescott has the Inca, the deluded noble savage, pointing to his god as evidence right at the time when the sun was going down, which in turn anticipates the doom of the Incas and God's triumph. (After all, Protestants had found no way around the fact that their God was the same as the Spaniards'.) Also, unlike Hakluyt, Prescott narrates in detail what happens to the book: "[Atahualpa] demanded of Valverde by what authority he had said these things. The friar pointed to the book which he held, as his authority. Atahualpa, taking it, turned over the pages a moment, then as the insult he had received probably flashed across his mind, he threw it down with vehemence" (Prescott 1998, 292) and asked for satisfaction for all the Spaniards' wrongdoings. Valverde, "greatly scandalized by the indignity offered to the sacred volume," picked it up, ran to Pizarro, and asked him to attack "the dog full of pride. . . , I absolve you" (Prescott 1998, 292).

That is, although Prescott reminds the reader that it was about the insult and the pope, not about the object, he concedes that Atahualpa did not treat the holy book as he should have and presents Valverde as reacting for just reasons—the offense to the "sacred volume." This seems to point to a larger contradiction. On the one hand, Prescott celebrates Atahualpa's doom: the foolish pointing at the Sun to prove his superiority just when he was fading, the mistreatment of the Bible and Valverde's reasonable reaction; on the other, he makes several attempts to excuse the Inca's behavior[31] and even uses the latter to reveal the Spaniards' foolish ideas.

The seeming contradiction vanishes when the broader image of the encounter is considered; the scene in Cajamarca reveals itself as a large act of foolishness and self-delusion by both Spaniards and Incas. Consequently, the reader becomes (together with Prescott) the only person who is beyond the spell and can see the truth inaccessible to all those in the plaza—the privilege of belonging to the second modernity.

On the one hand, Valverde's blindness and incapacity to recognize the absurd was part of the larger blindness affecting all Spaniards. Conquerors and priests are in Prescott's account fanatics of the "God of the battles," whom they invoked in a Mass before the encounter "to spread his shield over the soldiers" (i.e., the conquistadors), men who thought they were "fighting to extend the empire of the Cross" (Prescott 1998, 286). The key difference with the texts of the first modernity critical of the Spaniards lies in Prescott's nonattribution of consciousness: "whatever the vices of the Castilian cavalier, hypocrisy was not among the number. He felt that he was battling for the Cross, and under this conviction . . . *he was blind* to the baser motives which mingled with the enterprise" (Prescott 1998, 286, emphasis added). In other words, unlike in Hakluyt's accusation—ubiquitous in texts of the Black Legend—to Prescott the Spaniards were not hypocrites in their Christianity; they *deluded* themselves. The "baser motives" behind the Spaniards' blindness are—like in any text from Las Casas to the Black Legend—"a lurking appetite more potent than religion. . . , the love of gold" (Prescott 1998, 301).

On the other hand, even self-deluded and fanatical, the Spaniards were superior to the native peoples they conquered. Atahualpa was trapped by a reverse blindness, proper to his degree of civilization. In his four introductory ethnographic chapters Prescott praises the Incas' achievements but also signals the limits they could not escape: lack of individual initiative, a sign of civilization. As a result, when he moves to the actual historical plot Atahualpa's men are "a barbarian host" whose chaotic order makes it difficult to count (Prescott 1998, 286, n. 5)—despite their notorious order Prescott himself has highlighted—and the Inca was a "barbarian monarch" (Prescott 1998, 282). The point in the description of Atahualpa's barbarism is not so much illiteracy—as it was to sixteenth-century Spaniards—but a lack of the enlightened drive that would free men from the darkness of absolutism. The Inca, for instance, "was too absolute in his own empire easily to *suspect*" the Spaniards' plan; inventiveness was beyond him, "he could not *comprehend* the audacity of a few men" (Prescott 1998, 289, emphasis added). He was doomed to fail as was his god, to whom he pointed when responding to Valverde in a mistaken attempt at self-evidence.

Because blindness of one sort or the other affected everyone in Cajamarca, Prescott is ready to recognize the Spaniards' achievements and equally willing to point out the Incas' inferiority. A U.S. scholar in the mid-1800s, Prescott had nothing to fear from his predecessors in the evolutionary line that went from savagery to civilization. The Incas had achieved much but still were despotic and static; lacking free will, the cornerstone of innovation and improvement, they were doomed before the "civilization of the Europeans" (Prescott 1998, 127). That is why their empire "passed away and left no trace" (Prescott 1998, 126). The Spaniards, while part of that civilization and great adventurers, were prey to "that superstition which is the debasing characteristic of the times," the belief in divine intervention, "irreconcilable with rational criticism" (Prescott 1998, 132). The imperial, internal borders were clear to Prescott (1998, 143): "what a contrast did these children of Southern Europe present to the Anglo-Saxon races who scattered themselves along the great northern division of the western hemisphere!" While the former lived the "reality of romance" and understood religion as being that "of the Crusader," ready to spring in action, the latter "races" were driven neither by "avarice" nor "proselytism," but by "independence," which was to be achieved through "a life of frugality and toil" (Prescott 1998, 143). Hariot's doubts were far behind and similarities conveniently glossed over.

Once the scientific discourse replaced the religious one as guiding principle, the Anglo-Saxons could produce the same reality effect the Spaniards had in the 1500s. They knew how things *really* were. All that changed was the source guaranteeing the magical touch. English doubts and anxieties are over; not only had difference been established but it is a fundamental difference—epistemological in nature—that made Spaniards definitely inferior to them and close to Indians: neither could escape self-delusion. Prescott can then identify with the Spaniards as "white men" (the label he often uses for the conquerors, seldom "Christians") whose acts awakened awe in the "natives," because both others lagged behind him in the path to civilization. His account earnestly celebrates the achievements and shortfalls of his ancestors.

BORDER THINKING – THE EXTERNAL, COLONIAL CRITIQUE

So far I have delved into the western arguments that shaped accounts of Cajamarca, arguments that testify to the emergence of internal, imperial borders, and the game of reappropriation and difference they entailed. The movement from Xérez's to Las Casas's to Gómara's to Hakluyt's to Prescott's narrative of the events in the Cajamarca plaza speaks of the meandrous displacement of the first modernity by the second. However, for all their complexity, the critiques, additions, clarifications, and reappropriations examined are moves in a game in which all players not only share the rules but inhabit the same epistemological framework: Christianity, and its limited ontological options. I switch now to another kind of argument about Cajamarca, that which comes from the pen of intellectuals of Andean descent, and study how such arguments relate to Spanish ones and how they echo English ones. This will, in turn, speak of the emergence of external, colonial borders and make the limits of modernity—whether first or second—evident.

I argued above that Gómara's and Zárate's accounts of Cajamarca were a response to the internal Spanish critique; in an attempt to contest the party of the Indians' ideas they presented an extended version of the words Atahualpa and Valverde had exchanged. That is not true; or it is true only in part, and not the most revealing. I suggest that Gómara's and Zárate's narration of the dialogue was also an attempt to respond to another version of the events that did not fit the conquerors', one less powerful but more fundamental: that of Peruvian native intellectuals. Their critiques were less powerful because their "locus of enunciation" (Mignolo 1995) had no weight—it can even be argued that it did not exist as such, as only Christian European men could produce knowledge. Yet these intellectuals' critique was more fundamental because they questioned not the content—which Hakluyt did—but the form—which Hakluyt could not but the North Carolinian peoples Hariot encountered threatened to.

Studying these colonial dynamics reveals, ironically, that part of what happened in Europe as a result of Atahualpa's scene—including such classically European-viewed phenomena as the Reformation and counterreformation—was indebted to those who had always been objects, never subjects of that scene. This multidirectional pattern of influence points to the soundness of the current scholarly interest in reconceptualizing cultural and material fluxes as being more interactive than they have been understood in the traditional division of the globe in area studies, organized around oceanic basins, in this case the Atlantic (e.g., Bailyn 1996). But it also signals an early Spanish-Inca component of these fluxes, often overlooked as Atlantic studies tend to focus on the Anglo–French Caribbean colonial world.

As we saw, in the conquerors' accounts Atahualpa responds to Valverde's request to befriend the Christians by throwing away the sacred book. This disrespectful treatment of the book symbolizes the rejection of Christianity and provides the conquerors with a *casus belli*. It is because the interaction between the Inca and the friar is presented as clear and transparent that the conquerors' avenging acts are justified, and by some even celebrated. I want to question this transparency. In the early versions of the encounter Atahualpa says little in response to Valverde's opening words, but asks for the book in which what God had said was. I suggest that behind the Inca's attention to and handling of the book there is an epistemological disruption, which Spanish accounts silenced to avoid the threat of difference (because difference would mean the absence of transparency, therefore the absence of the invoked universal, therefore the absence of justification). Xérez, for instance, adds Atahualpa's failure to marvel before literacy, evident in his inability to open the book. Gómara and Zárate further improve the idea making Atahualpa's ignorance even more grotesque—he tried to listen to the book. But the exchange can be seen in a different light.

The earliest account that presents an Inca understanding of the scene was finished by 1551 by a Spaniard, Juan de Betanzos (1987), who was married to Cuxirimay Ocllo, an Inca princess of high rank. His narrative is composed largely of oral history from his wife's kin, who were close to Atahualpa. The account is written almost entirely from Atahualpa's side and includes what all Spanish accounts carefully try to erase: the uncertainty and guesswork proper to a contact process. As I argue in detail elsewhere (Lamana 2005), the uncertainty surrounding the Spaniards' status involved the possibility that they were *huacas*—a Quechua word for supernatural, powerful beings, often ancestors of particular groups. This possibility posed a political challenge to Atahualpa; as one function of his semidivine nature, the Inca was an intermediary between the natural and the supernatural. This uncertainty made it difficult to define a proper course of action and thus was still at work during the final encounter scene in Cajamarca.

Betanzos's narrative troubled the conquerors' on different accounts. There was no clear Inca capture plan beforehand; rather, different opinions were given about the status of the strange new people and views varied about what to do with them. Second, and more important for the sake of my argument, nothing was transparent, nor therefore intelligible, neither during the Spanish advance nor in Cajamarca's plaza. The encounter scene in Betanzos's text records not Valverde's words but his interpreter's. The friar approached Atahualpa alone, holding an open book, and began addressing the Inca,

> and the interpreter said that that father was son of the Sun, who sent him to tell him [Atahualpa] that he should not fight and should give obedience to the captain [Pizarro], who was a son of the Sun too; that it all was in that book, and thus it said it that painting—for the book. And as he said painting the Ynga asked for the book and took it in his hands, opened it, and as he saw the written lines he said: "This speaks and says that you are son of the Sun? I am son of the Sun too," and all his Indians answered . . . "thus is, *Çapa Ynga.*" And the Inca turned to say very loud that he also came from where the Sun was and saying this threw the book away. (Betanzos 1987, book II, chap. 22, p. 277)[32]

One can recognize coincidences with the early Spanish accounts. There is no long speech; neither Valverde's opening nor Atahualpa's response is elaborated. The clergyman asks Atahualpa to befriend and obey Pizarro and invokes their divine mission. The Inca in response asks for the book, examines it, and throws it away. The similarities end there. The exchanged words, transparent to a Christian, ceased to be so once translated. Since "god" was meaningless, the interpreter chose "sons of the Sun." This proved troublesome, as it is exactly what the Inca claimed to be. Instead of responding to Valverde's odd words, Atahualpa asked for the object that was their source. He asked for it and held it, but it failed to do what the interpreter promised: it remained silent.

The key to understanding the scene lies in translation and Andean categories of speaking beings. A different epistemology made events intelligible to the audience of the oral histories Betanzos was trying to marshal. The things "God/the Sun" said, his words, were in the book—that they were written was implicit to a Spaniard. Yet as a translation "written" was out of the question, since the Incas had no comparable writing system; "painting" (*quilca*) was the closest word to "book," but there were no images in the book, so the book *said* it. Among Andean polities the only object that could *say* something was a *huaca*. Although they most often spoke through their *porte-paroles*, in exceptional cases *huacas* did it directly. The Spaniards during their advance had claimed to have one *huaca*—God, who was superior to all others. Atahualpa was aware of this, the status of the Spaniards was unclear, and Valverde's words and the connection he made between them and his *huaca*/book made the Inca's reaction only reasonable. Rather than respond to the strange words of the alleged *huaca*'s *porte-parole*, he decided to confront the *huaca* itself. It was the long-awaited moment of truth. And yet, the *huaca*/book failed to perform; it remained silent. It deserved no special treatment, nor did the Spaniards' politicoreligious claim.

Atahualpa's response to Valverde makes explicit that neither the message (words like "God" or "written") nor the object (a book) that the conquerors claimed rendered the scene intelligible actually worked. As a result of this failure, there was no justification for the ensuing attack. I am not arguing that for the conquerors—or anyone on their side—this account of Cajamarca in and of itself proved problematic. If anything, Atahualpa's incapacity to understand that there was only one god and to pay respect to the sacred book only stressed the grandeur of the conquerors' deeds—the Indians' barbarism was one of the reasons the advocate of the conquerors/settlers' party cited in the 1552 meeting in Valladolid (Casas 1995b, 102–93). However, in light of Vitoria's and Las Casas's critiques, the conquerors' acts in Cajamarca were illegal: the Inca did not understand—as no one could because there were no divine signs. It followed that he neither rejected the faith nor paid any disrespect to the Bible.

Studied against the oral account registered by Betanzos, Zárate's and Gómara's elaborations cease to be a creative response to the internal Spanish critique and instead reveal the circulation of ideas already taking place at the external, imperial borders. Both Spanish accounts responded to the challenge narratives like Betanzos's posed by stressing, once again, that Atahualpa *did* understand—there was nothing confusing, therefore he consciously rejected Christianity. To do so both Spanish authors subverted the elements, keeping their visibility and changing their meaning. The version that has Atahualpa mocking God, pointing out that the Sun and the Moon did not die while Christ did, played on the translation problem (God = Sun). The same holds for both authors' account of the fact that Atahualpa asked for the book and wanted to listen to it: as presented in their accounts, it only stressed *his* barbarism, not *their* epistemological assumptions.[33] In this act of subversion and displacement, both chroniclers were more successful than Hariot; the English expeditionary could only express his estrangement upon seeing the native Carolinians' interest in the book itself, not co-opt it.

If, as we saw, the story did not rest in Europe, neither did it rest in colonial Peru. In particular, Andean border thinkers responded to Zárate's attempt at cooptation and control. In his 1,189-page critique of Spanish colonialism titled *Nueva Crónica y buen gobierno* (New chronicle and good government) (1987 [c. 1615]), the native intellectual Guamán Poma de Ayala narrated the scene at Cajamarca.[34] He chose a long version of the dialogue but explained Atahualpa's handling of the book along the lines of Betanzos's argument: "'Give it to me, the book, so that it will tell me that.' And . . . he began leafing through the pages of the said book [and said] 'What, how is it that it does not tell it to me? It does not even speak to me the said book!'" (Guamán Poma 1987, 385 [387], 392). Guamán Poma de Ayala used the same elements Zárate did but inserted again another epistemology, which made explicit to Andean eyes what had failed: the *huaca*/book. Testifying to the inextricably double-sided character of modernity/coloniality, and to the constant process of reappropriation and subversion it entails, Atahualpa's final response to the event echoed — many miles, loci of enunciation, and epistemological understandings away — Hakluyt's denunciation of the Spaniards' despicable treatment of English sacred texts: "Speaking with great majesty, sitting on his throne, the said Ynga Atagualpa flung the book from his hands" (Guamán Poma de Ayala 1987). However, unlike Hakluyt's, Guamán Poma de Ayala's writing did not have a political impact, much less effect changes in imperial policy. His letter remained unknown for some three hundred years until it was found in the royal library in Copenhagen, and even then it was found attractive because of its drawings, which were true curiosities, not because of its elaborate subversive message (Adorno 2000). Not only did Guamán Poma de Ayala's locus of enunciation make his letter excusable but its alternative epistemology was caught in the dilemma of being — by then — Christian; he had to accept the hegemonic rules of recognition, and only imply an other. This placed his account in the double-bind of being both different *and* sensible, what Salomon (1982) calls "chronicles of the impossible." From a western point of view, the *Nueva Crónica* reconfirmed the Indians' inferiority, as Atahualpa expected a book to talk. Paraphrasing Spivak's (1994, 105) well-known statement, Guamán Poma de Ayala (could but) could not speak.[35]

AFTERMATH — MODERNITY/COLONIALITY

The reader may have the impression that all these coming and goings, though perhaps interesting, involve people who lived a long time ago and come away with just the understanding that weird things happened to Spaniards and Incas. This would make room for a sense of detachment. The problem with that detachment is that it naturalizes contemporary practices and relations of power by making past ones a temporal other — very much what Prescott did. To counter this dissociation, I want to stress, as others do, that we still inhabit a modern/colonial world. In particular, current hegemonic projects build on the same elements and are guided by the same geopolitics as past ones; the same internal and external borders regulate the production of authoritative discourse. Let me give but one example.

The authors of present neocolonial projects present themselves as redeemers and are concerned mainly with internal critiques. Like the Spanish conquerors facing Atahualpa, U.S. President George W. Bush had to establish a *casus belli* for Iraq.[36] His answer was, like the Spanish, retaliation, presented also as spreading the light to the land of darkness. More straightforwardly, Bush announced with satisfaction that the attack was part of a new "crusade." What he took to be a self-evident good claim faced some problems. The Christian motive horrified many predominantly Muslim countries, as "crusade" equaled expansionist violence. More importantly, the crusade image troubled some of Bush's countrymen, although for different reasons. On March 9, 2003, right before the attack on Iraq was launched, Jimmy Carter published in the Sunday edition of the *New York Times* an opinion piece titled "Just War—Or a Just War?" The former U.S. president declared that "as a Christian" he had devoted time to studying the conditions for a war to be just (like Vitoria) and concluded that they had not been met (same again). For a war to be just there had to be a legal body authorizing the action and a just cause—avenging an offense. Authority (the pope) and cause (the throwing of the Bible) were also what sixteenth-century defenders of war wanted to establish. What Carter did not say is that these two principles were set by St. Augustine and St. Tomas Aquinas a long time ago, Christian authorities both Las Casas and Vitoria draw on.

Internal imperial borders are also visible today. The debate with actual consequences about the right to wage the Iraq war and ways to do it was not between the U.S. administration and the Iraqi (or any other) Muslim administration, but between the U.S. administration and the French. This is not a coincidence, since France is the cradle of the Enlightenment, the land of those who—Algiers and Indochina notwithstanding—disputed the United States' exclusivity as representative of "freedom" (as the English fought with the Spanish over "Christianity"). The debate entailed defining reality from a metropolitan point of view. While much of the world called the U.S. attack on Iraq an "invasion," the U.S. administration called it "liberation." The fight became bitter as the intelligent missiles did not succeed right away; in March 28, 2003, *Le Monde*'s cartoonist Pessin (fig. 7.1) pointed out what in many other countries than the United States was *evident* (very much as Atahualpa's imagined response was to Hakluyt):

7.1 Pessin, "Bon Dieu! Ils se laissent pas libérer facilement!!!" (Good God! They do not let themselves be liberated easily!!!). From *Le Monde*, March 28, 2003.

In a bitter moment of retaliation, the cafeteria of the U.S. Congress decided to rename one of its most popular dishes: from then on, "French Fries" were to be called "Liberation Fries." (Ice cream did not escape the same fate; "French Vanilla" followed suit.) But as usual, the nonWestern other remained the object of the debate, not the subject. English and Spaniards (and French and Dutch) had engaged in similar games of words about the events in Cajamarca.

In all cases, the (relevant) adversaries were either internal or external, but always western, never a post/colonial Other. The Iraqis—with the obvious differences that come from living in an interconnected world—had no visible say. And even if Las Casas and Carter criticized the official version, they never questioned the rightfulness and superiority of their respective imperial projects. Las Casas fought for the right path to conversion, Carter intended his critiques to "enhance our status as a champion of peace and justice" (Carter 2003). Neither doubted.

CHAPTER EIGHT

THE VIEW OF THE EMPIRE
FROM THE *ALTEPETL*

Nahua Historical and Global Imagination

SilverMoon and Michael Ennis

B ecause the Black Legend emerges from an interimperial rivalry, it focuses heavily on the image of the Spaniards as fanatical and rapacious
colonizers who utterly annihilated the native population. While Spanish critiques of their own imperial project—and the adoption of those critiques by
Anglo and American theorists—seem to justify the notion that native cultures were entirely destroyed, the historical record reveals a remarkable
amount of resilience among the peoples of Spanish America.[1] In other words,
the destruction of indigenous cultures does not necessarily result from Spanish colonialism. Rather, the erasure of the preconquest past comprises a potent aspect of the Black Legend. Indigenous cultures, epistemes, and practices have survived to this day despite the brutality of *European* colonialism.

This issue is at the heart of a recent debate about how to deal with the ca-
tastrophe of colonialism for indigenous peoples. Claude Lévi-Strauss notably criticized *The Cambridge History of the Native Peoples of the Americas* for
overly celebrating the surreptitious maintenance of some pre-Hispanic practices without sufficiently emphasizing the horrible tolls of colonialism.[2] These
projects are not mutually exclusive; one can acknowledge the horrors of colonialism while attending to and even lauding the perseverance of indigenous
peoples, all the more remarkable given the incredible material and cultural
pressures that continue to threaten their ways of life. Exploring how native
peoples deployed indigenous categories and forms of knowledge to comprehend and challenge Spanish colonialism as well as to foment an image of the
globe can join these two intellectual projects. This is more than simply an academic inquiry; it contributes to a genealogy of indigenous intellectual and
political activism that seeks to ground recent movements in their own obscured history and articulate them with the long history of globalization. In

150

this chapter, we explore the specific case of postconquest Nahua[3] politics, culture, and intellectual traditions in order to demonstrate the ways the Nahuas conceptualized colonialism and global politics.[4]

Before exploring some of the early roots of this genealogy, let us first look at the idea that Spanish colonialism either degraded or extinguished indigenous culture to underscore its salience to the Black Legend. Interestingly, this presumption serves both Spanish and British interests. For the Spanish, the degradation and disappearance of indigenous culture signifies a success of the mission. This idea is most evident as late as the twentieth century with the publication of Ricard's classic, but now-outdated, *The Spiritual Conquest of Mexico,*[5] which argues, based on mostly Spanish sources, that conversion to Christianity was thorough and quick, occurring within a generation of the conquest. More recent scholarship contradicts this general thesis and points to the difficulties of conversion and the translation of Christian categories into Amerindian languages. The work of Louise Burkhart is of particular interest in this vein.[6]

For British and American commentators, the notion of the degraded Indian is central to the critique of the Spanish insofar as it enables them to establish the superiority of their own colonial systems. This is most strikingly evident in John Lloyd Stephens' *Incidents of Travels in Yucatan* (1843), which provides an excellent example of the Black Legend in action. Although directly referring to the Maya rather than the Nahuas, Stephens generalizes his observations to apply to all indigenous peoples. He laments the degraded state that Spanish colonialism left the Maya in: "bound down and trained to the most abject submission, and looking up to the white man as a superior being. Could these be the descendents of that fierce people who made such bloody resistance to the Spanish conquerors?"[7] But this represents no mere compassion on Stephens' part; rather, Stephens fashions an image of the Spanish as corrupt and abusive, nicely coinciding with U.S. attempts to position itself as a just imperial power. It was, after all, the age of manifest destiny, and the United States was looking for whatever justification it could find to dispossess Mexico and Spain of their territories. At the time Stephens was writing, the Yucatan was attempting to align itself with the United States in a bid for its own independence from Mexico. For Stephens, the submissiveness of the Maya extends back through the colonial period. Referring to an account in 1582 that the Maya nobility lost interest in their titles, Stephens writes, "If at that early date the nobles no longer cared for their titles, it is not strange that the present inhabitants, nine generations removed, without any written language, borne down by three centuries of servitude, and toiling daily for scanty subsistence, are alike ignorant and indifferent concerning the history of their ancestors . . . it is my belief that among the whole mass of what are called Christianized Indians, there is not at this day one solitary tradition which can shed a ray of light upon any event in their history."[8] Ironically, a few years later the Caste War would break out, initiating more than sixty years of armed revolt by the Maya—a revolt deeply informed by Mayan beliefs and traditions. While this chapter addresses Nahua, rather than Maya, historical imagination in the colonial era, it seeks to counteract the beliefs so well articulated in Stephens (who refers to not only the Maya but the "whole mass of . . . Christianized Indians") by attesting to the diversity and potency of Nahua political and intellectual traditions under Spanish rule. As the title of this chapter suggests, we begin with the Nahua city-state, the *altepetl,* to explore one of the crucial lenses through which the Nahuas viewed Spanish colonialism and global politics.

THE *ALTEPETL*

Although we will eventually discuss specific texts and figures, we should first provide some background of the political categories that inform Nahua thought to show how specifically Nahua conceptions of politics aided in adapting to Spanish colonialism. One interesting trait of Nahua culture that enabled adaptability to colonial economic and political reorganization was the widespread existence of cellular organization, particularly of the chief political structure, the *altepetl.* Historian James Lockhart argues that the principle of cellular or modular organization can be seen as distinct from early modern Spanish counterparts and therefore considered to be of genuinely preconquest origin, "even when we can discover no direct evidence to that effect."[9] For Lockhart, distinctions between Spanish and Nahua civilizations stand out because they do so against a background of many commonalities, including but not limited to territorial states, state religion, the noble-commoner distinction, tax obligations, intensive agriculture and individual rights to land, etc. Furthermore, Lockhart contends, sensibly enough, "it would by no means be impossible to find some parallels in Spanish and generally European culture for the Nahua characteristics I will be discussing—it is a matter of degree and emphasis."[10] With these provisos out of the way, Lockhart goes on to elaborate his hypothesis:

> Outstanding is the Nahuas' tendency to create larger wholes by the aggregation of parts that remain relatively separate and self-contained, brought together by their common function and similarity, their place in some numerical or symmetrical arrangement, their rotational order, or

all three. This may be called cellular or modular organization . . . Note the similarity of the two master entities of Nahua civilization, the altepetl or state and the household. Each consists of subentities that function relatively independently, are a microcosm of the whole and could be the germ of a new entirely independent unit. Elaborate schemes of rotation and strict rotational order naturally characterize the long-continuing altepetl rather than the fleeting household (although in truth we are really in the dark about household-internal rotational schemes, which could very well have existed). At both levels, yet larger entities could be created with relative ease: at the state level, complex altepetl and imperial arrangements such as the "Triple Alliance" of Tenochtitlan, Tetzcoco, and Tlacopan; at the household level, "patios" around which were arranged several compound households (usually composed of relatives) functioning as a unit.[11]

Lockhart and others[12] have shown that the *altepetl* is composed of smaller subunits, interchangeably termed *calpolli* or *tlaxillacalli*. These smaller units— which form distinct regions or "neighborhoods" consisting of extended kinship groups—contain all of the aspects of the *altepetl* in general: political leadership (in the form of the *tlatoani* or speaker), ruling dynasty, and tutelary god. More strikingly, the composition of the *altepetl* follows a spatial organization that structurally contains its history: the respective *calpolli* are laid out according to a rotational pattern that follows the historical arrivals of each *calpolli* into the *altepetl.* The rotational order governs the functioning of the *altepetl,* where all communal functions and tasks are performed according to that rotation. The Nahuas based the payment of tribute on a rotation called the *coatequitl,* literally the serpentine tribute labor, poetically expressing the character of their political organization as it winds its way through time and space.

The disruption of the continuity of the *altepetl* structure constitutes one of the most severe and fundamental ruptures wrought by colonialism. Strikingly, the Primordial Titles[13] attest to the rupture that the *congregaciones*[14] caused. In those histories of the *altepetl,* the attempts at the reorganization of the *altepetl* often constitute a more fundamental rupture in the historical imagination than the conquest itself. That is, the disruption of the spatial organization of the *altepetl,* which as we have noted structurally contains its history, constitutes the "historical discontinuity" customarily imputed to the military conquest. The cellular composition of the *altepetl* facilitated the adaptation to the congregations precisely because the *calpolli* constitutes an internally coherent unit that could be appended to another *altepetl*'s structure and incorporated into its rotational scheme, a process Lockhart calls "hiving." This is not to say that the restructuring of the *altepetl* did not meet resistance. Robert Haskett cites several examples of petitions against the congregations.[15] Lockhart concisely explains the process as one of resistance and adaptation:

> For the altepetl, [hiving] was a perpetual threat; yet without the independence the scheme allowed to the proud and diverse subentities, it would have been impossible to persuade them to cooperate within the altepetl at all, and repeated splitting off from the parent entity was what had brought some altepetl, such as Tlaxcala, into existence. Cellular-modular organization gave the Nahua world great resilience in post-conquest times. Units seriously affected by demographic loss or Spanish reorganization always contained within themselves the means and the rationale to continue functioning. In the late colonial period, when times were becoming ever less propitious for larger altepetl units, the subunits not only made the adjustment but actively sought the independence to which they had tended from the beginning.[16]

So, what is seen as a natural state of affairs for family units—where children hive off to form new households—becomes a much more contentious matter for the larger sociopolitical structures. However, contention does not imply absolute rigidity, and Lockhart rightly points out the costs and benefits of the Nahuas's cellular social organization in confronting Spanish colonial policy.

In order to specify the *altepetl* as a Nahua construct, and not flatly analogous to a "city-state" or "*pueblo*," its cosmic and historical associations should be noted. Scholars often point to the complex relationship of the *altepetl* to the cosmos, which share a quadripartite configuration oriented to the cardinal directions. As Lockhart explains it, the structure of the *altepetl* and the universe mirror each other. He writes, "One might imagine that the *altepetl*'s archetypal division into four parts, often oriented to the cardinal directions, had its origins in Mesoamerican religion. Without doubt these aspects of sociopolitical organization coincided with religious-cosmological notions and had corresponding connotations for the Nahuas, but one could say just as well the Mesoamericans projected their own organization onto the cosmos, or that the cosmic and sociopolitical view coincided and interpenetrated."[17] This passage hints at the complex nature of representation in Nahua culture, trying first to grasp the *altepetl* as a representation of the universe, then suggesting that the reverse might be true, and finally relying on "coincidence" and "interpenetration" to describe the relation of the political to the cosmic. This is not a criticism of Lockhart; expressing these relationships in English presents unique challenges and he has done well insofar as he does so without recourse to the Nahuatl terminology. The relationship between the *altepetl* and the cosmos is best understood through the Nahua figural category of the *ixiptla*,[18] where the *altepetl* becomes a substantiation of the universe rather than its representation or model. *Ixiptla* translates variously as envelope, tree bark, image, messenger, idol, and even sacrificial victim, describing the manifold ways that "images" (a category that included individual humans) could embody or bear supernatural forces or *teotl*. As Serge Gruzinski explains, "The *ixiptla* could be the statue of a god . . . a divinity that appeared in a vision, a priest "representing" a deity by covering himself in adornments, or even a victim who turned into a god destined to be sacrificed."[19] For the Nahuas, artistic works were not "representations" but vehicles for communicating with other levels of the cosmos and substantiating divine forces for a variety of purposes. Although the comparison is not attested to in the sources, conceptualizing the *altepetl* as an *ixiptla* is a consistent extension of Nahuatl representational concepts. The current call to describe indigenous societies in their own terms can become stiflingly problematic if we take it to mean only describing exactly what indigenous people describe without using the concepts and language productively as valid categories of analysis.

Analogizing of the *altepetl*-cosmos relationship to that of the *ixiptla-teotl* reveals a crucial elision in Lockhart's comparison. The coincidence of *altepetl* and cosmology as described by Lockhart remains incomplete because he does not account for the fifth direction, the vertical center, the absence of which severely truncates the spatial arrangement of the Nahua cosmos. The Nahua cosmos contains thirteen layers above the earth (nine in some versions) and nine layers below. The earth is formed by the conjoining of lower and upper levels, counting as first in the numeration of both. Since the vertical direction communicates the terrestrial plane with the other layers of the universe, understanding the *altepetl* as spatially organized inclusive of the fifth direction reveals its relationship to the other layers of the universe. It is precisely the center-vertical direction that joins the earth, *tlalticpac*, to the rest of the universe, enabling the forces from other layers to be substantiated in the *ixiptla* and by extension for the universe to be substantiated in the *altepetl*.

Given the significance of the of the *altepetl* as a political structure that links Nahua history and cosmology, it makes sense that it plays a significant role in how the Nahuas understood the globe. The most impressive example of this comes in Chimalpahin's categorization of the world's cities as different kinds of *altepetl*.[20] Susan Schroeder's excellent analysis of Chimalpahin's texts reveals a fascinating array of descriptions of different cities around the world:

> Some examples include *tecpilalteptl* "lordly, noble city," which is used in reference to Seville (I-178–17), Mexico Tenochtitlan (I-153–13), and Amaquemacan (I-146–14). *Cemanahuac altepetl* "universal altepetl" describes the kingdom ruled by don Felipe, king of Spain (II-48–54). There are the big cities or *huey altepetl ciudades* of Aztlan (I-9–46), Amaquemacan (I-86–11), Mexico Tenochtitlan (II-22–47), Burgos (I-177–25), Plasencia (I-177–46), and Granada (I-177–51). Other "huey altepetl" include such diverse places as Vienna (II-135–35), Cairo (II-153–5), Tula (I-9–9), Babylon (II-159–43), Genoa (I-121–14), Rome (II-155–6), Salamanca (II-138–46), Texcoco (II-141–3), and Madrid. The latter is described as an *altepetl villa* (II-13–29) since in Spanish it bore the latter title rather than "ciudad." *Tlahtocaaltepetl* "kingly altepetl" refers to Peru (II-84–45) and Japan (II-92–46).[21]

This brief catalogue evinces Chimalpahin's broad knowledge and interest in the world, covering five continents and citing ancient cities such as Tula (the capital of the Toltecs in central Mexico) and Babylon. The wide-ranging use of the *altepetl* as a category demonstrates Chimalpahin's knowledge of world geopolitics as well as history. More importantly, it attests to his willingness and facility in using Nahua categories to understand and analyze the globe. Later in this chapter, we provide other examples of indigenous intellectuals' interests in geopolitics and global history. For now, it is sufficient to underscore the vitality of Nahua concepts in imagining a newly discovered world.

COLLABORATIVE HISTORY IN NEW SPAIN

While Nahua historical traditions such as annals and primordial titles attest to the ways indigenous communities employed Nahua categories and genres to create knowledge about their own local communities and their relation to the globe, Nahuas who lived and worked in intermediary orbits also produced knowledge about New Spain and about indigenous history for Spanish audiences. A glaring example of the creative power of New Spain's postconquest elite is their participation in the creation of the *Historia general de las cosas de la Nueva España*,[22] a work that is often, and shortsightedly, attributed only to the Franciscan Fray Bernardino de Sahagún. The information collected would eventually become a twelve-volume work, also known as the

Florentine Codex. This material was gathered from three areas of central New Spain: Tepepulco, Mexico-Tlatelolco, and Mexico-Tenochtitlan. Nahua leaders of those areas worked with the Franciscan, expressing their agency through their choice of informants and their selection of information to be shared. Fray Bernardino, who initiated the process, wrote about the steps taken in Tepepulco and Tlatelolco:

> In that town I had gathered all the principal people with their lord, who was called Diego de Mendoza. I asked them to grant me access to knowledgeable people of experience with whom I could talk, and who could explain the things I asked of them. . . . Another day, the lord and his principal people came and having made a very solemn speech . . . they assigned me as many as ten or twelve leading elders. They told me I could communicate with them, and they would give me answers to all that I would ask them . . . They gave me all the matters we discussed in pictures, for that was the writing they employed in ancient times. And the grammarians explain them in their language, writing the explanation at the bottom of the page.[23]

> [In Tlatelolco] They pointed to eight or ten principal people, chosen from the whole, very capable in their language and their old things, with whom, together with four or five students of the College . . . all that I brought written from Tepepulco was edited, verified, and to which additions were made.[24]

Sahagún's account does not imply any level of passivity on the part of the Nahua participants, or better, cocreators of the compendium. To the contrary, the Nahua elite, when faced with Sahagún's request for information, took their time in responding, stated their positions in a speech, granted permission, and offered those who would give answers. None of these were passive actions. In fact, the persistence of the indigenous people's attachment to their belief systems forced Sahagún to dedicate much of his adult life to what became his obsession: the eradication of those indigenous beliefs that he perceived as idolatrous. These *altepetl* leaders were not the only indigenous men taking positions in cultural preservation: the students of the *Colegio Imperial de Santa Cruz de Tlatelolco* also gathered information and learning from the selected elders. As will be discussed later, the students were also authors and translators in their own right.

The process necessary for the production of this encyclopedic work opened the doors for the Nahua leaders, informants, interpreters, and scholars to narrate their side of the story and to partake in the making of the new historiography as they had once participated in the construction of the old. It provided Nahua participants with an opportunity to mold the narrative around their interests, which were grounded in their preexisting categories and perspectives. It was fitting within Nahua tradition for the elite to decide "what to recover of the past and why."[25] The Nahua pre-Hispanic historian-priest was a specialist who "gather[ed] and explain[ed] the past to serve the interests of the *hueytlatoani,* or highest ruler."[26] Sahagún's role as the priest-recorder of Nahua traditions became the logical substitute for the historian-priest, but it remains possible that the students trained at the Colegio de Tlatelolco also held the same position in the eyes of many.

The compendium depended completely on the information that the Nahua elite saw fit to record and in the manner in which the students of the *colegio* recorded and translated it. Hence, Nahua participants retained access to the power of information and memory by collaborating with Sahagún's request to aid in the production of the *Historia.* They also were able to use this and other projects to insert their histories, lineages, and rights to rule and to land in the making of the postconquest manuscripts. Through the new script they made themselves heard.

As people under colonial rule the Nahuas faced several issues. The need to retain cultural cohesion—which was severely mediated by the demographic, psychological, religious, and cultural devastation of the epidemics—could only be accessed during early colonization through a preexisting indigenous understanding of the universe, including the cyclical conception of time and space. It is more than plausible that given the Nahuas's interpretation of events, they understood their subjugation as temporary. Things would eventually be as they once were. In fact, a famous proverb from the *Historia General* states that, "Another time it will be like this, another time things will be the same, some time, some place. What happened a long time ago, and which no longer happens, will be again, it will be done again, as it was in far-off times."[27] They also attempted integration and translation of the new faces of the supernatural through both their own concepts and the education received under the Franciscans. In other words, following pre-Hispanic tradition, they adopted the conquering Christian God, as they perceived him. They integrated the new religion and made it work for them. The result was, in the words of Louise Burkhart, a Nahua Christianity: "Out of their ambivalent position between indigenous and Spanish culture, between Nahuatl and Catholic religion, between their noble Nahua ancestry and their Franciscan surrogate fathers, these men articulated a set of solutions to the most glaring contradictions between Nahua and Catholic religion, solutions that fostered continuity between pre-conquest and colonial culture."[28]

This intellectual and social elite made a bid for personal and cultural survival through sophisticated subversive strategies. Through the retrospective writing of history and the historiographical redemption of an empire lost, they assimilated aspects of the outsider's world, including Sahagún himself. In addition, they willfully provided misinformation to the outsider. Perhaps the most significant aim of the participating Nahua elite was to establish the legitimacy of their pre-Hispanic status and its right to continuity in the new system. As Lockhart clearly explains, in a pre-Hispanic organizational model with a "general lack of clearly drawn polarities,"[29] one clear division did exist: there was a "sharp distinction between *pilli* or noble and *macehualli* or commoner."[30] This distinction was important enough to be "one of the . . . foundations of Nahua society and consciousness."[31] This fundamental rank definition formed the basis for the sort of information that the Nahua elite gave about themselves and others, where they placed emphasis, and how much information they dedicated to particular subjects. The Nahua elite vindicated their social status and made the compendium function in registers that made sense from within pre-Hispanic frameworks. The historical record served to validate, and perhaps clarify for the outsider, the upper class's definition of self and their connection to a particular *altepetl* and its history. Religion formed an intricate part of the writing of history, inseparable from the whole.

For example, The Tlatelolcans[32] "represented a position somewhat critical of the Aztec elite who conquered them nearly a century before."[33] This colored the information, particularly their version of the conquest, and arguably, it helped create the image of a weak Moctezuma: "When Moctezuma heard what the messengers said, how the Spaniards very much wanted to see him, he was filled with such anguish that he thought he should run away or hide,"[34] and again, "he was worried, filled with terror and fear."[35] After all, it was the Mexica-Tenochca proper that lost the empire. Distance from the losers might have helped the Tlatelolcans in their attempts to renegotiate power relations with the outsiders. Much of the information gathered in Tlatelolco, the merchant capital, also came from a particular subgroup of the elite, the *pochtecas,* or organized merchant class.[36] The rather specific nature of this group helped present the biased voice of people who "were active within the upper echelons of the governmental [and economic] system[s]; it says relatively little about the situation of the thousands of *pipiltin* who had little connection with the imperial court."[37] The specialized nature of the group also valorized their particular version of the Nahua world over others. It provided for the self-congratulatory definition of their particular class and of this group's rightful claim to leadership:

> After the merchants, having fought for four years, conquered the Province of *Anáhuac* . . . the most important among them said: Oh Mexican merchants! Already our Lord *Huitzilopochtli,* God of War, has done his job by helping us to conquer this Province . . . when they arrived to Mexico . . . they headed straight for the house of the lord *Ahuitzotzin* . . . having done this, one of them started to speak, telling him: Our lord . . . here at your feet we have place the bounty because your uncles the *pochtecas* who are here risked our heads and our lives . . . and although we call our selves merchants, we are more like captains and soldiers that with dissimulation went out conquering.[38]

The information gathered in Tenochtitlan-Tlatelolco gave greater value to merchant traditions, celebrations, and beliefs: "The informants [were] cultured and educated men of pre-Hispanic Mexico. However, the importance they g[a]ve to *Y[i]acatecuhtli* [Guiding God, God of Travelers], to travel, and to feasts given to the organized merchants make one suppose that at least some of them belonged to the merchant's guild."[39] These ten to twelve elders were not representative of the entire culture and can hardly be the source of a universal, or general, history. The interest of their participation resides on their particularity, not on their alleged representative status. The versions that they represented did not reflect the interests of the commoners, of women, of children, or of many of the specialized priests who had died at the hands of the Spaniards. They reflected the interests of elitist groups of men and, in Tenochtitlan-Tlatelolco, of a particular upper class, the merchants. But this was not entirely new for the Nahua; after all, before the conquest "the recording and reading of the past were the exclusive knowledge of the ruling class."[40]

The information given to Sahagún was particularly affected by the absence of an important informing group, the priests who held sacred knowledge. The copious materials in religious matters might have come from the perspective of novices or from the public perspectives of the ceremonies and celebrations. In a culture where memory and orality were extremely important, the power of handed-down knowledge cannot be ignored. As Inga Clendinnen has noted, "Few priests, easily identifiable as they were, survived the phobic hatred of the Spanish conquerors, and the destruction of their finely articulated ecclesiastic structure must have cast those few survivors into a social and cognitive void. Priestly doings were concealed from outsiders."⁴¹ However, some survived, as did their knowledge and stories.

NAHUA INTELLECTUAL PROJECTS

As mentioned earlier, one of the sites of production of the *Florentine Codex* was the School of Tlatelolco, which saw a variety of fascinating intellectual projects. It is worth detailing some of these projects briefly and naming the individuals who created them—often carelessly lumped together as a faceless group—to attest to the vibrancy of some of the work carried out there.⁴² The *Colegio Imperial de Santa Cruz de Tlatelolco* was officially inaugurated on January 6, 1536, as the first school for superior studies for indigenous boys in New Spain. Students of the college worked as communal leaders, scribes, translators, teachers, and writers in their own right. Sahagún wrote of the school, "After we came to this land to implant the Faith, we assembled the boys in our houses, as is said. And we began to teach them to read, write, and sing. And, as they did well in this, we then endeavored to put them to the study of grammar. For this training a college was formed in the city of México, in the Santiago Tlatilulco section, in which [college] were selected from all the neighboring villages and from all the provinces the most capable boys, best able to read and write. They slept and ate in the same college without leaving it, except few times."⁴³ The *colegiales*, often agglomerated as Sahagún's students, constituted a significant, if not the most significant, force in colonial dialectics. Young Nahua students, such as Antonio Valeriano of Azcapotzalco, Pedro de San Buenaventura from Cuauhtitlan, Martín Jacobita of the Barrio de Santa Ana in Tlatelolco, Andrés Leonardo from Tlatelolco, Alonso Vegerano from Cuauhtitlan, Mateo Ceverino de Arellano from Xochimilco, Agustin de la Fuente, Andres Leonardo from Tlatelolco, Diego de Grado from Tlatelolco, Bonifacio Maximiliano *vecino* of Tlatelolco, and Francisco Bautista de Contreras, who became Governor of Indians in Xochimilco and *vecino* of Cuernavaca, along with others, helped in fundamental ways to create many of the investigations of Nahuatl language and culture that survive today. Without the students these works would simply not have been possible, nor would our understanding of pre-Hispanic and colonial Nahua culture.

The students as a group were remarkably accomplished in letters and politics. One of them, Pedro Juan Antonio, went to Spain in 1568 to continue his studies at the University of Salamanca. Two others—Miguel from Cuauhtitlan and Juan Badiano from Xochimilco, both victims of the horrible plague of 1545—were wonderful Latinists and are well known to historians, botanists, and students of medicine today. Badiano wrote the Latin version of Martín de la Cruz's *Libellus de medicinalibus Indorum herbis*, a treatise on indigenous medical/botanical knowledge.[44] With Maturino Gilberti, the students also participated in the *Gramática* published in 1559, as well as in studies carried out by friars Juan de Gaona, Juan Bautista, and Alonso de Molina. Aside from scholarship on Nahuatl, the students translated numerous European texts such as Aesop's fables, Boethius's *The Consolation of Philosophy*, and Tomas de Kempis's *The Imitation of Christ*.[45] These men became expert language handlers and could cross between worlds. In March 1566, ten years before Ovid's works were first printed in Mexico City, Pedro Nazareo of Xaltocan quoted Ovid in a long letter to Philip II, "Munera, credi mihi, capiunt hominesque deosque: Pacatur donis Jupiter ipse datis. Quid sapiens faciet? Stultus munere gaudet. Ipse quoque accepto munere mitis erit." [Believe me, presents conquer men and gods. Gifts even pacify Jupiter. What should a wise man do? A gift delights a fool, and a present will soften a wise man too.][46] These men collaborated to create a period of textual production and reproduction to rival that "other" Renaissance, or at least to be a portentous if unacknowledged part of it. Walter Mignolo has named this locus of textual production the "Darker Side of the Renaissance," an infrequently acknowledged, yet no less constitutive, part of the development of modernity.[47]

The school was also, as Miguel Mathes demonstrated,[48] the first academic library of the Americas, holding titles by Plato, Aristotle, Plutarch, Caton, Cicero, St. Agustin, Aquinas, Vives, Nebrija, and Erasmus. The thought of what effect it might have had for the boys to become aware of Spain's own history and its subjugation under Roman rule is tantalizing, but surely they had first-rate teachers to learn this history from. For example, Sahagún had come to New Spain after studying at Salamanca. *Colegiales* composed and translated numerous other works. Furthermore, the students operated the press.

Proof of the school's success can be seen in the many enemies it developed among Spaniards. One of the most vociferous was the notary and *encomendero* Jeronimo López, who wrote to the king of Spain repeatedly to complain about the learning that the indigenous boys were exposed to and achieving. In one of his letters, dated February 25, 1545, he vehemently writes that the Franciscans are making the boys read widely and hence "they have come to know the whole beginning of our history and where we come from and how we were subjugated by the Romans and converted from paganism to the faith." This knowledge, López continues, "inspires them to say that we too came from the pagans and were subjected and defeated and subjugated and were subjects to the Romans and revolted and rebelled and were converted to baptism so very many years ago and are not even yet good Christians." However, perhaps worse still was the fact that these boys were informed about "the wars and troubles" that the king had "with France and the Turks," and the boys at the school were not the only ones who knew of those troubles.[49]

As López bitterly observed, this creative drive went beyond the school as indigenous and *mestizo* men took up the pen to record the history of their people. Men like Fernando de Alva Ixtlilxóchitl, Hernando de Alvarado Tezozomoc, Domingo Chimalpahin, and others had been connected with the school because of its role as an educational center. Many of the most beloved Franciscans spent considerable amount of time there because of its other resources, such as the library and press. Also, Nahua and *mestizo* historians, especially Chimalpahin, consulted the informants at the school.

ANNALS OF THE NAHUA WORLD

Even outside the politics of Mexico City, the interest in global events and history is evident. For example, the book of the guardians and governors of Cuauhtinchan (1519–1640) constitutes a series of accounts of things political, social, cultural, environmental, and religious that indigenous leaders and scribes thought important to record. The people of the Pueblo de San Juan Bautista Cuauhtinchan, near Puebla, were informed of the goings on of their environs, but what this text illuminates beyond any doubt is that the Nahuas also knew of events in the empire at large and incorporated world events into their accounts of events of the *altepetl*. Of course, they recorded matters of local interest such as elections, the effects of devastating epidemics throughout New Spain, and the terrible floods and earthquakes that hit the area and how they affected labor demands. But they also demonstrated their knowledge of events in Peru, the Philippines, and Spain as well as Rome, England, and Austria. They used the text to complain about the behavior or policies of priests, soldiers, and the viceroyalty at the same time that they complained about those who they called the enemy, "los ingleses." English pirate ships caused a freeze on shipments of goods from Spain with the result that "necessary things that [were] lacking" could not make it through and the prices on goods kept rising. When finally a few ships made it to New Spain, we are told that even the price of paper had become exorbitant.[50]

As with Chimalpahin, the leaders of Cuauhtinchan had detailed knowledge of and interest in global events, even if it is partially filtered through a Spanish lens. We are told how in 1532 "comenzó publicamente la herejía en Inglaterra por las pasiones y mal ejemplo del rey Enrique VIII" [heresy publicly began in England through the passions and bad example of King Henry the VIII] (41). It was indeed in 1532 that Henry VIII begun his separation from papal authority as he attempted to pressure the pope to consent to his divorce by threatening the annates paid to Rome by the clergy. Moreover, "Este año [1536] se rebeló la ciudad de Ginebra contra el duque de Saboya, su natural señor" [This year the city of Geneva rebelled against the Duke of Savoy, its rightful lord] (43). In 1536 Geneva declared its adhesion to the Reformation after overthrowing the Duke de Savoy from power, and the Geneva city council took a vote in May of that same year to leave behind the practices of Catholicism.

Of the problems facing the eastern edges of the empire, the annals inform us that in 1531, "fue Solimán, emperador de turcos, con poderoso ejército sobre la ciudad de Viena en Austria, salió a su encuentro el emperador Carlos V y el turco se retiró con pérdida y afrenta" [Soliman, emperor of the Turks, went with a powerful army upon the city of Vienna in Austria; the emperor Charles V came out to meet him and the Turk retreated with losses and affront](41). Sulayman had unsuccessfully besieged Vienna in 1529 but threatened Austria again in 1532 and 1541. Ferdinand I, younger brother to the Holy Roman Emperor Charles V, was then king of Bohemia (1526–1564). In 1531 Emperor Charles V had Ferdinand elected king of the Romans, an act that would make him the holy Roman emperor after Charles abdicated as emperor in 1558, although by all intents and purposes Ferdinand had been doing the job since 1556. More still, in 1535, "Tomó el emperador Carlos V por fuerza de armas la ciudad y reino de Túnez, venciendo al tirano Barbarroja que la poseía; la entregó a su propio rey y reservó para sí la fortaleza de la Goleta" [Emperor Charles V took by force of arms the city and kingdom of Tunis, defeating the tyrant Barbarossa, who had held it; he turned it over to its own king and reserved for himself the Goleta fortress] (43). Barbarossa, surname of the admiral of the Turkish fleet under Sulayman I, lost Tunis to Charles in 1535. As late as 1571, "Selin II, emperador de turcos, hizo mucho daño a los venecianos, les gano la isla y reyno de Chipre, e hiciera mucho daño a toda la cristiandad si no le hubiera desbaratado su armada en aquella famosa batalla naval del señor don Juan de Austria . . . el siete de octubre" [Selim II, emperor of the Turks, did much harm to the Venetians, won the island and kingdom of Cyprus, and would have done much damage to all of Christendom were his navy not defeated in that famous naval battle by don Juan of Austria . . . October seventh] (55). Selim II, Ottoman sultan, lost the battle of Lepanto on October 7, 1571, to the fleet of the Holy League commanded by John of Austria. This was a decisive battle because, although not the end of the Ottoman threat, it ensured that the Ottomans did not become rulers of the Mediterranean.

Since Spaniards, and specifically friars, would have brought almost all of the news into the community, it makes sense that it would slant toward episodes relevant to the Spanish empire. The annals show the Nahua leaders identifying as members of the empire, which is consistent with what we know of Nahua politics from other sources. The fact that the Nahuas were subjects of the Crown was used quite explicitly to seek protection from abusive *encomenderos* and priests by both Nahua elites and sympathetic priests. Some *altepetl* councils even took the approach of circumventing the courts and writing the crown directly with their grievances. For our purposes here, what is most significant remains witnessing the Nahuas using one of their own forms of recording history that predates the conquest (albeit in alphabetized form), annals, to articulate a nascent global perspective, a perspective seen as incongruous with a proper colonial order by many Spaniards.

CONCLUSION

All of the loci of indigenous intellectual production discussed in this chapter—from the general form of the *altepetl* to its specific historians—demonstrate the impetus and ability of the Nahuas to imagine and understand their own history and traditions within the larger colonial and global order. In many cases, doing so involved a direct act of critique of the supposed universalism of Spanish imperial rule and Christian dominion. Although our argument cannot offer a totally coherent or conclusive narrative about these situations of indigenous intellectual production, we can be satisfied with what Serge Gruzinski terms a necessarily "pointillist" approach to colonial history.[51] The fragmentary nature of the historical record combined with the surreptitious character of a good deal of Nahua cultural production during the colonial era leave many blind spots when trying to piece together any kind of genealogy or tradition. However, the points that we do see sufficiently affirm that, despite the horrors visited upon the Americas by Spanish colonialism, Nahua culture survived in forms exceeding the stereotype of a provincial peasantry. Out of those fragments, we can see the Nahuas using the remnants of preconquest histories and empires to actively understand and engage the New World they had discovered, from the contemporaneous imperial rivalries of the Mediterranean to the ancient splendors of Babylon.

In trying to open up our thinking about Nahua politics, history, and global consciousness, we hope to reimagine modernity as a global process. Such a conception of modernity demands the analysis and narration of the material and cultural contributions of peoples marginalized and devastated by colonialism, which figures so centrally to Europe's narrative of itself as rational, enlightened, and progressive. Although the Black Legend obscures the Nahua contributions to the forging of the modern world, such concepts as the *altepetl* continue to offer the possibility of imagining social and political life outside of Eurocentric frames. These contributions are all the more astounding for being made amid almost unimaginable losses.

CHAPTER NINE

"RACE" AND "CLASS" IN THE SPANISH COLONIES OF AMERICA

A Dynamic Social Perception

Yolanda Fabiola Orquera

When Spain implemented one of the first colonial programs of modernity in the Americas, the local population began to elaborate new cultural expressions to reinforce, reduce, or abrogate its effects. This chapter uses historical, pictorial, and literary work written by indigenous, *mestizo*, and white subjects who lived between the sixteenth and the nineteenth centuries to describe the functioning of the apparatus imposed over colonial subjects and the efforts made by them to subvert its violence.[1] The constant struggle for control of esthetic and historical representation implied that some cultural activities—like rituals and writing—often had to be performed in secrecy because of the official politics of suppression generated by a system in which racial classification was the preeminent criterion of differentiation.

Considering that "race and racism are social constructions" that pose the question of "who constructed them, when, for whom, and why," as the introduction to this book makes clear, this chapter deals with these issues indirectly. It does not analyze the genesis nor the early development of the idea of "race" in the Spanish colonies; others scholars have done this in a superb manner in this volume.[2] Rather, I focus on the cultural production of the colonized populations that were able to overcome racism, trying to understand how they manage to survive under extremely adverse conditions. To explore this subject I need to go beyond the Renaissance to examine its "informing pressure" through all the Spanish rule in the Americas.

Appreciation of the colonial cultural dynamism requires a model of analysis that contemplates diachronic and synchronic perspectives. Such a model would permit the replacement of evolutionary-linear narratives that culminated with Creole independence by the idea of multiple cultural layers whose types of interaction outline the difference between given periods of time.[3] In

167

this sense, I find Raymond Williams' conception of cultural history as a continuous interchange among dominant, emergent, and residual elements an accurate tool to analyze colonial situations.[4] In the case of the conquest of the Americas, Spain imposed its cognitive paradigm over local preexistent communities, using "scientific" reasons to refuse the validity of their forms of thinking and converting them into residual knowledge.

Behind Williams' proposal it is possible to read Mikhail Bakhtin's theory of the production and change of social meaning. In opposition to Saussure's point of view, the Russian theorist put emphasis on "language as activity, as practical consciousness" and on the "binary" character of the sign, rejecting the notions of arbitrariness and fixity of meaning. Focusing on the dialogic character of any statement, Bakhtin highlighted the fact that the relationship between form and content is dynamic, which characterizes the sign as *multi-accentual* and the social displacement of interpretation as *reaccentuation*.[5] Reaccentuations in the history of disciplines occur when one of the multiple variables that shape social perceptions suffers a significant change.[6]

The vitality of the colonial period can be considered the result of the permanent effort made by colonized people to read the archive available to them according to their needs in spite of, and on occasions behind the backs of, the imperial authorities. What interests me is how social changes deal with the structures instituted by the Crown and the Catholic Church; it is a matter of understanding, in Pierre Bourdieu's terms, the process of "breaking out of the cycle of symbolic reproduction."[7] If unequal conditions of access to the tools of cultural production generate social differences, classification systems create and shape social perception.[8] Thinking from a colonial context, social "distinction" is not only the result of the imposition of a set of concepts but also the consequence of a structure of power that appeals to racial classification to justify economic and cultural dominion over the local population. For this reason, there is a primary differentiation that distinguishes the Spanish elite, which possesses "legitimate" cultural capital, from the colonized, whose cultural capital is denied all validity on the bases of racial categories constructed to that purpose.[9] The question then, is how to describe the functioning of the cultural dynamism of the colonized: how does their system manage to survive under adverse conditions, what are their tools to create cultural artifacts, and in what terms does their power become evident?

To deal with this question, I introduce the concept of the capital of experience, inspired by and complementary to Bourdieu's cultural, symbolic, and legitimate capitals.[10] My concept focuses on the significance of the knowledge acquired by an individual or a collective subject during his/her/their life, plus what he, she, or they could have learned from progenitors or loved ones. The idea that a lived experience is valuable capital is old indeed: the institution of the "board of elders" that rules most traditional societies makes this evident. In my formulation, however, the criterion of value is new. While in traditional societies the elders are expected to understand the functioning of their social system and to help find solutions to problems that may arise, ensuring the continuity of the system, the capital of experience is exactly the opposite. Unlike the wisdom attributed to elders, this capital is not related to the amount of knowledge but to an ability to affect the quotidian and denaturalize a given order by shaking its foundations. It is not a way to fuel the ruling structures but is a deep rejection of all that implies the perpetuation of the naturalized, daily, subliminal, and physical violence that characterizes not only modern colonial but also postcolonial societies.

In consequence, the capital of experience is not an automatic result of the time that someone has been alive: it is shaped in the personal or interpersonal elaboration of a socially traumatic circumstance sufficient to confront human beings with the borders of their existence, opening up the nonsense of unquestioned rules and habits. The conflictive nature of these types of situations becomes visible when a social net is dismantled abruptly—in a war or an economical downfall—or when a group of people is forced to live in a new geographic context—through diasporas or exiles—or when hunger, sickness, poverty, or any other painful circumstance reaches an unbearable point.

Considering the physical and symbolic violence inherent to colonialism, the formation of a new type of knowledge is predictable. Built and enriched against dominant institutions, often in a language not understandable for the colonizers, this capital is not easily recognizable during its formative stage for two reasons: first, because it is frequently fed in secrecy, and second, because the members of a community educated within the dominant cognitive paradigm are not prepared to consider such manifestations as legitimate.[11] In fact, such an unnoticeable condition is its main strength because it makes this capital stronger, self-protecting, and ready to be empowered by residual practices, which help to elaborate the rationale of resistance and, eventually, to regain power.

The history of Bolivia provides a good example. Inspired by and contemporary with Tupac Amaru's revolution in the viceroyalty of Perú in 1780–1781, Túpac Katari led a powerful struggle in 1780–1781, demanding the restitution of the land, traditional clothing, and indigenous government. The revolution was suffocated and its ideas were interdicted, but they were kept alive among Aymara oral communities for two centuries, until the Katarista guerrilla movement restored its revolutionary spirit in the 1980s. In 2001 a proliferation of indigenous collective protests began that culminated successfully in 2005, when Evo Morales was elected president. In Morales's first speech, he incorporated Tupac Katari as part of the symbolic capital of the newly elected indigenous government.[12] In this case, the concept of "emergent" acquires the sense of recurrent and variable reinvigorations of the cultural practices of the original inhabitants of a colonized territory.

With the concept of the capital of experience defined and the type of cultural systems that interact in a colonial situation established, I next focus on social and racial criteria of sixteenth-century peninsular and indigenous societies; on the description of the formations that interact until the nineteenth century; and finally on the two levels of analysis necessary to appreciate the dynamics between the exclusivist nature of Spanish cultural politics in the Indies and indigenous cultural practices.[13]

THE ETHIC OF THE CONQUEST UNDER DEBATE: RACIAL AND SOCIAL CRITERIA

In response to internal and external critiques, Spain had to elaborate an ethical justification to set up the philosophic and legal bases of its empire. Around 1544 the emperor's chaplain and official chronicler, Juan Ginés de Sepúlveda, composed a work entitled *Democrates Secundus sive de justis causis belli apud Indos*. Based on the Augustinian argument that slavery is a punishment for a sin, he maintained that the violence against the American Indians was fair because they practiced human sacrifice and lacked other signs of a "civil condition." The Dominican missionary Bartolomé de Las Casas, in a particular reading of Aristoteles' *Politics*, affirmed that each human society occupied a place in a hierarchical scale according to the level of fulfillment of a set of requirements. The American Indians had achieved all their potential as pagans, but, unable to critique their culture from within, they practiced sacrifices. In consequence, sacrifice should be considered as a legitimate form of devotion, while conversion, historically inevitable, should be carried out through persuasion. The confrontation between Sepúlveda and Las Casas finally led to the debates of Valladolid, which took place in 1550.[14]

Taking into account the political context, I suggest that besides the theological conception of the conquered and the rivalry between theologians and rhetoricians, what was in play was the command of the colonial territories. Sepúlveda, educated in a protosecular, classic-inspired Italian humanism, argued in favor of the king and assigned to the New World the role of source of slave labor and economic extraction. Las Casas argues in favor of a neomedieval mode of colonialism, where the power over a new and devoted body of believers would remain in the hands of the church. Although the triumph of Las Casas's position preserved the humanity of the native inhabitants of the New World, it is not possible to ignore that it was embedded into a hyper-hierarchic social model, where the appraisal of the devout character of the other was necessary to implement a theocratic rule in the Indies. While for Sepúlveda the vanquished were reduced to a condition of instruments of economic extraction, for Las Casas they had to be admitted into the realm of his religion. Las Casas's stance softened the legal aspect of the Spanish rule but the creation of an emotional knot with a benevolent oppressor made this system more difficult to overcome. Therefore, the theory of pacific evangelization emphasized a sort of perverse message of liberation, because it required obedience to a religion emanated from an ultimately alien center.[15]

Neither Sepúlveda nor Las Casas could hear the point of view of the subjugated people. On the few occasions when they were consulted, as when their religious leaders were forced to defend their beliefs in front of the friars right after the military conquest of Mexico, the place given to their knowledge was that of superstition.[16] The dispute about the form of incorporation of the native inhabitants into the modern world was in fact a battle to legitimate one group over its opponents. Neither system was better for those to be subjugated; they would confront a violent and open exploitation in Sepúlveda's model or a persuasive and subtly perverse submission in that of Las Casas.

Although the logic that defines the limits between the self and the other is a constitutive factor of any given society, that logic in the case of the Spanish conquest presented an important novelty. It was the elaboration of a theory of "pure blood" that excluded the others as legitimate cultural producers.[17] Among the inhabitants of the Anahuac—the pre-Hispanic territory of present-day central Mexico—communities defeated in a war, even if they were enslaved or economically punished, were gradually "interwoven"—*entretejidos*—in the winners' society.[18] A clear example of this practice is the incorporation of the deities of the vanquished within the official rituals and myths of the victorious. The protocapitalist mode of production that propelled the Spanish conquest, however, did not conceive a cultural interaction of this type.

Extant social, political, religious, and other differences became opaque under the overwhelming violence of this conquest. By reducing the complete preexistent social structure to the most exploited level and destroying almost all of its written documents, the Spanish conquerors disavowed the conflicts that existed prior to their arrival. Mexicas, for instance, had a set of racial and social categories to place groups in their classificatory system. The *Codex Xólotl* distinguishes clearly the prestigious Toltecas, dedicated to artistic trades (pottery, jewelry, and painting) from the nomad Chichimecas, charac-

9.1 "Battle between Chichimecas (left)
and Toltecas (right)" from Codex
Xólotl. Notice how the ethnic warriors' origin is indicated in their clothing. Photograph: Bibliothèque na-
tionale de France.

terized by hunting activities.[19] Ethnic origin and social rank of each character
described in the *Codex Xólotl* are indicated by his or her clothing, such as the
white shawl for Toltecas and the coarse fur clothes for Chichimecas (fig. 9.1).

In indigenous pictorial documents, elite characters were represented sitting on top of reed grass while non-elites sat on the floor; the social belonging of a speaker was expressed in written texts by a color-based code and
verbally by a system of prefixes and suffixes (figs. 9.2 and 9.3). The *Codex
Mendoza* dedicates its third section to paintings of rulers, priests, warriors,
and artisans.[20] Of course such representations, produced by intellectuals educated in the most prestigious institution, the *Calmecac*, were not only a reflection of the distribution of power in the "real" world but a way to demonstrate that the current social organization, no matter the relationships of
domination that it implied, was natural and stable.[21]

In the modern colonial system, cognitive interweaving was not a possibility; to the contrary, the social structure was based on stressing of racial difference, which was constructed on Aristotelian bases and presented as natural human differences. The early and constantly increasing feeling of paranoia
among the elites, and of reluctant submission among the subjugated people,
reinforced racial conflicts. With the exception of the precolonial rulers, who

9.2 "Carpenter" (*quauhxinqui*), from Codex Mendoza, fol. 5v. This figure and figure 9.3 show characters from different social strata. Courtesy Bodleian Library, University of Oxford.

9.3 "Great Speaker" (*huey tlahtoani*), seated on *an icpalli,* from Codex Mendoza, fol. 70r. Courtesy Bodleian Library, University of Oxford.

were assimilated to the Spanish upper circles to help administer the new territories, the indigenous people were forced to occupy the bottom of the social pyramid, under poor whites. Their segment of the social structure was treated as an inevitable and passive remnant of the past that could facilitate the control of the people living according to their ancestral *habitus.*

PERIODIZING SOCIAL AND RACIAL PERSPECTIVES

Having outlined the cultural disarticulation produced by the conquest, I turn to describing its outcomes. I sketch out the distinctive characteristics of each formation of three main periods and the modifications that they go through according to their political contexts.

The First Period: Implementation of Colonial Rule

The first period is that of the implementation of colonial rule, characterized by the production of a theoretical corpus necessary to legitimate western practices in the New World and destroying or relegating previous conceptions of power to a marginal position. It extends from the conquest of the Americas through the beginning of the seventeenth century and includes the dominant, nonhegemonic emergent, and residual systems.

Given the need to justify the sudden possession of the Indies, the Spanish academic intellectuals created a dominant system that, appealing to ethnic, religious, and philosophical arguments, denied indigenous people access to political structures and legitimate capital. The work of highly educated authors like Gonzalo Fernández de Oviedo, Juan Ginés de Sepúlveda, Bartolomé de Las Casas, or Joseph de Acosta belongs to this system. As part of the political body, they were able to express their conflicting opinions about the colonial program and intervene in decision making about how to rule the empire and at the same time could print their manuscripts.[22]

Their works, devoted to understanding the culture of the colonized, are internally divided between fidelity to the Crown and the Catholic religion and an attraction to the material transmitted by the "informants," discussed below. In spite of the internal contradictions of these texts, I place them within the dominant system because their highly educated authors try to "understand" the indigenous logic and beliefs, not per se, or not to learn from them, but to better absorb them. As this corpus was alphabetically written, it was addressed to readers also interested in the conversion or the political domination of their original communities.

That interest was not a barrier to the emergence of a veiled sympathy for the culture analyzed. In fact, sympathetic writings took different forms: as a defense of the colonized within the limits of a colonial state (Las Casas), as a fascination for a bygone wisdom (Sahagún), or as an impulse to delve into forbidden beliefs (Durán). For this reason, the possibility of a "reading in reverse" is available. Like the Bakhtinian bivocal texts, these writings express an internal polemic with at least two voices defined by both their social and ethnic belonging.[23] The voice of the subject of the discourse, the "historian," has the institutional support to impose its power over the voice of the indigenous intellectuals, reduced to the category of "informants." But if the latter is objectified, it is not totally silenced; it is kept captive while the institutional apparatus can do so, or until its first meaning, given the appropriate historical circumstances, can be returned to the descendants of the original audience. These works, then, belong to the dominant system when they are read from the point of view of the ideology inscribed in the guiding comments and morals. If the readers are unsuccessfully Christianized indigenous people who remain rebellious toward the dominant discourse, these works become part of the residual system. The *Historia General* by Sahagún, for instance, may be read as its author proposes, as a way to know the "sickness" and mistakes of the people to be converted, or it may be conceived as a source of an encrypted wisdom.[24]

Among the conquerors there was also a nonhegemonic, emergent system, consisting of the works of nonacademic peninsular chroniclers like Pedro de Cieza de León, Bernal Díaz del Castillo, and Fray Ramón Pané. The upward technical and economic flow that characterized the fifteenth century had produced a social and cultural mobility whose inheritors were the self-educated chroniclers of the conquest. Logically, they are marked by the contradiction between their position of power as conquerors and their subordinated position as middle-low socially and culturally ranked subjects.

This corpus can be defined as an ideologically irreducible nucleus, because the never-solved tensions within peninsular social relations emerged in the tragic, melancholic, and disappointed tone of soldiers and low-ranked friars. The intellectual elite were not ready to include these expressions in any of the recognized disciplines, except as sources of information. Increasing restrictions were imposed by the political apparatus to prevent the publication of the works; in the best case, they were summarized by official historians, like the investigation about the *Taíno* people done by Fray Ramón Pané, which was used, not without disdain, by Bartolomé de Las Casas in his *Historia de las Indias.*

In a sense, the Spanish conquest was the consequence of a social explosion suffocated by a reinforced Catholicism that would lead toward the absolutism of the seventeenth century.[25] Propaganda about the conquest spread among middle- and low-ranked Iberian subjects. It centered on the promise of economic rewards and was a strategy to deflect uprisings inside the homeland, whereas propaganda disseminated among foreign powers and conquered peoples centered on religious issues and was a strategy to justify *a posteriori* the political decision of forcing a war to obtain economic benefits. Thus colonialism may be conceived as a military intervention of an external power on an alien territory motivated by internal disruptions and imbalances "resolved" by the externalization of violence.

Unlike the subjectivity of the colonized, shaped by the experience of an extreme exploitation, the social "identity" of the low-ranked people in the Iberian Peninsula of the early modern period was weaker. It was mainly shaped by the knowledge derived from trade, places of origin, and surviving pre-Catholic beliefs. Their revolts were focused on particular issues, like the rebellion led by Lope de Aguirre in the "Marañón" river in the early seventeenth century, who did not question the feudal-colonial system itself but the exclusion of the soldiers, self-perceived as low-ranked "vassals," from the new colonial nobility. Lope de Aguirre's case, like many of the episodes narrated by Bernal Díaz del Castillo in his chronicle, brings out the contradiction lodged in the mind of foot soldiers.[26] Although they remained faithful to Catholic beliefs and to the promise of economic rewards made by the Crown, they were deeply disappointed by the effects of the war, as it is expressed in some episodes of these authors' narratives.

The residual system, born right after the conquest, is formed by the remaining written materials and oral practices that kept the indigenous systems of knowledge alive and able to confront new social demands. The colonial situation gave rise to the *relaciones geográficas*, a set of alphabetic and pictorial answers to fifty questions ordered by the Crown in 1572 to obtain the necessary information to improve its economic benefits and administrative structure. In an astonishing reception, the indigenous communities took the questionnaire as a way to reshape their own perception of a threatening reality. The Nahuas, for instance, elaborated their reality as an effort to interweave with the conquerors, making evident that their mechanism of cultural inclusion was alive, even if it was not recognized by the dominant system. Many of the *relaciones*, then, far from being understood by their imperial addressees, were a living proof of the vitality and adaptability of nonwestern forms of thinking.[27] The same characteristics apply to the *títulos primordiales*, illustrated documents written in indigenous languages. They were produced in the second half of the seventeenth century or later and were intended to resemble sixteenth-century texts and to protect possession of the land for the communities settled on it.[28]

Finally, the few surviving "codices"—most of them produced right after the conquest—were collected first by learned direct descendants of their producers, like Fernando de Alva Ixtlilxóchitl in Mexico, and then by Creole scholars who had begun to consider them rare artistic pieces, like don Carlos de Sigüenza y Góngora. Other codices were reduced to feeding the exotic taste of the imperial elite, like the *Codex Mendoza*, a colonial reproduction of three Aztec records ordered by the viceroy Mendoza to be a gift to the Spanish king, Felipe II, or to feed the imperial administrative archives, like the *relaciones geográficas*. Emptied of the social functions for which they were conceived, their symbolic value was unavailable for the people linked to them. However, their anticolonial potential could become active once recuperated by the members of a resistant community.

The Second Period: Consolidation and Stratification

During the second period—from the second half of the seventeenth century to the second half of the eighteenth—the dominant system was consolidated, colonial institutions were tightened, and race replaced the socioeconomic factor as a criterion of stratification.

The dominant system in this period is characterized by an increasing homogeneity. The writing of low-rank conquerors that tried to emerge in the sixteenth century was soon neutralized and, with it, its threatening ideological potential. A program of neofeudalization boosted the integration of the few soldiers who survived the conquest into the peripheral nobility, assigning to some of them *encomiendas* and the new identity of "indianos."[29] A clear example of the suppression of the social conflicts among the colonizers is the disqualification by the official chronicler of the Indies, Antonio de Solís y Rivadeneira, of the history composed by Bernal Díaz del Castillo, because of his subordinate social rank and his preference for the representation of "vulgar" characters.[30]

The members of the emergent Creole system sought their own ideological identity within the dominant esthetic standards. Creoles took their distance with respect to the indigenous traditions by appropriating their ancient archive while disregarding the cultural practices of their descendants. In consonance with this tendency, the descendants of the Spanish colonizers deepened the process of neofeudalization by suppressing the critique of the conquest and erasing the popular backgrounds of their progenitors. For example, Bernal Diaz's son adds the aristocratic expression "del Castillo" to his father's last name in his manuscript and introduces other changes to reinforce that status.[31] In Mexico, the famously erudite don Carlos de Sigüenza y Góngora was one of the earliest collectors of indigenous codices, which reflects the formation of a social desire to possess a cultural object that has just become undecipherable and for that reason exotic; what is more important, it can give the prestige necessary to delineate the features of future Creole subjectivity. At the same time, he shows the first symptoms of a white paranoia in a testimony of the indigenous riots in Mexico City. On the other hand, when the sophisticated poet Sor Juana Inés de la Cruz composes *villancicos*, a popular religious genre, she introduces indigenous and black characters from her white high intellectual position, one albeit softened by the particular experience of a female writer in a male-dominated intellectual community.

The residual system in this period focuses its strategies on negotiating with, criticizing, or outwitting the colonial exclusion. While the Creoles were pushed up, the indigenous people were pushed down, reinforcing the tendency toward a relative social homogenization inside their communities, because inner conflicts were softened to increase the resistance to the violence deployed by Spanish conquerors.

A singular case is the alphabetic-pictorial text by the Andean writer Don Felipe Guamán Poma de Ayala, *Nueva Crónica y Buen Gobierno* (1615).[32] This work, unknown until the twentieth century, makes clear that reception of the epistemological imposition of the colonizers by the local population escaped the expectations of the colonizers. Guamán Poma de Ayala tried to save his ancestors' perception of the world by accepting the power of the Spanish crown and its religion but rejecting the authority of local administrators.[33] His work creates a symbolic capital appropriating, critically, the western tradition; its drawings deploy a witty look at the injustices denounced in the written parts, and in many cases they conceive an imagined reality. For example, in the representation of the "pontifical world," the Indies are centered on Cusco, the heart of the Inca territory, while Castile, the center of the Spanish empire, is placed in a subordinated position (fig. 9.4).

Another crucial intervention of this author is the representation of a new colonial subject by the figure of the indigenous "poor" (*el pobre indio*). A character dressed with a cloak, in a kneeling position with his hands folded as if in prayer, recreates the image of the humble good Christian who, in spite of his faithfulness and praiseworthiness, is a victim of the devastating effects of western colonialism on Andean societies. Ambition, avarice, and corruption of protocapitalist subjects are expressed by a serpent, a lion, a tiger, a cat, a fox, and a rat (fig. 9.5). Guamán Poma de Ayala's creative mind combines an Andean animalized perception of human beings' attitudes with the threatening zoological imagination spread by medieval bestiaries, represented by their large hoofs and tongues. New colonial subjects—*encomenderos, caciques,* priests, and bureaucrats—are described as "animals that do not have fear of God" that "skin the poor Indians in this kingdom and there is no remedy."[34]

Although inspired by Christian iconography, here the worn-out clothes make the concept of "poor" refer not to the spiritual sphere as much as to the new condition of economic indigence. The emergence of this subject demonstrates the moment when the artistic "structure of feelings" of the colonized—in Raymond Williams' terms—becomes permeated by a new suffering

9.4 "Pontifical world: The Indies of Peru and the kingdom of Castile" from Guamán Poma de Ayala's *El primer nueva corónica y buen gobierno* (1615/1616, 42). Notice how the two main Andean religious elements, the sun and the mountains, coexist with the western-ized diagram of the urban centers and how Peru is placed over Spain and Castile. Courtesy of the Royal Library, Copenhagen, Denmark. Guamán Poma's illustrated letter to Philip III of Spain, ms. GKS 2232 4° at the Royal Library of Denmark, is available at http://www.kb.dk/elib/mss/poma/.

9.5 "Six ungodly animals feared by the poor Indians of this kingdom" from Guamán Poma de Ayala's *El primer nueva corónica y buen gobierno* (1615/1616, 708). Courtesy of the Royal Library, Copenhagen, Denmark. Guamán Poma's illustrated letter to Philip III of Spain, ms. GKS 2232 4° at the Royal Library of Denmark, is available at http://www.kb.dk/elib/mss/poma/.

condition.[35] Such a condition is produced by the sudden socioeconomic debacle, the result of the violent imposition of a social structure perceived by one as a source of contention and perceived by another as an overwhelming threat. In spite of the official discourse of evangelization, Christian values were not practiced by colonial agents, who were interested in economic accumulation.

On the other hand, evangelization and alphabetic writing generated a desire for upward mobility in those whose achievement ultimately rendered this desire impossible to fulfill. An *indio ladino,* no matter how westernized, could not be recognized as an equal interlocutor by members of academic, religious, and political institutions. One of Guamán Poma de Ayala's figurative representations displays a scene as it might have happened, demonstrating how intense was this desire. He depicts himself conversing with Philip III, stating, "the author presents the chronicle in person to His Majesty" (fig. 9.6). However, a person-to-person encounter between a king and a colonized intellectual was, in fact, hindered by multiple relationships of domination — political, economic, social, and racial.[36] The scene has not only an esthetic but also a political purpose; paraphrasing J. L. Austin, Guamán Poma de Ayala uses a strategy of "making things with drawings" in the sense that, besides denouncing the crimes committed against indigenous peoples, he changes the terms of the colonial relationship in a graphic way. The author draws himself in a lower and submissive position, on his knees, but pointing upward with the forefinger of his right hand (like Jesus Christ's advising gesture in some paintings), in the attitude of giving answers, as the alphabetic text explains.

The drawings of *Nueva Crónica y Buen Gobierno* capture social changes that were not totally defined — what Williams calls "social experience in solution." When Guamán Poma de Ayala sketches the figure of a "poor Indian," he subsumes local racial specificities in the widely inclusive figure of the economically exploited subject. This is an early apprehension of the conflict between the sudden economic degradation of the colonized, a process whose increasing intensity would finally explode in the violent Andean uprising in 1780. The imaginary dialogue with the king is an early articulation of a decolonizing move that would only have a parallel in reality in present times, with Evo Morales's official visit to Spain.

But, as has been pointed out, the anchoring of western symbols and hierarchies in a preexistent *cosmovisión* was a common phenomenon among colonized communities. Other important expressions in this period are the orally transmitted narratives about the end of the pre-Spanish dominion and the return of previous forms of life that started to be shaped after the conquest.

9.6 "'The author Ayala' presents his *Corónica* to Philip III, King of Spain," from Guamán Poma de Ayala's *El primer nueva corónica y buen gobierno* (1615/1616, 975). Notice how the author places himself in an impossible scene. Courtesy of the Royal Library, Copenhagen, Denmark. Guamán Poma's illustrated letter to Philip III of Spain, ms. GKS 2232 4° at the Royal Library of Denmark, is available at http://www.kb.dk/elib/mss/poma/.

In a way, they are the answer to the tightening of the inquisitorial apparatus, determined to finish off remnant practices and types of knowledge associated with them.

Oral narratives of regression belong to popular, low, or nonwesternized sectors determined to resist. For example, the myth of the *Inkarry* (Inka-rey) maintains, in multiple versions, that the Andean society will be back once the head and the body of the Inca's corpse are reunited. In the central Mexico region, the "message of Cuauthemoc," which had been transmitted in secrecy for five centuries, announces the return of the Aztec times after the cycle of the Fifth Sun. Some Mayan oral narratives, like the sacred texts of *Pop Vuh* and several versions of the *Chilam Balam,* were the result of the desire to protect the legacy of the ancient symbolic capital from the continuous threat of the colonial agents. Treasured in secrecy, the sacred texts were "discovered" by Spanish speakers after the moment of their alphabetic record. With the help of these narratives, forbidden rituals were held in hidden places in a cohesive and consistent way by the same people forced to be baptized.

The Third Period: Emerging Violence

The third period includes the productions of the second half of the eighteenth century to the nineteenth century and is dominated by the violent emergence of the residual system. For the indigenous—and even more for the enslaved—the cynical nature of a benevolent evangelization was clear because of the shortages and punishments caused by racially discriminatory forced labor. Guamán Poma de Ayala's chronicle having been unknown by its contemporaries, the most politically effective text in the eighteenth century was Garcilaso de la Vega's *Comentarios Reales de los Incas,* a utopian reconstruction of the Inca state. The reading of this work and the use of Quechua among its native speakers allowed an articulation of a residual capital in an active-nostalgic mode. Túpac Amaru and other Andean leaders were able to elaborate theoretically the historical perspective of their people and recognize the power of their own capital of experience.[37] They pursued the transformation of the residual system into a dominant one, and the replacement of the channels of capital accumulation with the reestablishment of the Andean system, based on reciprocity. Their rebellion was militarily defeated, but its magnitude forced the conquerors to consider the indigenous as rivals, despite the dehumanizing condition attributed to them.

Maya communities in Yucatan confronted first the Spanish and then the Mexican militia for a long period of time, in the "Guerra de Castas" or Caste War (1855–1857) and the episode known as "La cruz parlante" (1851).[38]

They appealed to a strategy of inner cohesion based on the adoption of the adversaries' symbols and rituals into their own embedding practices.[39]

The strength of indigenous resistances, the consequence of long years of sedimentation, and the rearticulation of a new social and ethnic subjectivity in spite of sustained ethnic discrimination were parallel to the weakening of the colonial apparatus. Although it is important to distinguish the specific context, limitations, and consequences of the rebellions, it is crucial to consider the role of these movements in a cultural history. Their different political effects may be explained by the relationship with the Creole emergent system, in some cases more permeable to the indigenous discourse than in others. On a general level, the Creole cultural values looked for other European models as alternatives to the Spanish tradition; they were not able to recognize and incorporate the indigenous background. Only at the beginning of the nineteenth century do some points of contact between the residual and the emergent systems begin to appear. For example, the Mexican friar Servando Teresa de Mier, a member of the "neo-Aztec" movement, dared to write a polemical sermon to commemorate the Virgin of Guadalupe, resignifying the content encrypted in an ancient Mexican codex, while the Argentinean lawyer Manuel Belgrano proposed the restitution of the Inca dynasty for the new nation that he was helping to create.[40]

Works that appealed to an exclusively neoclassical esthetic became peripheral because they were further from the American reality. They followed an impulse to recreate bygone western icons, showing an incapacity to understand the residual-emerging expressions of the people. Neoclassicism can be taken as a way to neglect the emptiness, the nonsense, and the exhaustion of the political apparatus that legitimated it, whose structures were being shaken by both their oppressed communities and their European rivals.

DOUBLE COLONIAL PRACTICES

What is new in the capitalist colonial system is first, the idea of global power; second, the preeminence of a monetary economy that links the conquest of the Americas with a process of primitive accumulation; and third, the lack of an idea of incorporation of the vanquished into the legitimate capital of the conqueror. As Aníbal Quijano rightly observes, the Spanish conquest of the Americas implied the imposition of capitalism on a world scale, while modernity and coloniality became its constitutive axis until today.[41] However, as I have pointed out, neither the idea of conquest itself nor the idea of human hierarchies was new. American indigenous societies had their own fights and their own machinery to legitimize hierarchies, as do present-day democracies. For this reason, I would formulate the main novelty of the Spanish colonization as *the absolute denial of a valuable cultural capital for the colonized and the exclusion of any possibility of legitimization of their knowledge.* This means that while indigenous societies assimilated the practices of the conquered, the Spanish elite's theory of "pure blood" blocked any avenue of incorporation at the level of ideological production.[42] New rulers demanded the total submission to their own beliefs, even knowing that this would never be enough to incorporate the "other" as part of the "same."

This principle was concomitant with the disarticulation of previous socioeconomic systems that only subsisted at a residual level. On the contrary, in the case of noncolonial societies — those that did not suffer a colonial intervention for a long period of time or those that could truly overcome it — socioeconomic factors work as the main criterion of classification. Therefore, from a wider perspective, it is possible to infer that race works as the dominant criterion of classification in colonial societies, while socioeconomic factors gain power in noncolonial, or decolonized, societies. The last question to consider is how the interchanges between the dominant and residual systems may be compatible with a notion like that of exclusion. Considering the basic distinction between Europeans and their others, the model of perception that shaped the colonial regime was basically dual.[43] To keep this duality across three centuries in a continental extension, with the plural manifestations that I have just mentioned, imperial power created a hard ideological core. So two levels of analysis should be considered.

The first level describes original imbrications of elements inspired by the colonized and the colonizer's cultures in most of their expressions — linguistic, religious, gastronomic, musical, pictorial, customary, sexual, etc. The dark-skinned Virgin of Guadalupe of Mexico or the "Virgin del Cerro" in Potosí (whose red hill-shaped cloak is painted with minerals, animals, and plants) are good examples of the bicultural roots of colonial creation. Several scholars have analyzed the complexity of this mechanism, proposing different concepts to describe it. Among Latin-Americanists the application of the category of "mestizaje" to cultural artifacts — such as "literatura mestiza" — was questioned, because the idea of mixture makes difficult the appreciation of the inner components of a text. In the last twenty years, the concept of "transculturation" has been widely used, but also the ideas of a "heterogeneity" and a "contradictory totality" were proposed to highlight the internal conflict of these objects. More recently, the term "nepantlismo" has been introduced to refer to the "in between" position of indigenous subjects, refusing the idea of a harmonic coexistence of elements in texts written by them.[44]

The notion of "hybridism" deserves some attention. If in the present it often refers to the work of Homi Bhabha, I still think of it from the Bakhtinian sense; I find this more useful for thinking about the cognitive consequences of the bilingual contact that takes place, in a colonial context, among low-ranked people who are usually excluded from academic training. When Bakhtin describes the social origin of *carnavalesque* novels in the Renaissance, which were produced in Romance languages—like Rabelais' *Gargantua et Pantagruel* and Miguel de Cervantes's *Don Quijote de la Mancha*—he notices that popular cultures have a "centrifugal" movement, while elite writers follow a "centripetal" movement, remaining attached to academic knowledge, the official genre— the epic—and the prestigious language—Latin and Greek at that time.[45] This explains why Spanish soldiers let forbidden indigenous beliefs leak into their chronicles more frequently than writers like Ginés de Sepúlveda, who expresses his arguments in Latin and quotes the "authorities" to prove them. For their part, the conquered peoples were excluded from the use of imperial tools of communication—Spanish language, alphabetic writing, and the printing press—although some of them, such as indigenous elite writers, made a remarkable effort to register their traditions in the empire's codes.[46]

In consequence, from my point of view hybridism is the key surviving practice of low socially and racially ranked subjects; it is not totally absent among elite colonizers, but they seem to be determined to filter and control all that could work against the ruling power. Bartolomé de Las Casas's vigilant and censoring attitude against the poor friar Ramón Pané, who was far from fulfilling the official criterion for being a historian, illuminates this point. But, as I have tried to demonstrate, the fact that theoretical approaches were not recognized by the disciplinary canons did not cancel their powerful effects for the target audience. Writings, rituals, dances, singing, and a whole set of forbidden or rejected practices enjoyed a committed reception by their participants, sometimes rooted in understandable feelings of resentment, which explains why, instead of pacific mixtures, many colonial relationships triggered violent revolts.

The second level of analysis corresponds to the activities that imply production of ideology and knowledge, such as metadisciplinary discourses, religious dogmas, legal discourses, and people's stratification criteria. These activities, which imply political decisions, were not shared with the colonized nor the transcultured, nor was there even an internal contradiction in their articulation. These activities were part of a homogeneous corpus built exclusively on western concepts and implemented by colonizers. This corpus can be appreciated in the first and emblematic case of asymmetric dialogue between Catholic priests and Mexican *sátrapas*, whose answers were used to justify the sudden imposition of Catholicism. Garcilaso de la Vega's work suffered the consequence of this schizophrenic mechanism as well: if daily intercultural practices permitted its production, their theoretical implication—the rationality of the Inca's society—was far from being accepted.[47]

Finally, this distinction does not oppose hybrid praxis to pure theoretical production, but it does oppose intercultural, inclusive practices to an intracultural, exclusivist, self-protecting machine. The first level works in a highly dynamic way, generating unpredictable forms of cultural interchange that permit the formulation of political thoughts by the colonized and even low socially ranked colonizers, while the second tries to control and avoid the intervention of this knowledge in its network. Therefore in a colonial rule the first level is absorbed by a program designed to preserve the racial, social, and cognitive preeminence of the colonizer, ensuring the subordinated role of the Indies in the formative stage of capitalism.

To historicize the cultural expressions of the Indies it is necessary to consider the subjects whose records are available and study their interrelations. In this case, I have tried to draft a model based on indigenous, *mestizo*, Creole, and Spanish perspectives. Going beyond disciplinary limits, it is possible to see that often the dominant system is less active than the residual; that the latter may become emergent if its subjects can elaborate their suffering experience; that this elaboration helps to rebuild their own symbolic capital; and finally, that the colonized may formulate decolonizing programs to intervene in the constant reshaping of their societies.

CHAPTER TEN

UNFIXING RACE

Kathryn Burns

RACE [*RAZA*]. The caste of purebred horses, which are marked with brands to distinguish them. Race in cloth [means] the coarse thread that is distinct from the other threads in the weave . . . Race in lineage is understood to be bad [*se toma en mala parte*], as to have some Moorish or Jewish race.[1]

> Sebastián de Covarrubias Horozco, *Tesoro de la lengua castellana* (1611)

RACE [*RAZA*]. Caste or quality of one's origin or lineage. Speaking of men, generally understood to be bad. . . . [By the knightly rule] of Cal[atrava]: "We order and command that no one, of whatsoever quality and condition, be received into the said Order . . . unless he be a Gentleman . . . born of legitimate matrimony, and not of Jewish, Moorish, Heretic, nor Plebeian race. . . ."[2]

> Real Academia Española, *Diccionario de autoridades* (1726–1739)

What I consider in this chapter is the deep past of our keyword "race," a term that has long organized notions of fixity but has never itself been stable. My epigraphic borrowings from old dictionaries are meant to draw us into the subject of this instability—and the persistent racism that avails itself of categories even as they change.[3] Covarrubias gives us horses (and something like "breed"), cloth, and finally lineage, mentioning Moors and Jews, while the Real Academia's *Diccionario* homes in on origins and lineage. Jews and Moors also appear in the *Diccionario* in an embedded snippet of the rules of the prestigious Order of Calatrava, but in significantly augmented company: alongside the races of Heretics and Plebeians. Both definitions emphasize the term's negative associations ("se toma en mala parte").[4] And each differs strikingly from modern usages, rooted in scientific racism and the many ways it has been used and contested.[5]

What to make of such definitional drift? Here I use it to introduce arguments that will be the *hilos conductores*, the main themes, of this chapter: (1)

that the politics, categories, and practice of racism are historically specific, shaped by local struggles as well as far-flung imperial rivalries and the politics of state making; and (2) that important stakes are involved in making our work more sensitive, not just to these complex histories but to the ways in which they both do and do not relate to ours.[6] Scholars in many fields increasingly use the term "race" in scare quotes. This is a welcome move to unfix race — to signal that the categories we recognize as racial are not stable or panhistoric — but is only the beginning of a project we can take much further. The point of carefully historicizing racial usages is to understand better both early modern racisms and those of our time.[7]

Consider, for example, that one of the most potent racial insults one could hurl in early seventeenth-century Lima, Peru, was *judío* (Jew). Jews were stigmatized as "bad whites," *la mala casta blanca.*[8] This is a historically specific frame of reference, one Albert Sicroff calls "religious racism."[9] Its Iberian genealogy is quite involved and links together histories that exist on separate shelves of our libraries: those of Spanish Jews, many (though by no means all) of whom converted under pressure to Roman Catholicism after the anti-Jewish pogroms of 1391 and were known as *conversos,* and Spanish Muslims who did likewise, known as *moriscos.* By the early fifteenth century Old Christians increasingly regarded New Christian populations with deep suspicion.[10] A sincere convert could not be distinguished at a glance from a false or backsliding convert, and considerable anxiety centered on those Spaniards who allegedly still practiced in secret a faith they had renounced. The Spanish Inquisition was created in the 1480s primarily to discipline suspected "Judaizers" — people who were thought to practice Judaism clandestinely. And concern began to fix on the supposed cleanliness of people's bloodlines. More and more Spanish institutions and municipalities devised and enforced statutes that excluded those not descended from Old Christians.[11]

The Castilian politics of race circa 1492 thus hinged on the purity or impurity of one's Christianity, increasingly defined as a matter not simply of belief and practice but of inheritance, *limpieza de sangre* ("purity of blood") — something that could not be changed at the baptismal font. The intensifying persecution of those believed to be of impure Christian lineage was intimately related to the consolidation of the lineage of the Spanish absolutist state.[12] A militant, intolerant Christianity drove both processes. As the inquisitorial policing of distinctions between correct and heretical Christians got underway, the Spanish monarchs Isabel and Fernando were simultaneously campaigning to defeat the last Iberian stronghold of Islam, the kingdom of Granada. The year they succeeded, 1492, was also the year in which they obliged Spain's remaining Jews to convert to Christianity or emigrate. Ten

years later Muslims were given the same choice.[13] After another century of
tensions Philip III moved to expel all moriscos in 1609.

Thus during the years 1391 and 1609, the status of New Christians—who
were not recognizable at a glance but considered by Old Christians to be in-
eradicably tainted in their blood—became a white-hot political and cultural
issue in Spain. And militant Christianity, sharply defined against Spain's internal, demonized others, was part of the mental baggage that Columbus and
the Iberians who followed him brought along as they invaded and subjugated American peoples after 1492. Columbus's famous account of his first
voyage begins with the touchstone moment of the fall of Granada: "This present year of 1492 . . . I saw the Royal Standards of Your Highnesses placed
by force of arms on the towers of the Alhambra. . . ."[14] As for the Caribbean
people he encounters on the other side of the Atlantic, Columbus describes
them, in an eerie echo of conflicts just behind that foreshadowed conflicts
just ahead, as living in houses that "are all made like Moorish campaign tents
[*alfaneques*]."[15] (His own companions he refers to interchangeably as "Spaniards" and "Christians.") Cortés likewise wrote of Yucatecan houses with
rooms "small and low in the Moorish fashion."[16] As many historians have
noted, the horizon of conquest these men had in mind as they measured their
exploits was that of the Spanish *reconquista* and the cleansing of the realm of
their sovereigns from the stain of the "sects" of Moses and Mohammed.

Before long, in each American viceroyalty over which Spanish rule was
established, those suspected of secretly practicing their Jewish or Muslim
faith could be persecuted by an American office of the Spanish Inquisition—
and were, as Irene Silverblatt shows in the Lima case of Manuel Bautista
Pérez.[17] But to expel all non-Christians and suspicious converts was clearly
not an option. To the contrary: the Iberian monarchs by agreement with the
papacy were obliged to convert the natives of the Americas to Christianity.
One way or another, Iberians in the Americas were going to have to coexist
with an enormous population of "idolators" and brand new converts—just
the kind of people they had learned to despise back home.

Moreover, to stand any chance of success whatsoever, Iberians would need
the Americans' help. Assimilation was the initial framework the Spanish
Crown advocated during a few brief and experimental years. One royal decree went so far as to recommend that some Spaniards marry Indian women
and some Indian men marry Spanish women "[so] that they may communicate with and teach one another . . . and the Indians become men and women
of reason."[18] Proximity to Spaniards would give the latter a "good example"
of Christian conduct to follow, or so it was thought. When the dramatic news
from Las Casas and others showed just how badly things were going, how-

ever, royal advisors realized that a new course had to be charted. They gradually assembled the juridical fiction of "two republics," the *república de españoles* and its corresponding *república de indios*. These were propounded in a series of royal orders strikingly different from those issued not long before. By the 1570s, the Crown was betting on a strategy of physical segregation of Indians from non-Indians and the forced relocation or "reduction" (*reducción*) of the former into all-Indian towns.[19] Yet it is crucial to note that the overall goal of assimilation still held for the indigenous nobility, those whom Spaniards indiscriminately termed *caciques*.[20] Special schools were erected to convert the sons of native leaders to Christianity and give them a thoroughly Spanish upbringing. By the late sixteenth century, indigenous nobles were among the Spanish clergy's most enthusiastic new Christians (fig. 10.1).

However, the "two republics" model failed from its inception to keep Spaniards and indigenous peoples apart. As they settled in and erected towns, cities, and viceroyalties, Iberian immigrants — overwhelmingly male — brought with them numerous African slaves and peninsular slaves of African descent.[21] No one seemed to stay in the place the Crown had assigned. And as part of the violence of conquest and occupation, the invading Europeans and their allies took indigenous women as spoils of war, slaves, servants, and sometimes wives, appropriating to themselves access to native and enslaved women's bodies. Reports from the new viceroyalties mark new categories of people: *mestizo, mulato, zambo,* and so forth. These were not terms of self-identification but of convenient Spanish labeling. They gave Spanish authorities a linguistic handle on those who fit neither of the two republics — and who seemed, to their dismay, to threaten both with their disorderly conduct. These were Spaniards' impure New World others.

Were these new categories racial? They did not imply clear color lines.[22] But they did have to do with race in contemporary Castilian terms, as they referenced and linked the issues of blood (im)purity and fresh conversion to Christianity. These new labels — and that of "Indian" as well — were applied to people who, like the conversos and moriscos of Spain, were new converts (or their descendents), the better to delineate places for them in a well-governed society in which Christianization would, at least in theory, be assured by Christian masters and priests. While these designs never worked the way Spanish authorities intended, they can nevertheless be seen as driven by racial considerations in Castilian, period terms: the mission to impose Christianity and to extirpate religions considered false and heretical.[23]

But what exactly did new terms like *mestizo, mulato,* and *zambo* mean to those who were devising them in places like Peru or New Spain? What kinds of practices, choices, lifeways are hidden behind them? And can we see in

10.1 High-ranking Andeans are depicted by the Andean nobleman Felipe Guaman Poma de Ayala as good Christians, rosaries in hand. Redrawn from *El primer nueva corónica y buen gobierno,* 3 vols., eds. John V. Murra and Rolena Adorno (Mexico City: Siglo XXI, 1980), 2:710. Guaman Poma's illustrated letter to Philip III of Spain, ms. GKS 2232 4° at the Royal Library of Denmark, is available at http://www.kb.dk/elib/mss/poma/.

the written record any terms other than those used by Spaniards, perhaps subaltern usages? I consider these questions through the history of the Spanish terms that were being introduced and circulated in sixteenth-century Cuzco. Archivally it is hard to trace anything about Cuzco's history before midcentury because most of the paper trail has been scattered or lost.[24] But published chronicles are very rich and give us much to go on.

Take Part I, Book 9, chapter 31 of the *Comentarios reales* of Garcilaso de la Vega, el Inca, who was born in Cuzco in 1539: "New names for naming new generations" (*Nombres nuevos para nombrar diversas generaciones*). Himself the son of a Spanish father and Inca mother, Garcilaso focuses this section on mixture, beginning with laudatory comments on Spaniards and their slaves: "there [in America] from these two nations they have made others, mixed in all ways."[25] With this introduction, Garcilaso starts his inventory of categories with Spaniards, noting the distinction between those born in Spain and those born overseas. But what comes across strongly in this passage is the distinctions drawn (according to Garcilaso) by Africans:

> The children of Spanish men and women born there [in America] are called *criollo* or *criolla,* to indicate that they are born in the Indies. This name was invented by the blacks. . . . It means, among them, "a black born in the Indies." They invented it to differentiate those who go from here [Spain], and were born in Guinea, from those who were born there. Because they consider themselves more honorable and of better quality, for having been born in the fatherland [*patria*], than their children who were born in a foreign land. And the parents are offended if they are called criollos.
>
> Spaniards, for like reasons, have begun using this term for those born there, so that Spaniards and Africans born there are called *criollo* or *criolla.*[26]

Here the subjectivity attributed to African men and women is in the foreground; the Spaniards are copycats. And the term *criollo/a* refers to both Africans and Spaniards, the better to get across another criterion of difference and hierarchy that mattered: one's natal land or *patria.* Why did birthplace matter? Garcilaso indicates that it had to do with honor and quality, what contemporaries might also have described as *condición.*[27] And he means the honor and quality of unfree people, *siervos.* This remarkable passage thoroughly upends our racial expectations of Garcilaso's contemporaries and imagined readers. He gets us to understand "creoles" through the subjectivity of African men and women concerned with the defense of their honor (fig. 10.2).

Garcilaso continues by introducing the terms *mulato* and *mulata,* but not as the children of black and white parents, as our histories of colonial Latin America usually define them. By his account, "the child of a black man and an Indian woman — or of an Indian man and a black woman — is called a *mulato* or *mulata.* And their children are called *cholos.* This word is from the Barlovento islands. It means 'dog,' not of pure breed but of the very vicious *gozcones.* And Spaniards use it to defame and insult."[28] Garcilaso moves us further on the terrain of contemporary usage, pointing in the process to active trafficking in words over wide geographic expanses. Here impurity among those of African descent is not just stigmatized but bestialized (fig. 10.3).

He gets to his own background next: will we see more of the same? Garcilaso defines mestizos with reference to himself: "they call us mestizos, to say that we are mixed from both nations," Spanish and Indian.[29] He approaches this term much more personally. But note that the bounds of his sympathy have limits:

> It was imposed by the first Spaniards to have children in the Indies. And because the name [mestizo] was given us by our fathers according to their understanding, I call myself this with pride and am honored by it. In the Indies, however, if one of them is told 'you're a mestizo' or 'he's a mestizo,' they take it as an insult. This is why they have embraced with such enthusiasm the term *montañés* that was but one of the many affronts and insults a powerful man gave them in place of the term *mestizo.* And they fail to consider that although in Spain the name *montañés* is honorable, because of the privileges that were given to the natives of the mountains of Asturias and the Basques, calling anyone who was not born in those provinces by the same name is an abuse.[30]

So are these terms insults? According to Garcilaso, it depends who uses them, of whom, and where. He ironizes his kin (*parientes*) for readily referring to themselves as "highlanders" or "mountain people" when according to him this is an insult if used of anyone other than a Basque or Asturian. The equivalent term is likewise an insult in the Incas' language, he adds ("*sacharuna* . . . properly means 'savage'").[31] He thinks those he broadly defines as his relatives have been the unwitting dupes of a disrespectful "poderoso." Garcilaso himself prefers to (re)claim the term "mestizo" and draws this passage out even further to urge his relations to do the same: "My kinsmen, without understanding the malice of the man who imposed the name on them, take

ESPAÑOLES.
SOBERBIOSO, CRIOLLO
omestizo · omulafodesteRey[no]

enlos pueblos   criollos

10.2 Here Guaman Poma, a contemporary of Garcilaso de la Vega, el Inca, depicts *criollos* as Spaniards "who are raised on the milk of Indian and black women," and associates criollos with violence, judging them "worse than mestizos and mulattos and blacks." Redrawn from Murra and Adorno, eds., *El primer nueva corónica*, 2:510.

COREGIMIENTO
Õ EL COREGᵒ² COÑBÍDA

10.3 Guaman Poma, who was proud of his noble Andean heritage, also linked "lowness," impurity, and violence. Here he denounces the Spanish magistrate (*corregidor*) who upends proper order when he "invites lowly people to eat at his table—an Indian *mitayo* [tributary], a *mestizo*, a *mulato*—and he honors them." He elaborates further on "low people": "ruffians and thieves, liars, beggars, and drunks, Jews and Moors. . . . And in these people he confides his secrets and he converses with these mestizos and mulattos and blacks." Redrawn from Murra and Adorno, eds., *El primer nueva corónica*, 2:469.

pride in his affront, when they should reject and abominate it and call themselves what our fathers called us and not admit such new, insulting names."[32]

Garcilaso concludes his chapter on "new generations" by introducing
terms that I have never seen in any manuscript or, for that matter, any chronicle: *cuatralbo* for someone one part Indian and three parts Spanish and *tresalbo*
for someone three parts Indian and one part Spanish.[33] Perhaps these reflect
local usage that did not make it into wider circulation. Such terms — like *montañés*, which shows up in some late sixteenth-century Cuzco records — may
have had a range of reference limited to certain places and times.[34]

Because of his efforts to reposition terms in better usage, all the while insisting on their utter novelty and the racism that might invest them, Garcilaso unfixes race for us while grounding colonial racism in very particular
circumstances. He shows us the enormous historical and cultural chasms between his terms and how they operated, his Iberian contemporaries' terms,
and ours. This chapter is cited frequently, usually to make a point about Garcilaso's pride in his Spanish-Andean parentage and the losing struggle he
was waging to defend himself and his fellow mestizos from disrepute. Indeed
he was proud. Both his parents were nobles by the standards of their respective cultures, and very important people in Garcilaso's native city.[35] But
many of the terms he attempted to fix in Part I, Book 9, chapter 31 soon
drifted away, to catch on other meanings or disappear altogether. "Mestizo"
did replace "montañés," as Garcilaso wanted. But it did not lose its power-
fully disreputable connotations. And these had nothing to do with the supposed stain of Jewish or Muslim blood.

Or did they? The making of "mestizos" was a politically charged, historical process, as I have argued elsewhere, and Garcilaso engaged in it after
some strenuous fighting had already gone on around the term, both figura-
tively and literally.[36] It is worth noting that the "Indian mestizo" Garcilaso
himself went to war against moriscos for his king during the 1568 revolt in
Alpujarras.[37] This chapter is not the place to carry out a complete investigation of the late sixteenth-century history of what the term "mestizo/a" represented, but I would like to recap some of the investigations done in that direction and suggest why it is vital to situate them in an imperial context: that
of the expanding empire of Philip II. Mestizos might appear to us to have had
no possible blood relation to conversos or moriscos. But the point was still
debatable in the mid-sixteenth century, when some theorized that Indians
were descended from a lost tribe of Israel.[38] I argue that Philip II and his advisors must have linked in their minds the imperial dilemma of what to do
about all these fresh converts.

Mestizas and mestizos become visible at midcentury in royal decrees ordering Spaniards to *recogerlos:* to gather them together, educate and Christianize them, and impart to them "good customs" and, in the case of boys, a trade. Acting on these, Cuzco's city council members decided at midcentury to found a "monastery for mestizas"—a place where the daughters their companions had had with Andean women might be taken in and given a Christian upbringing. Resolving what to do about Cuzco's mestizos seems to have been much more complicated. As Garcilaso's age set grew up they were increasingly viewed as a threat. From the 1560s in Cuzco, Mexico City, and elsewhere, mestizos were singled out as the protagonists of plots to overturn royal authority. It was then that the term "mestizo" took on an especially sharp edge: Spanish authorities saw mestizos as a group of frustrated, armed, and dangerous aspirants to the legacies of their Spanish fathers.[39]

After this the royal orders came thick and fast. Mestizos were not to live in Indian pueblos, hold certain offices such as that of notary (*escribano*), or bear arms. Nor were they to be ordained as priests, a decision later reversed in law but not in practice.[40] Meanwhile, at precisely this time, Philip II was dealing with another newly converted population he saw as dangerous and restive: the moriscos whose numbers were concentrated in Granada. One rebellion had already occurred there in the mountainous Alpujarras region around 1500, in the wake of aggressive Christian efforts to force (and enforce) conversion. Enforcement thereafter had been lax. But by the late 1560s, Philip—concerned that the moriscos constituted a potential Ottoman "fifth column" capable of assisting his chief enemy, the Turks—determined to launch a fresh effort to wipe out Moorish customs.[41] Thus at the same time that he was receiving word of the "mestizo mutinies" in New Spain and Peru, he was ordering that moriscos undergo total acculturation, in dress, language, dance, rites, and customs. The result was another major rebellion in southern Spain, beginning December 23, 1568, known as the second revolt of Alpujarras. Philip cracked down even harder, ordering in a 1570 "bando de reducción" that moriscos be deported from Granada and the area be repopulated with Christians.[42]

In Cuzco, in January 1580, Bishop Sebastián de Lartaún wrote to his king with this turbulent imperial horizon in mind. Regarding a royal decree of 1578 that he had received ordering him not to ordain mestizos ("whom we here call montañeses") and to be sure that those already ordained were capable and trained, he responded that he had done his best. Some men had already been ordained by other bishops, wrote Lartaún, but as for himself, "I have only ordained about five, and to tell the truth that I owe Your Majesty, they are the best priests that I have in my Bishopric, although they do not know much on account of not having had higher education, but as far as evangelizing and living without scandal and knowing the [Quechua] language and living quietly, they do as they should."[43] He warned his king to consider carefully whether to remove such men from the priesthood, as they might decide to turn their hand to worse endeavors, having discovered that a virtuous life brought them nothing. Moreover, they were relatively free of greed—here Lartaún touches on the commercial activities ("tratos y grangerias") that he himself then stood accused of—and the native peoples were especially devoted to them. Finally, Lartaún concluded, "they [mestizos] should not be presumed to be like conversos and moriscos, because the latter have a law or sect which is considered rebellious and to which they are stubbornly obedient, some to that of Moses and the rest to that of Mohammad, whereas the natives of this land had none to which they might become so attached and devoted as they [the conversos and moriscos] to theirs, and thus . . . these mestizos should not be held in such suspicion as are conversos and moriscos."[44]

Bishop Lartaún, as rhetorically modest religious ethnographer, here places things in the perspective he knows is that of his monarch: how to defeat those rebelling against Christianity. The second Alpujarras uprising was still fresh in Philip II's mind. His desire to repress the ambitions and thwart the careers of mestizos can thus be seen as part of his wider crackdown on all relatively recent converts. If this is race in a period sense, it is also white-hot imperial politics at a moment of maximum tension between the Christian Spanish monarch and his Islamic Ottoman rival. The making of mestizos and other groups was clearly a social process that was at once extremely local and connected to a world-historic horizon of imperial rivalries—religious, political, military, and economic.

In conclusion, here I have suggested a framework for understanding sixteenth- and seventeenth-century Spanish-American racism that places it in local as well as imperial contexts, emphasizing not only Spanish, Amerindian, or African ancestry but the (im)purity of people's blood and the politics of Christian evangelization. We have much more to learn about racism in early colonial Peru and New Spain—particularly about the dehumanization of those of African or Afro-Peruvian ancestry to which Garcilaso alludes. Fear of perceived blackness seems to become increasingly salient in eighteenth-century (documented) racism, while earlier paradigmatic fears of Jewish/converso blood become less salient. But fear and loathing of "los negros" clearly existed earlier[45] (figs. 10.4 and 10.5). Take the 1654 Cuzco petition of Juan Francisco de Morales. He complained that he had been stripped of his weapons by an overzealous local official and jailed because he had tightly curled, dark hair.[46] This case sounds strikingly similar to the practice of

709

NEGROS
COMOLOSCRIOLLOS

negros hurtan plata sesus amos
para enganar alas yñs putas
y las negras criollas hurtan
para seruir asus galanes es
pañoles y negros

caymicudqya

apomay como

luxuria

como

10.4 Guaman Poma represents a "creolized" black who has stolen money from his master
to purchase the services of an indigenous prostitute. The man addresses the woman in
Quechua and Spanish and she responds in kind. Redrawn from Murra and Adorno,
eds., *El primer nueva corónica*, 2:669.

10.5 One casta painting from a Peruvian series of twenty sent to Carlos III by Peruvian
     Viceroy Amat in 1770. Its caption indicates, "Mulatta and Spaniard produce *Quarteron
     de Mulato.*" Guaman Poma had used the term much earlier: see Murra and Adorno, eds.,
     El primer nueva corónica, 2:668. Reproduced by permission of the Museo Nacional de
     Antropología, Madrid.

racism in the United States today by means of racial profiling. The official was
enforcing orders from above—"that no mulato or black shall wear a sword
nor other arms" (*que ningun mulato ni negro truxese espada ni otras armas*) —and
to him Morales appeared to be of African descent. Yet this 1654 incident also
sounds distinctly unlike racial profiling. The witnesses Morales brought to
testify on his behalf placed great stress on his legitimacy, and Morales won
the case because he was found to be "the son of Spaniards and legitimate."[47]
This incident of racism was embedded in connected notions of descent, appearance, and (il)legitimacy, which we have yet to fully understand.[48]

Historicizing race as I have tried to do here is not to deny that long-term
continuities can be traced in racist practice; certainly they can. My point is
that upstreaming contemporary notions of race to interpret colonial racism
can lead us to gloss over the very dynamics of difference and discrimination

we most want to understand. If we neglect the importance of conversion, for example, then difference shows up much more clearly between African slaves and Andean tributaries than between Iberian Jews and Old Christians. Africans and Andeans may have had much more in common in certain historical circumstances than we think.[49] And Spaniards (a term often misleadingly used interchangeably with "white" in the historiography) may have had a lot *less* in common with one another than we think, even viewing each other as incomprehensible savages. Basques, for example, were regarded by other Spaniards as walking stereotypes, while other sixteenth-century Europeans considered Spaniards "the most mingled, most uncertayne and most bastardly."[50]

It is far easier, given the early and midcolonial sources, to see things in relatively elite, Castilian terms than in any others.[51] We can too easily forget that our sources tell us only a certain part of much more complex histories. And obviously I am telling a very lopsided story here, if we think of the many terms native Americans, Africans, and their descendents must have used in sixteenth-century Cuzco and elsewhere for themselves and those who were attempting to rule them. Sometimes we can see these in colonial archives: for example, *puka kunka* ("red neck"), a term appearing in late eighteenth-century sources around the time of Túpac Amaru's rebellion, which seems to have been a common Quechua nickname for Spaniards.[52] What did the people whom the Spaniards lumped together as *indios, negros,* or *castas* call themselves in earlier centuries, and what kinds of distinctions did they draw? These understandings have barely begun to be investigated.[53] Archival traces of them may be few, but the questions are richly worth asking.

PART III

DUTCH DESIGNS

CHAPTER ELEVEN

DISCIPLINE AND LOVE
Linschoten and the *Estado da Índia*

Carmen Nocentelli

The Portuguese empire is considerably less familiar to the general public than the Spanish one, but the Portuguese have their own "Black Legend," too, which is in some ways a counterpart to that of the Spanish — namely of political corruption.

— George D. Winius, *The Black Legend of Portuguese India*

It was almost a commonplace among late nineteenth-century scholars that the Portuguese empire in India had succumbed to internal malaise. Symptoms of decay had appeared as early as 1515, claimed Richard S. Whiteway in 1899, and in short order the entire *Estado da Índia* — as the Asian territories under Portuguese rule used to be called — had degenerated into "a thoroughly vicious system worked by men more vicious even than itself."[1] In less than a century, echoed William W. Hunter, "the intensely military spirit" of the early conquerors had given way to "a reaction of profligacy and sloth."[2] Orientalists of various stripes concurred that the Portuguese had only themselves to blame for this decline, as at its very root was their peculiar penchant for racial and cultural mixing. "Experience and stern facts condemn . . . [such mixing] as a most delusive and treacherous political day dream," wrote Sir Richard Burton in 1851. "It has lost the Portuguese almost everything in Africa as well as Asia. May Heaven preserve our rulers from following their example!"[3] Luckily for Burton, something more tangible than heaven stood in the way: Britain's alleged racial "purity" would hardly allow for a repeat of Portugal's experience. A people's tolerance for interracialism, Whiteway explained reassuringly, was in itself merely the result of mongrelization. By the time Portugal conquered Asia, he noted, ongoing relations with Africa had already introduced into Portugal "alien strands of blood," so that the idea of "half-caste colonies was not unfamiliar to that nation as it would have been to some others" (176). The "Black Legend" of Portuguese India thus turns out to be a story not so much of decadence and corruption as of Portuguese "blackness"—a way of explaining imperial decline by means of racial inferiority.

As much nineteenth-century historiography implicitly acknowledges, the Portuguese Black Legend finds a foundational moment in the late sixteenth century, when a Dutchman named Jan Huygen van Linschoten published an account of his travels through the *Estado da Índia*. In 1583, Linschoten had joined the retinue of João Vicente da Fonseca, newly appointed to the Archbishopric of Goa. After half a decade of faithful service, however, Fonseca's untimely demise shattered Linschoten's every hope for preferment. Suddenly, India no longer looked as attractive, and Holland beckoned: "God had opened mine eies," he would write in later years, "and by my Lords death made me more cleare of Sight, & to call my native soile unto remembrance."[4] Back in his native country, Linschoten found himself under the wing of learned naturalist Bernardus Paludanus (Berent ten Broecke). Together, the two began to set in writing all the observations and information Linschoten had amassed during his stay abroad; the end result was the *Itinerario, Voyage ofte Schipvaert van Jan Huygen van Linschoten naer Oost ofte Portugaels Indien* (Itinerary, voyage or passage by Jan Huygen van Linschoten to the East or Portuguese Indies). This was a work of monumental proportions comprising three distinct parts: the *Itinerario* proper, which covered customs, religions, commodities, and just about every aspect of Portuguese Asia that was conceivable at the time; the *Beschrijvinghe van de gantsche Custe van Guinea* (Description of the whole coast of Guinea), a general survey of the coasts of Africa and America largely derived from Duarte Lopes, Filippo Pigafetta, Peter Martyr, Gonzalo Fernández de Oviedo, and Jean de Léry; and the *Reys-gheschrift van de Navigatien der Portugaloysers in Orienten* (Travel account of the navigations of the Portuguese to the Orient), which described the routes used by Portuguese mariners in the East. The *Reys-gheschrift* was the first part of the *Itinerario* to appear in print, having been prepared in great haste to accompany Cornelis de Houtman on his first voyage to the East Indies; the finished work, finely illustrated and complete with topographical charts, was published by Cornelis Claeszoon in 1596.

An instant bestseller, the *Itinerario* spread briskly across Europe. Within three years, it had been translated into Latin, English, and German; French translations followed in 1610, 1619, and 1638. With several Dutch reprints issued between 1604 and 1644, the *Itinerario* was probably the most widely circulated source on Asia throughout the early modern period.[5] Its dissemination lifted the veil of secrecy behind which the Portuguese had so carefully hidden their colonial possessions, exposing them once and for all to the covetous eyes of northern Europe. In addition, the *Itinerario* revealed to readers that the Portuguese had lost much of their wonted prowess. It graphically described the lack of discipline and seamanship reigning aboard their vessels, depicted the dilapidated state of their defenses, and deplored their complete disregard for "the common profit or the service of the king" (I, 203). In short, it portrayed a colonial system that not only was manifestly incapable of further expansion but also showed clear signs of contraction.[6] "There is no more [countries] in India won or new found out, but rather heere and there some places lost," noted Linschoten in this regard, adding that the Portuguese had "enough to doe, to hold that they have alreadie, [and to defende it from invasion]" (I, 203–4).

Linschoten was not the first, nor was he alone, in decrying the weakening of Portugal's empire. Strikingly similar views can be found in many other early modern sources, from João de Barros's and Fernão Lopes de Castanheda's histories to political exposés such as Diogo do Couto's *O soldado prático* (The experienced soldier) and Francisco Rodrigues Silveira's *Reformação da milícia e governo do Estado da Índia Oriental* (Reform of the military and governance of the state of East India). In these and other works, the last quarter of the sixteenth century appears to be characterized, if not by an actual decadence, at least by the acute and generalized perception of a crisis. In a 1585 letter to a friend, the Florentine merchant Filippo Sassetti—who resided in India roughly at the same time as Linschoten—likened the Portuguese in Asia to crumbs left on the tablecloth after a meal, writing, "Every year there come from Portugal 2500 or 3000 men and boys, as wretched as they can be; a quarter, a third, and sometimes a half of them are cast into the sea; those who make it alive are set on land: death or knavery comes and gathers them all and for the most part they come to a bad end, except for a few nobles or others who . . . rise one way or another."[7] Sassetti's bleak assessment finds ample corroboration in the writings of Couto and Silveira, both of whom served in India as soldiers in the late sixteenth century. Couto, in particular, is as critical of the *Estado da Índia*—with its "Babylonian confusion" of corruption, depravity, and greed—as he is contemptuous of his countrymen, noting that where the Indians once called them "Franks" (*Frangues*)—the Arab name for crusaders—they now called them "chickens" (*frângãos*) instead.[8] As George D. Winius has noted, Couto does not expound on the causes of this transformation, but Silveira does: because the viceroys routinely embezzled funds and left the troops unpaid, soldiers often dodged service or refused to fight. Even when this was not the case, many of the soldiers disappeared anyway, either dying of disease and malnutrition or intermarrying and blending into the Indian population. In the meantime, colonial officials pocketed their pay and requested new levies of men to be sent from Portugal.[9]

If the *Itinerario* reflects a vision of Portuguese Asia in some respects very similar to Sassetti's, Couto's, and Silveira's, in other respects it is as unique as Linschoten's subject position. In the second half of the sixteenth century, most of the laymen who left Europe for India did so either to trade, like Sassetti, or to fight, like Couto and Silveira. Linschoten, however, was neither a merchant nor a soldier. Moreover, neither Sassetti's letters nor Couto's and Silveira's exposés had been intended for general consumption, whereas the *Itinerario* was developed with a large public audience in mind. In this light, the passages in which Linschoten draws attention to Asian regions as yet "not discovered, nor by the Inhabitants themselves [well] knowne" (I, 111) can be read like an open invitation, suggesting — as Pieter A. Tiele has proposed — "that an energetic rival would have every chance to supplant" the Iberians.[10]

As a result, during the heyday of Dutch imperialism Linschoten was hailed in several quarters as a national hero, a colonial trailblazer consciously paving the way for his countrymen to follow. It is certainly not a coincidence that the *Linschoten–Vereeniging* (Linschoten Society), the Dutch equivalent of the British Hakluyt Society, was named after him. Yet we should be wary of reducing the *Itinerario* to any narrow ideological framework or nationalist agenda. For one, the incessant religious dissensions, central power vacuums, and frequent territorial shifts that beset the young Dutch Republic inevitably hindered the emergence of any defined sense of nationhood.[11] Moreover, the anti-Catholic sentiments that had animated and sustained the Dutch struggle for independence from Spain put people like Linschoten — who had been raised as a Catholic — in a particularly complex position.[12] Indeed, the *Itinerario* appears in many ways to be inflected less by a Dutch nationalist agenda than by the political tensions arising from the unification of the crowns of Spain and Portugal — and more specifically by Hapsburg attempts to reform the administration of Portuguese Asia "along lines more in keeping with Spanish precepts of empire."[13]

All the same, on his return from India Linschoten quickly renounced Catholicism and reneged loyalty to the Hapsburg crown, becoming a member of the Dutch Reformed Church and dedicating his work to staunchly Protestant, fiercely anti-Spanish authorities.[14] While this turnabout makes certain aspects of the *Itinerario* — such as Linschoten's admiration for the Spaniards or his self-identification as a citizen of Catholic Haarlem — rather puzzling, it may help explain certain sensibilities of the text, such as its rad-

ical ethic of social discipline and its program of voluntary subjugation of individual will to the common good.

HYBRIDITY AND DECADENCE

Chroniclers, merchants, and missionaries concerned with the seeming decadence of the *Estado da Índia* found in the "decline literature" of antiquity a
ready mold in which to cast their observations. The enervating power of the
"Orient" was already a trope in the Hellenistic and Roman republican periods. From 33 B.C. onward, Octavian's propaganda campaign against Antony
and Cleopatra exploited and further consolidated the existing prejudice,
crystallizing once and for all the stereotype of a lascivious and emasculating
East.[15] By the end of the first century A.D., the contraposition between East
and West was so familiar that the poet Statius could put the trope to new use,
turning imperviousness to Oriental pleasures into an index of moral fiber.[16]
Building on this tradition, early modern sources suggest that the *Estado da
Índia* was pushed to the brink of moral bankruptcy by overpowering Oriental influences. The "constant commerce with nations who have no knowledge
of the true God," remarked the Jesuit Giovanni Pietro Maffei, "has made it
easier for Europeans to learn each day some part of Asian lechery than teach
the natives any part of Christian sanctity and severity. To this corruption of
mores must be added the nature of the land . . . [which] extinguishes all martial vigor with the charms of leisure and the lure of pleasure."[17]

The *Itinerario* likewise connects the situation of the *Estado da Índia* with the
progressive entanglement of European settlers in Indian life. It tells how
the Portuguese have taken up the custom of the country, wearing lightweight
and colorful garments "so fine that you may see al their body through it" (I,
206), surrounding themselves with droves of slaves (I, 193), adopting local
diet and table manners—including the contemptible habit of eating everything "with their handes" (I, 207)—and incorporating local customs in virtually every aspect of their daily lives. Immigrants bound for India, noted a
French seventeenth-century traveler, threw their spoons overboard as soon
as they passed the Cape of Good Hope to symbolize their renunciation of
European manners and values.[18] While reports of this kind may well be metaphorical, they indicate the emergence of a "contact zone" culture marked by
reciprocal if highly asymmetrical exchanges.[19] Just as Portuguese values and
customs seeped into native Asia, Asian values and customs spread through
the *Estado da Índia*, giving rise to a repertoire of hybrid practices that sharply
distinguished the Portuguese in India from those at home.

Judging from contemporary accounts, one of the most ubiquitous—and perhaps most troublesome—signs of this hybridity was the portable litter or palanquin. According to the *Itinerario*, palanquins were preferred implements throughout Portuguese India, where they functioned both as vehicles of transportation and items of display. They served men and women alike and formed an integral part of the ceremonial processions that accompanied most special occasions (I, 196–98). Writing some time after his return to Florence in 1606, the Italian merchant Francesco Carletti described palanquins as sedans in which passengers sat "with the thighs and legs extended, as if on a bed, with cushions at the back and rugs beneath."[20] Linschoten did not provide glosses of any kind, yet the palanquin is one of the material objects most conspicuous in his account, being frequently mentioned and figuring in no less than five engravings.

Linschoten's fascination with the palanquin can perhaps be better appreciated in the context of the discourse that had been developing around it since the early sixteenth century. As an *object*—one made of this or that material, more or less ornate, carried by two or more bearers—the palanquin had been known in Europe for a long time, having been mentioned by Franciscan friar Giovanni de' Marignolli as early as the fourteenth century. As a *word*, however, it came to be known only in the sixteenth century, when the noun *palanquim*—a new coinage obtained by tacking a characteristic Portuguese nasal onto the East Indian vernacular *pālankī*—was imported from the contact zone.[21] The diffusion of this noun from about 1515 onward indicates a level of contact between colonizers and colonized sufficient for part of the latter's vernacular to make its way into the former's active vocabulary. In this sense, the Portuguese *palanquim* is literally a creation of the contact zone, where the vehicle itself came to define a dangerous site of hybridity. During the process of European expansion, the portable litter had come to be associated with weakness and effeminacy always implicitly opposed to the vigor and masculinity of the European conquerors. Martín Fernández de Figueroa, who served in various parts of the Portuguese Indies under Francisco de Almeida and Afonso de Albuquerque, reported with grim relish the death of a native lord who reached the battleground "in a fancy litter, like a lady." "This effeminate behavior"—Figueroa remarked—"seemed bad to everyone" and was certainly "a thing to be condemned in knights, for in courtly circles only honest love is to be permitted."[22]

Cultural prejudice notwithstanding, the palanquin spread rapidly among Portuguese settlers, soon replacing the horse and inviting scrutiny from colonial authorities. In 1591, a viceregal proclamation restricted use of the palanquin to persons "over 60 years of age," establishing stiff penalties for those who contravened: the vehicle and its belongings would be forfeited, a fine exacted, and the bearers condemned to the galleys.[23] In 1606, an ecclesiastical council declared the covered palanquin "prejudicial to the morality of the state," threatened excommunication on the clergy who used it, and urged the viceroy to prohibit it altogether.[24] All these prohibitions, however, achieved meager results, for when Roman aristocrat Pietro della Valle (1586–1652) visited the Malabar coast in 1623, he complained that even though in the territories of Portuguese India men were forbidden "to travel in palanquin, *as in good sooth too effeminate a proceeding,*" the prohibition was routinely ignored.[25]

The repeated, if ineffectual, attempts to curtail its diffusion suggest that the palanquin came to function both as a synecdoche for hybridity and a metaphor for the vulnerable instability of Western cultural identity. In a plate depicting how Portuguese men "cause themselves to be carried in Palamkins" (I, 205), for instance, Asian implements and objects are not merely juxtaposed to European ones, but dramatically shown to predominate (fig. 11.1). Placed squarely at the center of the composition, and defining its principal axes, palanquin and parasol cage and compress the reclining Portuguese, forcing him into a semifetal position. Within this grand but confined setting, even the sword and the hat, European articles denoting both racial and social standing, seem oddly out of place. Rather than on the man's head, the broad-brimmed hat sits on his lap, while the unsheathed sword rests awkwardly against his chest. The overall effect is one of weakness and enervation, markedly at odds with the power and vitality of the surrounding environment.

The fact that palanquins could be easily covered, thereby hiding the passenger from view, certainly did not make their use any more palatable. By allowing passengers to see without being seen, palanquins resisted the gaze of colonial authorities and inverted the "normal" asymmetries of power. The profound anxieties that this opaque mobility aroused are simultaneously revealed and deflected in contemporary records by reference to illicit desire: Francesco Carletti, for instance, noted that women found in the palanquin "a good mean" (*buono mezzano*)[26] to go about unseen and unrecognized, especially when they went "to visit men" (182). This characterization of the palanquin as a "mean" or go-between is in many ways paradigmatic of a more general anxiety concerning the evasive fluidity of the contact zone. At a time when statutory identity and geographical fixity were thought of as essential prerequisites of order, the mobility that palanquins afforded was regarded as promiscuous and the palanquin itself conceptualized as the site of a forbidden circulation of peoples, artifacts, and practices.

11.1 *Portuguese gentleman in a palanquin,* from Jan Huygen van Linschoten's *Itinerario.*
    Shaded by a parasol and surrounded by a large retinue of servants and slaves, the Por-
    tuguese man holds in his hands, as social and racial markers, a sword and a hat. The
    juxtaposition of these Western identifiers with the palanquin and the parasol indicates
    the cultural mixing that obtained in the contact zone. Courtesy of the John Carter
    Brown Library at Brown University.

DEGENERACY AND MISCEGENATION

While linking the decline of the *Estado da Índia* to a blurring of ethnoracial
distinctions, the *Itinerario* locates a crucial moment of such blurring in the
sexual traffic between European men and Asian women. Keeping erotic
desires in check seems to have been a major problem for the Europeans in
India, so much so that the apostolate of Francis Xavier and other Jesuit missionaries was partly devoted to the mission, as Ines G. Županov has observed, "of bringing back to the righteous path those Europeans whose souls
and bodies were imperiled by the Oriental environment." Almost every aspect of life in Asia seemed to conspire against moral purity and erotic restraint: writing from Japan in 1580, the Jesuit Alessandro Valignano blamed

the heat, the spicy diet, the "dishonest clothes," and the lax morality of native women for the loss of European virtue in the East.[27]

Clearly enraptured by the women of Portuguese India, Carletti devoted a long section of his *Ragionamenti* to their charms. Indeed, he confessed, it would be impossible for him to explain "how amorous, courteous, attractive, and clean" they really are "except by saying that in every way they lead all the women who have ever been or are endowed with similar graces, if not everywhere in the world, at least among those women whom I have seen and experienced in circumnavigating the whole world" (180). The passage turns the world into an erotic *Wunderkammer* where women of different nations and races are randomly juxtaposed, displaced from any proper context and ranked only according to the esthetic and libidinal pleasure they can afford the viewer. Carletti then invites the reader to share in this scopophilic exercise, dressing and undressing women in gauzes so fine and transparent that "one could say that they are naked from the waist up, and one sees all of the shoulders, the breasts, and the arms through the transparent bodice — and from the waist down one sees little less, as they display the outlines of the entire body" (181).

Passages of the *Itinerario* exhibit the same voyeuristic tendency, penetrating the walls of women's secluded quarters to disclose for the reader their virtually naked bodies. Within the house, Linschoten writes, women "goe bare headed with a wastcoate . . . that from their shoulders covereth [their] navels, and is so fine that you may see al their body through it, and downewardes they have nothing but a painted cloth wrapped thrée or foure times about [their] bodies" (I, 206). In the *Itinerario*, however, desire is never very far from derision: a few paragraphs later, Linschoten disparages Indian practices and ridicules the chewing of betel:

> The women are by nature very cleanelie and neat, as well in their houses as in apparell . . . they have a manner everie day to wash [themselves] all the body [over], from head to foote, and some times twyse [a day] . . . and as often as they ease themselves or make water, or [else] use the companie of their husbands, everie time they doe wash [themselves], were it a hundreth times a day and night: they are no great workers, but much delighted in swéet hearbs, and in perfumes and frankincense, and to rub their bodies and their foreheads with swéet sanders and such like woods . . . also the whole day long they [doe nothing, but sit and] chawe leaves [or hearbes], called Bettele, with chalke and a [certaine] fruit called Arrequa. . . . [T]hese 3 thinges they sit all the whole day chawing [in their mouthes], like oxen or kyne chawing the cud (I, 212–13).

The power of these female bodies to charm and seduce is acknowledged and then progressively obscured by an accumulation of suspect habits and inclinations. Even cleanness and tidiness figure, in this context, not as indexes of civility but rather as by-products of an idle, immoral existence. "The women are very luxurious and unchaste," claims the *Itinerario*, "for there are verie few among them, although they bee married, but they have besides their husbands one or two of those that are called souldiers, with whome they take their pleasures" (I, 209). The Portuguese have tried to curb their inordinate appetites by keeping them under lock and key: constantly guarded, women are rarely allowed in public, and then only if chaperoned and escorted. Within the home, they are segregated to separate quarters, where no man is allowed, no matter "howe néere kinsman [soever] he be unto them" (I, 209). Linschoten makes clear, however, that none of these measures has proven effective. Instead of enforcing chastity, segregation has compounded adultery with incest, for it is often the case "that the uncles sonne hath laine by his aunt, and the brother by the brothers wife, and the brother with his sister" (I, 209).

These sexual escapades present concrete risks for women: Portuguese law makes the murder of an adulteress a virtually negligible offense, and women too often lose their lives on the mere suspicion of inappropriate behavior. Yet, not even the fear of death can deter them from illicit liaisons; quite to the contrary, they hold that "there is no pleasanter death" than to die for love (II, 215). Bold and relentless in their evasion of domestic boundaries and custodial gazes, they do not hesitate to feed their husbands *datura* — a stupefying drug routinely associated with Indian licentiousness — so that in their presence "they may doe what they will" (I, 210).

It should be noted that Linschoten makes no distinction between "Indian" and "Portuguese" women, implying not only that conversion to Christianity has failed to curtail "Indian" lechery, but also that "Portuguese" women have found it easy to follow suit. A disquieting asymmetry is thereby revealed: the natives cannot be shorn of their innate ways by contact with the Europeans, yet the Europeans seem all too willing to "go native." As a group, the Portuguese residents of India are slowly but inexorably being obliterated, almost swallowed and absorbed into the very environment that — as conquerors and missionaries — they had deemed their mission to transform:

> The Portingales in India, are many of them marryed with the naturall borne women of the countrie, and the children procéeding of them are called Mesticos, that is, half countrimen. These Mesticos are commonlie of yelowish colour, notwithstanding there are manie women among them, that are faire and well formed. The children of the Portingales,

both boyes and gyrls, [which are] borne in India, are called Castisos, and are in all things like [unto] the Portingales, onely somewhat differing in colour, for they draw towards a yealow colour: the children of those Castisos are yealow, and altogether [like the] Mesticos, and the children of Mesticos are of colour and fashion like the naturall borne Countrimen . . . so that the posteritie of the Portingales, both men and women being in the third degrée, doe séeme to be naturall Indians, both in colour and fashion. (I, 183–84)

As scholars have pointed out, the most arresting feature of this passage is not the notion that through intermarriage the Portuguese "race" is progressively phagocytosed and eventually erased, but rather the suggestion that such erasure may occur even in the absence of interracial mingling.[28] The *castiços*, who are born in India of Portuguese parents, already "draw toward a yealow colour." Their children are indistinguishable from the *mestiços*, even though not a single drop of native blood may run through their veins.[29] In twinning the intimately linked fears of degeneracy and miscegenation, the *Itinerario* seems to anticipate central features of later eugenics discourse, according to which acquired cultural characteristics were as inheritable as skin color.

The racial mixing observed by Linschoten in late sixteenth-century Goa was partially the result of earlier colonial policies. During the first decades of expansion, the Portuguese Crown had not only condoned but actively encouraged interethnic unions by restricting emigration of European women and by providing financial incentives to mixed couples willing to tie the knot. Despite occasional shipments of "pure" Portuguese blood in the form of female orphans (known as "orfas-del-Rey"), intermarriage remained the rule rather than the exception throughout the seventeenth century and well into the eighteenth.[30] This does not mean, of course, that intermarriage was uniformly accepted; rather, it suggests that concerns about "purity of blood" were at least temporarily subordinated to the pragmatics of rule. Mixed marriages, in fact, were held to consolidate colonial penetration and promote conversion to Christianity, producing offspring that would bolster demographic and economic growth.

The *Itinerario*, however, paints a rather bleak picture of the results that intermarriage practices have achieved. Rather than assimilate the natives to European customs and values, mixed marriages have "Orientalized" the Portuguese, thus destroying them as a separate group. The lethal effects of such interbreeding find in the *Itinerario* a corporeal equivalent in the "bloody flixe" (dysentery), a primary cause of mortality among European colonists. The reason why so many of the settlers contract dysentery, Linschoten explains, is that they "use much company of women because ye land is naturall to provoke them therunto . . . for although men were of iron or stéele, the unchaste [life] of [a] woman, with her unsatiable lustes were able to grinde him to powder, and swéep him away like dust" (I, 236–37). This association between sex and dysentery is, as Ivo Kamps has remarked, a "disturbingly appropriate" one, for it precisely mirrors the moral situation of the *Estado da Índia*. While the disease can be seen as a metaphor for the socially and psychologically destabilizing effects of uncontrolled sexual appetites, the diarrhea that is symptomatic of it ominously forecasts the liquefaction of the Portuguese body politic.[31] By associating dysenteric bodies and cultural hybridity, personal conduct and race survival, management of desire and imperial rule, Linschoten's text highlights the risks that a lack of self-discipline may pose to the body politic.

In this perspective, the *Itinerario* is as much about the definition of a bourgeois sexuality triangulated by "degenerated" Europeans, mixed-bloods, and native others as it is about the failures of Portuguese India. For if the text explicitly disparages Asian and Eurasian women for their idleness, it does not spare the European settlers: "The Portingales . . . in India never worke," Linschoten notes, underscoring their indolent and ostentatious lifestyle (I, 187). And if the *Itinerario* makes no qualms about women's unruly sexuality, it also shows that Portuguese men are likewise unable to restrain their libidos. It depicts marriage ceremonies in India, for instance, as elaborate but brief affairs that often end with the bride and groom rushing to consummate at least "two houres before Sunne setting, not having the patience to stay so long as [we do] in these countries" (I, 198).

Although the Portuguese are the most immediate European target of Linschoten's critique, the *Itinerario* indicates that lack of discipline and scarce restraint were by no means problems confined to the Portuguese alone. Nowhere are the fatal effects of moral weakness more minutely illustrated than in the cautionary tale of Flemish diamond-polisher Frans Coningh (Francis King), his Eurasian wife, and her Portuguese lover. We first encounter the young Flemish jeweler as an apprentice merchant in Syria, where he immediately proves to be less adept at trading than at squandering his family fortune. Hoping to recoup his losses, he moves farther and farther away from home and deeper into Portuguese Asia. "Being young and without government" and "seeing himselfe so far distant" from his family, he once again throws thrift, prudence, and responsibility to the wind, "taking no other care, but onlie to [be merrie and] make good cheare so long, till in the end the whole stock was almost clean [spent and] consumed" (II, 205–6). Unable to repay his debts and unwilling to face the consequences of his actions, he de-

11.2 *The murder of Frans Coningh,* as depicted in Johann Theodor and Johann Israel
de Bry's *Tertia Pars Indiae Orientalis* (1601). In the upper left corner, Coningh's
unnamed wife and her lover, Antonio Fragoso, stab the Flemish jeweler as he lies
unconscious in his bed. In the lower right corner, the fateful couple flees with the
victim's valuables. Courtesy of the Newberry Library.

cides never to return home. While understandable—insolvency and bankruptcy were "sins" for which the Reformed Church reserved particularly
harsh punishment—this decision marks Coningh's ultimate fall from grace.
He marries a beautiful but wicked *mestiça* who cuckolds him for years, drugs
him with *datura,* and eventually murders him with the help of her Portuguese
lover (fig. 11.2).

Linschoten explains that he has set the story "downe at large, that hereby
men may the better perceyve the boldnesse and [filthie] lecherous mindes of
the Indian women, which are commonly all of one nature and disposition"
(II, 204). Yet the pedagogical thrust of the *exemplum* seems concerned less
with the lechery of Indian women than with establishing a causal connection
between Coningh's misfortunes and his moral shortcomings. Well before being betrayed by his wife and the man he considers his best friend, Coningh

is betrayed by his own "lack of government," that is, by his inability to perceive the limits of liberty and resist the temptations of lust and leisure. While idleness, dissipation, lewdness — in short, the low instincts of the body — were regarded in Europe as serious threats to the well-being of the body politic, they were even more dangerous in the periphery, where increased distance from the source of authority allowed European travelers and colonists the possibility of "forgetting themselves," neglecting their social and familial obligations, or even "betraying" their "true" cultural identity. Only a constant vigilance of the self could protect Europeans against the dangers of foreign enticement.

DOCILE BODIES, DISCIPLINED SELVES

Although Linschoten never ventured farther east than India, he included in his work information on Sumatra, Java, the Moluccas, China, and Japan. In the three chapters devoted to China, which are mostly derived from Juan González de Mendoza's *Historia de las cosas mas notables, ritos y costumbres del gran reyno de la China* (1585), the *Itinerario* enthusiastically describes an industrious and orderly nation in many ways resembling "the ancient Grecians and Romans" (I, 143). Education is so highly valued that no man is "estéemed or accounted of, for his birth, family or riches, but onely for his learning and knowledge" (I, 133); idleness is unknown, and no one is allowed to "travaile through the Country to begge" (I, 135). "Printing, painting, and gun-powder, with the furniture thereto belonging, have béene used in China many hundreth yeares past, and very common, so that it is with them out of memorie when they first began" (I, 142). In their mores and customs, in short, the Chinese rival and even surpass the most advanced of European societies.

Interestingly enough, the first chapter of this panegyric ends with a brief description of Chinese women: "The women goe verie richly apparelled . . . and estéeme it for a great beautifying [unto them] to have small féete, to the which end they use to binde their féete so fast when they are young, that they cannot grow to the full, whereby they can hardly goe, but in a manner halfe lame. Which custome the men have brought up, to let them from much going, for that they are verie jealous, and unmeasurable leacherous and unchast, yet is it estéemed a beautifying and comlinesse for the women" (I, 136–37). Here the *Itinerario* espouses a view already expressed by Mendoza, according to whom the practice of foot binding had been devised by men as a means of ensuring women's chastity. Far from inspiring revulsion, the custom of compressing women's feet so that they could hardly walk or stand was met by European commentators with almost unanimous admiration: indeed, given

11.3 Dress of the people of China, "a kingdom overflowing with all beauty and sumptuousness." From Sinschoteu's *Itinerario*. Courtesy of the John Carter Brown Library at Brown University.

the generalized association between women's mobility and unruly sexuality, foot binding was regarded as one of China's strong points. The German jurist Samuel von Pufendorf, for instance, referred to the practice with approbation,[32] and the Dominican friar Domingo Fernández Navarrete went so far as to propose that other countries would be well advised to follow suit: "The custom of swathing women's feet is very good for keeping females at home. It were no small benefit to them and their menfolk if it were also practised everywhere else too, not only in China."[33] In the specific case of the *Itinerario*, the Chinese practice of foot binding appears as one of several techniques of governance that mark the country as "civilized." Foot binding in fact ensures female chastity without spectacular violence or the threat of punishment; rather, it "corrects" women's errant desire by disciplining their bodies—and subjects both to the demands of the patriarchal state (fig. 11.3).

If the *Itinerario* places the Chinese clearly at the top of a hierarchy of Asian civility, Indian Brahmans—"the honestest and most estéemed nation amonge

[all] the Indian heathens" (I, 247)—are not too far behind:[34] skillful and sharp witted, they hold the most prestigious offices and enjoy such high regard that "the King doth nothing without their counsell and consent" (I, 247). They also serve as priests in Hindu temples and are venerated by the common people as prophets (I, 248). At this point, in a manner that is consistent with most contemporary European accounts about India, Linschoten relates in some detail the ceremony that takes place when a Brahman dies: friends and relatives build a pyre and place the corpse on it, singing songs of praise. Meanwhile, the widow distributes her worldly possessions among her friends and is exhorted to join her husband in death. She then throws herself willingly into the fire, where she is quickly consumed: "cometh his wife with Musike and [many of] her néerest frends, all singing certain prayses in commendation of her husbands life, putting her in comfort, and encouraging her to follow her husband, and goe with him into the other world. Then she taketh [al] her Jewels, and parteth them among her frends, and so with a chéerefull countenance, she leapeth into the fire, and is presently covered with wood and oyle: so she is quickly dead, and with her husbands bodie burned to ashes" (I, 249).

At first glance, Linschoten's description of *sati*—as *sahagamana* (Sanskrit for "keeping company") or widow sacrifice has come to be known in English since the eighteenth century—seems to ascribe to Brahman women a singular wifely devotion. Indeed, most sixteenth- and seventeenth-century commentators extolled *sati* in order to admonish, implicitly or explicitly, their readership. The Portuguese captain Antonio Galvão, for instance, mentioned *sati* as one of the reasons why Asian women "are very praiseworthy and exemplary for us."[35] Initially, Linschoten appears to be of a similar mind as Galvão, proposing *sati* as a striking counterpoint to the unbridled sexuality of the wives of the Portuguese. Soon, however, his account of *sati* takes an unexpected turn. Apparently in the attempt to explain the historical origin of the practice, the *Itinerario* evokes a distant past in which women's anarchic body natural had threatened the survival of the body politic: "The [first] cause . . . why the women are burnt with their husbandes, was (as the Indians themselves do say) that in time past, the women (as they are very leacherous and inconstant both by nature, and complexion) did poyson many of their husbands . . . thereby to have the better means to fulfill their lusts. Which the King perceiving . . . he made a law and ordayned, that when the dead bodies of men were buried, they shold also burne their wives with them, thereby to put them in feare, and so make them abstaine from poysoning of their husbands" (I, 251). The seemingly innocent parenthetical interpolation "as the Indians themselves do say" buttresses the power of received classical tradition with Linschoten's own authority as an ethnographical observer, precipitating Brahman wives into a bygone time in which they too were as lustful, deceitful, and murderous as their counterparts in Portuguese settlements.[36] Linschoten's etiology of *sahagamana* creates in this manner an Indian past that precisely mirrors the present of Portuguese Asia. Far from demonstrating an uncommon wifely devotion, *sati* reveals itself as an Indian version of Chinese foot binding: namely, a creation of the state intent on curbing and controlling the anarchy that threatens it from within.

As I have shown, the *Itinerario* goes to great lengths to underscore both the aberrant sexuality of Asian women and the threat it poses to the preservation of the *Estado da Índia.* Yet Linschoten also shows that neither the strategies of containment adopted by the colonists nor the regime of violence established by them have achieved results comparable to those obtained by the Chinese or the Brahmans. The Portuguese may segregate women in the innermost recesses of their homes, yet nearly all of these women have secret trysts, "which to effect, they use al the slights and practises [they can devise, by] sending out their slaves and baudes by night, and at extraordinary times, over walles, hedges, and ditches, how narrowlie [soever] they are kept [and looked unto]" (I, 209). Adulteresses may very well die at the hands of their husbands, yet no fear of retribution can deter them from taking "their filthie pleasures" (I, 212). Quite to the contrary, they insist that "there can be no better death, than to die in that manner, saying that so they are sacrificed for love, which they thinke to be a great honour [unto them]" (I, 212).

This is not the context to assess either the veracity of this affirmation or the possibility that Indian widows—for their part—may have actually faced *sahagamana* cheerfully. It will suffice, for the moment, to indicate that the two statements are intimately connected: the enshrinement of *sati* from "law" into custom is made possible, in fact, by the alleged inclination of Indian women toward love and sacrifice. In this perspective, *sati* is not an act of violence but an act of will—Brahman women "choose" to die on their husbands' pyres just as the wives of the Portuguese "choose" to sacrifice themselves for adulterous love. The substantial difference between the two lies in the *kind* of will that propels the action: in the case of the Brahman women, it is a will that has been "educated" and directed toward the preservation of the state (fig. 11.4).

I have dwelled on Linschoten's etiology and treatment of *sati* and foot binding to illustrate how the *Itinerario* constructs both practices as customs or traditions, and these, in turn, as *dressage* techniques that have in subjectivity their primary instrument and effect. In this respect, Chinese foot binding and Indian widow burning are training procedures that supersede mere

Brumenes cum mortuus est, fecundum corum legem crematur, uxor autem ejus, præ amore, fese vivam in ignem cum illo conjicit.

De Brumene doot wefende wort nae haer wet verbrant, en zyn vrouwe wt liefde haers mans, verbrant haer levendich met hem.

58 10 59

11.4 *Widow-burning* from Linschoten's *Itinerario*. Courtesy of the John Carter Brown Library at Brown University.

repression: they construct subjectivities that may discover anew the meaning of authority in their immanent freedom. External compulsion disap-
pears, remaining visible in discourse only as a vestige of the past, an original
"law" that no longer needs to be enforced. Contestable as it may be, this model
allows us to identify the intimate connection between the excessive, anarchic
sexuality of the women of Portuguese India and the normalized, productive
conjugal sexuality of Chinese and Brahman women. These mutually constituted polarities are essentially effects of the same discourse and define the
limits within which Europe came not only to imagine and represent Asia but
to imagine and represent *itself* in relation to Asia.

As we have seen, the *Itinerario* provides a rather unflattering portrait of the
Europeans in Asia. The failures of the *Estado da Índia* become even more blatant when placed side by side with the orderly and wealthy Chinese empire,
or when the oversexed women of Portuguese Asia are juxtaposed to foot-

bound Chinese women and loyal Brahman widows. The *Itinerario* suggests, however, that Europeans may have at their disposal a unique discursive instrument to represent the Orient and their own place in it — that of romance. In 1584, recounts Linschoten, there arrived in Goa the "queen of Ormus," a "faire white woman" who had married a Portuguese gentleman. Muslim by birth, she had come to India to be baptized. The conversion of elite figures was a prized objective of missionary activity, so the baptism of this personage would have received ample publicity. Yet the *Itinerario* turns the account of the queen's baptism into a full-fledged romance that is worth quoting in detail:

> At the same time the Queene of Ormus came to Goa, being of Mahomets religion, as all her auncesters had beene before her, and as then were contributarie to the Portingall. She caused her selfe to be christened, and was with great solemnitie brought into the Towne, where the Viceroy was her Godfather, and named her Donna Phillippa, after the King of Spaines name, being a faire white woman, very tall [and comely,] and with her likewise a brother of hers, being [verie] young, was also christened, and then with [one] Mathias Dalbuquerck that had been Captain of Ormus, she sailed to Portingall, to present her selfe to the king. She had married with a Portingall Gentleman called Anton. Dazeuedo Coutinho, to whome the king in regarde of his mariage gave the Captaineshippe of Ormus, which is worth above two hundred thousande duckets. . . . This Gentleman after hee had beene maried to the Queene about halfe a yeare, living very friendly and lovingly with her, hee caused a shippe to bee made, therewith to saile to Ormus, there to take order for the rentes and revenewes belonging to the Queene his wife: but his departure was so grievous unto her, that she desired him to take her with him, saying, that without him she could not live: but because he thought it not as then convenient, hee desired her to be content, promising to returne againe with all the speede he might. Whereuppon hee went to Bardes . . . about three myles off: and while hee continued there, staying for winde and weather, the Queene (as it is saide) tooke so great greefe for his departure, that she dyed, the same day that her husbande set saile and put to sea, to the great admiration of all the Countrey, and no lesse sorrowe, because shee was the first Queene in those countries that had beene christened, forsaking her kingdome and high estate, rather to die a Christian, and married with a meane Gentleman, then to live like a Queene under the lawe of Mahomet, and so was buried with great honor according to her estate. (II, 187–88)

In this account, interracial love is placed at the center of a circuitous route through which the forcible nature of European expansion in Asia is elided and colonial relations are naturalized. By granting the captainship of Hormuz to Antonio D'Azevedo Coutinho in virtue of his marriage, as if it were a dowry, King Philip II assumes the role of the bride's father. This fictive genealogy sets the "queen of Ormus" apart from her people and cuts her loose from her origins. The operation works on two levels: on one hand, it turns the queen into an honorary European; on the other, it simultaneously legitimizes Western patriarchy and Portuguese rule in Asia. This strategy allows Linschoten to present the Portuguese acquisition of Hormuz—brought to its knees only after intense and bloody confrontations—as a royal gift. Resistance to Portuguese rule is thereby erased and the conquest recast as a peaceful power transfer between the honorary father of the bride and her prospective husband.

The powerful nexus between marriage and baptism that subtends Linschoten's narrative bespeaks the relevance of both in the project of social and psychological engineering of the *Itinerario*. Marriage in particular came to function as a key factor in a moral taxonomy that distinguished not only Christians from non-Christians but also "redeemable" from "unredeemable" others. We can now begin to understand the complex and profound implications of the "queen of Ormus" romance. Her baptism indeed marks the moment of a radical transformation, but a transformation that had already been effected by her marriage to Coutinho. Baptism comes therefore to sanction a preexisting situation, the transformation of an eastern queen into "donna Phillippa," a bourgeois European wife. No longer a queen either in name or in practice, donna Phillippa relinquishes her public role to her new husband and withdraws into the domestic sphere; from now on, it will be her husband to act and speak for her or, as Linschoten puts it, "to take order for the rentes and revenewes" on her behalf. The *Itinerario* thus turns heterosexual love into a uniquely European *dressage* technique, one that precedes and in a sense replaces conversion to Christianity as an instrument for creating new colonial subjectivities. By encoding romantic love as an adequate compensation for powerlessness and objectification, the *Itinerario* legitimizes Western rule over a submissive and feminized Asia while offering symbolic relief from the political and economic disruption resulting from it. In doing so, it speaks to prospective European colonists as well as their wives, sisters, and daughters, instructing the latter in their true mission within patriarchy and depicting for the former the possible rewards that some—those endowed with the necessary self-restraint and the appropriate moral qualities—may derive from the Orient.

CHAPTER TWELVE

REREADING THEODORE DE BRY'S
BLACK LEGEND

Patricia Gravatt

Theodore de Bry's images of the New World, engravings that appear in
a six-volume collection of his work titled *America*, are so striking that for
many critics of the twentieth century they are more than simple illustrations;
they are Protestant propaganda.[1] According to these critics, de Bry, because
he is Flemish and Protestant, promotes the imperialism of the countries of
northern Europe and denounces the monopoly of Spanish Catholic colonization. Thus, they reason, his Indians are represented as innocent, peaceful, and helpless in order both to convince colonists to go the New World and
to emphasize the unjustifiable cruelty of the Spaniards.

If we add that de Bry publishes only Protestant texts or texts translated
by Protestants we could believe that de Bry's collection is one of the pillars
of the Black Legend.[2] However, when we read the prefaces written by de
Bry, we discover that his representation of the New World is more complex
than mere propaganda. The prefaces of the first five volumes of the collection (the sixth volume does not have a preface) throw a new light on his images and show that the engraver is more a Protestant philosopher than one
of the creators of the Black Legend. According to these prefaces, the Indians
are neither noble savages, serving as substitutes for persecuted Protestants,
nor reprobates, eternally cursed by God.[3] They are represented as human
beings with particular customs but with the same nature as other human beings. The Spaniards are not shown only as stereotypes of evil colonizers because they are Catholic and Spanish; they are also shown as human beings,
prisoners of their own greed, or idolatry, if we use de Bry's vocabulary. De
Bry's readers are European, educated people and collectors, perhaps merchants but also members of the bourgeoisie interested in the adventures of
the New World. They are presumably Protestant but not shown as the chosen, saved and without sins and thus entitled to judge others and to colonize

and evangelize the Indians. Rather, they are human beings who should learn lessons from the New World. In his prefaces, de Bry does not portray things in black and white. Neither does he project onto the New World the suffering of the Protestants. Rather, he sees the New World as a sort of mirror, a means of self-reflection, for the Europeans, who might thus examine their own nature.

DE BRY'S COLLECTION AS A PILLAR OF THE BLACK LEGEND

We know little about de Bry's life, but some elements could convince us that the engraver is anti-Spanish and anti-Catholic because he suffered personally from the Spaniards. He was born in Liège, Belgium, in 1528. He studied engraving at the academy of architecture, painting, and engraving founded by Lambert Lombard (1505–1565), a humanist artist, in Liège. This academy was renowned for its new ideas in art and religion. Lombard adhered to the theses of Luther, and de Bry seems to have converted to Protestantism while he was studying at the academy. In 1560, de Bry was in Strasbourg, where he married Catharina Esslinger. One year later, his first son, Jean-Theodore, was born there.[4] After Strasbourg, de Bry settled in Frankfurt, where he became a bookseller and a publisher. Early in his life he is ruined and writes, "I was the offspring of parents born to an honorable station, and was in affluent circumstances and in the first rank of the more honored inhabitants of Liège. But stripped of all these belongings by the accidents, cheats, and ill terms of fortune, and by the attacks of robbers, I had to contend against such adverse chance that only by my art could I fend for myself. Art alone remained to me of the ample patrimony left me by my parents. On that neither robbers nor rapacious thieves could lay hands. Art restored my former wealth and reputation and has never failed me, its unwearied devotee."[5]

The facts that de Bry is ruined and that he leaves Liège are often interpreted as being the result of religious persecutions and the origin of his presumed anti-Spanish sentiment. Stefan Lorant claims that de Bry is forced to flee Liège when "the Duke of Alba and his infamous Council of Blood was enforcing Phillip II's policy of ruthlessness against the Protestants in the Netherlands."[6] H. de Villenfagne affirms that de Bry is deprived of his wealth and banished from Liège in 1570 because he was part of a Lutheran sedition.[7] Yet there is no evidence that de Bry was obliged to leave Liège because of his religion and that he became the standard bearer of the Protestant cause.[8] First, almost all the students of Lombard's academy left their hometown and went to Brussels, Frankfurt, London, and Antwerp in order to practice and improve their art. Second, it is difficult to understand why de Bry would refer to the decisions of Catholic officials with expressions such as "accidents, cheats, and ill terms of fortune." Third, there is no record of a Lutheran sedition in 1570 in Liège. Finally, de Bry was no longer in his hometown in 1570.

It is not until the years between 1590 and 1596 that de Bry published *America*. The idea for the first volume of the collection was suggested by the English publisher Richard Haklyut. It consists of Thomas Harriot's account entitled *A Brief and True Report of the New Found Land of Virginia, directed to the investors, farmers and well wishers of the project of colonizing and planting there*, together with engravings of John White's drawings made in Virginia. The second volume, published in 1591, was also Hakluyt's idea. It consists of the diary written by the French Protestant Jacques Le Moyne de Morgues, who participated in the French expedition to Florida under Laudonnière in 1564, together with engravings of his watercolors of Floridians. In 1592, the third volume was published. It consists of passages of the *True History of his captivity* written by the German Protestant Hans Staden and passages of the French Calvinist Jean de Léry's *Histoire d'un voyage faict en la terre du Brésil*, together with engravings of woodcuts published in Staden's and Léry's works. Published between 1594 and 1596, the last three volumes were an edition of the Italian traveler Girolamo Benzoni's *Historia del Mondo Nuovo*, translated into Latin with commentary by the French Calvinist Urbain Chauveton. De Bry elaborates the woodcuts published in Benzoni's book and invents new ones.

While the first two volumes promote Protestant settlements in the New World, the third volume describes the culture of the cannibals. Only the last three volumes appear as an indictment of Spanish colonization, where the savagery of the Indians is eclipsed by the fierce barbarity of the Spaniards. Does this mean that de Bry's collection is a "machine de guerre," as Frank Lestringant puts it?[9]

THE POWER OF THE IMAGES

The first volumes show noble savages living in a golden age, ready to accept the presence of English or French Protestants among themselves. The last volumes show many innocent and helpless Indians who are victims of the barbarity of the Spaniards. In the first volume of the collection, de Bry shows portraits of Virginians, their manner of making boats, fishing, eating, their religion, and their dwellings. When we look at the portraits of a chieftain (fig. 12.1)[10] and a chief lady (fig. 12.2),[11] we note that de Bry uses a classical canon of proportion and body type. The anatomy reminds us of classical gods or heroes and the nudity seems to express the natural and innocent beauty of the creatures that lived in that golden age.[12] The backgrounds of these portraits, which show scenes of hunting and fishing, suggest both the benevolence of nature and a happy communal life. In the second volume, the Floridians are as handsome and well proportioned as the Virginians. Their life is depicted as being close to nature and happy, even though fourteen images out of forty-two represent wars and violence. Among the images of a happy life is "Storing their crops in the public granary" (fig. 12.3).[13] In the foreground, a group of men and women is carrying home fruits and vegetables in a canoe. Men are rowing elegantly. Their bodies are comparable to those of athletes. Women, with Venus-like hair, are seated comfortably in the rear and speak to each other. The water is calm and the canoe seems to move easily. In the background, we see a pleasant landscape, a granary on the riverbank and two other canoes. The composition and details of the image tell us about the abundance of nature and provide a portrait of well-organized and peaceful communal life. In the caption we read, "There [in the granary] the Indians store everything they wish to preserve, and there they go for supplies whenever they need anything—no one fears being cheated. Indeed, it would be good if among Christians there were as little greed to torment men's minds and hearts." This caption emphasizes harmony. The Floridians, living close to nature, are superior to the Christians in the sense that the latter are greedy. Floridian life is based on respect and trust, qualities that even the Christians have forgotten. In the image entitled "Floridians crossing over to an island on a pleasure trip" (fig. 12.4),[14] we see another scene of happiness. The landscape suggests that there is no danger. The shore is close and features some flowers, and the water is clear, pure, and "running no more than breast high," as the caption says. The three swimmers seem to enjoy themselves, and the mother carefully carries her children, the youngest one safe on her shoulder. She also carries a basket of fruits for the trip. The man who is not swimming carries a bow and a quiver in case of danger. This group of people seems rather happy and well organized. Each person has his own task. The image gives a sense of pleasure and innocence. Such scenes are possible because the Floridians have a very well-organized society. They have not only a strong and wise social and political hierarchy but also experts in agriculture, hunting, and fishing.

The only flaw in this report is the religion practiced by the Floridians. Like the Virginians, the Floridians adore idols, but this fact does not entirely tarnish the idyllic spectacle. With the Brazilian cannibals of the third volume, however, the view of the golden age is tarnished because of cannibalism. The cannibals are still healthy and handsome and their culture offers some

12.1. Theodore de Bry, *Admiranda narratio fida tamen, de commodis et incolarum. Ritibus Virginiae*, Pl. 3. Engraving. 1590.

12.2. Theodore de Bry, *Admiranda narratio fida tamen, de commodis et incolarum. Ritibus Virginiae*, Pl. 4. Engraving. 1590.

12.3. Theodore de Bry, *Brevis narratio eorum quae in Florida Americae provincia Gallis acciderunt*, Pl. 22. Engraving. 1591.

12.4. Theodore de Bry, *Brevis narratio eorum quae in Florida Americae provincia Gallis acciderunt*, Pl. 27. Engraving. 1591.

12.5. Theodore de Bry, *Americae Tertia Pars*, Pl. 13. Engraving. 1592.

characteristics of the golden age, but they eat human flesh. Most of the images of this third volume display contradictions. In "How the slave who had spoken ill of me was himself eaten" (fig. 12.5),[15] de Bry represents the four stages of the cannibal ritual. In the background, we see the preparation of the prisoner. The man is in a hammock to suggest that before the day of his execution he is well treated. The day of the execution, a woman, perhaps the wife he has been given during his detention, takes him to the second scene: the ritual execution. In the foreground, two men are cutting up the dead body, the young woman who took the prisoner to his execution is kneeling to pick up an arm, and a child is washing the head in a pond. Finally, to close the spectacle in the middle of the image, there is the symbolic grill on which the woman cooks human body parts. There are remarkable oxymorons in this image: the calm atmosphere in contrast to the violence of cannibalism; the child, symbol of innocence carrying the head, symbol of horror; the grace of the young woman and her actions. These oxymorons suggest that the Brazilians are no longer noble savages living in a golden age, but neither are they

12.6. Theodore de Bry, *Americae Pars Quarta*, Pl. 18. Engraving. 1594.

totally barbarous. Their cannibalism is a cultural and ritual practice that maintains social integrity. It is a feast that gathers the whole community.[16]

In the last three volumes the idyllic America turns into a form of Hell in which the Spaniards play the role of devils and the Indians the role of victims. In the fourth volume, we see how the Spanish attack an Indian village (fig. 12.6).[17] Armed and violent Spanish soldiers are killing unarmed and vulnerable victims who do not offer any resistance. The Spaniards have the situation under control. On the right, a fire traps the Indians, and those who can escape are killed by the Spaniards who are outside the stockade. On the left, soldiers rush in with their weapons and shoot in the direction of the village. In the foreground, the stockade surrounding the huts is destroyed, giving the Spaniards the opportunity to enter the village and to kill the men. Soldiers use swords, spears, or harquebus, and their gestures suggest cruelty. The violence of the Spaniards is emphasized by the fact that the Indians do not try to defend themselves. In the part of the village that is not yet invaded, we see the distress of the women and children who know that their death is

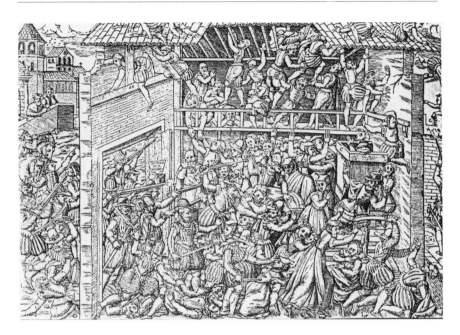

12.7. Tortorel and Perrissin, « Le massacre de Vassy ». *Quarante Tableaux*. Engraving. 1570.

near. Some of the women and children run and raise their arms, others are motionless, but all suggest helplessness.

Similar Catholic violence, of course, transpired elsewhere in the world. The situation and the emphasis on women and children are reminiscent of the representation of the massacre of Vassy depicted by two Protestant artists, Jacques Tortorel and Jean Perrissin (fig. 12.7).[18] The image represents the massacre by the Duke of Guise of a group of Protestants who are attending a service in a barn. The scene is densely packed and shows confusion. In the foreground, the soldiers rush into the barn with swords and firearms. They kill men, women, and children. On the floor, we see dead bodies. The emphasis is put on the violence toward women and children. In the middle, a soldier runs a woman through with a sword. Behind her, another woman kneels and prays, with her child embracing her, before being murdered. On the right, two women clasp their children to themselves. In the background, the minister is praying in the pulpit and many people are massed against the wall waiting for their death. They look frightened and helpless. Some men try to escape through the roof but the Catholics shoot them. The Protestants, like the Indians, are presented as innocent victims of the violence of furi-

12.8. Theodore de Bry, *Americae Pars Quarta,* Pl. 22. Engraving. 1594.

ous armed people who have decided to kill everybody. The massacres of the
Indians in the New World would clearly have recalled for Protestant readers
these very similar images of Catholic violence against Huguenots in France
and the ideological program shared between the Spanish and the French members of the Catholic League, such as the Duke of Guise.

But there are singular differences; in another image de Bry illustrates how
"Balboa orders Indians accused of sodomy to be eaten alive by dogs" (fig.
12.8).[19] The image is divided into two very distinct parts. At the top are the
Spaniards, in ceremonial dress and in conventional postures that symbolize
their dominance. Their eyes are looking down but express only indifference.
They do not seem to be affected by the horrifying spectacle that takes place
in front of them. They are imperturbable, as if on a pedestal. At the bottom
of the image is the horrible massacre. The Indians are reduced to food for
dogs. This is much more cruel than cannibalism. First, the victims are still
alive. Second, they are eaten by animals as a symbol of barbarity itself. De
Bry expresses this particular barbarity in symbolic details. The hounds that

attack men's heads are in a position of superiority. The faces of the Indians, who are still alive, suggest horror. Bones are lying on the ground. Two torn heads are lying in the foreground of the scene. One of them still bears the cruel marks of the massacre.[20]

Taken from the drawings of John White for the English, the first volume with its stereotype of the noble savage living in the golden age is clearly created to encourage Protestants to go to the New World. There are, indeed, no images of Europeans themselves in this series, even though the text and the paintings were done a full century after contact. Northern Europeans have nothing to fear from such peaceful and amiable peoples. The stereotype of the victim appears as an indictment of the unjust and criminal Spanish domination. Nevertheless, de Bry also shows that the natives of the New World can be violent among themselves and against the Spaniards. In the second volume, he illustrates the violence of Indian wars and the ill treatment they inflict on their enemies. In the third volume, he depicts the cruelty of cannibalism. In the final three volumes, he also shows how the Indians can take their revenge on the Spaniards.[21] We can thus say that sometimes the Indians adopt European forms of violence and that their revenge is just. They are, nevertheless, violent, and the barbarity of the Spaniards does not exonerate the Indians. In the fourth volume, de Bry shows how the Indians take revenge on the missionaries and other Spaniards in the province of Cumana (fig. 12.9).[22] The caption explains the circumstances of the event: "The Indian chiefs of the province of Cumana [port on the Caribbean, NE Venezuela], seeing that the Spanish captain d'Ocampo had gone off with most of the soldiery, agreed to rise in arms." The image shows a contrast between the luxuriance and peace of nature and the scene of massacre. In the background, we see the trees and huts of the village. On the left are the traditional Spanish vessel anchored in the bay and a boat on which the Spaniards try to flee. A last man is running toward this boat, lifting his arms for help, but two Indians are following him with their bows. A similar confrontation is taking place behind the major scene. The Indians run after their victim and are about to shoot arrows at his back. This suggests that the Indians are determined not to leave one person alive. In the foreground, seven Indians persecute two Spanish soldiers and two missionaries. The Indians look cruel and pitiless and use both bows and clubs. On the left, an Indian has just shot an arrow into the neck of a Spaniard while another Indian is going to kill a soldier with a club. On the right, an Indian, who is ready to strike a Spaniard with his club, has his foot on the head of his opponent, as he would do with an animal. The center of the image represents the murder of two monks by three Indians. The action is suspended at the moment of greatest intensity.

12.9. Theodore de Bry, *Americae Pars Quarta*, Pl. 16. Engraving. 1594.

The postures and the gazes of the Indians suggest extreme violence.[23] The bodies are bent, the torsos are elongated, the arms carry a club above the head or shoot an arrow, and the eyes are piercing. Such violence is almost inhuman and echoes the violence the Spaniards used previously on the Indians. The two monks are waiting for their death. One of them is trying vainly to avoid the stroke. The other one, quite the opposite, opens his hands to his martyrdom as if he were in ecstasy.[24]

From the point of view of the spectacular images alone, it is easy to understand why de Bry is considered one of the creators of the Black Legend. The texts he chose to print and images he published do in fact encourage Protestant colonization and condemn Spanish conquest. The Protestants, who believe that they are morally superior to the Catholic Spaniards, would bring the true God to America, whereas the Spaniards use the pretext of religion to destroy the newly discovered world and satisfy their greed. Even though the images of Indian violence demythologize the New World, it is easy to understand that de Bry's readers may well be happy that the Indians take their revenge on the Spaniards. Violence among the Indians themselves is perhaps more disturbing, but it could have been interpreted as a sign of cultural and moral inferiority by Europeans. Thus the Protestant readers, who believe in their superiority, could have been invited to reject both the Spaniards and the Indians as barbarians and "absolute others."[25]

WHY SHOULD ONE READ *AMERICA,* ACCORDING TO DE BRY'S PREFACES?

It is only when we read his prefaces that we discover how much de Bry's own perspective is not so much imperialistic and anti-Spanish as it is moral and philosophical. In terms of the weight of the whole set of volumes, the prefaces do not occupy much space. But, according to Gérard Genette, a preface is very important because it has a special hermeneutic value.[26] In the preface, Genette says, the author explains why and how a reader should read his book. Even if we admit with the critics of the twentieth century that the author is no sovereign over what he writes, we can say that the preface appears to be the only place where an author can tell his intentions and guide the reader.

In his prefaces, De Bry presents the specificity of each volume of his collection. He emphasizes the importance of the subject and, for the first two volumes, the importance of his support of it. Moreover, in order to emphasize the subject, he tries to reduce his own role. In each preface, he introduces himself and his sons only as serious craftsmen.

In the preface of the first volume he says, "Admiring, as I did, the paintings made of these people [Virginians], I wished to offer them to the public. This I have been able to do by the help of Master Richard Hakluyt of Oxford, a minister of God's word, who first encouraged me to publish the work."[27] He adds, "I and my sons have taken the most earnest pains in engraving them [the paintings] carefully on copper, since the subject is one of great importance." The expression "the subject is one of great importance" does not make clear the subject itself, but in previous sentences de Bry speaks about "the country and its inhabitants, their way of dressing, their manner of living, and their several habits." Is knowledge of Virginia the real subject? Why is it important? Because it must encourage English people to go to the New World and to colonize it, or because it shows to the Europeans other ways of living?

In the four other prefaces, de Bry clearly indicates the subject. In the preface of the second volume, he says, "I hope, dear reader, that you will receive with your whole heart the maps of this country and the narratives of its inhabitants, the way they live and their customs." In the preface of the third volume, he develops the differences among the Virginians, the Floridians, and the Brazilians. He says that he decided to publish this third volume in order to "clearly show the variety that exists among the savages, as much in their customs and their way of living as in their manner of dressing and adorning themselves." The prefaces of the fourth and fifth volumes define the subject as "the extraordinary events that happened in this recently discovered New World."

De Bry is aware of the criticism that can be made about the order of the first three volumes of the collection. He explains why there is no historical order in the first preface: "At the request of my friends, and because the memory of the recent feat is so fresh, I am publishing first the account of that part of the New World which the English call Virginia. If I were to regard the order of events, the history of Florida (which I already have in hand) should have first been published, since the French discovered and conquered that land in a notable victory long before the discovery of Virginia. However, I hope shortly to publish this work also." In the other prefaces, the engraver does not explain his choice because it becomes more and more clear that he does not want to publish a history of the New World. He wants to show different peoples and different events. The unity of the collection is given by the title, *America*, as if de Bry understood, as we do in the twenty-first century, that this New World was a continent with many different peoples and cultures. De Bry speaks about his "American histories" in his preface of the fifth volume. Another sign of unity is given at the beginning of the first preface and in the image of Adam and Eve with which the collection begins. De Bry writes in his preface, "Although, dear reader, on account of Adam's disobedience man was deprived of those good gifts with which he was endowed at the Creation, yet, as will be seen in the following account of the life of savage tribes, he still retained wit to provide for himself and to make whatever was necessary for his life and health-except the matter of his soul's health." To show, and to write about, Adam and Eve at the beginning of a collection about America is a clear sign that, for de Bry, the inhabitants of the New World are the same as the Europeans. They are not mythical creatures. They are human beings. They have the same human nature as any human beings. For de Bry, this means a corrupt nature and a common guilt owing to original sin. We understand that for him the Indians, the Spaniards, and all human beings have the same nature and are susceptible of similar sins.

As is common in the Renaissance, and especially in this kind of book, de Bry emphasizes the veracity of his work. He introduces himself as a publisher and an engraver. He tells his reader that he copied carefully and faithfully the images of White and those of Le Moyne and that he uses the images ". . . copied from life . . ." that he finds in Staden, Léry, and Benzoni. He explains that the translators, who translate the texts he publishes into Latin, are worthy of confidence. He also emphasizes that the authors of the texts he publishes are eyewitnesses. Eyewitnesses are perhaps not totally reliable, because, as Montaigne points it out, "it is important not only to see a thing but also how one sees it."[28] Nevertheless, in the Renaissance an eyewitness is more reliable than a cosmographer, who never leaves his office and writes from second- or third-hand documents. Even though veracity is important for de Bry, his collection is not only ethnological.

HOW SHOULD ONE READ *AMERICA*, ACCORDING TO DE BRY'S PREFACES?

De Bry clearly explains the origin of the collection. He introduces Hakluyt, who gave him the idea of the first two volumes, as a "minister of God's word." I already mentioned that Hakluyt gives de Bry the idea of the first two volumes. Notice that the engraver introduces the English publisher as a "minister of God's word." This remark must be important for de Bry. Does it give credibility to the publisher? Does it put the collection under God's protection? In the preface of the third volume, de Bry affirms, "I published, seized by a divine instinct, the first and the second part of *America* and I acquired, by a blessing of God, this History [of Brazil]." A reference to God is very common in Protestant prefaces in the Renaissance, but it seems that de Bry wants to emphasize that God not only helps and inspires him but also wants him to create this collection. If God is at the origin of this collection, we understand that it represents more than an entertainment.

De Bry defines his audience. He addresses his reader with the rhetorical formula "Dear reader" or "Benevolent reader." In the body of prefaces the engraver constantly uses the pronoun "we." Who are these "we?" Assuredly, they are Europeans; they are literate persons who read Latin and are interested in the New World. Finally, they are persons who believe in the same God as de Bry's God. In the fourth and fifth prefaces, de Bry uses the term "Christian." In the engraver's mind "Christian" most likely means "Protestant." Therefore, we can say that the collection addresses, first of all, Protestant readers. But does this necessarily make the collection Protestant propaganda?

De Bry explains his intentions in each preface. However, we observe an interesting progression over the five prefaces. In the first preface, he explains that his first goal is to give reliable and tangible information. In the second preface, he states two other goals: "Do not believe, benevolent reader, that we describe the history of the country of Virginia, published several months ago, and this other one, now, about the country of Florida, only in order to entertain you, even though this kind of history is very pleasant to men. First of all, we did it in order to give thanks wholeheartedly to God for the gifts we received from Him, showing his immeasurable and stupefying works. We also did it in order that God reveals and teaches us the path of salvation." The idea that this kind of book, showing new landscapes, new men, and new cultures, leads the readers to praise and to give thanks to God is common in Protestant books. For the Christians of the Renaissance, the world is a showcase of God's creation. The second idea, that the descriptions of the New World can teach the readers the way of salvation, implies that the readers are not definitively saved and that they can learn from otherness. De Bry's readers have the privilege of knowing God, something that the Floridians do not have up until now, but they still have to improve their lives.

In the third preface, de Bry adds, "God's care will appear even greater to those who do not lack common sense. If they consider how unhappy are these poor people [the Brazilians] who are deprived of the knowledge of God, they will fully find matter to give thanks to God and praise Him, He who, by a trait of his divine providence, opened the genuine path to salvation to them." In this passage the readers are clearly closer to God than the Brazilians. However, we cannot be sure that, for de Bry, the Brazilians are eternally cursed by God and incapable of being evangelized.[29] More generally, we do not know if, for de Bry, the hardships that the inhabitants of the New World endure from the Spaniards are a sign of God's damnation. However, we can affirm that, because of the unity of the human race, the example of the New World teaches the readers what they must avoid and what they must do. In the context of the first three prefaces, the readers must avoid idolatry, which means replacing God by gold, and must be content with what God granted them.

In the fourth preface, de Bry develops the lessons the readers can receive from the New World. He writes,

> If we examine ourselves, will we find that we are better than the Indians? We, to whom the authentic knowledge of God and eternal salvation has been revealed and shown by the Prophets and the Apostles, by our Lord Jesus Christ himself, the son of God, and by the eternal Word? I omit the numerous vices by which the Christians serve the Devil whom these barbarous peoples ignore; I will conceal the immoderate luxury that can be observed among us, in the way we cloth our bodies as well as in the way we prepare our food, which are completely unknown by those poor savages, who are content with what nature produces by itself. This forgotten, do not we, Christians, publicly deny God in order to serve and adore the Devil? Who does not subject himself to this de-

testable vice that is avarice? And that the Apostle calls idolatry? Does not the miser of gold and silver adore the Prince of this century instead of God? We, whose souls quiver with horror when we learn that the Devil is adored by those blinded men, do we not see the mote that is in their eyes without discerning the beam that is in ours?

De Bry uses five rhetorical questions in order to encourage his readers to rid themselves of prejudice. He does not seem to doubt that his coreligionists can be as bad as the Indians, but he wants his readers to acknowledge by themselves that, even though they are Christians, they are often no better than the Indians. On the one hand, the superiority of the Christians who have "the authentic knowledge of God" and to whom "eternal salvation has been revealed" is destroyed by an enumeration of vices. De Bry enumerates the "numerous vices by which the Christians serve the Devil," "the immoderate luxury that can be observed among us," and "the detestable vice that is avarice." On the other hand, the Indians are depicted with less negative expressions. De Bry says that "these barbarous peoples ignore" the vices of the Europeans. He reiterates: luxury is "completely unknown by those poor savages, who are content with what nature produces by itself." The Indians adore the devil and sometimes they are even possessed by him, but as de Bry shows, the Protestants also adore the devil. What is easy enough to apply to the Indians is much more difficult for the Christians to admit about themselves. Yet de Bry leads his readers, in Socratic fashion, to acknowledge that they are no better than the Indians. Furthermore, for de Bry the Christians or Protestants have no excuse for their vices because they know the true God and they know that they sin when they ignore God and his commands. If the readers think otherwise, it is only because they are blinded by prejudices. The readers should not judge the Spaniards too quickly either. De Bry continues:

> Let us not be too quick to condemn the Spaniards and let us first seriously examine ourselves, in order to see if we are truly better than they are. I have, in effect, known among Spaniards many men who were neither less pious nor less honest than those of any other nation. This I say without the slightest prejudice. Moreover, if the Spaniards have often behaved in a cruel, greedy, and unjust fashion in the Indies, we must not impute such a behavior to their nation but to the license of soldiers, who, as we know, behave with an equal cruelty whatever their nation of origin. Who ignores the numerous acts of violence perpetrated—and that are still committed now—by the French, German, and Italian soldiers and others in almost all campaigns and wars?

The beginning of this paragraph is similar to that of the previous one. De Bry exhorts his readers to be careful in their judgments. Then he affirms from his own experience that the Spaniards are "neither less pious nor less honest than those of any other nation." By comparing Spain with all nations, de Bry questions the prejudice that it is worse than other countries. Furthermore, de Bry chooses the two remarkable adjectives "pious" and "honest" to describe the Spaniards he knew. They are remarkable because they are the opposite of what we would expect in a work of Protestant propaganda. The engraver admits that the Spaniards "have often behaved in a cruel, greedy and unjust fashion" in the New World, but he adds, "we must not impute such a behavior to their nation but to the license of soldiers." With the expression "the license of soldiers," de Bry affirms clearly that neither religion nor national origin is responsible for cruelty. It is not because the Spanish soldiers are Catholic and Spanish that they are barbarous. Moreover, de Bry asks his readers to recognize "an equal cruelty" in the soldiers of any country. The conclusion is clear: for de Bry, the Spanish soldiers are cruel because they adore gold instead of adoring God. They are idolatrous, as are the Indians and the readers.

The preface ends on this last paragraph: "Who, therefore, as an equitable judge, will condemn a whole people for these crimes? May God allow that we learn to correct our ways by the example of others. May God grant that what we condemn in others, we correct it in us. First of all, may we stop our greed in order to be content with what God, in his generosity and bounty, granted us." A last time, de Bry tries to convince his readers not to condemn the Spaniards. God is the only one who can judge and condemn. Furthermore, the readers, as sinners, have to learn to correct their ways from the spectacle of the New World. From the conquistadors, the readers must learn to avoid greed, which is one of the worst kinds of idolatry for de Bry. From the Indians, the readers must learn to avoid idolatry and be content with what God grants them. Is this lesson an implicit condemnation of colonization? It is at least a warning against the dangers of greed. Thus, if colonization is governed by greed, we can assume that de Bry would condemn it.

If this paragraph does not convince the readers, de Bry adds a final argument in his fifth and last preface. As in all classical pieces of rhetoric, the author must frighten his readers in order to convince them. After he explains that the violent acts of the Spaniards come from "the two vilest vices of human race, which means ambition and craving for power," he writes, "Almighty God, in order to punish such an opprobrium, not only had them [the conquistadors] kill each other, but also, made them fall on foreign French pirates, who, pushed by resentment, attacked the Spaniards everywhere in the New World. They destroyed, devastated and set fire to cities and small villages. Thus they massacred and slaughtered many Spaniards." The purpose of this passage is to show the amplitude of God's punishment. Once again, de Bry wants to convince his readers that if they persist in their idolatry God will punish them, as he punishes the Spaniards. We note the accumulation of the verbs "kill each other," "destroy," "devastate," "set fire," "massacre," and "slaughter."

More than an indictment of the unjust Spanish domination of the New World or a promotion of Protestant colonization, de Bry's prefaces appear as a moral lesson. De Bry wants his readers not to allow their decisions to be governed by powers other than the true God. False gods, idolatry, greed, and the need for power are destructive for every human being. Thus, the readers are never explicitly called to colonize and evangelize the Indians. These ideas are not consistent with an interpretation of de Bry's work as an apologia for the Black Legend. There is some real contradiction between the messages of de Bry's prefaces and the texts and especially the powerful images he publishes. Such a contradiction allows us to think that de Bry's work may well have been as simplistically misinterpreted as has been Las Casas' *Brevísima relacion de la destruccion de las Indias*.[30] The Spanish are not the only guilty ones; all human beings must work to resist the temptations of greed, power, and the evils of violence.

PART IV

BELATED ENGLAND

CHAPTER THIRTEEN

WEST OF EDEN

American Gold, Spanish Greed, and the Discourses of
English Imperialism

Edmund Valentine Campos

Qui potest facere Mediam naturam, potest creare Mundos novos.

—Richard Eden

TREASURE ISLAND

In the middle of the sixteenth century Richard Eden brought news of the
New World to England through his translation of foreign works. His contributions include Sebastian Münster's *A treatyse of the newe India* (1553), Peter Martyr's *The Decades of the newe worlde or west India* (1554), and Martín de
Cortés's *The arte of navigation* (1561). While Eden is best known for his dedication as a translator of cosmographical material, he is perhaps less renowned
for his professional labors as an alchemist.[1] In a letter to William Cecil he recounts a wondrous experiment in which he outdoes Shakespeare's Prospero
by precipitating an island:

> I dissolved two substances in two waters. Then I put the waters togyther
> in a glasse, suffering them so to remayne for a tyme. Then I stilled of[f]
> the water frome the masse or *Chaos* lefte of them bothe. And put it on
> ageyn. And so dyd dyvers times. In fine, the masse being dissolved in the
> water, I lett it rest all night in a coulde place. In the morning, I found
> swymming on the water and in the myddest thereof, a little round Iland
> as brode as [a] riall or sumwhat more, with at the least a hundreth sylver
> trees abowt an ynche high, so perfectly formed with trunkes, stalkes,
> and leaves all most pure and glystering sylver, that I suppose no limne[r]
> or painter is able to conterfect the like.[2]

The letter is dated 1562 but the experiment was conducted years earlier, near the end of Edward VI's reign when Eden was contracted by the aristocrat Richard Whalley to discover the quintessence, a magical agent for generating unlimited specie. In David Gwyn's thorough essay on Eden's dual vocation as an alchemist and a cosmographer he notes that the translator and the scientific merchant circles he moved in displayed an enthusiastic (and potentially illegal) interest in the magical generation of gold.[3] Such pursuits sound fantastical and may seem hard to square with Eden's interest in new experiential knowledge characterizing the latest developments of cosmography and navigation, but as Tara Nummedal explains, alchemy took on a practical character in the sixteenth century. Hands-on philosophers commodified their technical skills and hired themselves out to Renaissance princes and other wealthy patrons applying the more practical aspects of their art to enterprises ranging from medicine to mining development.[4]

But what precisely had Eden "counterfected" in his cucurbit? A forested island? Or a silver coin? The language of the account resists definitive classification; rather, it seems to amalgamate Eden's interest in cosmography with his eccentric interest in alchemy such that the floating marvel would appear to represent a wishful fantasy of territorial acquisition made possible by the principles of natural philosophy. Given that England possessed no treasure islands of its own in the sixteenth century, could this episode be interpreted as a compensatory dream of counterfeit colonization in a microcosmic alembic? The numismatic measure of Eden's island is particularly revealing for it collapses mineral wealth (the superficial goal of alchemical practice) and expansion in a single token that was in itself a symbol of overseas domination. Eden's descriptive use of the Spanish *real* situates this experiment in a broader context of European colonization, for the *real* was the ubiquitous token of Spanish imperial success. The coin was stamped with a *rial* or "royal" inscription that not only guaranteed its "real" value as legitimate currency but also signaled Spain's transatlantic economic hegemony, for the *real* was often minted, as Eden well knew, from American silver.[5]

However legitimate it may be to interpret this reverie as a coded dream of colonial desire, it should still be read against the backdrop of the alchemical discourse that frames it. Indeed, any firm conclusions regarding Eden's attitude toward colonialism that one may draw from this example are shaken by Eden's failure to find a practical application for the phenomenon. His final comments to the secretary of state regarding the utility of such an island for the commonwealth, though suggestive, are inconclusive: "What this would have byn in fine, god knoweth, and not I. . . . And as touching these matters,

I have read a marvelous sentence in an olde written booke where these woordes are written: *Qui potest facere Mediam naturam, potest creare Mundos novos*".[6] What are the connections between natural philosophy's *Mundos novos* and the Spanish *nuevo mundo* that Eden made available to his English readers via his translations?

The political role of Eden's translations, especially *The Decades*, which was dedicated to Mary Tudor and Philip of Spain, has been the subject of much debate concerning whether the translator wanted his English audience to support the activities of Spain in the New World or to search for territory abroad in defiance of the Iberian monopoly on the Americas.[7] Eden's often-critiqued abandonment of Protestantism upon Mary's accession and his later arrest and imprisonment in 1555 upon suspicion of heresy makes such determinations even more complicated. My analysis engages this debate by reading Eden's translations through the scientific discourse of practical alchemy, especially as it relates to cosmography, travel, and foreign policy—a connection obtained not only in the experiment recounted above but also in Eden's decision to append his translation of *The Decades* with a partial translation of the *Pyrotechnia*, one of the most comprehensive Renaissance manuals on the behavior and treatment of metals.

In giving metallurgy an interpretive role in the apprehension of Eden's New World translations I hope to avoid what Andrew Hadfield calls "teleological reading," by which he means the tendency to situate early European responses to the New World, solely within the context of the large-scale process of colonialism.[8] Early texts such as Martyr's *De Orbe Novo Decades* resist monolithic interpretation as either pro- or anticolonial because they abound with "serious confusion regarding the value of their own and other cultures".[9] Hadfield's main example is an episode from the second decade in which Martyr finds himself in the uncomfortable position of narrating an encounter between gold-hungry conquistadores and the native peoples of Panama—an episode that reads like a condemnation of Spanish greed within the larger context of a treatise ostensibly devoted to exalting Spanish achievements. Hadfield sees Eden and Peter Martyr in analogous compromising and ambivalent positions as mediators of New World exploits. In the case of Eden, Hadfield believes that while his translation of the *De Orbe Novo Decades* holds out the Spaniards as exemplars of heroic behavior, it does so in an attempt to encourage national unity in the face of political critique stemming mainly from Protestant dissidents at home and abroad: Spanish "actions provide a recipe for unity and expansion and will provide internal and external cohesion illustrating that the forces of nationalism and colonialism cannot be easily separated."[10] As for the nagging image of the avaricious conquistador, Eden hopes that his English audience "will choose to be inspired by the hope for gold and empire, even if the motives for gain are transparently base."[11]

New World gold, momentarily uncoupled from the trope of greed and linked instead to the marginal interests of alchemy and metallurgy, is at the center of my treatment of Eden. By constellating translation, discovery, and alchemy I hope to remove Eden from a genealogy of political propaganda that might locate him in a prophetic line of descent heralding later Elizabethan colonial ideologues. By reading Eden alchemically I intend neither an apology for his support of colonialism nor a depoliticization of his cultural significance as a translator; rather, I hope to show that Eden the alchemist spoke an eccentric language of colonial expansion that makes it difficult to categorize the translator as either a Hispanophilic Marian conformist or a clandestine Protestant dissident working to bring about an independent English empire. Ultimately, alchemy's intervention in imperial thinking serves an indexical function marking the changes in colonial attitudes between the Marian and Elizabethan regimes that makes it impossible to surrender Eden's academic interest in mineral wealth to the first term of the totalizing conquistadorial motto of *gold, glory, and God.*

THE CHEMICAL WEDDING

Eden came of age in an era of economic crisis. The legacy of Henry VIII's lavish reign took its toll in the 1550s when the Crown, laden with debt, began to lower the value of currency while internal prices began to rise. Meanwhile the wool industry began to feel the long-term effects of the Henrician enclosure movements.[12] By 1551, it became clear that in order to compete in the wool trade, England would need to establish a reliable currency. The way to do this was to lower the value of currency yet again. As a result, a 50 percent devaluation was put into effect between May and August of that year.[13] The situation was exacerbated by the wars in France (1552–1556), which turned the exchange rate against England and caused currency to leave the country. At the heart of all of these problems was a simple lack of raw bullion.

The union of Mary Tudor and Philip of Spain offered hope of a solution: if only Spain's New World gold could become England's too. Prior to this Anglo-Spanish match, there seemed little hope that England might successfully claim a piece of American territory. In the "Epistle to the Reader" of *A treatyse of the newe India*[14] written just before Mary's succession, Eden cautiously expresses doubt as to whether England would be able to tread on the lands granted by papal donation to Charles V: "As for other landes and Ilandes in the west sea, where the Eagle (yet not in every place) hath so spled its winges, that other poore byrdes may not without offence seke theyr praye within the compasse of the same, I wyll speke nothing hereof, bycause I wold be loth to lay an egge, whereof other men might hatche a serpent."[15] The royal wedding altered this bleak perspective. According to the Latin dedication to the newlyweds in *The Decades*, Eden claims to have been so impressed by the procession of the royal couple into London that he felt compelled to memorialize the significance of the union. To honor the pair, he decided to publicize the discoveries and conquests of the Spaniards, all of which would become the joint inheritance of England should the royal pair have issue. But at thirty-seven, it was not very likely that Mary would bear children, and hence David Gwyn wonders if Eden really did imagine a future Anglo-Spanish dynasty or if this was simply "an adroit move, combining praise for the Spanish people and their rulers with the clear hint to the court that England's future prosperity lay in encouraging trade."[16]

Bearing Gwyn's supposition in mind and given Eden's mineral interests, it may be, however, that the translator was more deeply moved by a second procession that took place shortly after Philip's installation. A journal entry of a resident of the Tower of London records the delivery of Spanish bullion: "There came to the Tower in twenty carts made for the show, accompanied by certain Spaniards of the King's Guard, ninety-seven little chests, a yard long and four inches broad, of silver, which will make by estimation fifty thousand pounde."[17] The silver was from the Spanish mines in South America, and its importation and delivery was overseen by Augustín Zárate, a Spanish auditor of the Imperial mines. In the following year Zárate would publish his *Historia del descubrimiento y conquista del Perú* (1555, English 1574). Eden befriended Zárate, and in the preface to *The Decades*, he makes mention of this acquaintance and of the fabulous silver shipment in the same space where he observes the discrepancy between the economic conditions of England and Spain:

> But if I should here particularly and at large declare howe Inglande is in fewe yeares decayed and impoverysshed, and howe on the contrary parte Spayne is inryched, I shulde perrhappes displease more in descrybing the myserie of the one, then please other in expressynge the floryschynge state of the other, which by all reason is lyke dayly to increasse, aswell for the great rychesse that are yearely browght thyther from the Indies ... as I was credably informed by the woorthy and lerned gentleman Augustinus de Ceratta, Contador (that is) the auditour of the kynges myntes who had longe before byn surveyoure of the golde mynes

of Peru, and browght from these and from Rio de Plata. xiii. thousand pounde weyght of sylver which was coined to the Kynges use in the towre of Londin where never so much hath been at once as have been owlde officeres in the mynt doo affirme.[18]

Earlier in the dedicatory epistle of *A treatyse of the newe India,* Eden laments that were it not for the lack of "manly courage" on the part of early English explorers like Thomas Pert "it myghte happelye have comen to passe, that the riche treasurye called *Perurlaria,* (which is now in Spayne in the citie of Civile, and so named for that in it is kepte the infinite ryches brought thither from the new found land of Peru,) myght long since have bene in the towre of London, to the kinges great honoure and the welth of this realme."[19] This shipment then of Peruvian silver to the tower must have seemed to Eden like the partial fulfillment of a dream linking the Tower of London on the Thames to Seville's *Torre de oro* on the Guadalquivir.

Thanks to his acquaintance with Zárate and other Spaniards in Philip's retinue, Eden secured a job in the king's royal treasury at about the same time that *The Decades* was at press. This was not, however, Eden's first job working with metal. Under Henry VIII he worked in the royal treasury, but this job came to an end upon Edward's accession. At that time, in 1547, Eden was put to work in the royal distillery as a chemist. Around 1550–1552, Eden found himself unemployed. At this point he met Richard Whalley, who hired Eden to discover the secret to unlimited specie. While in Whalley's employ, he not only created his magical island but translated the *Pyrotechnia,* parts of which he would eventually incorporate into his translation of *The Decades.*[20]

VEIN PURSUITS

The *Pyrotechnia,* or *The Booke of Metals* as it was called by Eden, is just one of a number of supplementary texts included in Eden's rendition of *The Decades.* Peter Martyr's first three decades are followed by, among other things, portions of Gonzalo Fernández de Oviedo y Valdés's *Historia general y natural de las Indias;* López de Gómara's *Historia general de las Indias;* the voyage of Magellan; a papal bull granting Spain rights to the New World; and navigational pieces by Amerigo Vespucci, Andrea Corsali, and Alvise de Cadamosto. In remarking upon the heterogeneous nature of Eden's compilation, John Parker in *Books to Build an Empire* avers that "[p]erhaps the least pertinent portion of Eden's book was his translation from the *Pyrotechnia* of Vannucio Biringoccio."[21] While Parker does not consider *The Booke of Metals* a very good book to build an empire, clearly Eden felt it helpful for understanding the doings of the Spaniards in the Americas. Biringuccio's text marks the historical emergence of practical metallurgic literature intended for the treatment of metals for use and profit in an emerging capitalistic environment. Published in Venice in 1540, it concerns itself less with classical and medieval theories of metalworking and more with experimental precedent and contemporary technologies essential to the industrialization of metallurgic enterprises. Its scope is large, covering everything from mineral extraction, smelting, and bell casting to the making of fireworks. Certainly, the *Pyrotechnia* must have been among Prospero's books in Milan, and its inclusion in a miscellany of New World translations must have seemed utterly logical to the mineral-minded Eden.

Eden opens *The Booke of Metals* with a preface that makes reference to the classical Ages of Man, which may be in itself a reference to the New World, often understood as a version of the golden age "so named, not for the desyre that men had to golde, but for th[e] innocencie of lyvynge in those dayes, when Mars was of no poure, and men thought it crueltie by breakynge the bones of owre mother the earth, to open the way to the courte of infernal Pluto from thence to get golde and sylver the seedes of al mischiefes."[22] Even though Eden acknowledges the power of gold to blind men to virtue he nevertheless sees it as a necessary evil of the Iron Age in which he lived: "But syth it is nowe so that we shalbe inforced to seke ayde by that which was sumtymes a mischiefe, it resteth to use the matter as doo cunnynge phisitians that can mynister poyson in proportion with other thynges in such sorte qualyfyinge the maliciosnesse thereof, that none shall therby bee intoxicate."[23] In other words, practical knowledge of precious metals is offered as a homeopathic antidote for avarice.

Morality, though, is not Eden's priority in the preface. Instead, he devotes most of his energies to providing three practical justifications for the anomalous presence of this metallurgic text among others devoted to New World reports. The first reason addresses historical immediacy, aesthetics and economics: "[I]t seemeth to me a thynge undecent to reade so muche of golde and sylver, and to know lyttel or nothing of the natural generations thereof." Besides, he continues, "they are th[e] instruments of all artes, the prices of all thynges, the ornamentes of al dignities, and not the least portion of nature, whereby the co[n]te[m]plation of them is no less pleasaunte then necessary."[24] The second reason is expansionist: "that if in travaylyng strang and unknowen countreys any mans chaunce shalbe to arryve in such regions where he may knowe by th[e] information of th[e] inhabitauntes or otherwyse, that suche regions are frutefull of riche metals, he may not bee without sum judgement to make further searche for the same."[25] His third reason touches upon the general importance of translation as a tool for importing new knowledges into the vernacular: "that althowgh this owre realme of Englande be ful of metals not to bee contemned and much rycher then men suppose, yet is there fewwe or none in Englande that gave anye greate skyll thereof, or any thynge wrytten in owr tongue, whereby men maye bee well instructed of the generation and fynding of the same: as the lyke ignorance hath byn amonge us as touchynge Cosmographie and Navigations untyll I attempted to accordinge to the portion of my talente and simple lernynyge to open the fyrst dore to the enteraunce of this knoweleage into owre language"[26]

Eden's efforts to ally the search for precious metals to his New World translation effort are evident in all of his three major works of navigational material. In his early text, *A treatyse of the newe India,* he explains in the address to the reader that the European expansion into previously unknown lands is merely a repetition of King Solomon's overseas search for treasure. If, as Eden believes, the mythical land of Ophir is actually the newly (re)discovered portions of the globe where the heat of the equatorial sun engenders gold under the earth, then there is a venerable Biblical precedent for mineral expeditions. He surmises that the recent voyages of the Portuguese "greatly confyrme the trueth, of such thinges as are spoken of in this Boke, whereas the same perhappes to some men might otherwyse seme in maner incredible, yf the lyke had not been seen in tyme paste, and approued by auctoritie of most holy scripture, which declaring the great wysdom, ryches and noble viages of King Salomon, sayth that God gave him wisdom and understanding exceding muche, and a large heart, and that he prepared a nauie of shippes . . . which sayled to Ophir, and brought from thence. xxi. score hundreth (which is. xlii.M) weyght of golde."[27] In the general preface to *The Decades,* we witness a similar cyclical justification for mineral quests, only this time the case is a more worldly example of *translatio imperii* viewed as a series of mineral conquests: "Also Diodorus Siculus in the sixt booke of his *Bibliotheca* speakynge of Spayne (called by the Greekes Iberia) writeth that when in the mountaines named Pyrinei th[e] inhabitantes burnte up the wooddes, there ranne owt of the mountaynes as it were dyvers streames of pure sylver molten by the heate of the fyre. But the estimation and price of sylver being at those dayes to them unknowen, the Phenician marchauntes bought the same of them for thynges of smaule value: And carynge it into Grecia, Asia, and other countreys, got rychesse therby."[28] This story of eastern invaders trading trifles in return for precious metal sounds all too familiar. The implication here is that the Iberians were once like the Indians of the New World, surrendering gold in exchange for trinkets. In the continuation of this story the Phoenicians, having become very rich, established colonies in Spain. This wave of conquerors was followed by still another: "Lykewise when after-warde the Romans subdued the Iberians, the Italians which for the desyre of gaynes searched those metals, gotte great rychesse by the same."[29] Recount-ing past invasions and takeovers may sound like strange praise to bestow upon a contemporary empire, but as William Camden demonstrates decades later in his *Britannia*, the stamp of former subjugation guarantees the impe-rial maturity of a nation: "[Y]et however grievous this yoke [i.e. Roman rule] was, it prov'd of very good consequence to us. For together in it came the blessed doctrine of Christ Jesus, (of which hereafter,) upon the light of his glorious Empire, barbarism soon vanish'd among the Britains."[30] Elsewhere in Camden's chorographical tour of the British Isles he displays an anti-quarian interest in the remains of former conquerors. In one numismatic di-gression, he reiterates the civilizing influence of the Roman empire in his fanciful meditation upon a recovered Roman coin bearing the cameo of two-headed Janus, reputed by myth to have civilized the people of Latium. "Two-faced Janus, possibly because at that time, Britain began to be a little refined from its barbarity. For Janus is said to have first changed barbarity into good breeding; and for that reason . . . painted with two faces, as if he had ham-mered the same visage into quite another thing."[31] Coins then are metallic signs from imperial pasts that provide artefactual proof of an imperial future. In another, similar example concerning Spain, a rumor circulated that told of the finding of a Roman coin stamped with the head of Augustus in a South American gold mine. Like the images of two-headed eagles found elsewhere in the Americas, this coin was taken as evidence of a prior imperial occupa-tion. The Spaniards, seeing themselves as the inheritors of the Roman em-pire, embraced the coin as a testament to their right to reconquer the land.[32]

Mining and its outcome of gold and silver coins offer general models for colonization, models that can become discursively metaphorized. In *The Arte of navigation*, for example, Eden explicitly compares exploration to the ardu-ous task of prospecting. In both pursuits one must be attentive to signs. The tokens signaling inhabitable lands are

> not much unlyke to the shyning flowres of Marchasites [surface mineral deposits], which outwardly appearyng in minerall mountaynes, are signes and tokens wherby is conjectured what metal is conteyned therein, and whether the same is to be folowed or not. And although it sometyme so chaunce that such signes are fayleable, shewyng more in appearaunce then they conteyne in substaunce: yet are not such signes tokens, or shewes to be contemned, but rather earnestly to be folowed, forasmuch as it hath ben often proved and founde by experience, that by folowyng

the same, have ben founde great and riche mynes of metalles: as Georgius
Agricola in his bookes *De rebus metallicis,* doth largely declare and prove
by manye examples.[33]

This comparison evinces the powerful influence that the *Pyrotechnia* had on
Eden's understanding of the search for gold and its potential for enriching
the commonwealth, for it sounds very much like any number of examples that
Biringoccio offers of miners whose dedication and persistence ultimately pay
off.[34] Indeed the descriptions of mining and traveling seem virtually interchangeable. The uncertainty involved in the search for gold is also what
saves it from being interpreted as a greedy enterprise. This financial risk
common to both projects further links them as similar activities. The advice
to prospectors provided in *The Booke of Metals* is just as applicable to merchant adventurers: "He therefore that hath begune to digge a caue, let hym
determin to folowe it, puttinge away th[e] estimation of the baseness thereof,
and not to feare the streyghtnesse of the way, but rather to applye all his possible diligence withowt remorse, hopinge therby no lese to obteyne honour
and ryches, then to auoyde shame and infamie for omyttynge so profitable
an enterprise."[35] While it may seem odd to yoke the travel of voyaging with
the travail of prospecting, anyone familiar with Walter Ralegh's narrative
The Discoverie of Guiana (1596) will recall that the structure of the quest for
the elusive El Dorado is propelled by the finding of suggestive mineral clues
(*madre de oro*) that promise a profitable conclusion just over the next ridge,
beyond the next river, and so on.[36]

Ralegh's failure aside, the rewards for persistence, Eden believes, is colonial success. Did not the Iberian empires begin by a number of false starts?
"For in lyke maner all the late discoveries both of the Spanyardes and Por-
tugales, had theyr begynnyng of such small conjectures, with uncertyne
hope (as it were *preter spem sub spe*) untyl God and good happe, by the constant travayle and valiaunt mynde of such as fyrst attempted the same, gave
them to enjoye that they hoped for."[37] The relentless pursuit of profitable
lands when cast in this way transformed it into a noble pursuit free from the
taint of greed.[38]

ALL THAT GLITTERS . . .

Vannuccio Biringuccio probably would have frowned upon Eden's ideological deployment of his manual. In the first place, Biringuccio saw mining ventures as an alternative pursuit to warfare and, most notably, travel.[39] More
importantly, however, the Italian despised alchemists. In a lengthy diatribe

against their ilk that Eden conspicuously omits from his rendition, Biringuccio criticizes the alchemical quest for magical transmutation. "These men,"
he writes, "in order to arrive at such a port have equipped their vessels with
sails and hard working oarsmen and have sailed with guiding stars, trying
every possible course, and, finally submerged in the impossible (according
to my belief) not one of them to my knowledge has ever come to port."[40]
Biringuccio's treatise is a testament to experiential knowledge. As such, it derides unproven alchemical shortcuts that would bring about the quick and
easy generation and purification of metals. Blinded by greed, alchemists
naively think that they can bypass the technical methods of excavation, extraction, assaying, and smelting — not to mention the massive organization of
labor required to carry out these processes — that Biringuccio's manual takes
such pains to describe and explain: "But the great desire that they have to become rich causes them to gaze in the distance and hinders them from seeing
the intermediate steps because they are thinking only of the final result, fold-
ing about them the shadow of the happiness that they would derive from
such a thing."[41]

Eden's shortsightedness as an alchemical gold enthusiast leads him to
foreshorten the efforts involved in metallic acquisition. So, while he is quick
to compare exploration and prospecting as analogous labors, he is nevertheless unmindful of the day-to-day physical labor required to sustain mining as
a profitable and industrial enterprise. In one notable exception, Eden describes the mining efforts of the ancient Egyptians in a few brief passages
from the *Bibliotheca Historica* of Diodorus, which Eden appends to the end of
his translation of Biringuccio:

> The laboureres carrynge light before theyr for[e]heades, digge great
> stones owt of the myne, which they let fall on the ground. From this
> labour they never rest, inforced to contynual woorke with strokes and
> contumelious woordes. Children th[e] age of. xii [twelve] or. xiii [thir-
> teen] yeares or uppewarde, are divided into two companyes, whereof
> the one breake the stones into smaule pieces, and the other cary furth
> that which is broken. They that are past th[e] age of. xxx [thirty] yeares,
> receaue the sayd broken stones at theyr hands and beate them in vessels
> of stone with maules of iren, to the quantitie of tares or fytches: which
> afterward they caast into many milles, whereby the laboure of two or
> three women or owlde men to every mylle, they are grounde as smaule
> as meale. The fylthinesse of their bodies of these labourers, is apparent
> to all men. For not so muche as their privie members are couered with
> any thinge: And theyre bodies bysyde so fylthy, that no man can beholde

them withowt compassion of theyr miserie. But no pitie, no reste, no remission is graunted them, whether they bee men or women, younge or owlde, sycke or feeble: But are all with strokes inforced to continuall labour untyl the poore wretches faynt and often tymes dye for extreme debilitie: In so much that many of them for feare of theyr lyfe to coomme (which they thynke worse than the present payne) preferre death to lyfe.[42]

The odd thing about this pitiful scene of enforced servitude, child labor, and hopelessness is its utter removal from contemporary history. Scenarios similar to this one were being played out in Spanish America and yet Eden draws his example from a page of ancient history.

Others of Eden's generation, however, were quick to point out the heavy toll that enforced servitude in the mines took upon the Indians of the New World. This connection between mining and labor was central to a parallel discourse of gold that constituted a bitter critique of the Spanish in America. Bartolomé de las Casas was the most prominent voice in this regard. In his *Brevíssima relación de la destrución de las Indias* he describes the miserable conditions under which the Indians are forced to work:

> Now the . . . care that [the Spaniards] had of the [Indian men], was to send them unto the mines, to make them drein them out golde, which is an intollerable travell: and the women they bestowed into the countrey to their farmes, to manure and till the ground which is a sore travell. . . .They gave neither to one nor other, nought save grasses and such like thinges of no substance: in such sorte as the milke of the wives newe delivered of their childbyrth dryed up: and thus dyed in a small season, all the litle creature their young children. Further, by reason of the separation and not cohabitating of the men with their wives, the generation ceased between them. The men died with toyle and famine in the mineralles: these the women died of the same in the fieldes.[43]

Mining, then, became one of the most powerful tropes of genocide and the site of particularly vehement colonial critique. The English translation of Las Casas's tract was supplemented by the famous debate between Las Casas and Ginés de Sepúlveda over the spiritual status of the Indians. In the eighth remedy offered by Las Casas for the relief of the indigenous populations he makes specific reference to mining.

> The labour that they were put unto, was to drawe gold, whereof they had need have men of iron. For they must turne the mountaines 1000

times upside downe, digging and hewing the rockes, and washing, and clensing the gold it selfe in the rivers, where they shall continually stand in the water until they brust, and rent their bodies even in pieces. Also when the mines peradventure doe flow with water, then must they also besides all other laboures, drawe it out in their armes. To be briefe, the better to comprehend the labour that is emploid about gathering golde and silver, it may please your Majestie to consider, that heathen Emperours (except to death) never condemned the Martyres to greater tormentes, then to mining for metal.[44]

The cause of such misery Las Casas attributes to Spanish avarice: "The cause why the Spanishe have destroyed suche an infinite of soules, hath been onely, that they have helde it for their last hope and marke to gette golde . . . or for to say in a word, the cause hereof hath been their avarice and ambition."[45] The effects of Las Casas's discourse of labor and mining had far-reaching effects not merely for apprehending Spain's actions in the New World but also in Spain's actions in the Old World as well.

While Eden held out the Spaniards as exemplars — "Stoope Englande stoope, and learne to knowe thy lorde and master, as horses and other brute beastes are taught to doo" — others, in line with Las Casas, could not help but feel uncomfortable with the implications of bestial servitude present in such an exhortation.[46] Slavery was often associated with animal subjugation, and the term "brute" was used to qualify the indigenous peoples of the Americas. John Ponet, a Marian exile writing from Strassburg, railed against the English reversion to Catholicism and the union with Spain, which he viewed as a tyrannical threat to the nation. His political writings are concerned mostly with formulating a model of limited monarchy in a European context. From time to time, however, he looks to contemporary political developments overseas to illustrate his concerns for civil liberties and the protection of private property in Europe. From the following passage from *A Shorte Treatise of politicke power* it is clear that Ponet had read the *De Orbe Novo Decades* (perhaps Eden's translation of it) and considered the Indian fate in the Americas a grim prognostication of what would become of England under the Anglo-Spanish regime.

The people of that counterie whan the catholicke Spaniardes came thider, were simple and plaine men, and lived without great labour, the lande was naturally so pleintiful of all thinges, and continually the trees hade ripe frute in them. Whan the Spaniardes hade by flatterie put in their foote . . . they to get the golde that was ther, forced the people (that were not used to labour) to stande all the daie in the hotte sunne gathering

golde in the sande of the rivers. By this meanes a great nombre of them
(not used to suche paines) died, and a great nombre of them (seeing
them selves brought from so quiet a life to suche miserie and slaverie) of
desperacion killed them selves. . . . So that where at the comming thider
of the spaniardes, ther were accompted to be in that countrey nine hundred thousande persones, ther were in short time by this meanes so fewe
lefte, as Petre Martir (who was one of th[e] emperour Charles the fifthes
cou[n]cail there, and wrote this historie to th[e] emperour) saith, it was
a shame for him to name.[47]

The writings of men like Las Casas and Ponet were absorbed into what we
now call the Black Legend; that is, an anti-Spanish political discourse pack-
aged for widespread European distribution and consumption. Las Casas's
critique of Spain was so popular that it was excerpted, paraphrased, and
reprinted numerous times throughout the last quarter of the century and used
as wartime propaganda against the king of Spain.[48] By Elizabeth's reign, it was
clear that England had a national interest in declaiming the treatment of the
Indians. This propagandistic deployment of the Black Legend had the effect
of portraying Spanish perfidy in broad strokes. For example, England displayed little real interest in the complexities of Indian labor in New Spain or
the Andes, such as how the *encomienda* system functioned, the Andean tributary system (the *mita*), or freelance Indian labor.[49] Instead, England fed on the
raw image of the laboring *other* provided for them in political pamphlets and
visual representations. Certainly, part of England's obsessive protestations
toward Spanish gold lust was a cover for its own colonial desires. But above
and beyond straightforward colonial envy are far-reaching implications embedded in Ponet's political critique. The first is that England might become a
vassal of Spain; one of his final warnings to the reader is that the English will
be shipped over to the New World in chains to labor for the Spanish empire:
"Than [sic] shall [Spain] invade Englande, and [you] shalbe by shiploades
(if no worse happen unto you) caried into newe Spaine, and ther not lyve at
libertie . . . ye shal be tyed in chaynes, forced to rowe in the galie, to digge in
the mynes and to pike up the golde in the hotte sande."[50] The second is that
such vassalage would obscure the difference between the laboring other and
the English body (politic). The emphasis on gold lust and enforced labor
seemed to render the Amerindian visible in a way that was essential to England's political and racial conceptions of itself as a would-be overseas empire, especially at a time before the establishment of slave-based plantations
in North America. These investments in the Black Legend become glaringly
apparent in the moralizing literature of post-Armada publications.

DO YOU MINE?

No longer could New World gold be considered a noble pursuit during England's war with Spain that characterized Elizabethan foreign politics. Rather, it became the subject of political allegory cast in a moral register. Richard Hakluyt, Eden's counterpart in the proceeding generation of translators, flatly condemns gold as a motive for expansion: "Yet this dare I boldly affirme; first that a great number of them [i.e. the Spanish] have satisfied their fame-thirsty and gold-thirsty mindes with that reputation and wealth, which made all perils and misadventures seeme tolerable unto them."[51] In the lord treasurer's speech to Parliament in 1593, Burghley explains that the current conflict was different from previous international wars because in the past "neither party had any special advantage." Philip's American mines tipped the scales in Spain's favor. Burghley continues, "But now the case is altered. The King of Spain maketh these mighty wars by the means only of his Indies, not purposely to burn a town in France or England but to conquer all France, all England, all Ireland."[52]

John Lyly's *Midas* (1589/90) enacts the economic disparity between Spain and England onstage in an allegory of Anglo-Spanish politics with special emphasis on the way Spain's golden conquests in the New World provided a model for its ambitions in Europe. The title character, King Midas of Phrygia, an obvious stand-in for Philip II, is granted one wish by Bacchus at the opening of the play. Although the king is already in possession of rich gold mines, at the advice of his counselor, Mellacrites, Midas chooses gold over love and dominion, for with gold, one can buy the other two. As in the Greek myth, the Midas touch turns out to be a curse when the king realizes that he is unable to eat without his food turning to gold in his hands.

Eventually, Midas rids himself of the curse by bathing in a sacred river. Upon his return home, he stumbles on a music contest between Apollo and Pan. The gods decide to allow Midas to judge who is the better musician. Midas unwisely decides in Pan's favor. Angry, Apollo curses Midas with ass's ears. Embarrassed by yet another indiscretion, Midas attempts to make his way home unseen, whereupon he stumbles on a group of shepherds and eavesdrops on their conversation. The topic of their speech happens to be Midas himself, and in particular his desire for gold. Speaking with the artificially humble voice of the pastoral denizen, one shepherd condemns Midas's greed: "Well, then this I say, when a lion doth so much degenerate from princely kind that he will borrow of the beasts, I say he is no lion but a monster piec'd with the craftiness of the fox, the cruelty of the tiger, the ravening of the wolf, the dissembling of hyena, he is worthy also to have the ears of an ass" (IV.2.25–29).[53] Not only does this statement provide the audience with the symbolic meaning behind the ass's ears, it appears to echo one of the most famous lines of Las Casas's tract: "Upon these lambes so meeke, so qualified & endewed of their maker and creator, as hath bin said, entred the Spanish incontinent as they knewe them, as wolves, as lions, & as tigres most cruel of long time famished."[54]

This play is not merely an allegory of Spanish imperial greed, but also an English fantasy of Spanish remorse in which Midas repeatedly apologizes, usually in monologue, for his unnatural gold lust: "I, that did possess mines of gold, could not be contented till my mind were also a mine" (III.1.7). Moreover, it was not enough for England to criticize Spain's ambition in the New World, but as this play shows, England was asked to understand this ambition as something that threatened its own welfare as a state. Thus Lyly represents the commonly held belief that Philip's invasion of 1588 was an extension of Spain's American occupation. This is duly shown in one of Midas's many rueful monologues in which he repents having sent his navy against the island of Lesbos, for which we should read England. The description is rendered poetically as Philip's attempt to turn England into gold, or a profitable new territorial acquisition: "A bridge of gold did I mean to make in that island where all my navy could not make a breach. Those islands did I long to touch, that I might turn them to gold and myself to glory" (III.1.49–51). By the final act, all of Midas's misfortunes seem to stem from this ultimate act of aggression: "For stretching my hands to Lesbos, I find that all the gods have spurn'd at my practices, and those islands scorn'd them. My pride the gods disdain, my policy, men. My mines have been emptied by soldiers, my soldiers spoiled by wars, my wars without success because usurping, my usurping without end because my ambition without measure" (V.3.55–61).

Lesbos/England, of course, is free from ambition. The play insists on many occasions that England is not an island that will succumb to Spanish aggression in the way that other islands have. The conspicuous emphasis on islands suggests an implicit connection between the English isle and the landmasses of the New World often collectively referred to as islands. The patriotic imperative to contradistinguish the English from other conquered peoples is seen in many specimens of post-Armada ephemera. For example, in a popular political pamphlet Lord Burghley anonymously writes: "the [Spanish invaders] were so miserable [because] they thought the Conquest [of England] would be no more difficult than the overcomming of a nomber of naked Indians at the beginning of the Conquest thereof by King Ferdinand."[55]

In evading Midas's golden touch, England also evades the servitude that such a touch would imply. In many ways gold and silver acquired the stigma of servitude in a perverse reinterpretation of Thomas More's *Utopia*, in which slaves are shackled in gold. In Kim Hall's study of blackness in early modern economies, for example, she discusses the ways in which dark-skinned peoples were visually represented in heraldry and portraiture with badges of slavery forged of precious metals. But unlike More's fictional commonwealth in which such badges are meant to illustrate the Utopian disdain for material wealth, late English instances of such juxtapositions serve to register differences in status "between aristocratic white bodies, black servitude, and foreign wealth."[56] Theodore de Bry's engravings also helped make this iconic inscription of gold, dark skin, and labor in his several engravings of New World mining operations. In one poignant scene, the artist depicts African slaves extracting gold for their seated Spanish master (fig. 13.1). Another shows Peruvian metalworkers at their labors (fig. 13.2); yet another shows hunched Indian miners toiling in a tenebrous grotto in an ingenious cut-away perspective of the *Cerro Rico* of Potosí, the richest mountain in the Americas (fig. 13.3).

De Bry's images of Indian mining and metalworking find a literary counterpart in Book II of Edmund Spenser's *The Faerie Queene*, in which the poet takes the reader on an epic underground journey into a South American mine. In yet another moral allegory of Spanish greed, Spenser uses the Spanish treatment of the Indian as a way of marking the moral distance between the English and the Spanish, but also the racial difference between the Indian and the English. The hero of Book II is Sir Guyon, the elfin knight of temperance. Throughout this book, Guyon must continually test his continence by undergoing a series of physical and emotional temptations in what often feels like a romanticized American landscape.[57] In canto iv, he arrives at the entrance of Mammon's cave, where he is presented with a parody of New World excess:

> And round about him lay on euery side
> Great heapes of gold, that neuer could be spent:
> Of which some were rude owre, not purifide
> Of *Mulcibers* devouring element;
> Some others were driuen, and distent
> Into great Ingoes, and to wedges square;
> Some in round plates withouten moniment;
> But most were stampt, and in their metall bare
> The antique shapes of kings and kesars straunge & rare. (II.vii.5)

As David Read persuasively asserts, Mammon's cave is in fact a gold mine based on Spanish American accounts probably derived from Eden's translation

Ttritis, & penè abfumptis continuo labore Hifpaniolæ Infulæ incolis, Hifpani aliunde man-
cipia conquirere cœperunt, quorum minifterio in perfodiendis montibus, venisque metallicis perferutandis vterentur. Itaque redemptis fua pecunia, & accitis ex Guinea Quartæ
Africæ partis Prouincia mancipijs æthiopibus fiue Nigritis, illorum porrò opera vfi funt,
donec temporis fucceffu quidquid in ea Infula metallicarū venarū ineffet, exhaurirent. Nam vt Lufitani
eam Africæ partem quam ipfi Guineam (Incolæ Genni aut Genna appellant) fibi
fubiectam reddiderant; fingulis annis aliquot incolarum centurias
exteris nationibus diuendebant, quæ mancipiorum
vicem fupplerent.

A 2   Nigritæ

13.1 "African slaves mining gold" from Theodore de Bry's *America* VI, (1595). This item is
reproduced by permission of the Huntington Library, San Marino, California, call no.
122223.

AD CAP. XXII.

Peruanos valde induſtrios eſſe aurifabros.

 NTEQVAM Peruani ſub Ingarum imperium redigerentur, ea induſtria & politie quam nunc habent, deſtituebantur, vt ab ipſismet incolis intelleximus. Sed poſt quam Ingæ, hoc eſt, ſupre-mi illi Peruani regni Principes ipſis dominati ſunt, politiores & cultiores ſunt redditi. Nam In-gæilli valde delectabantur ornatiore ſupellectile, ſtatuis, & vaſis egregie fabrefactis: eam ob cauſam aurifabrorum officinas variis Regni ſui locis inſtituerunt, qui aurum & argentum in va-rias formas elaborarent. Et certe conſpecta ſunt vaſa ab ipſis fabrefacta tanta arte & induſtria, vt quotquot ea viderunt non potuerint non admirari, eoque magis, quod pauca inſtrumenta habeant, & exiguum apparatum ad ea quæ cum facilitate quadam elaborant, peragenda.

Occupato ab Hiſpanis eo Regno, conſpecta ſunt elegantia & admiranda vaſa de quibus (inquit Petruſ Cieca primæ partis Chronici Peruani cap. CXIIII) ſileo, quoniam ipſe non vidi. Illud tamen (pergit) affirmare poſſum, conſpexiſſe me illos duorum æreorum fragmentorum, & duorum aut trium lapidum nigrorum adminiculo, vaſa, fonticulos, candelabra tam affabre confeciſſe, vt noſtri aurifabri cum omnibus ſuis inſtrumentis ornatiora confi-cere vix poſſent. Ad metalla porro liquanda. duntaxat fornacula vtuntur ex luto conſtructa, in qua carbones poſi-ti incenduntur à viris circum fornaculam diſpoſitis, qui loco follium, arundinibus cauis flatu ignem excitant, vt materia vrceis impoſita liqueſcat, quam deinde eximentes, fabrorum præfectis tradunt.

Guaynacapam tradunt in theſauris ſuis habuiſſe aureas ſtatuas Gigantum magnitudine, ſed intus inanes, ex au-ro præterea & argento conflatas formas quadrupedum, auium, arborum & herbarum in ſuo regno naſcentium, ſi-militer omnis generis piſcium, vel quos mare regnum ſuum alluens vel flumina per illud labentia alerent. Ad-dunt inſuper, Ingas hortum quendam poſſediſſe in inſula quadam circa Punam, in quam nauigabant à curis ſoluti, vt genio indulgerent, cuius herbæ, flores, arbores ex auro & vrgento conflatæ eſſent. Hoc certum eſt, aurifabros iſtos, ſtatuas, idola, vaſa, clenodia, breuiter quæcunque ab ipſis requirerentur, elaboraſſe, ad ſua templa exornanda.

G 4   In

13.2 "Peruvian metal-workers" from Theodore de Bry's *America* VI, (1595). This item is reproduced by permission of the Huntington Library, San Marino, California, call no. 122209.

INDI, QVA ARTE AVRVM EX
MONTIBVS ERVANT.

 X POTOSSI *montanis, aurifodinis omnium ditißimis per o-*
mnem Indiã, aurum Indi hac arte effodiunt, qua in noſtris ferè
regionibus itidem factitant. Nã ex rupibus excindenda omnia
ſunt. Operarios in duos ordines diſpeſcunt. Quorum hi de die la-
borantes, noctu quieſcunt: illi noctu operis vacantes, interdiu dormiunt.
Quamuis nec diurnam nec nocturnam cæli facem videãt, ſed vniuerſim ſuc-
cenſis cereis opus habeant: Cum vltrà 150. orgias infra terram ſeſe demittant.
Nec tamen iſta tàm immenſa fodinarum profunditas impedit, quô minus
omne effoſſum æs ſuis dorſis foras efferre cogantur. Quem in vſum ſcalas ad-
hibent, ita ſtructas parataſqʒ, vt binæ ſibi ſemper cõiunctæ hæreant. Scalæ ve-
rò ex intortis boum coriis confectæ ſunt, quæ tranſuerſis radiis ligneis ſuffir-
mantur ita, vt ternis viris ſemper ex ordine deſcenſus vno latere, altero verò
totidem aſcenſus ſit. Cumqʒ in aſcenſus labore vtraqʒ manu ſcalas corripere
cogantur, ideo, qui illorum primus eſt, cereum ardentem de pollice religatum
geſtat. Porrò, quia meta aſcenſuris nimis longa eſt, iccirco in media via ſur-
recta quædã ſcamna ſunt, quibus onera ſua quadamtenus deponere poſſunt.

13.3 "Black slaves mining gold" (*Cerro Rico*, Potosí, Bolivia) from Theodore de Bry's *America*
V, (1595). This item is reproduced by permission of the Huntington Library, San
Marino, California, call no. 66985.

of the *De Orbe Novo Decades,* Zárate's history of Peru, or Las Casas' *Brevissima relación,* all of which were available to the poet by the early 1580s.[58] Guyon's challenge, of course, is to reject the wealth that Mammon places before him:

> Me list not (said the Elfin knight) receaue
> Thing offred, till I know it well be got,
> Ne wote I, but thou didst these goods bereaue
> From rightfull owner by vnrighteous lot,
> Or that bloud guiltnesse or guile them blot. (II.vii.19)

Eventually, we get a first-hand look at the rightful owners of this gold as Mammon leads the knight deeper into his plutonic realm. Despite Guyon's concern for indigenous property rights, any sympathy for the dispossessed is diffused in Spenser's chiaroscuro description of Mammon's demonic slaves at their hellish labors:

> Thence forward he him did led, and shortly brought
> Vnto another rowme, whose dore forthright,
> To him did open, as it had beene taught:
> Therein an hundred raunges weren pight,
> And hundred fornaces all burning bright;
> By every fornace many feends did bide,
> Deformed creatures, horrible in sight,
> And every feend his busie paines applide,
> To melt the golden metall, ready to be tride.
>
> One with great bellowes gathered fillin aire,
> And with forst wind the fewell did inflame;
> Another did the dying bronds repaire
> With yron toungs, and sprinckled oft the same
> With liquid waues, fiers Vulcans rage to tame,
> Who maistring them renewd his former heat;
> Some scumd the drosse, that from the metall came;
> Some stird the molten owre with ladles great;
> And every one did swinke and every one did sweat. (II.vii.35–36)

Read suggests that what we are witnessing here is a kind of New World first-contact encounter between Guyon and the native metalworkers, as the laboring hosts stop, stupefied at the sudden entrance of the exotic stranger.

But when as earthly wight they present saw,
Glistring in armes and battailous array,
From their whot worke they did themselues withdraw
To wonder at the sight: for till that day,
They neuer creature saw, that came that way.
Their staring eyes sparckling with feruent fire,
And vgly shapes did nigh the man dismay,
That were it not for shame, he would retire,
Till that him thus bespake their soueraigne Lord & sire. (II.vi.37)

Read's understanding of this episode as a moment of first contact depends on situating Guyon in the position of the Spanish explorer: "The effect is of Guyon incarnated as a Spaniard, but a Spaniard immaculately conceived, It is not so much a matter of temptation refused but of identity transcended."[59] I would emend this reading by placing Guyon in the position of the English, perpetually one step behind the Spaniard in the New World, for the enslavement of workers is already in place before the knight's arrival. In this way, Guyon does not represent a transcendent Spaniard so much as a morally superior Englishman free of avarice. Read against the backdrop of the Black Legend in England, this scene triangulates the Spaniard in Mammon, the Englishman in Guyon, and the Indian in laboring creatures so as to, once again, insert a moralized political difference between the Spaniard and the Englishman, and a racialized difference between the Englishman and the demonically rendered Indian. Both terms of difference seem necessary for situating the English hero at the apex of this triangle.

NEW GOLD STANDARDS

Ironically, the one means for acquiring gold that the Elizabethans found palatable proved to be as foreshortened and compensatory as Eden's distilled island coin, if not more effective. This method was piracy. Piracy and state-sanctioned privateering, was viewed as a justified and patriotic activity that not only lightened King Phillip's purse but also enriched the commonwealth thereby. Francis Drake and others were celebrated for relieving Spanish flotillas of their precious cargo as they crisscrossed the Atlantic. The virtue of piracy as an ideological alternative to straightforward territorial acquisition and enslavement of native populations was that it constituted a second-hand acquisition that removed the English from the dirty business of labor and exploitation. Numerous analogies were employed in the period to mark the distance between Indian exploitation and the fruits of industry. Robert

Greene's Armada pamphlet *The Spanish Masquerado* provides an example. In his celebration of the English Channel victory and Drake's Caribbean raids Greene sugarcoats the realities of New World wealth with mellifluous metaphor in this descriptive tableau of Spanish defeat.

> Sir Francis Drakes happie success in India [i.e. the Caribbean], and the late loss of their soveraignes fleete [i.e. the Armada], joined together sore daunted the mindes of the India generals, that they sit like men discontented in their heartes; to whom is objected (as in derision) the verses that Vergil wrote against Batillus. *Sic vos non vobis mellificatus Apes*. . . . Meaning that as the bees make honye themselves, yet not for themselves, but men reape it to their use, so the Spaniard digged out sweete honye from the golde mines, and Sir Francis Drake fetched it home to be tasted in England reaping his profite out of their labours.[60]

Greene's text makes clear that while it was convenient for Elizabethan England to adopt critical attitudes toward gold digging in the Americas, it does not, despite all, erase the fact that England openly praised the acquisition of New World wealth as long as such feats were seen as detrimental to ongoing Spanish expansion and free from the taint of first-hand labor exploitation. The genealogy of gold lust that I have attempted to trace from England's first glimpse of the New World via Richard Eden's translations to the allegorical representation of avarice of the Elizabethan era merely discovers the subterranean workings of the Black Legend, a discourse that enabled England to elaborate its own set of imperial imperatives. The desire for a golden empire, I would argue, never really faded in the time before England established permanent slave-based agrarian colonies, but was obscured over time by Elizabethan anti-Spanish propaganda that softened the harsh reality that England would never find a New World El Dorado.

CHAPTER FOURTEEN

BLACKENING "THE TURK" IN ROGER ASCHAM'S *A REPORT OF GERMANY*

Linda Bradley Salamon

I n the autumn of 1550, the regime of the boy-king Edward VI of England
dispatched to Holy Roman Emperor Charles V an embassy led by Sir
Richard Morison, a long-standing Tudor courtier. Morison's principal brief
seems to have been defending English diplomats' right to Protestant worship
abroad while contesting Mary Tudor's right to the Catholic Mass in England.
As his official secretary on this ill-starred venture rode Roger Ascham (1515?–
1568), a scrappily ambitious 35-year-old humanist who had received the patronage appointment through the good offices of Sir John Cheke, his former
university teacher. A sometime academic whose previous, short-term official
posts had been tutor to Edward and to Princess Elizabeth and the royal li-
brarianship, Ascham had no political or diplomatic experience. But his Latin
was fluent, his command of the new Italian penmanship was admired, his
Protestantism was fervent, and he could read newly fashionable Greek texts
like Herodotus with Morison in their leisure hours.[1] Given Morison's impoli-
tic audiences with Habsburg Emperor Charles, over the next months embassy members had ample time to observe the events that developed around
Charles's stumbling reign.[2] They traveled with the peripatetic imperial court
until August 1553, when, upon the death of King Edward and the forceful
ascension of Queen Mary, they took passage home. In those three years away
from England, Roger Ascham moved through a challenging world where
Catholics held hegemony. Inevitably he also formed what Edward Said (1994,
73) called a "collection of dreams, images, and vocabularies [for] what lies
east of the dividing line" in the Ottoman Empire under Suleyman the Magnificent, the major political and military threat to Habsburg power.[3] Traveling with Charles's court through the heart of Germany and Austria as close
to the Hungarian borderlands as Villach in Carinthia, despite Ascham's

scholarly and doctrinal preoccupations he had no choice but to imagine the strange world on the other side of that mid-sixteenth-century frontier.

In the final months of the embassy, Ascham began to draft an account of his observations as a first-time continental traveler (and the gleanings of a sociable, voracious gossip), initially as a letter to a friend. His unfinished production, the unofficial *A Report of Germany* composed in 1553, offers his analysis of Emperor Charles's many problems, including the danger from the Ottoman East. This virtually unnoticed text[4] was written decades before personal and commercial encounters between England and the Sublime Porte at Istanbul began to bring empirical information about contemporary Islam to Elizabethans. As Ascham wrote, construction of the "Mohammedan" world by Elizabethan and Jacobean travel writers and dramatists, informed by those contacts of the 1570s and 1580s, was not even on the horizon.[5] During the course of the sixteenth century, representation of the Turks was contingent on historical events to an extraordinary degree; to a careful observer at mid-century, Ottoman power could only seem ominous. With little concrete knowledge, then, Ascham created a "textual universe" (Said 1994, 52): anecdotes about fierce encounters between agents of the two major empires, Habsburg and Ottoman. His dark vision may be an illustration of what Kenneth Parker (1999, 3, 28) has wisely named "dis-orientation"; his larger purposes are not easy to discern.

In this chapter, I examine Ascham's narration of Turkish conduct in the contexts of its historical setting, its position within *A Report of Germany* as a whole, and its similarities to other representations of cultural and racial difference. I explore the figure of "the Turk" in *A Report* in both material and discursive terms, assessing its relation to Ascham's Protestant convictions, and I speculate about the knowledge and attitudes that he brought to his report. It is easy to suppose that his Turkish anecdotes are a form of propaganda, but such an assertion begs many questions, including the target at which he aims. As Andrew Hadfield (1998) has cogently demonstrated, discourses of early modern travelers—whether evoked by Ireland, the New World, or from around the globe—share many rhetorical functions, among them denigrating the barbarism of other places while instilling loyalty to the native state, combating the success of rival nations, and using representation of foreign otherness as a safely veiled critique of the closer to home. To position within this cultural field Ascham's armchair confrontation with a people that shocked him, then, I present his tone and diction in relation to the Black Legend about racialized encounters in the New World. Finally, to suggest how displaced representation of violent hostility circulated, I compare Ascham's construction of Turks to Michel de Montaigne's famous second-hand report of Brazilians and to images of Central American indigenes in the less-well-known collection of Theodore de Bry.

ASCHAM'S TURKS: TEXT IN HISTORICAL CONTEXT

The background for Ascham's narrative, as modern historians largely confirm, was a power struggle over North Africa. As the English embassy reached the continent, a 1545 truce between the empires of Suleyman I and the Habsburgs was about to expire.[6] *Before* the treaty ran out, Ascham explains, Charles's forces seized the strategic North African town of Mahdia[7] from Suleyman's corsair ally there. In response, and in vengeful mood, in 1551 Ottoman forces first took Tripoli, then feinted toward Malta, and came dangerously close to Sicily.[8] Ascham reports that, during the siege of Tripoli, the Turks violated a safe-conduct document for Christian inhabitants to leave the city that had been negotiated by the French ambassador.

> As soon as the Turks entered the town, they put old and young, man, woman, and child, to the sword; saving two hundred of the strongest men to be their galley slaves for ever. The general being asked why he kept no promise, made this answer: If the emperor had kept faith with my master for [Mahdia], I would not have broken with them of Tripoli; and therefore (saith he) with Christian men which care for no truth, promises may justly be broken. This Turkish cruelty was revenged this last year in Hungary, when like promise of life was made, and yet all put to the sword, the Christians bidding the Turks remember Tripoli. To such beastly cruelty the noble feats of arms be come unto betwixt the Christian men and the Turks.

Massacre, enslavement, revenge. Soon the conflict would move to another front, a Hungary divided between Habsburg and Ottoman rule. The stakes are raised as individuals suffer vividly imagined horrors. In the next move, Ascham relates,

> the basha of Buda [viceroy over the Ottoman province of Hungary] took in a skirmish a gentleman of the king of the Romans; for whose delivery, men for entreaty, and money for his ransom were sent to Buda. . . . [On the day appointed for the pasha's answer,] suddenly came out two hangmen, bare-armed, with great butcher's knives in their hands, bringing with them certain bandogs muzzled, kept hungry without meat of pur-

pose. The basha bade them do their feat: who, coming to the gentleman, stripped him naked, and bound him to a pillar; after with their knives they cut off his flesh by gobbets, and flung it to the dogs. Thus the poor gentleman suffered grief; not so tormented in feeling his flesh mangled with knives, as seeing himself piece-meal devoured by dogs. And thus, as long as he felt any pain, they cut him in collops; and after they let their dogs loose upon him to eat up the residue of him, that the grief which was ended in him, being dead, might yet continue in his friends looking on . . .

Not long after this, three Turks of good estimation and place were taken by the Christian men; for whose ransom great sums of gold were offered. Answer was made to the messenger, that all the gold in Turkey should not save them: and because ye Turks will eat no swine's flesh, you shall see if swine will eat any Turkish flesh. And so likewise great boars were kept hungry, and in sight of the messenger the three Turks were cut in collops and thrown amongst them. For these foul deeds I am not so angry with the Turks that began them, as I am sorry for the Christian men that follow them. (III, 12–13)

By any measure the physical violence of this passage is startling, considering the otherwise-sober *Report* and Ascham's writing generally.

It is Turkish focus on bodies, not ethics, that commands Ascham's sharpest attention. In the entire text of *A Report,* only in describing the cruel acts by Turks does the bookish Ascham cite a real (not metaphorical[9]) body, or pain, or any dimension of materiality except dinner. But in these anecdotes the reader's gaze is directed at bare arms, at a bound and expectant naked man, at gobbets of flesh[10]—the body has become a battleground between Christian and heathen. To add to the degradation, as in cannibalism the consumer becomes the consumed; Christians who are eaten by dogs are constituted as dogs, and Turks eaten by boars become swine.[11] Moreover, the reported torture includes a conscious edge of sadism: it invokes mental as well as physical pain. An unholy glee pervades the anonymous, passive-voiced Christian message: "And because ye Turks will eat no swine's flesh, you shall see if swine will eat any Turkish flesh." It is Roger Ascham who ventriloquizes that tone, although he ascribes it to vicious Habsburg warriors. But however he decries it, he as a listener to the story—and thus the reader of his *Report*—participates in horrified but detached gazing at despoiled bodies in what Le Mascrier's *Description de l'Egypte* (1735) calls "bizarre jouissance" (Said 1994, 103).

To unpack this moralized narrative, I need first to historicize the material events it describes. In 1542—less than a decade before Ascham's arrival on the continent—the armies of the Porte had extended the long-term Ottoman domination of the eastern Mediterranean and the Balkans by overrunning most of Hungary, including Buda; thus they were well positioned for a renewed march on Vienna. In an example of Machiavellian realpolitik that rather scandalizes Ascham, the deeply divided western Europeans—empire, nation-states, principalities—not only were open to pragmatic subversions from Suleyman but actively invited them. As Ascham relates, the Ottomans had forged an alliance of convenience with Charles's great temporal enemy, the France of Francois I and then Henri II; on the Mediterranean front, Charles's vassal the Prince of Salerno, failing to get the assistance he requested from the emperor, soon turned renegade to Suleyman's camp and (so Ascham heard rumored) commanded a sixty-three-ship fleet under the Ottomans (III, 28). To be sure, while the English embassy was still in place in 1552, Suleyman's troops were defeated in a skirmish in western Hungary, but that Habsburg victory was temporary. As Ascham's account halts, Suleyman was riding high, and Ottoman defeat in the battle of Lepanto lay almost twenty years in the future. The alliance of France with the sultan; many Christian warriors' defections and even conversion to Islam; the continuing trade between Europe and the Porte that, in England, led to the formation of the Levant Company in 1581—all these events subvert any simple binary between Christian Europe and the Ottomans as "occident" and "orient." Yet Ascham's report of this tumultuous period still accords the Turk a distinctive place: first among the personages whose political conduct he assigns a section heading.[12] The ostensible reason for this priority is simple chronology, for Ascham locates the beginning of Emperor Charles's plunge into near-universal animosity in the unprovoked seizure of Mahdia in 1550 (III, 14). But the Ottomans, active on both the Mediterranean and Balkan fronts, are nonetheless marked as the paramount concern of continental Europe.

The contestation between Charles V and the Ottomans is not, however, central to Ascham's overall narrative. The stated purpose of *A Report of Germany* is to explain how Charles came to be at odds with virtually every other player in the great game of international politics.[13] In analyzing the situation Ascham often expresses the goal of impartiality (III, 7, 10, 21, 30), which turns out to mean equal criticism of Charles V and Henri II. In something like high literary journalism combined with contemporary diplomatic history,[14] he not only narrates events but explains the causes for shifting political alliances. As an enthusiastic reader of Xenophon, Thucydides, Julius Caesar, Phillipe de Commines, and even Machiavelli, he follows antique models in aiming to write "exemplary" history in which events are driven by the character—very

14.1 Turkish soldiers "in their arrogance" preparing for an unsuccessful siege of the castle at Rhodes in the 1450s. From Bernhard von Breydenbach's *Die Reise ins Heilige Land: ein Reiseberich aus dem Jahre 1483*, 1486.

nearly by the virtues and vices—of leading political figures. (The raw anec-dotes about reciprocal cruelty between Turk and Christian, that is to say, di-verge considerably from his normal Plutarchan procedure.) In this vein As-cham assesses the actions, and offers word portraits when he can, of Charles V himself; Ottavio, Duke of Parma; Pope Julius III; Pedro, the Viceroy of Naples; Ferrante, the Prince of Salerno; Albrecht, the Markgraf of Bran-denburg; the emissary Lazarus Schwendi; Johann-Friedrich, Elector of Saxony; Maurice, the Duke of Saxony—and of course the Turk.

Throughout the text Suleyman I is never named, nor is he accorded rank by any such customary title as "sultan" or "grand seignior"; the only un-named western European in *A Report*, meanwhile, is the renegade prince of Salerno. The single designation "the great Turk himself" (III, 13) only adds portent to the gap. In a fashioning overwhelmingly familiar from later com-mentators, Ascham also uses "the Turk" as his normal referent for the entire geographico-politico-military complex that is the Ottoman Empire. He writes as if the act of naming would particularize, and perhaps legitimate, a looming presence, masculine but otherwise indistinct. In 1553, well before the happier Elizabethan contacts had begun, his lexicon essentializes the Ottomans, turning a nation-state into an indistinguishable mass of violent Asiatics, voiceless but implacable.[15] The vision, as evoked in contemporary graphical images,[16] is turbaned, scimitar armed, and almost identically featured—what Said called "patently foreign and distant . . . [yet] more rather than less familiar" (Said 1994, 58). Above all, these foreign men are treacherous: the first incident narrated is the ambush of Christian civilians supposedly retreating under guarantee of safe conduct.[17] The Ottoman general in this story, to be sure, attributes his violation of a solemn promise to retaliation for Charles V's prior abrogation of a truce. When the next gesture of reciprocation is a nearly identical Christian move to "put all to the sword" in Turkish territory, one possible implication is that the Christians learned such beastly behavior from the foreign horde whose cultural essence includes vengefulness.

Ascham appears to have a second thought about his report of Turkish cruelty. Immediately after that narrative, he notes the Venetian ambassador's opinion that "the great Turk himself (religion excepted) is a good and merciful, just and liberal prince, wise in making and true in performing any covenant" (III, 13)—exactly the qualities praised in the humanist *speculum principis*, explicitly including promise keeping. This is Suleyman the Magnificent, after all, and impartiality is a goal. But Ascham promptly erases that tempered image by characterizing the sultan's son Mustafa as cruel, false, greedy, extravagant, wily, a promise breaker, a warmonger, an oppressor of the poor, and a mocker of God.[18] Suleyman is thus the token exception that proves the rule of the Turkish essence. Suleyman's religious error and Mustafa's mockery of God are, somewhat surprisingly, the only references that connect the Turks to religion; like his humanist counterparts in Italy, Ascham inscribes the Ottoman Empire as a politicogeographic, rather than Islamic, power.[19]

A REPORT AS IDEOLOGY AND FACT

The character of the Turkish anecdotes marks them, at first glance, as obvious propaganda. Certainly Ascham intentionally selected these particular events—of all those he learned about in more than two years spent in German-speaking lands—to incorporate in his report to confidants, and certainly he is intentionally blackening the reputation of all participants in these two sorry stories. But is he, in his own voice, deliberately purveying a narrative of victimization that is designed to arouse righteous fury? All the analyses of this first-time traveler abroad are not only Anglocentric but often ingenuous;[20] when he remarks that only England and Venice were neutral in 1552 (III, 21), for instance, he seems oblivious to the enormous difference that Venice was positioned literally between empires, his England at the outer periphery of Europe. Any desire to involve Englishmen in a distant conflict is, in a provincial academic, highly implausible, and Ascham gives no evidence of reporting to Edward VI's advisors any suggestion of such an involvement—a report that would go far beyond his brief. This text is no *machine de guerre*.

No other motive for the violent images is immediately obvious. Is Ascham, with the credulity of diplomatic inexperience, claiming truth for reports gleaned from trusted sources who are in effect manipulating him? Epistemologically, what did he think he knew about the Turks, and how did he know it? Despite his numerous truth claims, should some elements of his report be attributed to his own imaginative revisioning? Whether Ascham had ever met a Turk, or indeed any Muslim, by 1553 cannot be determined (although he probably would have reported such an exciting occasion). While western ambassadors and traders from Genoa, Venice, Ragusa (modern Dubrovnik), and more recently France had long been received in Istanbul, a state of war existed between Suleyman and Charles throughout Ascham's stay on the continent, and traffic between them was unlikely. Although Anthony Jenkinson received the first recorded safe-conduct pass to travel through Ottoman lands for trade in 1553, English merchants did not have sustained contacts with Istanbul until around 1575, well after Ascham's death; the first longer-term Turkish diplomatic representative probably arrived in London no earlier than 1607. Ascham himself hoped—rather casually—to go to Turkey; as he was preparing to leave the Habsburg court, the Venetian ambassador (his trusted informant Marcantonio D'Anula) tantalized him by offering a place with Italians who were being dispatched to Constantinople, Damascus, or Cairo, but Ascham could not finance such a sojourn even if he seriously desired it.[21] Little or none of his construction, then, is based on first-hand acquaintance. And, in Stephen Greenblatt's term (1991, 139, 147), he had no go-between to play the legitimating and authenticating role in cultural translation.

But Ascham listened to a common discourse circulating at the Habsburg court. He gives every evidence of believing that the anecdotes about massacre of civilians and torture of captives were obtained from eyewitnesses, of whom he cites some fifteen throughout *A Report*.[22] As Lucette Valensi's study of sixteenth-century Venetian ambassadors' reports from Istanbul has shown, the Italians presented humanist-educated analyses that would be congenial to Ascham, and his text bears out that affinity. In regard to the specific stories about Turks, he names Monsieur Daramont, the French ambassador to the sultan, as the negotiator—hence potential eyewitness and auditor of reported speech—at the initial massacre outside Tripoli (III, 11–12). For the story of the Roman courtier fed to the dogs in Hungary, the most vivid in the sequence, Ascham supplies no source but offers the suggestive remark, "[His friends] were bade depart, and tell what they saw; who, ye may be sure, were in care enough to carry home with them such a cruel message" (III, 13). This indirect discourse implicates equally the messengers of the "in your face" taunt and its purported Ottoman author. (One possible *rapporteur* is Giambattista Gascaldo, the Habsburg general in Hungary [III, 59].)

And after all, the tales may be in large part veridical, just as the macro-events at Tripoli are historically accurate; as Jeremy Black has warned,[23] we forget at our peril that violence was endemic in early modern Europe. Some confirmation for Ascham's reportage comes from the letters he wrote from the road to his colleagues at St. John's College, Cambridge, almost two years before he drafted *A Report*, soon after the alleged events occurred. In this familiar correspondence, his narrative is more circumstantial. He sketches the political background, a regency in Habsburg Hungary; he identifies the protagonists more closely (a "gentleman of Ferdinand's court," quite likely Spanish, and "Belierboglie [i.e., *beylerbeyi*, the title of a provincial governor] Mahomet" [I, 309]); he quantifies numbers of troops, galleys, and "saddles of men at arms" (I, 311); of the slain and the captured; of the ducats offered in ransom. Truth seems to lie in these details. Moreover, Ascham is both skeptical and scrupulous, aware of the power of rumor, noting, "whether a promise of the delivery [of Mahdia back to the Turks] was either not made or not kept I cannot tell" (I, 310). And he concludes this section of a lengthy letter, "News were brought hither [from Malta], that many of the Turk's galleys were drowned by over-thwarting the seas; some said forty, some said sixteen, some nine; but the ambassador of Venice saith, that he heard in no letter that any ship took harm. And thus much of the Turk's stirs both by sea and land, as is most credibly known and confirmed to be true in this town and court" (I, 312). Such a measured conclusion underwrites the invincibility of the Ottoman navy; it also signifies Ascham's efforts at accuracy.

When Ascham comes to recast his newsy letters for a wider audience and (potential) publication, he has shaped his Turkish tale for greater effect. He reverses the order of the two anecdotes, placing the horrific Hungarian story in the later, more rhetorically effective position. Although time has passed and memory faded, he revitalizes the incidents: rather than simply narrating events as in his letters, he allows "the Turkish general," the pasha of Buda, and some anonymous Christians to speak, dramatically enacting their vengeful morality. The Turkish torturers and Christian boars, along with their acts, are described in greater detail and more expressive diction; passive voice gives way to active; new emphasis is given to the dread and pain of the primary victims; horrified on-lookers are specifically imagined. The more polished final version elicits less rational analysis and much more affective reaction. Ascham did not invent these anecdotes, and in his permanent record he simply heightened their impact.

ASCHAM'S INTELLECTUAL FORMATION

What, in the *mentalité* of a midcentury English intellectual, might underlie Ascham's receptivity to strong reports of the Turks and thus ground his vivid representation?[24] In the early Tudor years, circulating images of the Muslim other were at best confused. Hall's *Chronicle*, for instance, reports that Henry VIII appeared at the 1510 Shrove Sunday banquet armed with a scimitar and "appareled after Turkey fashion," accompanied by two ladies in headdress "like the Egipcians" with skins stained "to be nygros or blacke Mores" (Chew, 454–55 and n.) All that is missing is a Saracen. Distinctions among Middle Eastern and North African peoples were much clearer to the English by 1600 (Hadfield, 1998, 119, 160–61), but Ascham's writings do not yet make them. A kind man who, in *The Scholemaster* (1570), famously opposed violence in the form of beating schoolboys (III, 89, 96–97), he may simply have been struck by his first confrontation with the full horrors of war: a visceral awareness, albeit at second hand, that one's body might be placed completely beyond one's control.

Formation through schooling and practical experience is the obvious site to explore. But neither the school curriculum that he himself studied nor the revised, humanist curriculum that he passionately advocated in *The Scholemaster* opened much space for contemporary cultural geography. The royal council around Edward VI no doubt dispatched and received diplomatic state papers with some bearing on Ottoman affairs, but Ascham is discreet enough never to mention in *A Report* the correspondence he read or transcribed on Morison's behalf.[25] To be sure, Hakluyt reports English captains visiting Barbary ports in the early 1550s who might have brought news home, but the *Voyages* were not published until 1589–1600.

As for the scholarly knowledge of this bookish man, beyond extensive references to Xenophon as the model for princely conduct, Ascham's classical learning could offer little help in interpreting Turks; the Greeks and Romans had been confronted by different, pre-Islamic barbarians. He was translating Herodotus from the Greek with Morison as they traveled, but he cites the historian only briefly (III, 61) and omits his view of the Scythians, the Turks' protoancestors.[26] Ascham may have absorbed some "key discursive principles" such as the ostensible authority of eyewitnesses, but he never achieves the "multi-subjective, contingency-oriented account" (Greenblatt 1991, 123–26) that is Herodotus's great accomplishment. Meanwhile, the leading German humanist Philip Melancthon, whom Ascham greatly respected, had urged in 1537 that western princes should gain a good understanding of Turkish affairs because "we must fight the Turks, not only in defence of liberty, laws, and other refinements of civilization, but also for our religion, altars, and homes."[27] And certainly Ascham read what he could about recent Ottoman events: "the whole story of winning [Mahdia] ye may read when you list," he tells his friends and narratees, "being well written in Latin, by a Spaniard that was present at it" (III, 11). As he notes in *A Report* (III, 29–30, 41), he read critically the work of Luis de Avila, secretary of Ferrara, on earlier wars between Charles and his Protestant vassals. He is particularly fervid about Paolo Giovio, Bishop of Nocera, whose *Historiarum Sui Temporis Libri XLV* (1550–1552) he rejects out of hand as aiming "to deface the emperor, to flatter France, to spite England, to belie Germany, to praise the Turk, to keep up the pope" (III, 31).[28] As for local history, Ascham struggled with German, which might have been informative.[29] He knew no oriental languages, and the notion that Turks, or more generally the Arab world, might have a culture of their own to be consulted is inconceivable to him.[30] Apparently, Ascham had no intellectual access to the motives and practices of the Ottoman world. His grasp of savage atrocity derives from some other experience.

One final source for the animus in Ascham's Turkish anecdotes is available: some of his first-hand informants no doubt shared the centuries-old notion of crusading to rescue the eastern Mediterranean—now including Constantinople—from Muslims. The concept was still vital in the minds of Charles V, who saw himself as a new Charlemagne, and of successive popes. Ottoman cruelty, exaggerated or not, was readily made into fine propaganda for a new crusade. In England, however, the zenith of enthusiasm for crusading against the conquered Holy Land, along with other Muslim outposts, had probably been reached in the reign of Richard II.[31] Most important to Ascham, crusading was a Catholic movement; it was generally opposed by Protestant leaders, beginning with Luther, who initially considered violence in the name of the church an illicit form of Christian "works."[32] (Potential crusades, after all, were financed not only by levies added to church taxes but by the sale of indulgences—spiritual absolution offered as a commodity for as little as a hundredth of one's annual revenue [Housley, 1992, 412–15]— a *bete noire* of reformers as an aspect of the whole practice of penance.[33]) To be sure, during Ascham's stay in Habsburg lands, the ongoing war between Sicily and North Africa had in fact begun as an official crusade, declared and funded by Pope Paul III, who lent six galleys.

But Protestant Ascham never acknowledges that designation; *A Report* is altogether silent on the subject of crusading, even in the context of the martyred women and children in Tripoli. In Ascham's candid letters to Edward Raven, although he does not use the term "crusade" he is more forthcoming about the Ottomans as Emperor Charles's always-already enemy. Early on, "I wished to have a journey down Danubius through almost all of Europe, and I am afraid I shall have my wish . . . for it is thought here in a manner without doubt that we must all go [t]here against the great Turk" (I, 263); three months later, upon reaching Augsburg, "I think we shall go against the Turks this year, and if the emperor would go whither I would have him, he should never leave till he came to Constantinople" (I, 268). As time passed, Ascham's image of Charles's leadership dimmed: "Whether the Emperor go against the Turk, into Italy, into Spain, against Madenburge [*sic*], or come down into Flanders, it is not yet certain. We will go with him whithersoever he go, except he go to the devil" (I, 278). Like World War I soldiers after the Somme, Ascham's ardor for war cooled rapidly; faced with the reverses and horrors reported from the eastern front and the renewed challenges to Charles in the west, he simply stopped mentioning an offensive campaign against the Ottomans by a Catholic Christian force.

ASCHAM'S REPRESENTATION OF CATHOLIC POWERS

I contend that the real propaganda in *A Report of Germany* lies in a quite different inscription than Christian hostility to Islam. By subtle *bricolage* Ascham uses his Turkish anecdotes to intensify his critique of Charles V for provoking the Ottomans as only the first of many follies. The underlying opposition of Ascham's entire *tour d'horizon* in *A Report*—from his position near the leading edge of the advanced reforming party in England—is Protestant v. Catholic; confrontation with Ottoman immanence on the continent, however violent, unsettles that binary only briefly. In the sequence of anecdotes about treachery and torture, moreover, Ascham claims that he reprehends the Christian imitation of foul deeds more than the Turks' initiation of them.[34] (Christians, apparently, should love mercy, or at least leave vengeance to

God.) To be sure, the Christian actions are presented in a blander tone, in less detail, and with no attention to the suffering of the victims. But while the Ottoman troops' behavior is afforded modest justification, Christians who imitate them by invading and dismembering the bodies of the living appear to cross a line of dignity and humanity. Among the players in international politics, there is a clear scale of relative value: when Ascham wishes to denigrate the side changing of Henri II of France, in what he clearly intends as an escalation of disdain he derides the king's willingness to become "at once, by solemn league, protestant, popish, Turkish [capital *sic*], and devilish" (III, 55). The first and best choice is Protestant; below the Turks lie only demons — but the popish crew is next worst. In the tales of reciprocal cruelty, Ascham never explicitly points to the fact that all the Christian participants are Catholics, but his educated friends in England would be in no doubt.

For impartiality stops at the church door: Ascham makes no attempt to suppress his anti-Catholicism. His opening list of the principal topics in *A Report* includes "the double-dealing of Rome with all parties" (III, 5). Referring to the primary Catholic actors, he starts off by calling the pope (then Julius III) "the bishop of Rome," though gradual slippage to the conventional title begins soon. "Rome," he says, "is a shop always open to any mischief," and the pope has deliberately instigated the war between the Habsburgs and France (III, 17–20). "Julius Tertius is a knave," he quotes a courtier (III, 22). There is nothing good to be said of any pope; for no narrative purpose but scandal, Ascham accurately reports that Duke Pietro Alysio [actually Pier Ludovico] Farnese was Pope Paul III's son (III, 14).[35] The "papistical bishops" of German sees are equally blameworthy (III, 9, 36).

Charles V, as *Holy Roman* Emperor, is the next most potent Catholic figure, and Ascham scornfully notes his ostensible religious motivation: "as an obedient son of the church," albeit for his own secular reasons, Charles promised to "stretch out his arm and open his purse in that recovery of the church's rights" in Parma. The emperor even uses an ambitious former Protestant as informer so he "might the easilier overthrow the protestants and with them, God and his word" and "establish papistry in Germany with the sword," thus "defacing true religion, and tossing the world" (III, 18, 40, 45, 38). The explicit alignment of such a powerful man against Ascham's cause is automatically discrediting. And Charles's court is as treacherously violent as the Turks: "Being advised by some bloody counsellors that Duke Frederick's death should, by the terror of it, turn all the protestants from their religion, [the emperor] caused a writ to be made for the duke to be executed the next morning upon a solemn scaffold, in the sight of his wife, children, and the whole city of Wittenberg" (III, 41–42). State-sponsored terrorism, to be effective, requires eyewitnesses. On down the hierarchy, every Catholic ruler takes actions that are motivated by bad faith, greed, or pride,[36] although those—like Ottavio of Parma—who are mistreated by Charles may be justified or allowed saving graces (III, 14–16). Ascham rarely provides particulars about bad Catholic deeds, and his realist's tone implies not shock but Protestant rancor (e.g., III, 16, 23). Describing Lazarus Schwendi, an emissary (and spy) of Charles who had once studied in Basel, however, he lets out all the stops: "he fell to be a perverse and bloody papist: ever at hand in any cruel execution against the poor protestants" (III, 37)—Turk-like behavior.

Aside from anti-Protestantism, the chief motive that Ascham ascribes to Charles's actions (and those of Henri II of France as well) is "unkindness" (III, 9), presented as a contagion.[37] The term was defined by Thomas Elyot as "ingratitude," an Aristotelian negative quality in princes that is cited by Cicero and Machiavelli, among writers Ascham frequently notes (Ryan 1963, 170–71). Ascham privileges its implications of unnatural behavior toward "kind": a failure to fulfill the bonds of duty or responsibility—between ruler and vassal, between friends or relatives (III, 60)—like Lear's accusation of Cordelia as a "thankless child." Charles V is the primary practitioner; Albrecht of Brandenburg and Maurice of Saxony, who behave unkindly to Charles, are merely following suit. When Charles and others violate the claims of family and vassalage, they tear the social fabric. By contrast, Ascham criticizes the Turks only for cruelty, not for unkindness; the Ottomans live outside the traditional feudal system and cannot be expected to meet European standards.

On the other side Protestant leaders, in Ascham's representation, love learning and honor learned men, stand up for liberty and safeguard local governance. Albrecht the elder, Duke of Prussia, has founded the university at Koenigsberg (III, 31). Duke Johann-Friedrich, Elector of Saxony, although imprisoned for five years by Charles, is nobly stoic under threat of execution; exhibits wisdom, justice, courage, and temperance; has a bigger library than the Fuggers; recites history as table talk; and—despising cynics and busybodies—is himself an honest, humane plain speaker. Keeping his word is central to his integrity. No Catholic shows any such Platonic or humanistic qualities as this lengthy and fervent encomium (III, 41–44) attributes to Johann-Friedrich. Perhaps most telling are the lenient judgments, amounting to apologiae, that Ascham offers for the behavior of some Protestant nobles when a Catholic who acted similarly would be scourged. Albrecht of Brandenburg—an uncouth, easily offended spendthrift and conniver— still gets credited with courage, honesty, and "Honour" (III, 32–35). The overly ambitious Maurice, who betrays his own father-in-law and turns coats at least twice—clearly "unkind" behavior—is vindicated by his success against both the French and the Turks, and by his humiliation of Charles. In an effort at impartiality, Ascham weighs all the voices both against and for Maurice (who died in battle as *A Report* was being written) and concludes that "wise heads" found him humble, diligent, shrewd, discreet, brave, prepared to seek peace at the right moment, and "just in performing of covenants" (III, 54–60)—the *ne plus ultra*. Of course the Protestant princes are true followers of Christ who stand up for the gospel and, in one case, defend Luther (III, 28, 31, 37, 40). Some arm themselves "not to resist the emperor . . . but to keep God's religion up, if any by violence would put it down, refusing never, but requiring always to refer them and their doctrine to a lawful and free general council, where truth and religion might be fully tried . . . by the touchstone of God's canonical scriptures" (III, 45). The probable victor in such a trial by reason is not in doubt. What is mildly surprising is the restraint of Ascham's posture toward Catholics; Luther and later reformers initially saw the rise of Islam as a punishment from God for the church's iniquities.[38] Ascham makes such an elision at only one moment in the text: the Turkish anecdotes. It is the Catholic Charles V who sparks antagonism by breaking a truce, thus setting a precedent for the Ottoman breaking of a safe-conduct pass; it is Catholic Habsburg soldiers who take vengeance, both for Tripoli and for Ferdinand's man, when they feed not one but three Turks to swine.

The true villains of the text emerge gradually, as Spaniards come to play a special role in Ascham's review of untrustworthy behavior by Catholics. In his multiple listings of countries embroiled in the struggles (e.g., III, 7), he never names Spain; presumably, his well-informed readers would know that Spain was not a sovereign dependency of the Habsburg Empire but directly ruled by Charles. But the connection is made in Ascham's report of a Machiavellian move by Henri II: "The French king [encouraged by papal action] in the summer, 1551, proclaimed war against Charles king of Spain, abusing that name for a subtlety to separate the whole quarrel from the Empire" (III, 19). Spain has a powerful effect on Charles's policies, some of which are disastrous. "Men who know the truth" have privately told Ascham that the seizure of Mahdia—the first move in the whole imbroglio in North Africa—was undertaken to prevent the Turks from using it as a base to attack, indeed to become "too nigh and too homely a guest with [Charles] in Spain" (III, 11), from which Muslims had only recently been expelled.

The problem is less the country than its colonizing citizens; Ascham regularly describes the corps of courtiers surrounding Charles as Spaniards, imposed on resentful locals from Strassburg to Innsbruck. On this theme Albrecht of Brandenburg not only produced a text but, in a still-new development, "set it in print," listing among his grievances "the pride of the Spaniards, and the authority of strangers, which had now in their hands the seal of the empire, and in their swing the doing of all things, and at their commandment all such men's voices as were to be called the imperial diets; compelling the Germans in their own country to use strange tongues for their private suits, wherein they could say nothing at all, or nothing to the purpose; using *camera imperialis* at [Speyer] for a common key to open all men's coffers when they listed" (III, 28–29). In the colonized German lands, the Germans quite literally have no voice in their own affairs, and Spanish avarice holds sway. Maurice of Saxony was particularly hated by Spaniards who, "if he had lived . . . would . . . have driven all the Spaniards out of Germany." Now the local princes' remaining hope is Charles's nephew Maximilian, who Ascham speculates would have "the help of as many as hated the Spaniards, that is to say, almost any protestants and papists too in Germany" (III, 53). In his letters, Ascham comments personally on Spaniards with great disdain; early in his stay he blithely closes a familiar letter to Edward Raven, "the Germans [be set] upon god's doctrine; and the Spaniards also be the people of God, for all the world hates them," and a few weeks later he nastily notes, "upon Shrove Tuesday, at night, a wonderful sort of Spaniards did whip themselves naked through the streets, deep with sorrow" (I, 280, 285). They are the most Catholic of nations.

Perhaps most notable, of the many individuals portrayed in Ascham's exemplary history, those who behave most ignobly — in personal conduct and in governing the affairs of others — are almost invariably Spaniards. A Spaniard who had guarded Johann-Friedrich as Charles's prisoner produces "a brave Spanish brag" when fortune's wheel has so turned that he has become a guest in the elector's household; he is put in his place with a reminder that, on the earlier occasion, he stole a goblet (III, 44). The Duke of Alba offered "a supper [with] great cheer" to three German noblemen, then treacherously imprisoned one of them with a forged document (III, 51). These stories have the air of gossip that simply confirms its auditors' always-already views about the greed and hypocrisy of the arrogant men who surround and flatter the emperor. But the most Machiavellian player — the greatest villain of *A Report* — is Don Pedro de Toledo, the Viceroy of Naples, then ruled by the Aragonese. His reign is cruel, it is rapacious in "exactions of money without measure," it is corrupt in that suitors are admitted to his presence "by favour or money," it is arbitrary, and it lacks all transparency. Don Pedro's behavior inspires in Ascham his lengthiest digression, on the rule of law v. individual will and private enrichment, ornamented with examples from Cicero, Plato, Euripides, Xenophon, and the Bible (III, 23–24). Don Pedro "never could content his covetousness with money, nor satisfy his cruelty with blood" (III, 26). In one cautious, but particularly suggestive, remark, Don Pedro "used himself with much cruelty over the people of Naples . . . by *inquisition* of men's doings without order, and not only of men's doings, but also of men's outward lookings *and inward thinkings* using the least suspicion for a sufficient witness to *spoil* [i.e., torture] and to kill whomsoever he listeth" (III, 23–24; emphasis added).[39] The universal nightmare about Spain, after all, is torture and execution for suspect thoughts. Fortunately, early in 1553, God, Ascham says, took care of Don Pedro.

A *REPORT* AND THE BLACK LEGEND: TRANSCULTURAL VIOLENCE

Of course ideological differences between Spanish Catholic and English Protestant, and the heightened perceptions they aroused, crossed the Atlantic, along with the representational practices by which Europeans situated themselves in a changing world.[40] In this context, I claim *A Report of Germany* as a precursor of the Black Legend, England's version of *la leyenda negra*.[41] As Ascham traveled alertly with the Habsburg court, Bartolomé de Las Casas's *Brevissima Relacion de la Destruccion de las Indias* (1551) — arguably the mainspring for widespread acceptance of the Legend — although not yet translated into English was circulating in Spain, and Ascham could easily have heard its scandalous contents. In many of Las Casas's tales, not only violence and animal imagery but inscribed ironic relish resonate with Ascham's anecdotes from Hungary:

> The Spaniards . . . entered into towns, Boroughs, and Villages, sparing neither women with child, neither them that layed in, but that they ripped their bellies, and cut them in pieces, as if they had been opening of lambs shut up in the fold. They layed wagers with such as [who] with one thrust of a sword could paunch or bowel a man in the middest, or with one blow of the sword should most readily and deliverly cut off his head, or that would best pierce his entrails at one stroke. . . . Others they cast into the river laughing and mocking, and when they tumbled in the water they said, now shift for thyself, such a one's corpse. (Maltby 1971, 16)

The Spanish, that is to say, behave like Turks. Rumors of Las Casas's report are only one way that these violent images might have reached Ascham through what Greenblatt has called "mimetic circulation" (1991, 120). Until

Ascham visited Italy (a trip which *The Scholemaster*'s best-known passage [III, 147–63] confirms as a mind-changing experience for him[42]), he enjoyed the company of Venetians, and from them he might have absorbed echoes of cruel Spanish conduct, for instance in Naples in 1527. From his colleagues in the diplomatic corps he might have learned of the Latin epistles of the Italian humanist Peter Martyr d'Anghiera on the Spanish conquest of the New World, bringing the tale that clings persistently to the Black Legend that *conquistadores* fed Indians' babies to dogs (Maltby 1971, 17; Hadfield 1998, 94).

Whether or not Ascham had read or heard scandalous reports of New Spain, his representation of Spaniards in *A Report* emphasizes virtually all the Black Legend's major imputations: cruelty, treachery, haughtiness, greed. In his account of the Viceroy of Naples "greed plays counterpoint to atrocity" (Maltby 1971, 18), and the Inquisition even rears its head. From the traditional charges against Spaniards, Ascham omits only lechery. Given that absence, the qualities that characterize his Spaniards are remarkably similar to the essential Turk; indeed, Ascham's characterization of Suleyman's son Mustafa (with the exception of enmity to Christ) might suit a Spanish viceroy freed from the constraints of Europe. Read carefully, Ascham has sutured the evil of one ugly antagonist onto another, casting a pox on both their houses. The site of confrontation between Catholic and heathen, Hapsburg and Turk, I am arguing, can be displaced onto the confrontation between Spaniard and American indigene. Catholics on the eastern frontier with Turkey, copying the savage behavior of the enemy, are readily assimilated to *conquistadores;* Turks may be transposed to Indians. In the Black Legend of barbarity in the New World, as in Europe, violence is reciprocal, located not only in indigenous peoples but in the practices directed against those peoples by Spanish conquerors and colonizers, soldiers and priests. As Andrew Wheatcroft (2004, 127) has noticed, "the recent [Spanish] experience in mass conversion with the Muslims of Granada was carried forward into practice across the Atlantic." To justify Spanish aggression, both Muslims and native Americans were often anathematized as devils. Las Casas himself, while decrying the mistreatment of *indios* who had no prior chance or choice to become Christian, located them in the same discursive field as the "Moors" and Turks who are, by contrast, "persecutors of the Christian name and violent occupiers of the kingdoms of Christianity" and thus deserve war to the death.[43] Assessing texts from the early seventeenth century, Ivo Kamps and Jyostna Singh (2001, 3) usefully note that, in early modern cultural encounters, "self and other are not fixed in opposing positions but are rewritten through discursive and social interventions."

The suturing of eastern frontier to western colonization occurred in material, as well as textual, conditions. Because the Spanish were a powerful presence on both liminal edges of Christendom, similar policies and even actors at both sites are hardly surprising. The *encomienda* system of peonage in New Spain, against which Las Casas constantly lobbied, drew upon a scheme first devised for the management of property confiscated from the Moors of Al Andalus in the *reconquista* (Maltby 1971, 14, citing Chamberlain). Englishman Thomas Nicholas, who in 1578 would translate into English the *Cronica de Nueva España* of Cortes's chaplain Lopez de Gómara, had been an agent for the Levant Company, arrested by the Inquisition and held for five years.[44] Such hybridizing reactions to sixteenth-century difference reached around the globe: the Jesuit José de Acosta, whose writings were published by Theodore de Bry in 1598, analogized Aztec religious practices to those that had been recently observed in Japan (Bucher 1981, 19).

Experience of hostility and violence, incurred or enforced, circulates back into print. To my eyes, Ascham's report of the Christian soldier stripped naked by Turkish executioners and fed to hungry dogs summons the engraving in the *Grand Voyages* of Theodore de Bry's collection, often called *America*, that illustrates Balboa's troops humiliating Panamanians (see fig. 12.8, p. 234 above). This event, first reported by Peter Martyr in 1516, is repeated in Milanese adventurer Girolamo Benzoni's *Historia del Nuevo Mundo*, as reprinted in de Bry's fourth volume. The image shows near-naked Indian *berdaches* lying in the foreground being attacked by hounds, while above them in the picture plane stand elegantly dressed, disdainfully posed Spaniards—armed with sword and spear—who point, stare, and comment. In three of four cases, dogs attack the heads or, still more explicitly, the faces of Indian victims—not only the sites of their individuality but, in de Bry's representations of Brazilian anthropophagy, body parts of which the preparation and consumption is reserved to naturally inferior women.[45] As in Ascham's Turkish anecdotes, being eaten in the sight of one's torturers is especially degrading. The Black Spaniards are bearing eyewitness, and their gaze is also fixed on the sexual ambiguity hidden by the emphatic loincloths of two foregrounded *berdaches*.[46] To these multiply othered beings can be ascribed what Anthony Grafton (1992, 93) has named "nakedness, sodomy, cannibalism, the triad of inhuman customs that proved the Indians worthy only to be conquered." They create such anxiety in the breeches-and-hose that they must be placed below Spanish feet, untouchable, constructed as dogs by the parallel lines of human arms and animal forelegs. In Michael Alexander's collection of de Bry's engravings, the caption—written not by Benzoni but by a later collaborator, possibly a Protestant bookseller or translator (Bucher 1981, 26, 67) — reads as follows:

> The Spanish taught their hounds, fierce dogs, *to attack and devour the Indians as if they had been swine* in the space of time that one might say a Credo. These dogs wrought great destruction and slaughter, and forasmuch as sometimes, though seldom, when the Indians put to death some Spaniard upon good right and law of justice; they made a law between them that for one Spaniard they had to slay a hundred Indians.

> A certain Spaniard went one day to hunt deer or rabbits but found none and, worried lest his dogs should go hungry, he took a sweet little baby which he bereaved the mother of, and *cut off its arms and legs. These he chopped into small gobbets and fed them to the dogs*, and when all these morsels were thus dispatched, he cast the rest of the body or carcass into the kennel. (Bry 1976, 132; emphasis added)

Here again is the bizarre *jouissance* of animals devouring and thus further devaluing helpless bodies, here too in the service of Protestant propaganda. And like the reciprocity in Ascham, this text represents violence as committed by the Indians as well as the Spanish, albeit justly and minimally. In the attribution of cruelty, transatlantic transposition apparently became an easy slippage. Richard Knolles' 1603 *Generall Historie of the Turkes* describes Ottoman executions "when a prisoner, buried waist-deep in the earth, is made a target for bowmen" (Chew 1965, 114); thirty years earlier in "Of Cannibals," however, Montaigne (1957, 155) had said that the Brazilian indigenes learned exactly this practice from the Portuguese and use it because it is crueler than their own.

In the cultural field of mid-sixteenth-century representations of difference, the obvious touchstone is Montaigne, and indeed there are multiple intertextualities between Ascham's *Report* and "Of Cannibals" (1578–1580), although Montaigne's assessment of the Ottomans lies elsewhere.[47] Fundamentally for my argument, each writer presents the unknowable other from the optic of the European conflicts over religion spreading around him. Perhaps the most frequently quoted passage in Montaigne's essay is, "I think there is more barbarity in eating a man alive than in eating him dead; and in tearing by tortures and the rack a body still full of feeling, in roasting a man bit by bit, *in having him bitten and mangled by dogs and swine (as we have not only read but seen within fresh memory*, not among ancient enemies, but among neighbors and fellow citizens, and what is worse, *on the pretext of piety and religion*), than in roasting and eating him after he is dead" (Montaigne 1957, 155; emphasis added). Like Ascham, Montaigne attributes the worst tortures to interreligious hatred; in his case too (although more tacitly) the real division is between Catholic and Protestant. Because his essay too continuously seeks authoritative evidence to undergird his exotic claims, and because here he calls on recent memory, it may be safe to assume that, like Ascham, Montaigne thought an occasion of feeding a despised enemy to animals had actually occurred—at some time, to some body.

Both writers depict faceless men who are naked (not nude), stripped to a basic, vulnerable materiality, and both displace a portion of their despair over more local, Christian bodily cruelty onto heathen barbarians.[48] Both sets of strangers—the Turks and the "nations" of Brazil—are characterized as ferocious warriors who go beyond the pale in transgressions that produce high anxiety in the European imagination. Like Ascham, Montaigne reports of second hand wars that end not only in slaughter and bloodshed but in taunting, atrocity, and bodies displayed as trophies. Like Ascham's Turks, the Brazilian indigenes violate taboos that involve ghastly ingestion: the consumption of human flesh, albeit in a culturally coded practice that goes far beyond animals' hungry scavenging.[49] The victims of Montaigne's flesh eaters, prisoners of war captured from long-standing enemies who are themselves cannibals, mock their captors as they await execution by singing, essentially, "In eating me you consume your fathers and grandfathers who nourished me." Despite the exalted cultural meaning that Montaigne (1957, 158) ascribes to this song, to readers of *A Report of Germany* it carries an uncanny resonance of the Habsburg soldiers' taunt of Turkish flesh.

Montaigne goes beyond Ascham in his attempts to authenticate the truth about Brazilians from evidence and informants' reports; he interviews native South Americans who foolishly come to France (Montaigne 1957, 158–59). In fact, Montaigne's impressive effort to cast his mind into the world of the indigene—to make the strange familiar—is a move that is well beyond Ascham's intellectual reach. Ascham chastises (Catholic) Christians for reciprocating bad acts, but Montaigne can interrogate barbaric practices with a genuinely reflexive eye: "I am not sorry that we notice the barbarous horror of such acts, but I am heartily sorry that, judging their faults rightly, we should be so blind to our own" (Montaigne 1957, 155). To be sure, Montaigne writes from the safe distance of the Dordogne Valley, not the Austrian frontier; he describes preliterate people[50] in the process of being easily subdued and colonized, not a formidable military and political power near its apogee. But he can name the barbarism in Christian interreligious strife, as well as in strangers' cultural practices, with a clarity and assurance that elude Ascham. The mimetic circulation operating in multiple visions of barbarity that challenge Christian conduct, as well as ideology, reached the texts of two quite different humanists.

A REPORT'S LEGACY IN ENGLAND

Roger Ascham spent two-and-a-half years at the court of a major European player, the Holy Roman Empire. He was sufficiently acute to perceive that, while Charles V was comfortable juggling his Catholic and Protestant vassals and fencing with Henri II, his approach to the disciplined Ottomans was driven by fear (III, 10–11, 27). Conveying that perception, Ascham's anecdotes of Turkish and Christian bodies in conflict, set in a rhetorically potent position in his text, allow him to implicate the conduct of Charles's Spanish courtiers and viceroys. Confirming the attitude projected to him by German and Netherlandish princes, his strong Protestant perspective anticipates the English anti-Hispanism aroused by Philip II, and especially by the Duke of Alba, in their violent suppression of revolt in the Netherlands through events like the sack of Antwerp, some fifteen years after Ascham expressed his deep distaste. Observing the eastern frontier at the zenith of Suleyman's strength, Ascham conjured a vicious Turk who may stand in for the insolent and treacherous Catholic on the other side of the world. The *frisson* of his gaze at glistening bodies, ready to dare and do almost any cruelty, chimes with the reports of Las Casas, Zárate, and Hakluyt.

In 1553, nobody could foresee that the conflict on both frontiers of the Habsburg lands would end in hegemony for Catholic forces and a century of rivalry between the emerging English and Spanish empires. The brief, relatively early representations in *A Report of Germany* nonetheless helped to construct, at least in learned and court circles, the Tudor image of the inhuman Turk and the treacherous Spaniard. The manuscript survived the Marian years—when her marriage to Philip II required Ascham's self-censorship—to be published posthumously, perhaps buoyed by the success that same year of *The Scholemaster,* which the same printer issued. In 1571 George Gascoigne, who knew that volume well,[51] was invited to devise a masque with a Mediterranean flavor for a double wedding. He honored the famous victory of Lepanto with the tale of a soldier, ransomed from Turkish captivity, who warned

> How that the Christian[s'] enemye, the Turke that Prince of pride,
> Addressed had his power to swarm upon the Seas . . .

And that he made his vaunt, the greedy fishe to glut,
With gobs of Christian carcasses, in cruel pieces cut. (Gascoigne, I, 76)

Whatever his talents as a narrative poet, Gascoigne, author also of *The Spoyle of Antwerpe* and firm purveyor of the Black Legend, knew that the defeated Ottomans could be troped as feeders of Christian flesh to waiting animals (and threats to boys, and rapists).[52] But such triumphalism did not last long. When, barely a dozen years after Ascham's death, the queen whose letters he had transcribed began corresponding with two sultans and the leading woman of the seraglio, the English gaze at the Ottoman Empire had been transformed.[53] And England's contestation with Spain had become open warfare.

CHAPTER FIFTEEN

NATIONS INTO PERSONS

Jeffrey Knapp

Thus play I in one person many people,
And none contented.

—Shakespeare, *Richard II*

I want to consider the *backgrounding* of England in Elizabethan literature, by which I mean the often conspicuous subordination of a national plot to a psychological or sexual one. A good case in point is John Lyly's *Gallathea*, a play that Lyly wrote for his boy company around 1585. *Gallathea* begins with an English history lesson, the tale of England's invasion by the Danes, who enrage Neptune by destroying an English temple dedicated to him. Oddly, Neptune decides to take his revenge on the English, flooding the country as the Danes had just overrun it. Once his anger cools, however, Neptune limits his punishment of England to the incursions of the Agar, the tidal bore of the Humber River, to which the most beautiful virgin in the land is yearly sacrificed. We hear this story from the father of the beautiful virgin Gallathea, but we hear it because the father, Tityrus, is explaining how he plans to evade his civic duty and to outrage Neptune once more. Fearing that his daughter will be sacrificed, Tityrus has dressed her as a boy and sent her into the woods. The play follows Gallathea there: it backgrounds England by thrusting the nation's needs into the shadows and instead highlighting the erotic adventures of Gallathea, who falls in love with another beautiful virgin likewise hidden by her father and disguised as a boy. Recent criticism of *Gallathea* has focused nearly exclusively on Lyly's representation of cross-dressing and same-sex desire, and in a sense this scholarly disregard for the national plot that begins *Gallathea* accurately reflects the relative weighting of national and erotic issues in the play.[1] But commentators on the play have failed to ask why national issues should come to be subordinated to erotic ones in *Gallathea*, or why Lyly's sex comedy should bother to raise any national issues in the first place. What critics have overlooked, in short, is the *point* of backgrounding England in the play.

One might argue that, for Lyly and his fellow dramatists, such back-grounding was a practical necessity: the small size of acting companies made the dramatization of a nation's story impossible to sustain. As G. E. Bentley reminds us, "the lists, casts, prompt books, and Plots extant for the period 1590–1642 show that all the companies represented must have taken doubling for granted. Not only do the prompt books and Plots show most players as-suming more than one role, but several actors were required to represent four or five or even eight different characters." If theater companies had too few actors to play each part singly, how could these companies effectively portray a crowd, let alone a country? Sidney's *Defence of Poetry* (c. 1580) re-marks on the absurdity of contemporary plays that have "two Armies fly in, represented with four swords and bucklers," and Shakespeare famously ac-knowledges the problem in the choruses to *Henry V* (1599): "O for pity! —we shall much disgrace / With four or five most vile and ragged foils / (Right ill disposed, in brawl ridiculous) / The name of Agincourt."[2]

Yet a greater emphasis on persons rather than nations often figures in Eliz-abethan literature that operates under no such practical constraints, even in the poem that critics regularly characterize as England's national epic, Ed-mund Spenser's *The Faerie Queene* (1590). History lessons fare as poorly against love stories in *The Faerie Queene* as they do in *Gallathea*. The third book of *The Faerie Queene*, "The Legend of Britomartis, or Of Chastity," offers two such lessons; the first of them occurs after the heroine has fallen in love with the mirror image of another British knight, Arthegall. Merlin assures Britomart that she will eventually wed Arthegall and that from their union "a famous Progenie / Shall spring, out of the auncient *Trojan* blood," who "shall their conquests through all lands extend." Emboldened with a sense of patriotic as well as erotic purpose, Britomart rides off in search of her future husband, but she never meets him in the book, nor does Britain's imperial destiny ever materialize there. Instead, Britomart becomes entangled in the love stories of other persons. The second and final time the book lectures us on history, Britomart is seated at a dinner table with the old miser Malbecco, his young wife Hellenore, and the libertine knight Paridell, who tries to impress Hel-lenore by tracing his lineage back to fallen Troy. This invocation of Troy excites Britomart differently: she interrupts Paridell with a sudden paean to London as Troynovant. Paridell apologizes for having forgotten that another remnant of "the antique *Troian* stocke" had indeed branched off to Britain,

> But all the while, that he these speeches spent,
> Upon his lips hong faire Dame *Hellenore*,
> With vigilant regard, and dew attent,

Fashioning worlds of fancies evermore,
In her fraile wit, that now her quite forlore:
. . .
Which he perceiving, ever privily
In speaking, many false belgardes at her let fly.[3]

The second history lesson in book 3 of *The Faerie Queene* ends the way it began—as a sexual maneuver—and the next canto of the poem recounts Paridell's erotic success. We hear nothing more of Britain, or of Troynovant, for the rest of the book.

Throughout this chapter, I argue that such backgrounding of national to personal drama in Elizabethan literature represents not a dismissal of national concerns but rather a formulation or theorization of them that has hitherto escaped critical attention. The personal story of Britomart, for instance, has obvious national implications insofar as she will become queen of Britain. In his Letter to Raleigh, appended to the first edition of *The Faerie Queene*, Spenser repeatedly identifies the persons of monarchs with the body politic. "In the person of Cyrus and the Persians," Spenser writes, Xenophon "fashioned a government such as might best be"; "so have I labored to do in the person of Arthur," he adds, while the Fairy Queen herself will represent both "the most excellent and glorious person of our sovereign the Queen" and "her kingdom in Faery land."[4] For Spenser, monarchism seems to make nations and persons interchangeable.

Recent literary historians such as Peter Womack and Richard Helgerson would insist, however, that Spenser identifies kingdoms, not nations, with royal persons. In a monarchy, these critics maintain, the putative "unity of the realm" involves no collective will; it is merely "a reflection of the person of the monarch." But a nation is built on a "pluralist communal base," and therefore Elizabethan writers could encourage belief in an English nation only when they first opened a "conceptual gap" between England and its monarch by placing value on "some other interest or cultural formation" besides the king, such as "the nobility, the law, the land, the economy, the common people, the church."[5] Spenser accepts this logic to a degree: he too differentiates the nation from the monarch. Yet he finds this difference inscribed within the monarch, as the tension between her individual and her collective identities, her "two persons." And, while Spenser refuses to grant the monarch any monopoly on the self-complexity that allows her to represent the nation, he does see her as the incomparable exemplar of such self-complexity.[6] To Spenser's mind, the monarch constitutes a necessary if not a sufficient basis for explaining how a nation achieves unity and how that unity inheres in persons. Thanks in part to his monarchism, moreover, Spenser doubts whether any vehicles *besides* persons could ever serve as effective determinants of national identity. The story of persons regularly overwhelms the story of nations in *The Faerie Queene,* just as the poem shows that nations are regularly overwhelmed by invasion; yet Spenser also sees persons as rescuing national identity from the insecurity of physical borders and safely exporting national identity to an empire beyond those borders.

For Spenser as for Lyly, these great services to the nation come at some cost to the person. Benedict Anderson (1983) has famously asserted that a nation exists only when its individual members believe that it does: a nation is an "imagined" community, Anderson maintains, "because the members of even the smallest nation will never know most of their fellow-members, meet them, or even hear of them, and yet in the minds of each lives the image of their communion." Both Spenser and Lyly anticipate this theory of nationhood, but they take a stricter view of its implications than Anderson does. If a nation requires its members to harbor the thought of other members inside themselves, then a nation, both writers assume, must be built upon the self-alienation of its members. Even this apparent sacrifice, however, seems a gain to Lyly and Spenser: they take their own self-consciousness about the inward complexity of national identity as a strength that helps differentiate the English from the Spanish as rival colonizers and from the Irish as rivals to be colonized.

In the rest of this chapter, I offer detailed readings of the relation between persons and nations not only in *Gallathea* and book 3 of *The Faerie Queene* but also in Spenser's colonialist prose tract, "A View of the Present State of Ireland." I then turn to Shakespeare's Elizabethan history plays, in particular to *Richard II,* to show how these plays emphasize even more than Spenser and Lyly do the internally shattering effect of nations on persons. In the choruses to *Henry V,* Shakespeare exhorts his audience to transform a handful of actors into an army not by multiplying each actor in their thoughts but rather by *dividing* them: "Into a thousand parts divide one man, / And make imaginary puissance."[7] For the Elizabethan literary tradition I examine, the backgrounding of nation to person places the national story where it belongs — within the story of a person.

GALLATHEA

A simpler way to interpret the displacement of the national by the personal in *Gallathea* is to assume that the play treats English nationhood skeptically. After all, *Gallathea* begins by mocking the notion that the English can derive any reliable coherence or integrity as a nation, any "constancy" of identity, from their island.[8] Ocean borders did not prevent the Danish from conquering England. And, as the setting of the play on the Humber, a traditional river border between the northern and southern parts of the island, underscores, England was never fully demarcated by ocean borders in any case.[9] Now the Agar—the confluence of ocean and river borders—penetrates England. Tityrus portrays it as the monstrous consequence of Danish invasion, which ruined English faith that Neptune, the god of the ocean, was England's friend and patron. The Agar seems monstrous, above all, to the virgins who are "bound to endure" the "horror" of its incursions. But the Agar is at least a smaller threat to the nation than foreign armies or ocean floods; if it exposes the porousness of England's borders, the demonstration costs only one life. Indeed, Tityrus is not even sure that the virgin sacrificed to the Agar actually dies: "whether she be devoured of him, or conveyed to Neptune, or drowned between both, it is not permitted to know and incurreth danger to conjecture."[10] The threat of the Agar, Lyly stresses, is largely in the mind, a mind that prizes physical intactness above all else and that therefore views any physical penetration as a horror. In *Gallathea,* it may be a fantasy to regard the English isle as a guarantor of national identity, but it seems equally a fantasy to regard the "inconstancy" of English borders as somehow precluding national identity.

Yet what else beside the island can make England English? One plausible alternative, in the play, is "custom." Tityrus himself invokes it in his history lesson, although he presents it as no more reliable a determinant of nationhood than the island has been shown to be. First the Danes forced the English "people" to "change" their "custom" by destroying Neptune's temple; now Tityrus violates the new "custom of the country" by refusing to sacrifice his daughter. While various characters in the play regret that fathers have become "so overcareful" of "their children" as to "forget the safety of their country," the fact remains that the family proves more compelling to the doting Tityrus and his obedient daughter than the nation does. Yet not even kinship can weather Lyly's apparent skepticism about community in *Gallathea.* Through most of the play, the family is presented in privative terms, as a bond between father and daughter merely. Once Gallathea and Phyllida fall in love, even this limited attachment is thrown into question, eventually becoming so dubious as to seem illicit: in act four, after Tityrus and Phyllida's father Melebeus denounce each other for hiding their daughters, Tityrus claims that he saw Phyllida in Melebeus's arms, "whenas you gave her infinite kisses with affection I fear me more than fatherly."[11]

In the woods, Gallathea and Phyllida may be separated from their fathers as well as from their "countrymen," but they are not removed from all forms of community. Instead, they encounter the nymphs of Diana, who share the bond of being subjected to Diana, "the sovereign of all virtue and goddess of all virgins." After land, custom, and kinship, in other words, the play considers monarchy as a possible basis of collective identity. In comparison to these other determinants, Diana has the advantage of being constancy itself: her "thoughts are always answerable to her vows." But Cupid is wandering in the same woods, playing "truant" from his mother Venus, and the nymphs quickly prove susceptible to his influence. Diana's inability to stem this invasion of love reveals how her sovereign identity had only ever been imputed to her nymphs, not infused in them. As "Diana's train," the nymphs had achieved a collective identity only by the suppression or sacrifice of their own selves: "I have neither will nor leisure," says the first nymph Cupid meets, "but I will follow Diana in the chase, whose virgins are all chaste." So indifferent is Diana to the personal volition of her subjects that, when they fall in love, she immediately assumes that a rival sovereign now governs them: "Are Diana's nymphs become Venus' wantons?" she exclaims, "Is Diana's chase become Venus' court?" Telusa, the first nymph to bewail her lovelorn state, asks herself a similar question: "What new conceits, what strange contraries, breed in thy mind? Is thy Diana become a Venus?"[12] As Telusa's wonder at her "new conceits" suggests, however, Cupid has alienated the nymph from Diana not by enlisting her in Venus's camp but rather by surprising her with the novelty of her own desire.

If love disperses Diana's train, then, fragmenting it into individual persons, it also fragments the persons. Chief among the "strange contraries" that Telusa finds breeding in her mind is the perception of her own desire as a mystery. "Can there in years so young, in education so precise, in vows so holy, and in a heart so chaste enter either a strong desire or a wish or a wavering thought of love?" she soliloquizes. By invading her personal borders, love has rendered Telusa inconstant not merely to her sovereign but to herself. The next lovelorn nymph we meet, Eurota, similarly laments this loss of personal integrity or coherence: "I feel my thoughts unknit, mine eyes unstaid, my heart I know not how affected, or infected, my sleeps broken and full of dreams, my wakeness sad and full of sighs, myself in all things unlike myself." Significantly, Eurota mentions no broken vows to Diana. Love has alienated her from herself by making her feel within herself the desire for another person, the disguised Gallathea: "O eloquent Tityrus," she cries, "O credulous Eurota!" The surprise of the play is that this erotic bond, subverting Diana's monarchy, should form the basis for a new fellow feeling among the nymphs. Divided from themselves by their desire *for* another, the nymphs prove capable of recognizing the operations of a similar desire *in* another. "Thou hast told what I am in uttering what thyself is," Telusa remarks to Eurota. "These are my passions, Eurota, my unbridled passions": in dialogue rather than soliloquy, Telusa can interpret the "unbridled" nature of her desire as an incoherence that makes herself appear in others, and others in herself.[13]

When Phyllida and Gallathea fall in love and thereby join this sisterhood of Cupid's victims, the two would seem to have completed their defection from the national cause of virgin sacrifice that begins the play. By the end of *Gallathea,* however, the "common grief" of lovelorn women has persuaded Neptune to forego his "private grudge" and end his vengeful assaults on England's borders as well as virgins.[14] Neither land nor custom nor monarchy nor kinship prove capable of establishing England's integrity as a nation in *Gallathea;* that job is accomplished, paradoxically, by a narrative shift from nation to persons and then by a discovery of shared self-alienation in persons. Yet if the play defines community in England as a society of like-minded, love-minded people, where are the boundaries of that potentially limitless fellowship to be drawn, and how can it be called English?

The answer for Lyly seems to lie in the idiosyncratic form of love his play dramatizes. As the prologue to *Gallathea* explains, it is an erotics that Lyly expects his virgin queen to approve. "We [have] endeavored with all care that what we present your highness should neither offend in scene nor syllable, knowing that as in the ground where gold groweth nothing will prosper but gold, so in your majesty's mind, where nothing doth harbor but virtue, nothing can enter but virtue." Even as he abjects himself to Elizabeth, Lyly hints at the critique of virginity his play will launch: his aim, he implies, is to "enter" the queen's mind and thus make something grow there. "Yield, ladies, yield to love," Gallathea urges her audience in the epilogue. But the triumph of love in the play is made possible by Neptune's new hands-off treatment of virgins, which he adopts in exchange for a reconciliation between Venus and Diana. By implication, the love that the play arouses must be as virginal as it is erotic. Such a love feeds on sights—Telusa claims she was taken "by the eyes"—and sounds—Eurota claims she was taken "by the ears"—but it does not thrive on touching. For Lyly, so chaste a passion is best exemplified by the affection of one woman for another, enacted by one boy in relation to another. At the play's end, the invasive Neptune maintains that the desire of Gallathea and Phyllida for each other is "an idle choice, strange and foolish," with "no cause of affection," because it will allow neither virgin to be impregnated. In response, Venus promises to transform one of the couple into a man so as to make possible an "embrace" between them, but we never witness this metamorphosis in the play. Instead, to please Elizabeth, whose "judgment and favor" the prologue calls "our sun and shadow," Lyly restricts his portrayal of love to desires he represents as unconsummated.[15] In his view, it is this restriction, imposed by the will of a virgin monarch, that sets national boundaries to the erotic community of *Gallathea*.

Significantly, however, Elizabeth does not inspire the love she restricts, nor does the restriction work as she might intend. During the final scene of *Gallathea*, Venus laments that Diana has "clipp'd" Cupid's "wings," "quench'd" his "brands," "burnt" his "bow," and "broke" his "arrows," but Cupid assures his mother that these limitations have actually enhanced his powers: "I bear now mine arrows in mine eyes, my wings on my thoughts, my brands in my ears, my bow in my mouth, so as I can wound with looking, fly with thinking, burn with hearing, shoot with speaking."[16] Against Diana's will, her confinement of erotic passion to fanciful rather than physical intercourse gives love new and more various means to penetrate her nymphs. And Diana's subjects now experience a collective identity not through the imposition of her sovereign will but rather through a self-alienating sense of the difference between that will and the love wounds they share.

THE FAERIE QUEENE

During the history lesson she receives from Merlin, Britomart learns that her island will be invaded not just by the Danes, as in *Gallathea*, but by the Saxons and Normans too. As Spenser later moralizes in book 3 of *The Faerie Queene*, there is "no fort so fensible, no wals so strong, / But that continuall battery will rive." Unfortunately, any battery at all seems capable of penetrating Britain's island fortress: thanks to its pregnability, the British will be backgrounded as a story in their own country for eight hundred years. One wave of conquest after another will not overwhelm the British people entirely, however: Merlin foretells that they will rise again to rule their island, with the birth of Henry VII. Yet how can the British survive, subjected to so many invaders for so long? Britomart's personal story in *The Faerie Queene* is a proleptic test for her nation. By the time she hears Merlin's prophecies, her borders have already been invaded, by love for Arthegall: Cupid's dart has been "infixed . . . Within [her] bleeding bowells." Love's conquest of Britomart is the reason, moreover, she has come to Merlin and heard the story of her nation in the first place. Merlin explains to her that the internal wounds she now suffers are all to the good of her nation: they foreshadow her impregnation by Arthegall, which will generate the dynasty of kings that will ultimately produce Queen Elizabeth. Britomart's fate and the fate of her nation are thus complexly intertwined: first, insofar as her current loss of personal integrity and coherence prefigures Britain's future loss of national integrity through invasion; second, insofar as "a famous Progenee / Shall spring" from her womb to "revive the sleeping memorie" of the British; and third, insofar as Britomart must be invaded, as Britain will be invaded, so that the British nation can ultimately be restored to power.[17]

To the skeptical reader, these multiple correspondences between Britomart and her nation might seem little more than rhetorical tricks that enable Spenser to background the thorny question of British national identity to the more manageable drama of Britomart's quest for love and then pretend that Britomart's personal story magically resolves the national plight. Spenser anticipates such criticism and tries, as I have said, to substantiate the correspondences he draws between person and nation by insisting on the royalty of Britomart, from whom he derives his own "glorious Soveraines goodly auncestrye." But Spenser's aim in book 3 of *The Faerie Queene* is not to hide the scandal of his nation's broken borders behind a veil of rhetoric or of monarchism. Merlin's history lesson suggests that invasion can have a productive as well as destructive impact on nations: it can help them grow. Britomart learns that her progeny will revive the memory not merely of the British but also of the Trojans, whom Merlin reveals to be Britomart's ancestors. After their own country had been overrun, the Trojans traveled far beyond their original borders, and Spenser maintains that Britomart's "fruitfull Ofspring" will inherit the wanderlust of their forebears: they "shall their conquests through all lands extend."[18] In book 3 of *The Faerie Queene*, invasion transforms the concept of a nation from a fortress to an empire.

The second and final history lesson in book 3 grapples directly with this paradox that invasion can prove empowering to the invaded. Only disreputable characters, we find, or reputable characters in moments of weakness, equate a loss of impregnability with a loss of identity. The debauched Paridell describes the fall of Troy as an irremediable disgrace for Troy's survivors:

> *Troy*, that art now nought, but an idle name,
> And in thine ashes buried low dost lie,
> Though whilome far much greater then thy fame,
> Before that angry Gods, and cruell skie
> Upon thee heapt a direfull destinie,
> What boots it boast thy glorious descent,
> And fetch from heaven thy great Genealogie,
> Sith all thy worthy prayses being blent,
> Their of-spring hath embaste, and later glory shent.

Britomart, just as "lineally" descended from the Trojan "race" as Paridell is, responds quite differently to the story of Troy's fall. She asks Paridell to tell her about Aeneas, whose escape from Troy Paridell had not thought to mention, and when Paridell in his subsequent lecture reaches the founding of Rome, Britomart ecstatically interrupts him:

> There there (said *Britomart*) a fresh appeard
> The glory of the later world to spring,
> And *Troy* again out of her dust was reard,
> To sit in second seat of soveraigne king,
> Of all the world under her governing.
> But a third kingdome yet is to arise,
> Out of the *Trojans* scattered of-spring,
> That in all glory and great enterprise,
> Both first and second *Troy* shall dare to equalise.

Only if one identifies Troy with its "stately towres" does the fall of Troy mean the end of the Trojans. But Britomart, treating "race" and "nation" as synonymous, thinks of Troy as a people, not a place—and Troy's fall, however deplorable in itself, has to her mind "scattered" Trojan "of-spring" like seeds.[19] Where Paridell feels overwhelmed, Britomart proves inspired, for unless Troy's towers had gone up in flames, her own nation would never have been founded. In fact, it is only by regarding scatterable persons rather than fixed places as the privileged vessels of national identity that Britomart can envisage Britain as recapturing the Trojan legacy that counts—the expansiveness of a Trojan empire.

Yet if it is hard to see how the British can stay British after repeated invasions of their island fortress, it is equally difficult to grasp how the Trojans can stay Trojan after they have been scattered from Troy. Once again, Spenser offers Britomart's personal story as his elucidation of the national problem. A purported vessel of Trojan as well as British blood, Britomart on her love quest can allegorically represent wandering nations as well as penetrable ones. But the contrast between Paridell's and Britomart's accounts of Troy in canto 9 suggests that Spenser emphasizes a story of personal over national travails for more reasons than Britomart's mobility. Persons, in Spenser's view, sustain a nation's identity better than fortresses do. This is not to say that Spenser thinks of persons as more coherent guarantors of national identity than places are. After all, Britomart begins her quest self-alienated by "that fayre visage" of Arthegall "written in her hart."[20] Two cantos later, she must herself survive the backgrounding of her story, as Spenser drops her from the action and allows other characters—Marinell and Cymoent, Arthur and Florimell, Timias and Belphoebe—to take center stage. These rival characters threaten Britomart's prominence in her own book because they all share some erotic distress with her: they show that Britomart's troubles in love are not exclusively her own. When Britomart returns to the action, she meets Paridell and confronts the fact that her Trojan heritage is not exclusively her own either: she learns about that heritage from a foreigner, sees her own story in his, even sees her ancestry in his. But Paridell's story also underscores a crucial difference between himself and Britomart. Although they are "lineally extract" from the same roots, Paridell is *psychologically* weaker in the face of shattered borders than Britomart is. Armed with the knowledge of Merlin's prophecies, Britomart no longer regards herself as "embaste" by invasion. Instead, the consciousness that her identity is broken, impure, enlarges her: it enables her to find a national purpose in her love and ultimately to generate the offspring who will restore British sovereignty.

"A VIEW OF THE PRESENT STATE OF IRELAND"

Spenser is even more explicit about the value of broken borders in his imperialist tract, "A View of the Present State of Ireland" (1596).[21] Over the past few decades, critics have tended to misrepresent Spenser's account of race and nation in the "View." Its recent editors, for instance, reductively claim that Spenser portrays the colonized Irish as "implacably barbarous descendants of the Scythians." But one of Spenser's mouthpieces in the tract, Irenius, argues that Ireland has rather been "peopled" by "sundry people of different Conditions and manners": these include the Scythians, but also the Gauls, the Britons, the Saxons, and "the last and the greatest," the English.[22] For Irenius, Scythian roots alone cannot explain the bad reputation of the Irish as "the most barbarous nation in Christendom." Nor can the Irish "avoid" this "reproach" by inventing a counterlineage for themselves. As Irenius explains, the Irish "would derive themselves from the Spaniards whom they now see to be a very honorable people," yet "the Spaniard that now is, is come from as rude and savage nations" as the Irish. Indeed, the modern Spanish scarcely possess "any drop of the old Spanish blood left in them," inasmuch as they themselves have been conquered by the Romans; the Carthaginians; the Goths, Huns, and Vandals; the Scythians; and lastly the Moors, who, though expelled, have "left no pure drop of Spanish blood no nor of Roman nor Scythian." But then, Irenius continues, no European nation is free from such bastardizations of the blood: because the "Northern nations" of Goths, Huns, Vandals, and Scythians "spread themselves into all Countries in Christendom," "there is none," he maintains, "but hath some mixture and sprinkling if not thorough peopling of them." England is no exception to the rule, nor is

English national identity any more fixed than that of the Irish or the Spanish. According to Irenius, "the Chiefest abuses which are now in [Ireland] are grown" not from the Scythians but rather "from the English" who settled the country hundreds of years before, "and the English that were are now much more Lawless and Licentious than the very wild Irish."[23] For Irenius, then, there is no constancy or purity to any race or nation, including the English, who have developed into reputable and disreputable peoples just as Paridell and Britomart represent two different offshoots of the same Trojan "stocke."[24]

Rather than undermine Spenser's imperialism in the "View," as one might expect, this remarkably deconstructive approach to race and nation actually underwrites that imperialism. To the new English colonist Irenius, the savagery of the Old English betrays the seemingly embasing truth that "it is but even the other day since England grew Civil." Yet Irenius thinks that an awareness of England's own barbarous heritage is an imperial good, insofar as it helps English colonists detach themselves from their civilized homeland and mingle with barbarians. Because Ireland is, in Irenius's view, regrettably "full of her own nation that may not be rooted out," such an intermixture of invader and invaded constitutes the only sure means of successful colonization: "I think it best by an union of manners and Conformity of minds to bring them to be one people, and to put away the dislikeful Conceit both of th'one and th'other which will be by no means better than by there intermingling of them, that neither all the Irish may dwell together, nor all the English, but by translating of them and scattering them in small numbers among the English, not only to bring them by daily Conversation unto better liking of each other but also to make both of them less able to hurt."[25] Like Britomart, Irenius sees the "scattering" of peoples as the necessary precondition to empire.

Of course, the "conformity of minds" that Irenius envisions is a conformity to English ways of thinking. To preserve the hegemony of his own nation in Ireland, Irenius also places strict limits on colonial intermingling: he believes that "marrying with the Irish [is] most Carefully to be restrained." Coming as it does after Irenius's insistence that no European nation is purebred, this ban on miscegenation seems hard to fathom, except as a *Gallathea*-like concession to an ideal of sexual restraint imposed by Spenser's virgin queen. But Irenius takes pains to stress that his opposition to intermarriage has less to do with the threat of sexual than of psychic pollution. The problem, he claims, is that the characters of children "are first framed and fashioned" by their mothers. Even wet nurses have this shaping power over children, "for . . . the Child that sucketh the milk of the nurse must of necessity learn his first speech of her, the which being the first that is inured to his tongue is ever

after most pleasing unto him." By emphasizing the potentially corrupting influence of *surrogate* mothers, Spenser presents himself as having no more of
a stake in bloodline as a guarantor of national identity than he has in place.[26]
From his perspective, the wet nurse's power negatively underscores what
Britomart's difference from her fellow Trojan Paridell had positively demonstrated: that national identity depends on a frame of mind. Irenius's interlocutor Eudoxius is amazed by the degeneracy of the Old English: "Is it possible," he asks, "that any should so far grow out of frame that they should in
so short space quite forget their Country?" Irenius explains that the fault lies
neither in absence from England nor presence in Ireland but rather in "the
bad minds of the man, who having been brought up at home under a strait
rule of duty and obedience being always restrained by sharp penalties from
lewd behavior, so soon as they Come thither where they see laws more slackly
tended and the hard Constraint which they were used unto now slacked, they
grow more loose and Careless of their duty and as it is the nature of all men to
love liberty So they become Libertines."[27] According to Irenius, the English
colonist who grows barbarous in Ireland had never been civilized except by
the external "constraint" of law, culture, custom, whereas the colonist who
remains a civil Englishman in Ireland bears his nationality *within.*

Yet what enables the civil colonist to keep himself in an English frame of
mind?[28] The proem to *The Faerie Queene* suggests that the discipline of English
national identity requires devotion to England's monarch as the "true glorious type" of a specifically English personhood. But the "View" implies that
such faith in monarchism actually depends on the frame of mind it would
otherwise seem to inspire. Eudoxius initially resists Irenius's skepticism about
Spanish racial purity: "You speak very sharply *Irenius* in dishonor of the
Spaniard which some other boast to be the only brave nation under the sky."
Without reference to the Spanish king, Eudoxius nonetheless understands
the Spanish "nation" and "the Spaniard" to be interchangeable terms. He *per-
sonifies* the nation, and Irenius does the same in reply: "So surely he is a very
brave man neither is that which I speak any thing to his derogation for in that
I said he is a mingled people is no dispraise for aye there is no nation now in
Christendom nor much farther but is mingled and Compounded with others." "He is a mingled people": this strange phrase encapsulates Spenser's belief that a nation achieves whatever coherence it can be said to possess not
through place, laws, customs, institutions, or even race, but rather through
persons — or more precisely, through the *allegorization* of persons and therefore also through the will to read persons allegorically.

Monarchism is the strong form of this allegorization at work: as Irenius
tellingly puts it, "the only person" of the king often has more power "to Con-

tain the unruly people" than "an Army" does.[29] In its weaker forms, the consolidation of nations through persons in the "View" can sound merely rhetorical and expedient. Uncertain whether the "nation" that long ago invaded Ireland from Spain were "native *Spaniards,* or *Gauls* or *Africans* or *Goths* or some other of those Northern nations which did overspread all Christendom," Eudoxius nevertheless decides to label them "the Spaniard (for so we will call them what ever they were that Came from Spain)." In Irenius's account of the modern Spaniard as a mingled people, the implication that national identity is essentially a fiction becomes more explicit as Irenius goes on to explain why most other nations are equally impure: "there is no nation now in Christendom nor much farther but is mingled and Compounded with others, for it was a singular providence of god and a most admirable purpose of his wisdom to draw those Northern heathen nations down into these Christian parts where they might receive Christianity and to mingle nations so remote so miraculously to make as it were one kindred and blood of all people and each to have knowledge of him."[30] At the start of the *Faerie Queene* canto in which Britomart first learns British history, Spenser claims that "divine foresight" uses love to "effect" its purpose "in destined descents." But the divine purpose in favoring a lineage, we soon discover, is to mingle nations, not single them out. Merlin informs Britomart that, by "eternall providence," Britomart's offspring shall extend their conquests "Till universall peace compound all civill jarre." Paradoxically, the rebirth of the British nation is a major step toward this supranational goal. In returning the British to power, Henry VII will also forge "eternall union" in Britain "betweene the nations different afore," and this insular unification will anticipate the later compounding of more far-flung peoples into a transoceanic British empire.[31] Averting Lyly's problem of how to contain a fellowship of like-minded people within national boundaries, Spenser insists that a united Britain should itself be read allegorically, as a divine prefiguration of an ultimately universal conformity of minds. But this boundless fellowship begins in an even more circumscribed setting than the British island. It begins inside Britomart, so that Spenser can seem to base the imperial mingling of all people on nothing more particular to Britain than a psychological adjustment. Learning from Merlin's prophecies how to manage her self-estrangement, Britomart places herself in the providential frame of mind that sees the nation in the person.

RICHARD II

In *Richard II* (c. 1595) no less than in *Gallathea, The Faerie Queene,* and the "View," the backgrounding of nation to person coincides with doubts about

the constitutive power of national borders. This skepticism is easy to over-
look because *Richard II* contains the most famous celebration of English in-
sularity in the language:

> This royal throne of kings, this sceptred isle,
> This earth of majesty, this seat of Mars,
> This other Eden, demi-paradise,
> This fortress built by Nature for herself
> Against infection and the hand of war,
> This happy breed of men, this little world,
> This precious stone set in the silver sea,
> Which serves it in the office of a wall,
> Or as a moat defensive to a house,
> Against the envy of less happier lands;
> This blessed plot, this earth, this realm, this England,
> This nurse, this teeming womb of royal kings,
> Fear'd by their breed, and famous by their birth,
> Renowned for their deeds as far from home,
> For Christian service and true chivalry,
> As is the sepulcher in stubborn Jewry
> Of the world's ransom, blessed Mary's Son.

By the end of the play, Gaunt's son Bullingbrook has nevertheless invaded
the fortress isle and supplanted Richard. In sailing from France, moreover,
he effectively reenacts the Norman Conquest that put his bloodline on the
English throne in the first place. If England's royal breed are famous by
their birth, they are famous as invaders. Gaunt's very name indicates his foreign birth (in Ghent), while Richard's murderer refers to the dead king as
"Richard of Burdeaux."[32]

Critics have long noted how the story of England's disintegration in *Richard II* places increasing emphasis on Richard's character, and in the process
replaces a self-assured Richard with a self-alienated one. As Alvin Kernan
puts it, "Fate forces new identities on him, and since even in his own mind
man can find no stable identity, life becomes theatrical, a playing of many
roles in a constantly changing play."[33] But the growing psychological instability of Richard does more than reflect the instability of England's borders:
it also transforms that national problem into a personal one. In part, this transformation has been hidden from commentators by the seeming obviousness
of the special relationship between Richard and England in the play. Gaunt's
characterization of England as a "sceptred isle" bespeaks the monarchist as-

sumption, shared by Richard in the first half of the play, that king and country are one and the same: Richard claims that the very "earth" of England "shall have a feeling, and these stones / Prove armed soldiers, ere her native king / Shall falter under foul rebellion's arms."[34] Although Bullingbrook explodes this ideology, his invasion also paradoxically generates a new and more intensive sense of connection between England and Richard—who never was a "native king" in any case. During the second half of Shakespeare's play, Richard is invaded by English history. The warfare that England used to wage in France, which is first replaced by Richard's murder of Gloucester in Calais, which is in turn replaced by the duel between Bullingbrook and Mowbray, which is itself replaced by a struggle between Bullingbrook and Richard, ends up transformed into a strange series of contests between Richard and himself: first, there is Richard indecisive about retaining or surrendering his crown, then there is Richard reflected in a mirror he shatters, and finally there is Richard soliloquizing on the contradictory thoughts within his tortured mind.

Spenser, as we have seen, takes a surprisingly optimistic view of the broken borders shared by nation and character: he associates these twin collapses with imperial expansion. In *Richard II*, the tragic scene in which the fallen Richard is led to "Julius Caesar's ill-erected tower" and proclaimed "the model where old Troy did stand" has recognizably Spenserian implications.[35] First, the English isle could hardly be an impregnable "fortress," as Gaunt had claimed it was, if the invading Caesar had once built his own fortress within England. Second, Richard can seem to embody a heroic Trojan heritage only if England had already been invaded long before Caesar, by the Trojans fleeing from the collapse of their own national fortress. Third, the recollections of Caesar and Troy through the medium of Richard indicate that the truest "model" of a nation must be a person, not a fortress, as the mobile Romans and Trojans demonstrate. In short, the scene suggests that Shakespeare like Spenser is committed to rescuing national identity from a dependency on place and transplanting it to the more excursive vehicles of persons.

But Richard is no Britomart: old Troy *did* stand in him; now he too has fallen. Where Britomart had been forced to leave her island in order to find her future mate, Richard is at this point in the play being forced to leave his mate for a "little world" even more restrictive than his island—the walls of a prison cell. Britomart and Arthegall will eventually bear a race of kings; Richard, alone in his cell, will beget only "a generation of still-breeding thoughts," and none "contented." Conspicuously absent from Richard's story, as these comparisons suggest, is the erotic matrix of self-alienation in *Gallathea* and *The Faerie Queene* that had made the incoherence of the self seem a possible basis for national fellow feeling. An equally crucial change is the masculinity of the title character. Devotion to their monarch had encouraged Lyly and Spenser to treat women as the privileged vessels of national identity. At the same time, opposition to the queen's virginal exclusivity had also led both writers to stress that the invasion of women could ultimately generate the literal self-expansion, and communal gain, of pregnancy. If Lyly and Spenser thus invoke motherhood in order to legitimate their celebration of broken borders, they also worry that a maternal paradigm for national identity places physical and family limits on the conformity of minds that should result from broken borders. Consequently, both writers defer pregnancy in their narratives and articulate national identity instead through the medium of same-sex eroticism or an unfinished sexual quest. So compelling and yet so threatening does the connection between national identity and personal impregnation become for Spenser that the "View" portrays Irish mothers and even Irish wet nurses as deadly obstacles to the imposition of English hegemony on Ireland. Shakespeare's Richard represents the opposite threat: like the aging Elizabeth, he can produce no actual offspring. When Shakespeare infuses nation into person in *Richard II*, Richard's subsequent introspectiveness increasingly sets him apart from the other characters in the play. Bullingbrook may ruin Richard's assumption that he has sole title to the sceptered isle, but Richard's fall does make him the only person in England who can claim to have *been* king: "You may my glories and my state depose," he explains to Bullingbrook, "But not my griefs; still am I king of those." By internalizing England's disintegration, Richard has become thoroughly alienated from the nation whose fragmented character he now thoroughly embodies. "My grief," he declares, "lies all within."[36]

Kernan thinks that this new introspectiveness makes Richard more distinctive a dramatic creation too: "Richard changes from the formal, conventional style of the beginning of the play to a metaphysical style capable of handling irony and a reality in which the parts no longer mesh, capable of carrying intense agitation and the passionate effort of thought." Generalizing Kernan's claim, Joel Fineman treats the self-alienation of Shakespearean characters whose "parts no longer mesh" as the key to their "subjectivity effect," or "that psychologistic interiority for which and by means of which Shakespeare's major characters are often singled out."[37] In other words, while Richard's internal woes may estrange him from the rest of England, they also distinguish him in the eyes of many playgoers and readers as an incomparably Shakespearean achievement.

The notion that English writers are unusually sophisticated on the subject of broken identities seems implicit in Lyly and Spenser too. That notion fol-

lows from their shared emphasis on an insular and therefore apparently exclusive little English world that is nonetheless multinational and subject to
invasions. Where the Irish and the Spanish in Spenser's "View" "foolishly"
equate the nobilty of a nation with its purity, as Paridell does, Irenius like
Britomart sees no "derogation" in the impurity that results from invasions.
On the contrary, he thinks that a consciousness of themselves as "a mingled
people" gives the English a colonial edge. Lyly undermines the idea of English national purity from the start of *Gallathea.* In the happy past, as Tityrus
reports in the opening scene of the play, the English built a temple to Neptune
in order to protect those who "either ventured by long travel to see countries
or by great traffic to use merchandize." Even before the Danish invasion,
then, the English isle was no little world unto itself: the very worship of a Roman god had bespoken "traffic" with foreign countries. As Lyly puts it in the
prologue to his *Midas* (1590), "traffic and travel hath woven the nature of
all nations into ours."[38] *Gallathea* subsequently interweaves its first plot of
Roman-named characters with a second plot of English-named characters,
three boys shipwrecked in Lincolnshire. And Cupid begins his campaign of
wounding Diana's nymphs, generating a self-alienation in them to match the
larger cultural estrangement that allows Diana and himself to feel at home in
England in the first place.

Like Shakespeare, Lyly seems to have been professionally predisposed to
the representation of mixed or impure national identity. In the theater, as its
Renaissance critics loved to underscore, men "are always *acting others*, not
themselves." As one antitheatricalist put it, the player is a "Motley" in "mind"
as well as "fashion," his "profession" "compounded of all Natures, all humors,
all professions."[39] Gallathea and Phyllida do not need Cupid's darts in order
to fall for one another; disguise alone proves alienating, self-othering, enough
to make them lovers. Immediately before her first encounter with Phyllida,
Gallathea upbraids herself for practicing "deceit": "O, would the gods had
made me as I seem to be," she exclaims, "or that I might safely be what I seem
not!" Phyllida likewise insists that her disguise "will neither become my body
nor my mind." Yet for both girls the felt "unaptness" of their "apparel" leads
directly to a new "untamedness" in their "affections." As Phyllida reflects to
herself, "Art thou no sooner in the habit of a boy, but thou must be enamored
of a boy?" Deceit also unites the three boys in the play's second plot. Yet,
since they are boys and can never embody the literally social self-otherness
of pregnancy, deceit unites them more baldly than it does the virgins of the
first plot. The boys are also more radically dispossessed of any fixed identity than the disguised and hidden girls are: with "neither lands nor wit nor
masters nor honesty" to call their own, they decide that they "must live by

cozenage." In short, the boys achieve a collectively self-alienated identity not as fellow lovers but as fellow cheats: though brothers, they end up preferring a sense of themselves as "*cozens.*" And when, over Diana's objections, they take on the role of musical "consort" to the reconciliations that end the play, the boys underscore how an artful "roving" from fixed identity has become the new collective identity of the characters in the play, a distinctively *disin*tegral form of nationhood that Lyly suggests is best formulated and displayed in the theater.[40]

In the history plays that follow *Richard II,* Shakespeare too weighs the benefits of allying English national identity with theatrical self-otherness. The role-playing Prince Hal is not disabled by the thought of England's, or his own, internal fragmentation. On the contrary, he feels enlarged: as prince, he declares himself "of all humors," while as king he proclaims himself the rightful monarch of France as well as England. Many critics have noted Shakespeare's emphasis on the duplicity that enables Hal to turn disintegration into empire, but they have also tended to concede that Shakespeare's reservations about Hal fail to subvert the heroic effect of Hal's peculiarly unfixed character. Skepticism, it seems, cannot easily dislodge an identity that takes incoherence, or else an overt fiction of coherence, as its founding principle. It may be, then, that subsequent English nationalism inherited a significant part of its ideological resiliency from those Elizabethan writers who characterized their national identity as essentially motley. A century and a half later, after remarking on the exceptional heterogeneity of "manners and characters" in England, David Hume skeptically concludes that "the ENGLISH, of any people in the universe, have the least of a national character" — "unless," he adds, "this very singularity may pass for such."[41]

AFTERWORD

What Does the Black Legend Have to Do with Race?

Walter D. Mignolo

THE BLACK LEGEND AND THE EUROPEAN IMPERIAL DIFFERENCE

I have been asked the question, "What does the Black Legend Have to do with race?" several times in informal conversations about the title of this volume. I will attempt to answer the question here.[1]

The Black Legend is, as stated in the book's introduction, the twentieth-century name for a narrative that chastises Castilians for the brutality they committed in the New World, a narrative told from the perspective of England and dating back to the reign of Elizabeth I. What, indeed, does this legend have to do with discourses on race in the European Renaissance? Answering the question should begin by spelling out the assumptions underlying the interpretive concept of "race." There is already a debate in which several positions have been articulated, which I will summarize here briefly.

In western European countries, mainly in German and French scholarship, race is a concept that entered the vocabulary of the Western world during and after the Enlightenment. As such, race corresponds in time and in space with the New World order that emerged after the American Revolution in 1776 and the French Revolution in 1789. In Spanish (and Portuguese), in the Iberian Peninsula and in Ibero-América, race is *not* taken to be an invention of the Enlightenment in the countries north of the Pyrenees, but of the Renaissance. I would suggest that when the secular and scientific discourse on race (which covered up racism as ideology) was formed in the nineteenth century, the conceptual frame had already been in place since the Renaissance. What secular science and philosophy did in the nineteenth century was to translate and adapt the racial system put in place by theology in the sixteenth century. Theology served as the conceptual framework to argue "racial differences" in two directions simultaneously: First, Spain, and later England and France, distinguished themselves from the Muslims (in the north of Africa) and the "Turks" in the East (the Ottoman Empire). Second — and this is when the Black Legend comes into play — England distinguished itself from the Spaniards, who, the English said, had Moorish blood and acted as barbarians in the New World. About two centuries after the Black Legend was told and retold, Immanuel Kant stated as a fact that Spaniards had a non-European origin: "The Spaniard's bad side is that he does not learn from foreigners; that he does not travel in order to get acquainted with other nations; that he is centuries behind in the sciences. He resists any reform; he is proud of not having to work; he is of a romantic quality of spirit, as the bullfight shows; he is cruel, as the former auto-da-fé shows; *and he displays in his taste an origin that is partly non-European*" (Kant 1978, 231–32; emphasis added). Three general issues in the debate surrounding the concept of race could be summarized as follows:

1. Whether race should be linked to skin color and to the scientific classification of world races. This issue came out in nineteenth-century Europe (not in Russia or in the Ottoman Empire, nor in China or India). If it had become known in India (let us suppose) it would have been because of the British presence and not the concerns of learned men in the Mughal Empire. As Lal shows in chapter 3 of this volume, nothing like the racial discourses in the European Renaissance concerned the learned men of the Mughals.
2. Whether race should be understood in the terms by which social actors identified themselves, in terms of the identification that was bestowed upon them, or in terms of the power differential that interconnects both the imperial (theological, scientific, philosophical) allocation of meaning and the colonial subaltern relocation of meaning by social actors that have been classified from outside their own histories, that is, from the histories of imperial actors (see Burns, chap. 10; Silverblatt, chap. 6; and Lamana, chap. 7).
3. Whether "race" or "caste" was the better term to account for the hierarchical organization of people during the Renaissance and at what point in history "caste" became "race" (see Burns, chap. 10, and Nirenberg, chap. 4).

The idea we are trying (collectively) to advance in this book is that *race as racism* is a particular configuration that emerged in and during the European Renaissance as an intrinsic part of the consolidation of capitalism in the Atlantic economy and of Western expansion from the sixteenth century until today. In other words, race as racism goes hand in hand with the emergence of capitalism as a new form of economic organization: the massive appropriation of land and the massive exploitation of labor during the sixteenth and seventeenth centuries (in the hands of western Atlantic European empires) had as its main purpose the production of commodities for a global market. Racism emerged as a discourse to assert the superiority of Western Christians and as justification for land appropriation and exploitation of supposedly lesser human beings. Today racist discourse has a similar function in keeping Chinese and Iranian expansion at bay and criminalizing immigration in the United States and in Europe. The Black Legend is a piece in the puzzle of Renaissance discourse on race that put forward the imperial difference among European powers.

I will not engage in a debate with the three different positions outlined above. They are important, however, as the background of my meditations. My goal in this afterword is not a historical reconstruction and an evaluation of the available sources and the historical interpretations of those sources, but to ask two basic questions: (1) who was in a position to classify and to establish hierarchies of religion, blood, then of skin, and more recently of nations and languages and, again, religion; and (2) what are the purposes of those classifications, assuming that they are not simply an effort to tell the truth about world ontology? Below I review a series of interconnected and familiar events, avoiding both the words "caste" and "race." I return to them in the last section of the afterword, hoping to shed new light on current debates and provide a clear link between the Black Legend and the "discourse on race" in the European Renaissance and, on its darker side, the New World colonies.

RACISM, RELIGION, AND THE RENAISSANCE CONCEPT OF "HUMAN"

In the sixteenth century, Christian theology offered a frame and a conception of the human that took a particular turn in relation to coexisting civilizations (often called empires), like the Mughal and the Ottoman Sultanates, the Russian Tsarate, and the Incanate in the New World. Christian theological classification overruled, with time, all the others and served as the basic structures for the secular classification of races in the late eighteenth and nineteenth centuries.[2] In 1526, shortly after Charles I of Castile (Charles V of the Holy Roman Empire) ascended the throne, Babar (a descendent of Genghis Khan) was initiating the journey toward the foundation of the so-called Mughal Sultanate. Babar's son, Akbar, was the sultan of the Mughal Empire from 1556 to 1605, during almost the same years that Elizabeth I reigned in England and Philip II, son of Charles V, reigned in Spain (1556–1598). Suleyman the Magnificent extended his period of dominance and the preeminence of the Ottoman Sultanate (1520–1566), coexisting with the reign of Charles as Holy Roman Emperor (1519–1558) and king of Spain (1516–1556). While the Mughal and Ottoman sultanates coexisted (see Peirce, chap. 2, and Lal, chap. 3) during the sixteenth century with the emerging Spanish Empire, the Incanate in Tawantinsuyu and the Tlatoanate in Anahuac were destroyed, the former came to an end around 1548, twelve years after Francisco Pizarro set foot in the lands of Tawantinsuyu (see Silverblatt and Lamana), and the latter was destroyed in 1520, a few years after Hernán Cortés moved from the coast of Veracruz to Tlaxcala and finally to Mexico Tenochtitlan (see SilverMoon and Ennis, chap. 8). Last but not least, the Russian Tsarate was on its way—when Moscow was declared the Third Rome, toward 1520, after Muscovite Russia had ended its tributary dependence with the Golden Horde—to Ivan the Terrible (1530–1584). Thus, current debates about whether race is an eighteenth- and nineteenth-century discourse and whether in the sixteenth century caste was the proper system of classification assume that the classifications concocted by Renaissance men of letters or Enlightenment "philosophies" were universal. The system of classification and hierarchies during the Renaissance or during the Enlightenment was a local one in this precise sense: people in India, China, Ottoman, Tawantinsuyu, Anahuac, and so forth, certainly were part of the classification, but none of them, except Christian theologians, had any say in the classification, except to reclassify themselves for their own pride but with little effect in the organization of world power that was at stake.

Consequently, "discourses of difference in the Renaissance Empires" means, on the one hand, the Renaissance empires in Europe: the Hapsburg or Austro-Hungarian Empire, the Spanish and Portuguese empires, and the coming into being of the British Empire. On the other hand, the European Renaissance could be taken as a reference period for the emergence of several "empires," a general name extended after the name of the Roman emperor instead of, for example, the sultan or the tsar. This distinction is very important for the arguments advanced in this book for two reasons. The Black Legend is, first and foremost, an internal conflict in Europe and for that reason I will describe it as an *imperial internal difference.* But the narrators of the Black Legend, initiated and propelled by England, shared with the Spaniards the Christian cosmology that distinguished itself from the Muslims, the Turks, and the Russian Orthodox. That is, the Black Legend contributed to the reinforcement of an imperial divide that was already carried out by the Spanish kingdom of Charles I and the Spanish Empire under Philip II.

The chapters in this volume dealing with Spain and the New World in the sixteenth century agree on one basic principle regarding the outcome of a system of classification and hierarchy that emerged, as such, after 1492: the expulsion of the Moors and the Jews from the Iberian Peninsula. The "discovery" of the New World brought a different problem: if Jews and Moors were classified according to their belief in the wrong God, Indians (and later black Africans) had to be classified as having no religion. Although many Africans came from the vast region of Ethiopia and most likely were Muslims, their religious faith is not profusely documented. The fact is that, with time, whatever faith Africans brought with them, that faith did not hold, and new "religions" were created in each of the main colonial domains of the four imperial countries: Santería in Spanish domains, Voudou in French colonies, Candomblé in Portuguese Brazil, and Rastafarianism in the British Isles. Thus, the question of "purity of blood" acquired in the New World a meaning totally different from one it had had in the Iberian Peninsula. Nonetheless, the fact remains that with the double expulsion of Moors and Jews from the Iberian Peninsula, the New World brought a different dimension to the classificatory and hierarchical system. While in Spain, Jews and Muslims identified themselves with those labels, there were no "Indians" in the New World. To become "Indian" was a long and painful process for the diversity of people, the diversity of languages, the diversity of memories, and the diversity of rituals from today's southern Chile to today's Canada. And there were no "blacks" either. Africans transported to the New World from different regions of the continent had different languages, memories, and religions, yet all of them suddenly became blacks in the New World. In other words, whatever the system of classification in the Iberian Peninsula and in the New World, that system was controlled by Christian theology as the overarching and hegemonic frame of knowledge. Neither the "Turks" nor the Mughals nor the Christian Orthodox in Russia had any say in it — even less, of course, New World peoples and blacks.

Let us take a closer look at this first drawing of the sixteenth-century scenario in the Mediterranean and in the Atlantic. Three foundational articles for the logic of the articulation of race into racism at the end of the fifteenth and during the sixteenth century are Anibal Quijano's "Coloniality and Modernity/Rationality" (1992), Sylvia Wynter's "Beyond the Categories of the Master Conception: the Counterdoctrine of the Jamesian Poiesis" (1992), and Anibal Quijano and Immanuel Wallerstein's "Americanity as a Concept, or the Americas in the Modern-World System" (1992). These three articles have shifted radically the perspective and conceptualization of race/racism from the internal history of European modernity (Foucault) to the interrelated histories of modernity/coloniality. They have several common assumptions among them: (1) the reconfiguration of previous mutual conceptualizations among Christians, Moors, and Jews; (2) the new configuration between Christians, Indians, and blacks in the New World; (3) the interrelations between the first two reconfigurations; and, last but not least, (4) the translation of race into racism that took place in the sixteenth century that was—and still is—strictly related to the historical foundation of capitalism. This link was absent in coexisting sixteenth-century empires like the Mughal, the Ottoman, the Aztec, the Inca, the Chinese, and the emerging Russian. This was the "novelty" of the sixteenth century and the historical foundation of the racial colonial matrix whose logic is still at work today. The content has been changing but the logic remains quite the same: the Black Legend should be understood in this scenario as the historical foundation of a mild form of racism among European Christians and the north-south divide in Europe itself. But let us first discuss the translation of race into racism and the historical foundation of modernity/coloniality.

As is clearly explained in Burns's chapter 10 and Fuchs's chapter 5 (and underscored in the introduction), race was a concept that referred to a lineage, particularly as applied to horses. Horses had a distinction in Arabic history that they did not have among Christians. Thus, the fact that in Spanish dictionaries horses became the primary example of lineage—and still today, "pure blood" is an expression applied to horses with distinction that invaded the vocabulary in English and Spanish (*pura sangre inglesa, pura sangre española*)—is telling about the fact that animals were classified by "race" and people by "ethnicity" (Greek *ethnos*, Latin *gens* or *natio*). "Ethnicity" refers to a lineage of people for whom blood is not the only factor (one wonders when blood became a crucial factor to redefine ethnicity), but rather memories and common histories, languages, rituals, everyday practices, food, songs, and music were elements bonding a community of people through history. However, when Spanish Christians defined "race" on the exemplar of horses and added the slippage toward the human ("Race in [human] lineages is understood pejoratively, as having some Moorish or Jewish race . . ."), they planted the seed for the historical foundation of racism as a hierarchical classification of people. Racism, in other words, is not a question of blood or skin color but of a discursive classification entrenched in the foundation of modern/colonial (and capitalist) empires.

"Race" in the Covarrubias quotation is synonymous with "blood" and implies "religion"—that is, the wrong religion. In the New World the situation was different. There were no "people of the Book"; Christopher Columbus surmised that the people he met in the Caribbean were people with no religions. Later on, Spanish missionaries to the powerful Inca and Aztec "empires" had difficulties in figuring out what kind of "religions" were those that were so different from the three religions of the Book they were so used to. They decided that indeed people in the Tawantinsuyu and Anahuac lived in spiritual idolatry and under guidance of the devil. They assigned themselves the task of extirpating idolatry. Indians, therefore, were cast aside and placed in a different category from Jews and Moors. Thus, while in the Iberian Peninsula "conversos" and "moriscos" designated ex-Jews and ex-Moors who had converted to Christianity, in the New World the term "mestizo" was coined to identify an emerging population of mixed Spanish (and Portuguese) and Indian blood. In the process, "blacks" in the New World lost their European identification and relationship with the Moors. In fact, "Moor" was the identification of indigenous nomadic Berber people in North Africa who were converted to Islam around the seventh century. It came to mean Muslim people from Berber and Arab descent. The name itself, as is well known, comes from the Kingdom of Mauri (Mauritania), a province in the Roman Empire located in what is today North Africa and, more specifically, Morocco. As the Mauri were dark-skinned people from Africa, "Moor" was extended to African populations beyond the north of Africa. As Fuchs points out in her chapter, in the growing vocabulary of the Black Legend, Spaniards were sometimes pejoratively designated as Moors and as blacks. Shakespeare's "Moor of Venice" is indeed a black person, a "blackamoor" (type this word in Google, click on http://imageevent.com/bluboi/blackamoors, and you will understand what I mean).[3] Detached from that memory, blacks in the New World became, for European Christians, from the Spaniards to the British, related to slavery, and as slaves their memories and spiritual belonging were not taken into account. In the New World, blacks were not Moors but Ethiopians.[4] In the Spanish and Portuguese colonies a new word was coined—"mulatto/a"—to designate people of a new breed, a mixture of Spanish and Black.

Now we have the basic elements of the racial modern/colonial matrix. Christians placed themselves at the center—both as members of the right religion and of the hegemonic theological discourse and as white Spaniards and Portuguese.[5] On the one hand, we have Christians and, confronted with them, Moors and Jews. On the other, we have Spaniards and Portuguese and, confronted with them, Indians and blacks. In between the first triad, we have "conversos/as" and "moriscos/as." In between the second triad, we have "mestizos/as" and "mulattos/as." The first presupposed religion; in the second, religion is a nonexisting entity and so Spaniards and Portuguese in the New World become the substitute for Christians in the Iberian Peninsula. When, in the late eighteenth and early nineteenth centuries, the concept of race is reconfigured, it is reconfigured in a secular world. Thus, skin color began to replace blood as a racial marker.[6] Consequently, the peninsular triad was forgotten because it was based on religion, and the second triad was forgotten because it happened in the colonies—and that was not part of European history. Thus, today, scholars revisiting the concept of race—most of them in England, the United States, Germany, and France—start in the mid-eighteenth century. H. F. Augstein's edited volume, *Race. The origins of an Idea, 1760–1850* (1996), shows no *idea* of what happened before 1760, as if the *idea* really emerged in the heart of Europe (England, Germany, and France) without any relation to the European colonies since the sixteenth century. More to the point, and surprisingly funny, the first chapter from Buffon's *Natural History* is on what? On *the natural history of the horse*. There is no indication that the origin of the modern/colonial idea of race emerged when the lineage of the horse was linked to Christian notions of undesirable human beings, Moors and Jews. This double blindness among intellectuals and scholars from and in the heart of Europe is the (unintended) consequence of the Black Legend. Why?

Up to this point I have provided a sketchy summary of the idea of race/racism as it was articulated by Christian theologians in the Iberian Peninsula. Theology was the master epistemic frame, before secular philosophy and science grounded on the Cartesian epistemic shift (the ego-logy of "I think therefore I am" displaced the theo-logy of human rationality dependent on God's designs). Theology offered the tools to describe and classify people with the wrong religion and people without religion. Christianity was one among other world religions, but it was the *right* one. How was it decided? Because Christians made the classification on the basis of theology as the supreme Archimedean point from which the entire world could be observed and classified. Christians who were also Castilians and Portuguese in the New World were among Indians and blacks, but Castilians and Portuguese were superior to them as they controlled the discourse in which such hierarchy was established. Thus, theology allowed for a conceptualization of humanity for which Castilian and Portuguese were taken as exemplars of what human beings are supposed to be. But then came Elizabeth I, and with her the enactment of a discourse of race in England that was mainly directed against Spain. Of course, British men of letters and officers of the state did not look at the Ottoman Empire with friendly eyes either. Salamon in chapter 14 accounts for the tribulations of Roger Ascham at the frontier of the Hapsburg's dominion where the presence of the Turks was disturbingly felt. And with respect to the New World, England was more interested in following the Castilian example of empire building (see Campos, chap. 13) than in debating whether Indians and blacks were human beings. Thus, discourse of race in England during the European Renaissance does not contradict Spaniards' classification—on the contrary, England's target was the Spaniards in the same way that the Spaniards' targets were the Moors, Jews, Indians, and blacks. In other words, the Black

Legend is a racial discourse internal to Europe: the racialization of the Latin and Catholic south in the mouth and pen of the Anglo and Protestant north.

The logic of discourses on race during the European Renaissance that went hand in hand with the historical foundation of capitalism as a new economic formation could then be summarized as follows. Bartolomé de Las Casas offered a blueprint of this logic in his classification of "barbarians." An analysis of the logic of his classification shows a set of underlying principles. Long after the end of the Crusades, Christian Europe continued to be under pressure from the expanding Ottoman Empire. The Ottomans would achieve impressive victories, including the capture of Constantinople, the last outpost of the Roman Empire and spiritual center of Orthodox Christianity. Eventually, Western Christians would mount effective counterattacks and keep Ottoman forces out of central Europe, but for a long time the "Turkish Menace" would haunt European dreams. In the Iberian Peninsula, the racial difference between Christians on the one hand and Jews and Moors on the other follow two different principles. The Turks and the Moors were not, of course, the same in any Christian mind. However, they knew that the Moors had an imperial Islamic past and the Turks an imperial and bright present. Thus, calling the Turks and the Moors barbarians was a way to construct the *external imperial difference.* By external I mean that the difference was with non-Western non-Christians and, therefore, non-Europeans. And it was imperial because neither the Moors nor the Turks were colonized in the way Indians and black slaves were. Moors were expelled from Europe and the Turks were already in what would become Eurasia. The Jews were expelled, but most of them remained within Europe wherein, after the sixteenth century, they would have a remarkable presence and a tragic outcome: the Holocaust. On the characterization of the Jews (people without an empire or state), Christian theologians constructed the *internal colonial difference.* Aimé Césaire pointed out in his *Discourse on Colonialism* that Jews as the internal others in the Holocause were racially marked by the internal colonial difference, a difference that was traced at the end of the fifteenth century to their expulsion from the Christian Iberian Peninsula. Consequently, as Césaire observed, what European Christians could not forgive in Hitler is *"not the crime against man,* it is not *the humiliation of man as such,* it is the crime against the white man, the humiliation of the white man, and the fact that he applied to Europe colonialist procedures which until then had been reserved exclusively for the Arabs of Algeria, the 'coolies' of India and the 'niggers' of Africa" (Césaire 2000, 36). Interestingly enough, to understand how the coloniality of knowledge works, we should notice that even Césaire forgot about the Indians of the Americas.

"Internal" and "external" are not characterizations of an objective observer, from an Archimedean point of observation, who decides what is inside and what is outside in the objective reality of the world. Hegel's dictum, that the real is rational and the rational is real, is an obviously imperial statement that remains in the history of philosophy as the intricate connection between one rationality that corresponds with one reality: the reality of the imperial logic of the Archimedean point of view, whence race as racism is constructed and continues to survive. Both characterizations are a construction of Christian theological discourses (or theology-based discourses among men of letters and officers of the state) that I am reporting in a free-indirect style. There is not now, and cannot ever be, an Archimedean point at which the observer is not implied in the description of his or her observation. By describing the Christian point of view in a free-indirect style, I am at the same time speaking from the perspective of those who have been "racialized" and, in doing so, I am attempting to decolonize the structure and content of knowledge on race and racism that has been framed by Christian theology and by European secular science and philosophy. With this caveat in mind, let us then move to the construction of the external colonial difference. As you may have guessed, and the example of Césaire makes clear, Indians and blacks were "like" Jews (and as a matter of fact, the comparison between Indians and Jews—made by Spaniards and Creoles of Spanish descent—abound in the sixteenth century). Indians and blacks, like the Moors, were people alien to the sphere of Christianity. They were, in principle, external to Christianity. Thus, even if they were black Christians coming to the New World and, during the sixteenth century, Indians who converted to Christianity, Indian Christians and black Christians were still considered "different" from Spanish or Portuguese Christians. Indians became stateless people, for example, in Tawantinsuyu and Anahuac after the defeat of Atahualpa and Moctecuzoma (see Lamana and SilverMoon and Ennis). Indians and blacks were the target for the construction of the external colonial difference.

And where shall we place the Black Legend in this scheme? We are back in the sixteenth century. Philip II became king of Spain in 1556 and he would transform the kingdom he inherited from his father, Charles I, into the glorious moment of the Spanish Empire. With the death of Charles in 1558, the Hapsburg Empire began to lose clout in relation to an ascending Spanish Empire coming out from the margins of the Hapsburgs in the first half of the century. The Hapsburg or Austro-Hungarian Empire changed its role and function from the second half of the sixteenth century to its demise during WWI. It became a buffer zone where the Ottoman Empire was stopped, and it became a marginal region of Western Christendom now that the center of economy moved to the Atlantic, from Spain and Portugal to Holland and England. Vienna and Prague still today conserve the garb and the magnificence of imperial cities (while Moscow and Istanbul entered in a process of visible decay). Elizabeth I became Queen of England in 1558; Ivan the Terrible was the grand prince over all the Rus from 1533 and the first Russian tsar since 1547. Moscow as the Third Rome competes with and complements Istanbul (the Second Rome) and Rome proper. China and Beijing were far away but were the center of attraction in a world that had no center. It was Columbus and Western Christians who dreamed of Cipango, not the Chinese who desired the land of Christendom. For Chinese scholars and officers of the Ming Dynasty, Western Christendom was—if known at all—in the territory of the barbarians. It was in that scenario that Roger Ascham traveled from England to the limits with the lands of "the Turk" toward the middle of the sixteenth century and wrote a report that could be considered a blueprint of the Black Legend (see Salamon).

The advocates of the Black Legend employed the tropes already in place to describe and classify people in relation to a model or standard of humanity and turned them against Christian Spaniards at the height of the crisis of the Church in the middle of the Council of Trent.[7] By accusing Spaniards of being barbarians (for the atrocities they committed in the New World) and naming them Moors, blacks, and Sarracens (see Fuchs), no British men or women of letters confused the Spaniards with the Moors or the Turks, much less with blacks or Indians in the New World. The external imperial and colonial differences were maintained, as was the internal colonial difference: no Englishman or Englishwomen would fail to make the distinction between Christian and Jew. If the previous racial distinction were maintained, what was added was the internal imperial difference. The Black Legend inaugurated a racialized discourse within, that is, internal to, capitalist empires of the West. As is well known, the Black Legend was part of the political purposes of England of displacing Spain from its imperial domination. What the Black Legend does not mention, but that history and black intellectuals like Ottabah Cugoano made clear (see the introduction), is that the British were as brutal and greedy as the Spaniards. In fact, the Black Legend was part of an imperial conduct as well as discourse that we have seen at work since then in England to the present-day United States.

RACISM AND THE HISTORICAL FOUNDATION OF THE MODEL/COLONIAL WORLD

The Black Legend is a piece of a larger puzzle that transcends the particular moment of its origin. Gonzalo Lamana (chap. 7) traced its ramifications in the history of ideas that filtered into the United States in the nineteenth century and that informed popular narratives like William Prescott's *History of the Conquest of Peru* (1847). Notice also that Prescott's book was published one year before the signing of the Treaty of Guadalupe-Hidalgo that gave the United States possession of a vast territory previously belonging to Mexico. That is, the book was published at a moment in history when history repeats itself and the United States of the nineteenth century, like England of the mid-sixteenth century, is affirming its imperial ambitions, ambitions that had already been mapped by the discourse on race/racism during the European Renaissance, ambitions that have since given authority to imperial powers to reproduce themselves and to reproduce the sense of superiority of agents in a position of epistemic authority to classify the world. A few decades before Prescott, Hegel in Europe collected the legacies of the Black Legend and asserted the superiority of the heart of Europe that is, the three countries—England, France, and Germany—that in the nineteenth century consolidated and expanded Western capitalism and imperialism.

Hegel (1991, 102) was clear in capturing the unfolding of this story when he stated, at the end of his introduction to *The Philosophy of History*, that "the three sections of Europe require therefore a different basis of classification." And he went on to offer the following geopolitical map:

> 1. The first part is Southern Europe—looking towards the Mediterranean . . . North of the Pyrenees, mountain chains run through France, connected with the Alps that separate and cut off Italy from France and Germany. Greece also belongs to this part of Europe;
> 2. The second portion is the heart of Europe. . . . In this centre of Europe, France, Germany, and England are the principal countries.
> 3. The third, said Hegel, consists of the northeastern states of Europe—Poland, Russia, and the Slavonic Kingdoms. They came late into the series of historical states, and form and perpetuate the connection with Asia. In contrast with the physical singularities of the earlier division, these are already noticed, not present in a remarkable degree, but counterbalance each other.

Hegel talked about states but neglected to mention that the states of the heart of Europe are the new imperialism. He makes clear that the states of the heart of Europe are pure and clean, with no connection with Africa, as is the case of Spain and Portugal (that is why it is important for him to highlight Italy and Greece), and with no connections with Asia, like the northeastern states. It was in 1853 (a few years after Prescott's *History of the Conquest of Peru*) that Joseph Arthur, compte de Gobineau, published the new configuration of the discourse on race/racism, the discourse that would serve the purposes of the new Western empires. That treatise was titled *Essai sur l'inégalité des races humaines*.

The internal imperial difference that the Black Legend put in place had diminished its rhetoric through time, but not the lasting trace of what would become the marker of the heart of Europe and the foundation of white supremacy, as Prescott's history already indicates. In Europe today, England, France, and Germany are the strong players of the European Union. The Latin and Catholic south still forms an imperial core. England and the United States have joined forces, in spite of their differences, since Ronald Reagan and Margaret Thatcher opened the way to the fatal alliance of Tony Blair and George W. Bush. Five hundred years after the expulsion of the Moors from the Iberian Peninsula and five hundred years after the invasion and invention of America, Samuel Huntington identified the Moors as enemies of Western civilization and Hispanics (that is Latinos and Latinas) as a challenge to Anglo identity in the United States. Racism dies hard, and the specter of the Black Legend is still alive and well, contributing to diminishing Spaniards in Europe, marginalizing "Latins" in South America, and criminalizing Latinos and Latinas in the United States. If Indians were the victims of Spaniards that the Black Legend denounced, black slaves were the victims of England that the Black Legend hid under the cloak of Spanish barbarism.

However, none of the discourses on race/racism went uncontested. Imperial racialization was first contested by Waman Puma de Ayala in Peru in the late sixteenth and early seventeenth centuries, and then in the eighteenth century by Ottabah Cugoana in England, after he had been a slave in the Caribbean. Before Gobineau and before Prescott, Frederick Douglas in the nineteenth century published (in the United States) the *Narrative of the Life of Frederick Douglass, an American Slave, Written By Himself* (1845). Haitian Anténor Firmin published in 1885 in France a well-documented study against Gobineau. Firmin's book was titled *De l'égalité des races humaines* (1888). W. E. B. Du Bois and Frantz Fanon followed suit in the Americas; and Gloria Anzaldúa stood up as Latina to claim "for women of my race the Spirit shall speak." These voices of dissent not only contest the Black Legend but all imperial discourses on race and racism, including those of Spain, of which the Black Legend is one piece of the puzzle.

NOTES

Chapter One

1. Those modern practices emerged when the validity of a racial categorization began to be questioned, not in reference to black-white racism or anti-Semitism, but as a response to ideologies that posited a qualitative hierarchy between Caucasian peoples (Frederickson, *Racism*). Frederickson traces the historical study of racism back to the 1920's, to the refutation of theories of Nordic, Teutonic, or Aryan superiority (156–64).

2. For the use of castration to produce an imperial administrative caste, see Tsai, *The Eunuchs.*

3. Levathes, *When China Ruled the Seas*, 121.

4. For a discussion of nongovernmental, entrepreneurial Chinese traders, see Ptak, *China and the Asian Seas*, 35–44).

5. Kamen and Pérez, in *La imagen internacional* (56–63), paint the Black Legend, at least prior to the launching of the "Invincible Armada" against England in 1588, as an official rather than a popular propaganda war akin to that of the Soviet-U.S. Cold War, a one-sided argument to which Philip II did not contribute but which was fed by certain political and religious sectors in England.

6. In 1656, just after the Spanish colony at Jamaica fell to the English, John Philipps, a nephew of John Milton, published a translation of the *Brevíssima* entitled *The Tears of the Indians: Being an Historical and True Account of the Cruel Massacres and Slaughters of Above Twenty Millions of Innocent Peoples in the Islands of Hispaniola, Cuba, Jamaica, etc.*

7. Havelock, *The Literate Revolution;* a view from the other side, that is, from what Western literacy reduced to silence, is in Tedlock, *The Spoken World.*

8. The best-documented instance took place at Ma'arra an-Naman, in northern Syria. On sacking the city at the end of a long siege, the hungry Christian forces cooked and ate the bodies of Muslims and Jews they had killed on taking the city. The episode was recounted with various degrees of horror in three chronicles written shortly after the event. (Heng, *Empire of Magic*, 21–24).

9. Heng argues that the combination of history and fantasy in this Arthurian chronicles served three ends: (1) dealing with medieval Europe's first transnational imperial project, (2) giving shape to an emerging concept of the English nation, and (3) establishing an "emergent grammar of racial classification and hierarchy that appeared in the process of nation formation."

10. Cf. Pérez (*Historia de España*, 61–62), who denies the existence of intermarriage, which both Nirenberg and Menocal document.

11. The first group were the *Almoravides*, who invaded in 1086, followed by the *Almohades* in 1147.

12. "Los sucesos de 1391 deben interpretarse como una explosión de odio de clase, desviada contra los judíos y favorecida por la debilidad del poder." [The events of 1391 should be interpreted as an explosion of class hatred, rerouted against the Jews and favored by weakness of [monarchical] power.] (Pérez, *Historia de España*, 107).

13. The most celebrated example of this exchange is the case of Carlos I's appointment of a learned professor of peasant origins, Juan Martínez Siliceo, as archbishop of Toledo. When the aristocratic clergy rejected him, he retaliated by imposing blood purity requirements for posts in the ecclesiastical hierarchy at Toledo in 1547 (Pérez, *Historia de España*, 271, 293–94).

14. Covarrubias *Tesoro de la lengua* (716), defines "linaje" (lineage) as, "La descendencia de las casas y familias. Díjose a línea, porque van descendiendo de padres, hijos y nietos, etc., como por línea recta." [The descent line of houses and families. It comes from "line," because they descend from father to sons to grandsons, etc., as in a straight line.]

15. Dopico-Black, *Perfect Wives*.

16. See Hahn, "The Difference"; Kinoshita, "'Pagans Are Wrong'."

17. Menzies, *1421*, 50–56.

18. Levathes, *When China Ruled the Seas*, 79–80.

19. Shih-shan Henry Tsai's *Perpetual Happiness* simply assumes that Zeng He never made it to the Americas, but he does realize that the Chinese navy was far more advanced than anything Europe had to offer: "It is clear that in numbers, wealth . . . technology, and sophistication, the Ming Chinese surpassed both the Portuguese and the spaniards" (204–5).

20. For the Newport tower, see Menzies, *1421* (285–90).

21. For a discussion of the differences between Portuguese and Chinese trading networks in the Indian Ocean, see Ptak, *China and the Asian Seas*, esp. chaps. I and VI.

Chapter Two

1. For a case of early modern articulation of a Spanish "nation," see Dandelet, *Spanish Rome*, 113–21.

2. The term "Byzantium" was coined in 1557 from Byzantion, the ancient settlement near which Constantinople was founded, by the German scholar Hieronymus Wolf; see Evans, *Byzantium: Faith and Power*, 5.

3. Imber, *The Ottoman Empire*, chap. 3.

4. See Peirce, *The Imperial Harem*.

5. Kunt, *The Sultan's Servants*, 97.

6. Lowry, *The Nature of the Early Ottoman State*, chap. 7.

7. Imber, *The Ottoman Empire*, 130.

8. For a bibliography on the debate over *kul* status, see Demetriades, "Some Thoughts," 23, n. 1.

9. The literature on subject of military slavery is vast. See the article "Ghulam," *Encyclopedia of Islam*, second edition, for an introduction; for origins, see Crone, *Slaves on Horses*.

10. Demetriades, "Some Thoughts," 30–31.

11. I use the term "polyglot" rather "multiethnic" and "multireligious" because of the modern connotations of the latter, which are usually used in endorsement of the ultimate goal of human equality in difference. This is not a view the Ottomans would have endorsed in premodern times.

12. Matthee, "The Safavid-Ottoman Frontier."

13. Quoted in Dankoff, *An Ottoman Mentality*, 62–63.

14. Necipoğlu, "Süleyman the Magnificent."

15. Yérasimos, *La Fondation de Constantinople*, 221–22. For a general account of the Hapsburg-Ottoman rivalry, see Finkel, *Osman's Dream*, chap. 5.

16. Bayerle, "The Compromise at Zsitvatorok"; see also Köhbach, "*Çasar* oder *Imperator?*"

17. Bacqué-Grammont, "Une lettre d'İbrahim Paşa," 70, 81.

18. Oikonomides, "The Turks in Europe," 160.

19. Ibn Battuta, *The Travels*, vol. 2, 452.

20. I have been influenced in this view by the work of Walter Pohl and his colleagues in the European Science Foundation project on "The Transformation of the Roman World," especially Pohl and Reimitz, *Strategies of Distinction*.

21. Zachariadou, *Trade and Crusade*.

22. Beldiceanu-Steinherr, "La population non-musulmane de Bithynie," 7–22.

23. See Evans, *Byzantium: Faith and Power*, 374–75.

24. Reinert, "The Muslim Presence in Constantinople," 125–50.

25. Other meanings of "Rum" were "Greek-speaking Christian" (subjects of the eastern Roman empire) and the region around Sivas (Sebastea) in northeastern Anatolia.

26. Doukas, *Decline and Fall of Byzantium*, 136.

27. For the absurdly long lists of titles that were displayed in official correspondence by Charles V and Suleyman, see Bacqué-Grammont, "Une lettre d'İbrahim Paşa."

28. Vryonis, *The Decline of Medieval Hellenism*, 240–44.

29. Zachariadou, "Les 'janissaires' de l'empereur byzantin," 591–97.

30. Kunt, "Ethnic-Regional (*Cins*) Solidarity," 233–39.
31. On the Bektashi order, see Karamustafa, *God's Unruly Friends*, 83–84.
32. This point is well demonstrated in a provincial context by Watenpaugh, *The Image of an Ottoman City.*
33. Necipoğlu, "A Kanun for the State," 207.
34. Watenpaugh, *The Image of an Ottoman City.*
35. Stavrides, *The Sultan of Vezirs*, 294, quoting Tekin, "Fatih Devri Türk Edebiyatı," 184–85.
36. Gökbilgin, "İbrahim Paşa."
37. Quoted in Stavrides, *The Sultan of Vezirs*, 352–53.
38. Watenpaugh, *The Image of An Ottoman City*, 72.
39. Roe, *The Negotiations of Sir Thomas Roe*, 46.
40. See Veinstein, "Mehmet Pasha, Sokollu," *Encyclopedia of Islam*, second edition, vol. 9, 706–11. Sokollu's Bosnian patronage is fictionally chronicled in Andrič's epic *The Bridge on the Drina.*
41. On the diplomatic activities of the queen mothers, see Peirce, *The Imperial Harem*, chap. 8.
42. Sphrantzes, *The Fall of the Byzantine Empire*, 61.
43. Peçevi, *Tarih-i Peçevi*, vol. I, 30–31.
44. Peirce, *The Imperial Harem*, 77–79.
45. The phrase is Elliott's, *Imperial Spain*, 209.
46. Gibbons, *The Foundation of the Ottoman Empire.* See Kafadar, *Between Two Worlds*, especially chap. 1, for astute comments on the historiography of Ottoman origins.
47. For a fresh exploration of the regicide in the context of the several persons and groups interested in the disposition of the sultanate, see Tezcan, *Searching for Osman.* For the role of queen mothers in the politics of the regicide and succession in general, see Peirce, *The Imperial Harem*, 197, 232–33.
48. Tezcan, *Searching for Osman*, 191.
49. See the provocative comments of Piterburg on the anxiety inspired by the idea of "crossing over" from Istanbul/Europe to Anatolia, in *An Ottoman Tragedy*, Epilogue.

Chapter Three

A note on transliteration and citations: There is no standard system for transliteration from Persian into English. I have used the modified version of the *International Journal of Middle East Studies* as developed and used by Layla S. Diba and Maryam Ekhtiar for their edited volume, *Royal Persian Paintings: The Qajar Epoch, 1785–1925* (New York: I. B. Tauris, 1998). For better readability all diacritical marks have been removed. The original spellings have been retained in quotations. As a result, certain names appear with spellings in my text that differ from some spellings in the quotations. All information included in square brackets is mine.

1. Monserrate, *Commentary*, 202; I use the Blochmann's translation of *The A-in-I Akbari*, 3 vols. (Blochmann, *A'in-i Akbari*, I, 46). The Persian text used here is edited by Blochmann, *The Ain I Akbari by Abul Fazl I 'Allami*, 3 vols. (Blochmann, *Persian A'in*).

2. Gulbadan, *Ahval;* Beveridge, *Humayun*, Appendix A.

3. I use Beveridge's translation of *The Akbar Nama of Abu-l-Fazl;* Beveridge, *Akbarnama*, II, 76. The Persian text I use is that edited by Maulawi 'Abd-ur-Rahim, *Akbarnamah by Abul-Fazl*.

4. Beveridge, *Akbarnama*, II, 240.

5. Ibid., 242.

6. Badauni, *Muntakhab*, II, 59. Badauni, a severe critic of Akbar's policies, wrote his history in secret. The text was hidden but was copied and circulated after Akbar's death. Historians have found this chronicle a useful counter to the panegyric account of the court chronicler, Abu-l Fazl.

7. Nizam al-Din Ahmad, *Tabaqat*, II, 285.

8. Ibid.

9. Ibid. According to Beveridge, *Akbarnama*, it was Miran Mubarak Shah who wanted his daughter to be included among Akbar's *haram*, Nizam al-Din Ahmad, *Tabaqat*, II, 285, fn. 1.

10. Nath, *Private Life*, 23.

11. Beveridge, *Humayun*, Appendix A, 276. Nur al-Din Muhammad Chaghaniyani was the son of Sultan Husain Bayqura of Herat, whom Babur greatly admired. Similar considerations seem to underlie other royal marriages, such as the marriage of Akbar's sister, Bakhshi Banu, to Mirza Sharaf al-Din Husain, who (according to the *Akbarnama*) was of "very exalted lineage." So Akbar had given him a "lofty rank" in order to enable the *mirza* to be "a prop of the Sultanate" and gave him in marriage Bakhshi Banu Begum, who was the "Shahinshah's pure sister" (Beveridge, *Akbarnama*, II, 197). In the marriages of Akbar's daughters, Shakr-un-Nisa Begum and Khanim Sultan, the importance of illustrious connections is emphasized again (Beveridge, *Akbarnama*, III, 990, and Index, 43, 54, and 990). Jahangir, the son of Akbar from a Rajput princess, himself married into several Rajput households: to the daughter of Raja Bhagwan Das (son of Raja Bihari Mal of Amber) and to Jodhbai (the daughter of Mota Rai Udai Singh of Jodhpur), as well as to the daughter of Rai Raisingh of Bikaner. Similarly, Prince Sultan Danyal was married to the daughter of Rai Mal, who was the son of Rai Maldeo, a strong ally of Akbar (Blochmann, *A'in-i Akbari*, I, 330, 331, 474, 475).

12. See Srivastava, *Akbar the Great*, 62–63; Lal, *The Mughal Harem*, 25; Richards,

The Mughal Empire, 19–25; and Nath, *Private Life,* chap. III, to take only a few examples.

13. For an elaboration of this argument, see Lal, *Domesticity and Power,* chap. VI.

14. These different marital links also show the range of political connections that were deemed necessary for the making and maintenance of the empire. This process of political marriages would continue well after the empire was triumphantly and securely established; See Thackston, *Jahangirnama,* 6. Not surprisingly, doubts were expressed in various quarters about the legitimacy of the kinds of marriages being contracted and the kind of marriage network that the emperor was establishing. Badauni reports in the *Muntakhab-ut-Tavarikh* (II, 212) that there was an extended debate on the question of how many wives the emperor was allowed to have. For a detailed discussion of Akbar's marriages, see Lal, *Domesticity and Power,* 166–75.

15. For a more detailed account of these developments, see Lal, *Domesticity and Power,* chap. VI.

16. Lal, *Domesticity and Power,* especially chap. VI.

17. Blochmann, *A'in-i Akbari,* I, 9.

18. I discuss the meanings and implications of Fatehpur-Sikri as space more fully in Lal, *Domesticity and Power,* chap. VI. There is a wide range of architectural histories of Fatehpur-Sikri. The following compendiums might be excellent starting points for the reader: Rizvi and Flynn, *Fathpur-Sikri;* Brand and Lowry, *Fatehpur Sikri: A Source Book;* and Brand and Lowry, *Akbar's India.* For a recent detailed bibliography on Fatehpur-Sikri, see Juneja, *Architecture in Medieval India).*

19. In Babur's time, the *haram* is never discussed as an institutionalized entity but rather a well-regulated physical setup. The term almost always refers to the women. This begins to change in the texts from Humayun's time, where the *haram* is more regularly alluded to, but still in relation to the imperial women, the *haraman-i padshah* (Lal, *Domesticity and Power,* 105–11).

20. Blochmann, *A'in-i Akbari,* I, 45–46.

21. Ibid., 46–47.

22. Ibid.

23. Ibid, 47.

24. Beveridge, *Akbarnama,* III, 1008. The name of the "Shahinshah of Persia" is not clarified at the beginning of the letter. Judging by the time of the letter, the addressee should be Shah 'Abbas (1588–1629), a contemporary of Akbar.

25. Beveridge, *Akbarnama,* III, 1008.

26. Ibid, 1012.

27. Ibid, 1008.

28. See Campo, *The Other Sides of Paradise,* 19, and Peirce, *Imperial Harem,* 162, as examples.

29. Dehkhoda, "Loghatname," II, 3149.

30. Steingass, *Persian,* s.v. "bayt."

31. Campo, *The Other Sides of Paradise,* 9. The materials for the discussion that follows on the religious meanings of domestic spaces is taken from Campo, unless indicated otherwise.

32. Ibid, 13.

33. Ibid, 19.

34. Beveridge, *Akbarnama,* III, 1009.

35. Maulawi, *Akbarnamah,* II, 217; Beveridge, *Akbarnama,* II, 335.

36. Maulawi, *Akbarnamah,* II, 289; Beveridge, *Akbarnama,* II, 426.

37. Maulawi, *Akbarnamah,* I, 6; Beveridge, *Akbarnama,* I, 16.

38. Dehkhoda, "Loghatname," I, 82–98. There is another term, *Khanivadeh,* which has several meanings: *khandan, dudman, tabar, dudeh, khanivar;* see Dehkhoda, "Loghatname," I, 82–98. The term is used once in a discussion of the *'Ibadat Khana,* but the reference is not to Akbar's family, Beveridge, *Akbarnama,* III, 366; Maulawi, *Akbarnamah,* III, 253.

39. Blochmann, *Persian A'in,* 39. See also Blochmann, *A'in-i Akbari,* I, xxi.

40. Serjeant, "Haram and Hawtah," 43.

41. Ibid, 43–44.

42. Ibid, 50.

43. Bearman, *The Encyclopaedia of Islam,* 129.

44. Dehkhoda, "Loghatname," VI, 7786–89.

45. The pure and prophetic associations of the *haram* seem now to be deeply imbricated in the happenings recounted in the chronicles of the time. In a description of the arrival of the "chaste" royal women from Kabul to Hindustan (1557), the following words are used: the chaste ladies (*hazrat 'anayat*), *cupola of chastity* (*'Ismat qubab*), *cupola of chastity* (*'Ismat qubab*), and so on. See Beveridge, *Akbarnama,* II, 86; Maulawi, *Akbarnamah,* II, 54–57. Nizam al-Din Ahmad records the same event and uses the following expressions: "*Khalifa-i Ilahi*" for Akbar, "pavilion of chastity" for women; Nizam al-Din Ahmad, *Tabaqat,* II, 222.

46. Blochmann, *A'in-i Akbari,* I, *A'in* 15, 45; Blochmann, *Persian A'in,* I, 39.

47. On subsequent development of the notion of *purda* and the seclusion of women in the Islamic societies of the subcontinent, see Papanek and Minault, *Separate Worlds.*

48. Henry Beveridge suggests that Hamideh Banu's title must be translated as "rank" or "station," and not as "household," for it was given to her in her lifetime. See Beveridge, *Akbarnama,* I, 33, fn. 1. Annette Beveridge suggests that

Hamideh Banu's other name is posthumously given (Beveridge, *Humayun*, 83, fn. 1). According to Tirmizi, *Mughal Documents*, 30, the title was bestowed upon Hamideh Banu after her marriage. For a discussion on posthumous titles, see Thackston, *Jahangirnama*, xiii.

49. Beveridge, *Akbarnama*, II, 85.
50. Ibid., I, 130.
51. Ibid., III, 518. For details of the Begum, see Beveridge, *Humayun*, Appendix A, 214.
52. Beveridge, *Akbarnama*, I, 343.
53. Beveridge, *Akbarnama*, II, 502.
54. Ibid.
55. Ibid, 503.
56. Ibid, 503; Thackston, *Jahangirnama*, 21.
57. Beveridge, *Akbarnama*, II, 503.
58. Beveridge, *Akbarnama*, II, 507; Maulawi, *Akbarnamah*, II, 347.
59. Two of these illustrations are available in the Victoria and Albert Museum copy of the *Akbarnama:* "News of Selim's Birth being brought to Akbar" and "Rejoicings on the Birth of Prince Selim at Fatehpur." Victoria and Albert, *Akbarnama*, Ms. I. S. 2/1896, Acc. No. 115/117, and I. S. 2/1896, Acc. No. 78/117; Salim's birth also appears in the second series of *Akbarnama*, completed nearly ten years later. See the double-page composition by Lal at the Chester Beatty Library. Ms. no. 3, Fo. 142b and 143b. A folio at the British Library *Akbarnama*, Ms. Add. 26203, fo. 311a, shows "Daniyal as an infant with his mother (1572)." The folio corresponds to 1572, which is the year of Danyal's birth. The simplicity with which this folio is cast is worth noting, especially when compared to the scene of Salim's birth. The title of "Daniyal's birth" is taken from Titley, *Miniatures from Persian Manuscripts*, 2.
60. Beveridge, *Akbarnama*, II, 503.
61. For detailed discussion of the term, see Tirmizi, *Edicts*, Introduction, esp. xvii.
62. Tirmizi, *Edicts*, Persian text overlooking 10.
63. Ibid, xxii.
64. Beveridge, *Akbarnama*, II, 507–8. See also Badauni, *Muntakhab*, II, 124–25; Thackston, *Jahangirnama*, 4; and Nizam al-Din Ahmad, *Tabaqat*, II, 357–59.
65. Beveridge, *Akbarnama*, II, 509. Jahangir refers to her as Shahzadeh Khanum; Thackston, *Jahangirnama*, 37.
66. Beveridge, *Akbarnama*, II, 542–43. According to Abu-l Fazl, an order was issued that once Danyal became one month old, he should be conveyed to the town of Amber and committed to the care of the rani of Bihari Mal. Beveridge proposes that the transfer of Daniyal to the care of the rani would imply that the mother of Danyal was related to her (Ibid, 543, fn. 2). But this might well

have to do with the foster care of Danyal by the rani. Nizam al-Din Ahmad also records Murad's birth, Nizam al-Din Ahmad, *Tabaqat*, II, 360–61.

67. Beveridge, *Akbarnama*, II, 514–15. Badauni records the *qit'ah* of Mawlana Qasim Arsalan, composed especially for the occasion of Murad's birth. The first hemistich refers to the birth of Salim and the second to that of Murad; Badauni *Muntakhab*, II, 136.

68. Beveridge, *Akbarnama*, III, 661. Jahangir also records the births of Shahzadeh Khanum, Murad, and Danyal, all three born of "serving girls." No names or details of the mothers are given, Thackston, *Jahangirnama*, 37.

69. Correia-Afonso, *Letters*, 64.

70. Ibid, 65.

71. Ibid, 96.

72. Ibid, 348.

73. Beveridge, *Akbarnama*, III, 547.

74. Ibid., III, 709.

75. Ibid., III, 859.

76. Cited in Correia-Afonso, *Letters*, 65, fn 5.

77. The *Jahangirnama* records Ruqayya Sultan Begum as Akbar's "chief wife." (Thackston, *Jahangirnama*, 437) No more details may be found in the text regarding this status ascribed to Begum in reporting her death. The *A'in-i Akbari* calls her "Akbar's first wife" (*zan-i kalan*, better read as senior wife, Blochmann, *A'in-i Akbari*, I, 321), though not in the sense of the most important or "favourite" wife. See also Beveridge, *Humayun*, Appendix A, 274, "Ruqaiya Begam *Miranshahi*." Findly also calls Ruqayya Sultan Begum Akbar's "principle wife," Findly, *Nur Jahan*, 32.

78. Beveridge, *Akbarnama*, III, 571.

79. Ibid, III, 571, fn. 2; cf. Badauni, *Muntakhab*, II, 323.

80. Beveridge, *Akbarnama*, III, 572.

81. Ibid, Index, 2. For a discussion of the life of 'Abd-ul-Qaddus Gangoh, see especially Digby, "'Abd-al-Qaddus Gangohi (1456–1537 A.D.)."

82. Blochmann, *A'in-i Akbari*, I, 279–81.

83. Ibid., I, 282.

84. Beveridge, *Akbarnama*, III, 571–72, and fn. 2.

85. For details of Abu-l Fazl's murder, see Beveridge, *Akbarnama*, III, chap. CL.

86. Beveridge, *Akbarnama*, III, 1217.

87. Beveridge, *Akbarnama*, III, 1222–23. While Abu-l Fazl emphasizes the intervention of Hamideh Banu Begum and Gulbadan Begum, Muhammad Hadi, in his preface to the *Jahangirnama*, places more weight on Salimeh Sultan Begum's involvement in the affair of Salim (Thackston, *Jahangirnama*, 11).

88. Beveridge, *Akbarnama*, III, 351.

89. Beveridge, *Humayun*, Appendix. A, 275, "Sakina-banu Begam *Miran-shahi.*"

90. Subrahmanyam, "Structure or Process?" 298. Subrahmanyam suggests that "Mirza Hakim represented an alternative power-centre, and an alternative focus of authority and patronage to Akbar . . . even if the challenge from him did not wholly mature, we cannot dismiss it out of hand."

91. Subrahmanyam, "Structure or Process," 299.

92. Beveridge, *Akbarnama*, III, 352.

93. Ibid., III, 353.

94. Monserrate, *Commentary*, 135, fn. 207.

95. Ibid, 153, fn. 231.

96. Ibid., 75, fn. 121.

97. Ibid, 74–75.

98. *Hajj* has the following meanings: setting out, tending toward, going on a pilgrimage to Mecca, and performing the ceremonies there; see Steingass, *Persian*, s.v. "hajj."

99. Beveridge, *Akbarnama*, III, 205; see also *Muntakhab*, II, 216, 320. Hijaz refers to Mecca, Medina, and the adjacent territory; Steingass, *Persian*, 411.

100. Beveridge, *Akbarnama*, III, 205.

101. Ibid.

102. Ibid.

103. Ibid., III, 206. Beveridge actually translates two different dates of the women's departure: October 8 or 9, 1575 (Beveridge, *Akbarnama*, III, 206) and October 1576 (Beveridge, *Akbarnama*, III, 570, fn. 1).

104. Beveridge, *Akbarnama*, III, 569. There is some confusion about the dates of departure and return of Gulbadan and her companions. The date of their return is given as April 13, 1582, in the *Akbarnama* (Beveridge, *Akbarnama* III, 206, fn. 3.), which is clearly not compatible with the suggestion that the pilgrimage lasted three-and-a-half years. Henry Beveridge, the translator of the *Akbarnama*, works out this discrepancy by pointing to the confusion of the dates in the chronicles and concludes that it must have been about 1580 or beginning of 1581 when she might have started her homeward journey. Then the voyage to Surat, the detention in Gujarat, and the journey to Ajmer, where they performed a supplementary pilgrimage, and then on to Fatehpur-Sikri, would take another year (Beveridge, *Akbarnama*, III, 570, fn. 1).

105. For details of women who went on the *hajj*, see Lal, *Domesticity and Power*, 209–10.

106. The presence and support of senior women was clearly vital at many critical moments, and since many senior *haraman* were going away on the pilgrimage, it may have been decided that one or two of the most important should stay behind to support Akbar if the need arose. The event of Hamideh Banu

Begum taking charge of Delhi indicates that such possibilities always had to be taken into account. One might also suggest that Hamideh Banu did not accompany the pilgrims perhaps because of her old age. It should be noted, however, that she was fifty-one years or so in 1578 (born in 1527), at the time of the *hajj* and lived on for another twenty-six years (she died in 1604). For a brief biographical sketch of Hamideh Banu, see Beveridge, *Humayun*, 237–41.

107. Ibid, 71.
108. Beveridge, *Akbarnama*, III, 206.
109. Beveridge, *Humayun*, 71; Beveridge, *Akbarnama*, III, 206, fn. 2.
110. Ibid, 206, fn. 3.
111. Richards, in *Mughal Empire*, 30–31, observes that the *hajj* gave evidence of Akbar's "Islamic piety by actively organising and sponsoring an official pilgrimage to Mecca each year." The point about the emperor's sponsorship that several contemporary chroniclers (e.g., Badauni and Nizam al-Din Ahmad) as well as recent scholars (e.g., Farooqi, *Mughal-Ottoman Relations*) emphasize is also made evident in the Beveridge, *Akbarnama*. But what emerges in the official chronicle is the exceptional detail on royal women's endeavours, the complete omission of which, by Richards and others, is troubling.
112. Monserrate, *Commentary*, 167.
113. Ibid, 166, fn. 255.
114. *Muntakhab*, I, 480.
115. Beveridge, *Humayun*, 72.
116. Beveridge, *Akbarnama*, III, 207.
117. Ibid, III, 107.
118. See, for example, Badauni, *Muntakhab*, II, 200, 203, 204, 215, 219, 262, 294.
119. In 1617, Jahangir sent his sister, probably Shahzadeh Khanum, to Mecca (Roe, *Negotiations*, 418). Then Tavernier reports sometime later in the century that the queen of Bijapur had visited Isfahan on her way back from Mecca. See Findly, *Nur Jahan*, 121.

Chapter Four

1. See, *inter alia*, Banton, *Racial Theories*, ix; Langmuir, "Prolegomena," 691.
2. Salo Baron took an intermediate position, agreeing that medieval people did not have a conscious concept of race in its modern form but seeing real similarities between the ideologies. See Baron, *Modern Nationalism and Religion*, 276, n. 26, and 15, reformulated in Baron, *A Social and Religious History*, 84 ff. Kisch rejected this approach as well in Kisch, *The Jews of Medieval Germany*, 314–16 and 531, n. 60. The debate is summarized in Yerushalmi, 29.
3. Yerushalmi, *Assimilation and Racial Anti-Semitism*, is foundational. The line of argument is pursued further by Friedman, "Jewish Conversion," 3–31.

4. Elukin's argument is based on instances of the treatment of converts ranging from the first to the fifteenth century. See Elukin, "From Jew to Christian?", 171. One of the best known cases was addressed by Grabois, "From 'Theological' to 'Racial' Anti-Semitism," 1–16. For an important survey of medieval Christian attitudes toward converts from Judaism in the eleventh and twelfth century Rhineland see Haverkamp, *Geschichte der Juden*, who does not, however, engage the question of "racial anti-Semitism."

5. On this tendency in Netanyahu, *Origins*, see Nirenberg, "El sentido de la historia judía," 3–5.

6. Oberman, *Wurzeln des Antisemitismus*, 63. The bibliography on the question of anti-Judaism (nonracial) versus anti-Semitism (racial) is vast. See, *inter alia*, Herde, "Von der mittelalterlichen Judenfeindschaft"; Hoffmann, "Christlicher Antijudaismus"; Frey, "Vom Antijudaismus zum Antisemitismus"; Heil, "»Antijudaismus« und »Antisemitismus«." Langmuir posed the problem differently in *History, Religion, and Antisemitism*, positing a (medieval) shift between rational anti-Judaism and irrational anti-Semitism.

7. Bartlett, *The Making of Europe*, 197 (emphasis added).

8. Walz, "Der vormoderne Antisemitismus," offers an excellent review of some of the definitions of race proposed in the debate, as well as some new suggestions.

9. A criticism I would make of Rainer Walz. This tendency is manifest even in his otherwise excellent article "Rasse." On the other hand, neither is it very helpful to describe as racial every ideology that assigns to lineage a role in the production of identity, as many proponents of premodern "racism" do. Thus for Jouanna, race is an idea "according to which the qualities that classify an individual within society are hereditarily transmittable through blood." See Jouanna, *L'idée de race en France*, I, 1.

10. Hence some scholars like Barbara Fields entirely reject the explanatory value of "race" for American history. See Fields, "Ideology and Race."

11. The possibility of identifying genetic markers whose relative frequency varies markedly between specific populations is well known. See, for one example of such variation, Papiha, "Genetic Variation and Disease Susceptibility," on genetic differences in susceptibility to specific diseases between Anglo-Saxon populations and populations of immigrants from the Asian subcontinent in Britain. Anxiety about this possibility exploded recently in European accusations that Israel was building a "race" bomb that could target Arab populations with biological agents.

12. Hence arguments like that of David Romano, who states that "els antropòlegs seriosos . . . estableixen clarament que no hi ha races" and goes on to insist on the complete racial equality of Christians and Jews in medieval Catalonia, seem to me of limited utility. See Romano, "Característiques dels jueus," 15.

13. The population of Jews in the Crown of Aragon dropped from a high of between twenty-seven thousand and fifty thousand just before the massacres of 1391 to approximately nine thousand at the time of the expulsion of 1492 (and thereafter, of course, to zero). These figures, which are far below those offered by many historians, are meant primarily to illustrate the scale of the decline. They are taken from Riera, "Judíos y conversos," 78, who, however, provides no evidence for them. Kamen, in his self-consciously revisionist "The Mediterranean and the Expulsion of Spanish Jews in 1492," provides very similar numbers, but also adduces no evidence.

14. Though in this chapter I focus on the Jewish case, the same phenomenon applies to the historiography of Muslims in the Iberian Peninsula. Examples of racial language in the description of Christian-Muslim relations abound in Perceval, *Todos son uno;* see in particular 63.

15. See Von Ranke, *Fürsten und Völker,* 246.

16. "Locura es pensar que *batallas por la existencia,* luchas encarnizadas y seculares de razas, terminen de otro modo que con expulsiones o exterminios. La raza inferior sucumbe siempre y acaba por triunfar el principio de nacionalidad más fuerte y vigoroso," Menéndez y Pelayo, *Historia de los heterodoxos Españoles,* 379; cf. I, 410 and II, 381. Despite the Darwinian overtones of this passage, and though he everywhere utilizes the vocabulary of race, Menéndez Pelayo nevertheless also claims to reject some of the racial theories of his day (cf. I, 249: "Sin asentir en manera alguna a la teoría fatalista de las razas . . . los árabes . . . han sido y son muy poco dados a la filosofía. . . ."). Compare Henry Charles Lea, who argued that the Inquisition was an instrument of racism, based on racial categories; Lea, *A History of the Inquisition of Spain,* 126.

17. Castro, *The Spaniards,* 20. If such a faith lasted longer in Spain than it did in the rest of western Europe, this is partly because Franco's triumph allowed Falangist historians to continue celebrating the achievements of the "raza hispanica" for many years. But it should be added that the "faith . . . in biology continuity" of Spanish fascists had its own distinctive flavor. Primo de Rivera, for example, could proclaim, "España no se justifica por tener una lengua, ni por ser una raza, ni por ser un acervo de costumbres, sino que España se justifica por una vocación imperial para unir lenguas, para unir razas, para unir pueblos y para unir costumbres en un destino universal." Cited in Calleja and Nevado, *La hispanidad como instrumento de combate,* 27 f. Can we imagine a similar statement from a German fascist?

18. Quoted in Castro, *The Spaniards,* v. An approach common to Castro, see his *España en su historia, La realidad historica de españa, De la edad conflictiva, "Español," palabra extranjera,* and *The Spaniards.*

19. Castro, *La realidad historica de españa,* 5 of the 1965 introduction: "Un viraje mu-

cho más amplio será necesario para incluir en la historiografía futura la presencia positiva y decisiva de las castas (¡no razas!) mora y judía. Porque es notable la resistencia a aceptar que el problema español era de *castas* y no de *razas*, hoy sólo aplicable a quienes se distinguen, como dice el Diccionario de la Academia, 'por el color de su piel y otros caracteres.'" Compare, writing at the same time, López Martinez, "Teologia española," who saw the fifteenth-century drive toward assimilation as "un fenómeno casi biológico" (466). "Si añadimos la notoria eficacia de la raza hebrea para hacerse con las claves económicas del país, comprenderemos . . . que, a veces, por motivos immediatos aparentemente fútiles, se haga guerra sin cuartel" (467). "Como se ve, pretendía una discriminación semejante a la que, todavía en nuestros tiempos, se basa exclusivamente en motivos de raza o del color de la piel" (468).

20. A sloppy but stimulating treatment of racial and biological vocabulary in Spanish scholarship on Muslims in the Iberian Peninsula is Perceval, *Todos son uno*, esp. 48–78.

21. One might further complain that late medieval and early modern Spaniards were perfectly capable of believing that Jews and *conversos* were actually distingushed by physical characteristics, such as large noses. Lope de Vega pokes fun at precisely this belief in *Amar sin saber a quién*, 10, "Largas hay con hidalguía / y muchas cortas sin ella." See Malkiel, "Lope de Vega y los judíos," 88.

22. Villanueva, "El problema de los conversos," 61: "Por lo pronto, el problema de los cristianos nuevos no era, en absoluto, de indole *racial*, sino social, y secundariamente, religioso. No se pierda de vista que el converso no llevaba consigo en todo momento un estigma biológico indeleble. . . ."; Adeline Rucquoi, "Noblesse des conversos?" For a representative critique of "Anglo-Saxon" historiography on these grounds, albeit on a slightly different issue, see García-Arenal and Leroy, *Moros y judíos*, 13 f.: "El interés por la cuestión ha sido promovido principalmente por estudiosos anglosajones preocupados por problemas actuales de minorías dentro de sus propios países, y en ocasiones planteamientos u ópticas válidas para sociedades posteriores a los imperialismos occidentales han sido aplicadas a la Edad Media española con resultados deformantes y anacrónicos. Sobre todo ha hecho que se barajen conceptos muy semejantes a los de la vieja bibliografía polémica de finales del siglo pasado, conceptos que en este estudio se intentarán evitar." In García-Arenal, *Inquisición y moriscos*, 116, she suggests that although today anti-Muslim attitudes are racial, four centuries ago they were religious. On the question of an Anglo-American vision of Spanish history, see Galán Sánchez, *Una visión de la "decadencia española"*. Nevertheless the word "raza" is still applied to the Jews by Spanish historians writing today, for example, Gonzálvez Ruiz, "El

Bachiller Palma," 48: "Palma . . . guarda una natural vinculación con los hombres de su raza convertidos al cristianismo."

23. R. del Arco Garay, for example, could speak of a "raza Aragonesa," and José Plá of a "raza hispanica" which encompassed all of Spain and Latin America. See Arco Garay, *Figuras Aragonesas,* and Plá, *La misión internacional,* just two among countless examples.

24. Díez de Games, *El Victorial,* 17: ". . . desde la muerte de Alexandre acá nunca traición se hizo que no fuese judío o su linaxe." For the dating of these lines, see xiii.

25. "Dezir de miçer Francisco a las syete virtudes," lines 393–400, in Dutton and Gonzalez Cuenca, 316. Writing around 1432, Juan Alfonso de Baena also linked good kingship to the elimination of "Raza": "quitastes/del reyno todas las raças. . . ." See his "Desir que fiso Juan Alfonso de Baena," lines 1183–84, in *Cancionero de Juan Alfonso de Baena,* 766. The word in its origins seems also to have designated sexual defects and was in this sense used to refer to procuresses and prostitutes. Cf. *Cancionero* no. 496 (339, line 17) and (perhaps the earliest usage) no. 100, by Alfonso Álvarez de Villasandino (127, line 10). Against my view of this early association between "raza" and Judaism see Lida, "Un decir más de Francisco Imperial" and Spitzer, "Ratio>race." See also Corominas, *Diccionario crítico etimológico,* III, 1019–21, sub "raza." By the 1470s the word was so common in poetry that Pero Guillén included it in his *Gaya ciencia,* a handbook of rhymes for poets (along with other useful words like "marrano"). See Guillén de Segovia, *La gaya ciencia,* sub "raça."

26. Martínez de Toledo, *Arcipreste de Talavera,* chap. 18, 108: "así lo verás de cada día en los logares do bivieres, que el bueno e de buena raça todavía retrae do viene, e el desaventurado de vil raça e linaje, por grande que sea e mucho que tenga, nunca retraerá sinón a la vileza donde desçiende. . . . Por ende, quando los tales o las tales tienen poderío no usan dél como deven, como dize el enxiemplo: 'Vídose el perro en bragas de cerro, e non conosçió a su compañero.'"

27. Such knowledge long predated the Middle Ages, as a glance at Aristotle's *Historia Animalium* (7.6 on the resemblance of children to their parents, and cf. Aristotle, *On the Generation of Animals,* I.17–18), or Xenophon's *On Hunting* (III, VII on breeding of dogs), makes clear.

28. Dies, *Libre de la menescalia,* llib. I (Libre de cavalls), cap. 1 (Com deu ésser engendrat cavall): "car no ha animal nengú <que> tant semble ne retraga al pare en les bondats hi en les bellees, ni en la talla, ni en lo pèl, e axí per lo contrari. Axí que cové qui vol haver bona raça o casta de cavalls que sobretot cerch lo guarà o stalló que sia bo e bell e de bon pèl, e la egua gran e ben formada e de bon pèl." There is a forthcoming edition by Lluís Cifuentes in the series *Els*

Nostres Clàssics. For the Castilian translation by Martín Martínez de Ampiés, see Dies, *Libro de albeytería.* There is a transcription of the 1499 ed. by A. Cortijo and A. Gómez Moreno in the Archivo digital de manuscritos y textos españoles, Madrid (1992), disc I, number 32; lib. I (Libro de los cavallos), cap. 1 (En qué manera deve el cavallo ser engendrado): "El cavallo deve ser engendrado de garañón que haya buen pelo, y sea bien sano y muy enxuto de manos, canillas, rodillas y piedes. Y deve mirar en ésto mucho, que en él no haya mal vicio alguno, porque entre todos los animales no se falla otro que al padre tanto sea semejante en las bondades, belleza ni talle, ni en el pelo, y por el contrario en todo lo malo. Por ende, es muy necessario a qualquier persona que haver codicia raça o casta buena y fermosa cercar garañón muy escogido en pelo, tamaño y en la bondad, y la yegua creçida y bien formada y de buen pelo."

29. Covarrubias Orozco, *Tesoro de la lengua,* sub "raza": "La casta de cavallos castizos, a los quales señalan con hierro para que sean conocidos. . . . Raza, en los linages se toma en mala parte, como tener aguna raza de moro o judío." Examples of such usage are legion. A particularly famous one is that of Pineda, *Diálogos familiares* II, xxi, sec. 14: "Ningún cuerdo quiere muger con raza de judía ni de marrana."

30. The topic of medieval knowledge about animal breeding is only now beginning to be studied. See, for example, Gladitz, *Horse Breeding.* The well-known contribution of knowledge about animal breeding to the development of biological discourses about evolution in the eighteenth and nineteenth centuries suggests that for our purposes the topic would repay further research.

31. Sadoletus, *Sadoleto on Education,* 2: "Maxime autem in hoc laudanda Francisci Regis nostri sapientia est, et consilium summo principe dignum, qui quod caeteri fere in equis et canibus, ipse praecipue in uiris facit, ut prouidentiam omnem adhibeat, quo ex spectatis utrinque generibus electi in hoc sanctum foedus matrimonii conueniant, ut ex bonis parentibus nascatur progenies, que postea et Regi , et patriae possit esse utilis." Citied in Walz, "Der vormoderne Antisemitismus," 727. Bellay, "Ample Discours au Roy," 205, cit. Juanna, III, 1323: "Car si des bons chevaux et des bons chiens de chasse/Nous sommes si soigneux de conserver la race,/Combien plus doit un Roy soigneusement pourvoir/A la race, qui est son principal pouvoir?" I cite nonpenninsular texts in order to stress that, *pace* the Black Legend, there is nothing specifically Iberian about these strategies of naturalization. They are pan-European, as much Protestant as Catholic. See, for example, Luther, *Works,* LIII, 481, where he argues that the Jews' poisonous hatred "durch blut und fleisch, durch Marck und bein gangen, gantz und gar natur und leben worden ist. Und so wenig sie fleisch und blut, mark und bein können endern, so wenig können sie solchen stoltz und neid endern, Sie müssen so bleiben und verben."

32. Cf. Contini, "*Tombeau* de Leo Spitzer." Contini argued that Spitzer's derivation of Romance "raza" from Latin "ratio" was incorrect and drew the etymology from "haraz/haras," the breeding of horses, the stallion's deposit. The earliest use I know of in Castilian, however, has the term referring to a hoof disease in horses. See Borgognoni, *Libro de los Caballos,*: // La.x. titulo dela enfermedat. que dizen raza. // Faze se alos cauallos una malautia quel dizen Raça. Et faze se de sequedat dela unna.

33. Colegio Notarial de Barcelona, *Privilegios y ordenanzas históricos,* ACA:C 3124: 157r-v: "separatio aut differentia nulla fiat inter christianos a progenie seu natura et neophytos . . . et ex eis descendentes." The use of the word "by nature" to distinguish old Christians is significant.

34. "Et quoniam per gratiam baptismi cives sanctorum & domestici Dei efficiuntur, longeque dignius sit regenerari spiritu, quam nasci carne, hac edictali lege statuimus, ut civitatum & locorum, in quibus sacro baptismate regenerantur, privilegiis, libertatibus & immunitatibus gaudeant, quae ratione duntaxat nativitatis & originis alii consequuntur." Mansi, *Sacrorum conciliorum,* XXIX, 100.

35. Colegio Notarial de Barcelona, *Privilegios y ordenanzas históricos,* ACA:C 2592: 21r-22v, doc. 57; Sanahuja, *Lérida,* 103–110. See Riera, "Judíos y conversos," 86–87.

36. Beltrán de Heredia, "Las bulas de Nicolás V." Recall that the Council of Basel, loc. cit., had included an exhortation to the *conversos* that they marry old Christians: ". . . curent & studeant neophytos ipsos cum originariis Christianis matrimonio copulare."

37. Juan II, *Crónica,* 152; Netanyahu, *Origins,* 284–92.

38. Padilla, *Relación judeoconversa,* 60–67.

39. For a fuller exploration of the dialogic evolution of genealogical thinking among Jews, Christians, and converts in fifteenth-century Spain, see Nirenberg, "Mass Conversion."

40. On these changing notions of nobility see Rucquoi, "Noblesse des conversos?" and Rucquoi, "Etre noble en Espagne." On evolving chivalric ideology, see Rodríguez Velasco, *El debate.*

41. Valera, *Espejo de la verdadera nobleza,* 102–103: "si los convertidos . . . retienen la nobleza de su linaje después de christianos . . . en quál nasción tantos nobles fallarse pueden. . . . Dios . . . el qual este linaje escogió para sí por el más noble?" The converts' possession of the blood of Jesus and Mary remained a standard argument in defense of *converso* rights well into the sixteenth century. Apologizing for any embarrassment he might cause to the descendents of *conversos,* Llorente, the author of the first critical history of the Inquisition, used the same argument to insist that such descent was cause not for shame but for pride. See Llorente, *Historia crítica,* 24.

42. These accusations are taken from a fifteenth-century manuscript by an anony-
    mous author whose relationship to the Toledan rebels is unclear. See Juan II,
    "Privilegio," 26.

43. The statute is published by Baer, *Die Juden*, 315–17. On these texts see especially
    Ruano, "La 'Sentencia-Estatuto'"; "D. Pero Sarmiento"; and "El Memorial."

44. ASV, Reg. Vat. 470, fol. 201r-v (Simonsohn, *The Apostolic See*, 856). Krueger
    seems not to realize that Pedro is a *converso* in Krueger, "Conversion," 169 f.
    Pedro's logic here is not unlike that of the Catalan rabbi Salomon Ibn Adret,
    who, a century and a half earlier, had stipulated that the (Jewish) wife of a
    convert should "flee from him as from a serpent" in order to avoid giving birth
    to a *ben poris.*, a violent son, that is, a Christian who might oppress the Jews.
    Ibn Adret, *She'elot u-teshuvot*.

45. *Tratado del Alborayque*, BNM ms. 17567. The quote is from fol. 11r. Dwayne
    Carpenter is preparing a critical edition of the manuscript and printed ver-
    sions of this important text.

46. Once again these argumentative strategies seem to be quickly mirrored in
    Jewish sources. Shem Tov b. Joseph ibn Sem Tov, writing in the 1480s, made
    a similarly "metalurgical" argument: "If a person is of pure blood and has a
    noble lineage, he will give birth to a son like himself, and he who is ugly and
    stained (of blood?) will give birth to a son who is similar to him, for gold will
    give birth to gold and silver will give birth to silver and copper to copper, and
    if you find some rare instances that from lesser people sprang out greater ones,
    nevertheless in most cases what I have said is correct, and as you know, a sci-
    ence is not built on exceptions." Ibn Shem Tov, *Derashot*, 14a, col. b, cited in
    Gutwirth, "Lineage," 88.

47. A number of fourteenth-century polemics stressed the hybrid nature of the
    Jewish people. One influential tradition maintained that because Titus had
    put no Jewish women aboard the ships that carried the survivors of the siege
    of Jerusalem into the Diaspora, the males had taken Muslim or pagan women
    to wife, so that their descendents were not real Jews but only bastards, with
    no claim to the covenant. See Hernando i Delgado, "Un tractat anònim," 730;
    Millás Vallicrosa, "Un tratado anónimo," 28; and the Castilian polemic written
    around 1370 but preserved in a fifteenth-century manuscript: Biblioteca del
    Palacio, Ms. 1344, "Coloquio entre un Cristiano y un Judío," fols. 106r-v (in
    García Moreno, *Papers of the Medieval Hispanic Research Seminar*, 154–55).

48. *Fortalitium fidei, consideratio* ii, editio princeps Nurenberg (1494), fols. 79, col.
    d; see Meyuhas Ginio, *De bello iudaeorum*, 16–17. See also Netanyahu, *Origins*,
    83; Echevarria, *The Fortress of Faith*, 167.

49. The arrival of the *Tratado del Alborayque* in Guadalupe, for example, provoked a
    bitter schism that was later remembered by the friars as the defining moment

in relations between Old and New Christians in the monastery. Starr-Lebeau, "Guadalupe."

50. The scholarship on purity of blood statutes is too large to summarize here. Early and foundational contributions include Sicroff, *Les controverses des statuts;* Domínguez Ortiz, *La clase social;* Revah, "La controverse sur les statuts."

51. For the relator's text see Cartagena, *Defensorium,* 351–55. Note that though the relator condemns the anti-*converso* aspects of this genealogical approach, he nevertheless utilizes genealogical arguments as well, referring constantly to the converts as of the lineage of Christ. This seemingly contradictory strategy is common in pro-*converso* texts. On the relator see, *inter alia,* Round, "Politics, Style and Group Attitudes."

52. On Vives see De Vocht, "Rodrigo Manrique's Letter," 435. Non-Spaniards also developed this logic in order to present Spain as a hybrid, Jewish land. See, for example, Farinelli, *Marrano,* 53, 56, 66–67; Bataillon, *Erasmo y España,* I, 90, II, 74; Erasmus, *Opus epistolarum,* III, 6, 52; and above all Hillgarth, *The Mirror of Spain.*

53. The quotes are from Castro, *The Structure of Spanish History,* 542–43, 569. In a review of the Spanish version of the work (*España en su historia*) Malkiel mildly observed that Castro's approach resembled theories of cultural transmission discredited by association with National Socialism. In 1965 and 1980, to the contrary, Villanueva praised precisely these pages as "the most acute and fruitful of [Castro's] oeuvre." See Villanueva, "El problema de los conversos,"69. The piece originally appeared in a Castro Festschrift in 1965.

54. A convergence pointed out by Netanyahu in his *Toward the Inquisition,* chaps. 1 and 5. Sánchez-Albornoz, for example, cites approvingly Castro's arguments about the Jewish origins of the Inquisition, then invokes the vocabulary of race and of nineteenth-century racial theory in order to arrive at virtually identical conclusions about Jewish and *converso* attributes. See Sánchez-Albornoz, *España,* 16, 255.

55. Thus Villanueva, seeking to prove that the go-between is a "semitic" trope (ignoring such distinguished participants in the genre as Horace) writes of one author (Feliciano de Silva) that, although his ancestry is not certain, he "looks highly suspicious, given his marriage to a lady of known Jewish lineage and his life-long affinity with the *converso* literary milieu." See Villanueva, *"La Celestina* as Hispano-Semitic Anthropology," 452, n. 2. The association of particular intellectual positions or literary interests with "Judaizing," so prominent a feature of the Inquisition, has also become a prominent strategy of essentialization among a particular school of Spanish philologists in the United States. On this phenomenon, see Nirenberg, "Forum."

56. Castro expressed surprise at this in his introduction to *The Spaniards.*

57. Given Nietzsche's and Foucault's success in redefining the meaning of the term "genealogy," it is important to note that here and throughout I am using the term "genealogical" in its traditional, non-Foucauldian sense. Indeed the philogenetic historiographies this chapter describes are very much of the type they were reacting against. Following Nietzsche, Foucault (somewhat confusingly) used the term "genealogy" to describe his antithetical alternative to such historiographies, history as an "anti-genealogy" that does not "go back in time to restore an unbroken continuity that operates beyond the dispersion of forgotten things . . . [that] does not resemble the evolution of a species or map the destiny of a people." See Foucault, "Nietzsche, Genealogy, History," 154, 162; and Foucault, Il faut défendre, 10.

58. Frege, Die Grundlagen der Arithmetik, vii.

59. Foucault, Il faut défendre, 65.

60. I am aware that not only premodernists but also postmodernists and postcolonialists have castigated Foucault for his periodizations, some arguing for the persistence of "blood regimes" in the modern, for the existence of "sexual regimes" in the premodern, or against the notion of supercession itself.

61. Biddick, "The Cut of Genealogy," 453.

62. More dangerous, both because unlike Foucault she does not make the strategic nature of her argument explicit and because the logic of continuity inherent in "always already" is more prone to genealogical fantasies than the logic of disjuncture.

63. "Suum autem est metaphorae modum locutionis a proprietate sui quasi detorquere, detorquando quadammodo innovare, innovando quasi nuptiali amictu tegere, tegendo quasi praecio dignitatis vendere." Albert of Monte Casino, Alberici Casinensis, 45.

64. As Fredrikson implicitly suggests when he begins his Race: A Brief History, with a treatment of "limpieza de sangre."

65. Thus, for example, many of the Spanish scholars mentioned in these pages came to the conclusion that, whatever "raza" might be, it originated with the Jews. Already in the nineteenth century Marcelino Menéndez y Pelayo, considered the founding father of Spanish historiography, wrote that "the fanaticism of blood and race . . . we probably owe to the Jews"; see Menéndez y Pelayo, Epistolario, 408. See also Menéndez y Pelayo, Historia, i, 410; ii, 381. Within the context of Spanish history, the opinion has been embraced by writers as diverse as Américo Castro and his arch-enemy Claudio Sánchez Albornoz (see note 20 above). Conversely, an equally diverse group of Jewish scholars (which includes Yitzhak Baer, Cecil Roth, Haim Hillel Ben-Sason, Yosef Yerushalmi, Benzion Netanyahu, and Yosef Kaplan) has strenuously

argued the opposite thesis, that these ideas were invented by gentiles (in this case Iberian Christians) as a way of denying converts from Judaism full membership in the Christian spiritual and social communities they sought to enter. See Kaplan, "The Self-Definition," 128; Méchoulan, "The Importance of Hispanicity."

Chapter Five

I am grateful to Jodi Bilinkoff for her generous advice and assistance with this project.

1. For an account of these fluctuations, see the introduction to Hendricks and Parker, *Women*, and Hall, *Things of Darkness*.
2. See, for example, Davis, "Time Behind the Veil."
3. See, for example, Matar, *Turks, Moors and Englishmen*, 17; Vitkus, "Early Modern Orientalism"; Vitkus, "Introduction"; and Burton, "English Anxiety."
4. For more information on the museum, Casa Museo Arabe Yusuf al Burch, see http://www.camaracaceres.es/caceres/capital/museos/arabe/.
5. See Klor de Alva, "The Postcolonization."
6. The series by Georges Cirot on "Maurophilie littéraire" appeared in *Bulletin Hispanique* 40 (1938)–46 (1944).
7. Menéndez Pidal, *España y su historia*, vol. 2, 277: "La maurofilia, en fin, se hizo moda, maurofilia que está pidiendo un estudio especial por parte de los arabistas."
8. I am inspired here by the fine work on clothing and memory of Peter Stallybrass and Ann Rosalind Jones. Jones and Stallybrass, *Renaissance Clothing*.
9. For Moorish attire among Christians, see Bernís, "Modas moriscas," and Anderson, *Hispanic Costume*.
10. Bernís, "Modas moriscas."
11. Hieronimi Vicecomitis, cited in Bernís, "Modas moriscas," 201.
12. Sandoval, cited in Bernís, "Modas moriscas," 202.
13. Bernís, "Modas moriscas," 203.
14. Vital, *Premier Voyage*.
15. Bernís, "Modas moriscas," 203.
16. The term comes from Balibar, "The Nation Form."
17. For a related argument on the staging of Jews in medieval drama, see Clark and Sponsler, "Othered Bodies," and "Queer Play."
18. Ariosto, *Orlando Furioso*; see especially Canto 9.2.
19. Nader notes that the decoration of the palace, begun in 1485, included many Moorish elements: "In typical Castilian manner, the dukes did not distinguish among Muslim, ancient Roman, and modern European styles. Most surfaces

of the rooms were decorated in Muslim style: tile floors and wainscoting and inlaid wood ceilings, while Flemish tapestries covered the upper walls," Nader, *Power and Gender,* 9.

20. On the multiple cultural meanings of blackness, see Hall, *Things of Darkness.* As she notes in her introduction, "the culture recognized the possibilities of this language for the representation and categorization of perceived physical differences" (4), "I argue that descriptions of dark and light, rather than being mere indications of Elizabethan beauty standards or markers of moral categories, became in the early modern period the conduit through which the English began to formulate the notions of 'self' and 'other' so well known in Anglo-American racial discourses" (2).

21. For color-based racism in medieval and early modern Spain, see Sweet, "The Iberian Roots." While Sweet's reconstruction of the antecedents of modern racisms is important, I disagree with his assessment that "nearly all [Moors] were distinguishable from white Christians by their physical appearance" (150), and his account of *limpieza de sangre* as "based on skin color" (160) is highly misleading.

22. Cabrillana, *Documentos notariales.* The reference to "membrillo cocho" ("cooked quince") comes from document 304; the others are repeated throughout the collection.

23. See Pérez de Hita's depiction of the blonde Maleha in the second part of the *Guerras Civiles de Granada,* or Cervantes' fable of Spanish soldier-poets courting a blonde Moor in North Africa in "El amante liberal."

24. One of the most famous examples of this kind of satire is Cervantes' biting *entremés,* "El retablo de las maravillas," in which a trio of rogues convince an audience of small-town notables that they can only prove their *limpieza* by asserting that they can see the imaginary spectacle staged before them.

25. On passing and national identity, see Fuchs. *Passing for Spain.*

26. For the English construction of Spain as a racial other, see Griffin, "From Ethos to Ethnos," and Fuchs, "Spanish Lessons." Although Griffin chooses the term "ethnos," he is really concerned with "incipient racialist thought" (102) and the "ethno-essentializing spirit."

27. See Griffin, "From Ethos to Ethnos," 95–101.

28. Hall, *Things of Darkness,* suggests that the depiction of Spain as black might also inform material representations. In a chapter on court jewels, she describes the "black cameo" presented by Elizabeth to Francis Drake upon his triumphant return from raiding Spanish possessions. The cover shows a black male head superimposed on a white female one, leading Hall to speculate, "Anti-Spanish rhetoric in England often made note of Spain's ill-defined —

and therefore dubious—racial origins: these twin heads may be a sign of that mixture" (222).

29. Griffin, "From Ethos to Ethnos," 97.

30. Arnaud, "The Coppie of the Anti-Spaniard," 35.

31. Matar, *Turks, Moors and Englishmen,* 7–8.

32. Spenser's *A View of the Present State of Ireland,* which attempts to discredit any connection between Catholic Ireland and Spain, describes the latter as being "of all nations under heaven . . . the most mingled, most uncertayne and most bastardly" (59).

33. Daunce, "A Brief Discourse," 36.

34. Daunce, "A Brief Discourse," 31.

35. Casas, *The Spanish Colonie,* q2a, cited in Griffin, "From Ethos to Ethnos," 95.

36. See Fuchs, "Spanish Lessons," 55–58.

37. Boose, "The Getting of a Lawful Race," 39.

38. Greville, *The Prose Works,* 60. I am grateful to Benedict Robinson for this reference.

39. For the diplomatic relations between England and Morocco, see Matar, *Turks, Moors and Englishmen.*

Chapter Six

1. Many many thanks to the organizers of the "Black Legend" conference—Meg Greer, Maureen Quilligan, and Walter Mignolo—for inviting me to participate and for then being such good and persistent editors. This chapter is drawn from my book *Modern Inquisitions: Peru and the Colonial Origins of the Civilized World.* Some sections were also from my presidential address to the American Society of Ethnohistory (Silverblatt, "Colonial Conspiracies").

2. See Gibson, *The Black Legend.* Edward Said, certainly one of the most provocative, brilliant, and sensitive of postcolonial theorists, has also been hobbled by Black Legend reasoning. In a commentary comparing England and France with Spain, Said had this to say about Spanish colonialism, ". . . the major distinguishing characteristic of Western Empires (Roman, Spanish and Portuguese) was that the earlier empires were bent on loot, as Conrad puts it, on the transport of treasure from the colonies to Europe, with very little attention to development, organization, or system within the colonies themselves." See Said, *Culture and Imperialism,* 89.

3. Accusations that cut a little thin, given England's track record.

4. Kamen, *The Spanish Inquisition,* 305–6.

5. Kamen, *The Spanish Inquisition,* 306.

6. Helgerson, "Camoes, Hakluyt, and the Voyages of Two Nations," 51; and Lepore, *The Name of War,* 7–13.

7. Arendt, *The Origins of Totalitarianism*, ix.

8. "Contrary to the image—still widely current—of inquisitors as small-minded clerics . . . fanatically dedicated to the extirpation of heresy, in the sixteenth and seventeenth centuries, the inquisitors were an elite bureaucracy . . . in principal a bureaucracy not of the Church but of the State," Kamen, *The Spanish Inquisition*, 144.

9. Castañeda Delgado and Hernández Aparicio, *La inquisición de Lima*, vol. 1, pp. 12, 16, 50, 69, 114.

10. Through 1635, seven of nine Lima magistrates graduated to positions of higher authority; the other two ruined their chances because of "irregularities" on the job. See Castañeda Delgado and Hernández Aparicio, *La inquisición de Lima*, 3–9.

11. Kamen, *The Spanish Inquisition*, 193.

12. Kamen, *The Spanish Inquisition*, 193–213.

13. The Lima office of the Spanish Inquisition had jurisdiction over all of contemporary South America except present-day Colombia. Neither inquisitors nor their commissioners outside Lima had the kind of totalizing control that they are often projected as having (or that the tribunal wished it had). But I think it fair to say that the institution's presence was felt over a much broader region than might be expected given the limited personnel at the tribunal's disposal.

    There is an extensive literature on the Spanish Inquisition and a growing one on the Lima office. Some of the works I have consulted include Kamen, *The Spanish Inquisition;* Castañeda Delgado and Hernández Aparicio, *La inquisición de Lima;* Perez Villanueva and Escandell Bonet, *Historia de la Inquisicion;* Millar Carvacho, *Inquisición y sociedad;* Hampe Martínez, "Recent Works on the Inquisition"; Hampe Martínez, *Santo Oficio;* Mannarelli, *Hechiceras, beatas y expósitas;* Van Deusen, *Between the Sacred and the Worldly;* Palma, *Anales de la Inquisición;* Toribio Medina, *Historia del tribunal;* Perez Villanueva, *La Inquisicion Espanola;* Sanchez, *Mentalidad popular frente;* Lewin, *El Santo Oficio;* Caro Baroja, *Inquisición, brujería y criptojudaísmo.*

14. See Arendt, *The Origins of Totalitarianism*, ix, for her discussion of the west's "subterranean stream." She highlights two principles at its root, bureaucratic rule and race thinking. Also see Silverblatt, *Modern Inquisitions*, prologue.

15. Medina, *Historia del Tribunal*, vol. 2, 35.

16. Medina, *Historia del Tribunal*, vol. 2, 37

17. Henningsen, *The Witches' Advocate;* Levack, *The Witch-Hunt*, 201–6. Studies of colonial women accused of practicing witchcraft in the New World constitute a relatively small but growing field. See Manarelli, "Inquisicion y mujeres," for an important first examination of women tried for witchcraft in colonial Peru. See Karlsen's *The Devil in the Shape of a Women*, a pioneering analysis of the gen-

dered aspects of New England witchhunts of women of European descent. For important feminist analyses of witchcraft practices among Spaniards and mestizos in eighteenth-century Mexico, see Bejar, "Sex and Sin" and Bejar, "Sexual Witchcraft." For an analysis of indigenous women accused of practicing witchcraft in colonial Peru see Silverblatt, *Moon, Sun, and Witches*.

18. See, for example, Archivo Histórico Nacional (hereafter cited as AHN), Lib.1030, f.194v.

19. AHN, Lib.1030, f.201v.

20. AHN, Lib.1029, f.500v, 501.

21. AHN, Lib.1030, f.194v, 201v.

22. Moorish women were commonly held to be experts in occult matters, and Isabel de Espinosa, who left Seville to escape her husband, confessed that she learned how to tell the future from *moriscas* (women of Moorish descent). AHN, Lib.1028, f.233–34.

23. AHN, Inq, Lib.1028, f.502–5; one prayer also includes men who had been either hanged or decapitated. Their bones were considered very potent as well. Suardo mentions a mulato and *español* arrested with bones from hanged men that were to be used in witchcraft. Suardo, *Diario de Lima de Juan Antonio Suardo*, vol. 1, 231.

24. It was said that Ana de Castaneda, an accused witch, and the *tapadas* who accompanied her, had turned "the whole city of Potosi upside down . . . with her sorcery, tricks, and lies, and that even the convents of friars and nuns were not safe. . . ." AHN, Inq, Lib.1028, f.512, 514; also see AHN, Inq, Lib.1028, f.507–11.

25. AHN, Inq, Lib.1028, f.326. Feeling undone by the testimony against her, Francisca Gomez ended up turning herself in.

26. Although men were infrequently charged with witchcraft (they tended to be accused of blasphemy or of speaking heretical propositions), by 1622 two had been condemned for using sorcery to uncover another magical attraction of Indian life: *guacas*, the native burials, rumored to conceal vast quantities of treasure. Both men enjoyed substantial reputations as clairvoyants who could find lost property—from pilfered silver trays to stolen merchandise to escaped slaves, to the colony's "lost" property of underground Indian riches, AHN, Lib.1030, f.225. Senor Navarrete's fame extended to Lima's Indian artisans. Navarette was actually brought in front of the Inquisition because a native tailor charged him with taking a silver picture frame in payment for services (to find who had stolen bolts of cloth from his shop) that were never rendered. AHN, Inq, Lib.1030, f.225–225v.

27. Bartra, *Tercer Concilio Limense*.

28. AHN, Lib.1029, f.503v.

29. AHN, Inq, Lib.1030, f.194v, 201v.
30. AHN, Inq, Lib.1030, f.360.
31. AHN, Inq, Lib.1030, f.360v. Note that blacks and at times mulatas are often only listed by their first names in the record—an indication of their racial standing.
32. AHN, Inq, Lib.1030, f.360.
33. AHN, Inq, Lib.1030, f.360.
34. AHN, Inq, Lib.1030, f.361.
35. AHN, Inq, Lib.1030, f.361.
36. AHN, Inq, Lib.1030, f.360.
37. Although Catalina de Baena was penanced for engaging in withcraft, the court did not believe that the bones she brought had contributed to Isabel de Mendia's illness.AHN, Inq, Lib.1030, f.361–361v.
38. AHN, Lib.1030, f.381v. Another kind of clairvoyant made her way into colonial records, the *zahori*. At this period, as slave labor was becoming increasingly important to the Peruvian workforce, so were the divining gifts of women, and some men. The *zahori* often were forcibly taken to Peru from Africa.
39. AHN, Lib.1031, f.382.
40. See Fanon, *The Wretched*, and Taussig, *Shamanism*. A confusion of race and name got Catalina in trouble, when the wife of the royal lieutenant, Alferez— also named Francisca and also said to "have some mulata in her"—thought Catalina de Baena had been accusing her in the bone-excavation scandal. "Some mulata in her" must have been an important marker in the Andean mining region, one that not only bedeviled Catalina (who was threatened as a result) but bedeviled the wife of a very important local official. AHN, Inq, Lib.1030, f.360–361v.
41. AHN, Inq, Lib.1031, f.376, f.446v.
42. The trial records for accused witches during this time period are not to be found in the record group I am working with. Although witches were penanced, without the trial records I do not know of their beliefs until trial records appear again in 1646.
43. AHN, Inq, Lib.1031, f.332v.
44. AHN, Lib.1031, f.374v–375.
45. AHN, Lib.1031, f.399v. Also see AHN, Lib.1031, f.385v–86.
46. The racial confusions in her aliases were reflected in her murky geneology. At the first hearing, dona Luisa de Vargas claimed parents both "Old Christian and noble," but when arrested again ten years later, she was classed as a *quarterona de mulata*. AHN, Inq, Lib.1031, f.449v; AHN, Inq, Lib.1031, f.349v; AHN, Inq, Lib.1031, f.382.

47. AHN, Inq, Lib.1031, f.382v.

48. AHN, Inq, Lib.1031, f.386.

49. AHN, Inq, Lib.1031, f.383.

50. AHN, Inq, Lib.1031, f.382–87.

51. AHN, Inq, Lib.1031, f.382v–383.

52. AHN, Inq, Lib.1031, f.349v–350, f.385.

53. AHN, Inq, Lib.1031, f.384–384v; I do not know what literacy rates were for women, but I was surprised at the number of witches who seemed to know how to read and write.

54. AHN, Inq, Lib.1031, f.363v. This conjure was underlined in the text. Inga was also a common spelling for Inca.

55. AHN, Lib.1031, f.383. Accused witches, with similar stories—meeting in groups, praying to the Inca and using coca—are found through the rest of the seventeenth century. Some of the more insteresting cases include Antonia Abraca, AHN, Lib.1031, f.378; dona Anna Balleja, AHN, Lib.1031, f.388; Antonia de Urbina, AHN, Lib.1031, f.392; dona Petronilla de Guebara, AHN, Lib.1031, f.498; dona Ana de Sarate, AHN, Lib.1031, f.497; dona Josepha de Lievana, AHN, Lib.1031, f.498v; dona Magdalena Camacha, AHN, Lib.1031, f.499v; dona Catalina Pizarro, AHN, Lib.1031, f.501; Francisca Arias Rodriguez, Ibid., Lib.1032, f.178v; Francisca de Urriola, Ibid, Lib.1032, f. 188; Lorenza de Balderrama, Ibid, f.424; Maria Jurado, Ibid, f.181; Sabina Junto, Ibid, f.182; dona Maria Magdelena de Aliaga, Ibid, f.198.

56. AHN, Inq, Lib.1031, f.497, 498v.

57. AHN, Lib.1031, f.529v.

58. Silverblatt, *Moon, Sun, and Witches*, 169–81.

59. Regarding the concerns expressed by the Supreme Council in Madrid, see Medina, *Historia del Tribunal*, vol. 2, 163, n. 20. Kamen argued that in comparison to other European inquisitions, the Spanish Inquisition infrequently demanded capital punishment for heretical acts. See Kamen, *The Spanish Inquisition*, 198–203. However, Kamen also emphasized that crimes entailing the secret worship of non-Catholic religions were, by far, the most commonly punished by execution (ibid., 203–4). Scholars of the European witch-craze have also noted the relative restraint of the Spanish Inquisition: Henningsen, *The Witches' Advocate*; Levack, *The Witch-Hunt*, 201–6.

60. See AHN, Inq, Legajo 1647, no. 13.

61. I will be discussing Spanish anti-Semitism in greater detail in the pages that follow. Spanish anti-Semitic ideologies, however, were frequently engaged and shared by belief systems found throughout Europe. There is an enormous literature on European anti-Semitism during the medieval and early modern periods. For an excellent summary of the research on this subject in the early

modern Europe period, see Jaher, *A Scapegoat*, 1–81. Also see Oberman, *The Roots of Anti-Semitism;* Cohen, *Essential Papers;* Cohen, *The Friars;* and Katz, *Tradition and Crisis.* This edition of *Tradition and Crisis* includes a current bibliography compiled by Bernard Dov Cooperman.

62. During the last twenty years students of the processes of nation-state building, influenced by Antonio Gramsci, have been exploring the dynamics of class relations, state formation and cultural practices. Although these studies have, for the most part, investigated the roads to nation-state building and capitalist development, I believe Gramscian insights are germane to the early colonial state as it drove the making of our modern world. The literature on the cultural politics at the core of state-making has grown enormously, and I will cite here only a few of those works that have influenced my analysis: Corrigan and Sayer, *The Great Arch;* Thompson, "Eighteenth-Century English Society"; Williams, *Marxism and Literature;* Hall, "Old and New Identities,." Jean and John Comaroff have used Gramsci, along with Corrigan and Sayer, in their important discussions of the cultural dimensions of the English colonial state in South Africa. See Comaroff and Comaroff, *Ethnography;* Comaroff and Comaroff, *Of Revelation and Revolution.* See the following for a challenge to the assumption that the modernity began with the Enlightenment. These authors argue that the modern world has its origins in the colonization of the New World: Dussell, "Eurocentrism and Modernity"; Dussell, "Beyond Eurocentrism"; Quijano, "Colonialidad y Modernidad-Racionalidad."

63. AHN, Inq, Cartas, Rollo 9, f.7, letter from Don Leon de Alcayaga Lartaun to Muy Poderoso S., May 15, 1636.

64. Medina, *Historia del Tribunal,* vol. 2, 45–46.

65. See Kohut, "The Trial."

66. It has been estimated that after the Act of Expulsion, at least fifty thousand Jews—half of all those who left Spain—resettled in neighboring Portugal, swelling the percentage of Jews living there to one-fifth of the country's inhabitants. See Gitlitz, *Secrecy and Deceit,* 75. Estimates range from 50,000 to 120,000, with the lower end seeming most likely. See Kamen, *The Spanish Inquisition,* 287, for the number of Jews living in Portugal. In 1497 these emigrants again had to face the order to convert or be expelled. Most converted en masse, giving Portugal a coherent block of New Christians, many of whom retained their belief in Judaism and secretly practiced its rites. Scholars have stressed the significance of this early history of Portuguese Jews, converted as a block to Christianity, for New Christian communities. See Kamen, *The Spanish Inquisition,* 287–90; Yerushalmi, *From Spanish Court,* 1–51; Caro Baroja, *Los Judíos,* vol. 1, 207–26; Lockhart and Schwartz, *Early Latin America,* 225–26.

67. Elliott, *Imperial Spain*, 249–84, 337–49; Lockhart and Schwartz, *Early Latin America*, 221–27, 251; Gitlitz, *Secrecy and Deceit*, 43–46.

68. Beltrán y Rózpide, *Coleccion de las Memorias*, 13, 194–297; Suardo, *Diario de Lima de Juan Antonio Suardo*, 259–61.

69. The Spanish victory over the Dutch in Bahia was commemorated by Lope de Vega in his play *El Brazil Restituido*.

70. Though it is difficult to determine allegiances with great accuracy, evidence suggests that Brazil's New Christian population held divided loyalties: while some, principally crypto-Jews, might have sided with Holland, many, perhaps even the majority, fought to keep Brazil under Iberian control. See the excellent study by Novinsky, *Cristaos Novos na Bahia*. In a 1997 conference hosted by the John Carter Brown Library, "Jews and the Expansion of Europe: 1450–1800," Novinsky reiterated her belief that a significant proportion of New Christians remained loyal to Spain.

In a similar vein, a commonplace of the time (as well as today) held that Portuguese Jews had controlling interests in the Dutch West Indies Company. After a careful examination of company records, Jonathan Israel concluded that Jews never dominated the Dutch West Indies Company, even though some invested in it. See Israel, *Empires and Entrepôts*, 356, n. 2.

71. Kamen, *The Spanish Inquisition*, 42–43, 64–65, 290, 293–94, 297–98.

72. Gitlitz, *Secrecy and Deceit*, 61–62.

73. See AHN, Inq, Cartas, Rollo 9, f.51, letter from inquisitors Juan de Manozca, Andres Gaytan, Antonio de Castro y del Castillo to Muy P. Senor, May 18, 1636; also see Lockhart and Schwartz, *Early Latin America*, 250.

74. AHN, Inq, Lib.1031, Carta a Madrid.

75. Beltrán y Rózpide, *Coleccion de las Memorias*, 179.

76. Beltrán y Rózpide, *Coleccion de las Memorias*, 43.

77. Lewin, *El Santo Oficio*, 40.

78. Solorzano Pereira, *Politica Indiana*, Lib. I, tomo ii, 262.

79. Solorzano Pereira, *Politica Indiana*, Lib. I, tomo ii, 262.

80. AHN, Inq, Legajo 1647, no. 013, f.53v.

81. AHN, Inq, Legajo 1647, no.13, f.266.

82. AHN, Inq, Legajo 1647, no.13, f.53–53v. The parenthetical definition is part of the original testimony.

83. Arriaga, *The Extirpation*, 6.

84. Helgerson, "Camoes," 54.

85. Helgerson, "Camoes," 54.

86. Helgerson, "Camoes," 54.

87. The consequences of the Black Legend were felt way beyond the years England and Spain first locked horns. Contemporary Anglophone social theory,

for example, has consistently denied Spain a role in the creation of the modern world. They would argue that even if Spain had successfully conquered native peoples in the Americas, it was not capable of governing them in any way approximating a politically legitimate fashion. Spain dominated its colonies by brute force alone, rather than via any form of recognizable government. No less a scholar and activist than Edward Said considered Spanish rule in this way. See Said, *Culture and Imperialism*. For more on the Black Legend, see Gibson, *The Black Legend*.

Chapter Seven

1. For an understanding of modernity as a Euro-American process that began in the 1500s and is inextricable from Western colonialism, see Dussel (1998), Mignolo (2000a, 2000b), Escobar (2004). I focus here on some of the cultural dimensions of modernity and emphasize continuities but want to suggest neither that all imperial projects were equal nor that these dimensions are all that modernity is about.

2. "Yo soy sacerdote de Dios, y enseño a los christianos las cosas de Dios, y asimesmo vengo a enseñar a vosotros. Lo que yo enseño es lo que Dios nos habló, que está en este libro. Y por tanto, de parte de Dios y de los christianos te ruego que seas su amigo, porque así lo quiere Dios; y venirte ha bien dello; y ve a hablar con el Gobernador, que te está esperando." All translations are mine.

3. "Atabalipa dijo que le diese el libro para verle y él se lo dio cerrado; y no acertando Atabalipa a abrirle, el religioso estendió el brazo para lo abrir, y Atabaliba con gran desdén le dio un golpe en el brazo, no queriendo que lo abriese; y porfiando él mesmo a abrirlo, lo abrió; y no maravillándose de las letras ni del papel como otros indios, lo arrojó cinco o seis pasos de sí."

4. Nuremberg text: "Newe Zeitung Aus Hianien Und Italien." Venice text: "Copia delle lettere del Prefetto delle India." Lyon text: "Nouvelles certaines des isles du Perú." (Porras Barrenechea 1937, 28–44).

5. "e hablando el frayle las cosas de dios diole un libro de breviario que llevava havierto deziendo que lo mirasse y besasse que en aquel se contenia las cosas de dios y de nuestra fe y quel dicho cacique lo tomo e muy enojadamente lo echo e arrojo en el suelo començando a mostrar mucho enojo porque le havian entrado en su tierra."

6. "los christianos eran sus amigos y que el señor gouernador le queria mucho y que entrasse en su posada a verle. El cacique respondio que el no passaria mas adelante hasta que le bolbiessen los christianos todo lo que le hauian tomado en toda la tierra y que despues el haria todo lo que le viniesse en voluntad. Dexando el fraile aquellas platicas, con vn libro que traya en las manos le

empeco a dezir las cosas de Dios que le conuenian, pero el no las quiso tomar; pidiendo el libro el padre se lo dio pensando que lo queria besar; y el lo tomo y lo echo encima de su gente" (Sinclair 1929, 9).

7. *Diccionario de la Real Academia Española:* "Dar con lo cierto en lo dudoso, ignorado, u oculto."

8. See a summary of Vitoria's arguments in Manzano Manzano (1948, 61–82).

9. Even if after sustained dialogue and good example Indians continued to reject conversion it would be no cause for just war; they would just be in "mortal sin." (Vitoria 1947, 90)

10. "Si lo condenáis así ásperamente, escandalízanse; y los unos allegan al Papa y dicen que sois cismático porque ponéis duda en lo que el Papa hace; y los otros allegan al Emperador, que condenáis a Su Magestat y que condenáis la conquista de las Indias."

11. More than once, though, his scholarly opinion was requested by the Crown (see Heredia 1928, 163–64).

12. Las Casas's writing resulted in fourteen thick volumes (and those of his commentators in many more); I analyze here only what relates directly to the matter in question and was written before 1555.

13. In short, the text stated that God had created the world, that the pope was his representative, and that as such he had conceded the Spanish king *dominio* over the new lands. Depending on the response of a native lord—whether or not he recognized the Christian king—the door to pacific submission or a just war was juridically opened (for an English translation see Hanke 1938). I return to the text in the next section.

14. The *encomiendas* were neither abolished nor given in perpetuity with full jurisdiction, although the latter came very close to happening and was prevented not through scholarly arguments but through a very generous offer in cash by the party of the Indians, which outbid the settlers, paralyzing any final decision.

15. Oviedo's *Historia* was published several times during the author's life, as he kept adding new material. However, the complete version, which included the conquest of Peru, was published only in 1855.

16. Gómara's is a general history of the deeds of the Spaniards in the New World, while Zárate's focuses on the conquest of Peru alone. As is known, the pages relating to Peru in both texts are very similar.

17. "Dios trino y uno hizo de nada el mundo y formó al hombre de la tierra, que llamó Adán, del cual traemos origen y carne todos. Pecó Adán contra su criador por inobediencia, y en él cuantos después han nacido y nacerán, excepto Jesucristo, que, siendo verdadero Dios, bajó del cielo a nacer de María virgen, por redimir el linaje humano del pecado. Murió en semejante cruz que ésta,

y por eso la doramos. Resucitó el tercero día, subió en cuarenta días al cielo, dejando por su vicario en la tierra a San Pedro y a sus sucesores, que llaman papas; los cuales habían dado al potentísimo rey de España la conquista y conversión de aquellas tierras; y así viene ahora Francisco Pizarro a rogaros seáis amigos y tributarios del rey de España, emperador de romanos, monarca del mundo, y obedezcáis al papa y recibáis la fe de Cristo, si la creyéredes, que es santísima, y la que vos tenés es falsísima. Y sabed que haciendo lo contrario os daremos guerra y quitaremos los ídolos, para que dejéis la engañosa religión de vuestros muchos y falsos dioses."

18. "no quería tributar siendo libre, ni oír que hubiese otro mayor señor que él; empero, que holgaría de ser amigo del emperador y conocerle, ca debía ser gran príncipe, pues enviaba tantos ejércitos como decían por el mundo, que no obedecería al papa, porque daba lo ajeno y por no dejar a quien nunca vio el reino que fue de su padre. Y en cuanto a la religión, dijo que muy buena era la suya, y que bien se hallaba con ella, y que no quería un menos debía poner en disputa cosa tan antigua y aprobada; que Cristo murió y el Sol y la Luna nunca morían."

19. The need for understanding was explicitly mentioned in the body of the *Requerimiento;* the lack of communication was also part of Las Casas's and Vitoria's critiques of the conquerors' acts.

20. For an erudite study of Hakluyt's sources, see Quinn and Quinn (1993).

21. Sir Francis Drake, another pioneer of the English empire, less politically sophisticated than Raleigh, called the pope simply "the Antichrist" (Hillgarth 2000, 379).

22. In the opinion of a Spanish nobleman in 1550s London, "these English are barbarous people and great heretics, with no soul or conscience or fear of God and His Saints" (Hillgarth 2000, 352).

23. That Hariot's outrage was an attempt to build difference becomes clear if one considers that Walter Raleigh—Hakluyt's and Hariot's master—in his account of his attempt to discover El Dorado (1928 [1595]), makes plain that the search for gold was his main goal, dignified, though, by preempting the Spaniards.

24. All data from searches in WorldCat; accessed 01/25/07.

25. Many of which Spanish scholars, in a late-imperial impulse, began publishing soon in massive collections of documents that attested the Crown's civilizing efforts—to mention only the most important, the 1864–1884, forty-two-volume *Colección de documentos inéditos relativos al descubrimiento, conquista y colonización de las posesiones españolas en América y Oceanía, sacados, en su mayor parte, del Real Archivo de Indias,* and its 1885–1932, twenty-five-volume sequel, the *Colección de documentos inéditos relativos al descubrimiento, conquista y organización de las antiguas posesiones españolas de Ultramar.*

26. For instance, Trueba y Cosio's 1830 *History of the Conquest of Peru* builds by and large on the accounts of Lope de Gómara, Zárate, Garcilaso, and Herrera.

27. None of which was in Cajamarca. Naharro does not date his account, but he mentions the chronicler Herrera, whose *Historia General* was published in 1610–1615.

28. It follows Naharro's edition of Gómara, making Valverde's words more pacific (there is no threat at the end); Prescott, in turn, added some sentences that made it more Catholic-like than either Spanish original.

29. The first part, concerning the emperor, is a free translation of Naharro, which is, in turn, a good rephrasing of Gómara. Gómara: "que no quería tributar siendo libre, ni oír que hubiese otro mayor señor que él; empero, que holgaría de ser amigo del emperador y conocerle, ca debía de ser gran príncipe, pues enviaba tantos ejércitos como decían por el mundo" (1991, 171). Naharro: "no quiero tributar a nadie, que soy libre y señor de mi tierra y vasallos, ni tampoco creo que hay otro mayor señor que yo en el mundo: si bien no disgustaré de ser amigo de ese emperador que decís, cuya potencia conozco de haberos enviado a una tierra tan distante de la vuestra, que no ha llegado jamás a mi noticia" (1917, 201).

30. Naharro: "Obedecer a ese que llamáis Papa, no me está bien, porque debe de ser loco, puesto que da lo que es mío y no suyo . . . cuanto a la religión, no quiero más que la que tengo" (1917, 201). Gómara: "que no obedecería al papa, porque daba lo ajeno y por no dejar a quien nunca vio el reino que fue de su padre. Y en cuanto a la religión, dijo que muy buena era la suya, y que bien se hallaba con ella, y que no quería ni menos debía poner en disputa cosa tan antigua y aprobada; y que Cristo murió y el Sol y la Luna nunca morían" (1991, 171).

31. Notice, for instance, how Atahualpa's failure to marvel when exposed to literacy, a legitimating strategy present in Xérez, Zárate, and Gómara, is almost imperceptible in Prescott's account.

32. "Y la lengua dijo que aquel padre era hijo del sol y que le enviaba el sol a él a le decir que no pelease y que le diese obediencia al capitán que también era hijo del sol, que allí estaba en aquel libro aquello, y que ansí lo decía aquella pintura por el libro; e como dijo pintura pidió el Ynga el libro y tomólo en sus manos abriólo y como él viese los renglones de la letra dijo: '¿Esto habla y esto dice que eres hijo del sol? Yo soy también hijo del sol.' Respondieron a esto sus indios y dijeron en alta voz todos juntos: 'ansí es Capa Ynga.' Y tornó a decir el Ynga en alta voz que también él venía de donde el sol estaba, y diciendo esto arrojó el libro por ahí."

33. Among other clues of Zárate's/Gómara's knowledge of Inca views of the conquest, the most salient appears in the descriptions of the Spanish swords.

Gómara: "they girded on some shining splints, like the ones their women used to knit" (Gómara 1991, chap. 113, 169). Betanzos: the Spaniards "gird on certain sashes . . . and from these sashes they bring hanging a certain piece of silver that resembles these sticks that women stick into their warps to tighten what they are knitting" (1987, book II, chap. 17, p. 253). I choose this clue because swords—unlike horses or fire guns—are secondary elements and because of the way in which they are made sense of.

34. For Guamán Poma de Ayala's uses of Zárate, see Adorno (2000, 15–35) and MacCormack (1991, 151).

35. As Beverley points out (1998, 306), a subaltern subject cannot talk (in this case literally write) in a way that effectively alters the relations of power that make him or her such. For the writing strategies of several Andean intellectuals regarding the events in Cajamarca, see Seed (1991) and MacCormack (1989).

36. I am neither an expert on the Middle East nor endorsing the idea that the war in Iraq is in all aspects equal to the Spanish conquest; I do suggest though, against representations of current times as a different period marked by the western achievement of (self-evident) civilization, that there are many continuities and that neoimperial dynamics owe much—consciously or unconsciously—to the plain old imperial ones.

Chapter Eight

1. See the introduction to this volume for a discussion of the British adoption of an internal critique Spanish colonialism by Las Casas.

2. In fact, this is a somewhat tame representation of the debate, which became virulent, with accusations of holocaust denial. See Lévi-Strauss (2001) and Schwartz's reply (2002).

3. The Nahuas are, simply, the group of people indigenous to central Mexico who speak Nahuatl. They are popularly termed the "Aztecs," although this denotes more specifically the Nahuas of the valley of Mexico who created the tribute-based empire that fell to Cortés.

4. For this chapter we draw on the work of several scholars of postconquest Nahua society and culture as well as our research into primary documents. The last twenty-five years have seen many important works on the Nahuas, and specifically Nahua views of and adaptation to, colonization. Of chief importance here are Lockhart (1991, 1992), Schroeder (1991), Haskett (1991), Burkhart (1989, 1991), Wood (2003).

5. Ricard (1966).

6. See especially *The Slippery Earth* (1989) and *Before Guadalupe* (2001).

7. Stephens (1996, 44).

8. Stephens (1996, 276).
9. Lockhart (1992, 436).
10. Lockhart (1992, 436).
11. Lockhart (1992, 436).
12. See especially León Portilla (1992) and Haskett (1991).
13. The Primordial Titles are town histories that appeared throughout the central Mexican altiplano in the late seventeenth century. These complex texts are still the subject of considerable debate as to their intended use, origins, and relative accuracy; however, their interest as Nahua representations of history is undeniable.
14. *Las congregaciones* were attempts by the Crown beginning in the late sixteenth century to concentrate indigenous populations in the wake of plagues to evangelize and organize labor more efficiently.
15. Haskett (1991, 3–8).
16. Lockhart (1992, 438).
17. Lockhart (1992, 440).
18. See Gruzinski (2001) for a detailed explanation of the *ixiptla* and its role in colonial misunderstandings.
19. Gruzinski (2001, 50).
20. Chimalpahin was a Nahua annalist and diarist who wrote in Nahuatl in the early 1600s.
21. Schroeder (1991, 120).
22. The *Historia General* is a twelve-volume encyclopedia of Nahua culture and surely the richest and most thorough source about precontact Nahua culture. Among other things, the text contains information about the calendar, moral rhetoric, rulership, cosmology, geography, history, and an account of Cortés' invasion. Versions were prepared in Nahuatl and Spanish.
23. Sahagún (1985, vol. I, book II, 105–6). Original wording: "En el dicho pueblo [Tepepulco] hize juntar todos los principales con el señor del pueblo, que se llamaba don Diego de Mendoza. . . . [L]es pedí que me dieran personas hábiles y experimentadas, con quien pudiese platicar y me supiesen dar razón de lo que les preguntase. Ellos me respondieron que se hablaría cerca de lo propuesto, y que otro día me responderían. . . . Otro día vinieron el señor con los principales, y hecho un solemne parlamento, como ellos entonces usaban hacer, señaláronme hasta diez o doce principales ancianos, y dijéronme que con aquellos podía comunicar y que ellos me darían razón de todo lo que les preguntase. . . . Todas las cosas que conferimos me las dieron por pinturas, que aquella era la escritura que ellos antiguamente usaban, y los gramáticos las declararon en su lengua, escribiendo la declaración al pie de la pintura."
24. Sahagún (1985, vol. I, book II, 106). Original wording: "[In Tlatelolco] me

señalaron hasta ocho o diez principales, escogidos entre todos, muy hábiles en su lengua y en las cosas de sus antiguallas, con los cuales, con cuatro o cinco collegiales . . . se enmendó, declaró, y añadió todo lo que de Tepepulco traje escrito."

25. Florescano (1994, 39).

26. Florescano (1994, 30).

27. Sahagún, *Florentine Codex*, as quoted by Florescano (1994, 28). Also in López Austin (1980, 65).

28. Burkhart (1991, 2).

29. Lockhart (1992, 440).

30. Lockhart (1992, 441).

31. Lockhart (1992, 441).

32. Tlatelolco was once an independent *altepetl*, which joined with the more powerful Tenochtitlan to form one city, the chief partner in the Aztec Triple Alliance. However, the Tlatelolcans maintained a strong sense of pride in their city.

33. Carrasco (1982, 48).

34. Sahagún (1985, vol. V, book XII, 35). Original wording: "Cuando oía Mochecuzoma la relación de los mensajeros, cómo los españoles preguntaban mucho de él, y que deseaban mucho de verle, angustiábase en gran manera, pensó de huir o esconderse."

35. Sahagún(1985, vol. V, book XII, 95). Original wording: "[E]staba preocupado; lleno de terror, de miedo."

36. Alfredo López Austin in Edmonson (1974, 140).

37. Calnek (1974, 190).

38. Sahagún (1985, vol. III, book IX, 17–18). Original wording: "Despúes que los mercaderes, peleando por espacio de cuatro años, conquistaron la provincia de Anáhuac . . . tomó la mano el más principal de ellos y dijo: ¡Oh mercaderes mexicanos! Ya nuestro señor Huitzilopochtli, dios de la guerra, ha hecho su oficio en favorecernos en que hayamos conquistado esta provincia. . . . Y como hubieron llegado a México . . . fuéronse derechos a la casa del señor Ahuitzotzin . . . Habiendo hecho esto, comenzó uno de ellos a hablar al señor diciendole: 'Señor nuestro . . . aquí en tu presencia hemos puesto el precio, porque tus tíos los pochtecas que estamos aquí pusimos nuestras cabezas y vidas a riesgo . . . que aunque nos llamamos mercaderes y lo parecemos, somos capitanes y soldados, que disimuladamente andamos a conquistar."

39. Alfredo López Austin in Edmonson (1974, 124).

40. Florescano (1994, 41).

41. Clendinnen (1991, 129–30).

42. For more information on the school and its students see SilverMoon (2007).

43. Sahagún (1985, vol. II, book X, 165). Original wording: "Luego que venimos a esta tierra a plantar la fe juntamos (a) los muchachos en nuestras casas, como está dicho, y les comenzamos (a enseñar) a leer y escribir y cantar, y como salieron bien con esto, procuramos luego de ponerlos en el estudio de la Gramática, para el cual ejercicio se hizo un Colegio en la ciudad de México en la parte de Santiago del Tlatilulco, en el cual de todos los pueblos comarcanos y de todas las provincias se escogieron los muchachos más hábiles, y que mejor sabían leer y escribir, los cuales dormían y comían en el mismo Colegio sin salir fuera sino pocas veces."

44. Mathes (1982, 26–27); Gruzinski (1993).

45. Kobayashi (1985, 250–71); Mathes (1982, 24–27).

46. From Ovid's *Ars Amatoria* (The Art of Love), in Osorio Romero (1979). Gruzinski (2002, 94–95).

47. Mignolo (1995).

48. Mathes (1982). For works on the college see Gonzalbo Aizpuru (2000) and Kobayashi (1985).

49. Paso y Troncoso (1939).

50. The next paragraphs quote liberally from the annals, so we will put page numbers parenthetically directly in the text. The source is Medina Lima (1995). Information complaining about the activity of pirates and the ensuing consequences can be found in pages 126–27. In 1629, we are told, they await ships that would bring "ropa, lencería y vinos y otras cosas necesarias de que carece esta tierra, porque hoy, 20 de diciembre, vale 12 y 13 reales una vara de mal ruan, y cuatro tomies la mano de papel y a este modo todas las cosas." The price of paper then goes up in 1630, "por el mes de febrero" when, we are told, "Mas los géneros siempre van subiendo, porque hoy día vale seis reales la mano de papel y todo lo demás" (131).

51. Gruzinski (2001).

Chapter Nine

1. The consideration of the role played by any other ethnic or social actor in this long-term period would certainly bring useful and necessary adjustments.

2. Particularly the chapters by Burns, "Unfixing Race," and Nierenberg, "Race and the Middle Ages."

3. At present, the discourse of "independence" is being questioned because it meant the imposition of a new type of domination, where Creoles were the mediators between a neocolonial power, usually French or English, and indigenous, *mestizo,* and black populations. See, among others, Flores Apaza et al., *El hombre que volvió a nacer.*

4. He develops this issue in Williams, *Marxism and Literature.*

5. Mikhail Bakhtin introduces this notion under his pen name, V. N. Vološinov, in *Marxism and the Philosophy of Language*. See as well Bakhtin, "El problema de los géneros discursivos," 248–94. Williams refers to Bakhtin's contributions in *Marxism and Literature*, 35–44.

6. This kind of sociocognitive move may certainly explain the aim of this book; in the same vein, I focus on the three main moments of reaccentuation that I observe during Spanish rule.

7. Bourdieu, "Social Space and the Genesis of 'Classes,'" 245.

8. In *Distinction*, 179, Bourdieu says, "What is at stake in the struggles about the meaning of the social world is power over the classificatory schemes and systems which are the bases of the representations of the groups and therefore of their mobilization and demobilization: the evocative power of an utterance which puts things in a different light (as happens, for example, when a single word, such as 'paternalism' changes the whole experience of a social relationship) or which modifies the schemes of perception, shows something else, other properties, previously unnoticed or relegated to the background. . . ." I would add that instead of "mobilizations," the rigidity of the colonial structure produces hidden resistances or open revolutions to either locally suspend or openly refuse the ruling mechanism of perception and the system that supports it.

9. The vast Creole elite jargon to call rightless people survived in the modern nations; for example, words like "indio," "mulato" and "negro" are all included in the pejorative sense of "chusma," used by the Argentinean writer Esteban de Echeverría, to refer to the workers of Buenos Aires's meat market in "El matadero." See Flemming, ed., *El matadero/La Cautiva*.

10. See Bourdieu, "La production," and Bourdieu, "Sur le pouvoir symbolique."

11. Unless their sensibility has been mediated by a critical elaboration of a familiar, witnessed, or directly lived trauma.

12. A rich analysis of this topic is Mamani Ramírez, "Simbología y poder indígena." See as well Albó, "From MNRistas to Kataristas to Katari."

13. With reservations regarding the idea of "weak" and "strong" systems, I find inspiring the theory of "poly-systems" elaborated by Itamar Even-Zohar, on the basis of the study of the Hebreo-Yiddish literary system. See Even-Zohar, "Interference in Dependent Literary Polysystems," and Even-Zohar, "Polysystem Theory."

14. Pagden analyzes the debate in *The Fall of Natural Man*. So also does Hanke, *All Mankind Is One*. Late in his life Las Casas suggested that the king of Spain should restore the New World to the original inhabitants, who should remain Catholics.

15. I have analyzed these conflicting ideologies in Orquera, "Guardianes de la

verdad." It is focused on the Aristotelian background of Gonzalo Fernández de Oviedo, which coincides at several points with Sepúlveda's views. My main argument is that Oviedo's polemic with Bartolomé de Las Casas, apparently related to a geographical matter (the possibility that Las Indias were the mythical region "Las Hespérides"), is in fact a veiled ideological struggle.

16. There is a transcription of this episode in Duverger, *La conversión*.

17. Mignolo comments on this issue in his introduction to *Local Histories/Global Designs*. I also think of his concept of "knowledge" when I use this word.

18. I take the concept of "interweaving" from Durán's *Historia de las Indias*. According to Durán, the low-ranked Aztecs tried, in vain, to convince their rulers not to pursue the war against the neighbor city, Azcapotzalco; they preferred to obtain forgiveness and permission to "interweave" with its inhabitants. From the low-ranked people's discourse can be gathered that this was a frequent option to end armed conflicts. This practice also explains the appropriation of the most Tolteca prestigious deity, Quetzalcóatl, by the rulers of Tenochtitlán, what Alfredo López Austin shows in *Hombre-Dios: religión y política en el mundo nahuatl*.

19. Dibble, *The Codex Xólotl*.

20. I use the edition by Berdan and Rieff Anawalt. Bernardino de Sahagún and his "informants" give a detailed account of the ethnic origins and trades of each group in *Historia General*. This work also give some interesting details on the social improvement of artisans of luxury objects in Tenochtitlán, which was at the peak of its power when the Spanish arrived.

21. From an original perspective, López Austin examines the Nahuas's conception of the human body to understand the functioning and points of friction of their society, whose future developments were cut short by the Spanish irruption. See López Austin, *Cuerpo Humano*. Acknowledgment of the inconsistencies of the Aztec society, whose regime was imposed upon by violence over most of the Anahuac's population at the end of the fifteenth century, would allow a glimpse at the internal problems undergone by the local communities before the Spanish conquest and the kind of alternatives that were interrupted by its rule.

22. Some of their works could be censored, but this did not affect their academic (and social) rank as stipulated by each discipline. Regarding the politics of censorship in the Indies, there is a classic article by Friede, "La censura española."

23. Bakhtin has developed this topic in *Problems of Dostoevsky's Poetics*.

24. See Sahagún's prologue to *Historia General*.

25. This phenomenon has been studied by, among others, Maravall, *La cultura del barroco*, and Rodríguez, *Teoría e Historia*.

26. I have analyzed this particular case in Orquera, *Los castillos decrépitos*. See the chronicle by Díaz del Castillo, *Historia verdadera*, edited by Miguel León Portilla.

27. For a description of this typical colonial genre see Acuña's introduction *to Relaciones Geográficas*. See also Gruzinsky, *La Colonisation*, chap. 2.

28. Further details on this topic can be found in Gruzinsky, *La Colonisation*, chap. 3, and Mignolo, *The Darker Side*, chap. 5.

29. Important contributions in this respect are the work by Himmerich y Valencia, *The Encomenderos*, and by Nutini, *The Wages of the Conquest*, 48 and 155.

30. The criterion established by Solís y Rivadeneira was prevalent until the XVIII century. See Solís y Rivadeneira, *Historia de la Conquista*, chap. 2.

31. See Sáenz de Santa María, *Historia de una historia*, 87–100.

32. My edition is translated by Pease (1993).

33. I follow here Adorno's study, *Cronista y Príncipe*, 70–74. On Inca economic organization, there is a classic work by Murra, *Waman Puma*.

34. Guamán Poma de Ayala's analysis is consistent with that of Bartolomé de Las Casas, which makes Adorno think that he may have been somehow in contact with the Dominican's ideas. See Adorno, *Guamán Poma*.

35. This concept is introduced in chap. 9 of Williams, *Marxism and Literature*.

36. In fact the manuscript was "discovered" in the Ancient Collection of the Royal Library of Copenhagen in 1908, and it was never known by Felipe III. The specific reasons why it was not printed and why it ended up in Copenhagen remain an enigma. See Adorno, *Cronista y Príncipe*, 47–61.

37. For Túpac Amaru's letters see Lienhard, *Cartas*, 254–74. Stern examines this issue in "The Age of Andean Resurrection."

38. Lienhard, *Cartas*, 128–42.

39. Lienhard, *Cartas*, 128–29.

40. About Mier's case, there is an article by Jara, "The Inscription of Creole Consciousness." This friar was prosecuted and punished after his sermon, although he managed to return to Mexico, fight against Spain, and be part of the first Creole government.

41. "En breve, con América (Latina) el capitalismo se hace mundial, eurocentrado y la colonialidad y la modernidad se instalan asociadas como los ejes constitutivos de su específico patrón de poder, que subsiste hasta hoy." Quijano, "Colonialidad." Quijano and Wallerstein affirm that the creation of the the Americas as a "geosocial entity" in the sixteenth century was the "constitutive act of the modern world-system" in "Americanity." Mignolo develops this point in *Local Histories/Global Designs*.

42. It is important to remind the reader here that I refer to the specific case of the Spanish colonization of the Americas, which would correspond to what Ashis

Nandy calls "first colonization" or "traditional oppression." Although Nandy's study is based on Indian "second colonization" or "modern oppression"—a case that does not apply to my concept of "exclusion"—I would like to mention two important points of contact with my perspective. The first one is the idea that Indians "become participants in a moral and cognitive venture against oppression," what I have tried to demonstrate in the struggle of the residual system to arise and be accepted as valid. The second is that the West "would make sense to the non-West in terms of the non-West's experience of suffering." In my view, this experience becomes a powerful capital that proves, as Nandy would say, that the colonized "have emerged less innocent" from that experience. See the preface to Nandy, *The Intimate Enemy.*

43. If the well-known dichotomy between "civilización y barbarie" postulated by the Argentinean essayist Domingo Faustino Sarmiento shows the persistence of this dualism in the new nations' intellectuality, Jose Marti's defense of other subjectivities opens up a sensibility that would gradually give birth to the formulation of decolonizing political projects in the twentieth century.

44. Some key texts on this issue are Ortiz, *Cuban Counterpoint,* Rama, *Transculturación narrativa,* Cornejo-Polar, "El indigenismo y las literaturas heterogéneas," Cornejo-Polar, "Literatura peruana," and Cornejo-Polar, *Escribir en el aire.* Also Lienhard offers a useful introduction in *La voz y su huella.* Velazco proposes the concept of "nepantlismo" in "Historiografía y etnicidad emergente." It is inspired by an indigenous quotation taken from Diego Durán's *Historia de las Indias de Nueva España,* like the one of "entretejido" that I have introduced before. Notice what I have pointed out in the description of the first period's dominant system: if Spanish intellectuals condemned indigenous knowledge and beliefs, they were permeable to their expressions. The cases that recreate oral speech offer a hardly explored venue to understand structures of feelings and thinking in the Americas right before the conquest. Mignolo's idea of "border thinking" seems to be close to mine of "theoretical elaboration" in the sense that they challenge the "cultures of scholarship." However, "border thinking" means a "rearticulation of the colonial difference" characteristic of the present, whose ideal would be "diversality as a universal project." I sustain that in modern colonial situations diversality was prevented because they are based on open oppression. To expand on Mignolo's point, see *Local Histories/Global Designs,* chap. 7.

45. Bakhtin postulates this theory in *Rabelais and His World.*

46. Of course in the colonial baroque period there were works that represented local characters, like the *villancicos* written by Sor Juana Inés de la Cruz. However, these were playful exercises that did not imply a significant change in the social and cultural perception of the other, a sensibility that would only

emerge among Creole intellectuals in the late nineteenth century, with writers like José Martí and the Peruvian indigenist Clorinda Matto de Turner.

47. This double discourse explains as well why the term "mestizo" could never acquire the positive value attributed to it by Garcilaso: being a highly educated writer, he was allowed to propose a linguistic interpretation, but being a son of an indigenous woman, his intervention could never affect the classificatory system. On this failed attempt to change the meaning (reaccentuate) of the word "mestizo," see Burns, "Unfixing Race," chap. 10 of this volume.

Chapter Ten

1. Covarrubias, *Tesoro de la lengua*, 896–97: "La casta de cavallos castizos, a los quales señalan con hierro para que sean conocidos. Raza en el paño, la hilaza que diferencia de los demás hilos de la trama. . . . Raza, en los linages se toma en mala parte, como tener alguna raza de moro o judio."

2. "Casta o calidad del origen o linage. Hablando de los hombres, se toma mui regularmente en mala parte. . . . Defin. de Cal[atrava]: 'Ordenamos y mandamos que ninguna persona, de qualquiera calidad y condición que fuere, sea recibida a la dicha Orden . . . sino fuere Hijodalgo . . . y de legitimo matrimonio nacido, y que no le toque *raza* de Judio, Moro, Herege, ni Villano. . . .'"

3. See Fields, "On Rogues and Geldings," on why it is not enough to proclaim "race" a social construction. The move to study "race" rather than "racism," Fields argues, constitutes "the great evasion of American historical literature, as of American history itself. . . . That substitution, as I have written elsewhere, 'transforms the act of a subject into an attribute of an object.' Disguised as race, racism becomes something African-Americans are, rather than something racists do." See also Fields, "Whiteness, Racism, and Identity." As Nelson Manrique points out in *Vinieron los Sarracenos*, 563, "La 'naturalización' de las desigualdades sociales, atribuyéndolas a la biología es, lo reiteramos una vez más, la esencia del discurso racista."

4. Compare Covarrubias's definition of *casta* ("caste"), *Tesoro de la lengua*, 316, which is more closely associated with purity: "Vale linage noble y castizo, el que es de buena línea y decendencia; no embargante que dezimos es de buena casta, y mala casta. . . . Castizos llamamos a los que son de buen linage y casta."

5. Contemporary U.S. usage, while very much in flux, still keys on skin color as a mark of race, and especially virulent racism targets those perceived to be of African descent. To be sure, Covarrubias and other far-flung speakers of the Castilians' language did mark skin color as a criterion of difference—but in sixteenth-century Castilian racism a person's color and his or her race were not the same thing (see Covarrubias's definition of *negro* in *Tesoro de la lengua*, 826); other criteria of difference were in play. A large and growing interdisci-

plinary literature examines the early modern coordinates of race thinking. See for example Floyd-Wilson, *English Ethnicity and Race*, on the humors, climate, and geography, or what Wilson calls "geohumoralism." Manrique's *Vinieron los Sarracenos* gives an excellent extended account of the mental horizons of the Europeans who invaded, named, and colonized America.

6. Of course "ours" is plural; different readers will draw on different repertoires of associations for race/*raza* and racism/*racismo*. In any case, drawing connections to the present, and the histories we embrace in it, seems all the more important since the events of September 11, 2001, have been used to stoke racist fear and loathing that reinscribes religious and cultural otherness as a crucial criterion of difference. See Said's eloquent preface to the twenty-fifth anniversary edition of *Orientalism*.

7. Race is among our keywords in the sense that Williams explains in *Keywords*, 13: such words locate "a problem of *vocabulary*, in two senses: the available and developing meanings of known words . . . and the explicit but as often implicit connections which people were making, in what seemed to me, again and again, particular formations of meaning—ways not only of discussing but of seeing many of our central experiences." Williams recognizes that "[o]f course the issues could not all be understood simply by analysis of the words. . . . But most of them, I found, could not really be thought through, and some of them, I believe, cannot even be focused unless we are conscious of the words as elements of the problems."

8. See Gose, "Priests, Petty Disputes and Purity of Blood," and Silverblatt, "New Christians and New World Fears." Both Gose and Silverblatt rely on records of the Lima Inquisition, which was charged with rooting out suspected practitioners of Judaism. However, ordinary trial records over matters totally unrelated to Judaism or the Inquisition also indicate "Jew" was used in the late sixteenth and early seventeenth centuries as an especially potent insult.

9. Sicroff, "Spanish Anti-Judaism."

10. They were especially suspicious of conversos (also known by the derogatory term *marranos*), about whom a large scholarly literature exists. See Sicroff, *Los estatutos de limpieza de sangre*, 51–56, on the 1449 Toledo "sublevación anticonversa" and its sequels, including the promulgation in 1449 of the first statute of blood purity (*limpieza de sangre*) in Spain. Further conflict in Toledo in 1467 occasioned "doble conflicto entre conversos y cristianos viejos, y conversos contra judíos" (88). See also Nirenberg's excellent "Enmity and Assimilation"; he argues that "the conversions of tens of thousands of Jews in the generation between 1391 and 1418 transformed the sacred and social worlds in which they occurred" (139).

11. It would be a mistake to see these historical processes as linear or uniform

across Spain; more careful work like Martz's recent study, *A Network of Converso Families*, is needed. Many conversos were accepted as Christians to the
point of being able to marry well among Old Christians. But as Martz points
out, the institution of blood purity statutes "raised the stakes" for conversos;
"acceptance of Christianity was an attainable goal, but demonstrating a lineage untouched by any Jewish ancestors was not" (401).

12. Anderson does not note the connection in his discussion of Spain in *Lineages*,
60–84, but it has been noted many times; see Elliott's *Imperial Spain* and Manrique's *Vinieron los Sarracenos*.

13. According to Fletcher in *Moorish Spain*, 167, it was not much of a choice:
"Since emigration was permitted only on payment of a fairly substantial sum
to the government and on other widely acceptable conditions—for example,
emigrants had to leave their children behind—it proved an unrealistic option
for most Muslims."

14. Columbus, *The Diario*, 17.

15. Columbus, *The Diario*, 93; see also 121. A mountaintop seen along the way reminds Columbus of "a pretty mosque" (123). Manrique, *Vinieron los Sarracenos*,
29–35, gives a more extended analysis of the invading Europeans' ready recourse to "categorías mentales . . . profundamente permeadas por el contacto
cultural con los musulmanes y, a un nivel menos evidente pero igualmente im-
portante, con los judíos" (34).

16. Cortés, *Hernán Cortés: Letters*, 30.

17. Silverblatt, "New Christians and New World Fears."

18. Konetzke, *Colección de documentos*, 1:12–13.

19. As Mörner points out in *La corona española*, 27–36, the Crown had come to fear
the influence of Spaniards' and other non-Indians' "bad example" on an indigenous population they considered weak and susceptible.

20. Overemphasis of the "dual republic system" can obscure this important
continuity.

21. Before the mid-seventeenth century, large numbers of African slaves were
brought to New Spain and Peru. See Bennett, *Africans in Colonial Mexico*, and
Bowser, *The African Slave*.

22. Many unrecognized children born to a Spanish father and Andean mother, for
example, "grew up with their mothers as Indians," while others received better
treatment from their fathers and grew up more or less as Spaniards. See Lockhart, *Spanish Peru*, 166–67.

23. Proof of *limpieza de sangre* came to mean in Spanish America that one not only
had no Jewish or Moorish ancestry but no blood connection to New Christians. For example, in the documentation Alonso Beltrán Lucero presented to
obtain a notarial post (Sevilla, Archivo General de Indias, Lima, 178, n. 12

[1573], expediente 2, f. 1v.), witnesses were asked to testify that Beltrán
Lucero (a Spaniard from Moguer) and his parents, grandparents, and great-
grandparents "an sido y son cristianos viejos, de linpia y honrrada generazion
y no son de los nuevamente convertidos a nuestra santa fe catolica judios moros ni [h]erexes hijos ni nietos de quemados ni reconciliados ni de persona que
p[ublica]mente ayan traydo sanbenito y por tales cristianos viejos y descendi-
ente dellos an sido y son abidos y tenidos y comunmente reputados. . . ."

24. Notarial records, for example, are nonexistent for Cuzco before 1560, and
    only a few notarial *protocolos* date to that decade.

25. "De estas dos naciones se han hecho allá [i.e. en Indias] otras, mezcladas de
    todas maneras." NB: In the 1966 English edition Harold Livermore translated
    this chapter's heading as "New names for various racial groups," and used the
    term "race" or "racial" where Garcilaso wrote of "generaciones" and "naciones."

26. Garcilaso de la Vega, *Comentarios Reales*, vol. 2, 627, trans. mine: "A los hijos de
    español y de española nacidos allá dicen *criollo* or *criolla*, por decir que son
    nacidos en Indias. Es nombre que lo inventaron los negros. . . . Quiere decir,
    entre ellos, "negro nacido en Indias." Inventáronlo para diferenciar los que
    van de acá [i.e. España], nacidos en Guinea, de los que nacen allá. Porque se
    tienen por más honrados y de más calidad por haber nacido en la patria, que
    no sus hijos porque nacieron en la ajena. Y los padres se ofenden si les llaman
    criollos. Los españoles, por la semejanza, han introducido este nombre en su
    lenguaje para nombrar los nacidos allá, de manera que al español y al guineo
    nacidos allá les llaman *criollos* y *criollas*."

27. Covarrubias, *Tesoro de la lengua*, 347, gives, among various meanings, "Condi-
    ción, estado; como si es rico o pobre, noble o plebeyo."

28. Garcilaso de la Vega, *Comentarios Reales*, vol. 2, 627, trans. mine: "Al hijo de ne-
    gro y de india—o de indio y de negra—dicen *mulato* y *mulata*. A los hijos de es-
    tos llaman *cholo*. Es vocablo de las islas de Barlovento. Quiere decir 'perro,' no
    de los castizos sino de los muy bellacos gozcones. Y los españoles usan de él
    por infamia y vituperio." The "islas de Barlovento" are the windward islands
    of the Caribbean. "Gozcones" may be "gozques," which Covarrubias defines in
    Tesoro de la lengua, 652, as a corrupted line of once-noble dogs: "se perdió y bas-
    tardeó, demanera que ya los gozques son unos perrillos que crían gente pobre
    y baxa."

29. Garcilaso de la Vega, *Comentarios Reales*, vol. 2, 627: "Nos llaman *mestizos*, por
    decir que somos mezclados de ambas naciones."

30. Garcilaso de la Vega, *Comentarios Reales*, vol. 2, 627–28: "Fue impuesto por los
    primeros españoles que tuvieron hijos en Indias. Y por ser nombre impuesto
    por nuestros padres y por su significación me lo llamo yo a boca llena y me
    honro con él. Aunque en Indias si a uno de ellos le dicen 'sois un mestizo' o 'es

un mestizo' lo toman por menosprecio. De donde nació que hayan abrazado con grandísimo gusto el nombre *montañés* que, entre otras afrentas y menosprecios que de ellos hizo, un poderoso les impuso en lugar del nombre *mestizo*. Y no consideran que aunque en España el nombre *montañés* sea apellido honroso, por los privilegios que se dieron a los naturales de las montañas de Asturias y Vizcaya, llamándoselo a otro cualquiera que no sea natural de aquellas provincias es nombre vituperioso."

31. Garcilaso de la Vega, *Comentarios Reales*, vol. 2, 628: "Y en la lengua general del Perú para decir 'montañés' dicen *sacharuna*, que en propia significación quiere decir 'salvaje.'"

32. Garcilaso de la Vega, *Comentarios Reales*, vol. 2, 628: "Y mis parientes, no entendiendo la malicia del imponedor, se precian de su afrenta, debiéndola de huir y abominar y llamarse como nuestros padres nos llamaban y no recibir nuevos nombres afrentosos, etc." However, Schwartz and Salomon indicate in "New Peoples and New Kinds of People," 483, that "[i]n Paraguay, eastern Upper Peru, and Ecuador, *montañés* — which suggests backlander or countryman, and which also may have been associated with an area of Spain that resisted Moorish rule — became the more polite term for people of mixed origin. It won some acceptance among the people it labeled." Lane, in *Quito 1599*, specifies that *montañés* was "usually reserved for Andean-Europeans born of a church-sanctioned marriage" (3) but suggests it was not (or not necessarily) a term of self-reference.

33. Garcilaso de la Vega, *Comentarios Reales*, vol. 2, 628. This is very different from the much-cited eighteenth-century repertoire of *pinturas de castas* or "caste paintings," in which *castizo/a* is the standard designation for the former and *coyote* for the latter.

34. Corregimiento, Causas ordinarias, Legajo 2 (1587–1602), expediente 46 (1595), cuaderno 25: "Pareció Juan Tupia regidor de la parroquia de Belén, y dió queja de Don Gerónimo Chanca Topa y contando el caso dijo que el dicho día como regidor le mandó que acudiese a la obra de la iglesia [al cual] se resistió y le maltrató juntamente con unos montañeses sobrinos suyos y le rompieron la camiseta y así lo manifestó ante el dicho juez y pidió a su merced le mande castigar." A later complaint involved an "india china." Local Andean-Castilian usages seem to come out here, as translated by Don Juan Callapiña and other "indios ladinos" who acted as Quechua-to-Spanish translators (though it is not possible to be sure the words are those of plaintiffs rather than those attributed to them by translators and scribes.)

35. His father, Sebastián, was legitimate, related to the noble house of the Duke of Feria, and among the earliest Spanish authorities in the Inca city. His mother, Chimpu Ocllo, was related to the Inca Huayna Capac. On Garcilaso's Petrar-

chism in colonial context see Greene, "'This Phrasis is Continuous,'" and Greene, *Unrequited Conquests;* on resonances of Quechua orality in Garcilaso's best-known text, see Mazzotti, *Coros Mestizos del Inca Garcilaso.*

36. Burns, "Gender and the Politics of Mestizaje." In Peru the term was forged in times of war, and as Lockhart notes in *Spanish Peru,* 167, "it is hard to separate Spaniards' feelings about racial mixture, as it affected the mestizos, from their position on legitimacy, for ninety-five per cent of the first generation of mestizos were illegitimate." Yet for Spaniards trying to make it in the opportunistic milieu of mid-sixteenth-century Cuzco, there was not necessarily a stigma/problem attached to marrying a mestiza, particularly the daughters of leading Spaniards. Not everyone was trying hard to avoid any taint from new converts.

37. Garcilaso de la Vega, *The Florida of the Inca:* "[Garcilaso] was again in Spain in 1568, for when the Moriscos of Alpujarra were forced into rebellion by the obstinacy of the King, Garcilaso took part in their subjugation" (xxix).

38. Stolcke, "Invaded Women," 279. Among those who believed Indians were Jews was the Dominican friar Diego Durán; see his *History of the Indies of New Spain.* For a refutation of such thinking see the work, originally published in 1590, of de Acosta, *Natural and Moral History of the Indies,* 69–71.

39. Burns, "Gender and the Politics of Mestizaje." Not much is known about the so-called Cuzco "mutiny" of 1567, which seems to have involved plotters of various kinds, although it was pinned on the mestizos. Documentation is found in the Archivo General de Indias, 1086; see Martínez, "Un motín de mestizos en el Perú (1567)." On an alleged mestizo mutiny in Potosí, see AGI, Patronato, ramo 5 (1586).

40. See Mörner, *La corona española y los foráneos,* 106.

41. Fletcher, *Moorish Spain,* 167–69; Hess, "The Moriscos."

42. According to Fletcher, *Moorish Spain,* 168, "a large number of persons, perhaps in the region of 100,000–150,000, were forcibly resettled elsewhere" in Spain. This ended rebellion in Alpujarras, "but only at the cost of spreading the Morisco problem throughout the kingdom of Castile." Expulsion of the moriscos followed in 1609–1614, and "it is reckoned that something like 300,000 people were expelled" from Spain.

43. Lisson, *La Iglesia de España en el Perú,* vol. 10, 824: "[H]abré ordenado solo cinco y para tratar la verdad que debo digo a vuestra Magestad que son los mejores clerigos que tengo en mi Ovispado dado caso que no saben mucho por no haber estudiado facultades mayores pero en lo que toca a hazer doctrina y vivir sin escandalo y saber la lengua general y vivir sin menos nota hacen lo que deben." I am very grateful to Alan Durston for bringing this document to my attention.

44. Lisson, *La Iglesia de España en el Perú,* vol. 10, 824: "dellos no se debe presumir lo que de confesos [i.e. conversos] y moriscos por que estos tales tienen ley o secta a lo que dicen rrebelada a que estan con mucha porfia obedientes los unos a la de Moysen (sic) y los otros a la de Mahoma y los naturales desta tierra ninguna tuvieron a que puedan estar tan afectados y vendidos como ellos a la suya y asi a mi poco entender y juicio no se debe tener tanto recelo destos mestizos como de los confesos y moriscos."

45. Martínez, "The Black Blood of New Spain," begins by analyzing the brutal deaths in 1612 of "thirty-five blacks and mulattoes" punished for "an alleged conspiracy by blacks in central Mexico to rebel against their masters" (479).

46. "Porque tengo el cavello crespo y algo moreno": in ARC, Corregimiento, Causas ordinarias, legajo 14 (1651–54), expediente 283 (1654), "Autos de información que presenta Juan Francisco de Morales, natural de Los Reyes, declarando no ser mulato ni negro, y ser hijo de españoles."

47. "Es hijo legítimo de . . . españoles y vecinos de la ciudad de Los Reyes, y como a tal su hijo legítimo les vio criarlo y alimentarle y reconocerle por tal llamandole de hijo y él a ellos de padres, por cuya causa sabe que . . . no es mulato sino español hijo de españoles."

48. The rarity of legitimacy in midcolonial Cuzco is striking in the available parish registers in the Archivo Arzobispal del Cuzco but has yet to be studied. On illegitimacy in midcolonial Lima, see Mannarelli, *Pecados públicos.*

49. See O'Toole, "Inventing Difference."

50. Hendricks and Parker, Introduction to *Women, "Race," and Writing,* 300, citing Jones and Stallybrass, "Dismantling Irena," 159–60.

51. *Pinturas de castas* provide a good example: these used to be treated almost as though they were snapshots. Lately scholars have focused on their intended audience and who prepared and circulated these artistic statements. Many canvases were made for a Spanish or Mexican creole elite; see Katzew, *Casta Painting;* Carrera, *Imagining Identity in New Spain;* Estenssoro, "Los colores de la plebe." As Cope points out in *The Limits of Racial Discrimination,* "[w]e should not assume that subordinate groups are passive recipients of elite ideology" (4). Elites seem to have been much more interested in drawing and circulating "racial" distinctions and categories than plebeians.

52. On the complicated definition of "Spaniard" from an indigenous perspective, see Szeminski, "Why Kill the Spaniard," and Thomson, "Was There Race in Colonial Latin America?" unpublished ms.

53. For excellent work in this direction see O'Toole, "Inventing Difference"; Lokken, "Marriage as Slave Emancipation." Also Graubart, "Hybrid Thinking," which begins with the figure of an "Indian servant, mestizo youth" in the

1613 Lima census, and discusses the archival figure of the "mestizo/a en hábitos de indio/a" and dress as a marker of identity.

Chapter Eleven

I wish to express my gratitude to the mentors and colleagues who have read and commented on earlier drafts. Of these, special thanks go to Aeron Hunt, David Karmon, Stephen Orgel, Courtney Quaintance, Sam Truett, and the readers of the University of Chicago Press.

1. Whiteway, *The Rise of Portuguese Power*, 297.
2. Hunter, *A History of British India*, vol. 1, 156.
3. Burton, *Goa and the Blue Mountains*, 88; see also Van den Berg, *Uit de dagen der Compagnie*. On the racial etiology of Portugal's imperial decline, see Subrahmanyam, "The 'Kaffirs of Europe,'" and Pearson, *The Portuguese in India*, 103.
4. Linschoten, *The Voyage*, vol. 2, 217. All quotations are drawn from this edition, which is based on the first English translation of 1598. The editors have enclosed in square brackets words or phrases that appear in the 1598 translation but have no equivalent in the Dutch original.
5. Tiele, "Introduction," xl; Koeman, *Jan Huygen van Linschoten*, esp. 41–46.
6. Masselman, *The Cradle of Colonialism*, 73; Kamps, "Colonizing the Colonizer," 160. Although Kamps's argument differs from mine, I am greatly indebted to his perceptive reading of several key passages of the *Itinerario*.
7. Sassetti, *Lettere dall'India*, 78; translation mine.
8. Couto, *O soldado prático*, 4, xxiii.
9. Winius, "The Portuguese Asian 'Decadência' Revisited," 112–13.
10. Tiele, "Introduction," xl.
11. Kamps, "Colonizing the Colonizer," 163.
12. Gorski, "The Protestant Ethic Revisited," 276–77.
13. Frank, "The Images of Jan Huygen van Linschoten," 48. As Frank points out, the very appointment of Linschoten's employer to the Archbishopric of Goa was part of a larger plan for colonial reform.
14. Parr, *Jan van Linschoten*, 188.
15. Hamer, *Signs of Cleopatra*, 20.
16. Parker, "Ex Oriente Luxuria," 40.
17. Maffei, *Le istorie delle Indie orientali*, vol. 1, 361; translation mine.
18. Pyrard de Laval, *The Voyage*, vol. 2 (1), 121.
19. I borrow the term "contact zone" from Pratt's *Imperial Eyes*, where it is intended as a "space in which peoples geographically and historically separated come into contact with each other and establish ongoing relations, usually involving conditions of coercion, radical inequality, and intractable conflict" (6).

20. Carletti, *Ragionamenti,* 181–82. All quotations are drawn from this edition; translations are based on Herbert Weinstock's English edition with modifications.

21. Yule and Cordier, *Cathay and the Way Thither,* 241; Yule and Burnell, *Hobson-Jobson,* 659.

22. Fernández de Figueroa, *A Spaniard in the Portuguese Indies,* 104.

23. Rivara, *Archivo Portuguez-Oriental,* vol. 3, 324–25.

24. Rivara, *Archivo Portuguez-Oriental,* vol. 4, 273. This edict probably remained unimplemented; the citizenry of Goa, in fact, found the idea that "palanquins should travel in such a fashion that it could be seen who was in them" utterly odious and begged the king "to make no new rule." See Rivara, *Archivo Portuguez-Oriental,* vol. 1 (2), 186.

25. Della Valle, *The Travels,* vol. 1, 31. Emphasis added.

26. I have deliberately adopted the obsolete "mean" as a way of rendering both the clandestine implications and the erotic connotation of the Italian "mezzano." My most obvious reference is Chaucer's *Troilus and Cryseide,* where the procurer Pandarus defines himself "a meane,/As maken women unto men to comen."

27. Županov, "Lust, Marriage and Free Will," 210; Wicki, *Documenta Indica,* vol. 13, 271–72.

28. Kamps, "Colonizing the Colonizer," 169.

29. Originally reserved for the offspring of European fathers and Eurasian mothers (*mestiças*), from the early seventeenth century onward the term *castiço* came to denote "Portuguese born in India without any infusion of Asian blood." See Boxer, *Race Relations,* 63, and Dalgado, *Glossário Luso-Asiático,* vol. 1, 229.

30. Boxer, *Race Relations,* 62.

31. Kamps, "Colonizing the Colonizer," 173.

32. Pufendorf, *De jure naturae et gentium libri octo,* VI, I, 10.

33. Fernández Navarrete, *The Travels and Controversies,* vol. 1, 162.

34. For an intriguing analysis of the *Itinerario*'s plates and their role in the construction of a hierarchy of Asian civility, see Boogaart, *Civil and Corrupt Asia,* esp. 9–17.

35. Galvão, *A Treatise on the Moluccas,* 89.

36. The earliest known account linking *sati* to female lechery and murderousness dates back to the Greek historian Diodorus Siculus (first century B.C.). See Majumdar, *Classical Accounts of India,* 240–41.

Chapter Twelve

1. Bucher, *Icon and Conquest;* Duchet, *L'Amérique de Théodore de Bry;* Duviols, *L'Amérique espagnole vue et rêvée;* Lestringant, *Le huguenot et le sauvage;* Lorant, *The New World.* For these critics, de Bry uses dramatization and hyperbole in order to convince his Protestant readers that Spanish cruelty is unique and that a Protestant colonization would be gentler and more spiritual.

2.   We only speak about the first six volumes of the collection entitled *America*, published in Frankfurt between 1590 and 1596 during Theodore de Bry's life. The collection possesses twelve volumes. The volumes published after de Bry's death are the work of his sons and grandson-in-law.

3.   The Protestants often use the stereotype of the noble savage in order to emphasize the barbarity of the Spanish domination. They also use the idea of God's malediction of the Indians. This so-called malediction allows them to show the uselessness and illegality of the Spanish conquest. See Gliozzi, *Adam et le Nouveau Monde*.

4.   Livet and Rapp, *Strasbourg au coeur religieux*, 297–307.

5.   Cited in Lorant, *The New World*, 30.

6.   Lorant, *The New World*, 30.

7.   Villenfagne, *Mélanges de littérature et d'histoire*, 150.

8.   Gossiaux, "L'iconographie,", 99–169. We must also notice that William S. Maltby never mentions de Bry as one of the creators of the Black Legend, even though four engravings by de Bry appear as illustration of his *The Development of Anti-Spanish Sentiment*.

9.   Lestringant, "L'automne des cannibales."

10. Vol. I, plate 3.

11. Vol. I, plate 4.

12. The gestures are not classical. There are no ancient sculptures with folded arms or one hand on the hip. The hand on the hip is a feature of the Renaissance that suggests "boldness or control, and therefore the self-defined masculine role, at once protective and controlling, in the contemporary society and in the microcosm of the family." Spicer, "The Renaissance Elbow."

13. Vol. II, plate 22.

14. Vol. II, plate 27.

15. Vol. III, plate 13.

16. Whereas, during the wars of religion, European cannibalism is a sign of social confusion, a sign that the community is being torn apart.

17. Vol. IV, plate 18.

18. Jacques Tortorel and Jean Perrissin engrave a series of forty images without narratives in order to show the Catholic cruelty against the Huguenots that occurs in France between 1559 and 1570. The series is entitled *Histoires diverses qui sont mémorables touchant les guerres, massacres et troubles advenus en France en ces dernières années*, published in 1570. Musée Carnavalet, Paris.

19. Vol. IV, plate 22.

20. There is a similar barbarity in the images that illustrate the 1598 de Bry's version of Las Casas's *Brevisima relacion de la destruccion de las Indias* (*Narratio regionum Indicarum per Hispanos quosdam devastatarum verissima*). However,

de Bry's sons explain to their readers in the preface that they "illustrated this work not so much in order to show the vices of the Spaniards but above all to show that these vices are also yours [the readers']."

21. There are seven images of Indian violence and revenge against the Spaniards and fifteen images of Spanish violence against the Indians.

22. Vol. IV, plate 16.

23. This is the archetypal gesture of violence that we see in the representations of the cannibals in Etienne Delaune's *Mêlée de guerriers nus*, in Vespucci's travels, in Thevet's *Singularités de la France Antarctique*, and in other engravings by de Bry.

24. On this idea that the pictures of violence borrow motifs from Christian symbolism, see Puppi, *Les supplices dans l'art*, and Edgerton, *Pictures and Punishment*.

25. By "absolute others" we mean that there is no possible comparison between the Protestant readers and either the Spaniards or the Indians. In de Bry's prefaces, however, we note a constant effort to draw comparisons among the readers, the Spaniards, and the Indians. De Bry encourages his readers to see the Indians and the Spaniards as the "others," different and yet identical. This idea of a possible comparison leads to the concept of the unity of human race, which appears at the beginning of the collection. The first engraving of the first volume is a representation of Adam and Eve when Eve is picking the apple. Moreover, at the end of the same volume, de Bry publishes five representations of Picts. De Bry explains that he publishes these images in order to show that the inhabitants of Great Britain were, in the past, as savage as the Virginians.

26. Genette, *Seuils*.

27. All the translations of the prefaces are mine.

28. Montaigne, *Essais*, I, 14.

29. If the Brazilians were incapable of being evangelized, colonization would make no sense, as, like the Spaniards, the Protestants use the pretext of evangelizing in order to justify colonization. Having said this, it is not clear whether or not de Bry agrees with any colonization.

30. On this idea that Las Casas's work is misinterpreted, see Bumas, "The Cannibal Butcher Shop."

Chapter Thirteen

1. A full account of Eden's alchemical labors is recounted in Gwyn, "Richard Eden."

2. Eden, in Arber, *The First Three English Books*, xliv. All references to Eden are from this edition.

3. Magical forgery seems to have run in the Eden family. Gwyn notes that one

Thomas Eden, perhaps Richard's uncle, was implicated in magical forgery. Gwyn, "Richard Eden," 18.

4. See Nummedal, "Practical Alchemy."

5. For more on the significations of the Spanish *real*, see Shell, *Art and Money*, 10.

6. Eden, in Arber, *The First Three English Books*, xliv.

7. This debate is found in Hadfield, "Peter Martyr," Hamlin, "On Reading Early Accounts" and Jowett, "'Monsters and Straunge Births.'"

8. Hadfield, "Peter Martyr," 2.

9. Hadfield, "Peter Martyr," 19.

10. Hadfield, "Peter Martyr," 17.

11. Hadfield, "Peter Martyr," 16.

12. For a concise summary of England's money problems, see Gwyn, "Richard Eden," 21.

13. Parker, *Books to Build an Empire*, 37.

14. *A Treatise of the new India* is a translation of the fifth book of Münster's *Cosmographiae Universalis*, which tells of Iberian voyages to the East Indies and includes summaries of Columbus's and Vespucci's journeys.

15. Eden, *A treatyse of the newe India*, in Arber, *The First Three English Books*, 9.

16. Gwyn, "Richard Eden," 29.

17. Quoted in Arber, *The First Three English Books*, xxxix.

18. Eden, *The Decades*, in Arber, *The First Three English Books*, 54.

19. Eden, *A treatyse of the newe India*, in Arber, *The First Three English Books*, 6.

20. Apparently Eden had translated twenty-two chapters of the *Pyrotechnia* but lost them when he lent out the manuscript. When it came time to translate *The Decades* he only retranslated the first three chapters.

21. Parker, *Books to Build an Empire*, 48.

22. Eden, *The Decades*, in Arber, *The First Three English Books*, 355.

23. Eden, *The Decades*, in Arber, *The First Three English Books*, 355.

24. Eden, *The Decades*, in Arber, *The First Three English Books*, 355.

25. Eden, *The Decades*, in Arber, *The First Three English Books*, 355.

26. Eden, *The Decades*, in Arber, *The First Three English Books*, 355.

27. Eden, *A treatyse of the newe India*, in Arber, *The First Three English Books*, 6.

28. Eden, *The Decades*, in Arber, *The First Three English Books*, 54,

29. Eden, *The Decades*, in Arber, *The First Three English Books*, 54,

30. Camden, *Britannia*, 65.

31. Camden, *Britannia*, 87.

32. Romm, "New World," 97–98. See also Gilbert, *The Voyaging*, 137.

33. Eden, in Arber, *The First Three English Books*, xli.

34. For example, "And being nowe comme to this harde stone after they had susteyned so great charges byside the travayle of both of mynde and body, if

they shulde then have left theyre enterprise, they shulde not have come to such ryches whereby they have obteyned many commodoties aswell profitable for themselves as also for theyr lordes and princes, theyre countrey, theyr kinsfolkes and famelie" (Eden, *The Decades,* in Arber, *The First Three English Books,* 360).

35. Eden, *The Decades,* in Arber, *The First Three English Books,* 361.
36. For an excellent analysis of the structure of Ralegh's narrative, see Fuller, "Ralegh's Fugitive Gold."
37. Eden, in Arber, *The First Three English Books,* xli.
38. Other examples in which Eden praises the search for wealth tempered by "uncertain hope of gain":

> But as this covetousnesse is to bee reproved, so is the liberalitie of such to be commended as have byn at greate coaste and charges in settynge forward suche viages: wherein not onely the marchauntes of London, but also divers noble men and gentlemen aswell of the counsayle as other, which bothe with theyr money and furtheraunce otherwise have furnyshed and sent furth certeyne shyppes for the discoverynge of suche landes and regions as were heretofore unknowen, have herein deserved immortall fame, for as much as in such attemptes and daungerous vyages, they have shewed no small liberalitie uppon uncerteyne hope of gayne: wherein they have deserved so much the greater prayse as theyr intent seemed to bee rather to further honest enterprises then for respecte of vantage (Eden, *The Decades,* in Arber, *The First Three English Books,* 59).

> See also the preface to *The Arte of Navigation,* where Eden lavishes praise on the members of the Muscovy Company, whose voyages proved far from lucrative: "The whiche thyng doubtelesse is the more to your commendation, in that it maye hereby apppeare that you have attempted the same rather for knowledge and vertues sake, then for covetousness of gaynes: as is furthermore well knowen by your fyrste viages of discoverye attempted to Cathaye by the Northeast seas, upon certen losse and detriment, for uncerteyne hope of gaynes . . ." (Quoted in Arber, *The First Three English Books,* xli).

39. Eden, *The Decades,* in Arber, *The First Three English Books,* 360.
40. Biringuccio, *Pyrotechnia,* 36.
41. Biringuccio, *Pyrotechnia,* 39.
42. Eden, *The Decades,* in Arber, *The First Three English Books,* 369.
43. Casas, *The Spanish colonie,* sig. B3^r.
44. Casas, *The Spanish colonie,* sig. P2^v.
45. Casas, *The Spanish colonie,* sig. A3^r.
46. Eden, *The Decades,* in Arber, *The First Three English Books,* 52. For more on how England equated the state of slavery to animal subjugation, see Jordan, *White Over Black,* 54.

47. Ponet, *A Shorte Treatise*, 93–94. Ponet also used the example of Spain in the Americas to condemn, in addition to forced servitude, the unlawful appropriation of lands and private property by a usurping tyrant:

> But let us ymagine an untruthe, that all the subjectes goodes were the princes, and that he might take tham at his pleasure. Let us ymagine, that subjectes were only carnall men without the knowlage a[n]d feare of God. Yea a[n]d let it be graunted also, that they were spoiled of all their armour, and great garisones set in every place to kepe them in obeisaunce, so that they had not wherewith to redresse their i[n]juries, as nature wolde cou[n]sail them: were this a waie to make the people labour, whan others should take the bread out of their mouthe? wolde they desiere to live, to be in such miserie them selves? wolde they desire to increace the world with children, whan they knewe that they should be lefte in worse case than unreasonable beastes? No surely, and that ye maie see by the worke of nature in the people of the west Indies, now called newe Spain: who knewe of Christ nothing at all, and of God no more than nature taught them (Ponet, *A Shorte Treatise*, 93).

48. Maltby, *The Black Legend in England*, 12ff.
49. For more on the various types of Indian mine labor in the Andes, see Bakewell, *Miners of the Red Mountain*.
50. Ponet, *A Shorte Treatise*, 167.
51. Hakluyt, "Preface to the Second Edition, 1598," vol. 1, xliii.
52. Quoted in MacCaffrey, *Elizabeth I*, 74.
53. Lyly, *Gallathea and Midas*.
54. Casas, *The Spanish colonie*, sig. A1ᵛ.
55. Burghley, *The copie of a letter*, 3.
56. Hall, *Things of Darkness*, 19.
57. The American feel of Book II of Spenser's *The Faerie Queene* is established early in the proem in which Spenser uses the recently discovered New World as proof of the existence of Faerie Land:

> But let that man with better sence aduize,
> That of the world least part to vs is red:
> And dayly how through hardy enterprize,
> Many great Regions are discouered,
> Which to late age were neuer mentioned.
> Who ever heard of th'Indian *Peru?*
> The *Amazons* huge river now found trew?
> Or fruitfullest *Virginia* who did ever vew? (II. proem 2).

58. Read, "Hunger for Gold." I would like to acknowledge the appearance of this article in Read's subsequent and excellent book on Spenser. In its revised and

expanded form, his chapter on Guyon and Mammon shares some similarities with my present analysis. Unfortunately, his book has come to my attention too late for me to give it the critical attention it deserves. See Read's *Temperate Conquests.*

59. Read, "Hunger for Gold," 220. See also Maureen Quilligan, "On the Renaissance Epic: Spenser and Slavery," *SAQ,* 100.4 (2001), 15–39.

60. Greene, *The Spanish Masquerado,* 282–83.

Chapter Fourteen

1. Ryan, *Roger Ascham,* 132–35. In almost every respect—particularly its assessment of *A Report of Germany* as sixteenth-century historiography—Ryan's authoritative life and works is invaluable; for biographical details my work depends upon it.

   Cheke, Ascham's teacher in the revived study of Greek secular and patristic literature at St. John's College, Cambridge, left the Regius Professorship to become tutor to Edward VI and, later, privy councilor. Long-time ally through slippery times (and briefly brother-in-law) of William Cecil, another St. John's man, Cheke was directly or indirectly responsible for every public appointment Ascham held except the Latin secretaryship to Queen Mary. He is the recipient of many of Ascham's letters from "Germany," in which silence reveals Ascham's discretion about court politics.

2. More than two months after the arrival of the Morison embassy in Augsburg, on January 3, 1551, Ascham wrote to his friend Edward Raven, "I have seen the Emperor twice, first . . . in his privy chamber, at our first coming. . . . I saw him also on St. Andrew's day, sitting at dinner at the feast of Golden Fleece" (I, 267)—the latter occasion far from a private audience for Morison. The ambassador addressed his brief with *trop de zele;* Ascham's defensive comment confirms that Morison's skill was called into question: "My lord surely is a witty man, and serves his God, his king, and his country, nobl[y] here. If ye hear any thing to the contrary, be bold, Edward, of my word to reprove it" (I, 282–83). For an account of Morison's undiplomatic blunder and the reaction of Edward VI's council, see Ryan, *Roger Ascham,* 132–34.

   On October 1, 1552, Ascham reported back to Morison on the failure of his delegated mission to M. d'Arras, Charles's chief of staff, to request an audience on grounds that England was more important than Portugal (whose ambassador had been received) and that Morison needed to "make a good reckoning at home, of [his] duty abroad" (I, 334–37). Ascham was tartly rebuffed (with an oblique comment on Edward VI's tolerance of bad French actions) and warned that in future Morison should write, not send a messenger.

3. It is impossible to enter this discursive field, even in the early modern period, without acknowledging Said's quarter-century-old intuition, and I appropriate

some fundamental aspects of his conception, not least recognition that the imperialist reach of European culture was grounded in discourse as much as in military/political power (but cf. Greenblatt, *Possessions*, 54). As Bruce Robbins ("Edward Said's Culture," 1) observes, "Edward Said has in large part created the audience by which he is now enjoyed—which is also the audience that now questions and contests him, the contest being an indispensable part of the enjoyment." Said's own position[s] changed over time ("Orientalism Reconsidered"; cf. Brennan, "The Illusion of a Future"); as "traveling theory," the book's impact continues. My argument—focused on an era one hundred fifty years earlier than the moment when, in Said's analysis, the British and French intellectual construction of the Islamic world arose—borrows from Said's second, "more general meaning" of orientalism as "a style of thought" (*Orientalism*, 2).

Although postcolonialism derived some of its early impetus from Said's work, it has become a very different enterprise as critical practice. I associate my inquiry with recent studies exploring postcolonialism atemporally such as Davis, "Time Behind the Veil" and Ganim, "Native Studies."

4.   Because I make extensive reference to Ascham's letters, for convenience I have quoted throughout from the Giles edition of *The Whole Works of Roger Ascham* of 1864–1865, of which a modern reprint (1965) is available; all quotations from Ascham, drawn from that edition, are cited by volume and page. *A Report of Germany* was most recently reprinted in Ascham, *The English Works*, which may be more accessible.

The scant Ascham scholarship of the last quarter-century has concentrated on his critical esthetic, his Ciceronian lexicon, and his appealing *Toxophilus*, a treatise on archery. I have not found *A Report of Germany* cited in any discussion of Anglo-Turkish contacts or literary relations. Ryan (*Roger Ascham*, 171–73) treats the narrative about Turkish conduct only briefly. Beck (*From the Rising*, 30) quotes a summary sentence from the anecdotes but misascribes it to the conquest of Rhodes. An early, short portion of this paper was presented at the conference "Between Empires: Orientalism before 1600" at Trinity College, Cambridge, July12–15, 2001. My final argument was immeasurably aided by "Rereading the Black Legend: The Discourses of Racial Difference in the Renaissance Empires" at Duke University, April 18–20, 2003.

5.   Among recent publications on the theme of cultural representations of the Ottomans in English texts, I have found particularly helpful Matar's *Turks, Moors, and Englishmen*, his *Islam in Britain*, Vitkus's "Early Modern Orientalism," and his "Trafficking with the Turk." For the presence of Turks in English drama, see *Three Turk Plays*; for narratives of Turks, see Parker, *Early Modern Tales*. On the broader field of travel discourse, see Hadfield's seminal *Literature*.

The entire field is indebted to Chew's *The Crescent and The Rose*; though critical practices have advanced since he wrote, Chew offers a comprehensive archive of Tudor citations of matters Islamic, and his imaginative epilogue (541–49) rewards rereading.

6. Modern historians' presentations of this treaty depend on their focus: Shaw, interested in the Ottomans, explains it clearly and circumstantially (*History*, 103); Imber narrates both its function and its violation without analysis (*The Ottomans*, 54–55); Maltby's *Reign of Charles V*, presumably drawing on Habsburg archives, notes only a strategic retreat by Charles following a serious defeat and a need to focus on Germany (47–48); other historians with a European ocular report nothing. Shaw holds that the temporary truce became a permanent treaty — with violation more serious — on the death of Francois I in 1546. One explanation for the variance may lie in Shaw's wry comment (*History*, 98) on an earlier situation: "the sultan learned what many of his successors were to find out in later years: that infidel [i.e., Christian] friends would abandon all agreements when it suited their interests in Europe to do so."

    A comprehensive historical analysis of events in Hungary in the 1540s and 1550s is difficult to find: for western European historians, the required Turkish and Hungarian languages are difficult; for Magyar nationalists the occupation is a troubling issue; for Turkish historians Hungary is a peripheral province; in the forty-year communist era, when social history took hold in the West, the Ottoman period was read locally in an ideological way. For a survey of Hungarian historiography on the period, see David and Fodor, "Hungarian Studies," esp. 314–27, 337–39.

7. In the sixteenth century, the town of Mahdia was often called "Africa"; to avoid confusion, I have consistently used the modern name, including within Ascham's text. Similarly, I use "Islam" (not recorded in English usage until 1613) and "Muslim" rather than the sixteenth-century "Mohammedan," in various spellings.

8. My principal sources for the political events in Ascham's text and their broad background include Brandi's old but authoritative biography, *The Emperor Charles V*; the wonderfully readable work of Wheatcroft, who knows both the Habsburg and the Ottoman worlds; Shaw, *The Rise and Decline*; Kafadar, *Between Two Worlds*; Imber, *The Ottomans*; Maltby, *The Reign of Charles V*; Coles, *The Ottoman Impact on Europe*; Rodríguez-Salgado, *The Changing Face of Empire*; Skilliter, *William Harborne*; and the extensive scholarship on the late crusades of Norman Housley and Jonathan Riley-Smith. Ascham's description of historical events appears to be largely accurate by modern standards, in outline and often in detail; historians agree, for instance, that Maurice of Saxony, as Protestant prince and military leader, was indeed central to Charles V's difficulties.

9. Assuming the standard trope of the body politic, Ascham presents discord in public affairs as a feverish sickness; in the worst case, the body of Naples was "so inwardly distempered" that it almost "burst forth into a foul sore" (III, 10, 26) of open rebellion. He also characterizes the pope as a brewer, broacher, and drinker of the beverage that causes trouble (III, 18, 20).

10. The strongly envisioned image of the body being tortured is the most orientalist moment of Ascham's anecdotes. Gerome's painting *The Snake Charmer* (c. 1870), selected as the cover art for the 1995 reissue of *Orientalism*, draws a picture similar to Ascham's: the nude, emphatically rounded rear view of a young boy—his upper body wreathed by a snake the head of which he holds in his hand, gazed upon frontally by a reclining, aged oriental despot—invites a reading of pederasty. Said, while detaching himself from the sensuality of the images that historical/academic orientalists present, nevertheless supplies quotation and interpretation of knowing comments by Flaubert (who offers examples of exhibitionism, bestiality, and masturbation on a single page, *Orientalism*, 103), Richard Burton (though largely praised, cited for "often prurient interventions," *Orientalism*, 196), Lord Cromer (commenting on "intimate friendship," *Orientalism*, 211), T. E. Lawrence (noting "the Semitic capacity for enjoyment . . . lust and self-denial," *Orientalism*, 241), Leon Mugniery (on "powerful sex drive," *Orientalism*, 311), and, pointedly, Bernard Lewis (*Orientalism*, 314–15). Subsequent inquiries into orientalism in literature and art history leave much less to the imagination. On the literary-historical reality behind some of the imputed imagery, see Rowson, "Two Homoerotic Narratives."

    Behind the violence that Ascham uncannily narrates may lie some awareness in England of Ottoman practices like circumcision and castration—especially, perhaps, of such treatment for Christian youths who became favored cadres of the sultans' regime through *devsirme,* the tax of promising young boys exacted from the conquered Balkans. Italian humanist exhortations to crusade after 1453, cast as classical orations, often cited the *devsirme* among Ottoman crimes (Housley, *Crusades,* 385). No later than the early twelfth century, a purported letter from the Byzantine emperor, forged further west, initiated western sexualized stereotyping of Muslims by citing Turks' raping women by mounting them like animals, circumcising boys and youths, and sodomizing men, including clergy (Trexler, *Sex and Conquest* 50, citing Boswell, 367–68).

11. It may be relevant that medieval Christian polemics against the Prophet Muhammad—essentially carnivalized versions of a saint's life—often claimed that his dead body was devoured by dogs or, more frequently, pigs (Daniel, *Islam and the West,* 104–05, 241–42). Ascham could conceivably have seen the

version of Geraldus Cambrensis or the one that "Matthew Paris personally worked into the St.Albans Chronicle, under the year 622" (Daniel, *Islam and the West*, 104); however, circulation of the calumny was very wide.

12. Whenever Ascham lists the four great powers—the Empire, the pope, France, and the Ottomans—he always puts the Turks first (III, 5, 7, 27, 54); compare a letter to his scholar friend Johannes Sturm, where the listing is clearly an insult (I, 274).

13. For the modern reader the term "great game" has nineteenth-century connotations of conflicts involving Britain in Muslim Central Asia, yet Ascham—who enjoyed gambling—presents Pope Julius III as a player who "takes up the game," "makes sport," "hazards Parma on the main chance," and "makes the two princes better sport and fresher game" (III, 20–21).

14. Valensi's discussion of the structure and intellectual perspective, as well as content, of Venetian ambassadors' reports on the Ottomans suggests that Ascham may have modeled *A Report* on a semirecognized genre—one that he discovered in the diplomatic corps at Charles V's court.

15. Vitkus ("Trafficking," 47) presents a similar strand in the later extensive literature on travels to the Levant: admiration for a "masculine force capable of maintaining a strict order and discipline" including "spectacular punishment and assassination"; he quotes Sir Henry Blount (1636) on "Empaling, Gaunching, Flaying alive, cutting off by the Waste with a red hot iron," etc. In passages not published until the twentieth century, Fynes Moryson's *An Itinerary*, based on his visit to Istanbul in 1597 at the end of an extended "grand tour," reports a still more extensive catalogue of "Judgments Corporall and Capitall" to discipline and punish; he provides descriptions of two that he witnessed in a level of detail to match Ascham (Hadfield, *Amazons*, 170–72).

Although Ascham anticipates such travel narratives by a half-century, it is inevitable that—as Ottoman invasions of southeastern Europe posed an ever-increasing threat—word circulated about the effectiveness of Turkish military organization, with its uniform dress, ordered ranks, and martial music to keep troops in line. Imagining such discipline no doubt sparked in a pikeman or musketeer anxieties about janissaries who never retreat, know no fear or boundaries of self, and willingly act as cannon fodder. For a crisp report on Turkish forces and their administration, see Housley (*Crusades*, 71–72); on the image presented in the detailed reports prepared by sixteenth-century Venetian ambassadors to the Ottoman court, including on military structures, see Valensi, "The Making," esp. 180–81.

16. See Coles' (*The Ottoman Impact*) copious illustrations from contemporary prints, especially plates 3, 4, 6, and 52, which Ascham could conceivably have seen, and plate 72, which demonstrates the (common) diachronic appropria-

tion of earlier monstrous horrors—in this case, the Romans' massacre of the innocents—to illustrate Turkish unnatural cruelty. Bernhard von Breydenbach's *Reise ins Heilige Land* (1486) includes a woodcut (41) of "turci" on horseback entering battle, three in turbans, at least two carrying crossbows, and the two whose lower bodies are visible wearing skirted robes and playing a wind instrument and drums. (See fig. 14.1.)

17. This guarantee may have been a form of *aman,* a safe-conduct pass that any Muslim—not just the sultan—could unilaterally grant to nontaxpaying residents of or passers through the Ottoman world; it is a significant step below an *ahdname,* the formal document in which sultans granted trading privileges, and rights to organize themselves as a body, to foreigners (Skilliter, *William Harborne,* 2, 9–10, 97–98; she includes many examples). The emphatic functional role of such documents underlines the cultural importance in Ottoman society of making and keeping promises.

18. Mustafa is the son whom, in 1553, Suleyman ordered assassinated, probably at the behest of his Russian concubine Hurrem Sultan ("Roxelana"), to secure the throne for her son—a story told in England as early as William Painter's 1566 *The Palace of Pleasure* (Chew, *The Crescent,* 498,) originally *The Cytie of Cyvelitie* (Hadfield, *Literature,* 149).

19. On Italian humanists' views of the Ottomans, see Bisaha's valuable chapter, "'New Barbarian,'"esp. 189–96; they generally cast Turks as book-destroying Goths and Vandals, clearly secular barbarians.

20. Letter to Edward Raven, January 20, 1551: "This know, there is no country here to be compared for all things with England. Beef is little, lean, tough, and dear, mutton likewise; a rare thing to see a hundred sheep in a flock. Capons be lean and little; pigeons naught; partridge as ill, black, and tough," etc.; "The Emperor's palace is overmatched with many of the king's houses in England" (I, 250, 245). Letter of February 23, 1551: "England need fear no outward enemies. The lusty lads surely be in England. I have seen on a Sunday more likely men walking in Paul's church than I ever yet saw in [Augsburg,] where lieth an Emperor with a garrison, three kings, a queen, three princes, a number of dukes, &c" (I, 279).

More significantly, after appraising skilled historians, Ascham concludes, "England hath matter, and England hath men furnished with all abilities to write; who, if they would, might bring both like praise unto themselves, and like profit to others, as [Xenophon and Caesar] hath done" (III, 8).

21. Ascham's ambitions are highly contingent. Before he had been gone from England five months, he was writing to private friends of his hope "to see England shortly, God willing"; "if I can get leave of my lord ambassador, surely . . . I will come home at Michaelmas" (I, 280, 286). Although he expresses

willingness to take on another foreign post (and confidence of his ability to contribute), his major incentive is clearly to "get a living" otherwise unavailable to him (I, 269). After a year, "I never loved [Cambridge] so well as I do at this day" (I, 302); in the many letters with which he showers first Cecil, then Sir William Petre and Bishop Gardiner of Mary's council, about his prospects on return to England, further foreign travel is the third of three posts that he proposes—the first being a free appointment at Cambridge (where he had been Greek orator) with little to do (e.g., I, 332–33). He eventually received his second choice of a court post: the Latin secretaryship to Mary.

22. I had completed my earlier work on Ascham, including his emphasis on what he has personally witnessed or learned from witnesses—and indeed my work on Montaigne's use of multiple sources of authority—before I read Greenblatt's theorization, immediately inspired by Mandeville, of the role of "eye witnessing" in taking discursive possession of the western hemisphere (*Possessions*, 122–48), which greatly enriched my thinking. Greenblatt (*Possessions*, 68) draws upon the analysis of de Certeau, extensively using his reading of Herodotus. Herodotus no doubt referred to the Greek term *theoroi*, or contemplative spectators; the related noun *theoria*, for the act of gazing, eventually led to modern "theory" (Nightingale, *Spectacles*).

23. Black, *The Origins of War*, 1; he quotes Michael Howard's mordant remark that in the sixteenth-century war was a seasonal form of hunting (*The Origins of War*, 5).

24. The general absence of skepticism in mid-sixteenth-century Europe deserves note; confronted for the first time with phenomena like rhinoceri, even the educated were ready to accept as plausible the "men whose heads grow beneath their shoulders," based in the Greek ethnographic tradition of monstrous races that, following Pliny, drew renewed attention in the early days of print (Grafton, *New Worlds*, 34–37, 70–72). As Vitkus remarks in this context ("Early Modern Orientalism," 209), "The distinction between story and history, fiction and fact, legend and chronicle, was not a clear one."

25. In his correspondence about his career with Cecil, then principal secretary to Edward VI, Ascham remarks, "Sir, if I might be so bold, I doubt not but your mastership is well ware in seeing our letters fitly deciphered, lest the *fallax* of composition and division [create errors if words are incorrectly joined or separated]; and because I perceive this in ciphering, I think other may perhaps light upon the same in deciphering" (I, 329)—an indication of the effort given to maintaining secrecy in correspondence. In his long, early letter to Raven he explains that he cannot send more news "because I know so much; and being in this room that I am, I must needs keep them close" (I, 265). Discretion of another sort is apparent in Ascham's careful request for permission to "some-

time as occasion serveth talk with the Pope's Nuncio's men, as I do with other agents and Italians here. Hitherto I have not, nor would not do it, for still I knew not whether I might do it or no, nor hereafter will not attempt it, except your wisdom from home would warrant me thereunto. . . . I would trust so to observe my talk as I should get more of some of them, than any of those should win of me" (I, 330–31.) Seeking cover for talking to papists, he seems to imply the possibility of intelligence gathering.

For the value of Ascham's post as a source of information, note Bacon's advice, in "Of Travel," to a young man on the grand tour: "As for the acquaintance, which is to be sought in *Travaile;* That which is most of all profitable, is Acquaintance with the Secretaries, and Employd Men of Ambassadours; For so in *Travailing* in one Country he shall sucke the Experience of many" (quoted in Hadfield, *Amazons,* 34).

26. Heath explores the Renaissance debate on the descent of Turks: from ancient Trojans, or—the view of Aeneas Silvius (later Pope Pius II)—from Scythians. Such humanist intellectual precedent connects Turks to unclean, forbidden ingestion, for Scythians "ate detestable things: the flesh of mares, wolves,vultures, and what is even more horrifying, aborted human fetuses" (Bisaha, "'New Barbarian,'" 195)—the latter a form of tribal cannibalism.

27. Beck (*From the Rising,* 20), citing Setton, "Lutheranism." Via his colleague Johannes Sturm, Ascham quotes Melancthon on Johann-Friedrich, Elector of Saxony, as a more extensive reader and writer than both Melancthon himself and another leading Wittenberg scholar (III, 43)—flattery of a Protestant champion, perhaps. But Ascham regreted Melancthon's advocacy to the German Protestant princes of Charles V's compromise of 1548; he preferred the unyielding urban Protestants of Augsburg (Ryan, *Roger Ascham,* 128).

On early English scholarship about the Middle East, see Parker, *Early Modern Tales,* 3–6 and notes. Setton (*Hostility,* 14) holds that knowledge of Arabic declined markedly in Europe between the mid-fourteenth and mid-seventeenth centuries.

28. Ascham saw (and perhaps purchased) the Latin edition of the *Historiarum* in Speyer in October 1551 (I, 258). Giovio also wrote *Commentario de le cosi de Turchi* (1531; Latin trans. 1533; English trans. by Peter Ashton, 1546), which, contrary to Ascham's fervor, contrasted Christian heroism with Turkish barbarism. Largely interested in military history, Giovio has been called "the first great journalist in the field of history writing" (Parry, "Renaissance," 289), in part for his diligent efforts to gather detailed, first-hand information from an international array of princes, soldiers, ambassadors, ransomed captives, travelers, and papal correspondents, from listeners to Suleyman, from Charles V himself on the Tunis campaign of 1535, and—near his death—from Moorish

sailors in the harbor. His reports on Suleyman's campaigns (1520–1566) are
unequalled in the West and often confirmed (Parry, "Renaissance," 283–88;
von Ranke, *Fürsten,* validates his informative value). Giovio saw a different
side of the Turk from Ascham's reports; for instance, he records the famous
visit to the Porte of Giovanni Bellini, at the invitation of Mehmet II, "to draw
forth his own princlye portraiture" (Chew, *The Crescent,* 479n.) *Mutatis mutan-
dis,* Giovio's goals, and his use of oral resources, might be expected to appeal to
the author of *A Report.* But Ascham reproaches Giovio as a historian for hatred
and flattery, both telling untruths and suppressing hard facts (*A Report,* 4) —
presumably concerning the regimes opposite to Ascham's preferences.

    The only other books available to have served as sources for Ascham's
Turkish construction at this early date may be Geuffroy's *Estat,* which takes a
condescending tone that is a far cry from Ascham; an irrelevant two-and-a-
half-page chapter in Boorde's *Introduction of Knowledg* (c. 1548); and Cambini's
Two Commentaries (Beck, *From the Rising,* 24). Ascham cites none of them.

29. Letter to Raven, May 1551: "For understanding of the Italian I am [meetly]
    well; but surely I drink Dutch better than I speak Dutch" (I, 285; see also I,
    280). In *A Report,* a lengthy anecdote about the betrayal of the Protestant
    Landgraf of Hesse turns on the difference between *ewig* and *einig,* altered by
    the stroke of a pen; Ascham must ask for "the very words in Dutch" (III, 51)
    to be written into his notebook, so he may understand the trick. Thus he was
    unable to read the virulent anti-Turkish *Fleugschriften* published in the 1530s
    and 1540s, with their "tabloid-style atrocity stories" (Housley, *Crusades,* 385)
    that intentionally aroused *Teurchenfurcht* and exhorted readers to defense of
    civilization against the new barbarians. Though intended for popular audi-
    ences, their "news," songs, etc., of course circulated among court figures as well.

30. To defend a high level of education for well-born men in *The Scholemaster,*
    Ascham cites the learned François I and remarks that the contrary "opinion is
    not French, but plain Turkish" (III, 135) — an all-purpose code for barbarism.

31. Throughout the desultory crusade campaigns — and crushing defeats — of the
    fifteenth century, "English participation in actual crusading had become mini-
    mal . . . and the government either remained neutral or actually obstructed
    preaching" that advocated it (Housley, *Crusades,* 411). Although "the crusade
    as a serious military venture aroused more publicity and discussion in the
    years 1517-'20 than it had for decades" (*Crusades,* 126), made more effective
    by circulation in print rather than preaching, Henry VIII's alliance of the
    1520s with the vocal crusader Charles was strained in the 1530s by the king's
    "great matter" of divorcing Charles's aunt.

32. Erasmus, whom Ascham revered as "the ornament," "the honour of learning
    in our time" (III, 214, 317), despised the hypocrisy and extortion of crusade

planning almost as much as the violence of war; in *Consultatio,* written when the threat to Vienna was greatest, his abhorrence of both military destructiveness and church financing gives way with grave reluctance to the need to contain Ottoman advances — preferably by conversion, if necessary by secular resistance, but with the ultimate goal of peace (Housley, "A Necessary Evil?" 267–69, 273).

33. Housley, *Crusades,* 132–33. See also Riley-Smith, (*Oxford History,* 12 [citing Setton, *Hostility*]) in a splendid overview of crusading and its impact on society. On the continent there was a long history of crusade songs describing the predations of Muslims; it is possible that Spaniards who reported the torture in Budapest knew the mid-thirteenth-century "Ay, Iherusalem!" — the only such song in Spanish that survives — with its descriptions of Christians watching "their sons roasted . . . their wives' breasts sliced off while they are still living," and so on, all committed by "Moorish dogs . . . helped by those of Babylon" (Routledge, "Songs," 107).

34. The sentiment echoes the pointed comment of the condemned Thomas More, whose learning and virtue Ascham greatly admired (see *Report* III, 6), in *Dialogue* that no Turk is so cruel to Christians as are false Christians — those fallen from the faith, such as Protestants.

35. In private letters Ascham is still more irreverent, in high Lutheran style. "Pope Julius is a very king. He hath made a boy of his kitchen, an ape-keeper, cardinal de Monte, whereof he was cardinal himself. Men now say, *Parturiunt montes, nascetur simian turpis*" (I, 279). His speculations when the Council of Trent is not reconvened for political reasons, and when papal stratagems are clearly failing (I, 278, 312), amount to *Schadenfreude.*

36. For example, both Henri II and Charles V offer patent bribes (III, 9, 18), the French ambassador flatly lies (III, 19), the French join the Turks in piracy (III, 21), and oppressed Neapolitans — made landless outcasts by the viceroy — turn highwaymen (III, 26).

37. Ascham attributes this foundational concept to Sir Thomas Wyatt (III, 9) who spent two years as ambassador in Toledo in the 1530s in a vain attempt to reconcile the England of Henry VIII to the Spain of Charles V (Knapp, *An Empire,* 8–9, 36–41); what Ascham knew of Wyatt's ambiguously sad view of an isolated England cannot be determined.

    The Protestant uncle-nephew pair of Johann-Friedrich and Maurice of Saxony are also reciprocally "unkind," but Maurice's bad public behavior is virtually excused by Johann-Friedrich's rumored private behavior (III, 46); Maurice's motive, thickly described, is said to be ambition (III, 47). In a more modern touch, Henri II uses money as bait when he angles for vassals to whom Charles V has behaved "unkindly" (III, 9). In addition to the broken bonds of traditional order, Ascham offers a tacit implication of Catholic cowardice—another violation of the feudal code—in his comment that Charles's court could not bear the hot breath of the Protestant Maurice (III, 58), who disrupted an early convocation of the Council of Trent when his armies "brought such fear to the bishops . . . that they ran every one far away from thence, with such speed as they never durst hitherto speak of meeting [in Innsbruck] again" (III, 55). They were following Charles, who would later retreat hastily from Villach, Ascham says, when a Turkish attack was only rumored.

38. Ever since Wycliffe, would-be reformers had pointed to parallel flaws in Islam and in the Roman church; Catholics, to be sure, reversed the equation of heresies (Southern, *Western Views*, 77–83, 104–06; Vitkus, "Early Modern Orientalism," 211–14). For an introduction to the large literature on Catholic v. Protestant sectarianism in the early construction of Islam, see Setton, *Western Hostility to Islam*. A letter from Queen Elizabeth to Murad III, for instance, suggests a natural alliance between England and the Porte against "idolaters"; on the Catholic side, the Ottomans were said to have saved the reformation by opening a second front against the papal forces.

39. On only two points of interpretation does Ascham differ radically from the consensus of modern historians: the characters and conduct of Don Pedro—who defended Neapolitans from excessive taxation, built public works, and campaigned against *banditi* (Maltby, *Reign*, 17, 47, 93)—and of Suleyman's son Mustafa, "universally loved" in Istanbul (Valensi, "The Making," 185), whose execution was a severe loss to competent rule in the Ottoman Empire (Shaw, *History*, 108–109). In both cases Ascham constructed images for the men he most despised: a hegemonic Spaniard and a hegemonic Turk.

40. Southern, an early scholar of England's encounter with the Muslim world, comments that after the mid-sixteenth century, western Europeans "turned their thoughts from Islam to the Indies . . . as westward the course of Empire took its way" (*Western Views*, 107). Trexler (*Sex and Conquest*, xi) trenchantly makes a similar connection: "Having just completed their conquest of the allegedly 'effeminate' Moors, Iberian warriors now an ocean away faced feathered warriors and, fearing them, called them women." For comparison between different encounters, east and west, see the ground-breaking work of Matar (e.g., *Turks*, ix–x). Parker (*Early Modern Tales*, 233–38) has constructed an illuminating parallel timeline that puts events in England, in publication history, in the Ottoman world, and in the western hemisphere in the same time frame. Hadfield (*Literature*, 265–66) points to the intertextuality of travel writing and colonial writing.

41. Perhaps not formally named until Juderías's coinage in 1912, the Black Legend of powerful anti-Hispanist propaganda was recognized no later than Quevedo's 1604 *España Defendida* (Maltby, *Legend*, 3, in a book to which I am greatly indebted for the Spanish textual history behind the Legend). Its precise origin is subject to polemical debate—not a contest that I can enter. "It is necessary to recall that it is a legend and not a myth. It sprang, as legends do, from actual events" (Maltby, *Legend*, 10–11).

42. Hadfield (*Literature*, 4, 18, 48) quite rightly uses Ascham as his touchstone for negative sixteenth-century views on the impact—the "corrupting pointlessness"—of foreign travel. Ascham's famous ten-day journey to Venice was a side-trip in the closing months of his three-year sojourn at the Hapsburg court, a side-trip about which *A Report* is silent. The experience obviously stunned him, completely reversing the delight that his letters reflect in his journey across the Low Countries and up the Rhine and undermining the instructive observations he made of everything from Roman antiquities to land use. Ryan (*Roger Ascham*, 120)—also rightly—calls Ascham's letters "one of the finest specimens of realistic travel writing from the Tudor period." The ironies are obvious.

43. Casas, *Apolegetica*, 1039; cited by Wheatcroft in *Infidels*, which includes contestation with *moriscos* in Spain (131–52) in its sweeping survey of Christian relations with Islam through 9/11 and the United States' invasion of Iraq in 2003. Wheatcroft effectively uses Greenblatt's *Learning to Curse* in the deployment of linguistic and graphic propaganda to create hatred on both sides.

44. Nicholas may be cast as a Greenblattian go-between, a "servant of the great representational machine" (*Possessions*, 145) as he crosses from Englishman in the Levant to Englishman in the power of the Inquisition to circulator to his countrymen of the discourse of Gómara and the more revelatory Zárate, who disdained Indians.

45. Two already-detached heads also interrupt the bottom of the picture plane, entering the viewer's space. Bernadette Bucher's structuralist analysis of Tupinamba practice—as represented in the engravings of de Bry's volume 3— has shown that brains, like viscera, are soft, "white" food, boiled rather than grilled like the "red" trunk and limbs allotted primarily to men. See Bucher, *Icon and Conquest*, plates 2–4; ethnographic reports, she notes (58, 110), do not confirm these and other visual distinctions.

     Copies of de Bry's texts are rare. Bibliographical information, including a history and description of Benzoni's work, a brief biography, and an assessment of the notes added by Chauvenet, the translator into both Latin and French for de Bry's collections, is available in Camus, *Memoire*, 69–83; his discussion of the engravings adds little. Duchet, however, in *L'Amérique*, 9–46, reads the images beyond sheer ethnographic value, with a Foucauldian sensibility for their function as archive; the volume does not include the consumption of the *berdaches*.

46. Alexander's selection from de Bry's illustrations and the relevant texts that accompany them includes reports by at least six western observers of cross-dressed or transgendered men fulfilling defined, often devalued roles (Bry, *Discovering*, 1976); some of the commentators are both curious and sympathetic about indigenous peoples and their plight. See Trexler, *Sex and Conquest*, esp. 64–95; apparently he draws the term *berdache* for permanently transvested males in the Americas from Williams (*The Spirit*); he notes (*Sex and Conquest*, 40) its similarity to the Arabic *bardadj*, used for male prostitutes in the thirteenth and fourteenth centuries. Trexler's book emphasizes the use of sexual acts to punish and humiliate, including circumcision of fallen victims. In de Bry's engraving, the *berdaches* are not only effeminized but transformed from their traditional role as food bearers into food.

   Ironically, one twentieth-century anthropologist suggests that the Spaniards misinterpreted as sodomites/hermaphrodites the large percentage, among the Cuna of Panama, of albinos (Bucher, *Icon and Conquest*, 200).

47. The comparison that follows is my own, although Ryan (*Roger Ascham*, 121) generously compares *A Report* to Montaigne's "celebrated journal" of his trip to Italy in terms of keen alertness and skepticism about legend. While "Of Cannibals" does not cite the Turks, the always-curious Montaigne took an interest in Ottoman history and military prowess: "The strongest state that we see in the world at present is that of the Turks, a people equally trained to esteem arms and despise letters" ("Of Pedantry," 106). Selim I, he says in "Against Do-Nothingness" (513), believed generals should lead their troops into battle; three recent stay-at-home sultans have harmed the empire (an early start to the *grand récit* of "sick man of Europe"). In narratives about specific sultans, Montaigne also represents Turks as fatalists ("Of Virtue," 536–37), shrewd colonizers ("Of the Greatness of Rome," 520), and cruel conquerors. Although he describes some Turkish tortures that are predictably similar to the Black Legend, Montaigne notes that "The most hideous tortures to see are not always the hardest to endure" ("Cowardice, Mother of Cruelty," 530). His comments on Ottomans almost all appear at or very near the end of an essay, and all are late interpolations following the first two editions of the *Essays*. The last praises the military discipline of the Turks, whose soldiers do not pillage civilians or their property on pain of extreme penalties ("Of Physiognomy," 797). In general, his views of the Ottomans are measured and informed.

Given Montaigne's associative compositional practice, it is suggestive that six paragraphs later, he also writes "The Hungarians, very bellicose fighters, did not in olden times pursue their advantage beyond putting the enemy at their mercy" ("Of Physiognomy," 156). Ethnographically, it is difficult to surmise what Montaigne might mean by "Hungarian," when the territory was divided between a Christian kingdom with fealty to the Holy Roman Empire and an Ottoman suzerainty, with Scythians in a mythical background.

48. Montaigne begins "Of Cannibals" with some scholarly play on the relative nature of barbarism since ancient Greece (150). Ascham refers to a North African domain as "Barbaria" (he never uses the term "Berber") and to "a heathen king" who was Charles V's ally in the region (III, 11).

Certeau's stimulating discussion of the operations by which Montaigne attempts to capture the elusive bodies of the cannibals in speech, then discourse (*Heterologies*, 70–79), takes note of the representation of savage society as a single, unified body not unlike Ascham's "Turk."

49. A full discussion of the representation of cannibalism, extensively analyzed in recent years by anthropologists and cultural critics, is beyond the scope of this study. An interpretation relevant to my argument is Taussig's: "the image of the person-eating Indian [is chosen] to represent that fear of being consumed by a wild, unknown, half-sensed uncertainty" (*Shamanism*, 105). See Greenblatt, *Possessions*, 71–72, 113–14, 134–36.

Representation of the anxieties inherent in cross-cultural consumption takes an ironic turn in a caption to an engraving in Benzoni's report of the Balboa campaign: "Along most of the coast of Darien they are accustomed to eat human flesh, though some were afraid to eat the flesh of Spaniards, thinking that even in their bodies it might do them harm. Those they caught alive, in particular the captain, they used to tie up by their hands and feet. Then they would throw them to the ground and pour molten gold into their mouths saying 'Eat, eat gold, Christian.'" The engraving is graphic (Bry, *Discovering*, 137).

50. I cite illiteracy as the initial assumption of the *conquistadores*, and their chroniclers such as José de Acosta, who believed they had contacted peoples without a written language and therefore without a history. See the seminal work of Mignolo, *The Darker Side*, esp. chaps. 2 and 3. The principal modern claim for the disadvantage caused by Mexican "illiteracy" is made by Todorov, *The Conquest*. For a brilliant assessment of miscommunication, verbal and otherwise, "in the long and terrible conversation of war (123)" when Cortes took Tenochtitlan, see Clendinnen, "Cortes, Signs, and the Conquest of Mexico."

51. See Salamon, "Gascoigne's *Glasse*," "Gascoigne's Globe."

52. Once again Turkish cruelty is reciprocated by Christians. After Gascoigne's Christian warriors successfully besieged Famagusta, among other indignities

its Ottoman governor was "flayd quicke" and "his ears cut from his head"; soon after, a Turkish captain,

His head from shoulders cut, upon a Pike did stand,
The which Don John of Austrye helde in his triumphant hand.
(Gascoigne, I, 80, 82)

('Don John' was a Habsburg Catholic, the illegitimate son of Charles V.) Concerning the Spanish, Gascoigne writes in *The Spoil of Antwerp* that their "barbarous cruelty, insolence, rapes, spoils, incests, and sacrileges committed in sundry other places, might yield sufficient matter without the lawful remembrance of this their late stratagem" (Gascoigne, II, 587). That is the Black Legend in full efflorescence.

53. For the staying power of representations of the cruel Turk, consult Ivo Andrič's *The Bridge on the Drina* (1945): the practices of Ottoman servants who arrive in Bosnia in the 1520s to build the titular bridge include the murder of twin children of a retarded woman and the torture of a peasant, first by fiery hot chains and then by anal impalement. These legendary incidents, depicted by Andrič as retained in folk memory across the centuries, are the most physically vivid events in the novel.

Chapter Fifteen

1. See, for example. Rackin, "Androgyny"; Jankowski, "'Where there can be no cause of affection'"; Shannon, "Nature's Bias"; Wixson, "Cross-Dressing"; and Dooley, "Inversion." Critics who do mention the national plot of *Gallathea* have bound it exclusively to the sexual plot of the virgin queen, as in Vanhoutte's "Sacrifice, Violence and the Virgin Queen."

2. Bentley, *The Profession*, 242; Sidney, *The Defence*, 121; Shakespeare, *Henry V,* 4.chorus.49–50 (all Shakespeare citations will refer to the *Riverside*).

3. Spenser, *The Faerie Queene* (hereafter *FQ*), 3.3.22–23, 3.9.47 and 52.

4. Spenser, Letter to Raleigh, in *FQ*, 716. Drawing on Cicero, Sidney in the *Defence* writes that Xenophon gives us "*effigiem justi imperii*, the portraiture of a just empire under the name of *Cyrus* (as *Cicero* saith of him)" (91). Meres quotes this passage from Sidney without attribution in his *Palladis Tamia*, 280r.

5. Womack, "Imagining Communities," 137; Helgerson, *Forms of Nationhood*, 5, 114, 10.

6. *FQ*, 716. While Spenser's references to royal personhood in the Letter to Raleigh have been much discussed, critics have had less to say about the broader complexity of the term "person" throughout Spenser's work and in E. K.'s notes to *The Shepheardes Calender*. Lyly too uses "person" variously over the course of *Gallathea*. For instance, both Gallathea and Phyllida lose confi-

dence in their intuitive understanding of "person" as they reckon with their new homoerotic desire: see 2.1.16–18 and 3.2.17–18.

These literary instances aside, "person" was a complex term in a variety of Elizabethan discourses, including common usage in both English and Latin. For conceptions of "person" in monarchic discourse, see Kantorowicz, *The King's Two Bodies*, Axton, *The Queen's Two Bodies*, and Hutson, "Not the King's Two Bodies," 166–98. In the theological discourse of the time, discussions of "person" revolved around the Trinity as well as Peter's claim that God is no respecter of persons; see Shuger, *Habits of Thought*, 93–105.

7.   Anderson, *Imagined Communities*, 15; *Henry V,* prol.24–25.

8.   For references to constancy in the play, see Lyly, *Gallathea* (acted c. 1585, publ. 1592), in *Gallathea and Midas*, 1.1.19, 5.3.33, and 132.

9.   The Humber, which lies well south of the Scottish border, nevertheless figures as that border in two key moments of British history. The first is when Brutus divides his realm among his three sons; for an Elizabethan reference, see, for example, Prise and Lloyd, "A Description of Cambria," 1–2. The second occasion is when Gorbudoc divides his realm between his two sons; see, for example, Sackville and Norton, *Gorbudoc* (acted 1561, publ. 1565), 1.2.345–47. A reference to the Gorbudoc legend by Hugh Latimer in a sermon of 1550 indicates how the Humber could still serve as an informal demarcator of England from Scotland: "Mark in the Chronicles of England. Two brethren have reigned jointly together, the one on this side Humber, and the other beyond Humber in Scotland & all that way" (*Certayn Godly Sermons*, 125v).

10.   *Gallathea*, 1.1.51–52 and 54–56.

11.   *Gallathea*, 1.1.20 and 66, 4.3.3–4, 4.1.38–39.

12.   *Gallathea*, 1.1.37, 5.2.40–41, 3.4.31–32, 2.2.9, 1.2.6 and 23–24, 3.4.1–2 and 56–57, 3.1.1–2.

13.   *Gallathea*, 3.1.8–11, 50–53, 65, and 55–56.

14.   *Gallathea*, 5.3.73–74.

15.   *Gallathea*, prol.13–18, epil.4–5, 3.1.59–65, 5.3.131–33 and 148, prol.3–4.

16.   *Gallathea*, 5.3.95–100.

17.   *FQ,* 3.10.10, 2.39, and 3.22.

18.   *FQ,* 3.3.4 and 23.

19.   *FQ,* 3.9.33, 34, 38, 44, 38, 44.

20.   *FQ,* 3.2.29.

21.   I use the short title "View" to refer to the manuscript version of Spenser's tract in *Spenser's Prose Works*, 41–231.

22.   Hadfield and Maley, *A View of the State of Ireland* by Edmund Spenser (an edition of the first [1633] publication), xx; Spenser, "View," 82, 96. According to Hadfield in his essay "Briton and Scythian," the *View* presents Ireland's later

invaders as only incidentally shaping the modern Irish: "it is the Scythians who really define [them]" (401). Cf. Hadfield's *Edmund Spenser's Irish Experience*, 102. The implication is that Irenius treats the Irish as *racially* Scythian, yet Irenius invokes the Scythians in discussing the origins of Irish "Customs" only ("View," 81), and he cites Irish customs that derive from "the Spaniards the Gauls the Britons" as well as "the old English" (113). Moreover, Irenius aims to prove only that "the Irish are very *Scots* or *Scythes* **originally** though sithens intermingled with many other nations repairing and joining unto them" ("View," 107; emphasis added in bold). To Spenser's mind, such distant origins do not make the Irish barbarous (let alone "implacably" so), any more than the ancient Scythian presence in England means that the modern English must be savage also. Eudoxius points out that the Irish should in any case not feel "dishonored" by descent from the Scythians and Gauls, who were "two as mighty nations as ever the world brought forth" ("View," 92).

   In his overview of Renaissance English attitudes toward the Irish, Canny persuasively argues that the English generally regarded the Irish as "anthropologically"—which is to say, *culturally*—"inferior" (*The Elizabethan Conquest of Ireland*, 121–36). The theory that Spenser holds a racial account of Irish identity has been somewhat misleadingly associated with Stephen Greenblatt's influential discussion of the "View" in *Renaissance Self-Fashioning*, 184–88. For a more direct claim that the "View" presents the Irish as a "racial other," see Carroll, "The Construction of Gender."

23. Spenser, "View," 90–91 and 113. According to Canny, Spenser's invective against the Old English was a "novelty" in English disquisitions on Ireland; see Canny's "Introduction: Spenser and Reform in Ireland," 20.

24. My point about the instability of national identity in the "View" has been anticipated by both Richard McCabe and Barbara Fuchs; see McCabe, "Ireland"; and Fuchs, "Spanish Lessons." Fuchs speaks of Spenser's "ambivalence" ("Spanish Lessons," 53) about sharply defining national identity, while McCabe sees a "contradiction" between Spenser's moral and colonial conceptions of national identity: "Moral allegory has a strong tendency to internalize its enemies whereas colonial allegory is inherently resistant to any suggestion of kinship between 'self' and 'other' for fear of compromising the sense of autonomous identity that the contrast functions to sustain" ("Ireland," 64–65). In my view, however, Fuchs and McCabe underestimate Spenser's skepticism toward national identity, which he regards as a historically and rhetorically useful but ultimately untenable concept. I would not deny, however, that Spenser repeatedly expresses a deeper commitment to national identity than his principles allow.

   For an entirely different account of a barbarism in the "View" that crosses national lines, see Shuger, "Irishmen."

25. Spenser, "View," 118, 211–12.

26. Spenser, "View," 120, 119. Greenblatt draws the opposite conclusion: that "the evil metamorphosis caused by Irish wetnurses is completed by miscegenation" (*Renaissance Self-fashioning*, 185).

27. Spenser, "View," 115, 211.

28. When speculating whether the rebellious Earl of Tyrone would ever "frame himself to subjection" ("View," 166), Irenius presents a frame of mind as an act of will rather than a genetic inheritance. According to Irenius, the Irish colonial enterprise should itself be considered a "framing as it were in the forge" (146). Greenblatt remarks, "the colonial violence inflicted upon the Irish is at the same time the force that fashions the identity of the English" (*Renaissance Self-Fashioning*, 188). In "Significant Spaces,", Grenfell discusses the "frame" as a cartographic metaphor in the "View" (3–4).

29. *FQ*, Proem.4; Spenser, "View," 92 and 55.

30. Spenser, "View," 84, 94, 92. Eudoxius too sees "a wonderful providence" in "this mingling of nations" (95).

31. *FQ*, 3.3.2, 3.3.24, 3.3.23, 3.3.49. Anderson is thus mistaken when he claims that "the most messianic nationalists do not dream of a day when all the members of the human race will join their nation" (*Imagined Communities*, 16).

32. Shakespeare, *Richard II* (acted c. 1595, publ. 1597), 2.1.40–56 and 5.6.33. See Knapp, *Shakespeare's Tribe*, 81–85.

33. Kernan, "The Henriad," 276.

34. *Richard II*, 3.2.24–26.

35. *Richard II*, 5.1.2 and 11.

36. *Richard II*, 5.5.9, 8, 11; 4.1.192–93 and 295.

37. Kernan, "Henriad," 276; Fineman, "The Sound of O in *Othello*," 150.

38. Spenser, "View," 91–92; *Gallathea*, 1.1.15–16; Lyly, *Midas* (acted 1590, publ. 1592), in *Gallathea and Midas*, prol.13–14.

39. Prynne, *Histrio-mastix*, 156; Cocke, in John Stephens, *Satyrical Essayes* (1615), quoted in *The Elizabethan Stage*, , 4.255–57.

40. *Gallathea*, 2.1.3–5, 1.3.16, 2.5.2–4, 1.4.38–39, 5.1.71 (my emphasis), 5.3.190, 1.4.93.

41. *1 Henry IV*, 2.4.92; Hume, "Of National Characters," , 1.251–52.

Afterword

1. For an overview of the subject, see Gibson, *The Black Legend*. During the same period, the debate between two noted Hispanists, Benjamin Keenan and Lewis Hanke, is instructive. See Keenan, "The Black Legend Revisited," Hanke, "A Modest Proposal," and Keenan, "The White Legend Revisited."

2. I am assuming here a principle shared by many scholars and intellectuals in

and from Latin America, chiefly as charted in many works by Enrique Dussel and Eduardo Mendieta. There are differences many times with scholars in religion in Europe and the United States. That is simply due to the fact that the past is not the same from each of the local histories and sensibilities I just mentioned. For "us" (those who think from the history, sensibility, and conceptual frames of colonial South America and the Caribbean), the assumption is that Christian theology was, in the sixteenth century, what secular philosophy and sciences were in the nineteenth, in the history of western Christendom and secular Europe. Of course Christian theology was not homogeneous. It is very simple: the diversity of Christian theological discourses in order to be recognized as Christian theological discourses have to have something in common and to distinguish themselves from Jewish and Muslim theology. Juan Ginés de Sepúlveda, Francisco de Vitoria, and Bartolomé de las Casas have considerable differences among themselves. But, alas, the differences were articulated within Christian and not Muslim theology.

3. In England, and in Shakespeare, the meaning of Moor was far from precise. See Bartels, "Making More of the Moor."

4. Alonso de Sandoval—a Creole in the viceroyalty of Nueva Granada (today Colombia and Venezuela) published during the first half of the seventeenth century *De instauranda Aethiopum salute: Naturaleza, policia sagrada i profana, costumbres i ritos, disciplina i catechismo evangelico de todos etiopes* (1627, 1647). I owe this information to Eduardo Restrepo (graduate student, Anthropology, University of North Carolina, writing his dissertation on this work). For a general overview of Sandoval's treatise, see Beer, "Alonso de Sandoval."

5. I explored this issue at certain length in Mignolo, "The Markers of Race."

6. How Christians became white in the Spanish colonies has been superbly documented and theorized by Colombian philosopher Santiago Cástro-Gómez in his recent book, *La Hybris del Punto Cero.*

7. The nineteenth ecumenical council opened at Trent on December 13, 1545, and closed there on December 4, 1563. Its main object was the definitive determination of the doctrines of the Church in answer to the heresies of the Protestants; a further object was the execution of a thorough reform of the inner life of the Church by removing the numerous abuses that had developed in it.

BIBLIOGRAPHY

Note: The bibliography is offered in the spirit of further exploration, not exhaustive inclusivity or specific citation. Because the range of reference among the chapters included in this volume is broader than the usual academic volume focused on a more restricted set of archives, we offer not merely the titles referred to in the individual chapters but also the wider specific contexts in which those chapters develop their arguments. Because the value of the volume is, we think, the juxtaposition of very different languages, we have organized the bibliography under thematic headings, trying to keep the juxtaposition, for example, of materials about New World exploration with Islamic expansion as close as possible. We have also included, by specific design, untranslated texts, hoping by this means to demonstrate that the world thought in many more languages than English during the Renaissance, and therefore to remember this crucial fact in the very form of this bibliography.

ANTHOLOGIES, BIBLIOGRAPHIES, AND REFERENCE TEXTS

Bearman, P., et al., eds. *The Encyclopaedia of Islam,* 2nd ed. 12 vols. Leiden: Brill, 1960–2005.

Brunner, Otto, et al., eds. *Geschichtliche Grundbegriffe: Historisches Lexicon zur politisch-sozialen Sprache in Deutschland.* 8 vols. Stuttgart: E. Klett, 1984.

Corominas, J. *Diccionario crítico etimológico de la lengua castellana.* Madrid: Gredos, 1954.

Covarrubias [Orozco], Sebastián de. *Tesoro de la lengua castellana o española.* Edited by Martín de Riquer. Barcelona: Editorial Alta Fulla, 1989.

Dalgado, Sebastião R. *Glossário Luso-Asiático.* 2 vols. Coimbra: Imprensa da Universidade, 1919–1921.

Dehkhoda, Aliakbar. "Loghatname, 1879–1955." In *Encyclopedic Dictionary,* edited by Mohammad Mo'in and Ja'far Shahidi. 14 vols. Tehran: Chapkhanah-I Mu'ssasah-i Isharat va Chap-i Danishgah, 1994.

Hampe Martínez, Teodoro. "Recent Works on the Inquisition and Peruvian Colonial Society, 1570–1820." *Latin American Research Review* 31, no. 2 (1996): 43–63.

Mo'in, Mohammad and Ja'far Shahidi, eds. *Loghatname, 1879–1955 (Encyclopedic Dictionary).* 14 vols. Tehran: Mu'assasah-'i Intisharat va Chap-i Danishgah-i Tihran: ba hamkari-i Intisharat-i Rawzanah, 1993–1994.

Real Academia Española. *Diccionario de Autoridades.* 3 vols. Madrid: Editorial Gredos, 1979.

Steingass, F. A. *Comprehensive Persian-English Dictionary.* New Delhi: Trubner Collo-
    quials Series, 1981.

Tirmizi, S. A. I. *Mughal Documents.* Delhi: Manohar, 1989.

Walz, R. "Rasse." In *Geschichtliche Grundbegriffe: Historisches Lexicon zur politisch-
    sozialen Sprache in Deutschland,* 135–78, edited by Otto Brunner, et al. Stuttgart:
    E. Klett, 1984.

Williams, Raymond. *Keywords: A Vocabulary of Culture and Society.* New York: Oxford
    University Press, 1976.

Yule, Sir Henry, and Arthur C. Burnell. *Hobson-Jobson.* Delhi: Munshiram
    Manoharlal, 1968.

Zea, Leopoldo, ed. *Fuentes de la Cultura Latinoamericana.* México: Tierra Firme, 1993.

PRIMARY SOURCES

Classical Texts

Aristotle. *Historia Animalium.* Translated by A. L. Peck. Cambridge, MA: Harvard
    University Press, 1965–1991.

Aristotle. *On the Generation of Animals.* Translated by A. L. Peck. Cambridge, MA:
    Harvard University Press, 1953.

Xenophon. *On Hunting.* Translated and edited by A. A. Phillips and M. M. Will-
    cock. Warminster, England: Aris & Phillips, 1999.

East Indies/Asia

Badauni. *Muntakhabu-t-tawarikh.* 3 vols. Translated and edited by George S. A.
    Ranking, W. H. Lowe, and Sir Wolseley Haig (1884–1925). Delhi: Idarah-i-
    Adabiyat-i-Delli, 1986.

Battuta, Ibn. *The Travels of Ibn Battuta.* Translated and edited by H. A. R. Gibb.
    London: Cambridge Univeristy Press, 1962.

Beveridge, H., trans. *The Akbar Nama of Abu-l-Fazl,* vols. I–III (1902–1939);
    reprint, Delhi, Low Price Publications, 1993.

Burton, Richard. *Goa and the Blue Mountains; or Six Months of Sick Leave.* Berkeley:
    University of California Press, 1991.

Carletti, Francesco. *My Voyage around the World.* Translated by Herbert Weinstock.
    New York: Pantheon Books, 1964.

Carletti, Francesco. *Ragionamenti del mio viaggio intorno al mondo.* Torino: Giulio
    Einaudi Editore, 1989.

Correia-Afonso, John, ed. *Letters from the Mughal Court: the First Jesuit Mission to
    Akbar, 1580–1583.* Bombay: Gujarat Sahitya Prakash, Anand, 1980.

Couto, Diogo do. *O soldado prático.* Edited by M. Rodrigues Lapa. Lisbon: Livraria
    Sá da Costa, 1954.

Della Valle, Pietro. *The Travels of Pietro della Valle in India.* 2 vols. Translated by George Havers and edited by Edward Grey. New York: B. Franklin, 1967.

Blochmann, H., trans. *The A-in-I Akbari* by Abdul Fazl I 'Allami. 3 vols. Edited by H. S. Jarrett. Calcutta: Royal Asiatic Society, 1993.

Blochmann, H., ed. *The Ain I Akbari by Abul Fazl I 'Allami,* vols I–III. Calcutta, The Asiatic Society, 1872–1877.

Fernández de Figueroa, Martín. *A Spaniard in the Portuguese Indies: The Narrative of Martín Fernández de Figueroa.* Translated by James McKenna. Cambridge, MA: Harvard University Press, 1967.

Fernández Navarrete, Domingo. *The Travels and Controversies of Friar Domingo Navarrete.* 2 vols. Translated and edited by J. S. Cummings. London: The Hakluyt Society, 1960.

Galvão, Antonio. *A Treatise on the Moluccas.* Translated and edited by Hubert Jacobs. Rome: Jesuit Historical Institute, 1977.

González de Mendoza, Juan. *Historia de las cosas mas notables, ritos y costumbres del gran reyno de la China.* Madrid: M. Aguilar, 1944.

Gulbadan, Banu Begum. *Ahval-i Humayun Badshah.* British Library MS. Or.166.

Beveridge, Annette Susannah, (trans. *The History of Humayun: Humayun Nama* by Banu Begum Gulbadan. Delhi: Low Price Publications, 1994.

Linschoten, Jan Huygen van. *The voyage of John Huyghen van Linschoten to the East Indies.* 2 vols. Edited by Arthur C. Burnell and Pieter A. Tiele. London: The Hakluyt Society, 1885.

Maffei, Giovanni Pietro. *Le istorie delle Indie Orientali.* 2 vols. Translated by Francesco Serdonati. Bergamo: Pietro Lancellotti, 1749.

Majumdar, Ramesh C., ed. *The Classical Accounts of India.* Calcutta: Firma KLM, 1960.

Maulawi 'Abd-ur-Rahim, *Akbarnamah by Abul-Fazl I Mubarak I 'Allami,* vols. I–III. Calcutta, The Asiatic Society, 1873–1886.

Monserrate, Antonio. *The Commentary of Father Monserrate, S. J. on his Journey to the Court of Akbar.* Translated by J. S. Hoyland and edited by S. N. Banerjee. London: Oxford University Press, 1922.

Pyrard de Laval, François. *The Voyage of François Pyrard of Laval to the East Indies.* 2 vols. in 3 parts. Translated by Albert Gray. London: The Hakluyt Society, 1877–1890.

Nizam al-Din Ahmad. *The Tabaqat-i Akbari of Khwajah Nizammudin Ahmad.* 3 vols. Translated by B. De and Baini Prasad (1936). Delhi: Low Price Publications, 1992.

Rivara, J. H. da Cunha, ed. *Archivo Portuguez-Oriental.* 6 vols. in 10 parts. Nova-Goa: Impreusa Nacional, 1857–1877.

Sassetti, Filippo. *Lettere dall'India, 1583–1588.* Edited by Adele Dei. Rome: Salerno Editrice, 1995.

Silveira, Francisco Rodrigues. *Reformação da milícia e governo do Estado da Índia Oriental.* Edited by Benjamin N. Teensma. Lisbon: Fundação Oriente, 1996.

Thackston, W. M., trans. *The Jahangirnama Memoirs of Jahangir, Emperor of India.* New York: Oxford University Press, 1999.

Tiele, Pieter A. "Introduction." In Jan Huygen van Linschoten, *The voyage of John Huyghen van Linschoten to the East Indies*, vol. 1, xxiii–xlvi. Edited by Arthur C. Burnell. London: The Hakluyt Society, 1885.

Wicki, Joseph, ed. *Documenta Indica*, 18 vols. Rome: Jesuit Historical Institute, 1948–1988.

Yule, Sir Henry, and Henry Cordier, eds. *Cathay and the Way Thither.* London: The Hakluyt Society, 1914.

England and North America

Arber, Edward, ed. *The first three English books on America. 1511–1555 A.D. Being chiefly translations, compilations, &c., by Richard Eden, from the writings, maps, &c., of Pietro Martire, of Anghiera (1455–1526) Sebastian Münster, the cosmographer (1489–1552) Sebastian Cabot, of Bristol (1474–1557) with extracts, &c., from the works of other Spanish, Italian, and German writers of the time.* Westminster, U.K.: A. Constable and Co., 1895.

Ascham, Roger. *The Whole Works.* 3 vols. Edited by J. A. Giles. London: John Russell Smith, 1864.

Ascham, Roger. *The Letters of Roger Ascham and Others.* In Roger Ascham, *The Whole Works*, vol. I, edited by J. A. Giles. London: John Russell Smith, 1864.

Ascham, Roger. *A Report and Discourse of the Affairs and State of Germany.* In *The Whole Works*, vol. III, edited by J. A. Giles. London: John Russell Smith, 1864.

Ascham, Roger. *The English Works.* Edited by William Aldiss Wright. Cambridge, U.K.: Cambridge University Press, 1904.

Ascham, Roger. *The Scholemaster.* In *The Whole Works*, vol. III, edited by J. A. Giles. London: John Russell Smith, 1864.

Behn, Aphra. *Oroonoko.* Edited by Janet Todd. London: Penguin, 2003.

Boorde, Andrew. *The Fyrst Boke of the Introduction of Knowledge.* London: N. T. Trübner and Co., 1870.

Burghley, William Cecil, Lord. *The copie of a letter sent out of England to Don Bernardin Mendoza ambassadour in France for the King of Spaine.* London: I. Vautrollier for Richard Field, 1588.

Camden, William. *Britannia.* Translated by Philemon Holland. London: F.K.R.Y. and I.L. for William Apsley, 1637.

Cortés, Hernán. *The Arte of Navigation.* Translated by Richard Eden. London: William Stansby for John Tapp, 1615.

Donne, John. *Complete English Poems.* Edited by J. M. Dent. London: Everyman's Library, 1994.

Donne, John. *Sermons*. Edited by George R. Potter and Evelyn M. Simpson. Berkeley: University of California Press, 1953–1962.

Elizabeth I, Queen of England. *Collected Works*. Edited by Leah S. Marcus et al. Chicago: University of Chicago Press, 2002.

Elyot, Thomas. *The Castle of Health*. New York: Scholars' Facsimilies and Reprints, 1936.

Fletcher, John. *The Island Princess* [electronic resource]. Cambridge, MA: Chadwyck-Healey, 1994.

Foxe, John. *Actes and Monuments: Facsimile of John Foxe's Book of Martyrs, 1583* [electronic resource]. Edited by David G. Newcombe and Michael Pidd. Oxford: Oxford University Press, 2001.

Gage, Thomas. *The English American: A New Survey of the West Indies, 1648*. Edited by A. P. Newton. Guatemala City: El Patio, 1946.

Gascoigne, George. *The Complete Works*. 2 vols. Edited by John W. Cunliffe. New York: Greenwood Press, 1969.

Gilbert, Humphrey. *The Voyaging and Colonizing Efforts of Humphrey Gilbert*. Edited by David Beers Quinn. London: The Hakluyt Society, 1940.

Greene, Robert. *The Spanish Masquerado*. In *The Life and Complete Works of Robert Greene, M.A.*, vol. V, 282–83, edited by Alexander B. Grosart. London: Hazell, Watson and Viney, 1881–1883.

Greville, Fulke. *The Prose Works of Fulke Greville, Lord Brooke*. Edited by John Gouws. Oxford: Clarendon, 1986.

Hadfield, Andrew, ed. *Amazons, Savages, and Machiavels; Travel and Colonial Writing in England, 1550–1630: An Anthology*. Oxford: Oxford University Press, 2001.

Hakluyt, Richard. *The Original Writings and Correspondence of the Two Richard Hakluyts*. Edited by Eva G. R. Taylor. London: The Hakluyt Society, 1935.

Hakluyt, Richard. *A Particuler Discourse Concerninge the Greate Necessitie . . . by the Westerne Discouries Lately Attempted, Written in the Yere 1584*. Edited by David B. Quinn and Alison M. Quinn. London: The Hakluyt Society, 1993.

Hakluyt, Richard. *The Principall Navigations, Voiages, and Discoveries of the English Nation. Imprinted at London, 1589*. Cambridge, U.K.: The Hakluyt Society, 1965.

Hall, Edward. *The Union of the Noble and Ilustre Famelies of Lancastre and York*. London: Richard Grafton, 1550.

Hariot, Thomas. *A briefe and true report of the new found land of Virginia of the commodities and of the nature and manners of the naturall inhabitants*. 1590.

Heywood, Thomas. *The Fair Maid of the West I and II*. Edited by Robert K. Turner, Jr. Lincoln, NE: Bison Books, 1967.

Jonson, Ben. *Two Royall Masques: The One of Blacknesse and the Other of Beautie*. London: Thomas Thorpe, 1608.

Knolles, Richard. *Generall Historie of the Turkes*. London: Adam Islip, 1603.

Kyd, Thomas. *The Spanish Tragedy.* Edited by J. R. Mulryne. New York: Norton, 1989.

Latimer, Hugh. *Certayn Godly Sermons.* London: John Day, 1562.

Lyly, John. *Gallathea and Midas.* Edited by Anne Begor Lancashire. Lincoln: University of Nebraska Press, 1969.

Martyr, Peter. *The Decades of the Newe Worlde or West India.* Translated by Richard Eden. New York: Readex Microprint, 1966.

Meres, Francis. *Palladis Tamia.* New York: Scholars' Facsimiles & Reprints, 1938.

Milton, John. *Paradise Lost.* Edited by Stephen Orgel and Jonathan Goldberg. New York: Oxford University Press, 2005.

More, Thomas. *Utopia.* Edited by George M. Logan and Roger M. Adams. Cambridge Texts in the History of Political Thought. New York: Cambridge University Press, 2002.

More, Thomas. *Dialogue of Comfort Against Tribulation.* Edited by Frank Manley. New Haven, CT: Yale University Press, 1977.

Moryson, Fynes. *An Itinerary Containing His Ten Yeeres Travell.* Glasgow: J. MacLehose, 1907–1908.

Münster, Sebastian. *A Treatyse of the Newe India.* Translated by Richard Eden. New York: Redex Microprint, 1966.

Nashe, Thomas. *The Unfortunate Traveller.* In *The Unfortunate Traveller and Other Works,* edited by J. B. Steane. Harmondsworth, Penguin, 1985.

Parker, Kenneth, ed. *Early Modern Tales of Orient; A Critical Anthology.* New York: Routledge, 1999.

Ponet, John. *A Shorte Treatise of Politicke Power.* In *John Ponet (1516?–1556), Advocate of Limited Monarchy,* edited by Winthrop S. Hudson. Chicago: University of Chicago Press, 1942: 93–94.

Prise, John and Humphrey Lloyd. *The Historie of Cambria, Now Called Wales,* by Caradoc of Llancarvan. Translated by H. Lhoyd and edited by David Powel. London: Rafe Newberie and Henrie Denham, 1584.

Prynne, William. *Histrio-mastix.* London: E. A[llde, Augustine Mathewes, Thomas Cotes], and W[illiam] I[ones]., 1633.

Purchas, Samuel. *Hakluytus Posthumus, or, Purchas His Pilgrimes.* 20 vols. Glasgow: J. MacLehose and Sons, 1905–1907.

Quinn, David B., ed. *The Roanoke Voyages.* 2 vols. London: The Hakluyt Society, 1955.

Raleigh, Sir Walter. *The Discoverie of the Large and Bewtiful Empire of Guiana.* Edited by V. T. Harlow. London: The Argonaut Press, 1928.

Sackville, Thomas, and Thomas Norton. *Gorbudoc.* Edited by Irby B. Cauthen, Jr. Lincoln: University of Nebraska Press, 1970.

Shakespeare, William. *The Riverside Shakespeare,* 2nd ed. Edited by G. Blakemore Evans et al. Boston: Houghton Mifflin, 1997.

Sidney, Philip. *The Defence of Poesie.* In *Defence of Poesie, Astrophil and Stella, and Other Writings,* edited by Elizabeth Porges Watson. London: J. M. Dent, 1997.

Spenser, Edmund. *The Faerie Queene.* Edited by A.C. Hamilton et al. London: Longman, 2001.

Spenser, Edmund. "A Vewe of the Present State of Irelande" (MS 1596). In Rudolf Gottfried, ed., *Spenser's Prose Works.* Baltimore: Johns Hopkins University Press, 1949.

Spenser, Edmund. *A View of the State of Ireland.* Edited by Andrew Hadfield and Willy Maley. Oxford: Blackwell, 1997.

Vitkus, Daniel, ed. *Three Turk Plays from Early Modern England.* New York: Columbia University Press, 2000.

Webster, John. *The White Devil.* New York: Norton, 1996.

White, John. *The New World. The First Pictures of America.* Edited by Stefan Lorant. New York: Duell, Sloan and Pierce, 1964.

Israel/Jewish Diaspora

Millás Vallicrosa, J. M. "Un tratado anónimo de polémica contra los judíos." *Sefarad* 13 (1953).

Anonymous, "Coloquio entre un Cristiano y un Judío." Biblioteca del Palacio, Ms. 1344, fols. 106r–106v.

Ibn Adret, Salomon. *She'elot u-teshuvot,* no. 1162.

Ibn Shem Tov, Shem Tov b. Joseph. *Derashot al ha-Torah.* Jerusalem: Makor Publishing, Ltd., 1974.

Ottoman Empire

Bacqué-Grammont, Jean-Louis. "Une lettre d'Ibrahim PasQa à Charles-Quint." In *Comité international d'études pré-ottomans et ottomans,* 70, 81. Leiden: Brill, 1987.

Doukas. *Decline and Fall of Byzantium to the Ottoman Turks.* Translated and Edited by Harry J. Magoulias. Detroit: Wayne State University Press, 1975.

Peçevi, Ibrahim. *Tarih-i Peçevi.* 2 vols. Istanbul: Matba'ai Amire, 1865–1867.

Roe, Sir Thomas. *The Negotiations of Sir Thomas Roe in his Embassy to the Ottoman Porte.* London: Samuel Richardson, 1740.

Spain, New Spain, and Peru

Pope Alexander VI. *Inter Caetera,* Papal Bull of May 4, 1493. In Frances Gardiner Davenport, ed., *European Treaties Bearing on the History of the United States and its Dependencies to 1648,* 75–78. Washington, DC: Carnegie Institution, 1917.

Acosta, José de. *Natural and Moral History of the Indies.* Edited by Jane E. Mangan. Durham, NC: Duke University Press, 2002.

Acuña, René, ed. *Relaciones geográficas del siglo xvi: México.* México: Universidad Autónoma de México, 1985.

Alva Ixtlilxóchitl, Fernando de. *Obras históricas.* México: Universidad Autónoma De México, Instituto De Investigaciones Históricas, 1975.

Alvarado Tezozómoc, F. *Crónica Mexicayotl.* México: Impr. Universitaria, 1949.

Baena, Juan Alfonso de. *Cancionero de Juan Alfonso de Baena.* Edited by B. Dutton and J. Gonzalez Cuenca. Madrid: Visor Libros, 1993.

Bartra, Enrique, ed. *Tercer concilio limense, 1582–1583.* Lima, 1982.

Beer, M. E. "Alonso de Sandoval: Seventeenth-Century Merchant of the Gospel." [accessed 2/26/07.] http://www.kislakfoundation.org/prize/199702.html.

Beltrán y Rózpide, Ricardo, ed. *Coleccion de las memorias o relaciones que escribieron los virreyes del Peru acerca del estado.* Madrid: Impreso del Asilo de Huérfanos del S. C. de Jesús, 1921.

Benzoni, Girolamo. *Historia del mundo nuevo.* Madrid: Alianza, 1989.

Berdan, Frances F., and Patricia Rieff Anawalt, eds. *The Codex Mendoza.* 4 vols. Berkeley: University of California Press, 1993.

Betanzos, Juan de. *Suma y narración de los Incas.* Cochabamba, Bolivia: Fondo Rotatorio Editoria, 1992.

Borgognoni, Teodorico. *Libro de los caballos,* Ms. Escorial b-IV-31. In *Electronic Texts and Concordances of the Madison Corpus of Early Spanish Manuscripts and Printings* [CD-ROM]. Prepared by John ONeill. New York: Hispanic Seminary of Medieval Studies, 1999.

Núñez Cabeza de Vaca, Álvar. *La Relación, o, Naufragios.* Edited by Martin A. Favata and José B. Fernández. Potomac, MD: Scripta Humanistica, 1986.

Núñez Cabeza de Vaca, Álvar. *The Account.* Translated by Martin A. Favata and José B. Fernández. Houston: Arte Público, 1993.

Cabrillana, Nicolás, ed. *Documentos notariales referentes a los moriscos 1569–71.* Archivo Histórico Provincial de Almería. Granada: Universidad de Granada, 1978.

Calnek, Edward E. "The Sahagún Texts as a Source of Sociological Information." In *Sixteenth Century Mexico: The Work of Sahagún,* edited by Munro S. Edmonson, 189–204. Albuquerque, NM: University of New Mexico Press, 2000.

Cartagena, Alonso de. *Defensorium unitatis christianae.* Edited by P. Manuel Alonso. Madrid: Escuela de Estudios Hebraicos, 1943.

Casas, Bartolomé de las. *Apologética historia sumaria.* Edited by Edmundo O'Gorman. 3rd ed. 2 vols. México, 1967.

Casas, Bartolomé de las. *Obras completas.* 14 vols. Edited by Paulino Castañeda Delgado. Madrid: Alianza Editorial, 1988–1998.

Casas, Bartolomé de las. "Aquí se contiene una disputa o controversia . . . en la villa de Valladolid." In *Obras completas,* vol. 10, 102–93, edited by Paulino Castañeda Delgado. Madrid: Alianza Editorial, 1995.

Casas, Bartolomé de las. *The Only Way*. Edited by Helen Rand Parish and translated by Francis Patrick Sullivan, S.J. New York: Paulist Press, 1992.

Casas, Bartolomé de las. *The Spanish Colonie*. Translated by MMS. London: Thomas Dawson, 1583.

Casas, Bartolomé de las. *Tyrannies et cruautez des Espagnols, perpetrees ès Indes Occidentales*. Translated by Jacques de Miggrode. Antwerp, 1578.

Casas, Bartolomé de las. *The Tears of the Indians: Being an Historical and True Account of the Cruel Massacres and Slaughters of Above Twenty Millions of Innocent Peoples in the Islands of Hispaniola, Cuba, Jamaica, etc*. Translated by John Philipps. London: J. C. Nath, 1656.

Cervantes Saavedra, Miguel de. *El amante liberal*. Edited by Florencio Sevilla Arroyo. Alicante, Spain: Biblioteca Virtual Miguel de Cervantes, 2001. http://www.cervantesvirtual.com/index.shtml.

Cervantes Saavedra, Miguel de. *Don Quixote de la Mancha*. Edited by Francisco Rico. Madrid: Real Academia Española, 2004.

Chimalpahin Cuauhtlehuanitzin, Domingo Francisco De San Antonio Munon. *Codex Chimalpahin*. Translated and edited by Arthur J. O. Anderson and Susan Schroeder. Norman: University of Oklahoma Press, 1997.

Cieza de León, Pedro de. *Descubrimiento y conquista del Perú*. Edited by Carmelo Sáenz de Santa María. Madrid: Historia 16, 1986.

Colegio Notarial de Barcelona. *Privilegios y ordenanzas históricos de los notarios de Barcelona*. Edited by R. Noguera Guzmán and J. M. Madurell Marimón. Barcelona, 1965.

Columbus, Christopher. *The Diario of Christopher Columbus's First Voyage to America 1492–1493, abstracted by Fray Bartolomé de Las Casas*. Transcribed and translated by Oliver Dunn and James E. Kelley, Jr. Norman: University of Oklahoma Press, 1989.

Cortés, Hernán. *Cartas de relación*. Edited by Mario Hernández. Madrid: Historia 16, 1985.

Cortés, Hernán. *Hernán Cortés: Letters from Mexico*. Translated and edited by Anthony Pagden. New Haven, CT: Yale University Press, 1986.

Daunce, Edward. *A Brief Discourse of the Spanish State, with a Dialogue annexed intituled Philobasilis*. London: Richard Field, 1590.

Díaz del Castillo, Bernal. *Historia Verdadera de la Conquista de la Nueva España*, 2 vols. Edited by Miguel León Portilla. Madrid: Historia 16, 1984.

Dibble, Charles E., ed. *The Codex Xólotl*. México: Publicaciones del Instituto de Historia and University of Utah, 1951.

Dies, Manuel. *Libro de albeytería*. Zaragoza: Pablo Hurus, 1495.

Dies, Manuel. *Libre de la menescalia*. Biblioteca General i Històrica de la Universitat de València, ms. 631.

Díez de Games, Gutierre. *El Victorial.* Edited by J. de Mata Carriazo. Madrid: Espasa-Calpe, 1940.

Durán, Diego. *Historia de las Indias de Nueva España e islas de Tierra Firme.* Edited by Angel María Garibay. México: Porrúa, 1967.

Durán, Diego. *History of the Indies of New Spain.* Translated by Doris Heyden. Norman: University of Oklahoma Press, 1994.

Edmonson, Munro S., ed. *The Book of Counsel: The Popol Vuh of the Quiche Maya of Guatemala.* New Orleans: Tulane University Press, 1971.

Fernández de Oviedo y Valdés, Gonzalo. *Historia general y natural de las Indias.* Edited by Juan Pérez de Tudela Bueso. Madrid: Ediciones Atlas, 1992.

Fernández Retamar, Roberto. *Calibán. Apuntes sobre la cultura en nuestra América.* Buenos Aires: Editorial la Pleyade, 1973.

Fernández Retamar, Roberto. *Caliban and Other Essays.* Translated by Edward Baker. Minneapolis: University of Minnesota Press, 1989.

Flemming, Leonor, ed. *El matadero/La Cautiva,* by Esteban Echeverría. Madrid: Cátedra, 1993 [1838–1840].

García Moreno, A. *Papers of the Medieval Hispanic Research Seminar,* no. 40. London: University of London, 2003.

Garcilaso de la Vega, el Inca. *Historia general del Perú.* In *Obras completas del Inca Garcilaso de la Vega,* vols. 134–35, edited by Carmelo Sáenz de Santa María. Biblioteca de Autores Españoles (continuation). Madrid: Ediciones Atlas, 1960.

Garcilaso de la Vega, el Inca. *Comentarios reales de los Incas.* 2 vols. Edited by Carlos Araníbar. Lima: Fondo de Cultura Económica, 1991.

Garcilaso de la Vega, el Inca. *The Florida of the Inca.* Translated by John and Jeannette Varner. Austin: University of Texas Press, 1951.

Ginés de Sepúlveda, Juan. *Tratado sobre las justas causas de la guerra contra los Indios.* Edited by Marcelino Menéndez de Pelayo and Manuel García-Pelayo. México: Fondo de Cultura Económica, 1941.

Guillén de Segovia, Pero. *La gaya ciencia de P. Guillén de Segovia.* 2 vols. Edited by L. Casas Homs. Madrid: Consejo Superior de Investigaciones Científicas, 1962.

Guaman Poma de Ayala, Felipe. *Nueva crónica y buen gobierno.* 3 vols. Edited by John V. Murra et al. México: Siglo XXI, 1987.

Guaman Poma de Ayala, Felipe. *El primer nueva corónica y buen gobierno (1615/1616).* Edited by Rolena Adorno. Copenhagen: The Royal Library of Denmark, GKS 2232 4°. http://www.kb.dk/elib/mss/poma/.

Guaman Poma de Ayala, Felipe. *Nueva crónica y buen gobierno.* 3 vols. Translated by Franklin Pease. México: Fondo de Cultura Económica, 1993.

Hernando i Delgado, Josep. "Un tractat anònim *Adversus iudaeos* en català." In *Paraula i història. Miscel·lània P. Basili Rubí.* Barcelona, 1986.

Herrera y Tordesillas, Antonio de. *Historia general de los hechos de los castellanos en las islas y tierrafirme del mar océano.* 4 vols. Edited by Mariano Cuesta Domingo. Madrid: Universidad Complutense de Madrid, 1991.

Isabel and Ferdinand, *Treaty between Spain and Portugal concluded at Tordesillas; June 7, 1494.* In *European Treaties Bearing on the History of the United States to 1648,* edited by Frances Gardiner Davenport. Washington, DC: The Carnegie Institution, 1917.

Juan II, King of Castile and Leon. *Crónica del halconero de Juan II.* Edited by J. de Mata Carriazo. Madrid: Espasa-Calpe, 1946.

Juan II, King of Castile and Leon. "Privilegio de Don Juan II en favor de un Hidalgo." *Biblioteca de Autores Españoles,* vol. 176, 25–28. Madrid, 1964.

Kaplan, Josef. "The Self-Definition of the Sephardic Jews of Western Europe and Their Relation to the Alien and the Stranger." In *Crisis and Creativity in the Sephardic World, 1391–1648,* edited by Benjamin Gampel. New York: Columbia University Press, 1997.

Lienhard, Martin. *Cartas, crónicas y manifiestos de la conquista.* Caracas: Ayacucho, 1992.

López de Gómara, Francisco. *Historia general de las Indias y Vida de Hernán Cortés.* Edited by Jorge Gurria Lacroix. Caracas: Biblioteca Ayacucho, 1991.

Mariana, Juan de. *Historia general de España.* Edited by Eduardo Chao. Madrid: Gaspar y Roig, 1848–1851.

Martínez de Toledo, Alfonso. *Arcipreste de Talavera: o, Corbacho.* Edited by Michael Gerli. Madrid: Cátedra, 1992.

Medina Lima, C. *Libro de Los guardianes y gobernadores de Cuauhtinchan (1519–1640).* México: CIESAS, 1995.

Menéndez y Pelayo, Marcelino. "17 Oct. 1887." In *Epistolario de Valera y Menéndez Pelayo.* Madrid: Espasa, 1946.

Monardes, Nicolas. *Joyfull Newes Out of the Newe found Worlde.* Translated by John Frampton. London: Willyam Norton, 1577.

Muñoz Camargo, D. L. Reyes García, et al. *Historia de Tlaxcala: Ms. 210 de la Biblioteca Nacional de París.* Tlaxcala, México: Gobierno del Estado de Tlaxcal, Centro de Investigaciones y Estudios Superiores en Antropología Social Universidad Autónoma de Tlaxcala, 1998.

Naharro, Pedro. "Relación de los hechos de los españoles . . . marqués Francisco Pizarro." In *Colección de libros y documentos referentes a la historia del Perú,* vol. 4, 189–213, edited by Horacio H. Urteaga and Carlos A. Romero. Lima: Imprenta y Librería Sanmarti y Cía., 1917.

Palacios Rubios, Juan López de. *Requerimiento.* In *La idea de justicia en la conquista de América,* 37–239, edited by Luciano Pereña Madrid: MAPFRE, 1992.

Paso y Troncoso, Francisco de. *Epistolatio de Nueva España,* vol. 4. México: Editorial Porrúa, 1939.

Pérez de Hita, Ginés. *Guerras civiles de Granada.* Edited by Paula Blanchard-Demouge. Madrid: Imp. de E. Bailly-Baillière, 1913–1915.

Pineda, Juan de. *Diálogos familiares de la agricultura cristiana.* 5 vols. Madrid: Editorial Atlas, 1963.

Pizarro, Hernando. "Carta de Hernando Pizarro a los oidores de la audiencia de Santo Domingo." In *Tres testigos de la conquista del Perú,* 51–69, edited by El Conde de Canillejos. Buenos Aires: Espasa-Calpe, 1952.

Porras Barrenechea, Raúl, ed. *Las relaciones primitivas de la conquista del Perú.* Paris: Imprimeries Les Presses Modernes, 1937.

Quevedo, Francisco. *España defendida y los tiempos de ahora.* Edited by R. Selden Rose. Madrid: 1916.

Sahagún, B. D. *Historia general de las cosas de Nueva España.* Barcelona: Círculo de Lectores, 1985.

Sahagún, B. D. *Adiciones, Apéndice a la postilla; y Ejercicio cotidiano.* Edited by A. J. O. Anderson. México: Universidad Nacional Autónoma de México Instituto de Investigaciones Históricas, 1993.

Sahagún, B. D. *Coloquios y Doctrina Cristiana: Con que los doce frailes de San Francisco, enviados por el Papa Adriano VI y por el Emperador Carlos V, convirtieron a los Indios de la Nueva España. En lengua mexicana y española. Los diálogos de 1524.* Edited by M. León Portilla. México, Universidad Nacional Autónoma De México Fundación De Investigaciones Sociales, 1986.

Sahagún, Bernardino de. *Historia de General de las Cosas de Nueva España.* Edited by Juan Carlos Temprano. Madrid: Historia 16, 1990.

Sancho, Pero. "Relación destinada a SM de cuanto ha sucedido en la conquista y pacificación . . . y la prisión del cacique Atabalipa." In *La relación de Pero Sancho,* 60–215, edited by Luis A. Arocena. Buenos Aires: Plus Ultra, 1986.

Sandoval, Alonso de. *De instauranda Aethiopum salute: Naturaleza, policia sagrada i profana, costumbres i ritos, disciplina i catechismo evangelico de todos etiopes.* Bogotá: Empresa Nacional de Publicaciones, 1956.

Sinclair, Joseph H. *The conquest of Peru as Recorded by a Member of the Pizarro Expedition.* Facsimile edition. New York: The New York Public Library, 1929.

Solís y Rivadeneira, Antonio de. *Historia de la conquista de México, población y progresos de la América Septentrional, conocida por el nombre de Nueva España.* México: Porrúa, 1988.

Solorzano Pereira, Juan de. *Politica Indiana* [1647] in *Biblioteca de Autores Espanoles,* vols. 252–56. Madrid, 1972.

Suardo, Juan Antonio. *Diario de Lima de Juan Antonio Suardo (1629–1639)*. 2 vols. Lima: Editorial Lumen, 1936.

Sta. Teresa de Avila, *Libro de la Vida*. Edited by Damaso Chicharro. Madrid: Cátedra, 1997. *Tratado del Alborayque*, BNM ms. 17567.

Valera, Diego de. *Espejo de la verdadera nobleza*. Edited by Mario Penna. *Prosistas castellanos del siglo xv, Biblioteca de Autores Españoles*, vol. 116. Madrid: 1959.

Vega, Lope de. *Amar sin saber a quién*. Edited by Carmen Bravo-Villasante. Salamanca: Anaya, 1967.

Vega, Lope de. *Comedias americanas: El nuevo mundo descubierto por Cristóbal Colon; El Brasil restituído*. Buenos Aires: Editorial Poseidón, 1943.

Vitoria, Francisco de. *Political Writings*. Edited by Anthony Pagden and Jeremy Lawrance. Cambridge, U.K.: Cambridge Univeristy Press, 1991.

Vitoria, Francisco de. *Relecciones sobre los indios y el derecho de guerra*. Edited by Armando D. Pirotto. Buenos Aires: Espasa Calpe Argentina, 1947.

Vocht, Henry de. "Rodrigo Manrique's Letter to Vives," in *Monumenta Humanistica Lovaniensia: Texts and Studies about Louvain Humanists in the First Half of the XVIth Century: Erasmus, Vives, Porpius, Clenardus, Goes, Moringus*. Louvain.

Xérez, Francisco de. *Verdadera relación de la conquista del Perú*. Edited by Concepción Bravo Guerreira. Madrid: Historia 16, 1985.

Zárate, Agustín de. *Historia del descubrimiento y conquista del Perú*. Edited by Franklin Pease G. Y. and Teodoro Hampe Martínez. Lima: Pontifica Universidad Católica del Perú, 1995.

Other European

Albert of Monte Casino. Alberici Casineasis flores rhetorici. Edited by Mauro Inguanez and Henry Matthew Willard. Montecassino, 1938.

Ariosto, Ludovico. *Orlando Furioso*. Vicenza: Mondadori, 1976.

Arnaud, Antoine (supposed author). "The Coppie of the Anti-Spaniard." London: John Wolfe, 1590.

Bellay, Joachim du. "Ample Discours au Roy sur le Faict des quatre Estats du Royaume de France" In *Oeuvres poétiques*, edited by Henri Chamard, vol. 6. Paris: Nizet, 1982.

Biringuccio, Vannoccio. *Pyrotechnia*. Translated by Cyril Stanley Smith and Martha Teach Gnudi. Cambridge, MA: MIT Press, 1959.

Breydenbach, Bernhard von. *Die Reise ins Heilige Land*. Edited by Elisabeth Geck. Wiesbaden: Guido Pressler, 1961.

Bry, Theodore de. *Discovering the New World*. Edited by Michael Alexander. New York: Harper and Row, 1976.

Cambini, Andrea. *Two Commentaries. The One of the Originall of the Turks. The Other of the Warre of the Turks Against George Scanderbeg.* Translated by John Shute (1562). New York: Da Capo, 1970.

Davis, James C., ed. *The Pursuit of Power: Venetian Ambassadors' Reports on Turkey, France and Spain in the Age of Philip II, 1560–1660.* New York: Harper & Row, 1970.

Duchet, Michèle, ed. *L'Amérique de Théodore de Bry: Une Collection de Voyages Protestante du XVIe Siècle; Quatre Etudes d'Iconographie.* Paris: Editions du CNRS, 1987.

Erasmus, Desiderius. *Consultatio de bello Turcis inferendo.* In *Collected Works of Erasmus,* vol. 64, edited by Dominic Baker-Smith. Toronto: University of Toronto Press, 2005.

Erasmus, Desiderius. *Opus epistolarum.* 12 vols. Oxford: Oxford University Press, 1906–1958.

Farinelli, A. *Marrano (Storia di un vituperio).* Geneva: Olschki, 1925.

Geuffroy, Antoine. *The Order of the Greate Turckes Courte.* Translated by Richard Grafton. London, 1542.

Giovio, Paolo. Bishop of Nocera. *Historiarum Sui Temporis Libri XLV.* Florence, 1560.

Giovio, Paolo. *Commentario de le cosi de Turchi.* Vinegia, 1531.

Léry, Jean de. *Histoire d'un voyage fait en la terre du Brésil.* Edited by Jean-Claude Morisot and Louis Necker. Geneva: Droz, 1975.

Léry, Jean de. *Voyage to the Land of Brazil.* Translated and edited by Janet Whatley. Berkeley: University of California Press, 1990.

Le Mascrier, Jean-Baptiste. *Description de l'Egypte.* Paris: Louis Genneau and Jacques Rollin, 1735.

Luther, Martin. *Works.* Edited by Jaroslav Pelikan. Saint Louis: Concordia, 1955–1986.

Mansi, J. D. *Sacrorum conciliorum nova et amplissima collectio.* Graz: Akademische Druck- u. Verlagsanstalt, 1960–1961.

Montaigne, Michel de. *The Complete Works.* Translated by Donald M. Frame. Stanford: Stanford University Press, 1957.

Pufendorf, Samuel Freiherr von. *De jure naturae et gentium libri octo.* Oxford: Clarendon Press, 1934.

Sadoletus, Jacobus. *Sadoleto on Education: A Translation of the De pueris recte instituendis.* Edited by E. T. Campagnac and K. Forbes. London: Oxford University Press, 1916.

Thevet, André. *Le Brésil d'André Thevet: Les singularités de la France antarctique (1557).* Edited by Franck Lestringant. Paris: Chandeigne, 1997.

Tortorel, Jacques, and Jean Perrissin. *Histoires diverses qui sont mémorables touchant les guerres, massacres et troubles advenus en France en ces dernières années.* Geneva: Jean de Laon, 1569.

Vecellio, Cesare. *Habiti antichi et moderni: Vecellio's 1590 Costume Book.* Trans. Ann R. Jones and Margaret Rosenthal. London: Thames and Hudson, 2008.

Vespucci, Amerigo. *The First Four Voyages of Amerigo Vespucci: Reprinted in facsimile and translated from the rare original edition (Florence, 1505–6)*. London: B. Quaritch, 1893.

Vital, Laurent. *Premier Voyage de Charles-Quint en Espagne, de 1517 à 1518,* vol. III, 149. In *Collection des Voyages des Souverains des Pays-Bas*. 3 vols, edited by Gachard and Piot. Brussels: F. Hayez, 1881.

GENERAL HISTORIES

Adanir, Fikret and Suraiya Faroqhi, eds. *The Ottomans and the Balkans; A Discussion of Historiography*. Boston: Brill Academic Press, 2002.

Ahrweiler, H., and A. E. Laiou, eds. *Studies on the Internal Diaspora of the Byzantine Empire*. Washington, DC: Dumbarton Oaks, 1998.

Anderson, Ruth Matilda. *Hispanic Costume 1480–1530*. New York: The Hispanic Society of America, 1979.

Arnoldsson, Sverker. *La leyenda negra: estudios sobre sus orígenes*, vol. LXVI. Göteborg: Göteborgs Universitets Arsskrift, 1960.

Arendt, Hannah. *The Origins of Totalitarianism*. New York: Harcourt Brace, 1973.

Bailyn, Bernard. "The Idea of Atlantic History." *Itinerario* 20, no. 1 (1996): 19–44.

Bartlett, Robert. *The Making of Europe: Conquest, Colonization, and Cultural Change, 950–1350*. Princeton: Princeton University Press, 1993.

Bartlett, Robert. "Medieval and Modern Concepts of Race and Ethnicity." *The Journal of Medieval and Early Modern Studies* 31, no. 1, (2001): 39–56.

Beck, Brandon. *From the Rising of the Sun: English Images of the Ottoman Empire to 1775*. New York: Peter Lang, 1987.

Beldiceanu-Steinherr, Irène. "La population non-musulmane de Bithynie (deuxième moitie du XIVes. - première moitie du XVes.)." In *The Ottoman Emirate (1300–1389)*, 7–22. Heraklion: Crete University Press, 1993.

Bentley, G. E. *The Profession of Player in Shakespeare's Time*. Princeton: Princeton University Press, 1984.

Black, Jeremy, ed. *The Origins of War in Early Modern Europe*. Edinburgh: J. Donald, 1987.

Blanks, David R., ed. *Images of the Other: Europe and the Muslim World before 1700*. Cairo: The American University of Cairo Press, 1997.

Boxer, Charles R. *The Dutch Seaborne Empire, 1600–1800*. London: Hutchinson, 1965.

Boxer, Charles R. *The Portuguese Seaborne Empire, 1415–1825*. New York: Knopf, 1969.

Brandi, Karl. *The Emperor Charles V: The Growth and Destiny of a Man and of a World Empire*. Translated by C. V. Wedgwood. London: Jonathan Cape, 1949.

Browne, Walden. *Sahagún and the Transition to Modernity*. Norman: University of Oklahoma Press, 2000.

Canny, Nicholas. *The Elizabeth Conquest of Ireland.* Hassocks: Harvester Press, 1976.

Caro Baroja, Julio. *Los Judíos en la España moderna y contemporánea.* Madrid: Ediciones Arión, 1962.

Castañeda Delgado, Paulino and Pilar Hernández Aparicio. *La inquisición de Lima.* 3 vols. Madrid, Demos, 1989.

Castro, Américo. *España en su historia: cristianos, moros y judíos.* Buenos Aires: Editorial Losada, 1948.

Castro, Américo, *The Structure of Spanish History.* Translated by Edmund L. King. Princeton: Princeton University Press, 1954.

Castro, Américo. *La realidad histórica de España.* México: Porrúa, 1954.

Castro, Américo. *De la edad conflictiva.* Madrid: Taurus, 1963.

Castro, Américo. *"Español," palabra extranjera: razones y motivos.* Madrid: Taurus, 1970.

Castro, Américo. *The Spaniards: an Introduction to their History.* Translated by Willard F. King and Selma Margaretten. Berkeley: University of California Press, 1971.

Chamberlain, R. S. *Castilian Backgrounds of the Repartimiento-Encomienda.* Washington, DC: Carnegie Institution Publications, 1939.

Chew, Samuel C. *The Crescent and The Rose: Islam and England during the Renaissance.* New York: Octagon Books, 1965.

Clendinnen, Inga. *Aztecs: An Interpretation.* New York: Cambridge University Press, 1991.

Clendinnen, Inga. "Cortes, Signs, and the Conquest of Mexico." In *The Transmission of Culture in Early Modern Europe,* edited by Anthony Grafton and Ann Blair, 87–130. Cambridge, MA: Belknap, 1992.

Cohen, Jeffrey Jerome, ed. *The Postcolonial Middle Ages.* New York: Palgrave, 2000.

Coles, Paul. *The Ottoman Impact on Europe.* London: Thames and Hudson, 1968.

Comaroff, John and Jean. *Ethnography and the Historical Imagination.* Boulder: University of Colorado Press, 1992.

Corrigan, Philip and Derek Sayer. *The Great Arch.* Oxford: Blackwell, 1985.

Dandelet, Thomas James. *Spanish Rome 1500–1700.* Heraklion: Crete University Press, 2001.

Daniel, Norman. *Islam and the West; The Making of an Image.* Edinburgh: Edinburgh University Press, 1980.

David, Geza, and Pal Fodor. "Hungarian Studies in Ottoman History." In *The Ottomans and the Balkans,* edited by Fikret Adanir and Suraiya Faroqhi, 305–49. Boston: Brill Academic Press, 2000.

Davis, James C. *The Pursuit of Power: Venetian Ambassadors Reports on Turkey, France, and Spain in the Age of Philip II.* New York: Harper and Row, 1970.

D'Olwer, L. N. *Fray Bernardino De Sahagún (1499–1590).* México: Instituto Panamericano De Geografía E Historia, 1952.

Demetriades, Vassilis. "Some Thoughts on the Origin of the Devşirme," in *The Ottoman Emirate (1300–1389)*, edited by E. Zachariadou, 23 nl. Heraklion: Crete University Press, 1993.

Edmonson, Munro. S., ed. *Sixteenth-Century Mexico: The Work of Sahagún*. Albuquerque: University of New Mexico Press, 1974.

Elliott, John H. *Imperial Spain 1469–1716*. New York: St. Martin's, 1963.

Findly, Ellison Banks. *Nur Jahan, Empress of Mughal India*. New York: Oxford University Press, 1993.

Finkel, Caroline. *Osman's Dream: The Story of the Ottoman Empire 1300–1923*. London: Basic Books, 2005.

Fletcher, Richard. *Moorish Spain*. Berkeley: University of California Press, 1992.

Florescano, E. *Memory, Myth, and Time in Mexico: From the Aztecs to Independence*. Austin: University of Texas Press, 1994.

Frederickson, George M. *Racism: A Short History*. Princeton: Princeton University Press, 2002.

Friede, Juan. "La censura española del siglo XVI y los libros de historia de América." *Revista de Historia de América* 47 (1959): 45–94.

Gibbons, Herbert A. *The Foundation of the Ottoman Empire: A History of the Osmanlis up to the Death of Bayezid (1300–1403)*. New York: The Century Co., 1916.

Gibson, Charles, ed. *The Black Legend: Anti-Spanish Attitudes in the Old World and the New*. New York: Alfred A. Knopf, 1971.

Gladitz, Charles. *Horse Breeding in the Medieval World*. Dublin: Four Courts, 1999.

Grafton, Anthony. *New Worlds, Ancient Texts: The Power of Tradition and the Shock of Discovery*. Cambridge, MA: Belknap, 1992.

Grafton, Anthony, and Ann Blair, eds. *The Transmission of Culture in Early Modern Europe*. Philadelphia: University of Pennsylvania Press, 1990.

Gruzinksi, Serge. *Images At War: Mexico from Columbus to Blade Runner, 1492–2019*. Durham, NC, Duke University Press, 2001.

Gwyn, David. "Richard Eden: Cosmographer and Alchemist." *The Sixteenth Century Journal* 15, no. 1 (1984): 13–34.

Hadfield, Andrew. "Briton and Scythian: Tudor Representations of Irish Origins." *Irish Historical Studies* 28 (1993): 390–408.

Hadfield, Andrew. *Edmund Spenser's Irish Experience: Wilde Fruit and Salvage Soyl*. Oxford: Clarendon Press, 1997.

Hampe Martínez, Teodoro. "Agustín de Zárate, contador y cronista indiano (estudio biográfico)." In Agustín de Zárate, *Historia del descubrimiento y conquista del Perú*, LI–CII. Lima: Pontificia Universidad Católica del Perú, 1995.

Hampe Martínez, Teodoro. *Santo Oficio e historia colonial: aproximaciones al Tribunal de la Inquisición de Lima (1570–1820)*. Lima: Ediciones del Congreso del Perú, 1998.

Hanke, Lewis. "A Modest Proposal for a Moratorium on Grand Generalizations:

Some Thoughts on the Black Legend." *Hispanic American Historical Review*, 51, no. 1 (1971): 112–27.

Heath, Michael J. "Renaissance Scholarship and the Origin of the Turks." *Bibliotheque d'Humanisme et Renaissance* XLI (1979): 453–71.

Hegel. George. *The Philosophy of History.* Translated by J. Sibree. Buffalo, NY: Prometheus Books, 1991.

Henningsen, Gustav. *The Witches' Advocate: Basque Witchcraft and the Spanish Inquisition, 1609–1614.* Reno: University of Nevada Press, 1980.

Hess, C. "The Moriscos: An Ottoman Fifth Column in XVI-Century Spain." *American Historical Review* 74 (1968): 1–25.

Hillgarth, J. N. *The Mirror of Spain, 1500–1700.* Ann Arbor: University of Michigan Press, 2000.

Himmerich y Valencia, Robert. *The Encomenderos of New Spain 1521–1555.* Austin: University of Texas Press, 1991.

Housley, Norman. "A Necessary Evil? Erasmus, the Crusade, and War against the Turks." In *Crusading and Warfare in Medieval and Renaissance Europe.* Ashgate, U.K.: Aldershot Press, 2001.

Housley, Norman. *Crusading and Warfare in Medieval and Renaissance Europe.* Ashgate, U.K.: Aldershot Press, 2001.

Housley, Norman. *The Later Crusades.* Oxford, U.K.: Oxford University Press, 1992.

Hunter, William W. *A History of British India.* 2 vols. London: Longmans, Green and Co., 1899.

Imber, Colin. *The Ottoman Empire, 1300–1650: The Structures of Power.* New York: Macmillan, 2002.

Inalcik, Halil, and Cemal Kafadar, eds. *Suleyman the Second and His Time.* Istanbul: Isis Press, 1993.

Jaher, Frederic Cople. *A Scapegoat in the New Wilderness.* Cambridge, MA: Harvard University Press, 1994.

Juderías, Julián. *La leyenda negra. Estudios acerca del concepto de España en el extranjero.* Madrid: Editora Nacional, 1967.

Kafadar, Cemal. *Between Two Worlds: The Construction of the Ottoman State.* Berkeley: University of California Press, 1995.

Kail, Owen C. *The Dutch in India.* Delhi: Macmillan India, 1981.

Kamen, Henry. *Empire: How Spain Became a World Power, 1492–1763.* New York: Perennial, 2004.

Kamen, Henry. *Philip of Spain.* New Haven: Yale University Press, 1997.

Kamen, Henry. *The Spanish Inquisition: A Historical Revision.* New Haven: Yale University Press, 1998.

Kamen, Henry, and Joseph Pérez. *La imagen internacional de la España de Felipe II: 'legende negra' o conflicto de intereses.* Valladolid: Universidad de Valladolid, 1980.

Kant, Immanuel. *Anthropology from a Pragmatic Point of View.* Translated by Victor L. Dowdell. Carbondale: Souther Illinois University Press, 1978.

Kant, Immanuel. *Observations on the Feeling of the Beautiful and the Sublime.* Translated by John T. Goldthwait. Berkeley: University of California Press, 1991.

Keenan, Benjamin. "The Black Legend Revisited: Assumptions and Realities." *Hispanic American Historical Review* 49, no. 4 (1969): 703–19.

Keenan, Benjamin. "The White Legend Revisited: A Reply to Professor Hanke's Modest Proposal." *Hispanic American Historical Review* 51, no. 2 (1971): 336–55.

Klor De Alva, J. J., H. B. Nicholson, et al. *The Work of Bernardino de Sahagun, Pioneer Ethnographer of Sixteenth-Century Aztec Mexico.* Austin: University of Texas Press, 1998.

Kohut, George Alexander. "The Trial of Francisco Maldonado de Silva." *American Jewish Historical Society* 11 (1903): 166–67.

Konetzke, Richard. *Colección de documentos para la historia de la formación social de Hispanoamérica, 1493–1810,* 3 vols. Madrid: Consejo Superior de Investigaciones Científicas, 1953–1962.

Lal, Kishori S. *The Mughal Harem.* Delhi: Aditya Prakashan, 1988.

Langmuir, Gavin. *History, Religion, and Antisemitism.* Berkeley: University of California Press, 1990.

Lea, Henry Charles. *A History of the Inquisition of Spain,* vol 1. New York: Macmillan, 1906.

Lepore, Jill. *The Name of War: King Philip's War and the Origins of American Identity.* New York: Random House, 1999.

Levack, Brian. *The Witch-Hunt in Early Modern Europe.* New York: Longman, 1987.

Levathes, Louise. *When China Ruled the Seas: The Treasure Fleet of the Dragon Throne 1405–1433.* New York: Simon and Schuster, 1994.

Lewis, Bernard, and P. M. Holt, eds. *Historians of the Middle East.* London: Oxford University Press, 1962.

Llorente, Juan Antonio. *Historia crítica de la Inquisición de España.* Barcelona: Oliva, 1835–1836.

Lockhart, James, and Stuart B. Schwartz. *Early Latin America: A History of Colonial Spanish America and Brazil.* New York: Cambridge University Press, 1983.

Lockhart, James. *The Men of Cajamarca: A Social and Biographical Study of the First Conquerors of Peru.* Austin: University of Texas Press, 1972.

Lockhart, James. *Spanish Peru 1532–1560: A Colonial Society.* Madison: University of Wisconsin Press, 1968.

Lowry, Heath W. *The Nature of the Early Ottoman State.* Albany: State University of New York Press, 2003.

Maltby, William S. *The Black Legend in England: The Development of Anti-Spanish Sentiment, 1558–1660.* Durham, NC: Duke University Press, 1971.

Maltby, William. *The Reign of Charles V.* New York: Palgrave, 2002.

Manzano Manzano. *La incorporación de las Indias en la corona de Castilla.* Madrid: Ediciones de cultura Hispánica, 1948.

Marx, Karl. *Capital.* London: J. M. Dent and Sons, 1946.

Matar, Nabil. *Islam in Britain, 1558–1685.* Cambridge, U.K.: Cambridge University Press, 1998.

Matar, Nabil. *Turks, Moors, and Englishmen in the Age of Discovery.* New York: Columbia University Press, 1999.

Menéndez Pidal, Ramón. *España y su historia.* 2 vols. Madrid: Minotauro, 1957.

Menéndez y Pelayo, Marcelino. *Historia de los heterodoxos españoles.* 7 vols. Madrid: V. Suárez, 1911–1932.

Menzies, Gavin. *1421: The Year China Discovered America.* New York: Morrow, 2002.

Millar Carvacho, Rene. *Inquisición y sociedad en el virreinato peruano: estudios sobre el tribunal de la Inquisición de Lima.* Lima: Instituto Riva-Agüero, Pontificia Universidad Católica del Perú, 1998.

Nath, R. *Private Life of the Mughals of India, 1526–1803 A.D.* Jaipur: Historical Research Documentation Programme, 1994.

Netanyahu, Benzion. *Toward the Inquisition: Essays on Jewish and Converso History in Late Medieval Spain.* Ithaca, NY: Cornell University Press, 1997.

Nutini, Hugo. *The Wages of the Conquest: The Mexican Aristocracy in the Context of Western Aristocracies.* Ann Arbor: University of Michigan Press, 1995.

Oikonomides, Nicolas. "The Turks in Europe (1305–13) and the Serbs in Asia Minor (1313)." In *The Ottoman Emirate (1300–1389),* 160, edited by E. Zachariadou. Heraklion: Crete University Press, 1993.

Palma, Ricardo. *Anales de la Inquisición de Lima.* Madrid: Ediciones del Congreso de la República, 1997.

Parr, Charles McKew. *Jan van Linschoten: the Dutch Marco Polo.* New York: Thomas Y. Crowell Co., 1964.

Parry, V. J. "Renaissance Historical Literature in Relation to the Near and Middle East." In *Historians of the Middle East,* edited by Bernard Lewis and P. M. Holt. London: Oxford University Press, 1962.

Pearson, M. N. *The Portuguese in India.* Cambridge, U.K.: Cambridge University Press, 1987.

Pease, G. Y., Franklin. *Las crónicas y los Andes.* Lima: Pontifica Universidad Católica del Perú–Fondo de Cultura Económica, 1995.

Pérez, Joseph. *Historia de España.* Barcelona: Crítica, 2000.

Pérez Villanueva, Joaquin and Bartolome Escandell Bonet, eds. *Historia de la Inquisicion en España y America.* 3 vols. Madrid: Biblioteca de Autores Cristianos: Centro de Estudios Inquisitoriales, 1984.

Pérez Villanueva, Joaquin, ed., *La Inquisición Española: nueva visión, nuevos horizontes.* Madrid: Siglo Veintiuno de España, 1980.

Piterburg, Gabriel. *An Ottoman Tragedy: History and Historiography at Play.* Berkeley: University of California Press, 2003.

Pogo, Alexander. "The Anonymous *La conquista del Peru* (Seville 1534) and the *Libro vltimo del Svmmario delle Indie Occidentali* (Venice, October 1534)." *Proceedings of the American Academy of Arts and Sciences* 64, no. 8 (1930): 177–286.

Porras Barrenechea, Raúl. *Los cronistas del Perú (1528–1650) y otros ensayos.* Edited by Franklin Pease, G. Y. Lima: Banco de Crédito del Perú, 1986.

Prescott, William H. *History of the Conquest of Peru.* New York: The Modern Library, 1998.

Quinn, David B., and Alison M. Quinn. "Introduction." In Richard Hakluyt, *A Particuler Discourse Concerninge the Greate Necessitie . . . by the Westerne Discouries Lately Attempted, Written in the Yere 1584,* XV–XXXI. London: The Hakluyt Society, 1993.

Rabasa, José. *Inventing America: Spanish Historiography and the Formation of Eurocentrism.* Norman: University of Oklahoma Press, 1993.

Rabasa, José. *Franciscans and Dominicans under the Gaze of Tlacuilo: Plural-World Dwelling in an Indian Pictorial Codex.* Morrison Library Inaugural Address Series, 1998.

Reyes García, Luis. *Anales de Juan Bautista: ¿Cómo te confundes? ¿Acaso no somos conquistados?* México: CIESAS, 2001.

Richards, John F. *The Mughal Empire.* New York: Cambridge University Press, 1993.

Riley-Smith, Jonathan. *The First Crusade and the Idea of Crusading.* London: Athlone, 1986.

Riley-Smith, Jonathan, ed. *The Oxford Illustrated History of the Crusades.* New York: Oxford University Press, 1997.

Rodríguez-Salgado, Mia J. *The Changing Face of Empire; Charles V, Philip II, and Habsburg Authority, 1551–1559.* New York: Cambridge University Press, 1988.

Rodríguez Velasco, J.D. *El debate sobre la caballería en el siglo xv: la tratadística caballeresca castellana en su marco europeo.* Salamanca: Consejería de Educación y Cultura, 1996.

Routledge, Michael. "Songs." In *The Oxford Illustrated History of the Crusades,* 94–111, edited by Jonathan Riley-Smith. New York: Oxford University Press, 1997.

Salomon, Frank. "Chronicles of the Impossible." In *From Oral to Written Expression,* 11–39, edited by Rolena Adorno. Syracuse: Syracuse University Press, 1982.

Sáenz de Santa María, Carmelo. *Historia de una historia. La crónica de Bernal Díaz del Castillo.* Madrid: Instituto Gonzalo Fernández de Oviedo, 1984.

Sánchez-Albornoz, Claudio. *España: un enigma histórico*. Buenos Aires: Editorial Sudamericana, 1956.

Schroeder, Susan. *Chimalpahin and the Kingdoms of Chalco*. Tucson: University of Arizona Press, 1991.

Seed, Patricia. *Ceremonies of Possession in Europe's Conquest of the New World, 1492–1640*. Cambridge: Cambridge University Press, 1995.

Seed, Patricia. "'Failing to Marvel.' Atahualpa's encounter with the Word." *Latin American Research Review* 26, no. 1 (1991): 7–32.

Setton, Kenneth M. "Lutheranism and the Turkish Peril." *Balkan Studies* 3 (1962): 133–168.

Setton, Kenneth M. *Western Hostility to Islam and the Prophecies of Turkish Doom*. Philadelphia: American Philosophical Society, 1992.

Shaw, Stanford J. *History of the Ottoman Empire and Modern Turkey*, vol. 1. In *The Empire of The Gazis, 1280–1808: The Rise and Decline of the Ottoman Empire*. New York: Cambridge University Press, 1976.

Silverblatt, Irene. *Modern Inquisitions: Peru and the Colonial Origins of the Civilized World*. Durham, NC: Duke University Press, 2004.

SilverMoon. "The Emergence of a New Nahua Intellectual Elite." PhD diss., Duke University, 2007.

Skilliter, S. A. *William Harborne and the Trade with Turkey, 1578–1582*. London: Oxford University Press, 1977.

Southern, R. W. *Western Views of Islam in the Middle Ages*. Cambridge, MA: Harvard University Press, 1962.

Sphrantzes, George. *The Fall of the Byzantine Empire*. Translated by M. Philippides. Amherst: Univeristy of Massachussetts Press, 1980.

Srivastava, A. L. *Akbar the Great: Political History, 1542–1605*, vol. I. Agra: Shiva Lal Agarwala & Co., 1962.

Stephens, J. L. *Incidents of Travel in Yucatan*. Washington, DC: Smithsonian Institution, 1996.

Subrahmanyam, Sanjay. *The Portuguese Empire in Asia, 1500–1700*. New York: Longman, 1993.

Thompson, E. P. "Eighteenth-Century English Society: Class Structure without Class?" *Social History* 3, no. 1 (1978): 133–65.

Toribio Medina, José. *Historia del Tribunal de la Inquisición de Lima, 1569–1820*. Santiago de Chile: Fondo Histórico y Bibliográfico, 1956.

Toribio Medina, José. *Historia del tribunal del Santo oficio de la inquisicion de Lima (1569–1820)*. 2 vols. Santiago: Impr. Gutenberg, 1887.

Trueba y Cosio, Telésforo. *History of the Conquest of Peru by the Spaniards*. Edinburgh: Constable and Co. and Hurst, Chance and Co., 1830.

Tsai, Shih-shan Henry. *The Eunuchs in the Ming Dynasty.* New York: State University of New York Press, l996.

Vatin, Nicolas, and Gilles Veinstein. *Le Sérail ébranlé: essai sur les morts, depositions et avènements des sultans ottomans XIV–XIX siècle.* Paris: Fayard, 2003.

Wheatcroft, Andrew. *The Habsburgs: Embodying Empire.* London: Viking, 1995.

Wheatcroft, Andrew. *Infidels: The Conflict Between Christendom and Islam, 638–2002.* New York: Random House, 2004.

Wheatcroft, Andrew. *The Ottomans: Dissolving Images.* London: Viking, 1993.

Whiteway, Richard S. *The Rise of Portuguese Power in India, 1497–1550.* Westminster: A. Constable, 1899.

Williams, Walter. *The Spirit and the Flesh; Sexual Diversity in American Indian Culture.* Boston: Beacon, 1986.

Wright, J. W., Jr., and Everett K. Rowson. *Homoeroticism in Classical Arabic Literature.* New York: Columbia University Press, 1997.

Zachariadou, E. ed. *The Ottoman Emirate (1300–1389).* Heraklion: Crete University Press, 1993.

Zavala, Silvio. *La encomienda indiana.* México: Editorial Porrúa, 1992.

ART/ARCHITECTURE

Boogaart, Ernst van den. *Civil and Corrupt Asia: Images and Text in the* Itinerario *and the* Icones *of Jan Huygen van Linschoten.* Chicago: University of Chicago Press, 2003.

Brand, Michael, and Glenn Lowry. *Akbar's India: Art from the Mughal City of Victory.* London: Sotheby Parke Bernet Publications, 1986.

Brand, Michael, and Glenn Lowry. *Fatehpur Sikri: A Source Book.* Cambridge, MA: Harvard University Press, 1985.

Bucher, Bernadette. *Icon and Conquest: A Structural Analysis of the Illustrations of De Bry's Great Voyages.* Translated by Basia Gulati. Chicago: University of Chicago Press, 1981.

Carrera, Magali M. *Imagining Identity in New Spain: Race, Lineage, and the Colonial Body in Portraiture and Casta Paintings.* Austin: University of Texas Press, 2003.

Edgerton, Samuel Y. *Pictures and Punishment: Art and Criminal Prosecution during the Florentine Renaissance.* Ithaca, NY: Cornell University Press, 1985.

Frank, Bill. "The Images of Jan Huygen van Linschoten." In *India & Portugal: Cultural Interactions,* 47–69, edited by Jose Pereira and Pratapaditya Pal. Mumbai: Marg Publications, 2001.

Gossiaux, Pol-P. "L'iconographie des *Grands Voyages.*" In *Protestantisme aux frontiers. La réforme dans le duché de Limbourg et dans la principauté de Liège (XVIe–XIXe siècles).* Aubel: Librairie ancienne et moderne Pierre M. Gason, 1985.

Juneja, Monica, ed. *Architecture in Medieval India*. Delhi: Permanent Black, 2001.

Katzew, Ilona. *Casta Painting: Images of Race in Eighteenth-Century Mexico*. New Haven, CT: Yale University Press, 2004.

Necipoğlu, Gülru. "A Kanun for the State, A Canon for the Arts: Conceptualizing the Classical Synthesis of Ottoman Art and Architecture." In *Soliman le Magnifique et son temps*, edited by Gilles Veinstein. Paris: Ecoles du Louvre, 1992.

Necipoğlu, Gülru. "Süleyman the Magnificent and the Representation of Power in the Context of Ottoman-Hapsburg-Papal Rivalry." *Art Bulletin* 71, no. 3 (1989): 401–427.

Parent, Alain. *La Renaissance et le Nouveau Monde*. Québec: Gouvernement du Québec, 1984.

Puppi, Lionnello. *Les suplices dans l'art*. Paris: Larousse, 1991.

Rizvi, S. A. A., and V. J. Flynn, *Fathpur-Sikri*. Bombay: D. B. Taraporevala Sons, 1975.

Shell, Marc. *Art and Money*. Chicago: University of Chicago Press, 1995.

Spicer, Joaneath. "The Renaissance Elbow." In *A Cultural History of Gesture*, 84–128, edited by Jan M. Bremmer. Ithaca, NY: Cornell University Press, 1992.

Titley, Norah M. *Miniatures from Persian Manuscripts: A Catalogue and Subject Index of Paintings from Persia, India, and Turkey in the British Library and the British Museum*. London: British Museum Publications, 1977.

Watenpaugh, Heghnar Zeitlian. *The Image of an Ottoman City: Imperial Architecture and Urban Experience in Aleppo in the 16th and 17th Centuries*. Leiden: Brill, 2004.

Yérasimos, Stéphane. *La Fondation de Constantinople et de Sainte Sophie dans les Traditions Turques: Légendes d'Empire*. Paris: Adrien Maisonneuve, 1990.

COLONIALISM/COLONIALITY

Adorno, Rolena. *Guaman Poma: Writing and Resistance in Colonial Peru*. Austin: University of Texas Press, 2000.

Anderson, A. J. O., F. Berdan, et al. *Beyond The Codices: The Nahua View of Colonial Mexico*. Berkeley: University of California Press, 1976.

Anderson, Benedict. *Imagined Communities: Reflections on the Origin and Spread of Nationalism*. London: Verso, 1991.

Bartolovich, Crystal and Neil Lazarus, eds. *Marxism, Modernity, and Postcolonial Studies*. Cambridge: Cambridge University Press, 2002.

Beltrán de Heredia, Vicente. "Ideas del maestro Francisco de Vitoria anteriores a las Relecciones 'De Indis' acerca de la colonización de América, según documentos inéditos." *Anuario de la asociación Francisco de Vitoria* 2 (1929–1930): 23–68.

Beltrán de Heredia, Vicente. *Los manuscritos del Maestro Fray Francisco de Vitoria, O.P.* Biblioteca de Tomistas Españoles, vol. 4. Valencia: Real Convento de Predicadores, 1928.

Beverley, John. "Theses on Subalternity, Representation and Politics." *Postcolonial Studies* 1, no. 3 (1998): 305–19.

Bhabha, Homi K. *The Location of Culture*. London: Routledge, 1994.

Bravo Guerreira, Concepción. "Introducción." In *Verdadera relación de la conquista del Perú*, 7–54, edited by Francisco de Xérez. Madrid: Historia 16, 1985.

Carrasco, David. *Quetzalcoatl and the Irony of Empire: Myths and Prophecies in the Aztec Tradition*. Chicago: University of Chicago Press, 1982.

Césaire, Aimé. *Discourse on Colonialism*. Translated by Joan Pinkham. New York: Monthly Review Press, 2000.

Coates, Timothy J. *Convicts and Orphans: Forced and State-Sponsored Colonizers in the Portuguese Empire, 1550–1755*. Stanford: Stanford University Press, 2001.

Cooper, Frederick, and Ann L. Stoler. "Between Metropole and Colony: Rethinking a Research Agenda." In *Tensions of Empire: Colonial Cultures in a Bourgeois World*, 1–56. Berkeley: University of California Press, 1997.

Dussel, Enrique. "Beyond Eurocentrism. The World-System and the Limits of Modernity." In *The Cultures of Globalization*, 3–31, edited by Frederic Jameson and Masao Miyoshi. Durham, NC: Duke University Press, 1998.

Escobar, Arturo. "Beyond the Third World: Imperial Globality, Global Coloniality and Anti-Globalisation Social Movements." *Third World Quarterly* 25, no. 1 (2004): 207–30.

Fanon, Frantz. *Les damnés de la terre*. Paris: F. Maspero, 1961.

Fanon, Frantz. *The Wretched of the Earth*. New York: Grove, 1968.

Fernández Retamar, Roberto. "Nuestra América y el Occidente." In *Para el perfil definitivo del hombre*, 222–50. La Habana: Editorial Letras Cubanas, 1974.

Flores Apaza, Policarpio, Fernando Montes, Elizabeth Andia, and Fernando Huanacuni. *El hombre que volvió a nacer: vida, saberes y reflexiones de un amawt'a de Tiwanaku*. La Paz: Plural Editores/CID and Universidad de la Cordillera, 1999.

Fuller, Mary. "Ralegh's Fugitive Gold: Reference and Deferral in *The Discoverie of Guiana*." In *New World Encounters*, 218–40, edited by Stephen Greeblatt. Berkeley: University of California Press, 1993.

Ganim, John M. "Native Studies: Orientalism and Medievalism." In *The Postcolonial Middle Ages*, edited by Jeffrey Jerome Cohen, 123–34. New York: Palgrave, 2000.

Graubart, Karen. "Hybrid Thinking: Bringing Postcolonial Theory to Colonial Latin American Economic History." In *Postcolonialism Meets Economics*, 215–34, edited by Eiman O. Zein-Elabdin and S. Charusheela. New York: Routledge, 2004.

Greene, Roland. "'This Phrasis is Continuous': Love and Empire in 1590." *Journal of Hispanic Philology* 16, no. 3 (1992): 237–52.

Greene, Roland. *Unrequited Conquests: Love and Empire in the Colonial Americas*. Chicago: University of Chicago Press, 1999.

Gruzinski, Serge. *La colonisation de l'imaginarie. Sociétés indigènes et occidentalisation dans le Mexique espagnol, xvi–xviii siècles.* Paris: Gallimard, 1988.

Gruzinski, Serge. *The Conquest of Mexico: The Incorporation of Indian Societies into the Western World, 16th–18th Centuries.* Cambridge, MA: Blackwell, 1993.

Gruzinski, Serge. *The Mestizo Mind: The Intellectual Dynamics of Colonization and Globalization.* New York: Routledge, 2002.

Gruzinski, Serge, and Heather MacLean. *Images at War: Mexico from Columbus to Blade Runner (1492–2019), Latin America and Otherwise.* Durham, NC: Duke University Press, 2001.

Hanke, Lewis. *La humanidad es una.* México: Fondo de Cultura Económica, 1985.

Hanke, Lewis. *The Spanish Struggle for Justice in the Conquest of America.* Boston: Little, Brown, 1965.

Hanke, Lewis. "The 'Requerimiento' and Its Interpreters." *Revista de Historia de América* 1 (1938): 25–34.

Helgerson, Richard. "Camões, Hakluyt, and the voyages of Two Nations." In *Colonialism and Culture,* 27–63, edited by Nicholas B. Dirks. Ann Arbor: University of Michigan Press, 1991.

Jara, René. "The Inscription of Creole Consciousness: Fray Servando Teresa de Mier." In *1492–1992: Re/Discovering Colonial Writing,* edited by René Jara and Nicholas Spadachini. Minneapolis: University of Minnesota Press, 1989.

Klor de Alva, J. Jorge. "The Postcolonization of the (Latin) American Experience." In *After Colonialism: Imperial Histories and Postcolonial Displacements,* edited by Gyan Prakash. Princeton: Princeton University Press, 1995.

Lamana, Gonzalo. "Beyond Exotization and Likeness: Alterity and the Production of Sense in a Colonial Encounter." *Comparative Studies in Society and History* 47, no. 1 (2005): 4–39.

Lemistre, Annie. "Les origines du requerimiento." *Mélanges de la Casa de Velázquez* 6 (1970): 161–209.

León Portilla, Miguel. *The Aztec Image of Self and Society: An Introduction to Nahua Culture.* Translated by José Jorge Klor de Alva. Salt Lake City: University of Utah Press, 1992.

Lestringant, Frank. *Le huguenot et le sauvage: l'Amérique et la controverse coloniale en France au temps des guerres de religion.* Paris: Aux amateurs de livres, 1990.

Lockhart, J. *Nahuas and Spaniards: Postconquest Central Mexican History and Philology.* Stanford: Stanford University Press, 1991.

Lockhart, J. *The Nahuas after the Conquest: A Social and Cultural History of the Indians of Central Mexico, Sixteenth through Eighteenth Centuries.* Stanford: Stanford University Press, 1992.

Mamani Ramírez, Pablo. "Simbología y poder indígena: Después de los Kataris-Amarus, Willkas: los Mallkus en los nuevos levantamientos indígenas." In *El*

Rugir de las Multitudes: la Fuerza de los Levantamientos Indígenas en Bolivia/Qulla-suyu, 95–110. La Paz: Ediciones Yachaywasi, 2004.

Mannarelli, Maria Emma. "Inquiscion y mujeres: Las hechiceras en el Peru durante el siglo XVII." *Revista Andina* (1985), Vol. 3, 141–56

Martínez, María Elena. "The Black Blood of New Spain: Limpieza de Sangre, Racial Violence, and Gendered Power in Early Colonial Mexico." *The William and Mary Quarterly* 61, no. 3 (2004): 479–520.

Masselman, George. *The Cradle of Colonialism*. New Haven: Yale University Press, 1963.

Mignolo, Walter. *Local Histories/Global Designs: Coloniality, Subaltern Knowledges, and Border Thinking*. Princeton: Princeton University Press, 2000.

Mignolo, Walter. *The Darker Side of the Renaissance: Literacy, Territoriality, and Colonization*. Ann Arbor: University of Michigan Press, 1995.

Mignolo, Walter. "The Many Faces of Cosmo-Polis: Border Thinking and Critical Cosmopolitanism." *Public Culture* 12, no. 3 (2000): 721–48.

Mignolo, Walter. "The Markers of Race: Knowledge and the Differential/Colonial Accumulation of Meaning." *Neohelicon. Acta Comparationis Litterarum Universarum*, XXX, no. 1 (2003): 89–102.

Nandy, Ashis. *The Intimate Enemy. Loss and Recovery of Self Under Colonialism*. In *Exiled at Home*. Oxford, U.K.: Oxford University Press, 1988 (1983).

O'Gorman, Edmundo. *Invention of America: An Inquiry into the Historical Nature of the New World and the Meaning of Its History*. Bloomington: Indiana University Press, 1961.

Ortiz, Renato. *Cuban Counterpoint: Tobacco and Sugar*. Durham, NC: Duke University Press, 1995 (1940).

Pagden, Anthony. *Lords of All the World: Ideologies of Empire in Spain, Britain and France, c. 1500–c.1800*. New Haven, CT: Yale University Press, 1995.

Parker, John. *Books to Build an Empire*. Amsterdam: N. Israel, 1965.

Pratt, Mary Louise. *Imperial Eyes: Travel Writing and Transculturation*. New York: Routledge, 1992.

Quijano, Anibal. "Coloniality and Modernity/Rationality." In *Globalizations and Modernities*, edited by G. Therborn. Stockholm: FRN, 1992.

Quijano, Anibal. "Colonialidad y Modernidad-Racionalidad." In *Los Conquistados: 1492 y la poblacion indigena de las Americas*, edited by Heraclio Bonilla. Bogota: Tercer Mundo, 1992.

Quijano, Aníbal. "Colonialidad del poder y clasificación social." *Journal of World-Systems Research* 2 (2000): 342–86.

Quijano, Aníbal, and Immanuel Wallerstein. "Americanity as a Concept, or the Americas in the Modern-World System." *ISSAI* 134 (1992): 549–57.

Rabasa, José. *Writing Violence on the Northern Frontier: The Historiography of Sixteenth-*

Century New Mexico and Florida and the Legacy of Conquest. Durham, NC: Duke University Press, 2000.

Romm, James. "New World and '*novos orbes*': Seneca in the Renaissance Debate over Ancient Knowledge of the Americas." In *The Classical Tradition and the Americas,* vol. 1, 97–98, edited by Wolfgang Haase and Meyer Reinhold. Berlin: Walter de Gruyter, 1994.

Said, Edward. *Culture and Imperialism.* New York: Knopf, 1993.

Silverblatt, Irene. "Colonial Conspiracies." *Ethnohistory* 53, no. 2 (2006): 259–80.

Spivak, Gayatri. "Can the Subaltern Speak?" In *Colonial Discourse and Post-Colonial Theory: A Reader,* 66–111, edited by Patrick Williams and Laura Chrisman. New York: Columbia University Press, 1994.

Taussig, Michael. *Shamanism, Colonialism, and the Wild Man.* Chicago: University of Chicago Press, 1987.

Todorov, Tzvetan. *La conquête de l'Amérique: la question de l'autre.* Paris: Seuil, 1982.

Todorov, Tzvetan. *The Conquest of America: The Question of the Other.* Translated by Richard Howard. New York: Harper & Row, 1984.

Velazco, Salvador. "Historiografía y etnicidad emergente en el México colonial: Fernando de Alva Ixtlilxóchitl, Diego Muñoz Camargo y Hernando Alvarado Tezozómoc." *Mesoamérica* 38 (1999): 1–31.

Wesseling, H. L. *The European Colonial Empires, 1815–1919.* New York: Pearson, 2004.

Winius, George D. "The Portuguese Asian 'Decadência' revisited." In *Empire in Transition: The Portuguese World in the Time of Camões,* 223–36, edited by Alfred Hower and Richard A. Preto-Rodas. Gainesville: University of Florida Press, 1985.

Wolf, Eric R. *Europe and the People without History.* Berkeley: University of California Press, 1982.

Wood, S. G. *Transcending Conquest: Nahua Views of Spanish Colonial Mexico.* Norman: University of Oklahoma Press, 2003.

Wynter, Sylvia. "Beyond the Categories of the Master Conception: the Counter-doctrine of the Jamesian Poiesis." In *C. L. R. James's Caribbean,* 63–91, edited by Henry and Paul Buhle. Durham, NC: Duke University Press, 1992.

DOMESTICITY/FAMILY

Bernís, Carmen. "Modas moriscas en la sociedad cristiana española del siglo XV y principios del XVI." *Boletín de la Real Academia de la Historia* 144 (1959): 199–228.

Campo, Juan Eduardo. *The Other Sides of Paradise: Explorations into the Religious Meanings of Domestic Space in Islam.* New York: Columbia University Press, 1991.

Gutwirth, E. "Lineage in XVth Century Hispano-Jewish Thought," *Miscelanea de estudios arabes y hebraicos* 34 (1985): 85–91.

Jones, Ann Rosalind, and Peter Stallybrass. *Renaissance Clothing and the Materials of Memory.* Cambridge, U.K.: Cambridge University Press, 2000.

Lal, Ruby. *Domesticity and Power in the Early Mughal World.* New York: Cambridge University Press, 2005.

Lokken, Paul. "Marriage as Slave Emancipation in Seventeenth-Century Rural Guatemala." *The Americas* 58, no. 2 (October 2001): 175–200.

Mannarelli, María Emma. *Pecados públicos: La ilegitimidad en Lima, siglo XVII.* Lima: Ediciones Flora Tristán, 1993.

Martz, Linda. *A Network of Converso Families in Early Modern Toledo.* Ann Arbor: University of Michigan Press, 2003.

Županov, Ines G. "Lust, Marriage and Free Will: Jesuit Critique of Paganism in South India (Seventeenth Century)." *Studies in History* 16, no. 2 (2000): 199–200.

EDUCATION

Biddick, Kathleen. "The Cut of Genealogy: Pedagogy in the Blood." *Journal of Medieval and Early Modern Studies* Fall (2000): 449–62.

Gonzalbo Aizpuru, Pilar. *Historia de la educación en la época colonial: El mundo indígena.* México: El Colegio de México, 2000.

Kobayashi, José María. *La educación como conquista: empresa franciscana en México.* México: El Colegio de México, 1985.

Mathes, W. Michael. *Santa Cruz de Tlatelolco: La Primera Biblioteca Académica de las Américas.* México: Secretaría de Relaciones Exteriores, 1982.

GENDER/SEXUALITY

Bejar, Ruth. "Sex and Sin, Witchcraft and the Devil in Late Colonial Mexico." *American Ethnologist* 14 (1987): 35–55.

Bejar, Ruth. "Sexual Witchcraft, Colonialism, and Women's Powers: Views from the Mexican Inquisition." In *Sexuality and Marriage in Colonial Latin America,* 178–206, edited by Asunción Lavrín. Lincoln: University of Nebraska Press, 1989.

Boose, Lynda E. "The Getting of a Lawful Race: Racial Discourse in Early Modern England and the Unrepresentable Black Woman." In *Women, "Race," and Writing in the Early Modern Period,* edited by Margo Hendricks and Patricia Parker. New York: Routledge, 1994.

Burns, Kathryn. "Gender and the Politics of Mestizaje." *Hispanic American Historical Review* 78, no. 1 (February 1998): 5–44.

Carroll, Clare. "The Construction of Gender and the Cultural and Political Other in *The Faerie Queene* 5 and *A View of the Present State of Ireland:* the Critics, the Context, and the Case of Radigund." *Criticism* 32 (1990): 163–92.

Clark, Robert L. A., and Claire Sponsler. "Queer Play: The Cultural Work of Crossdressing in Medieval Drama." *New Literary History* 28 (1997): 319–44.

Dooley, Mark. "Inversion, Metamorphosis, and Sexual Difference: Female Same-Sex Desire in Ovid and Lyly." In *Ovid and the Renaissance Body*, 59–76, edited by Goran V. Stanivukovic. Toronto: University of Toronto Press, 2001.

Dopico-Black, Georgina. *Perfect Wives, Other Women: Adultery and Inquisition in Early Modern Spain*. Durham, NC: Duke University Press, 2001.

Fields, Barbara J. "On Rogues and Geldings." *American Historical Review* 108, no. 5 (December 2003): 1397–1405.

Hamer, Mary. *Signs of Cleopatra: History, Politics, Representation*. New York: Routledge, 1993.

Hendricks, Margo, and Patricia Parker, eds. *Women, "Race," and Writing in the Early Modern Period*. New York: Routledge, 1994.

Jankowski, Theodora A. "'Where there can be no cause of affection': Redefining Virgins, Their Desires, and Their Pleasures in John Lyly's *Gallathea*." In *Feminist Readings of Early Modern Culture: Emerging Subjects*, 253–74, edited by Valerie Traub et al. Cambridge, U.K.: Cambridge University Press, 1996.

Jones, Ann Rosalind, and Peter Stallybrass. "Dismantling Irena: The Sexualizing of Ireland in Early Modern England." In *Nationalisms and Sexualities*, edited by Andrew Parker et al. London: Routledge, 1992.

Karlsen, Carol. *The Devil in the Shape of a Woman: Witchcraft in Colonial New England*. New York: Norton, 1987.

Kinoshita, Sharon. "'Pagans are wrong and Christians are right': Alterity, Gender, and Nation in the *Chanson de Roland*." *The Journal of Medieval and Early Modern Studies* 31: 1 (2001): 79–111.

Mannarelli, Maria Emma. "Inquisicion y mujeres: las hechiceras en el Peru durante el siglo XVII." *Revista Andina* 3 (1985): 141–56.

Mannarelli, Maria Emma. *Hechiceras, beatas y expósitas: mujeres y poder inquisitorial en Lima*. Lima: Ediciones del Congreso del Perú, 1998.

Nader, Helen, ed., *Power and Gender in Renaissance Spain: Eight Women of the Mendoza Family, 1450–1650*. Urbana: University of Illinois Press, 2004.

Osorio Romero, Ignacio. *Colegios y profesores Jesuitas que enseñaron latín en Nueva España, 1572–1767*. Mexico City: Universidad Nacional Autónoma de México, 1979.

Papanek, Hanna, and Gail Minault, eds., *Separate Worlds: Studies of Purdah in South Asia*. Columbia, MO: South Asia Books, 1982.

Peirce, Leslie. *The Imperial Harem: Women and Sovereignty in the Ottoman Empire*. New York: Oxford University Press, 1993.

Rackin, Phyllis. "Androgyny, Mimesis, and the Marriage of the Boy Heroine on the English Stage." *PMLA* 102 (1987): 29–41.

Rowson, Everett K. "Two Homoerotic Narratives from Mamluk Literature: al-Safadi's *Law'at al-shaki* and Ibn Daniyal's *al-Mutayyam*." In *Homoeroticism in*

Classical Arabic Literature, 158–91, edited by J. W. Wright and Everett K. Rowson. New York: Columbia University Press, 1997.

Serjeant, R.B. "Haram and Hawtah, the Sacred Enclave in Arabia." In *Melanges Taba Husain,* edited by Abdurrahman Badawi. Le Caire: 1962.

Shannon, Laurie. "Nature's Bias: Renaissance Homonormativity and Elizabethan Comic Likeness." *Modern Philology* 98 (2000): 183–210.

Silverblatt, Irene. *Moon, Sun, and Witches: Gender Ideologies and Class in Inca and Colonial Peru.* Princeton: Princeton University Press, 1987.

Stolcke, Verena. "Invaded Women: Gender, Race, and Class in the Formation of Colonial Society." In *Women, "Race," and Writing in the Early Modern Period,* 272, edited by Margo Hendricks and Patricia A. Parker. New York: Routledge, 1994.

Tirmizi, S. A. I. *Edicts from the Mughal Harem.* Delhi: Idarah-i Adabiyat-i Delli, 1979.

Trexler, Richard C. *Sex and Conquest; Gendered Violence, Political Order, and the European Conquest of the Americas.* Cambridge, U.K.: Polity Press, 1995.

Vanhoutte, Jacqueline A. "Sacrifice, Violence and the Virgin Queen in Lyly's *Gallathea.*" *Cahiers Élisabéthains* 49 (1996): 1–14.

Williams, Walter. *The Spirit and the Flesh: Sexual Diversity in American Indian Culture.* Boston: Beacon Press, 1986.

Wixson, Christopher. "Cross-Dressing and John Lyly's *Gallathea.*" *Studies in English Literature* 41 (2001): 241–54.

Zilfi, Madeline C., ed. *Women in the Ottoman Empire: Middle Eastern Women in the Early Modern Era.* Leiden: Brill, 1997.

LAW/GOVERNMENT

Albó, Xavier. "From MNRistas to Kataristas to Katari." In *Resistance, Rebellion and Consciousness in the Andean Peasant World, 18th to 20th Centuries,* edited by Steve J. Stern. Madison: University of Wisconsin Press, 1987.

Anderson, Perry. *Lineages of the Absolutist State.* New York: Verso, 1979.

Axton, Marie. *The Queen's Two Bodies: Drama and the Elizabethan Succession.* London: Royal Historical Society, 1977.

Balibar, Etienne. "The Nation Form: History and Ideology." In *Race, Nation, Class: Ambiguous Identities,* 86–106, edited by Etienne Balibar and Immanuel Wallerstein and translated by Chris Turner. London: Verso, 1991.

Bayerle, Gustav. "The compromise at Zsitvatorok." *Archivum Ottomanicum* 6 (1980): 101–14.

Carter, Jimmy. "Just War—Or a Just War?" *New York Times,* March 9, 2003.

Crone, Patrica. *Slaves on Horses: The Evolution of the Islamic Polity.* New York: Cambridge University Press, 1980.

Dankoff, Robert. *An Ottoman Mentality: The World of Evliya Çelebi.* Leiden: Brill, 2004.

Farooqi, N. R. "Mughal-Ottoman Relations: A Study of Political and Diplomatic Relations between Mughal India and the Ottoman Empire, 1556–1748." PhD diss., University of Wisconsin, 1986.

Foucault, Michel. "Afterword. The Subject and Power." In *Michel Foucault: Beyond Structuralism and Hermeneutics,* 208–26, edited by Hubert L. Dreyfus and Paul Rabinow. Chicago: University of Chicago Press, 1982.

Gökbilgin, M. Tayyib. "İbrahim Paşa." *İslam Ansiklopedisi* 5, no. 2 (1968): 908–15.

Gruzinski, Serge. *Man-Gods In the Mexican Highlands: Indian Power and Colonial Society, 1520–1800.* Stanford: Stanford University Press, 1989.

Haskett, R. S. *Indigenous Rulers: An Ethnohistory of Town Government in Colonial Cuernavaca.* Albuquerque: University of New Mexico Press, 1991.

Helgerson, Richard. *Forms of Nationhood: The Elizabethan Writing of England.* Chicago: University of Chicago Press, 1992.

Hutson, Lorna. "Not the King's Two Bodies: Reading the 'Body Politic' in Shakespeare's *Henry IV,* Parts 1 and 2." In *Rhetoric and Law in Early Modern Europe,* 166–98. New Haven, CT: Yale University Press, 2001.

Kafadar, Cemal. *Between Two Worlds: The Construction of the Ottoman State.* Berkeley: University of California Press, 1995.

Kantorowicz, Ernst. *The King's Two Bodies: A Study in Medieval Political Theology.* Princeton: Princeton University Press, 1957.

Köhbach, Markus. "*Çasar* oder *Imperator?* Zur Titulatur der römischen Kaiser durch die Osmanen nach dem Vertrag von Zsitva-Torok." *Wiener Zeitschrift für die Kunde des Morgenlandes* 82 (1992): 223–34.

Kunt, Metin. *The Sultan's Servants: The Transformation of Ottoman Provincial Government, 1550–1650.* New York: Columbia University Press, 1983.

Lewin, Boleslao. *El Santo Oficio en America y el mas grande proceso inquisitorial en el Peru.* Buenos Aires: Sociedad Hebraica Argentina, 1950.

Lynch, John. *Latin America between Colony and Nation. Selected Essays.* New York: Palgrave, 2001.

MacCaffrey, Wallace T. *Elizabeth I: War and Politics 1588–1603.* Princeton: Princeton University Press, 1992.

Matthee, Rudi. "The Safavid-Ottoman frontier: Iraq-i Arab as Seen by the Safavids." *International Journal of Turkish Studies* 9, nos. 1–2 (2003): 157–73.

Mörner, Magnus. *La corona española y los foráneos en los pueblos de indios de América.* Stockholm: Instituto de Estudios Ibero-Americanos, 1970.

Murra, John. *Waman Puma. La organización económica del estado inca.* México: Siglo XXI, 1978.

Ranke, Leopold von. *Fürsten und Völker von Süd-Europa im sechzehnten und siebzehnten Jahrhundert,* vol. I. Berlin: Duncker und Humblot, 1837.

Stavrides, Theoharis. *The Sultan of Vezirs: The Life and Times of the Ottoman Grand Vezir Mahmud Pasha Angelovic (1453–1471)*. Leiden: Brill, 2001.

Stern, Steve, ed. *Resistance, Rebellion and Consciousness in the Andean Peasant World, 18th to 20th Centuries*. Madison: University of Wisconsin Press, 1987.

Tezcan, Baki. "Searching for Osman: A Reassessment of the Deposition of the Ottoman Sultan Osman II (1618–1622)." PhD diss., Princeton University, 2001.

Tsai, Shih-shan Henry. *Perpetual Happiness: The Ming Emperor Yongle*. Seattle: University of Washington Press, 2001.

Valensi, Lucette. "The Making of a Political Paradigm: The Ottoman State and Oriental Despotism." In *The Transmission of Culture in Early Modern Europe*, edited by Anthony Grafton and Ann Blair, 173–203. Philadelphia: University of Pennsylvania Press, 1990.

Veinstein, Gilles. "Mehmet Pasha, Sokollu." In *Encyclopedia of Islam*, 2d ed., edited by P. J. Bearman, T. Bianquis, C. E. Bosworth, E. van Donzel, and W. P. Heinrichs. Leiden, The Netherlands: Brill, 1960–2005.

Womack, Peter. "Imagining Communities: Theatres and the English Nation in the Sixteenth Century." In *Culture and History 1350–1600: Essays on English Communities, Identities and Writing*, edited by David Aers. Detroit: Wayne State University Press, 1992.

LITERARY AND CULTURAL STUDIES

Adorno, Rolena. *Cronista y Príncipe: la obra de don Felipe Guaman Poma de Ayala*. Lima: Fondo Editorial de la Pontificia Universidad Católica del Perú, 1989.

Adorno, Rolena. "Nuevas perspectivas en los estudios coloniales hispanoamericanos." *Revista de Crítica literaria latinoamericana* 28 (1988): 11–27.

Andrews, Walter, and Mehmet Kalpakli. *The Age of the Beloveds: Love and the Beloved in Early-Modern Ottoman and European Culture and Society*. Durham, NC: Duke University Press, 2005.

Andrič, Ivo. *The Bridge on the Drina*. Translated by Lovett Edwards. New York: Macmillan, 1959.

Bakhtin, M. "El problema de los géneros discursivos." In *Estética de la creación verbal*. Mexico: Siglo XXI, 1989.

Bakhtin, M. *Problems of Dostoevsky's Poetics*. Translated by R. W. Rotsel. Ann Arbor: University of Michigan Press, 1973.

Bakhtin, M. *Rabelais and His World*. Bloomington: Indiana University Press, 1984 (1965).

Barfoot, C. C., and Theo D'haen, eds. *Oriental Prospects; Western Literature and the Lure of the East*. Amsterdam: Rodopi, 1998.

Bartels, Emily C. "Making More of the Moor: Aaron, Othello, and Renaissance Refashionings of Race." *Shakespeare Quarterly* 41, no. 4 (1990): 433–52.

Bataillon, M. *Erasmo y España*. 2 vols. México: Fondo de Cultura Económica, 1950.

Bisaha, Nancy. "'New Barbarian' or Worthy Adversary? Humanist Constructs of the Ottoman Turks in Fifteenth-Century Italy." In *Western Views of Islam in Medieval and Early Modern Europe*, edited by Michael Frassetto and David R. Blanks, 185–205. New York: St. Martin's Press, 1999.

Bourdieu, Pierre. *Distinction: A Social Critique of the Judgement of Taste*. Cambridge, MA: Harvard University Press, 2000 (1979).

Bourdieu, Pierre. "La production et la reproduction de la langue légitime." In *Ce que parler veut dire: l'économie des échanges linguistiques*, 23–58. Paris: Librairie Artheme Fayard, 1982.

Bourdieu, Pierre. "Social Space and the Genesis of 'Classes.'" In *Language and Symbolic Power*. Cambridge, MA: Harvard University Press, 1991.

Bourdieu, Pierre. "Sur le pouvoir symbolique." *Annales* 32, no. 3 (1977): 405–11.

Brennan, Timothy. "The Illusion of a Future: *Orientalism* as Traveling Theory." *Critical Inquiry* 26 (2000): 558–83.

Camus, A-G. *Memoire sur La Collection des Grands et Petits Voyages*. Paris: Baudouin, 1802.

Canny, Nicholas. "Introduction: Spenser and Reform in Ireland." In *Spenser and Ireland: An Interdisciplinary Approach*, edited by Patricia Coughlan, ed. Cork: Cork University Press, 1989.

Certeau, Michel de. *Heterologies*. Translated by Brian Massumi. Minneapolis: University of Minnesota Press, 1985.

Certeau, Michel de. "Montaigne's 'Of Cannibals': The Savage 'I.'" In *Heterologies*. Translated by Brian Massumi. Minneapolis: University of Minnesota Press, 1985.

Chambers, E. K., ed. *The Elizabethan Stage*. 4 vols. Oxford: Clarendon Press, 1923.

Clendinnen, Inga. *Ambivalent Conquests: Maya and Spaniard in Yucatan, 1517–1570*. New York: Cambridge University Press, 1987.

Cornejo-Polar, Antonio. "El indigenismo y las literaturas heterogéneas: su doble estatuto socio-cultural." *Revista de Crítica Literaria Latinoamericana* 7–8 (1978): 7–21.

Cornejo-Polar, Antonio. *Escribir en el aire. Ensayo sobre la heterogeneidad socio-cultural en las literaturas andinas*. Lima: Editorial horizonte, 1994.

Cornejo-Polar, Antonio. "Literatura peruana: Totalidad contradictoria." *Revista de Crítica Literaria Latinoamericana* 18 (1983): 7–51.

Davis, Kathleen. "Time behind the Veil." In *The Postcolonial Middle Ages*, edited by Jeffrey Jerome Cohen, 104–122. New York: Palgrave, 2000.

Dussell, Enrique. "Eurocentrism and Modernity." *boundary* 2 (1993).

Dussell, Enrique. "Beyond Eurocentrism." In *The Cultures of Globalization*, edited by Fredric Jameson and Masao Miyoshi. Durham, NC: Duke University Press, 1998.

Duviols, Jean Paul. *L'Amérique espagnole vue et rêvée. Les livres de voyages de Christophe Colomb à Bougainville.* Paris: Editions Promodis, 1985.

Even-Zohar, Itamar. "Interference in Dependent Literary Polysystems." *Poetics Today* 11, no. 1 (1990): 79–84.

Even-Zohar, Itamar. "Polysystem Theory." *Poetics Today* 11, no. 1 (1990): 9–26.

Fineman, Joel. "The Sound of *O* in *Othello*: The Real of the Tragedy of Desire." In *The Subjectivity Effect in Western Literary Tradition: Essays Toward the Release of Shakespeare's Will.* Cambridge, MA: MIT Press, 1991.

Foucault, Michel. "Nietzsche, Genealogy, History." In *Language, Counter-Memory, Practice,* edited by D. Bouchard. Ithaca, NY: Cornell University Press, 1977.

Foucault, Michel. *Il faut défendre la société: Cours au Collège de France, 1976.* Paris: Seuil/Gallimard, 1997.

Frege, Gottlob. *Die Grundlagen der Arithmetik.* Breslau: W. Koebner, 1884. Translated by J. L. Austin. *The Foundations of Arithmetic: A logico-mathematical enquiry into the concept of number.* London: Blackwell, 1974.

Fuchs, Barbara. *Passing for Spain: Cervantes and the Fictions of Identity.* Urbana: University of Illinois Press, 2003.

Fuchs, Barbara. "Spanish Lessons: Spenser and the Irish Moriscos." *Studies in English Literature* 42, no. 1 (Winter 2002): 43–62.

Fuchs, Barbara. *Mimesis and Empire: The New World, Islam, and European Studies.* New York: Cambridge University Press, 2001.

Fuller, Mary C. *Voyages in Print: English Travel to America, 1576–1624.* New York: Cambridge University Press, 1995.

Genette, Gérard. *Seuils.* Paris: Editions du Seuil, 1987.

González, José Manuel. *Spanish Studies in Shakespeare and His Contemporaries.* Newark: University of Delaware Press, 2006.

Greenblatt, Stephen. *Renaissance Self-Fashioning: From More to Shakespeare.* Chicago: University of Chicago Press, 1980.

Greenblatt, Stephen. *Learning to Curse: Essays in Early Modern Culture.* New York: Routledge, 1990.

Greenblatt, Stephen. *Marvelous Possessions: The Wonder of the New World.* Chicago: University of Chicago Press, 1991.

Grenfell, Joanne Woolway. "Significant Spaces in Edmund Spenser's *View of the Present State of Ireland*." *Early Modern Literary Studies* 6 (1998): 1–21.

Guzmán, María de. *Spain's Long Shadow: The Black Legend, Off-Whiteness, and Anglo-American Empire.* Minneapolis: University of Minnesota Press, 2005.

Hadfield, Andrew. "Peter Martyr, Richard Eden and the New World: Reading, Experience and Translation." *Connotations* 5, no. 1 (1995/96): 1–22.

Hadfield, Andrew. *Literature, Travel, and Colonial Writing in the English Renaissance, 1545–1625.* Oxford, U.K.: Clarendon, 1998.

Hall, Kim F. *Things of Darkness: Economies of Race and Gender in Early Modern England.* Ithaca, NY: Cornell University Press, 1995.

Hamlin, William. "On Reading Early Accounts of the New World." *Connotations* 6, no. 1 (1996–1997): 46–50.

Havelock, Eric A. *The Literate Revolution in Greece and its Cultural Consequences.* Princeton: Princeton University Press, 1982.

Helgerson, Richard. "Camoes, Hakluyt, and the Voyages of Two Nations." In *Colonialism and Culture,* edited by Nicholas B. Dirks. Ann Arbor: University of Michigan Press, 1992.

Hulme, Peter. *Colonial Encounters: Europe and the Native Caribbean, 1492–1797.* New York: Methuen, 1986.

Hutson, Lorna. "Not the King's Two Bodies: Reading the 'Body Politic' in Shakespeare's *Henry II,* Parts 1 and 2." In *Rhetoric and Early Modern Europe.* Ed. Victoria Kahn and Lorna Hutson. New Haven: Yale University Press, 2001. 166–98.

Jowett, Claire. "'Monsters and Straunge Births': The Politics of Richard Eden. A Response to Andrew Hadfield." *Connotations* 6, no. 1 (1996–1997): 51–63.

Kamps, Ivo. "Colonizing the Colonizer: A Dutchman in Asia Portuguesa." In Ivo Kamps and Jyotsna G. Singh, eds. *Travel Knowledge; European "Discoveries" in the Early Modern Period,* 160–81. New York: Palgrave, 2001.

Kamps, Ivo, and Jyotsna G. Singh, eds. *Travel Knowledge; European "Discoveries" in the Early Modern Period.* New York: Palgrave, 2001.

Kernan, Alvin. "The Henriad: Shakespeare's Major History Plays." In *The Revels History of English Drama,* vol. 3, edited by J. Leeds Barroll et al. London: Methuen, 1975.

Kliman, Bernice W., and Rick J. Santos. *Latin American Shakespeares.* Madison, NJ: Fairleigh Dickinson University Press, 2005.

Knapp, Jeffrey. *An Empire Nowhere: England, America, and Literature from* Utopia *to* The Tempest. Berkeley: University of California Press, 1992.

Koeman, C. *Jan Huygen van Linschoten.* Lisbon: Instituto de Investigação Científica Tropical, 1984.

Lestringant, Frank. "L'automne des cannibales ou les outils de la conquête." In *L'Amérique de Théodore de Bry: une collection de voyages protestante au XVIe siècle.* Paris: Editions du CNRS, 1987.

Lévi-Strauss, Claude. "Amériques." *L'Homme* 158–59 (2001): 439–42.

Lienhard, Martin. *La voz y su huella.* La Habana: Casa de las Américas, 1990.

López Austin, Alfredo. *Cuerpo Humano e Ideología: las concepciones de los antiguos nahuas.* México: Universidad Nacional Autónoma de México, 1980.

López Austin, Alfredo. *The Human Body and Ideology: Concepts of the Ancient Nahuas.* Salt Lake City: University of Utah Press, 1988.

MacCormack, Sabine. "Atahualpa and the Book." *Dispositio* 14, nos. 36–38 (1989): 141–68.

Macfie, A. L., ed. *Orientalism: A Reader.* New York: New York University Press, 2000.

Maravall, José Antonio. *La cultura del barroco: Análisis de una estructura histórica.* Barcelona: Ariel, 1986.

Márquez Villanueva, Francisco. "*La Celestina* as Hispano-Semitic Anthropology." *Revue de Littérature Comparée* 61 (1987): 425–53.

Mazzotti, José Antonio. *Coros Mestizos del Inca Garcilaso: Resonancias Andinas.* México: Fondo de Cultura Económica, 1996.

McCabe, Richard. "Ireland: Policy, Poetics and Parody." In *The Cambridge Companion to Spenser,* 60–78, edited by Andrew Hadfield. Cambridge, U.K.: Cambridge University Press, 2001.

Mignolo, Walter. "La lengua, la letra, el territorio (o la crisis de los estudios literarios coloniales)." *Dispositio* 28–29 (1986): 137–61.

Nightingale, Andrea W. *Spectacles of Truth in Classical Greek Philosophy; Theoria in its Cultural Context.* Cambridge, U.K.: Cambridge University Press, 2006.

Orquera, Yolanda Fabiola. "Guardianes de la verdad: narración e ideología en la polémica Oviedo/Las Casas," Paper presented at a meeting of the Latin American Studies Association Miami, 2000.

Orquera, Yolanda Fabiola. *Los castillos decrépitos o "La Historia Verdadera," de Bernal Díaz del Castillo: una indagación de las relaciones entre cultura popular y cultura letrada.* San Miguel de Tucumán: Universidad Nacional de Tucumán, 1996.

Orr, Bridget. *Empire on the English Stage, 1660–1714.* New York: Cambridge University Press, 2001.

Palmer, Patricia. *Language and Conquest in Early Modern Ireland.* New York: Cambridge University Press, 2001.

Pizarro, Ana, ed. *La literatura latinoamericana como proceso.* Buenos Aires: Centro Editor de América Latina, 1985.

Quilligan, Maureen. "Freedom, Service, and the Trade in Slaves: The Problem of Labor in *Paradise Lost.*" *Subject and Object in Renaissance Culture.* Ed. Margreta de Grazia, Maureen Quilligan and Peter Stallybrass. Cambridge: Cambridge University Press, 1992.

Quilligan, Maureen. On the Renaissance Epic: Spenser and Slavery." *South Atlantic Quarterly,* 100. (2001), 15–39.

Quint, David. *Epic and Empire: Politics and Generic Form from Virgil to Milton.* Princeton: Princeton University Press, 1993.

Rama, Angel. *Transculturación narrativa de América Latina.* México: Siglo XXI, 1982.

Raman, Shankar. *Framing "India": The Colonial Imaginary in Early Modern Culture.* Stanford: Stanford University Press, 2001.

Reiss, Timothy. *Knowledge, Discovery, and Imagination in Early Modern Europe: The Rise of Aesthetic Rationalism.* New York: Cambridge University Press, 1997.

Robbins, Bruce, et al. "Edward Said's Culture and Imperialism." *Social Text* 16 (1994): 1–24.

Rodríguez, Juan Carlos. *Teoría e Historia de la Producción ideológica: Las primeras literaturas burguesas.* Madrid: Akal, 1990.

Roth, Cecil. "Marranos and Racial Anti-Semitism: A Study in Parallels." *Jewish Social Studies* 2 (1940): 239–48.

Round, Nicholas. "Politics, Style and Group Attitudes in the *Instrucción del Relator.*" *Bulletin of Hispanic Studies* 46 (1969): 289–319.

Ryan, Lawrence. *Roger Ascham.* Stanford: Stanford University Press 1963.

Said, Edward W. *Orientalism.* New York: Vintage, 1994.

Said, Edward W. "Orientalism Reconsidered." *Cultural Critique* 1 (1985): 89–107.

Said, Edward W. *The World, The Text, and The Critic.* Cambridge, MA: Harvard University Press, 1983.

Salamon, Linda Bradley. "A Face in *The Glasse:* Gascoigne's *Glasse of Governement* Re-examined," *Studies in Philology* 81 (1974): 47–71.

Salamon, Linda Bradley. "Gascoigne's Globe: The Spoyle of Antwerpe and the Black Legend of Spain" *Early Modern Literary Studies* 13 (2007).

Schwartz, Stuart B. "Denounced by Lévi-Strauss." *The Americas* 59, no. 1 (2002): 1–8.

Singh, Jyostna G. "History or Colonial Ethnography? The Ideological Formation of Edward Terry's A Voyage to East India (1655 & 1665) and The Merchants and Mariners Preservation and Thanksgiving (1649)." In *Travel Knowledge; European "Discoveries" in the Early Modern Period,* 197–207. New York: Palgrave, 2001.

Tedlock, Dennis. *The Spoken World and the Work of Interpretation.* Philadelphia: University of Pennsylvanis Press, 1983.

Tekin, Gönül. "Fatih Devri Türk Edebiyatı." In *Istanbul Armağanı,* 184–85. Istanbul, 1995.

Van Deusen, Nancy E. *Between the Sacred and the Worldly: the Institutional and Cultural Practice of Recogimiento in Colonial Lima.* Stanford: Stanford University Press, 2001.

Villenfagne, H. de. *Mélanges de littérature et d'histoire.* Liège: J. Desoer, 1788.

Vitkus, Daniel J. "Early Modern Orientalism: Representations of Islam in Sixteenth- and Seventeenth-Century Europe." In *Western Views of Islam in Medieval and Early Modern Europe,* edited by Michael Frassetto and David R. Blanks, 207–30. New York: St. Martin's Press, 1999.

Vitkus, Daniel J. "Trafficking with the Turk." In *Travel Knowledge; European "Discoveries" in the Early Modern Period,* 35–52, edited by Ivo Kamps and Jyotsna Singh. New York: Palgrave, 2001.

Vološinov, V. N. [Mikhail Bakhtin]. *Marxism and the Philosophy of Language.* Cambridge, MA: Harvard University Press, 2000 (1929).

Williams, Raymond. *Marxism and Literature.* Oxford: Oxford University Press, 1978.

RACE/ETHNICITY

Arco Garay, R. del. *Figuras aragonesas: El genio de la raza.* Zaragoza, 1913.

Augstein, Hannah Franziska, ed. *Race: The Origins of an Idea, 1760–1850.* South Bend, IN: St. Augustine's Press, 1996.

Banton, Michael. *Racial Theories.* Cambridge, U.K.: Cambridge University Press, 1998.

Bartlett, Robert. "Medieval and Modern Concepts of Race and Ethnicity." *The Journal of Medieval and Early Modern Studies* 31, no. 1 (2001): 39–56.

Bennett, Herman L. *Africans in Colonial Mexico: Absolutism, Christianity, and Afro-Creole Consciousness, 1570–1640.* Bloomington: Indiana University Press, 2003.

Boxer, Charles R. *Race Relations in the Portuguese Colonial Empire, 1415–1825.* Oxford, U.K.: Clarendon Press, 1963.

Cirot, Georges. "La Maurophilie Littéraire en Espagne au XVIe Siecle." *Bulletin Hispanique* 31 (1929); 40–44 (1938–1942); 46 (1944).

Clark, Robert L. A., and Claire Sponsler. "Othered Bodies: Racial Cross-Dressing in the *Mistere de la Sainte Hostie* and the Croxton *Play of the Sacrament.*" *Journal of Medieval and Early Modern Studies* 29, no. 1 (1999): 61–87.

Cohen, Jeffrey Jerome. "On Saracen Enjoyment: Some Fantasies of Race in Late Medieval France and England." *The Journal of Medieval and Early Modern Studies* 31, no. 1 (2001): 113–46.

Cope, R. Douglas. *The Limits of Racial Discrimination: Plebeian Society in Colonial Mexico City, 1660–1720.* Madison: University of Wisconsin Press, 1994.

Domínguez Ortiz, Antonio. *La clase social de los conversos en Castilla en la Edad Moderna.* Madrid: Consejo Superior de Investigaciones Científicas, 1955.

Estenssoro, Juan Carlos. "Los colores de la plebe: razón y mestizaje en el Perú colonial." In *Los cuadros de mestizaje del Virrey Amat: La representación etnográfica en el Perú colonial,* 66–107. Lima: Museo de Arte de Lima, 2000.

Fields, Barbara. "Whiteness, Racism, and Identity." *International Labor and Working-Class History* 60 (Fall 2001): 48–56.

Fields, Barbara. "Ideology and Race in American History." In *Region, Race, and Reconstruction: Essays in Honor of C. Vann Woodward,* 143–77, edited by J. Morgan Kousser and James M. McPherson. New York: Oxford University Press, 1982.

Firmin, Joseph-Anténor. *De l'égalité des races humaines.* Edited by Jean Métellus. Montreal: Mémoire d'encrier, 2005.

Floyd-Wilson, Mary. *English Ethnicity and Race in Early Modern Drama.* New York: Cambridge University Press, 2003.

Frassetto, Michael, and David R. Blanks, eds. *Western Views of Islam in Medieval and Early Modern Europe: Perceptions of Other.* New York: St. Martin's Press, 1999.

Fredrickson, George. *Racism: A Short History.* Princeton: Princeton University Press, 2002.

Frey, Winfried. "Vom Antijudaismus zum Antisemitismus. Ein antijüdisches Pasquill von 1606 und seine Quellen." *Daphnis* 18 (1989): 251–79.

Fuchs, Barbara. "Spanish Lessons: Spenser and the Irish Moriscos." *Studies in English Literature* 42 (2002): 43–62.

Hahn, Thomas. "The Difference the Middle Ages Makes: Color and Race before the Modern World." *The Journal of Medieval and Early Modern Studies* 31, no. 1 (2001): 1–37.

Heil, Johannes. "»Antijudaismus« und »Antisemitismus« - Begriffe als Bedeutungsträger." *Jahrbuch für Antisemitismusforschung* 6 (1997): 91–114.

Heng, Geraldine. *Empire of Magic: Medieval Romance and the Politics of Cultural Fantasy*. New York: Columbia University Press, 2003.

Herde, P. "Von der mittelalterlichen Judenfeindschaft zum modernen Antisemitismus." In *Geschichte und Kultur des Judentums*, edited by K. Müller and K. Wittstadt. Würzburg, 1988.

Hoffmann, Christhard. "Christlicher Antijudaismus und moderner Antisemitismus. Zusammenhänge und Differenzen als Problem der historischen Antisemitismusforschung." In *Christlicher Antijudaismus und Antisemitismus. Theologische und kirchliche Programme Deutscher Christen*, 293–317, edited by Leonore Siegele-Wenschkewitz. Frankfurt, 1994.

Hume, David. "Of National Characters." In *Essays Moral, Political, and Literary*, edited by T. H. Green and T. H. Grose. New York: Longmans, Green & Co., 1898.

Galán Sánchez, Ángel. *Una visión de la "decadencia española": la historiografía anglosajona sobre mudéjares y moriscos*. Málaga, 1991.

Gobineau, Joseph-Arthur (Comte de). *Essai sur l'inégalité des races humaines*. Paris: Éditions Pierre Belfond, 1967.

Gonzalez Calleja, E., and F. Limon Nevado. *La hispanidad como instrumento de combate: raza e imperio en la prensa franquista durante la guerra civil española*. Madrid: Consejo Superior de Investigaciones Científicas, 1988.

Griffin, Eric. "From Ethos to Ethnos: Hispanizing 'the Spaniard' in the Old World and the New." *Early Modernities*, a special issue of *CR: The New Centennial Review* 2, no. 1 (Spring 2002): 69–116.

Hall, Stuart. "Old and New Identities, Old and New Ethnicities." In *Culture, Globalization, and the World System: Contemporary Conditions for the Representation of Identity*, edited by Anthony D. King. Minneapolis: University of Minnesota Press, 1997.

Jordan, William Chester. "Why "Race"?" *The Journal of Medieval and Early Modern Studies* 31, no. 1 (2001): 165–73.

Jordan, Winthrop. *White over Black, American Attitudes Towards the Negro, 1550–1812*. Chapel Hill: University of North Carolina Press, 1968.

Jouanna, Arlette. *L'idee de race en France au XVIème siècle (1498–1614)*. 3 vols. Lille: Atelier reproduction des thèses, Université de Lille III, 1976.

Kamen, Henry. "The Mediterranean and the Expulsion of Spanish Jews in 1492." *Past and Present* 119 (1988): 30–55.

Kunt, I. Metin. "Ethnic-regional (*Cins*) Solidarity in the Seventeenth-century Ottoman Establishment." *International Journal of Middle East Studies* 9 (1974): 233–39.

Lida, María Rosa. "Un decir más de Francisco Imperial: Respuesta a Fernán Pérez de Guzmán." *Nueva Revista de Filología Hispánica* 1 (1947): 170–77.

López Martínez, Héctor. "Un motín de mestizos en el Perú (1567)." *Revista de Indias* 24 (1964): 367–81.

O'Toole, Rachel Sarah. "Inventing Difference: Africans, Indians, and the Antecedents of 'Race' in Colonial Peru (1580s–1720s)." PhD diss., University of North Carolina at Chapel Hill, 2001.

Pagden, Anthony. *The Fall of Natural Man: The American Indian and the Origins of Comparative Ethnology*. Cambridge: Cambridge University Press, 1982.

Papiha, S. S. "Genetic variation and Disease Susceptibility in NCWP [New Commonwealth with Pakistani] Groups in Britain." *New Community* 13 (1987): 373–83.

Perceval, José María. *Todos son uno. Arquetipos, xenofobia y racismo. La imagen del morisco en la Monarquía Española durante los siglos XVI y XVII*. Almería: Instituto de Estudios Almerensis, 1997.

Plá, José. *La misión internacional de la raza hispánica*. Madrid: El Sol, 1928.

Pohl, W., and H. Reimitz, eds. *Strategies of Distinction: The Construction of Ethnic Communities, 300–800*. Leiden: Brill, 1993.

Revah, I. S. "La controverse sur les statuts de pureté de sang." *Bulletin hispanique* 63 (1971).

Schwartz, Stuart B., and Frank Salomon. "New Peoples and New Kinds of People: Adaptation, Readjustment, and Ethnogenesis in South American Indigenous Societies (Colonial Era)." In *Cambridge History of the Native Peoples of the Americas*, vol. III, no. 2, 483, edited by Bruce G. Trigger. New York: Cambridge University Press, 1999.

Shuger, Debora. "Irishmen, Aristocrats, and Other White Barbarians." *Renaissance Quarterly* 50 (1997): 494–525.

Sicroff, A. *Les controverses des statuts de "pureté de sang" en Espagne du xve au xviie siècle*. Paris: Didier, 1960.

Sicroff, Albert A. *Los estatutos de limpieza de sangre: Controversias entre los siglos XVI y XVII*. Madrid: Taurus, 1985.

Spitzer, Leo. "Ratio>race," In *Essays in Historical Semantics*. New York: Russell, 1948.

Stoler, Ann L. *Race and the Education of Desire*. Durham, NC: Duke University Press, 1995.

Subrahmanyam, Sanjay. "The 'Kaffirs of Europe': A Comment on Portugal and the Historiography of European Expansion in Asia." *Studies in History* 9, no. 1 (1993): 131–46.

Sweet, James H. "The Iberian Roots of American Racist Thought." *Constructing Race: Differentiating Peoples in the Early Modern World, The William and Mary Quarterly* 54, no. 1 (January 1997): 143–66.

Thomson, Sinclair. "Was There Race in Colonial Latin America? Identifying Selves and Others in the Insurgent Andes." In *Race, Culture, and Power in the Andes and Mesoamerica: From "Purity of Blood" to Indigenous Social Movements*, edited by Laura Gotkowitz. Volume under consideration by Duke University Press.

Walz, R. "Der vormoderne Antisemitismus: Religiöser Fanatismus oder Rassenwahn?" *Historische Zeitschrift* 260 (1995): 719–48.

Yerushalmi, Yosef Hayim. *Assimilation and Racial Anti-Semitism: the Iberian and the German Models*. New York: Leo Baeck Institute, 1982.

RELIGION

Arriaga, Father Pablo José de. *The Extirpation of Idolatry in Peru*. Translated by L.Clark Keating. Lexington: University of Kentucky Press, 1968.

Baer, Yitzhak. *Die Juden im christlichen Spanien*. Westmead, UK: Gregg International Publishers, 1970.

Baron, Salo. *Modern Nationalism and Religion*. New York: Harper, 1947.

Baron, Salo. *A Social and Religious History of the Jews*, vol. 13. New York: Columbia University Press, 1969.

Beltrán de Heredia, V. "Las bulas de Nicolás V acerca de los conversos de Castilla." *Sefarad* 21 (1961): 37–38.

Benito Ruano, Eloy. "La 'Sentencia-Estatuto' de Pero Sarmiento contra los conversos Toledanos." *Revista de la Universidad de Madrid* 6 (1957): 277–306.

Benito Ruano, Eloy. "D. Pero Sarmiento, repostero mayor de Juan II de Castilla." *Hispania* 17 (1957): 483–54.

Benito Ruano, Eloy. "El Memorial del bachiller Marcos García de Mora contra los conversos." *Sefarad* 17 (1957): 314–51.

Bumas, E. Shaskan. "The cannibal Butcher Shop. Protestant Uses of las Casas's Brevisima relación in Europe and American Colonies." *Early American Literature* 35 (2000): 107–36.

Burkhart, L. M. *The Slippery Earth: Nahua-Christian Moral Dialogue In Sixteenth-Century Mexico*. Tucson: University of Arizona Press, 1989.

Burkhart, L. M. "Encounter of Religions. The Indigenization of Christianity: The Nahua Scholar-Interpreters." *Occasional papers in Latin American Studies* 13 (1991).

Burkhart, L. M. *Holy Wednesday: A Nahua Drama from Early Colonial Mexico.* Philadelphia: University of Pennsylvania Press, 1996.

Burkhart, L. M. *Before Guadalupe: The Virgin Mary in Early Colonial Nahuatl Literature.* Albany, N.Y.: Institute for Mesoamerican Studies University at Albany, distributed by University of Texas Press, 2001.

Burton, Jonathan. "English Anxiety and the Muslim Power of Conversion: Five Perspectives on 'Turning Turk' in Early Modern Texts." *Journal for Early Modern Cultural Studies,* A Special Issue on Representations of Islam and the East, 1 (Spring/Summer 2002) v–viii.

Caro Baroja, Julio. *Inquisición, brujería y criptojudaísmo.* Barcelona: Ediciones Ariel, 1972.

Chew, Samuel. *The Crescent and The Rose; Islam and England during the Renaissance.* New York: Octagon Books, 1965.

Cohen, Jeremy, ed. *Essential Papers on Judaism and Christianity in Conflict from Late Antiquity to the Reformation.* New York: New York University Press, 1991.

Cohen, Jeremy. *The Friars and the Jews: the Evolution of Medieval Anti-Judaism.* Ithaca, NY: Cornell University Press, 1982.

Comaroff, John and Jean. *Of Revelation and Revolution: Christianity, Colonialism, and Consciousness in South Africa.* 2 vols. Chicago: University of Chicago Press, 1991–1997.

Contini, Gianfranco. "*Tombeau* de Leo Spitzer." In *Varianti e altra linguistica. Una raccolta di saggi (1938–1968),* 651–60. Turin: Einaudi, 1970.

Daniel, Norman. *Islam and the West; The Making of an Image.* Edinburgh: Edinburgh University Press, 1980.

Digby, Simon. "'Abd-al-Qaddus Gangohi (1456–1537 A.D.): The Personality and Attitudes of a Medieval Indian Sufi." *Medieval India: A Miscellany,* 3 (1975): 1–66.

Duverger, Christian. *La conversión de los indios de Nueva España.* México: Fondo de Cultura Económica, 1993.

Echevarria, Ana. *The Fortress of Faith: The Attitude toward Muslims in Fifteenth-Century Spain.* Leiden: Brill, 1999.

Elukin, Jonathan. "From Jew to Christian? Conversion and Immutability in Medieval Europe." In *Varieties of Religious Conversion in the Middle Ages,* 171–89, edited by J. Muldoon. Gainesville: University of Florida Press, 1997.

Evans, Helen C. ed., *Byzantium: Faith and Power (1261–1557).* New Haven, CT: Yale University Press, 2004.

Friedman, J. "Jewish Conversion, the Spanish Pure Blood Laws, and Reformation: A Revisionist View of Racial and Religious Anti-Semitism." *Sixteenth Century Journal* 18 (1987): 3–31.

García-Arenal, Mercedes, and Béatrice Leroy. *Moros y judíos en Navarra en la baja Edad Media.* Madrid: Hiperión, 1984.

García-Arenal, Mercedes. *Inquisición y moriscos, los procesos del Tribunal de Cuenca.* Madrid: Siglo XXI, 1983.

Gitlitz, David M. *Secrecy and Deceit: The Religion of the Crypto-Jews.* Philadelphia: Jewish Publication Society, 1996.

Gliozzi, Giuliano. *Adam et le Nouveau Monde.* Lecques: Théétète éditions, 2000.

Gonzálvez Ruiz, R. "El Bachiller Palma y su obra de polémica proconversa." *"Qu'un sang impur . . ." Les Conversos et le pouvoir en Espagne à la fin du moyen âge. Etudes Hispaniques* 23 (1997).

Gorski, Philip S. "The Protestant Ethic Revisited: Disciplinary Revolution and State Formation in Holland and Prussia." *American Journal of Sociology* 99, no. 2 (1993): 265–316.

Gose, Peter. "Priests, Petty Disputes and Purity of Blood: Unauthorized Threats to Old Christian Status in 17th Century Lima." Unpublished manuscript.

Grabois, Aryeh. "From 'Theological' to 'Racial' anti-Semitism: the Controversy over the 'Jewish' Pope in the Twelfth Century." *Zion* 47 (1982): 1–16.

Hanke, Lewis. *All Mankind is One: A Study of the Disputation Between Bartolomé de Las Casas and Juan Ginés de Sepúlveda in 1550 on the Intellectual and Religious Capacity of the American Indians.* De Kalb: Northern Illinois University Press, 1974.

Haverkamp, Alfred. *Geschichte der Juden im Mittelalter von der Nordsee bisuz den Südalpen: kommentiertes Kartenwerk.* Hannover: Hahnsche Buchhandlung, 2002.

Israel, Jonathan. *Empires and Entrepôts: The Dutch, the Spanish Empire, and the Jews, 1585–1713.* Roncevert, WV: Hambledon Press, 1990.

Jackson, R. H. and E. D. Castillo. *Indians, Franciscans, and Spanish Colonization: The Impact of the Mission System On California Indians.* Albuquerque: University of New Mexico Press, 1995.

Karamustafa, Ahmet. *God's Unruly Friends: Dervish Groups in the Islamic Later Middle Period, 1200–1550.* Salt Lake City: University of Utah Press, 1994.

Katz, Jacob. *Tradition and Crisis: Jewish Society at the End of the Middle Ages.* Translated by Bernard Dov Cooperman. New York: New York University Press, 1993.

Kisch, Guido. *The Jews in Medieval Germany: A Study of their Legal and Social Status.* Chicago: University of Chicago Press, 1949.

Klaus, Susanne. *Uprooted Christianity: The Preaching of the Christian Doctrine in Mexico Based on Franciscan Sermons of the 16th Century Written in Nahuatl.* Schwaben, Germany: Saurwein, 1999.

Knapp, Jeffrey. *Shakespeare's Tribe: Church, Nation, and Theater in Renaissance England.* Chicago: University of Chicago Press, 2002.

Krueger, S. "Conversion and Medieval Sexual, Religious, and Racial Categories." In *Constructing Medieval Sexuality,* 158–79, edited by Karma Lochrie et al. Minneapolis: University of Minnesota Press, 1997.

Langmuir, Gavin. "Prolegomena to any present analysis of hostility against Jews." *Social science information = Information sur les sciences sociales* 15 (1976): 689–727.

Lida de Malkiel, M.R. "Lope de Vega y los judíos." *Bulletin hispanique* 75 (1973): 73–112.

Lisson, Emilio, ed. *La Iglesia de España en el Perú.* 23 vols. Sevilla, 1943–1947.

Livet, G., and F. Rapp. *Strasbourg au coeur religieux du XVIe siècle.* Strasbourg: Librairie Istra, 1977.

López Austin, Alfredo. *Hombre-Dios: religión y política en el mundo nahuatl.* Mexico: Universidad Nacional Autónoma de México, Instituto de Investigaciones Históricas, 1973.

López Martinez, N. "Teologia española de la convivencia a mediados del siglo XV." In *Repertorio de las Ciencias Eclesiásticas de España, vol. 1, Siglos III–XVI*, 465–76. Salamanca: Instituto de la Historia de la Teología Española, 1967.

Manrique, Nelson. *Vinieron los sarracenos: El universo mental de la conquista de América.* Lima: DESCO, 1993.

Márquez Villanueva, F. "El problema de los conversos: Cuatro puntos cardinals." *Hispania judaica* 1 (1980): 51–75.

Matar, Nabil. *Islam in Britain, 1558–1685.* Cambridge, UK: Cambridge University Press, 1998.

Marín Padilla, E. *Relación judeoconversa durante la segunda mitad del siglo XV en Aragón: La Ley.* Madrid: E. Marín Padilla, 1988.

Méchoulan, H. "The Importance of Hispanicity in Jewish Orthodoxy and Heterodoxy in Seventeenth-Century Amsterdam." In *In Iberia and Beyond: Hispanic Jews Between Cultures*, 353–372, edited by B. Cooperman. Newark: University of Delaware Press, 1998.

Menocal, María Rosa. *Ornament of the World: How Muslims, Jews, and Christians Created a Culture of Tolerance in Medieval Spain.* Boston: Little, Brown, 2002.

Meyuhas Ginio, Alisa. *De bello iudaeorum: Fray Alonso de Espina y su Fortalitium fidei.* Salamanca: Fontes Iudaeorum Regni Castellae VIII, 1998.

Netanyahu, Benzion. *The Origins of the Inquisition in Fifteenth Century Spain.* New York: Random House, 1995.

Nirenberg, David. *Communities of Violence: Persecution of Minorities in the Middle Ages.* Princeton: Princeton University Press, 1996.

Nirenberg, David. "El sentido de la historia judía." *Revista de libros* 28 (April 1999): 3–5.

Nirenberg, David. "Forum: Inflecting the *converso* voice." *La corónica* 25, no. 2 (1997): 183–85.

Nirenberg, David. "Enmity and Assimilation: Jews, Christians, and Converts in Medieval Spain." *Common Knowledge* 9, no. 1 (2003): 137–55.

Nirenberg, David. "Mass Conversion and Genealogical Mentalities: Jews and Christians in Fifteenth-Centruy Spain." *Past and Present* 174 (2002): 3–41.

Novinsky, Anita. *Crisaos novos na Bahia.* Sao Paolo, 1976.

Oberman, Heiko Augustinus. *The Roots of Anti-Semitism in the Age of Renaissance and Reformation.* Translated by James I. Porter. Philadelphia: Fortress, 1984.

Oberman, Heiko Augustinus. *Wurzeln des Antisemitismus. Christenangst und Judenplage im Zeitalter von Humanismus und Reformation.* Berlin: Brunnen-Verlag, 1983.

Reinert, Stephen W. "The Muslim Presence in Constantinople, 9th–15th Centuries: Some Preliminary Observations." In *Studies on the Internal Diaspora of the Byzantine Empire,* 125–50, edited by H. Ahrweiler and A. E. Laiou. Washington, DC: Dumbarton Oaks, 1998.

Ricard, Robert. *The Spiritual Conquest of Mexico: An Essay on the Apostolate and the Evangelizing Methods of the Mendicant Orders in New Spain, 1523–1572.* Translated by Lesley Byrd Simpson. Berkeley: University of California Press, 1966.

Riera, J. "Judíos y conversos en los reinos de la Corona de Aragón durante el siglo XV." In *La expulsión de los judíos de España,* 71–90, edited by Luís Suárez Fernández. Madrid: MAPRFRE, 1992.

Romano, David. "Característiques dels jueus en relació amb els cristians en els estats hispànics." In *Jornades d'història dels jueus a Catalunya,* 9–27, edited by J. Alegret. Girona: Ayntamiento de Girona, 1987.

Rucquoi, Adelina. "Noblesse des conversos?" *"Qu'un sang impur . . ." Les Conversos et le pouvoir en Espagne à la find du moyen âge. Etudes Hispaniques* 23 (1997): 89–108.

Rucquoi, A. "Etre noble en Espagne aux XIVᵉ–XVIᵉ siècles." In *Nobilitas. Funktion und Repräsentation des Adels in Alteuropa,* 273–98, edited by O. Oexle and W. Paravicini. Göttingen: Vandenhoeck & Ruprecht, 1997.

Sanahuja, Fray Pedro. *Lérida en sus luchas por la fe (judíos, moros, conversos, Inquisición, moriscos).* Lleida: Fora de collecció, 1946.

Sánchez, Ana. "Mentalidad popular frente a ideologia oficial: El Santo Oficio en Lima y los casos de hechiceria (siglo xvii)." In *Poder y violencia en los Andes,* edited by E. Urbano. Lima: Centro de Estudios Regionales Bartolomé de las Casas, 1991.

Shuger, Debora. *Habits of Thought in the English Renaissance: Religion, Politics, and the Dominant Culture.* Berkeley: University of California Press, 1990.

Sicroff, Albert A. "Spanish Anti-Judaism: A Case of Religious Racism." In *Encuentros and Desencuentros: Spanish Jewish Cultural Interaction Throughout History,* 589–613, edited by Carlos Carrete Parrondo et al. Tel Aviv: University Publishing Projects, 2000.

Silverblatt, Irene. "New Christians and New World Fears." *Comparative Studies in Society and History* 42, no. 3 (2000): 524–46.

Simonsohn, Shlomo. *The Apostolic See and the Jews: 1394–1464,* no. 856. Toronto: Pontifical Institute of Mediaeval Studies, 1989.

Southern, R. W. *Western Views of Islam in the Middle Ages.* Cambridge. MA: Harvard University Press, 1962.

Starr-Lebeau, G. "Guadalupe: Political Authority and Religious Identity in Fifteenth-Century Spain." PhD diss., University of Michigan, 1996.

Vitkus, Daniel. "Early Modern Orientalism: Representations of Islam in Sixteenth- and Seventeenth-Century Europe." In *Western Views of Islam in Medieval and Early Modern Europe,* 203–7, edited by David R. Blanks and Michael Frassetto. New York: St. Martin's Press, 1999.

Vitkus, Daniel. "Introduction: Toward a New Globalism in Early Modern Studies." *Journal for Early Modern Cultural Studies,* A Special Issue on Representations of Islam and the East, 2, no. 1 (Spring/Summer 2002): v–viii.

Vryonis, Spyros. *The Decline of Medieval Hellenism in Asia Minor and the Process of Islamization from the Eleventh through the Fifteenth Century.* Berkeley: University of California Press, 1971.

Yerushalmi, Yosef Hayim. *From Spanish Court to Italian Ghetto: Isaac Cardoso: A Study in Seventeenth-Century Marranism and Jewish Apologetics.* New York: Columbia University Press, 1971.

SLAVERY/SLAVE TRADE

Bearman, P. J., T. Bianquis, C. E. Bosworth, E. van Donzel, and W. P. Heinrichs, eds. "Ghulam." In *Encyclopedia of Islam.* Leiden, The Netherlands: Brill, 1960–2005.

Bakewell, Peter. *Miners of the Red Mountain: Indian Labor in Potosí, 1545–1650.* Albuquerque: University of New Mexico Press, 1984.

Bowser, Frederick P. *The African Slave in Colonial Peru, 1524–1650.* Stanford: Stanford University Press, 1974.

Crone, Patrica. *Slaves on Horses: The Evolution of the Islamic Polity.* New York: Cambridge University Press, 1980.

Cugoano, Ottabah. *Thoughts and Sentiments on the Evil of Slavery and Other Writings.* Edited by Vincent Carretta. New York: Penguin, 1999.

Douglass, Frederick. *Narrative of the Life of Frederick Douglass, an American Slave, Written By Himself.* Edited by David W. Blight. Boston: Bedford St. Martin's, 2003.

Hazlewood, Nick. *The Queene's Slave Trader: John Hawkyns, Elizabeth I, and the Trafficking in Human Souls.* New York: Harper, 2004.

Zachariadou, Elizavet. "Les 'janissaires' de l'empereur byzantin." In *Studia Turcologica Memoriae Alexii Bombacci Dicata,* 591–97, edited by A. Gallotta. Naples: Istituto Universitario Orientale, 1982.

TRADE

Berg, N. P. van den. *Uit de dagen der Compagnie.* Haarlem: Willink, 1904.

Nummedal, Tara E. "Practical Alchemy and Commercial Exchange in the Holy Roman Empire." In *Merchants and Marvels: Commerce, Science, and Art in Early Modern Europe*, 201–222, edited by Pamela Smith and Paula Findlen. New York: Routledge, 2002.

Parker, Grant. "Ex Oriente Luxuria: Indian Commodities and Roman Experience." *Journal of Economic and Social History of the Orient* 45, no. 1 (2002): 40–95.

Ptak, Roderich. *China and the Asian Seas: Trade, Travel, and Visions of the Others (1400–1750).* Aldershot, UK: Ashgate, 1998.

Reed, David T. "Hunger for Gold: Guyon, Mammon's Cave, and the New World Treasure." *English Literary Renaissance* 20.2 (1990): 209–32.

Skilliter, S. A. *William Harborne and the Trade with Turkey, 1578–1582.* London: Oxford University Press, 1977.

Zachariadou, Elizavet. *Trade and Crusade: Venetian Crete and the Emirates of Menteshe and Aydin (1300–1415).* Venice: Istituto ellenico di studi bizantini e postbizantini di Venezia per tutti i paesi del mondo, 1983.

CONTRIBUTORS

Kathryn Burns is associate professor of history at the University of North Carolina at Chapel Hill. She is the author of *Colonial Habits: Convents and the Spiritual Economy of Cuzco, Peru* (1999) and is currently working on scribes, writing, and power in colonial Peru.

Edmund Valentine Campos is visiting assistant professor of English at Dartmouth College. He studies exploration, discovery, and transatlantic imperialism in the early modern period.

Michael Ennis is an adjunct assistant professor of English at Elon University and a former Fulbright García-Robles Scholar. He works on Mesoamerican literature and culture. He is the author of a dissertation titled "Historicizing Nahua Utopias."

Barbara Fuchs is professor of Romance languages at the University of Pennsylvania. She is author of *Mimesis and Empire: The New World, Islam and European Identitites* (2001), *Passing for Spain: Cervantes and the Fictions of Identity* (2003), and *Romance* (2004).

Patricia Gravatt is assistant professor of French at Ithaca College. She is the author of *L'Eglise et l'esclavage* (2003) and *Le Nouveau Monde et le Vieux Monde* (2006).

Margaret R. Greer is professor of Spanish and chair of Romance studies at Duke University. Her publications include *The Play of Power: Mythological Court Dramas of Pedro Calderón de la Barca* (1991), *María de Zayas Tells Baroque Tales of Love and the Cruelty of Men* (2000), and *Decolonizing the Middle Ages* (2000), edited with John Dagenais. She is working on a book on early modern Spanish tragedy.

Jeffrey Knapp is professor of English at the University of California at Berkeley. He is the author of *An Empire Nowhere: England, America, and Literature from "Utopia" to "The Tempest"* (1992) and *Shakespeare's Tribe: Church, Nation, and Theater in Renaissance England* (2002). He is currently writing a companion volume to *Shakespeare's Tribe*, entitled *Shakespeare Only*.

Ruby Lal is associate professor in the Department of Middle Eastern and South Asian Studies at Emory University. She is author of *Domesticity and Power in the Early Mughal World* (2005).

Gonzalo Lamana is assistant professor of Hispanic languages and literatures at the University of Pittsburgh. He has written several essays on Andean colonialism, among them "Beyond Exotization and Likeness," which appeared in *Comparative Studies in Society and History,* and "Definir y Dominar," which received the honorable mention for the Franklin Pease G. Y. Memorial Award for best essay published in the *Colonial Latin American Review* (2001–2002). His forthcoming book will be published by Duke University Press.

Walter D. Mignolo is William H. Wannamaker Professor and Director, Center for Global Studies and the Humanities, at Duke University. He is the author of *The Darker Side of the Renaissance: Literacy, Territoriality and Colonization* (1995), *Local Histories/Global Designs: Coloniality, Subaltern Knowledge and Border Thinking* (2000), and *The Idea of Latin America* (2005). His latest book, *Coloniality and the De-Colonial Reason* is forthcoming.

David Nirenberg is professor in the Committee on Social Thought at the University of Chicago. Author of *Communities of Violence: Persecution of Minorities in the Middle Ages* (1996), he is currently working on a study of the collapse of religious pluralism in late medieval Spain and on history of the Jew as a figure of thought from ancient Egypt to the present.

Carmen Nocentelli is assistant professor of English and comparative literature at the University of New Mexico. She is currently completing a manuscript on the intersection of race and sexuality in early modern European culture.

Yolanda Fabiola Orquera is a researcher at the National Council of Scientific and Technical Research of Argentina (CONICET), to which she returned after completing her Ph.D. in Spanish at Duke University. She is the author of *Los Castillos decrépitos, o la "Historia Verdadera" de Bernal Díaz del Castillo* (1996), an essay that won first prize in the National Competition of the Secretary of Culture of Argentina in 1995.

Leslie Peirce is the Silver Professor of History and Middle Eastern and Islamic Studies at New York University. She is the author of *The Imperial Harem: Women and Sovereignty in the Ottoman Empire* (1993) and *Morality Tales: Law and Gender in the Ottoman Court of Aintab* (2003).

Maureen Quilligan is R. Florence Brinkley Professor of English at Duke University. Having served as one of the editors of *Rewriting the Renaissance: Discourses of Sexual Difference in Early Modern Europe* (1986), she has published articles on the Renaissance epic and New World slavery, and is currently at work on a book about women rulers in the Renaissance.

Linda Bradley Salamon, professor of English at George Washington University, co-edited (with Arthur Kinney) and wrote the monograph for *Nicholas Hilliard's Art of Limning* (1983). Her most recent publications are "Vagabond Veterans: The Rogueish Company of Martin Guerre and *Henry V*" in *Rogues and Early Modern Literary Culture* (2004) and "Screening Evil through History:

Rope, Compulsion, Scarface, Richard III" in *The Changing Face of Evil in Film and Television* (2007).

Irene Silverblatt is professor of cultural anthropology and history at Duke University. She is the author of *Moon, Sun, and Witches: Gender Ideologies and Class in Inca and Colonial Peru* (1987) and *Modern Inquisitions: Peru and the Colonial Origins of the Civilized World* (2004).

SilverMoon received her Ph.D. from the Department of History at Duke University and is a former Fulbright García-Robles Scholar. She is a lecturer of history at North Carolina State University. She wrote her dissertation about the students of the School of Tlatelolco, titled "The Emergence of a New Nahua Intellectual Elite: Access to Power Positions through the Imperial College de Santa Cruz de Tlatelolco."

INDEX